WALLACE-HOMESTEAD
PRICE GUIDE TO ANTIQUES
AND PATTERN GLASS
SEVENTH EDITION

Edited by Robert W. Miller

Other books by Robert W. Miller

American Primitives
The Art Glass Basket
Clock Guide Identification with Prices
Clock Guide Identification with Prices, Book II
Fabulous Houston Museum
Mary Gregory and Her Glass
Oriental Primer
Pictorial Guide to Early American Tools and Implements
Wallace-Homestead Flea Market Price Guide
Wallace-Homestead Price Guide to Dolls
Wallace-Homestead Price Guide to Toys

Copyright© 1981
Wallace-Homestead Book Company

ISBN 0-87069-305-0
Library of Congress Catalog No. 74-84521

Cover photograph: Perry Struse, West Des Moines, Iowa
Antiques courtesy of: Wilbur and Opal Williams
The China Closet, Engelbert House
1910 Army Post Road Des Moines, Iowa

Other photography: Tom Needham, Panama City Beach, Florida
Marshall Thurman, Knoxville, Tennessee, and
John Shuman III, Pottstown, Pennsylvania

Published by

Wallace-Homestead Book Company
1912 Grand Avenue
Des Moines, Iowa 50309

Contents

Introduction

We wish we could tell you differently, but the prices in this Seventh Edition, WALLACE-HOMESTEAD PRICE GUIDE TO ANTIQUES & PATTERN GLASS are like all the other prices, worldwide — absolutely crazy!

It would be nice as we enter into a new decade to be able to tell you that the cost of food, clothing, fuel, and, yes, antiques, are leveling off, but you know better than that. So, we'll ask you to use this Seventh Edition as a *guide* because that's exactly what it is.

Certainly, our competitors are going to tell you that ten minutes before their price guide went to press all their prices were updated. Well, if you like telephone books spewed out by a computer, all well and good. But, the truth is, *no one* can keep up with today's rapidly changing prices. We try as hard as we know how to keep you abreast of what's collectible today but, we also ask your indulgence.

AND we ask you to compare. Which price guide has *more* categories, *more* photos, *more* information? Tells you how to buy by mail? How to buy at auction? Where to get that broken vase repaired? Where to find out about your family's heritage? Which? Where? **Right here**, in this Seventh Edition of the WALLACE-HOMESTEAD PRICE GUIDE TO ANTIQUES & PATTERN GLASS, that's where!

We know our split-price system works because everyone else is copying it. Also, if you'll compare *our* price guide with a few of the others, you'll notice that when we estab-lish new categories it isn't too long before all the others are listing those *same* categories. That's fine with us, imitation is the sincerest form of flattery.

Further, we have no quarrel with some of those "cheapie" price guides that sell for $1.50 or thereabouts. They should know what their price guide is worth.

We don't try to hide the fact that our WALLACE-HOMESTEAD PRICE GUIDE TO ANTIQUES & PATTERN GLASS is aimed at the beginning collector and/or the beginner dealer. We also know thousands of established dealers who highly recommend our price guide because of the realistic, up-to-date pricing, the ever-expanding categories, newest trends, etc. Certainly, they use price guides, but as a *guide* and not as the final word! And, anyone who says differently is not telling you the truth.

If you've purchased this Seventh Edition, WALLACE-HOMESTEAD PRICE GUIDE TO ANTIQUES & PATTERN GLASS, you've purchased the best, and for that we thank you. Although every effort has been made to avoid errors, the editor and the publisher cannot be held responsible for any errors in typography or in judgment as applied to prices given in this book.

Constructive criticism is always welcome because that's how we make each edition of this price guide better than the last. But, once again, bear with us because we aren't responsible for the crazy things prices are do-ing. We hope you understand and we thank you sincerely.

How to Buy by Mail

One of the most popular methods of buying and selling antiques is through the U.S. mails. Most antiques publications, whether weekly or monthly, will not knowingly accept advertisements from dishonest people. Unfortunately, some questionable ads slip by the editors, and for that reason we list here some basic rules to follow when you decide to buy or sell by mail.

1. The licensed antiques dealer should guarantee the condition and the authenticity of the merchandise in his ad. This same rule applies to an individual advertising a particular item for sale.

2. When you decide to purchase something that is advertised in one of the many antiques publications, mail your check at once and ALWAYS include a SAE (stamped-and-addressed-envelope) in the event the item you order has already been sold. Don't expect the dealer to pay the postage when returning your check. If you especially desire the item, telephone the seller, person-to-person; also, for faster service, send a certified check or money order. Your personal check may be good locally, but a dealer who doesn't know you has every right to wait until your check clears his bank before mailing you your merchandise.

3. Ask for "five-day approval." You won't always get it, but if you do you have the right to return the merchandise if you aren't satisfied.

4. UNPACK CAREFULLY! Careless unwrapping of merchandise can cost you money, and don't be foolish enough to think you can blame your mistake on the post office. If the post office is responsible, that's one thing—trying to cheat them is a sad mistake!

5. PACK CAREFULLY! If you're filling an order, that extra paper and extra time taken can save you lots of grief when the buyer notifies you that your merchandise arrived in a damaged and/or broken condition. If you do receive damaged and/or broken merchandise, save all the wrapping and take the package immediately to your local post office and file a claim. Save the nasty notes and give those responsible time to make good on your purchase.

6. Remember also that "buying by mail" does not include United Parcel Service. Check with the bus lines. With respect to saving the wrapping or filing a claim, if you are mailing and/or shipping by bus. Call them and ask what requirements they have for handling your package.

7. Misrepresented merchandise is just that, and you should take every action to get your money back. First, write to the person or persons from whom you made your purchase, sending your letter by Registered Letter, Return Receipt Requested. It may cost you a little more but you'll know your letter of complaint was received. If your letter fails to get action, check with your local post office to see what, if any, action can be taken. Also, write to the publisher of the publication from which you ordered your merchandise. Save the sarcasm and nasty threats—you may end up being sued for libel. Most publications are sincere and will honestly try to get your money back. They won't be in business long if they don't.

8. Don't be afraid to order by mail. It's big business and those using the mails to defraud usually end up in court. Reading the advertisement carefully **BEFORE** you order can save you a lot of trouble. Buy with confidence and be fair if a disagreement arises between you and the buyer and/or seller. If you're still not satisfied, then follow suggestions in No. 7 above.

How to Buy at Auctions

Whether you're buying at Sotheby Park Bernet, Adam Wecheler & Sons, or Richard A. Bourne Co., to mention just a few of the top auction houses in this country, it doesn't mean a thing unless you understand the chant of the auctioneer,

Few auctioneer's chants are the same. To the uninitiated, it's all a bunch of unintelligible gibberish. Also, the rules of buying vary from state to state, so here are a few basic rules to help you when you attend you first auction:

1. Learn how to bid **BEFORE** you bid by listening to the auctioneer's chant for a time, keeping in mind that innocent scratching of your ear or nose or a casual wave to a friend across the aisle may purchase you a genuine toilet seat!

2. You can bid by voice or by the wave of a hand; those known to the auctioneer may bid by a slight nod of the head or some other pre-arranged signal with the auctioneer. It depends upon the particular auction.

3. Most auction houses will not be responsible for the correctness of description, authenticity, genuineness or condition of the property being sold, so go early and look over the items being offered. When an auctioneer says, "It looks like walnut!" he's not saying it *is* walnut. You may be buying a piece of furniture made of poplar. Know what you're buying!

4. The highest bid accepted by the auctioneer is usually the buyer, but if there's a dispute between two bidders, the auctioneer will usually reopen the bidding, but only between disputing bidders. Then, when the hammer falls, the person with the highest bid is the buyer and thereafter the property is the purchaser's sole risk and responsibility. At most auctions, someone will usually assist you in loading your purchases. Some auction houses will put what you've purchased in a warehouse, at your expense, if you don't claim it within a specified period of time.

5. At an unrestricted sale, or a sale without reserve, the consignors of the items being sold are not supposed to bid. If the consignors bid back their own items, they still pay the full sales commission.

6. Most auctioneers reserve the right to refuse a bid if it is not commensurate with the value of the article or if the next bid is merely a nominal advance over the previous bid. It's the auctioneer's job to get as much as he can for an item, and he's not going to injure the sale by accepting too-low bids.

7. Be knowledgeable from the beginning. Go to the auction in time to get a bidder's number and a good seat. Popular auctioneers with a following will usually fill the house long before the auction begins.

8. Most auction houses will accept your personal check, locally, but if you're attending an auction out-of-town, arrange beforehand for credit or take travelers' checks.

There is a National Association of Auctioneers and most states have their own organizations. It's fun to buy by auction and they're becoming more and more popular because of the lure of "instant cash" to the seller. Most auction houses charge 15 percent of the gross. If you're interested in selling your merchandise by auction, find a reliable firm with which to do business. And, as in any other business transaction, read the contract **BEFORE** you sign it and understand what it says before you sign it.

How to Buy from Mail Auction Houses

More and more mail auction houses are popping up in the field of antiques and collectibles, and, as the rules seem rather confusing to us, we thought we'd list a few and let you judge for yourself.

One firm states that the highest bidder wins at the highest bid sent in. This firm doesn't allow phone calls and there are no reductions given over lower underbidders.

Another mail auction house reduces winning high bids to 10 percent above the second highest bid, except that no bid will be reduced by more than 20 percent, and bids under $5 are not lowered. Phone calls are allowed by this house, and the caller is given the current high bid which, if the caller chooses to overbid, must be topped by a minimum of 10 percent.

Still another firm sells to the highest bidder except that if more than 15 percent separates the high bid from the next highest, the high bid is reduced by a maximum of 15 percent. During the last two days callers are given the current high bid and are allowed to raise it in 15 percent increments if they have previously bid on the item. Otherwise they must raise by 20 percent.

Sounds like a high stakes crap game at Las Vegas and, as we said, it does sound confusing. But mail auction houses are here to stay, so if you're interested in buying antiques and collectibles by this method, learn the rules *before* you bid.

Auction Galleries

One of the most-asked questions is, "How do I find a reliable auction gallery?" Well, you can try the Yellow Pages; ask a trustworthy antiques dealer. We've listed a few auction galleries for your consideration. Obviously, there are many other reliable galleries, nationwide.

Courtesy demands that you first correspond with the particular gallery, always enclosing a S.A.S.E. Don't be insulted if the gallery isn't interested in your item(s); try another one. And, if you have only a few things to sell, try a local antiques dealer or a local auctioneer.

Philip E. Fitanides
Hooksett, NH 03106

C.G. Sloan & Co., Inc.
715 13 St. NW
Washington, DC 20005

Tom Sapp Auction Co.
Springfield, IL

Woody Auctions
Douglas, KS 67039

Christie's, USA
867 Madison Ave
New York, NY 10021

James E. Wilson & Son
1019 Airport Rd.
Hot Springs, AR 71901

Sotheby Park Bernet
980 Madison Ave
New York, NY 10021

Gene Harris
Marshalltown, IA 50158

P-B 84 (Park Bernet)
171 E 84 St.
New York, NY

Stumpf Auction Company
Mascoutah, IL

Adam A. Weschler & Son
905 E St. NW
Washington, DC 20004

Broughton Auction Co.
1645 S. Tejou
Colorado, Springs, CO 80906

Garth's Auctions, Inc.
2690 Stratford Rd
Delaware, OH 43015

The Summer Auction Service
Owatonna, MN 55060

California Book Auction Galleries
270 McAllister St.
San Francisco, CA 94102

West Coast Auction Co.
Anaheim, CA

Morton's Auction Exchange, Inc.
643 Magazine St.
New Orleans, LA 70130

Dunning's Auction Service
755 Church Rd.
Elgin, IL 60120

Col. Marty Higgenbotham
1702 Edgewood Dr.
Lakeland, FL 33803

Milwaukee Auction Galleries
5466 N Port Washington Rd.
Milwaukee, WI 53217

Trade Winds Auction Gallery
58 Wolcott Rd.
Akron, OH 44313

Richard A. Bourne Co.
Hyannis Port, MA 02647

Schrader Galleries
211 3rd St. South
St. Petersburg, FL 33701

Black Bros., Ltd.
Carlisle, PA 17013

Urich's Auction Gallery
3628 Washington Ave.
Fort Myers, FL 30901

Louis Aronoff
1117 Vine St.
Cincinnati, OH 45210

ABCD Auction Gallery
1 N. Clarendon Rd.
Avondale Estates, GA 30002
(Atlanta Metro area)

Browner Art Co., Ltd.
Margate, FL 33068

Clements Antiques
Hixson, TN

E. & M. Alexander, Inc.
1285 N. Post Oak Rd.
Houston, TX 77055

Robert W. Skinner, Inc.
Bolton, MA 01740

Atlanta Galleries
1405 Spring St. NW
Atlanta, GA

Richard's Auction Gallery
527 E. Locust
Des Moines, IA

Repairs, Services, Where-to-Buy

Every year hundreds of letters arrive, asking, "Where can I get my china vase repaired?" or "Who can find me such-and-such a book?" etc., etc. So here are a few folks who may be able to help you solve your particular problem. **PLEASE: always** inquire first and **always** enclose a S.A.S.E. (Self-Addressed-Stamped-Envelope). Some catalogs are free; others cost a nominal fee. Also, some of these firms are wholesale only. So **inquire first!** Want your service listed? Drop us a line, we answer **our** mail! (S.A.S.E., **Please!**)

A
Aladdin lamp parts 47
Antique fabrics, textiles restored 104
Antiques appraisals, professional 35
Antiques, repair 46
Art & frame repair books 20
Artifacts repair 63
Art instruction books 20
Art repair 46, 80, 95, 103, 110
B
Barometer restoration 2
Basketmaking materials 69
Bellows repair, restoration 64
Bible repair 22
Bisque repair, 16, 91, 117
Blacksmith 58
Bookbinding 22
Book search 10
Bottle cleaners—brushes 61, 62
Brass bed parts 26
Brass repair 46
C
Calligraphy supplies 92
Candleholders, wrought iron 14
Carnival Glass repair 16
Cash register parts 123, 126
Chair cane supplies 13, 39, 17, 69

China repair 16, 21, 63, 71, 91, 95, 96, 97, 98, 117
Clock dials 115
Clock dials redone 25, 103
Clock parts 48, 87, 116
Clock repair 48, 52, 108, 114
Cloisonne repair 99
Cup and saucer holders 47
D
Demography service 57
Doll, antique reproductions 38
Doll bodies 38, 42
Doll bodies, ceramic 41
Doll collectors' display frames 33
Dolls, complete supplies for 38
Doll eyes 27, 38
Dolls, glass domes for 14
Doll head repair 21, 63, 71, 117
Doll jewelry 38
Doll patterns 38, 43
Doll repair 16, 117
Doll stands 14, 38
Doll wigs 38
Dollhouse plan books 38
Dollhouse plans 38
E
Easels, cup & saucer 14
Easels plastic & wood 14
Easels, plate 14
Escutcheon pulls 13
Escutcheons, brass 13
Eyes, glass (doll, bird, fish, animal) 27
F
Figurine repair 71, 95, 103
Flow Blue matching service 118
Frame repair 20
Furniture restoration 37, 125
(Look in your Yellow Pages.)
G
Genealogical help 24, 57, 60
Glass, curved, for china cabinets, 1, 29

Repairs, Services, Where-to-Find Them

1. B & L Antiquerie
   25011 Little Mack
   St. Clair Shores, MI 48080
2. Henry F. Witzenberger
   15 Po Lane
   Hicksville, NY 11801
3. T-K Michael Stained Glass
   28200 Florence
   St. Clair Shores, MI 48081
4. LEMiniatures
   2615 Gravenstein Hwy.
   Sebastopol, CA 95472
5. Studio Hannah
   Star Route A, Box 93
   Flemington, NJ 08822
6. Thompsons
   Back Meadows Rd.
   Damariscotta, ME 04543
7. Wilson Bergerud
   30 Herring St.
   Harrington Park, NJ 07640
8. Hector Olszewski
   140 W. Houston
   New York, NY 10003
9. Globes by Chick
   328 Danville Pike
   Hillsboro, OH 45133
10. COLONIAL "out-of-print" Book Service
    23 E. 4 St.
    New York, NY 10003
11. Horton Brasses
    Box 95
    Cromwell, CT 06416
12. Nowell's Inc.
    Box 164
    Sausalito, CA 94965
13. Noel Wise Antiques
    6503 St. Claudia Ave.
    Arabi, LA 70032
14. T & B Sales Co.
    Box 30
    Old Hickory, TN 37138
15. Al Meekins
    PO Box 161
    Collingswood, NJ 08108
16. "My Grandfather's Shop" LTD
    940 Sligo Ave.
    Silver Springs, MD 20910
17. Ronald's Woodcarving
    434 W. 4 St.
    W. Islip, NY 11795
18. Morgan, Dept. A03K11
    915 E. Ky.
    Louisville, KY 40204
19. Antique Trunk Supply Co.
    3706 W. 169 St.
    Cleveland, OH 44111
20. J & S Co.
    PO Box 4840
    Chattanooga, TN 37405
21. Sierra Studios
    PO Box 1005
    Oak Park, IL 60304
22. Paul W. Bowser
    1618 W. Main St.
    New Lebanon, OH 45345
23. Les Gould
    391 Tremont Pl.
    Orange, NJ 07050
24. The Genealogical Helper
    526 N. Main St.
    Logan, UT 84321
25. Mike Wells
    30½ W. Wheelock St.
    Hanover, NH 03755
26. The Bedpost
    RD 1, Box 155
    Pen Argyl, PA 18072

27. Schoepfer Eyes
    138 W. 31 St.
    New York, NY 10001
28. Wood & Leather Craft
    RD 1
    Long Eddy, NY 12760
29. Same address as #1
30. Constantine
    2050 Eastchester Rd.
    Bronx, NY 10461
31. Whittemore-Durgin
    Box H2065
    Hanover, NH 02339
32. PECO
    PO Box 777
    Smithville, TX 78957
33. Replica Products
    610 57 St.
    Vienna, WV 26105
34. Trans World Trading Co.
    509 S. Cross
    Robinson, IL 62454
35. Appraisers Association of America, Inc.
    60 East 42 St.
    New York, NY 10017
    (NOTE: a Membership Directory is available at a cost of $3 to those people seeking the services of a professional appraiser)
36. Mildred E. Webster
    Box 37114
    Los Angeles, CA 90037
37. Adams Antiques
    426 Main Ave.
    Northport, AL 35476

    Harris Woodcarving
    120 E. Main St.
    Falconer, NY 14733

    John Martin Antiques
    Route 3
    Clarksville, GA 30523

    Sack Conservation Co., Inc.
    15 E. 57 St.
    New York, NY 10022
38. Doll & Craft World
    125 8 St.
    Brooklyn, NY 11215
39. Waymar, Inc.
    6015 S. Lindbergh
    St. Louis, MO 63123
40. Gaston Wood Finishes, Inc
    3630 E. 10 St.
    Bloomington, IN 47401
41. Seeley's Ceramic Service, Inc.
    9 River St.
    Oneonta, NY 13820
42. Dolls By Rene
    8228 Allport
    Sante Fe Springs, CA 90670
43. Costume Quarterly
    38 Middlesex Dr.
    Brentwood, MO 63144
44. Jeannette Strauss
    3705 Chapel Forge Dr.
    Bowie, MD 20715
45. John J. Mesterhazy
    12917 Westwood Lane
    Omaha, NB 68144
46. Hess Repairs
    200 Park Ave. S.
    New York, NY 10003
47. Williams' Antiques
    Albion, IL 62806
48. BMS Materials
    Box 222
    Windsor, NY 13865
49. Hardwood Grove Mfg.
    Box 200, Rt. 2
    West Fork, AR 72774
50. Pat & Hanks Antiques
    410 Don Tyler
    Dewey, OK 74029
51. DiPonziano & Assoc.
    Box 23356
    San Jose, CA 95153
52. Bill E. Berger
    29 E. 12 St.
    New York, NY 10003
53. Museum Services
    Box 119
    Hingham, MA 02043
54. American Assoc. of Conservators
    1250 E. Ridgewood Ave.
    Ridgewood, NJ 07450
55. Graphics International
    PO Box 13292, Station E
    Oakland, CA 94661
56. Ms. Micheline Masse
    Stock Market Information Services, Inc.
    Montreal, Canada

57. Accelerated Indexing Systems, Inc.
    3346 S. Orchard Dr.
    Bountiful, UT 84010
58. Michael Sissman
    Buttonshop Rd.
    Williamsburg, MA 01096
    (hand-forged hardware)
59. Pandora's Quilt Museum
    2014 Old Philadelphia Pike
    Lancaster, PA 17602
60. Genealogical Bookshelf
    Box 468
    New York, NY 10028
61. John Crary
    RD 1
    Canton, NY 13617
62. W.H.M.
    2686 McAllister
    San Francisco, CA 94118
63. Donna Vernal
    217 E. First
    Waconia, MN 55387
64. Sandy Ritchie
    Rt. 1, Box 17
    Scottsville, VA 24590
65. Clark Mfg. Co.
    Rt. 2
    Raymore, MO 64083
66. Wallin Forge
    Rt. 1, Box 65
    Sparta, KY 41086
67. The Sobys
    Box 180
    W. Springs, IL 60558
68. Irvin Hoover
    RD 1
    Mt. Pleasant Mills, PA, 17853
69. The Canery
    250 Brookstown Ave.
    Winston-Salem, NC 27101
70. Haviland Corner Matching Service
    Box 82
    Belmont, CA 94002
71. Berkley, Inc.
    2011 Hermitage Ave.
    Wheaton, MD 20902
72. Helt's Antiques
    Durhamville, NY 13054

73. Strawflower, Inc.
    801 W. Eldorado
    Decatur, IL 62522
74. House of Antiques
    202 N. 5th St.
    Springfield, IL 62701
75. Helen Lawler
    Rt. 1, Box 334
    Blytheville, AR 72315
76. Antique Hardware Co.
    Box 877
    Redondo Beach, CA 90277
77. Porter Music Box Co.
    5 Mound St.
    Randolph, VT 05060
78. DB Musical Restorations
    230 Lakeview Ave NE
    Atlanta, GA 30305
79. The Shade Tree
    1318 S. Peoria Ave.
    Tulsa, OK 74120
80. Peter Michaels
    1922 South Rd.
    Baltimore, MD 21209
81. Nicholas Fiscina
    20-17 Jackson Ave.
    W. Islip, NY 11795
82. Neumann Miller
    5482 Lakeview
    Yorba Linda, CA 92686
83. Karl Frick
    940 Canon Rd.
    Santa Barbara, CA 93110
84. Doe's Treasures
    Box 6505
    Providence, RI 02940
85. Marleda's
    Box 2308
    San Bernadino, CA 92406
86. Bob McCumber
    201 Carriage Dr.
    Glastonbury, CT 06033
87. Warden's Clock Supply
    103 N. Boling
    Claremont, OK 70017
88. Musical Americana
    354 E. Campbell
    Campbell, CA 95008

89. William D. Gilstrap
Rt. 2
Bevier, MO 63532

90. Vintage Patterns II
5304 Thrasher Dr.
Cincinnati, OH 45239

91. McKenzie Art Restoration Studio
2907 E. Monte Vista Dr.
Tucson, AZ

92. Calligraphic Ink
Crystal City Underground
Arlington, VA 22202

93. Emerson Hardwood Co.
2279 NW Front Ave.
Portland, OR 90710

94. Glass Masters Guild
621 6th Ave.
New York, NY

95. Paul Baron Co.
2825 E. College Ave.
Decatur, GA 30030

96. Grady Stewart
2019 Sansome St.
Philadelphia, PA 19103

97. All-Art Restorers
140 W. 57 St.
New York, NY 10019

98. Rikki's Studio
2256 Coral Way
Miami, FL 33145

99. Mr. William and Co.
14 Garfield Place
Cincinnati, OH 45202

100. Bostonia Furniture Co.
183 Friend St.
Boston, MA 02114

101. Marcey Medgepeth,
Rt. 179
Ringoes, NJ 08551

102. W.B. Lewis
231 Chatham Ave.
Pooler, GA 31322

103. Dorothy Briggs
410 Ethan Allen Ave.
Takoma Park, MD 20012

104. Helene Von Rosenstiel
88 Prospect Park West
Brooklyn, NY 11215

105. Rosemary Evans
9303 McKinney
Loveland, OH 45140

106. Billard's Old Telephones
21710 Regnart Rd.
Cupertino, CA 95014

107. Ritter & Son
Box 907
Campbell, CA 95008

108. Heritage Clocks of Mass.
Box 336
Sturbridge, MA 01566

109. Antique Music Box
1015 S. Teljon
Colorado Springs, CO 80906

110. The Broderick Gallery
119 Allandale St.
Jamaica Plain, MA 02130

111. Howard's Stained Glass
2602 S. 11 St.
Gadsden, AL 35901

112. American Lamp
100 Elm Hill Pk.
Nashville, TN 37210

113. Eleanor Sopp
15144 Chamisal
Ballwin, MO 63011

114. The Yankee Drummer
23 Burnham Rd.
Hudson, NH 03051

115. TEC Specialties
Box 909
Smyrna, GA 30081

116. Modern Technical Tools
Box 681
Hicksville, NY 11801

117. Wedgwood Studio
2522 N 52 St.
Phoenix, AZ 85008

118. Elaine L. Mooza
286 Wilson Ave.
Rumford, RI 02916

119. White's
Box 680
Newberg, OR 97132

120. Jacquelynn's China
4770 N. Oakland Ave.
Milwaukee, WI 53211

121. Oscar Black
1940 Old Taneytown Rd.
Westminster, MD 21157

122. Mrs. Emily Troutman
     325 N. 6 St.
     Reading, PA 19601
123. Bob Depenbrok
     6638 Van Noord Ave.
     No. Hollywood, CA 91606
124. Pie Galinat
     41 Perry St.
     New York, NY 10014
125. Stephen W. Weston
     Winthrop, ME

126. Sam Robins
     8211 Kostner
     Skokie, IL 60076
127. James Broaddus
     1635 S. 4th
     Terre Haute, IN 47802
128. Silver Plated Flatware Matching
     Service
     142 Hampshire Rd.
     Waterloo, IA 50701

Clubs to Join;
Publications to Subscribe to

It is sincerely hoped that you will find this section of the 6th Edition, WALLACE-HOMESTEAD PRICE GUIDE TO ANTIQUES & PATTERN GLASS, useful. Always correspond before sending money, etc. And, don't forget to include a stamped envelope for a speedy answer. We hope that new friendships will be formed and that you will benefit from the information given here. But, we cannot be held responsible for any situation arising between you and any of the organizations listed herein. Want to list your club? Write — we answer all our mail.

1. 1977 Quilt Shop Directory
   (over 200 dealers — $3)
   Box 6722
   Tucson, Arizona 85733
2. Bottle News
   (nice publication — $7.50 yr.)
   Kermit, Texas 79745
3. Doll News
   (UFDC)
   552 W. Lakeshore Dr.
   Lincoln, Nebraska 68528
4. International Postcard Collectors
   6380 Wilshire Blvd., Suite 907
   Los Angeles, Calif. 90048

5. Avon Collectors Club Newsletter
   (Free — 24¢ S.A.S.E.)
   8149 Laurel Grove
   N. Hollywood, Calif. 91605
6. Heisey Collectors of America, Inc.
   PO Box 27
   Newark, Ohio 43055
7. Jugates
   (Pres. & VP Collectibles)
   Box 5322
   Eugene, Oreg. 97405
8. Marble Collectors Society
   (the shootin' kind)
   Box 222
   Trumbull, Conn. 06611
9. American Paperweight Guild
   Box 177
   Atlantic City, N.J. 08404
10. Tin Container Collectors
    Box 4555
    Denver, Colo. 80204
11. American Antiques Art Assoc.
    6213 Joyce Dr.
    Washington, DC 20031
12. National Toothpick Holder Collectors
    7726 Carrleigh Pkwy.
    Springfield, Va. 22152

13. National Carnival Glass Assoc.
    (dues — $4 yearly)
    3142 S. 35 St.
    LaCrosse, Wis. 54601
14. Books on antiques & collectibles
    (free list)
    Wallace-Homestead Book Co.
    1912 Grand Ave
    Des Moines, Iowa 50305
15. Goebel Collectors' Club
    (Hummel figurines)
    105 White Plains Rd.
    Tarrytown, N.Y. 10591
16. Genealogical Helper
    (fine publication — $11 yr.)
    526 Main St
    Logan, Utah 84321
17. Belleek Collector's Newsletter
    (quarterly — $10 yr.)
    Box 371
    La Mesa, Calif. 92041
18. Lithopane Collectors Club
    2032 Robinwood
    Toledo, Ohio 43620
19. The Coin Slot ($20 yearly)
    (antique coin amusements magazine)
    Box 612
    Wheatridge, Colo. 80033
20. Genealogical Bookshelf
    Box 468
    New York, N.Y. 10028
21. Accelerated Indexing Systems, Inc.
    3346 S. Orchard Dr.
    Bountiful, Utah 84010
    (consulting services on Genealogy, Paleography, Demography)
22. Stein Collectors International
    PO Box 16326
    St. Paul, Minn. 55116
23. Antique Bottle Collecting (British)
    Chapel House Farm
    Newport Rd.
    Albrighton, NR. Wolverhampton
    Staffordshire, England
24. Collectibles Monthly ($5 per year)
    PO Box 2023
    York, Pa. 17405
25. Political Collector ($4.50 per year)
    503 Madison
    York, Pa. 17404

26. Scout Memorabilia
    1000 Golfview
    Glenview, Ill. 60025
27. Old Toy Soldier Newsletter
    209 N. Lombard
    Oak Park, Ill. 60302
28. World's Fair Collectors Society
    148 Poplar
    Garden City, N.Y. 11530
29. Antique Valentines Association
    PO Box 288
    Colts Neck, N.J. 07722
30. Nat'l. Assoc. of Paper & Advertising
    Collectors
    Box 471
    Columbia, Pa. 17512
31. Music Box Society
    Box 202, Rt. 3
    Morgantown, Ind. 96160
32. American Graniteware Assoc.
    Box 65
    Downers Grove, Ill. 60515
33. Universal Autograph Collectors Club
    PO Box 467
    Rockville Centre, N.Y. 11571
34. Bottle Opener Collectors
    c/o Don Bull
    63 October Lane
    Trumbull, Conn. 06611
35. Cloisonne Collectors Club
    PO Box 48248
    Los Angeles, Calif. 90048
36. Paper Dolls: PDQ
    3135 Oakcrest Dr.
    Hollywood, Calif. 90068
37. Elongated Coin Collectors
    c/o John Spadone
    4872 NW 171 Terr.
    Miami, Fla.
38. Antique Valentines Assoc.
    PO Box 178
    Marlboro, N.J. 07746
39. Gumball Vendor
    Box 758
    Kentfield, Calif. 94904
40. The Oriental Journal
    Box 94
    Little Neck, N.Y. 11363

41. Paper Doll News Letter
    Box O, Buckland Station
    Manchester, Conn. 06040
42. International Rose O'Neill Club
    Branson, Mo.
43. American Cut Glass Assoc.
    Box 4481
    Huntsville, Ala. 35802
44. Rathkamp Matchcover Society
    638 Stark Dr.
    Mt. Pleasant, Tex. 75455
45. Toothpick Holder Collectors
    c/o J. Ender
    Red Arrow H'way
    Sawyer, Mich.
46. Whistle Collectors
    c/o R.J. Fornwalt
    GPO Box 1807
    New York, N.Y. 10001
47. Animal License Collectors
    c/o Karen Rose
    4420 Wisconsin
    Tampa, Fla. 33616
48. Sugar Packet Collectors
    c/o Harold Bearce
    603 E 105 St.
    Kansas City, Mo.
49. Spark Club Collectors
    Box 2229
    Ann Arbor, Mich. 48106
50. Military Vehicle Collectors Club
    Box 33697
    Thornton, Colo. 80233
51. Pencil Collectors Society
    603 E 105 St.
    Kansas City, Mo. 64131
52. Hatpin & Hatpin Holders Collectors
    15237 Chanera Ave.
    Gardena, Calif. 90249
53. Paperweight News
    761 Chestnut St.
    Santa Cruz, Calif. 95060
54. "Hummel" Collectors Club
    Box 257
    Yardley, Pa. 19067
55. Pen Collectors
    Box 413
    Clearwater, Fla. 33517
56. Political Collectors Newspaper
    503 Madison Ave.
    York, Pa. 17404
57. Convertible Lovers (autos) of America,
    Ltd.
    Box 187
    Center Rutland, Vt. 05736
58. Human Hair Jewelry, RJF
    GPO Box 1807
    New York, N.Y. 10001
59. American Philatelist (stamp collecting)
    5932 N 14th Place
    Phoenix, Ariz. 85014
60. Antique Phonograph Monthly
    3400 Snyder Ave.
    Brooklyn, N.Y. 11203
61. Military Collectors News
    Box 7582
    Tulsa, Okla. 74105
62. Quilters Newsletter
    Box 394
    Wheat Ridge, Colo. 80033

For a more complete list of clubs, try Robert D. Connolly's, *The New Collectors Directory*, PO Box 1275, San Luis Obispo, Calif. 93406. Also, Bob's *Paper Collectibles* is worthy of note if you're into autographs, books, labels, etc. Available from Books Americana, Florence, Alabama.

Acknowledgments

"Thanks!" to John A. Shuman III of Pottstown, Pennsylvania, for his fine photography. John's *Art Glass Sampler,* a pictorial guide to fifty-seven diversified types of Art Glass from around the world is well worth $12.95. A price guide is also available. It's a Wallace-Homestead publication. Those of us in this industry who know of what we speak all agree that the *Art Glass Sampler* is an exceptionally fine book with beautiful photographs and well-researched material.

Once again we'd like to thank the following people, firms, and institutions for all their help in making the Seventh Edition of the *Wallace-Homestead Price Guide to Antiques and Pattern Glass,* the BEST price guide on the market today.

The Houston Antique Museum, Chattanooga, Tennessee
The McClung Museum, Knoxville, Tennessee
The Bradford Exchange, Chicago, Illinois
Poor Richard's Antiques, Pensacola, Florida
The Collector's Haven, Panama City, Florida
The Franklin Mint, Franklin Center, Pennsylvania
Brown Pelican Antiques, Panama City, Florida
The Gallery of Art, Panama City, Florida
The Clock & Gift Shop, Panama City, Florida
Fowler's Trade Mart, Panama City, Florida
Panama City Antiques, Etc., Panama City, Florida
Euna's Antiques & Gifts, Panama City, Florida
Doll & Craft World, Brooklyn, New York
Bottle News, Kermit, Texas
American Collector, Kermit, Texas
The Yesterday Shop, Panama City, Florida
Richard R. Corser, Phelps, New York
Robert G. Hall, Dover-Foxcroft, Maine

Robert & Cynthia Baker, Providence, Rhode Island
Glentiques, Ltd., Glenford, New York
Little Hundred Gallery, Charlotte, North Carolina
William L. Scolnik, Paramus, New Jersey
Elmwood Record Sales, Elmwood, Connecticut
Wilbur S. Munyon, Van Nuys, California
Ken & Esther Owings, Memphis, Tennessee
Sage House Antiques, Blandford, Massachusetts
Donn Pearlman, Skokie, Illinois
Mrs. Louise A. Sarni, Pottstown, Pennsylvania
Mrs. Nancy S. Tunnicliffe, Pottstown, Pennsylvania
Mr. & Mrs. William J. Weiss, Pottstown, Pennsylvania
Mr. William O'Brien, Dunmore Pennsylvania
Mrs. Jane Clymer, Bethlehem, Pennsylvania
Mrs. Ann Reinert, Macungie, Pennsylvania
Mrs. Marion T. Hunter, Spring City, Pennsylvania
Mr. Richard Wright, Spring City, Pennsylvania
Mr. Barton L. Seltmann, Pottstown, Pennsylvania
James S. Maxwell, Sr., Alexandria, Virginia
Peter Wienstein, Montreal, Quebec, Canada
Bob's Place, Clinton, Iowa
Lawson's Antiques, Salem, Illinois
Kramer Gallery, St. Paul, Minnesota
Frances Edwards Antiques, Algonquin, Illinois
The Liberty Tool Company, Liberty Village, Maine
Wee Barn Antiques, Thomaston, Maine
Simpson's Antiques, New London, New Hampshire
Eagle's Nest Antiques, Rutland, Vermont
Bill Egleston, Inc., Marshalltown, Iowa
Warren Nussbaum, Flushing, New York
Kandis, Ripon, California
Mark L. Pahlow, Los Angeles, California
Frank D. Guarino, De Bary, Florida
Old Piano Roll Auction, Los Angeles, California
Harvey Miller, Tucson, Arizona
Mort Packman, Philadelphia, Pennsylvania
Jack M. Kline, Indianapolis, Indiana
Walt Johnson's Extravaganza, Des Moines, Iowa
Nancy Johnson's The Library, Des Moines, Iowa
Don Brown's Lamplighter Books, Leon, Iowa
And the entire staff, Wallace-Homestead Book Company, Des Moines, Iowa.

Section of General Antiques

ABC (Alphabet) Plates

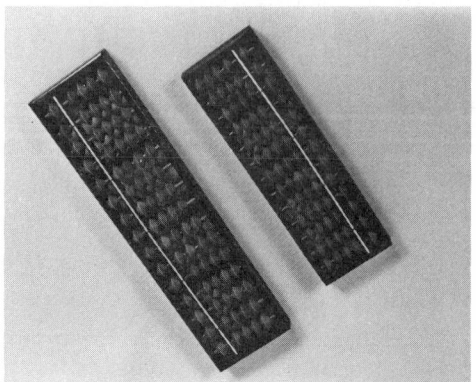

Abacus

ABC (Alphabet) Plates

These plates were made for children, late 19th, early 20th century. The alphabet was around the border, the center decorations consisting of proverbs, animals, etc. They were made of glass, ceramics, tin, pewter. Now being reproduced in glass.

Ceramic:
Black-faced children, riddle on front (ill.)	$ 43 -	53
Brownies, Palmer Cox, 1896	37 -	47
Capitol, Washington, D.C.	30 -	40
Clock face center	40 -	50
Dick Whittington and his Cat	26 -	36
Franklin proverbs (Meakin)	38 -	48
Punch and Judy (Allerton & Co.)	38 -	48

Glass:
Elephant center, 6"	28 -	38
Frosted Stork, Iowa City	40 -	50
Hen and chicks	34 -	44
Little Bo Peep	30 -	40
Star center	25 -	35

Pewter:
Pigs-in-Pen	55 -	65
Tower of London, dated 1805	80 -	85

Tin:
Aesop's Fable; Fox and Crow	26 -	36
Hey Diddle Diddle	29 -	38
Jumbo	40 -	50
Mary Had a Little Lamb	38 -	48
Who Killed Cock Robin	48 -	58

Abacus

Used by the Chinese for centuries, it's simply a counting frame with movable wooden beads. The older ones are collectible today.

Teakwood frame & beads, brass rods	$ 28 -	38
Ornate teakwood frame inlaid with mother-of-pearl, beads, brass rods (ill.)	30 -	40
Ebony frame and beads, brass rods (ill.)	28 -	38

Adams China

William Adams & Sons were famous for their American scenes on blue and pink china. The firm was founded in the 1650s at Stoke-on-Trent, England, and is still in business. Their "Dr. Syntax" series is well known.

Bowl, Chinese decor, 11½" diameter	$ 50 -	60
Cup/saucer, Rose pattern, late (ill.)	60 -	70
Cup/saucer, pink, floral scenes	60 -	70
Cup plate, vegetables, marked Adams on bottom	40 -	50
Dish, vegetable, Schenectady on Mohawk River, pink, 10" diameter	100 -	120

Adams China

Plate, bird, by James Audubon,
  black-on-white, 10½" diameter   65 - 75
Plate, Columbus Landing, blue/
  pink, 9" diameter . . . .   80 - 90
Plate, view near Conway, N.H.,
  9" diameter . . . .   80 - 90
Platter, Lake Champlain, pink,
  14" diameter . . . .   115 - 140
Tureen, soup, farm scene blue/
  white, Ironstone . . . .   98 - 115

Adams Rose Pattern China

Adams Rose Pattern China

Decorated with bright red roses and green leaves on a white background, made by various members of the Adams family from 1820 on; still in business. In the early 1900s a variation of the original was made with a darker background—almost a "dirty" white. This type is worth about one-half the older type. We'll refer to the newer as Late. Various marks, all with word Adams; also,

after 1891 Made in England was added. Earlier pieces have only England.

Bowl, 7" diameter, late	$ 50 - 60
Cracker jar, black basalt, silver lid and bail, classical scenes . . .	135 - 150
Creamer	
a. Early	160 - 170
b. Late	85 - 95
Cup/saucer, scalloped edge	
a. Early	135 - 150
b. Late, plain edge	70 - 80
Pitcher, milk (ill.), 16" high	800 - 850
Plate, 10" diameter, winter scene, holly border	90 - 110
Sugar bowl, 6¼" high	
a. Early, "wood"	185 - 200
b. Late	100 - 110
Teapot	
a. Early, 8"	230 - 265
b. Late, 5"	115 - 130

Advertising Items

Advertising Items

Chromolithography, the process of printing on tin, and the development of celluloid for buttons and mirrors created a new field for advertisers at the turn of the century. Most items were given away free to customers.

Booklets:
Barker's (liniment)
  "Komic" Picture
  Souvenir . . . . $ 4 - 6
Hartman Magazine of
  Health . . . .   4 - 6
Pe-Ru-Na coloring
  book . . . .   5 - 8
Buttons:
Campbell Soup,
  celluloid . . . .   5 - 7
Cascaret, "All going
  out - - -," celluloid . .   14 - 20
Ceresota Flour,
  celluloid . . . .   4 - 6
Studebaker, "Used
  the world over,"
  celluloid . . . .   5 - 9

21   (continued)

Whitehead & Hoag	
Co., celluloid	4 - 7

Clickers:

Buster Brown Shoes .	5 - 8
Dr. Pepper (with celluloid button) . . .	27 - 35
H.J. Heinz Co.	4 - 7
Hires Root Beer	4 - 6
Lava Soap	5 - 7

Postcards:

The postcard became legal mailing matter in the 1870s. Every manufacturer in the world used them to advertise their products. The value depends on the subject matter.

Containers:

Adams Spearmint Chewing Gum, tin .	22 - 28
Lucky Strike cigarette box, tin	6 - 9
Roly-Poly tobacco, tin	190+
Weideman coffee, tin .	5 - 7
Whitman's candy box, tin (ill.)	9- -14

Mirrors:

Ballard's Obelisk (flour)	10 - 15
Bell Roasted Coffee . .	13 - 16
Bromo-Seltzer	27 - 35
Gillette Safety Razors	11 - 15
Holland Furnaces . . .	13 - 16
Moller Pianos & Organs	8 - 13
Shawmut Rubbers . . .	8 - 12
Standard Oil Company	9 - 14
Worth Hats	14 - 18

Paperweights:

Burr & Co., coach builders, glass	13 - 17
Crawford Shoes, glass	11 - 16
Firestone Tires, glass	11 - 18
Plume & Atwood Mfg. Co., glass	11 - 16

Paper Items:

Cigar box labels, any make	1 - 2 each
Herrick's Pills & Plasters, wall poster	11 - 17
Magazine advertisements, 1920s-1930s	50¢ - 75¢ each
Maltine, bookmark . .	5 - 8
Pearline Pills	3 - 5
Piper-Heidsieck notebook	4 - 6
RCA fan, cardboard .	8 - 11
Wrigley's Gum calendar, cardboard, 1927	5 - 8

Yellow Kid Ginger	
Wafers, box labels .	16 - 24 each

Metal Signs:

Armour Meats, 13" x 19"	60 - 70
Cherry Sparkle, 6" x 13"	12 - 19
Dr. Brown's Cel-Ray, 5" x 10"	8 - 12
Drink Orange Crush, 16" x 22"	17 - 23
Gillette Safety Razors, 6" x 13" . . .	9 - 15
Pepsums Stomach Soothers, 5" x 9" . .	13 - 20
Sen-Sen Chewing Gum, 6" x 6"	33 - 40

Agata Glass

Made in 1887 by the New England Glass Company, for less than a year. The glass item to be ornamented was first coated with a metallic stain or mineral color (of color desired) then spattered with alcohol, benzene or naphtha. When this evaporated, it left a mottled surface on the glassware. Don't confuse the genuine with a marbled ware called Akro Agate.

Bowl, 3" high	$1,750 - 2,200
Celery vase, pink	1,600 - 1,800
Cruet, multi-mottling	1,650 - 1,800
Sugar bowl, blue/green, 4½" high	1,900 - 2,100
Toothpick holder, four way . .	850 - 1,000
Tumbler, pink	800 - 950
Vase, lily, 11½"	1,500 - 1,700

Agate Glass

Agate Glass

Eugene Rousseau originated this glass in the 1870s; later it was made by other companies. Gold and other metallic oxides were used in the glass batch to achieve the agate effect.

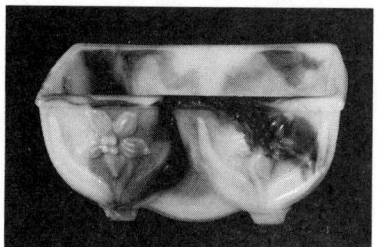
Akro Agate Glass

Akro Agate Glass

The Akro Agate Glass Company didn't get around to making glass until 1932. Before that, in 1911, they were jobbers for a marble company in Ohio. In 1914 they moved to Clarksburg, West Virginia, and made their own marbles. They made various types of glass in several colors until they went out of business in the late 1940s.

Ashtray, leaf-shaped	$ 11 -	17
Bowl, green slag	13 -	23
Cigarette holder	10 -	18
Creamer, 3″ high, blue	13 -	24
Dish, shell-shaped, green	8 -	16
Match holder, green, white, black	15 -	20
Planter, blue/white (ill.)	18 -	25
Powder jar, dog, white	27 -	35
Tumbler, green/white	15 -	24
Vase, green and white	19 -	27
Vase, small, orange and white	16 -	21
Vase, blue, 6″ high	15 -	24

Albums

Albums

Cherished photographs were kept in ornate albums in the mid-to-late Victorian era. Usually velvet-covered with metal hinges.

Average price . . . . $55 - 70

Alcohol Collectibles

"Demon Rum," Carrie Nation — today, jugs, bottles, advertising material — all being collected, and the older the better.

Whiskey jug, Doulton, Lambeth, England, 1854 (ill.)	$ 90 - 100	
Tin advertising sign, "Hampton's Rye," early 1900s	35 -	45
Jack Daniel advertising folder (ill.)	50¢ -	1

Albums

23

(continued)

Alcohol Collectibles

Brown-Forman Distillers
  decanter w/stopper, late 1800s   55 - 65
Old Tucker decanter, late 1800s .   68 - 75
Wooden whiskey case, Hanover
  Rye, Cincinnati, late 1800s ...   28 - 38
Old Crow paper fan, collapsible
  type ....   6 - 9
Bacardi rum, 1 gallon, in wicker
  container, 1878, Cuba ....   45 - 55
"Hand" vase, Brown-Forman,
  Louisville, late 1800s ....   45 - 55
Metal serving tray, Hayner's
  Distillery, 1879 ....   35 - 45
Hanover Rye "shot" glass
  (salesman's sample) ....   15 - 23
Cloth tape measure, "No. 7 Gin,"
  late 1800s ....   5 - 9

Alexandrite Glass

Thomas Webb & Sons, England, made this beautiful glass at the beginning of the 20th century. It shades from pale yellow to rose, then to blue. Stevens & Williams, England also produced it, using the cut-through method to achieve their effect. A ware somewhat similar to the above also was made by Moser of Carlsbad, Czechoslovakia.

Goblet, amethyst, signed
  Moser .... $ 150 - 200
Match holder, 2½" diameter,
  signed Webb ....   650 - 750
Plate, 6", 7" diameter, Webb .   700 - 800
Plate, 8" diameter, signed
  Moser ....   100 - 125
Rose bowl, 2" diameter,
  fuchsia, signed Webb ..... 1,400 - 1,750
Toothpick holder, ITP, amber,
  Webb .... 1,550 - 1,800
Wine, 3½" high, Webb .....   225 - 260
Wine, 4" high, Stevens &
  Williams ....   225 - 260

Almanacs

Great fun to collect and even more fun to read. What didn't our illustrious ancestors believe in?

Almanacs

Centaur Almanac, 1874, pub-
  lished by J.B. Rose, New York $ 10 - 15
Morning, Noon & Night, 1871-2,
  P.H. Drake & Co's Plantation
  Bitters ....   12 - 19
Ayer's American Almanac, 1876,
  published by Dr. J.C. Ayer &
  Co. (ill.) ....   15 - 25
Vinegar Bitters Almanac, 1879 ..   10 - 15
The Gardener's Almanac, 1852,
  by Comstock, Ferre & Co.,
  Connecticut ....   14 - 23
Leavitt's Farmer's Almanac,
  1893, Concord, N.H. ....   15 - 25
New England Almanack, 1795,
  New London ....   26 - 37
Old Farmer's Almanack, 1853,
  published by Jenks, Hickling
  & Swan ....   22 - 32
Old Farmer's Almanac (no 'k'),
  1868, published by Brewer
  & Tileston ....   9 - 14
Poor Richard's Almanac, 1834,
  Tobias Ostrander ....   20 - 30
B.F. Goodrich Farmer's
  Handbook and Almanac, 1948   7 - 15
Farmer's Almanac, 1849, Boston   12 - 18
Watkins Almanac and Home
  Book, 1939 ....   7 - 15
Miner's Almanac, 1873,
  Pittsburgh ....   9 - 17
Pocket Almanac and Account
  Book, by Brown's Iron
  Bitters, 1889 ....   8 - 16
Ford Home Almanac and Facts
  Book, 1939, Ford Motor Co. ..   6 - 12
Tarrytown Argus Almanac, 1874   8 - 16
Dr. Miles New Weather Almanac
  and Hand Book, Miles
  Laboratory, 1937 ....   6 - 12
Rawleigh's Good Health Guide
  Almanac Cook Book, 1927 ...   8 - 16
The Ladies' Birthday Almanac,
  1960 (ill.) ....   7 - 15

Amberina

Amberina

Amberina

Patented in 1883 for the Libbey brothers and their New England Glass Company, Amberina was made by placing a small amount of gold in a transparent amber glass batch. The article was formed, then allowed to cool below a glowing red heat; then specific parts were reheated at the glory hole. This caused the finished product to be shaded from amber to ruby red. Genuine Amberina is scarce today. "ITP" means Inverted Thumbprint. Lots of repros!

Art glass basket	$ 700 -	800
Bowl, diamond optic, 4¼" dia.	170 -	195
Bowl, diamond-quilted, 4½" dia.	165 -	195
Bowl, finger, ruffled, 4" dia. . .	195 -	220
Bowl, fluted, applied handles, 4¾" dia.	245 -	285
Castor, pickle, ITP, footed silver plateholder	500 -	575
Candlesticks, pair, 14" high . .	240 -	285

Celery, diamond-quilted, 6" high	290 -	340
Celery, daisy & button, 5" high	285 -	340
Compote, wafer base, signed "Libbey," 8" dia.	370 -	425
Compote, diamond optic, 8" dia.	340 -	370
Creamer, ITP, clear handle, 4½" high	195 -	275
Creamer, daisy & button, 6" high (ill.)	180 -	190
Creamer, amber handle, 4½" high	220 -	260
Cruet, ITP, cut glass stopper, 7" high	225 -	245
Cruet, diamond-quilted, c.g. stopper, 6¾" high	275 -	310
Cup/saucer, both signed "Libbey"	160 -	195
Cup, punch, set of 12, all signed "Libbey"	1,700 -	1,950
Cup, punch, baby ITP	115 -	130
Cup, punch, herringbone, clear handle	140 -	155
Decanter, 14½" high, blown glass stopper	450 -	575
Decanter, 12½" high, ITP, blown glass stopper	430 -	465
Decanter, 12" high, cut glass stopper	470 -	495
Mug, amber handle	110 -	135
Mug, swirled, diamond, clear handle	140 -	220
Mug, child's, clear handle . . .	90 -	100
Parfait, ITP	145 -	195
Pitcher, water, applied rope handle, 9" high	400 -	450
Pitcher, water, clear handle, fuchsia, 9½" high	220 -	275
Pitcher, milk, ITP, 10" high . .	240 -	295
Pitcher, diamond-quilted, 9¾" high, clear handle	250 -	295
Pitcher, applied, twisted handle, diamond optic, 9" high	295 -	350
Plate, 7½" dia.	100 -	115
Plate, diamond-quilted, 7¼" dia.	115 -	130
Plate, fluted edge, signed "Libbey" in pontil	135 -	175
Salt/pepper shakers, 4" high, pewter tops	185 -	210
Salt/pepper shakers, 4½" high, ITP, pewter tops	220 -	245
Salt/pepper shakers, 4" high, expanded diamond, p. tops	215 -	230
Salt, master, 1½" high, ruffled edge	120 -	140
Salt, master, 1½" high, diamond-quilted	120 -	140

(continued)

Sauce, daisy & button, 4¼" dia., expanded diamond . . .	140 -	180
Sauce, diamond-quilted, 4½" dia.	145 -	195
Sauce, diamond optic, 4½" dia.	120 -	180
Sugar bowl, 5" high, double handles, ITP	325 -	360
Sugar bowl, 4¾" high, diamond-quilted	315 -	345
Sugar bowl, 4½" high, single handle	310 -	325
Sugar bowl, 4½" high, double handles	300 -	315
Toothpick holder, daisy & button, 3" high	170 -	190
Toothpick holder, diamond-quilted, 3¼" high	185 -	210
Toothpick holder, ITP, 3½" high	190 -	215
Toothpick holder, trefoil, 3½" high	215 -	240
Tumbler, 4¼" high	95 -	115
Tumbler, diamond-quilted, 4" high	115 -	140
Tumbler, baby ITP, 3¾" high	90 -	110
Tumbler, expanded diamond, 4" high	92 -	125
Tumbler, enameled flowers, 4¼" high	110 -	125
Vase, fuchsia, signed "Libbey," 10" high	310 -	340
Vase, ITP, 9" high	165 -	180
Vase, lily-shaped, in silver plateholder, 7½" high	315 -	340
Vase, Jack-in-the-pulpit, signed "Libbey," 14½" high	400 -	425
Vase, ribbed, 10" high	325 -	355
Vase, hobnail, 7¼" high.	275 -	315
Vase, blown, with ribs, applied amber glass, rigaree at the neck (ill.)	165 -	185

Amethyst Glass

Amethyst Glass

A dark purple glass. Sandwich made a lot of it after the Civil War.

Barber bottle, castle scene, pewter cap	$ 60 -	68
Bowl, finger, rough pontil, 6" dia.	20 -	30
Candleholders, pair, 7" high	30 -	40
Compote, clear stem, 6½" high . .	22 -	32
Dish, bird decor, 5" dia.	17 -	25

Flask, cornucopia/eagle, rough pontil, one-half pint, 5" high . .	145 - 160
Lamp, kerosene-type, 8" high, original brass collar	52 - 62
Mug, child's, Little Bo Peep, 4" high, handled	42 - 60
Paperweight, triangular, floral enamels, 5½" long (ill.)	19 - 28
Pitcher, water, enameled flowers, ferns, 6" high	37 - 48
Plate, 6" dia., Mary Gregory	100 - 125
Sauce, Millersburg, 2½" deep . . .	32 - 44
Vase, enameled flowers, 5" high, pair	55 - 70
Vase, enameled design, possibly Sandwich	65 - 75
Vase, etched flowers, 7" high . . .	42 - 52
Wine, bell-shaped, clear stem, 3½" high, set of 6	48 - 58

Amphora

A two-handled Greek vessel for holding wine, oil, etc. Originally made in 720 to 1200 in Rhineland villages as containers for wine which was exported to Britain and certain Baltic countries. What you find today in shops was made by Teplitz in Germany in the late 1800s.

Basket, flowers in relief, 7½" high, signed	$210 - 250
Urn, 15" high, green/gold, blue trim, signed "Amphora"	250 - 275
Urn, applied flowers, gold handles, 9" high	168 - 182
Vase, applied flowers, gray/white, gold handles, 9" high	130 - 165
Vase, gold/green, pink leaf decor, signed "Amphora" with crown	140 - 175
Vase, brown/green, jewel trim, 11¼" high	115 - 130
Vase, yellow flowers, 7¾" high, signed	180 - 220
Vase, floral decor, 8½" high, signed "Amphora" with crown	210 - 240
Vase, red/white/green, flowers, 10" high	110 - 125

Andirons

Dogs, as they were called in the earlier days, were usually made of wrought iron. Blacksmiths made them to personal order for the housewife. Brass andirons were known in America as early as 1740; even Paul Revere made a few.

Brass, ball top, 19th century, pair	$250 - 300
Brass, Georgian, pair, 17" high . .	550 - 625

Andirons

Brass, poodles, early 19th
century, pair . . . . 350 - 400
Wrought iron, 15" high, hand-
forged, early 19th century, pair 140 - 190
Wrought iron, 17" high, ring top,
late 18th century (ill.) . . . . 110 - 130

Animal Collectibles

Collectors are finding everything from
elephant-feet wastebaskets to stuffed mice.
The older the better.

Plaster lion on teakwood
pedestal, 9½" high, late
1800s (ill.) . . . . $ 28 - 40
Wastebasket made from
elephant's foot, early 20th
century . . . . 225 - 265
Tiger's skin, complete with
head and paws, late 1800s . 1,200 - 1,500
Zebra hide, felt-lined . . . . 350 - 450
Stuffed mongoose "attack-
ing" stuffed cobra . . . . 120 - 140
Stuffed moose head . . . . 300 - 400
Stuffed water buffalo's head,
47" rack . . . . 550 - 700
Brass lion's head door
knocker, mid-1800s . . . . . . 135 - 185

Animal Dishes (Covered)

These covered dishes were made in clear,
colored, and opal (milk) glass; also of pottery,
usually from the Staffordshire district,
England. They've been around for over 200
years and have been reproduced in every size
and shape without exception. Prices shown
are for the old and genuine. One of the finest
collections in the United States is at the
Houston Museum, Chattanooga, Tennessee.

Cat, white milk glass . . . . $160 - 185
Camel, 2 humps, white milk glass 130 - 165
Chick-in-egg-in-sleigh, white milk
glass . . . . 75 - 95
Cow-shape cover, caramel slag
(goes over butter) . . . . 140 - 170
Dog, purple slag . . . . 125 - 150
Ducks; clear glass, 6½" . . . . 65 - 75
frosted glass, 6½" . . . . 75 - 85
milk glass, white, 5" . . . . 88 - 110
multicolored (ill.) . . . . 130 - 150
Eagle, milk glass . . . . 100 - 125
Fish on skiff, 7" diameter,
milk glass . . . . 55 - 75
Hens, colored glass:
5" and 6", dark amber and
light amber . . . . 125 - 175
6½" and 7" diameter, frosted . 65 - 80
Hens, milk glass:
5", white, Bakewell, Pears
cross on bottom, wicker nest . . 58 - 70
5", white with blue head (ill.) . . 65 - 80
7", white, lacy nest . . . . 170 - 195
7", white, lacy nest, caramel
flecked . . . . 170 - 185
Lamb, hexagon base, white . . . . 70 - 80
Quail, white milk glass . . . . 72 - 82
Rabbits; milk glass, 5½"
same, mule-eared . . . . 85 - 110
Robin on nest, basketweave base,
white milk glass . . . . 128 - 140
Swans:
5", blue . . . . 110 - 125
6", Staffordshire . . . . 255 - 295
7", Sandwich milk glass, pr. . . 325 - 350
Turkey, hen, 9", Leeds . . . . 280 - 320

Animal Collectibles

Animal Dishes (Covered)

"Apostle" Pitcher

"Apostle" Pitchers

Embossed figures of the Apostles set within Gothic window frames, they were first made at Creussen, Germany, in the 17th century. Daniel Greatbach made one of Parian ware for the American Pottery Company, Jersey City. An Apostle cuspidor was made by the Congress Hill Pottery Company about the same time.

Cuspidor	$ 275 - 350
Pitcher, 17th century (ill.) ...	1,400 - 1,600
Pitcher, Parian ware, American	475 - 525

"Apostle" Spoons

Of all spoon designs, this is the most famous. In the 15th and 16th centuries the first ones were made of pewter and silver. At the tip of each spoon was the figure of an Apostle. 12 Apostles and 1 spoon of Jesus made a set. Few sets of the original exist, but many reproductions, adaptations, what-have-you, are on the market today. Reproductions were first made in the 1850s. Careful!

Apothecary Collectibles

Apothecary funnel, copper, has hanging ring, 9" high	$ 16 -	27
Apothecary funnel, glass, 7½" high	7 -	12
Breast pump, has rubber suction ball, 4" high	3 -	8
Cork press, lever-type, 4 different sizes, 9" long	45 -	60
Counter scale, 2 large brass pans, full set of weights	130 -	150
Display case, tin/wood, 3 drawers	60 -	85
Drug mill, looks like small coffee grinder	45 -	55

Apothecary Collectibles

Hand scale, in wooden box, full set of weights	20 -	30
Hydrometer jar, hand blown, 12" high	8 -	15
Mentholatum lamp, brass, glass bowl, 6½" high	12 -	19
Mortar and pestle, brass	75 -	85
Mortar and pestle, porcelain (ill.) .	20 -	30
Pill roller, wood, 3" dia.	15 -	20
Sterlizer, tin, looks like a coffee percolater, 8" high	18 -	25

Appliances

Appliances

Some go back into the early 1800s, such as the wooden clothes wringer. Others came into vogue at the turn of the century, such as the hand-operated vacuum cleaner.

These old appliances are being collected today as decorative items for kitchen, den, whatever.

Clothes wringer, hand-made, early 1800s (ill.)	$ 40 -	50
Electric iron, early 1900s	15 -	20
Electric fan, GE, 1915, table model, still runs	25 -	35
Vacuum cleaner, hand-operated .	30 -	37
Washing machine, hand-operated, wooden, late 1800s ..	52 -	62

Art Deco

Art Deco or Art Moderne was a style beginning after the Paris Exposition of 1925.

Art Deco

It was the first "modern design," Lincoln's Zephyr being a classic example. It has contrasting colors and wild lines, etc. It was popular until World War II and is now coming back into vogue.

Compote, metal/glass, 19″ high (ill.)	$115 - 140
Cup, handled, green/blue, 3½″ high	21 - 31
Desk clock, marble and cloisonne, luminous hands	50 - 60
Dressing table set, cameo glass, inlaid silver, nudes, 1931	95 - 110
Elephant head incense burner	15 - 23
Figurine, ape in "thinking" pose, bronze, 12″ high	125 - 150
Figurine, dancing girl, partially nude, bronze, 10″ high	125 - 145
Figurine, lovers, bronze on marble pedestal, French	65 - 80
Lamp, "Dutch silver" (pot metal), kneeling black dancer, glass shade	70 - 80
Lamp, naked man holding nude woman overhead, bronze, glass ball shade	130 - 150

Mirror, hand, 11″ long, nude figure in relief on back	39 - 50
Statuette, tubular metals, cubism design, dated 1934 on bottom	52 - 70
Vase, frosted lion over dead lamb, marble and glass, French 1930s	90 - 110
Vase, black glass, silver holder, Italian, 14″ high	125 - 145
Vase, blue and red geometric design, 16½″ high, French	80 - 90
Wall plaque, glass and cloisonne, nude figures, 8″ × 15″	95 - 110

Art Glass Baskets

During the late 19th and early 20th centuries these beautiful, handmade baskets were always produced by hand and in every type glass. Expensive then, out-of-sight today, the Houston Museum has one of the finest collections in the world. See specific type glass for prices.

Art Glass Sampler

A comprehensive guide written by John A. Shuman III, covers 57 types of art glass with hundreds of photos in b&w, 8 color pages, $12.95. Available from Wallace-Homestead Book Co., 1912 Grand Ave., Des Moines, Iowa, or better bookstores everywhere. A marvelous book and a *must* for any serious art glass collector!

Art Nouveau

Rebelling against the "accepted forms" of art, Art Nouveau was in vogue in the late 1800s, then until just before World War I. Tiffany collectors revived it and today it's highly collectible, being found in metal, wood,

Art Glass Baskets

29

(continued)

Art Nouveau

glass. Surface decoration is one of its identifying marks.

Bookends, nudes, sterling silver, pr.	$ 75 - 90
Bookmark, 2" high	29 - 38
Bowl, flower, Galle style, deep cut	115 - 140
Box, jewelry, footed, sterling silver, 4½" square	50 - 60
Brush, sterling silver (ill.)	95 - 150
Buckle (also brooch), women's profile, silver	23 - 33
Buttonhook, silver, entwining snake, 8" long	20 - 28
Buttonhook, sterling silver (ill.)	45 - 60
Cigarette case, chased copper, birds in relief, enamel-lined	70 - 80
Clock, desk type, nude nymph, in metal case	45 - 55
Figurine, nude male, Dresden porcelain, 14" high	165 - 180
Figurine, dancing figure, bronze, 11" high, marble pedestal	130 - 150
Flask, sterling silver, nude lovers on beach	250 - 300
Inkwell, devil's tail as penholder, bronze, 2½" square	45 - 55
Lamp, nudes holding 2 glass shades, 14" high, electrified	200 - 225
Lamp, young girl holding cigarette, cast iron base, 12" high	65 - 75
Match holder (ill.)	25 - 32
Pin, profile of lovers, copper-on-brass	22 - 32
Pin, angel, brass (ill.)	13 - 20
Pin, girl on horseback, brass (ill.)	15 - 20
Spoons, sterling silver, embossed figures, each	85 - 125
Tray, brass, reclining nude on beach, relief, 15" dia.	75 - 85
Tray, sterling silver, heart-shaped, initialed BHM, fluted rim	95 - 150
Tray, pin, reclining figures on couch, 14" dia.	40 - 50
Vase, amberina-type glass, in holder, 9" high	45 - 55

Art Nouveau

Vase, Tiffany type, iridescent, bronze holder, 14" high	95 - 110
Vase, pewter, autos racing, 13" high	75 - 90
Vase, pottery, flowers & butterflies in relief, 10" high	40 - 48

Audubon Prints

Audubon Prints

Audubon originals, the engravings, are priceless today. The Havell edition, 1827-1838; the "Quadrupeds of America" series in 1844—all highly-collectible today. Many reproductions since 1915. Careful!

All prints listed here are from the Havell and Son edition, London, completed in 1838.

Plate #	Subject	
4	Purple Finch	$ 925 - 975
12	Baltimore Oriole	3,900 - 4,300
25	Song Sparrow	925 - 975
31	White-headed Eagle	4,000 - 4,500
40	American Redstart	925 - 950
51	Red-tailed Hawk	2,900 - 3,200

30

65	Rathbone Warbler ..	900 - 975
74	Indigo Bird	1,600 - 1,800
90	Black-and-White	
	Creeper	800 - 900
101	Raven	3,200 - 3,500
115	Wood Pewee	875 - 950
133	Black Poll Warbler ..	975 - 1,100
139	Field Sparrow	725 - 800
148	Pine Swamp Warbler	825 - 875
155	Black-throated Blue	
	Warbler	875 - 950
164	Tawny Thrush	1,100 - 1,200
179	Wood Wren	800 - 850
187	Boat-tailed Grackle..	2,200 - 2,400
205	Virginia Rail	1,450 - 1,650
211	Great Blue Heron . . .	3,900 - 4,200
232	Hooded Merganser ..	3,000 - 3,400
265	Puff-breasted	
	Sandpiper	1,100 - 1,300
287	Ivory Gull	1,700 - 1,900
311	White Pelican	4,000 - 4,200
333	Green Heron	2,600 - 2,800
367	Band-tailed Pigeon ..	2,000 - 2,100
382	Sharp-tailed Grouse .	3,000 - 3,400
395	Audubon's Warbler .	1,800 - 2,000
401	Red-breasted	
	Merganser	3,600 - 3,800
409	Havell's Tern	1,200 - 1,400
432	Burrowing Owl	2,200 - 2,400

All prints listed here are from the Bien Edition, done in 1860 by Julius Bien in New York. All are full-sized plates.

18	Swallow-tailed Hawk	1,600 - 1,800
34	Barn Owl	2,300 - 2,500
57	Great Crested	
	Flycatcher	375 - 425
90	Yellow Redpoll	450 - 500
124	Lesser Marsh Hen ..	400 - 450
163	Henslow's Bunting ..	375 - 425
189	Song Sparrow	400 - 450
226	Fish Crow	1,500 - 1,650
244	Yellow-breasted Chat	900 - 975
293	Ruffed Grouse	1,800 - 1,900
358	Glossy Ibis	1,600 - 1,850
465	Great Auk	1,900 - 2,200

Austrian, General

Many small potteries produced beautiful porcelain and pottery in Austria during the 19th century, some being financed by money from America; others manufacturing wares with American names only for export to America only. Carlsbad was the center for many of these firms. **Specific firms are listed alphabetically in this Guide.**

Vase, 10¾″ high, flowers,
gilded, handled, "Carlsbad"
(ill.) . . . . $70 - 88

Austrian, General

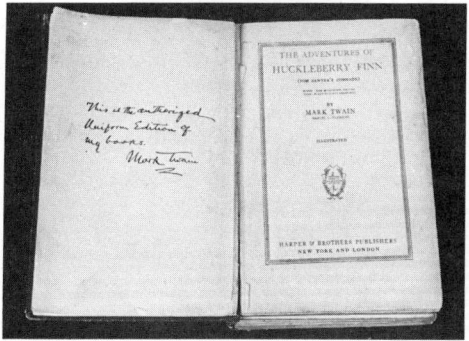

Autographs

Autographs (Philography)

The signatures of "known" people are always in demand by collectors. Keep in mind that governors, presidents, and the like, seldom signed routine documents, leaving this menial task to clerks. Prices quoted here are for genuine signatures only. "Holographs" are letters written entirely by the hand of the signer of the letter. In the case of presidential letters, these are very valuable. A JFK "holograph" would bring upwards of $6,000 today!

Arnold, Benedict (patriot/
traitor, Revolutionary
War) . . . . $ 4,300 - 4,800
Caruso, Enrico, opera star
of the 1920s . . . . 375 - 425
Cody, "Buffalo Bill,"
program signature . . . . . 60 - 70
Coolidge, Calvin, signed
when campaigning
through New England .. 175 - 200
Davis, Jefferson, note
declining invitation to
supper party . . . . 300 - 350

31

(continued)

Eisenhower, Dwight D., note of thanks during World War II	270 -	310
Grant, U.S. giving Sherman final approval to march to the sea	7,000 -	7,800
Grant, Ulysses S., letter of regrets for boy killed during war	650 -	750
Hancock, John, Bendict Arnold's commission as Major General	9,500 - 10,800	
Hancock, John, Benedict Arnold's commission as Major General	9,500 - 10,800	
Hitler, Adolph, signed document (careful of repros here)	1,900+	
Jackson, Andrew, inviting friend to horse race at Hermitage, Nashville . . .	275 -	325
Lincoln, Abraham, note to Union General	900 -	1,200
Lincoln's Gettysburg Address, handwritten copy	60,000 - 70,000	
Lincoln, handwritten letters, 1846, poems to friend	31,000 - 35,000	
Lipton, Thomas, of tea fame, 1713 (ill.)	35 -	45
Revere, Paul, hand-written signed document	70,000 - 75,000	
Roosevelt, Franklin, presidential stationery, to senator, 1935	200 -	250
Roosevelt, Teddy, letter of regrets to banquet invitation	400 -	475
Twain, Mark (if original) . .	850 -	1,000
Washington, George (if all his signatures are as authentic as the beds he was supposed to have slept in, forget it!)		

Automobiles

Automobiles

In 1947 the Antique Automobile Club of America set up a system whereby buses, motorcycles, cars, fire engines, etc., made before 1930 would be classified as authentic antique vehicles. Generally, those cars from 1930 to 1948 are considered Classics. All prices listed here are for autos in "restored" condition.

Apperson, Jack Rabbit runabout, 1914, 6-cylinder	$21,500 - 24,000
Auburn, 6-cylinder touring, 1912	10,500 - 12,000
Auburn, touring, 1917	9,700 - 10,900
Buick, 2-cylinder, chain drive, 1905	12,900 - 16,000
Buick, Model E runabout, 1908	12,200 - 12,900
Buick, Model 10 surrey, 1910	13,500 - 15,000
Buick, roadster, 1914	12,500 - 14,500
Buick, 4-passenger coupe, 1922	6,100 - 6,700
Buick, special cabriole, 1936	10,000 - 11,500
Cadillac, roadster, 1904 . . .	21,000 - 23,500
Cadillac, toy tonneau, 1910	20,000 - 22,000
Cadillac, V-8, touring, 1916	19,700 - 20,900
Cadillac, sport roadster, 1923	19,000 - 22,000
Cadillac, Series 61 convertible sedan, 1939	19,000 - 22,000
Chalmers, touring car, 1909	10,500 - 12,000
Chandler, sport touring, 1921	15,300 - 15,800
Chandler, 2-door sedan, 1926	5,500 - 7,000
Chevrolet, Baby Grand roadster, 1913	12,000 - 14,000
Chevrolet, roadster, 1913 .	11,500 - 13,500
Chevrolet, touring car, 1916	10,700 - 12,600
Chevrolet, 490 roadster, 1921	7,000 - 8,000
Chevrolet, touring car, 1927	8,500 - 9,500
Chevrolet, sport roadster, side mounts, 1929	14,000 - 16,000
Chevrolet, standard sedan, 1935	6,400 - 7,500
Chevrolet, standard coupe, 1937	5,500 - 6,500
Chrysler, 6-cylinder sport phaeton, 1925	11,800 - 13,500
Chrysler, Model 50 coupe, 1926	5,700 - 6,800
Chrysler, 72 cabriolet, 1928	12,000 - 12,900
Chrysler, 6-cylinder coupe, 1934	6,800 - 7,900
Cole, 5-passenger, V-8, touring, 1916	12,300 - 12,800

Columbia Electric, Victoria, 1904	8,200 - 9,000
Columbia Electric, Victoria, 1907	10,200 - 10,750
Crane-Simplex, touring car, 1912	25,000 - 28,000
Dodge, touring, 1915	6,300 - 6,900
Dodge, roadster, 1917	5,700 - 6,800
Dodge, touring car, 1922 . .	6,200 - 7,000
Dodge, coupe, 1937	5,500 - 7,000
Duesenberg, dual cowl phaeton, 1921	110,000+
Duesenberg, phaeton, 1924	155,000+
Durant, 6-cylinder touring, 1923	6,800 - 7,300
Essex, 2-door coach, 1921 .	7,400 - 8,000
Essex, Boattail Speedster, 1927	12,000 - 13,500
Flanders, touring, 1911 . . .	11,800 - 12,900
Franklin, roadster, 1910 . .	9,900 - 10,900
Franklin, touring, 1917 . . .	11,300 - 12,200
Graham-Paige, 6-cylinder coupe, 1929	7,000 - 8,400
Hispano Suiza, touring car, 1910	19,400 - 22,000
Hupmobile, coupe, 1910 . .	9,400 - 10,400
Hupmobile, roadster, 1913	10,000 - 11,300
Hupmobile, sedan, 1925 . .	6,800 - 7,400
International, high wheel auto buggy, 1908	8,000 - 8,500
Isotta-Franschini, tourer, 1914	25,500 - 27,000
Jordan, Playboy roadster, 1920	11,000 - 12,200
Jordan, 8-cylinder sedan, 1927	7,800 - 8,500
Lafayette Nash, 2-door sedan, 1936	5,000 - 5,600
LaSalle, rumble seat coupe, 1935	9,600 - 10,500
LaSalle, opera coupe, side mounts, 1936	8,500 - 8,900
Lincoln, LeLand touring, 1922	18,000 - 20,000
Lincoln, limousine, 1924 . .	11,500 - 12,600
Lincoln-Zephyr, convertible sedan, 1939	14,800 - 17,000
Lincoln-Zephyr, convertible coupe, 1941	13,500 - 15,000
Locomobile, roadster, 1910	19,000 - 21,000
Locomobile, laundelette coupe, 1915	21,800 - 23,500
Locomobile, sport touring, 1922	30,000 - 33,000
Marmon, speedster, 1911 .	24,500 - 26,000
Marmon, Model 34 touring, 1916	18,700 - 20,600
Marmon, Model E 75 touring, 1924	14,700 - 16,000
Marmon, 8-70 convertible coupe, 1931	15,400 - 15,800

Maxwell, 2-cylinder roadster, 1903	10,800 - 11,800
Maxwell, roadster, 1912 . .	10,900 - 12,100
Mercedes, 2-passenger racer, 4-cylinder (ill.)	90,000+
Mercedes, touring car, 1912	31,000 - 33,000
Mercer, raceabout, 1913 . .	140,000+
Mercer, sporting, 1915 . . .	40,000 - 45,000
Moon, touring car, 1922 . .	10,800 - 11,900
Nash, touring car, 1921 . . .	8,200 - 9,000
Nash, Special 6 sedan, 1926	6,400 - 7,700
Nash, 400 touring, 1929 . .	7,700 - 8,900
Oakland, 6-cylinder touring, 1913	15,400 - 16,000
Oakland, touring, 1923 . . .	10,900 - 11,900
Oldsmobile, roadster, 1901	8,000 - 8,700
Oldsmobile, touring, 1918 .	7,800 - 8,800
Oldsmobile, V-8 sport touring, 1928	7,800 - 8,400
Overland, roadster, 1911 . .	10,900 - 11,900
Overland, Model 85 touring, 1917	7,300 - 7,900
Packard, 4-cylinder roadster, 1909	34,000+
Packard, Twin-Six, 7-passenger touring, 1915	36,000+
Packard, 7-passenger limousine, 1922	11,000 - 11,800
Packard, 8-cylinder, 120C sedan, 1936	8,700 - 9,700
Pierce-Arrow, Great Arrow, 1907	32,000+
Pierce-Arrow, Model 38 touring, 1914	25,000 - 26,000
Pierce-Arrow, 7-passenger touring, 1922	25,300 - 26,500
Rambler, 2-cylinder touring, 1905	16,700 - 17,800
Regal, underslung coupe, 1913	16,500 - 17,800
Reo, 1-cylinder runabout, 1904	7,900 - 9,000
Reo, 4-cylinder touring, 1910	11,800 - 12,900
Rolls-Royce, roadster Silver Ghost, 1910	95,000+
Rolls-Royce, landaulet, 1914	70,000+
Rolls-Royce, tourer, 1920 .	85,000+
Rolls-Royce, Model 20 touring, 1923	40,000+
Sears, motor buggy, 1907 .	9,500 - 10,000
Singer, LeMans roadster, 1933	6,200 - 6,900
Stanley Steamer, runabout, 1904	13,500 - 14,700
Stanley Steamer, touring car, 1908	20,200 - 21,700
Stevens-Duryea, roadster, 1909	28,000 - 31,000

(continued)

Studebaker, roadster, 1911   10,400 - 11,700
Studebaker, Model 25
  touring, 1913 . . . .   11,200 - 12,500
Studebaker, doctor's
  coupe, 1924 . . . .   7,500 - 8,400
Stutz, Bearcat roadster,
  1914 . . . .   57,000 - 62,000
Stutz, Bearcat speedster,
  1919 . . . .   55,000+
Stutz, 6-cylinder touring,
  1924 . . . .   16,800 - 17,700
Thomas, roadster, 1909 . . .   27,500 - 30,000
Winton, touring car, 1917 .   18,700 - 19,800
Winton, 4-passenger
  touring, 1921 . . . .   23,000 - 24,600
Winton, 7-passenger
  touring, 1923 . . . .   21,700 - 22,800

Obviously, there are hundreds of other automobiles. Sorry if we've missed your model.

Automobiliana

From 1900 until 1930 over 1,500 different makes of automobiles were manufactured in the United States. Practically every part of the car is collectible today, especially items such as radiator caps and emblems, dashboard clocks, brass head lamps, hubcaps, etc.

Automobiliana

Advertisement, Goodrich
  "Safety Tread" Tires, 1914 . . . $ 14 - 24
Advertisement, Metz "22"—$475
  —The Gearless Car, 1913 . . . . .   24 - 33
Advertisement, Dragon Touring
  Car—"The motor that motes,"
  1907 . . . .   33 - 43
Advertisement, Murine ("A tonic
  for the 'auto eye' "), 1907 . . . . .   29 - 39
Advertisement, Aerocar Motor
  Co.—"There's No Getting
  Away," 1908 . . . .   32 - 42
Advertisement, Midland Motor
  Co., Moline, Illinois, 1910 . . . . .   25 - 35
Auto Blue Books, 1909 through
  1919, each . . . .   25 - 35

Auto Green Books, 1915 through
  1926, each . . . .   17 - 25
Auto Wiring Manual, Abbot-
  Detroit cars, 1910-1914 . . . . . .   42 - 50
Book, GET OUT AND GET
  UNDER, 1913, illustrated . . . .   40 - 45
Book, SALESMAN'S
  CADILLAC, 1913 . . . .   47 - 58
Book, THE OPEN ROAD, 1914 .   40 - 50
Book, THE EASY ROUTE TO
  CALIFORNIA, 1911 . . . . . .   75 - 90
Carbide tank for 1909 Ford
  Model-T . . . .   155 - 175
Carbide tank for 1912 Cadillac .   210 - 240
Dashboard clock for 1914 Pierce
  Arrow . . . .   78 - 88
Dashboard clock for 1916
  Packard . . . .   78 - 88
Emblems: average price, each . . .   25 - 38
  Buick   Cadillac   McFarlan   Stutz
  Oakland   Kleiber   DaVis   Overland
  Franklin   Essex   DeLage
Bail handle light, brass, 1909
  Hupmobile . . . .   325 - 400
Headlight, 1916 Buick . . . .   140 - 165
Horn, double twist, brass, bulb-
  type, 1908 Maxwell . . . .   120 - 160
License plates, enamel-over-
  metal, 1909-1916, average price   33 - 55
Magazine CAR LIFE, 1916, 12
  issues, all . . . .   145 - 160
Motor meter (forerunner of the
  speedometer), 1912 Marmon . .   90 - 110
Motor meter, 1913 Mercer . . . . .   130 - 150
Motor meter, 1914 Columbia . . .   65 - 75
Owner's manual, 1908 Rolls
  Royce . . . .   200 - 250
Owner's manual, 1914 Stutz
  "Bearcat" . . . .   160 - 200
Poster, "1913 Auto Show,
  Chicago," 15" × 20", paper . . .   160 - 190
Radiator cap ornament, knight
  with lance . . . .   75 - 85
Radiator cap ornament, Lady
  Ascot, Rolls Royce, silver, 1911   350 - 400
Road map showing routes to
  Chicago from New York City,
  1909 . . . .   62 - 72
Sales catalogs, General Motors'
  cars, 1916-1925, all . . . .   300 - 375
Signature of Ramsey E. Olds,
  creator of the Reo and the
  Oldsmobile, 1909 . . . .   27 - 37
Spark plug for 1909 Saxon . . . . .   15 - 23
Spark coil for 1910 Model-T;
  still works . . . .   67 - 77
Vases, used in back seat of 1913
  Cadillac limousine, pair, cut
  glass . . . .   88 - 110
Vases, cut glass, used in back
  seat of 1912 Locomobile limo . .   90 - 125

Aventurine Glass

A yellowish glass in which there are large numbers of small crystals of copper. Fairly collectible today, though Fostoria Glass Company, Moundsville, West Virginia, has reproduced a fair imitation in recent years.

Bowl, ruffled edges, 6″ diameter .	110 - 130
Pitcher, 6″ high, clear applied handle	130 - 160
Rose bowl, 3″ high	120 - 145
Vase, fluted top, 10″ high	185 - 200
Vase, flowers, ruffled lip, 11½″ high	189 - 220

Aviation

Aviation

Anything "aeronautical" from World War I to World War II is collectible today. Pilots' wings, both wars, charts, old wooden propellers, emblems; even the old World War I planes bring huge prices today.

Arm patches, squadron, 8th Air Force, etc., each	$1.50- 4
Wooden propeller, clock in center, WWI	175 - 225
Leather pilot's helmet, goggles attached, 1930s	45 - 55
Leather pilot's jacket, Chinese/ C.B.I. Theater flag on back, WWII	110 - 135
Tail insignia, French Spad 13, WWI, 28″ high	160 - 195
Airmail pilot's chart, Pittsburgto-Chicago, 1934	60 - 75
Theatre poster, "The Dawn Patrol," 1930	35 - 45
Pewter mug marked "Royal Flying Corps, 1916"	90 - 105
Sterling silver pilot's wings, WWII	40 - 50
Squadron insignia, taken from old hangar, England WWI . . .	250 - 325

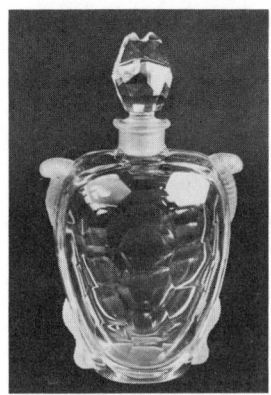

Baccarat Glass

Baccarat Glass

French, by La Compagnie Des Cristalleries De Baccarat; they also had a factory in Alsace-Lorraine. Factory started in 1765. Famous for their cane and Millefiori paperweights, 1860 to 1880. Careful! Excellent fakes coming into the U.S. Know your dealer if you're after a genuine paperweight.

Bell, clear-cut . . . . $	38 -	52
Bobeche (wax catchers on candlesticks), lacy, pair . . .	50 -	60
Bottle, perfume, cut and polished crystal, stylized turtle with frosted feet, c. 1900, 4¼″ high (ill.)	240 -	260
Bottle, perfume, blue trim, pair	69 -	79
Bowl, Depose, Rubina color . .	265 -	285
Candleholder, diamond point, 7″ high	35 -	45
Chandelier, 12-light, drip pan, amethyst head chain	1,100 - 1,400	
Cologne, Pink Swirl, cut stopper	32 -	43
Compote, green, swirl, pedestal	130 -	160
Decanter, bronze, scroll design	95 -	120
Goblet, lacy, 1850s, signed . .	135 -	150
Ice bucket, Pink Swirl	145 -	165
Ink stand, script design, signed	85 -	100
Lamp base, cameo, flowers . .	240 -	285
Paperweight, red/periwinkle, star cut base, 2½″ diameter, signed and dated "B1850"	1,600 - 2,200	
Paperweight, salmon pink, double clematis, 3½″ dia., signed and dated "B1848" .	1,700 - 2,300	
Paperweight, Sulfide, Pope John, star cut base	250 -	265

35

(continued)

Paperweight, wheat, flowers,
star cut base, approxi-
mately 2½" diameter . . . . .   2,500+
Pitcher, water, 6 glasses,
Amberina . . . .   465 -   565
Vase, stick type, cameo, floral
decor, 11" high . . . .   280 -   325

Again, PLEASE don't let a bunch of prices lull you into thinking you know genuine Baccarat paperweights. It's one thing to list a hundred or more with prices, but can you tell the old from the new?

Baggage Stickers

Baggage Stickers

Years ago, when it was fun to travel, hotels and steamship lines pasted colorful stickers on your steamer trunks, etc. I'll never forget the "Flying Scot" and the "Orient Express," among others.

Baggage sticker, in good
condition . . . . $ 1 -   2

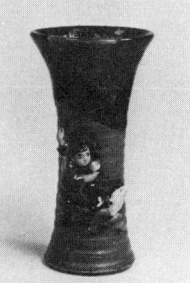

Banko Ware

Banko Ware

Some call it Poo Ware; it comes from Korea and originated in the 1840-1910 period though Korean potters have been making pottery for centuries. The molded, applied figures around the piece usually tell a story.

Teapot, green ground, applied
figures, 6½" high . . . . $240 - 260

Vase, red, applied figures, 8" high   80 - 90
Vase, red/black glaze, applied
figures (ill.), 5½" high . . . .   65 -   75

Banks, Mechanical

Banks that "do something" when you insert a coin are called mechanical. There were over 300 different kinds made in this country from the 1870s until the early 1900s. There are many reproductions on the market today, some so good it's difficult to tell the old from the new, especially when the new bank has been "aged" by chipping its paint or fading it with an infra red lamp. Rare banks are expensive so know your subject **before** you buy!

Acrobat . . . . $	725 -	775
Afghanistan	750 -	850
Always did 'spise a mule (ill.)	175 -	200
Artillery, 8-sided block house	1,300 -	1,550
Atlas	755 -	900
Bad Accident	350 -	400
Bank Teller	4,800 -	5,200
Baseball Player	70 -	85
Bowery	6,400 -	6,800
Bowing man in cupola	2,300 -	2,600
Breadwinner	2,700 -	3,000
Butting Ram	1,700 -	2,000
Cabin	250 -	275
Calamity	2,300 -	2,450
Called Out	4,200 -	4,400
Calumet Bank (tin)	160 -	170
Cat and Mouse	425 -	475
Chandlers Bank	360 -	385
Chief Big Moon	450 -	475
Chimpanzee	825 -	900
Chinaman in Boat	5,300 -	5,500
Chinaman with Queue, tin .	875 -	925
Circus	2,800 -	3,250
Clever Dick (tin)	925 -	975
Clown and Dog (tin)	1,400 -	1,650
Clown on Globe	475 -	550
Confectionery Store	1,800 -	2,100
Creedmore	195 -	265
Dapper Dan	450 -	500
Darktown Battery	425 -	450
Dinah with Sleeve	150 -	175
Ding Dong Bell (tin)	3,200 -	3,450
Dog Charges Boy	390 -	430
Dog on Turntable	150 -	170
Dog, Speaking	225 -	255
Dog Trees Cat	5,000 -	5,300
Dog with Tray	825 -	875
Donkey	250 -	275
Eagle and Eaglets (ill.)	225 -	275
Electric Safe	355 -	400

Eagle and Eaglets	....	225 - 275		Always did 'spise a mule	....	175 - 200

Elephant, 3 Stars	210 -	240	Minstrel, tin	180 -	240
Elephant, Light of Asia	1,500 -	1,700	Monkey and Organ		
Elephant Wiggles	70 -	90	Grinder	130 -	165
Football Bank	1,300 -	1,500	Monkey and Parrot (tin)	300 -	365
Freedman's Bank, desk	11,500 -	12,000	Mosque	240 -	285
Frog and Serpent (tin)	5,400 -	5,650	Music Bank (tin)	475 -	500
Frog on Rock	195 -	240	National Bank	470 -	500
Frog on Stump	190 -	260	North Pole	4,000 -	4,400
Gem	190 -	210	Owl with Book, slot in book	150 -	170
Giant	4,700 -	5,000	Paddy and His Pig	425 -	475
Girl Skipping Rope		3,400+	Panorama Bank	1,200 -	1,450
Globe on Arc	180 -	220	Patronize The Blind	1,400 -	1,650
Guessing Bank	925 -	960	Pegleg Beggar	600 -	700
Hall's Excelsior	95 -	125	Picture Gallery	1,900 -	2,200
Hall's Lilliput	178 -	240	Pig in High Chair	300 -	350
Hen, Setting	580 -	620	Popeye Knockout Bank	375 -	450
Hindu with Turban	650 -	750	Preacher in Pulpit	8,200 -	8,600
Hold the Fort	940 -	985	Professor Pugfrog	1,600 -	1,900
Home	275 -	320	Pump and Bucket	650 -	725
Hoop-La	380 -	420	Punch and Judy (iron and		
Humpty Dumpty	220 -	260	tin)	1,400 -	1,700
Indian Shooting Bear	310 -	340	Punch and Judy, small or		
John Bull's Money Box	2,900 -	3,300	large letters	260 -	285
Jolly Nigger, Butterfly Tie	170 -	195	Queen Victoria	5,000 -	5,500
(I abhor THAT word BUT			Rabbit in Cabbage	170 -	200
that's the original name)			Rabbit, standing, on round		
Jonah and the Whale	725 -	825	base	250 -	290
Kiltie Bank	725 -	800	Red Riding Hood	5,500 -	5,800
Leap Frog	450 -	500	Rival	6,000 -	6,400
Liberty Bell	320 -	365	Roller Skating Rink	4,800 -	5,000
Little High Hat	725 -	765	Rooster	138 -	175
Little Joe	120 -	165	Saluting Sailor (tin)	640 -	750
Magic Safe (tin)	275 -	300	Sambo	425 -	475
Magician	580 -	635	Santa Claus at Chimney	340 -	385
Mammy and Child	520 -	600	Scotsman (tin)	260 -	285
Mason and Hod Carrier	700 -	775	Sentry Bank (tin)	750 -	800
Merry-Go-Round	4,900 -	5,400	Shoot the Chute	3,700 -	4,000
Mickey Mouse (tin)	1,300 -	1,600	Signal Cabin (tin)	410 -	440
Mikado	4,600 -	5,000	Speaking Dog	400 -	450

(continued)

Stump Speaker	355 -	400
Tabby Bank	235 -	285
Tammany	95 -	130
Teddy and the Bear	270 -	300
Tiger (tin)	875 -	975
Time Is Money	2,000 -	2,400
Tower Bank	1,900 -	2,200
Trick Pony	250 -	300
Turtle	4,800 -	5,200
Uncle Remus	1,200 -	1,500
Uncle Sam	375 -	425
Watch Bank	375 -	425
William Tell	220 -	280
Wimbleton	3,000 -	3,300
Windmill (tin)	145 -	170
Wireless (tin)	220 -	265
Woodpecker	1,800 -	2,000

Lion and Monkeys ...... 400 - 475

Ferris Wheel Bank .... 3,400+

Tank and Cannon Bank .... 375 - 450

Banks, Still

Banks, Still

These banks don't have any moving parts. Usually cast in the shape of buildings, animal figures, etc., the same advice holds true for these as does for the "mechanical." The General Pershing is being heavily reproduced, as are others.

Aunt Jemima with Spoon	$ 75 -	85
Bank Building, 5" high (ill.)	60 -	70
Baseball Player	85 -	100
Battleship Maine	135 -	150
Black Beauty	80 -	90
Blackamoor	72 -	82
Boy Scout	80 -	90
Buffalo, standing	75 -	85
Buster and Tige	165 -	185
Cat, sitting	60 -	65
Campbell Kids	230 -	255
Deer with Antlers	60 -	70
Dog, 5" long	45 -	54
Donkey with Saddle	120 -	140
Duck	165 -	175
Empire State Building	65 -	75
Horseshoe	65 -	75
Indian Head, Maiden	68 -	78
Liberty Bell, Carnival Glass	45 -	55
Lion, Large	82 -	92
Lion on Wheels	90 -	110
Little Daisy	48 -	58
Mailbox, green	35 -	45
Owl	120 -	130
Negro Mammy	63 -	72
Presto #426	52 -	62
Radio	60 -	70

Rooster #187	68 - 78	Bird on Stump, 4¾" high	58 - 68
Shell, World War I	39 - 49	Cat w/Ball, 2½" high	50 - 60
Soldier, W.W. I	80 - 90	Red Goose Shoes, 3¾" high	50 - 55
Standing Elephant	40 - 50	Dog w/Pack, 3¾" high	57 - 67
Statue of Liberty	70 - 78	Dog "Candy Container," 3¾"	
Teddy Bear	62 - 72	high (ill.)	28 - 38
Thrifty Pig	32 - 42	Rearing Horse, "Beauty," 5"	
Tiger	35 - 45	high, on oval base	49 - 59
Turkey	50 - 58	Prancing Horse w/Belly Band,	
Uncle Sam, Cash Register	65 - 75	4½" high	47 - 57
Humpty Dumpty, tin, 5½" high	30 - 40	Two Kids (goats), 4½" high	115 - 135
F.D. Roosevelt, die cast	38 - 48	Resting Camel, 2½" high	110 - 120
Captain Kidd, 5½" high	135 - 160	Feed My Sheep, pot metal,	
Mickey Mouse, aluminum 8¾"		3" high	32 - 42
high	120 - 135	Pig w/Bow Tie, 3" high	68 - 78
Poor Tired Tim, tin, 5" high	54 - 64	Yellow Cab, 4" high	175 - 225
Elephant on Tub, 5¼" high	60 - 70	Trolley Car w/People, 3" high	90 - 110
Elephant w/Howdah, 4¾" high	48 - 58	Trolley Car without People,	
Jumbo Savings Bank, English,		3" high	85 - 110
tin, 5¼" high	30 - 38	Graf Zeppelin w/Wheels, 8" long	110 - 120

Banks, Still   Photograph: Louis S. Filles

ROW 1

Taft and Sherman—Political	$115 - 130
Sailor, small, 5½" high	58 - 68
Golliwog (English)	100 - 115
Santa Holding a Tree, 5½" high	88 - 98
Capitalist	76 - 85
Owl on square base	56 - 66
Bear Stealing Pig, 5½" high	158 - 170
Bird on Stump	54 - 64

ROW 2

Independence Hall, 9" high	$110 - 130
Light House	82 - 90
Panorama	56 - 66
Bank Building	42 - 51

39   (continued)

Banks, Still

ROW 3

Liberty Bell on base	$ 60 - 70	Independence Hall (3 banks in one)	149 - 168
Liberty Bell	52 - 62		

Banks, Still

Bank Building, 3½" high	$ 30 - 40	Lion on Tub	63 - 73
Bank Building, 4½" high	58 - 68	Tower Bank	36 - 46
Bank Building, 5½" high	58 - 68	Bank Building, 11" high	56 - 63
Horse on Tub	65 - 75	Bank Building, 7" high	44 - 54
Small Lion	48 - 58		

Banks, Still, Pottery

The crudest types were made centuries ago when someone wanted a container in which to bury valuables. They were usually made of fire-hardened clay and they remained popular until replaced by the iron banks in the mid-1800s.

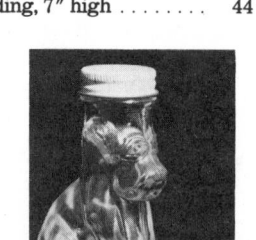

Banks, Still,

Bear, sitting, 5½"	$40 - 45
Bird	30 - 40
Buffalo	35 - 45
Corn	60 - 70
Gourd	50 - 60
Lion's head	35 - 45
Pig, blue	30 - 35
Rooster, standing	35 - 45
Tree stump	23 - 30
Teddy Roosevelt	95 - 110
Zeppelin	45 - 55

Barbed Wire

Barbed Wire

First patented in the late 1800s, there were more than 600 kinds. It had a great effect on the cattle business in the West. It's very collectible today. Rare, one-of-a-kind pieces bring upwards of $100 for 18 inches! Also called "devil's rope."

Common variety, 18"	$ 1 - 2

Up to $350 for rare pieces

Basalt

Barometers

Barometers, Chronometers

Used for indicating the weather, barometers go back to the 11th century. A great many of the older ones still work. If you find a Louis XVI, ormolu-mounted, $10,000 is about right!

Banjo shape case, floral medallions, mahogany	$140 -	190
Banjo, silvered dial, rosewood, English	280 -	340
Banjo, inlaid rosewood, 1860s	165 -	185
Banjo, mahogany, John Berwinger	85 -	95
Desk style, brass case, German	55 -	70
Desk style, brass dial, English 8" high	30 -	40
Hygrometer, thermometer, spirit level, Joseph Alexander	180 -	220
Stick type, George III, Edinburgh, 40" high, operating .	280 -	320
Stick type, ivory register dial, rosewood, inlaid, London . .	190 -	220
Stick type, American, mid-19th century	350 -	455
Wall, circular, register dial, gilt, inlaid rosewood, 45" high	325 -	360
Chronometer, "Whyte Thompson & Co.," gimbled, double cased	950 -	1,200

Basalt

Wedgwood made this pottery in the late 18th century. It was also made in ancient times and is a black, vitreous pottery, shiny inside, glossy on the outside. It's rather expensive. Look for Wedgwood impressed in the bottom if you want the genuine.

Bowl, 9½" dia., sterling silver rim	$235 - 275
Bowl, 12" diameter, acanthus decor, marked Wedgwood	260 - 300
Bust, Shakespeare, circa 1800, marked Wedgwood	400 - 450
Bust, John Dryden, 14" high (ill.)	350 - 400
Candlesticks, 13¼" high, pair . . .	230 - 265
Chalice, beaded pedestal base, marked Wedgwood	210 - 240
Coffeepot, 9" high	175 - 200
Creamer, black	65 - 80
Medallions, 2¼" × 2¾", marked Wedgwood and Bentley, George III and Queen Charlotte, pair	575 - 625
Pitcher, Flaxman figures in relief around base, leaves/grapes border at top, 6¾" high	185 - 210
Sugar bowl, covered, black	200 - 225
Teapot, usual marking, classic design	240 - 270
Tea set, sugar, creamer, pot, tray, flower motif, all	350 - 425
Vase, 7" high, circa 1890, marked Wedgwood England, pair	235 - 275

Baseball Cards

Baseball Cards

The first baseball cards were issued in 1886 by Old Judge cigarets. Some of the rarest are Honus Wagner ($1,200+), Eddie Plank ($350-400) and Napoleon Lajoie ($300-350). Other companies, such as Glendale Meats, Signal Oil, and Tip Top Bread, put out these cards on a regional basis at the turn of the century.

Average cost: 50¢ to $1.50 for modern type. For the "rare" type—what you pay is what it's worth to you!

41

Basketry

Basketry

The beautiful and delicate work done by the Indians of our continent is highly collectible today. Their thoughts and attitudes are woven into these magnificent objects.

Tlingit rattletop, Greek Key design, 4″ high, c. 1920s . . . $	295 -	350
Tlingit rattletop, 4″ x 5″, c. 1900s	375 -	425
Eskimo, openwork design, 13″ high, c. late 1800s	295 -	340
Eskimo, willow, "fern root" design, 11″ high, c. 1930s . .	150 -	190
Aleut, yarn used for color, 7½″ high, c. 1900s	2,000 -	2,500
(Baskets from the Aleutian Islands sometimes have 40 stitches to the inch—highly collectible!)	400 -	500
Aleut bottle w/goblet	425 -	475
Reed-woven, 2″ high, Guatemala, new	50¢ -	$1
Tsimshian, spruce root w/aniline dyed design, 1920s	110 -	160
Skokomish, typical rim design of dogs	190 -	250
Western Apache, tray, 19″ wide, Geometric Star design, c. 1920	525 -	565
San Carlos, tray, 15″ dia., willow, Devil's Claw design, c. 1920	650 -	750
Yavapai, tray, 14½″ dia., willow, typical design, c. 1900s	765 -	815
Makah covered box, eagle motif, red/blue (ill.)	235 -	265
Pima, coiled bowl, 9″ high, willow, Devil's Claw design, c. 1930s	125 -	160
Moki, w/handle and cover, 6½″ high, 3 colors, (rare) (ill.)	320 -	375

Pima, olla storage, willow, Devil's Claw, c. 1925	90 -	120
Hopi coil, yucca fiber, deer design, c. 1930s	130 -	165
Navajo, tray, wedding-type, 15″ dia., willow, c. 1930s . . .	110 -	145
Walapai, twined, rabbit brush, 8½″ high, aniline dyed, c. 1930s	75 -	95
Chemehuevi (Southern California), coil, quill design, c. 1930s	525 -	600
Nez Perce Fez, fully beaded, 8¼″ high, c. 1910	825 -	900
Yokut (Tulare), coiled bowl, deer design, 4″ dia., c. 1920s	225 -	275
Yokut, bottleneck, yarn and feathers woven into shoulder, c. 1920s	1.200 - 1.400

Battersea Enamel

Battersea Enamel

Stephen Janssen made this exquisite enamel work at Battersea, England, for only 5 or 6 years, 1750-1755. Knobs, jewel and patch boxes, lids, etc. A lot was made after 1755 in Staffordshire district, but the true Battersea was made for 6 years at most. It is reproduced in France today.

Box, blue base, Love Is Eternal . $400 - 450
Box, angel motif, 2″ x 3″	450 - 525
Box, 3″ x 2″, Pixies	450 - 500
Box, blue/yellow, floral, 4″ square	450 - 525
Box, green enamel, white inside, pear shape, 2″ x 3 1/2″	400 - 425
Box, "Love is Thine," 2 3/4″ x 2 1/8″	475 - 525
Box, patch, rose base, white lid, family coat-of-arms	400 - 450
Box, patch, Mother on lid	310 - 360
Box, hunters chasing fox, 2″ x 4″	340 - 375
Box, green/blue, bird decor, 1 1/2″ x 2″	425 - 485
Box, 3″ x 4 1/2″, red/green, lid . . .	500 - 550

Bavarian, General

The small firms which produced ceramics in Bavaria have long since disappeared. Who made those pieces you find today, simply marked Bavaria on the bottom? Few records

42

Bavarian, General

were kept, so we'll probably never know.
Look for specific factories listed alphabetically in this Guide.

Berry set, hand-painted flowers,
  pink, green . . . . $ 30 - 40
Bread plate, yellow roses, red
  border, 11″ long . . . . 27 - 37
Chocolate pot, roses, gilt trim,
  handled, with lid . . . . 40 - 50
Candy dish, Dresden-type
  flowers, pink, blue . . . . 28 - 38
Castor jug, vinegar/oil, red rose,
  green background . . . . 18 - 28
Hatpin holder, pink and yellow
  flowers, 8″ high . . . . 25 - 35
Powder box, violets in blue and
  lavender, gilt edge . . . . 50 - 60
Plate, flowers, garden scene, gilt
  edge, 7″ diameter . . . . 15 - 22
Plate, white, gold (center left
  vacant for amateur painter) . . . 22 - 32
Plates, 4 fruit, pastoral scenes,
  signed "PUNCH – Z. S. & Co.,
  Bavaria," 9½″ dia. (ill.), each . . 65 - 75
Platter, pink roses around border,
  10″ long . . . . 34 - 44
Sugar bowl, multicolored flowers,
  handled lid . . . . 42 - 52
Teapot, pink and green floral
  decorations, 5″ high, lid . . . . . . 24 - 33
Vase, gold and red roses, gilt
  lip, 6½″ high . . . . 28 - 38

Beaded Bags

They were popular in the early to middle
Victorian era.

Beads, tapestry scene, silk lined,
  silver frame at top with silver
  chain, late 1800s . . . . $ 24 - 34

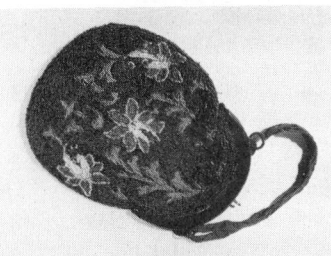

Beaded Bags

Black glass beads, silver frame at
  top with silver chain, late 1800s   26 - 36
Cloth, beaded flowers sewn into
  material, late 1800s (ill.) . . . . . .   10 - 18
Garnet beads, opera-type back,
  snap catch, 5″ wide, mid-1800s   62 - 70
Green glass beads, drawstring
  type, late 1800s . . . .   28 - 37
Jade-colored glass beads, tortoise
  shell frame, shell link handle . .   34 - 44
Red, blue, gold, black, silk cords,
  peacocks and eyes (ill.) . . . .   25 - 35
Silk bag, embroidered bead
  initials, silver frame and chain,
  late 1800s . . . .   25 - 35

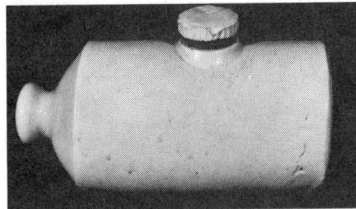

Bed (and Foot) Warmers

Bed (and Foot) Warmers

The earliest pans had iron handles. Usually
what you find in shops today have a wooden
handle and brass pan with cover. Reproductions are abundant! Coals from the fireplace
were placed in the pan and put under the

43

(continued)

covers to warm the bed. Other bed warmers were made of soapstone, heated in the oven, then placed at the foot of the bed under the covers. The earliest buggy foot warmers were metal with a drawer for coals. Pottery heaters held hot water. Being reproduced in brass and copper.

Brass bed warmer, walnut handle, English, 1800s	$250 - 285
Buggy-type, moleskin covered metal handles	40 - 50
Ceramic, c. 1890s (ill.)	48 - 55
Ceramic, Bennington type	175 - 210
Soapstone foot warmer, bail handle, early 1900s	30 - 40
Stoneware, blue/gray, Logan County Pottery Company	50 - 60
Tin foot warmer, charcoal drawer, carpet-covered	45 - 50

Belleek

Made from feldspathic clay in County Fermanagh, Northern Ireland, Belleek was first made in 1857. The most characteristic productions are shell pieces and similar forms, supported by coral branches. Perhaps the loveliest are the openwork basket pieces. A real porcelain, the result of the simple vitrification of feldspar and china clay, it is extremely light and thin with a creamy, ivory surface and an iridescent luster. The typical Belleek mark consists of a hound, harp, tower, and shamrock, with the name **Belleek** on a ribbon underneath, printed in black, light and dark blue, brown, red, or green. Most original Belleek had this trademark. Look for marine plants, seashells, dolphins, coral designs, Echinus (sea urchin), Limpet (coneshaped shell of shellfish), Tridacna (clam); also shamrock decorations. A glittering iridescent glaze resembling mother-of-pearl is another way to identify this fine pottery. Made continuously from 1857 to 1941, a black mark was used in conjunction with the hound, harp, etc. Production stopped in 1941, beginning again in 1946, when a green mark was instituted. A "Belleek-type" was made in America by several factories in the 1880s and 1890s—Ott & Brewer, Trenton, N.J., using "O. & B." in a circle; Cook Pottery Company, using "Eturia" and three feathers; Willets Mfg. Co., using a "W" in the form of a snake; The American Art China Works, using "R.E.Co./China/Trenton" as a mark. Lenox, Inc. in Trenton, probably made the best of the American "Belleek," stopping production just before WWI. Confused? Then, know the genuine BEFORE you buy!

Animal, swan, black mark, 3" high	$130 - 170
Animal, dog, black mark, 4½" long	115 - 130
Basket, openwork, twisted handle, black mark, 8"	165 - 180
Basket, openwork, woven bottom, black mark, 8½" dia.	175 - 200
Basket, openwork, woven bottom, 10½" dia.	80 - 90
Bowl, finger, green mark, 4¾" dia.	68 - 78
Bowl, fruit, "Lenox," 5½" dia.	55 - 65
Bowl, round, openwork, woven bottom, black mark, 7" dia.	200 - 260
Creamer, Echinus pattern, black mark, 4½" high	58 - 68
Creamer, mermaid, black mark, 5" high	58 - 70
Creamer, Tridacna pattern, 4¾" high	57 - 66

Belleek

Belleek

Cup/saucer, Limpet pattern, black mark	125 - 165
Cup/saucer, Shamrock, green mark	120 - 145
Cup/saucer, Tridacna pattern, green mark	90 - 115
Dish, openwork, applied roses, black mark, 5" dia.	62 - 72
Dish, dolphin pattern, green mark, 5½" dia. . . .	58 - 68
Hatpin holder, seashells, 6" high, "O. & B."	43 - 53
Honey jar, beehive shape, green mark, 4½" high (ill.)	55 - 65
Mug, Shamrock pattern, green mark, 6" high	61 - 70
Mug, pink lustre, "R.E.A. Co."	38 - 48
Pig, sitting, yellow/white, 3" high, green mark	58 - 70
Picture frame, black mark, 8" x 10"	160 - 175
Pitcher, swirling seaweed, black mark, 7½" high . .	80 - 90
Pitcher, Limpet pattern, 6¾" high, green mark . .	85 - 125
Pitcher, monk drinking, "W" mark	61 - 71
Plate, Limpet, black mark, 4½" dia.	47 - 56
Plate, mermaid, green mark, 6" dia.	38 - 48
Platter, Shamrock, 11" long, green mark	75 - 90
Salts, 6 individual, shell and coral, black mark . .	110 - 130 all
Sugar bowl, "W" mark, blue/green, 4" high	40 - 47
Sugar bowl, "Lenox" mark, cream/white, 5" high	36 - 43
Sugar bowl, "Etruria" mark, blue/white, 4¾" high	37 - 46
Tea set, mermaid, "Lenox" mark	340 - 400
Tea set, Neptune, "W" mark	260 - 300
Tray, bread, Neptune, green mark, 11½" long .	80 - 90
Vase, applied floral, green mark, 9½" high	120 - 150
Vase, diamond-faceted tripod, dog-paw feet, black mark, 9" high	245 - 270
Vase, "W" mark, 8½" high, flower pattern	80 - 95
Vase, "W" mark, white/ yellow, floral design, 7" high	57 - 67

Vase, "Etruria" mark, blue/yellow, flowers, 6½" high	48 - 57

Bellows

Bellows

Usually made of wood with leather trim, they blew air on the smithy's coals or household fire. Some ornately carved, others painted. They go back into the dim shadows of time.

Brass covered wood, leather bellows, tavern scene in relief, mid-1880s	$140 - 170
Hand-carved, ornate wooden bellows, leather good, German, dated 1742	150 - 165
Ornately painted wooden bellows, Satan blowing on coals, dated 1735, East Hampton, Connecticut	172 - 182
Smithy bellows, 5' long, good leather, and all parts, mid-1800s	140 - 165
Wood body, leather bellows, brass tacks, carved, mid-1800s works (ill.)	80 - 90
Wooden bellows, leather good, brass tacks, strap for hanging .	62 - 72

Bells

Bells

Going back to ancient times, bells have been made in all sizes and shapes and have been used for calling to worship, alerting the town during Indian raids, and, of course, tolling in the New Year. Glass, brass, iron, wood, paper, just about every material has been used to make them. Some of the finest made in this country were and are still being

(continued)

made at the East Hampton (Connecticut) Bell
Factory.

Brass, burnished, 14 on leather
   strap, 1″ diameter (ill.) . . . . . . $ 95 - 145
Brass calf bell on leather strap,
   3″ diameter . . . . 45 - 50
Brass, wooden handle, 8½″ high . 38 - 40
Chinese brass gong, dragon in
   relief . . . . 65 - 75
Cowbell, brass plated, 6″ long,
   original clapper . . . . 35 - 45
Cowbell, leather collar, original
   clapper . . . . 42 - 52
Same, brass . . . . 45 - 55
Same, copper . . . . 43 - 54
Dinner chimes, railroad-type,
   with mallet . . . . 58 - 68
Dinner, sterling silver, handle,
   4″ long . . . . 25 - 35
Door, pull type, brass . . . . 15 - 22
Elephant bell, inlaid enamel,
   17″ high . . . . 95 - 125
Farm, cast iron, 26″ diameter,
   goes on post . . . . 300 - 350
Farm, cast iron, 20″ diameter . . . 250 - 300
Hand, brass, 4″ diameter . . . . . . 20 - 28
Hand, brass, 7½″ diameter,
   12″ high . . . . 60 - 70
Hand, schoolmaster, brass,
   wooden handle, 6″ diameter,
   10″ high . . . . 90 - 110
Hand, teacher, brass, 5″ high . . . 52 - 62
India brass (look out for repro-
   ductions!) 3″ high (ill.) . . . . 15 - 19
Iron church bell, 24″ diameter . . . 450 - 600
Locomotive, steam whistle-type,
   brass frame and rack, 16″
   diameter, 23″ high . . . . 850 - 950
Mission bell, Mexican . . . . 275 - 350
Plantation, brass, dated 1877,
   8″ high . . . . 39 - 49
Ship, brass, dated 1858 . . . . 95 - 110
Ship, brass, 7″ high . . . . 175 - 225
Sleigh, 24 on new leather strap,
   burnished, graduated sizes . 475 - 575
Sleigh, 36 on new leather reins,
   burnished, small size . . . . 325 - 375
Sleigh, 20, original leather,
   burnished . . . . 425 - 475
Store, on heavy coiled spring . . . 32 - 41
Trolley car, 9½″ diameter . . . . . . 75 - 90

Bells, Glass

Amber, clear handle, 11″ high . . . $120 - 135
Bristol glass, clear handle . . . . . . 85 - 100
Burmese, clear handle (rare) . . . . 375 - 425
Carnival, marigold, 8″ high . . . . . 38 - 44
Cranberry, 12″ to top of handle . . 125 - 140
Cut glass (ill.) . . . . 70 - 80
Milk glass, 7″ high . . . . 70 - 80

Bells, Glass

Nailsea, clear handle . . . . 145 - 160
Ruby glass, red handle . . . . 50 - 60
Tiffany, clear handle (rare) . . . . . 350 - 400
Venetian Latticino, multicolored,
   6″ high . . . . 145 - 165
Look out for reproductions from Europe!

Belt Buckles

Belt Buckles

Made of 14 karat gold, silver plate, sterling,
engraved, plain. Just about everyone wore a
belt.

14K Gold, ornate, inscribed,
   Lightweight Champion, 1915 . $750 - 900
Gold-plated, rodeo type (ill.) . . . . 40 - 50
Ladies' "buckle" type (ill.) . . . . . . 15 - 20
Silver-plated, initialed or plain,
   many types . . . . 12 - 20
Sterling silver, Navy Wings, St.
   Christopher's Medal, World
   War II . . . . 175 - 250
Turquoise and silver inlaid,
   handmade by Navajos . . . . 200 - 250

Bennington Pottery

Parian, porcelain, stonewares, Rockingham-Bennington—all were made at Bennington, Vermont, from 1793, the first wares being lead-glazed. The Rockingham-Bennington type ware was also produced by several other Vermont potteries, at Dorset, St. Johnsbury, and Middlebury. Some was also made in Baltimore, Maryland, and today it's difficult to give complete credit to Bennington for everything they made, although certain experts still try to do so.

Bennington type bedpan, mottled brown glaze	$130 - 150
Bennington type bowl, mottled brown glaze, 7½" dia.	75 - 90
Bennington type bowl, octagonal, 13" dia.	120 - 150
Bottle, Coachman, mottled brown glaze, 10½" high	500 - 600
Bottle, flask-type, mottled brown glaze, 9" high	140 - 180
Cake mold, 8¾" dia.	63 - 73
Cake mold, 9½" dia.	70 - 80
Candlesticks, pair, mottled brown glaze, 11" high	180 - 210
Churn, mottled brown glaze, wooden lid and dasher	175 - 225
Creamer, cow, mottled brown glaze (ill.)	160 - 170
Cuspidor, enamel, flint, 1849, 7½" dia.	90 - 110
Cuspidor, shell pattern, mottled brown glaze, 8½" dia.	90 - 120
Doorknobs, 2 in set, mottled brown glaze	55 - 70 pr.
Flask, book-shaped "Departed Spirits," mottled brown glaze	178 - 210
Flask, ½ quart, tavern scene, mottled brown glaze	130 - 150
Foot warmer, holds 1 gal., mottled brown glaze	160 - 175
Frame, picture, blue/green/brown, flint enamel	185 - 195
Inkwell, usual color, 4 quill holes, raised design	180 - 200
Inkwell, dog's head, Rockingham glaze	115 - 130
Jug, 2 gal., blue/green, flint enamel	85 - 95
Jug, 1½ gal., mottled brown glaze, 9½" high	130 - 150
Mug, frog in bottom	150 - 170
Mug, birds in relief	62 - 72
Mug, Rockingham glaze, 6" high	90 - 115
Pitcher, Parian ware, paneled vine and flower, rare	450 - 500
Pitcher, tulip & heart, flint enamel, 8¼" high	120 - 130
Pitcher, castle scene, 8¾" high, Rockingham glaze	300 - 320
Plates, 8¼", 9", 9¼", 9¾", mottled brown glaze, av. price	75 - 120 ea.
Pudding mold, tulip in bottom, Rockingham glaze, 6½" dia.	95 - 110
Teapot, 2 qt., mottled brown glaze	115 - 150
Tobacco jar, covered, 11" high, mottled brown glaze	180 - 220
Toby mug, mottled brown glaze, U.S. Pottery Co., c. 1850	120 - 140
Toby mug, pint, Jolly Good Fellow, 6½", brown glaze	345 - 385
Vase, ear-of-corn-shaped, 7¼" high, mottled brown glaze	84 - 95
Vase, tulip in relief, flint enamel, 7½" high	210 - 230

Bennington Pottery

ILLUSTRATED PIECES:

Top: Hound-handled pitchers (space between head and paws makes it original)	550 - 650 ea.
Bottom: Hound-handled pitcher, "B2" in relief on bottom (rare)	1,100 - 1,400
Lower left: Zachary Taylor pitcher, Rockingham glaze, 13¼" high (rare)	2,500+
Lower right: Cow creamer, mottled brown glaze	140 - 170

Note: The illustrated pieces can be seen at the Houston Museum in Chattanooga, Tennessee. Few museums own the Zachary Taylor pitcher!

Bibles

Don't worry too much about finding a King James Version or a 15th century Gutenberg printed before 1456. On the other hand, there are many "family" Bibles turning up in shops

47

(continued)

Bible

today. Many have their backs broken as this was where money and valuable papers were stored. Did you know The Old Testament contains 39 books, 929 chapters, 23,214 verses, 592,439 words, 2,738,100 letters? You didn't? Well, the New Testament contains 27 books, 260 chapters, 7,950 verses, 182,253 words and 933,380 letters! Also, the name of Jehovah or Lord occurs 6,855 times in the Old Testament and the word "and" occurs in the Old Testament 35,643 times!

Embossed leather-bound, brass hinge, c. early 1800s (ill.)	$ 80 - 90
Large, leatherbound, brass hinges, good condition, mid-1800s	65 - 80
Miniature, 150 pages, microscopic print	50 - 60
Small, carrying size, good condition, mid-1800s	20 - 30

Bicycle Ribbons

Photo Courtesy Hake's Americana & Collectibles

Bicycles

A Frenchman named de Sivrac called it a **celerifere** as early as 1690; in 1779, Blanchard and Magurier called theirs a **velocipede**. Later, around 1815, a German baron improved

The Columbia Road Bicycle

it, calling his a **Draisine**. Curricle, Boneshakers, and finally the change from iron to rubber-rimmed wheels. In 1877, the famous English bicycle, **Ordinary**, showed up in America. Then a man named Pope changed it all with his **Columbia** high wheeler. When John Dunlap invented the pneumatic tire in 1889, "bikers," worldwide, were off and pedaling.

Accessories:

Advertising mirror, National Bicycles	$ 30 - 35
Advertising mirror, Zimmy Bicycles	27 - 33
Advertising pin, metal, Spalding	12 - 20
Advertising charm, brass, Corbin Brake	10 - 18
Catalogue, Stearns Bicycle, c. 1900	43 - 53
Lapel stud, enamel, League of American Wheelmen (L.A.W.), 1898	8 - 12
Lapel stud, enamel, Crown Cycles, La Porte, Inc.	8 - 12
Lapel stud, enamel, Alpha Cycle Co., Philadelphia	8 - 12
Lapel stud, enamel, L.A.W., Mass. Div., Spring Meet, Boston 1896	8 - 12
Lapel stud, enamel, Laclede Mfg. Co. (LaTour), St. Louis	8 - 12
Ribbons (ill.)	9 - 14 ea.
Stickpin, Corbin Brake	10 - 14
Stickpin, New Departure Coaster Brake	10 - 14
Tray, brass and porcelain, Columbia Bicycles	17 - 25

BICYCLES:

Columbia, ladies', 1896, wood rims, studded tires, works	400 - 450
Columbia, Road Model (ill.)	1,200 - 1,400
Columbia, Tourist Model, 1899, complete, good condition	300 - 350
Crescent, still works	300 - 350
Draisine, 1815	3,100 - 3,300
Iver Johnson, sprocket type, 1915, still works	120 - 140
Star, 1885	975 - 1,400

Bing and Grondahl

A porcelain factory established at Copenhagen, Denmark, by Harold Bing in 1853. Famous for their stoneware and earthenware, as well as their porcelain, they achieved fame in the early 1900s for their Christmas plates. See CHRISTMAS PLATES.

Bisque

Bisque

Unglazed china describes it perfectly. Fired only a single time to harden the china, the pieces were then decorated with colors. Primarily a product of Europe, it was also made in the U.S. Some of the bisque-type figurines coming in from Japan are of excellent craftsmanship and too many people are being fooled by unscrupulous dealers. **Please, know your dealer!**

Baby in diaper swing	$ 25 -	35
Bathing Beauty	62 -	72
Black potty babe	35 -	45
Boy and dog, 12" high	56 -	66
Boy and girl on pedestal, 10½" high, pair	60 -	70
Boy, girl, seated, holding basket, 10½" high, pair	85 -	95
Boy on potty	24 -	34
Boy with hat, 7" high (ill.)	43 -	52

Bisque

Boy with dog and gun	55 -	65
Cupid with bow and arrow	48 -	58
Dog with puppies	40 -	48
Epergne, flower pickers, 4 in group	33 -	43
Girl holding kitten	56 -	66
Girl toothpick holder (ill.)	36 -	43
Gray-striped cat, gold colored bow	29 -	39
Kitten with drum	32 -	41
Maid in Victorian dress, 7½" high	48 -	58
Orphan Annie and Sandy vase	45 -	55
Pair, Victorian man and lady	155 -	175
Peasant boy, pipe in mouth	45 -	55
Piano baby with cat (or dog)	130 -	150
Plaque, in relief, farmyard scene	110 -	125
Tobacco jar, dark girl, kerchief forms cover	48 -	58
Toothbrush holder, two kittens	26 -	36
Toothpick shoe	22 -	32
Vase, 7" high, boy playing music for girl, green/blue (ill.)	65 -	75
Woman feeding white rooster	26 -	36

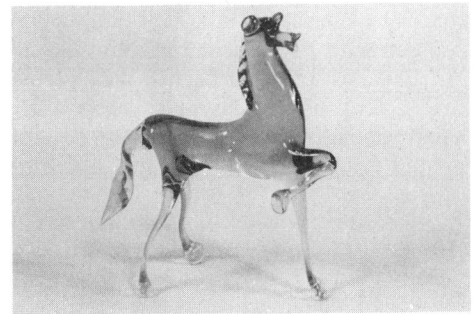

Blown Glass Animals

(continued)

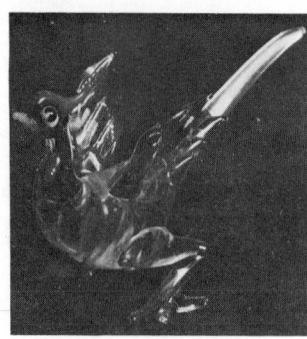

Blown Glass Animals

Blown Glass Animals

These delicate little "creatures" were given away by glassblowers; also sold at expositions, county fairs, etc. Lots of them around and bringing brisk prices when found in perfect condition. Those illustrated here are not old, but keep looking.

Boehm Porcelains

Boehm Porcelains

Edward Marshall Boehm made his first pottery figures near Trenton, New Jersey, in 1949. Before he passed away in January of 1969, his beautiful birds, animals, flowers, etc., were known, worldwide. Today, many fine museums throughout the world include Mr. Boehm's works as part of their permanent collections. Today, his works bring huge prices, when authenticated, and rightfully so!

BIRDS:

American Eagle, large,
1957, 18" × 15" . . . . $ 9,500 - 10,500
American Eagle, small,
1957, 15" × 12" . . . . 6,900 - 7,400
Blue Grosbeak, 1969,
11" × 10" × 7" . . . . 1,400 - 1,700
Bob White Quail, pr., 1953,
female, 7"; male, 8" . . . . 8,300 - 8,500

Golden Oriental Pheasant,
1954, 6" × 21" . . . . 32,000 - 33,500
Nuthatch, 1963, 11" × 16" 425 - 450
Robin, 1964, 13" × 8" . . . . 5,200 - 5,600
Tern, Common (ill.), 1968,
16" × 12" × 14" . . . . . . 6,100 - 6,400
Western Meadowlark,
1971, 13" × 9" . . . . 2,300 - 2,500
Young American Eagle,
1969, 9½" × 6" × 7" . . . 2,200 - 2,400

ANIMALS:

Angus Bull, 1950,
5" × 8¼" . . . . 2,400 - 2,600
Beagle, 1952, 7" × 6¼" . . 675 - 775
Chipmunk, preening, 1959,
3" . . . . 1,700 - 1,900
Fawn, 1954, 3" × 4" . . . . . 875 - 975
Lion Cub, 1954, 4½" × 5" . 1,000 - 1,300
Raccoons, 1971,
11" × 11" × 10" . . . . . . 1,700 - 1,900
Tiger, 1952, 6" × 15" . . . . 2,600 - 2,800

FLOWERS:

Daisies, yellow, 1971,
8" × 8" × 6" . . . . 275 - 325
Swan Centerpiece,
6" × 22" × 9" . . . . 1,850 - 2,000

PAINTINGS:

Cockatoo and Flowers,
1971, 18½" × 15½" . . . 3,700 - 4,100
Mockingbirds, pr., 1970,
12" × 15" . . . . 2,700 - 2,950

PLATES:

European Bird Plates, set
of 8, 10" dia. . . . . 475 - 575 all
Tropical Fish Plate, 1955,
10" dia. . . . . 3,800 - 4,000

DECORATIVE PIECES:

Apollo, 7½" × 3½", 1953 . 775 - 850
Choir Boy, 1949, 4½" . . . . 350 - 425
Cupid with Flute, 1954,
5¼" . . . . 600 - 675
Mercury, 1953, 7½" × 4" . 700 - 800
Pope John XXIII, 1960,
10" . . . . 1,600 - 1,800
Tulip Pitcher, 1956, 6½" . . 3,200 - 3,500
Venus, 1953, 8" . . . . 700 - 800

BOOKS:

Boehm's Birds, 1960,
8" × 10¾" . . . . 475 - 525
EMB 1913-1969, deluxe
edition, 9" × 12", 1970 . 170 - 200

Bohemian Glass

Ruby-colored, flashed, stained, in blue, yellow, green, other colors; 1870s until early 1900s, most sought after today. Originally made in Bohemia which is now part of Czechoslovakia. Hundreds of reproductions on the market. Careful!

Bohemian Glass

Caster set, 4 bottles, ruby-
colored, etched landscapes . . . . $160 - 170
Compote, red, grapevine motif,
6½" high, cov. . . . . 110 - 130
Decanter (ill.) . . . . 60 - 70
Decanter, 6 small glasses, deer,
forest, etched, yellow . . . . 175 - 200
Goblet, dog chasing deer, etched,
yellow . . . . 40 - 50
Goblet, footed, flower scene,
yellow flashed, 7" high . . . . . . 60 - 65
Lustres, pair, crystal prisms,
15" high . . . . 175 - 190
Pitcher, deer and castle, 6
tumblers, ruby flashed . . . . . . 98 - 115
Pitcher, grape pattern, ruby
flashed, 12½" high . . . . 105 - 115
Rose petal jar, painted figure,
ruby flashed, 8" high . . . . 55 - 65
Tumbler, deer, etched, green . . . . 48 - 58
Vase, deer and castle, blue,
10" high, pair . . . . 87 - 97
Vase, birds and flowers, red,
etched, 11" high . . . . 115 - 130
Water set, leaf and grape motif,
ruby, etched, 7 pieces . . . . 140 - 155

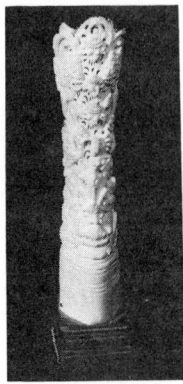

Bone

Bone

So much of this is being sold as ivory, especially the pieces flooding in from the Orient. But, because so much of it is around, collectors are now buying same. If you're going to spend huge sums for genuine ivory, have a qualified jeweler test it. Sulphuric acid applied to vegetable ivory, others, will cause a pink coloring in about 10 minutes. This can be removed by washing with water. The acid has no effect on genuine ivory. REPEAT: let an expert do it—**any** acid is dangerous!

Bone China

This is made from clay with the ashes of birds' bones or other small animals ground up and added to the clay to give it added strength.

Bone Dishes

Bone Dishes

In the late 1800s, it was considered fashionable to eat fowl with your fingers. These dishes were held close to the mouth to put the bones and other unedible material into. Haviland, Rosenthal, etc. made them from the mid-1700s on. Today, people use them for ashtrays. Price depends on who made them.

Book Matches

In the 1850s sheets of thin wooden matches appeared on the market. In 1897, the Diamond Match Company produced them in folder form with advertisements on the outside. Today, millions of advertisers use them to sell their products. There are countless thousands of collectors saving them today. Any and all are collectible. If you begin a collection, it's a good idea to remove the matches before putting them in an album.

Common—usually purchased in
bulk (per thousand) . . . . $ 10 - 16
Early 1900s—usually purchased
in bulk (per hundred) . . . . 19 - 26

Bookends

Bookmark

Books

Bookends

For years they were considered fashionable. Made from every type of material. All kinds are showing up at shops and shows—from the sublime to the ridiculous.

Bison, 6" x 6", late 1800s . . . . $	165 -	180
Bronze tigers on marble bases, 5" × 2½", late 1800s	100 -	120
Cast (pot metal) dog heads, 4" sq., pre-WWI	20 -	30
Copper ships, lead-weighted bases, 6" × 3¼", 1900s . . .	40 -	50
Elephants, rearing, bronze, 1890s, 8½" x 6"	180 -	200
Indians, brass, on wood base, 6" x 8"	145 -	160
Ivory elephants, teakwood bases, 6" high, 1890s	120 -	140
Jade Foo dogs, ebony bases, 5" × 3", mid-1800s	1,100 - 1,400	
Lincoln, bust, copper, 1880s, 7" x 9½"	165 -	180
Monkeys-at-play, carved wood, 6" × 4", early 1900s .	35 -	45
Owl-on-limb, brass, 7½" x 9" .	55 -	65
Painted iron, flowers (ill.)	28 -	38
Pelicans, carved wood, 6½" x 7"	40 -	50
Porcelain, Japan, 5½" high, 1930s	30 -	40
Quartz birds, copper bases, 4½" × 3½", 1900s	80 -	90
Reclining nudes, brass bases, 6½" × 3", 1900s	95 -	110
Roosters, painted, on wood base, 8" x 7"	45 -	55
Tigers, bronze, late 1800s, 6½" x 9"	150 -	160

Bookmarks

Used for just that; silk, leather, paper, etc. A "fun" collectible, and there are lots of old ones around. See—Stevengraphs.

Books

Soft clay cylinders, wax slates, papyrus scrolls, the degreased skins of cows and goats—a few ancient "books," going back before time immemorial. When Gutenberg (or was it Koster?) invented the printing press, things changed for the better in the book business. If you're looking for out-of-print books, Colonel "out-of-print" Book Service, Inc., 23 E. 4th St., New York, N.Y. 10003, is tops in its field.

Addison, Joseph, *The Free-Holder*, London, 1716 . . $	100 -	150
Ade, George, *Fables in Slang*, Chicago, 1900 . . .	35 -	45
Agee, James, *Permit Me Voyage*, New Haven, 1934	270 -	300
Alcott, Louisa M., *Little Men*, Boston	165 -	190
Alger, Horatio, Jr., *Do and Dare*, Philadelphia, no date (ill.)	30 -	40
Alger, Horatio, *Ragged Dick*, Boston, 1868, 1st ed.	525 -	575
Anderson, H.C., *Tales for Children*, London, 1891	12 -	22
Anderson, Sherwood, *Winesburg, Ohio*, New York, 1919	95 -	110
Anderson, Sherwood, *Perhaps Women*, New York, 1930s	70 -	80
Arnold, Matthew, *Alaric at Rome*, London, 1893 .	100 -	110
Auden, W.H., *Spain*, London, 1937	23 -	33
Austen, Jane, *Sense & Sensibility*, London, 1813 (3 vols.)	175 -	195
Bisset, J., *The Orphan Boy*, 1799	28 -	38

Bacon, Francis, *Certaine
Considerations,* 1640 . . .   160 -   175
(was he Shakespeare's
"ghost writer?")
Beecher, Henry Ward, *Nor-
wood,* New York, 1874 . .   58 -   68
Beerbohm, Max, *Things
Old & New,* London, 1923   42 -   50
Buck, Pearl, *Dragon Seed,*
1942, 1st ed., New York .   12 -   21
Buck, Pearl, *The Good
Earth,* New York, 2nd ed.   15 -   25
Caldwell, Taylor, *This Side
of Innocence,* New York,
1946 . . . .   10 -   15
Cather, Willa, *Obscure
Destinies,* New York,
1932 . . . .   45 -   55
Clemens, Samuel Lang-
horne ("Mark Twain"),
*Tom Sawyer, The Prince
& the Pauper, A Connec-
ticut Yankee in King Ar-
thur's Court*—a few of
the many books by a
great man, a great
writer. His works bring
hundreds of dollars.
Know your dealer!
Conrad, Joseph, *A Set of
Six,* London, 1908 (one of
Poland's greatest
writers) . . . .   65 -   75
Crane, Stephen, *The Red
Badge of Courage,* New
York, 1895 . . . .   60 -   70
Crane, *The Little Regi-
ment,* New York, 1896 . .   52 -   62
Cruikshank, George, *The
Humorist,* London, 1822
(he illustrated many of
Charles Dickens' books) .   110 -   130
DeFoe, Daniel—he wrote
many books but his *The
Life & Strange Surpris-
ing Adventures of Robin-
son Crusoe, of New York,
Mariner,* printed in Lon-
don 1719, was his most
famous and most valu-
able. Published in two
volumes, it's a rare, rare
find! . . . .   14,000 - 16,000
A few other books writ-
ten by DeFoe are *Mem-
oirs of Count Tariff*
(350-400), *Advice to the
People of Great Britain*
(175-200) and *The
History of the Wars*
(225-275)

Du Maurier, Daphne,
Rebecca, New York 1938   10 -   15
Grey, Zane, *The Lost
Wagon Train,* New York,
1936 . . . .   10 -   15
The greatest western
writer of them all! Ned
Buntline, eat your heart
out!
Hersey, John, *The Wall,*
New York, 1950 . . . .   15 -   22
Lindbergh, Charles, *We*
(Lindy, a kitten and "The
Spirit of St. Louis"—the
rest is in the history
books), New York, 1927 .   15 -   25
Lindbergh, Anne Morrow,
North to the Orient, New
York, 1935 . . . .   15 -   27
Tarkington, Booth, *Seven-
teen,* New York, 1916,
1st ed. . . . .   15 -   25
Trench, P.C., *Tiger Hunt-
ing,* London, 1836 . . . . .   150 -   160
Wescott, *David Harum,*
New York, 1898 (remem-
ber the movie with Will
Rogers?) . . . .   18 -   28
Wouk, Herman, *The Caine
Mutiny,* Garden City,
1952 . . . .   14 -   23

Obviously, there are millions of old books in every
type of shop, at flea markets (you mean you
haven't bought a copy of my FLEA MARKET
PRICE GUIDE, $6.95), in attics and basements,
etc.

Boot Scrapers

Boot Scrapers

Usually set in the brick or cement of the
front porch, the sharp blade was used to

(continued)

remove the mud or snow from the soles of the boots. Early 1800s to mid-1900s.

Antique car, brass . . . . $ 95 - 110
Long-backed horse, iron . . . . 28 - 37
Bristle brushes in metal frame . . 40 - 50
Cast iron, bristle brush (ill.) . . . . 24 - 34
Cast iron, plain, still usable . . . . . 16 - 29
Whale's belly, cast iron (rare) . . . 85 - 120

Bootjacks

Bootjacks

"Naughtie Nellie" and the "Beetle" are two of the most collectible, though both are being reproduced. They were then and are still being used to remove tight boots. Usually in wood or cast iron.

American bulldog, folding pistol, brass . . . . $ 70 - 80
Same, except iron . . . . 50 - 60
Beetle, harp-shaped, iron . . . . . . 50 - 60
Beetle, brass . . . . 83 - 95
Bettle, iron . . . . 23 - 33
Bull, cast iron . . . . 75 - 85
Cricket, cast iron, 10½" . . . . 22 - 30
Cap pistol, cast iron . . . . 40 - 50
Naughty Nellie, brass . . . . 75 - 90
Naughty Nellie, cast iron (ill.) . . . 40 - 48
Vine, cast iron, 11½" . . . . 17 - 25
Wood, hand-carved cherry (ill.) . . 33 - 43
Wood, hand-carved, lady's leg . . . 32 - 42

Being reproduced in Cricket, Naughty Nellie, Pistol. Probably others.

Bottles

APOTHECARY

Brown porcelain, label. 7" high . . $ 17 - 23
Brown, blown, gold label, 8½" high . . . . 18 - 22
Clear, blown, stopper, 8" high . . . 16 - 20
Capsicum on porcelain label, blown, 10½" high . . . . 18 - 22
Bulbous, salesman's sample, fancy base, 11" high . . . . 23 - 30
Clear, blown, Tinc, Orsc on label, 12" high . . . . 18 - 24

Apothecary Bottle

Blown, Masson's Guaranteed on label, 14" high . . . . 21 - 30
Blown, Self Cure on label, 15" high . . . . 20 - 25
Blown, squat green, 5" high (ill.) . . . . 18 - 23
Brown, Extr. Strict on label, ground stopper, 15¼" high . . . 20 - 25

ARDOS

Clock . . . . 40 - 45
Green Duck . . . . 40 - 45
Rocker . . . . 26 - 33

AVON

Alpine flask, full & boxed . . . . . 50 - 58
Antique telephone, 1969 . . . . 11 - 15
Apothecary jar, 1965 . . . . 16 - 19
Bath, Seasons, 1967 . . . . 7 - 9
Bath urn, clear . . . . 8 - 11
Bath urn, milk glass, 1966 . . . . . 19 - 26
Bay rum jug . . . . 11 - 16
Bay rum keg, 1962 . . . . 19 - 25
Boot, gold top, label . . . . 7 - 11
Boot, silver top, 1965 . . . . 8 - 12
Bud vase, 1962 . . . . 12 - 20
Bud vase, 1966 . . . . 9 - 14
Bud vase, 1968 . . . . 12 - 17
Candleholder, Christmas, frosted, apple, 1967 . . . . 10 - 15
Candlestick, Christmas, Charisma cologne, 4 oz, red/gold (ill.) . . . . 9 - 13
Casey's lantern, amber, green, red . . . . 14 - 21
Christmas ornaments—angel, balls, candle, icicle, sparkler, tree . . . . 12 - 19
Daylight Shaving Time, 1968-70, 6 oz. . . . . 9 - 12
Decanter—inkwell, owl . . . . 6 - 10
Dollars and Scents, 1966 . . . . 20 - 26
Forever Spring—cologne, cream sachet, perfume, powder sachet 12 - 20
Gavel, 1967, 6 oz. . . . . 15 - 25
Gold Cadillac . . . . 10 - 15
Greek goddess . . . . 10 - 16
Keynote, label . . . . 12 - 17
Nearness—body powder, toilet water . . . . 18 - 26

Pony post—short, tall, label	9 - 17
Quaintance—cologne, cream lotion, powder sachet, 1949 ...	50 - 60
Quaintance diary, 1949	95 - 115
Silver stein, 6 oz., 8 oz..........	10 - 15

Avon Bottle

Snail, boxed, label	9 - 15
Stagecoach embossed, 2 oz., 4 oz.	10 - 15
Topaze cream lotion, label	8 - 16
Topaze Gem perfume, glass stopper	120 - 135
Viking horn................	18 - 30
Kitten Little cologne, 1973	3 - 4
Warrior head, blue and silver, frosted label..............	13 - 23
Western Choice (steer horns) pair	19 - 30
Wild Rose—cream lotion, cream sachet, toilet water	20 - 28
Windjammer, printed label	8 - 16

BALLANTINE (whiskey)

Duck	22 - 32
Fisherman..................	19 - 27
Golf Bag	14 - 24
Knight, silver	18 - 29

Barber Bottles

BARBER (clear, colored or milk glass)

Amber....................	60 - 70
Amethyst	70 - 80
Apple green, painted flowers (ill.)	40 - 50
Bay rum, amethyst, etched, pewter spout	78 - 88
Cobalt, pewter stopper	56 - 65
Cranberry, Mary Gregory figure, pewter stopper	152 - 170
Carnival, marigold, metal stopper	65 - 70
Cut glass, sterling silver stopper, initialed	75 - 85
Hobnail, honey amber, stopper ..	65 - 75
Mary Gregory (ill.)............	140 - 155
Milk glass, octagon base, stopper	62 - 72
Sandwich glass, amethyst, silver stopper	144 - 153
Spanish Lace, blue, stopper	38 - 48
Swirled Rib, ITP, amber	71 - 80
Tiffany Glass, sterling silver stopper, initialed BJM	375 - 425

BEER

Milk glass, 9″ high .... $	21 - 32
Red, quart..................	12 - 17
Schmidt, original label, quart ...	17 - 27
Olive green, quart	8 - 16

BISCHOFF

Bell tower, 1959............. $	40 - 50
Boy: Chinese, Spanish.........	45 - 55
Egyptian vase: single, double ...	40 - 50
Fish bottle ashtray	21 - 31
Grecian vase: decanter	16 - 26
Nigerian mask...............	22 - 29
Red Clown..................	24 - 34
Senorita	25 - 35

BITTERS

From the 1860s until the early 1900s, various concoctions of herbs were mixed with alcohol (sometimes as much as 80%) and peddled as get-wells, feel-betters. More than one gal, fighting Demon Gin, got her pep, probably unknowingly, after sipping her husband's bitters.

Atwood's jaundice, screw top, aqua.................... $	36 - 46
Brown's iron, honey amber	33 - 43
Clark's sherry wine, aqua	111 - 119
Cole Brothers	32 - 42
Electric, embossed	47 - 56
Goff's herb, embossed, aqua	28 - 38
Pinkerston's Wahoo and Claisaya bitters, amber	56 - 66
Prickly ash, quart, amber	80 - 90
Tippecanoe, amber	115 - 130
Willards Golden Seal, aqua	72 - 82
Yerba Buena, amber, flask	110 - 118

BOLS

Ballerina .... $	16 - 26
Cream de menthe, Delft	21 - 31
Dutch: boy, girl..............	28 - 38

BORGHINI

Dog .... $	23 - 33

55

(continued)

Ford car, recent, old . . . . 12 - 17
Horse's head . . . . 17 - 26
Nubian girl . . . . 9 - 15
Santa Maria . . . . 7 - 12

EZRA BROOKS
Antique cannon . . . . $ 20 - 27
Bucket of blood . . . . 22 - 32
Cable cars, 3 colors, each . . . . 17 - 27
Clown on drum, short, tall . . . . . 68 - 80
Dueling pistol . . . . 17 - 27
Churchill bust . . . . 15 - 25
Grizzly bear . . . . 12 - 24
Gun series (4) . . . . 28 - 38
Harold's Club dice . . . . 16 - 26
Kentucky gentleman . . . . 22 - 32
Mr. Foremost . . . . 22 - 32
Oil derrick (gusher) . . . . 18 - 28
Potbelly stove . . . . 16 - 27
Queen of hearts . . . . 16 - 27
Reno arch . . . . 12 - 21
Trout and fly . . . . 17 - 27
Wheat shocker, Kansas . . . . 26 - 36

J.W. DANT
Alamo (black) . . . . $ 15 - 22
Bobwhite . . . . 26 - 36
Crossing the Delaware . . . . 16 - 27
Field birds (Chukar partridge,
etc.) each . . . . 15 - 26
Indianapolis 500 . . . . 19 - 28
Patrick Henry . . . . 16 - 26

GEORGE DICKEL
Golf club, large . . . . $ 19 - 29
Golf club, miniature . . . . 7 - 12
Powderhorn . . . . 17 - 27

FIGURALS
Black bear, Smirnoff vodka . . . . $ 18 - 30
Brown owl . . . . 16 - 25
Christmas tree, star stopper . . . . 140+
Crying baby, clear, 6½" high . . . 40 - 50

Figural Bottle

Elephant (used as bank) . . . . . . 9 - 16
Face, 12" high (ill.) . . . . 45 - 50
Fish, ashtray . . . . 26 - 36
George Washington bust,
miniature . . . . 24 - 34
Guitar, brown . . . . 9 - 18
Hunter, lady, pr. . . . . 32 - 42
Lincoln (used as bank) . . . . 12 - 22
Queen Elizabeth II . . . . 16 - 26
River Queen boat . . . . 17 - 26
Violin, blue . . . . 48 - 54
Watchtower bell . . . . 27 - 38

GARNIER
Bellows . . . . $ 18 - 26
Bullfighter . . . . 20 - 35
Cardinal . . . . 21 - 33
Duck . . . . 22 - 34
Indian . . . . 19 - 32
Locomotive . . . . 18 - 30
New Mexico road runner . . . . . . 16 - 30
Parrot . . . . 31 - 42
Pheasant . . . . 19 - 33
Quail . . . . 17 - 29
Ship scene . . . . 18 - 30

GRENADIER, Soldiers
Colonial series, five so far,
military in nature . . . . $ 19 - 30

HOUSE OF KOSHU
Daughter . . . . $ 19 - 27
Golden pagoda . . . . 16 - 30
Pink geisha . . . . 50 - 60
Princess . . . . 17 - 31
Two lovers . . . . 12 - 21
White pagoda . . . . 22 - 36

JIM BEAM
The Jim Beam bottles have created quite a
sensation in the bottle field. Several books
are available on these highly-collectible bottles. The Jim Beams listed here are for identification purposes.

CENTENNIAL SERIES
Alaska Purchase (1966) . . . . $ 22 - 38
Baseball . . . . 18 - 34
Civil War: North, South, each . . . 48 - 58
Laramie . . . . 14 - 24
Preakness . . . . 15 - 23
St. Louis Arch, 1964 . . . . 32 - 41
Santa Fe, 1960 . . . . 255 - 275

CUSTOMER SPECIALTIES
Cal-Neva . . . . $ 16 - 24
First National Bank of Chicago,
1964, has recently been "counter-
feited"—be careful here! Orig-
inal, 1964 . . . . 3,500+
Foremost, black and gold, gray
and gold . . . . 162 - 184
Foremost, pink speckled beauty . 700 - 800
Harold's Club: 12 bottles made so
far with more to come. They
vary in range, price-wise, from

56

20 to 275. Do know with whom you're doing business!

Harold's Club, blue slot machine .	21 -	32
Harold's Club, man in a barrel, No. 1, 1957	520 - 560	
Harold's Club, VIP Executive, 1967, 1968, 1969, 1970, 1971 . .	65 - 195	

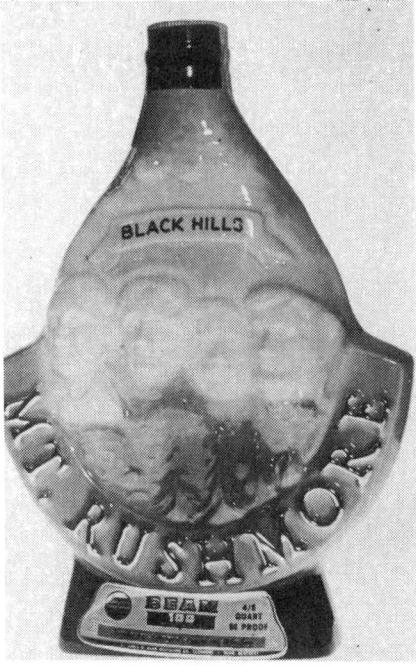

Jim Beam

EXECUTIVE SERIES

Royal porcelain, 1955	$250 -	275
Royal Di Monte, 1957	90 -	110
Blue cherub, 1960	100 -	120
Royal rose, 1963	62 -	74
Marbled fantasy, 1965	85 -	95
Prestige, 1967	34 -	50
Presidential, 1968	19 -	29

POLITICAL SERIES

Ashtrays, Elephant and Donkey, all years, pair	$ 31 -	41
Boxers, pair	41 -	50
Clowns, pair	22 -	33

REGAL CHINA SERIES

Arizona tombstone	$ 21 -	31
Black canasta, 1956	17 -	30
Broadmoor Hotel	12 -	30
Cable car, 1968	15 -	25
Grand Canyon, 1969	21 -	34
Kentucky Cardinal, 1973 trophy .	35 -	44
Oatmeal jug	61 -	70
Pony Express	11 -	21
Scotch bell ringer	20 -	34
Thailand	9 -	17
Yosemite	10 -	18

STATE SERIES

Alaska Star, 1958, 1964, 1965 . . .	$105 - 120	
Hawaii, 1959, 1967	74 -	90
Kentucky Derby, black head, 1967	20 -	30
Nebraska	20 -	29
North Dakota	110 - 130	
West Virginia Centennial	150 - 170	

TROPHY SERIES

Doe, 1963, 1967	$ 47 -	57
Dog, 1959	74 -	86
Fish, 1965	50 -	63
Horses, three colors, each	34 -	48
Ram	210 - 230	
Woodpecker	16 -	29

GLASS SPECIALTIES

Cannon	$ 17 -	29
Cleopatra, rust, 1962	24 -	32
Dancing Scot, short, 1963	47 -	58
Dancing Scot, tall, 1963	16 -	29
Delft blue, Delft rose	12 -	24
Mark Antony, 1962	24 -	36
Pin: gold top, white top, wooden top	12 -	27
Pyrex coffee warmers, 1954, four colors	16 -	27
Royal Emperor	12 -	24
Royal Reserve	12 -	22
Smoked Crystal, 1964	14 -	24

DOCTORS

In the late 1800s many "doctors" promised their product would cure everything from falling hair to falling arches. (Alcohol was the base, and some users touched every one!)

Dr. Baker's Pain Relief, aqua, pint	$ 10 -	20

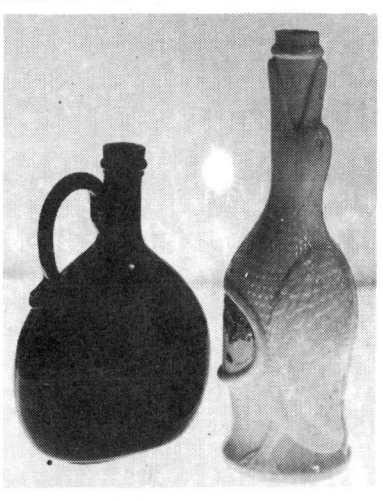

Chestnut Flask   **Duck Bottle**

Dr. Baxter's Benevolent Pro-
tector, green, pint . . . .   11 - 19
Dr. Churchill's Hypophosphite
Pectoral . . . .   10 - 22
Dr. Kennedy's Prairie Weed . . . .   26 - 36
Dr. Kilmer's Swamp Root Kidney
Cure . . . .   12 - 24
Dr. Miles Nervene . . . .   10 - 20
Dr. Caldwell's Syrup Pepsin, aqua   12 - 19
Dr. Pepper's (indented letters) . .   11 - 22
Dr. Wistar's Balsam . . . .   32 - 42
Dr. Woods Sarsaparilla and
Wild Cherry . . . .   74 - 90

LUXARDO
Bacchus . . . . $ 12 - 21
Clock . . . .   16 - 30
Dolphin . . . .   50 - 62
Gondola . . . .   10 - 20
Miss Luxardo . . . .   21 - 33
Santa Maria . . . .   22 - 33
Tapa Print . . . .   12 - 21
Zodiac . . . .   28 - 38

MEDICINE
Bird's lung cure, aqua . . . . $ 10 - 21
Davis vegetable compound . . . . .   26 - 38
Hall's catarrh cure, aqua . . . . . .   10 - 20
Lydia Pinkham (most famous) . .   12 - 21
Moxie Nerve, aqua . . . .   18 - 27
River Swamp chill and fever cure   74 - 84
Shiloh's consumption cure, aqua .   10 - 20

MINERAL WATERS
Buffalo Lithia Water, green,
quart . . . . $ 18 - 29
Congress and Empire 'E', pint . .   24 - 36
Empire Water, quart . . . .   34 - 44
Hathorn Spring, quart . . . .   29 - 43
Saratoga Red Spring, pint . . . . .   40 - 50
John Ryan, cobalt, pint . . . .   30 - 40
Clark and White, olive green,
quart . . . .   36 - 44
Gettysburg, green, quart . . . . . .   50 - 64
Mississquoi Springs, brown,
pint and quart . . . .   38 - 48

MINIATURES
Ardo Paestum . . . . $ 8 - 17
Borghini black cat . . . .   12 - 21
Borghini candleholder . . . .   15 - 25
Borghini candlelamp . . . .   14 - 25
Borghini redbird . . . .   8 - 17
Drioli cat . . . .   16 - 27
Drioli dog . . . .   16 - 26
Drioli duck . . . .   14 - 28
Irish Mist soldier . . . .   8 - 15
Larson's Viking ship, china . . . .   19 - 28
Larson's Viking ship, glass . . . . .   16 - 27
Ryenbende: churn, cruet, oil
lamp, shoe . . . .   9 - 21

OLD FITZGERALD CABIN STILL
Candlelight, pair . . . . $ 24 - 34
California . . . .   16 - 29

Santa Claus   **Uncle Sam**

Fish . . . .   8 - 16
Florentine . . . .   17 - 26
Gold coaster . . . .   21 - 31
Hillbilly: pint, fifth, 1969 . . . . . .   12 - 22
Lexington . . . .   10 - 20
Quail . . . .   11 - 24
Sons of Erin, 1969 . . . .   16 - 26
Tournament, 1963 . . . .   19 - 28
Tree of Life . . . .   15 - 24
Venetian . . . .   9 - 18
Weller masterpiece . . . .   41 - 60

PERFUME
Cut glass, Harvard cut, silver cap $ 36 - 46
Black amethyst, marked
'Guerlain' France . . . .   18 - 30
Bulbous, sterling silver overlay,
7" high . . . .   75 - 90
Crystal, silver overlay, floral,
birds . . . .   72 - 86
Diamonds, sunbursts, cut glass .   42 - 52
Hobnail pattern, clear . . . .   12 - 21
Pelican, Germany, porcelain . . . .   16 - 26
Lalique, rectangular . . . .   42 - 54
Silver overlay, leaf decor,
ball stopper . . . .   19 - 29
Thousand-eye, bulbous . . . .   24 - 34

POISON
Amber, 3-sided, riffled,
marked Poison . . . . $ 14 - 26
Cobalt, 3-sided, riffled,
marked Poison . . . .   18 - 28

Skull and Crossbones, embossed
Poison on all sides . . . .   24 - 34

SODA AND SARSAPARILLA

Ayers compound extract
sarsaparilla, aqua . . . .$ 9 - 17
Babcock's sarsaparilla, aqua . . . .   56 - 60
Bull's sarsaparilla, plain, aqua . .   76 - 90
Coca-Cola, dated 1909, Knoxville,
brown . . . .   19 - 30
Dana's sarsaparilla, Bangor,
Maine, aqua . . . .   21 - 36
DeWitt's sarsaparilla, aqua . . . .   27 - 33
Dr. Green's sarsaparilla, clear . . .   16 - 28
Joy's sarsaparilla, aqua . . . .   27 - 38
Rodway's sarsaparilla, aqua . . . .   26 - 34
Scoville's unembossed, aqua . . . .   16 - 29
Verner's ginger ale, embossed
seal . . . .   12 - 18

WHISKEY AND OTHER SPIRITS

Belle of Anderson, milk glass . . . $115 - 132
Binninger's Regulator, clock
shape, amber . . . .   520 - 570

Whiskey Flask

Binninger's Peach Brandy jug . .   270 - 310
Binninger's barrel-shaped
whiskey, amber . . . .   480 - 525
Chestnut Grove whiskey, pint . .   170 - 200
Deep Spring, Tennessee, whiskey   22 - 32
Golden Wedding, 1933 . . . .   12 - 22
Hart, John and Company,
figural, amber . . . .   37 - 46
Hayner Distilling Company,
Dayton, St. Louis, clear . . . . . .   12 - 21
Jo-Jo Monogram, labeled, pint
and quart . . . .   68 - 76
Lady's Leg, amethyst, green or
amber . . . .   66 - 76
Lighthouse figural, C.T. Morris,
amber, quart . . . .   115 - 126
Mallard Distilling, Baltimore and
NYC, violin-shaped . . . .   30 - 42
Miller's Game Cock, Boston . . . .   16 - 26
Jessie Moore's whiskey, amber,
fifth . . . .   58 - 70
Whitney, 1800s (ill.) . . . .   170 - 190

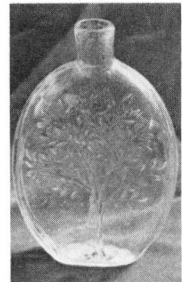
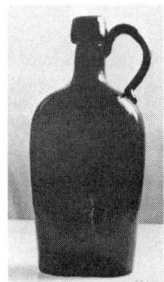

Whiskey Flasks

Whiskey (New)
I.W. Harper / Seagrams

Spring-winter, aqua, ½ pt., (ill.) . .   195 - 220
Old Grey Mare (ill.), amber . . . . .   110 - 140
E. G. Booz Cabin whiskey—an
original would be worth upwards of $300, but it was
reproduced in the 1920s, a
perfect duplication EXCEPT
FOR ONE THING, the orig-
inal has a period (.) after the
word Whiskey on the "roof" of
the bottle. Careful! The 1960s
reproduction is so obvious, it
should fool no one.
Old Charter Pure Rye . . . .   18 - 29
Old Quaker, embossed anchor
bottom, clear, pint . . . .   40 - 55
Paul Jones (printed on bottom),
amber, pint . . . .   19 - 24
Quaker Maid, amber . . . .   32 - 40
Van Denebergh, gin . . . .   110 - 130

MISCELLANEOUS

Anderson's Dermador . . . . $ 14 - 22
Pickle barrel, emerald green . . . .   24 - 34
Binocular-shaped, black, quart . .   12 - 20
Extracts bottle, blue . . . .   10 - 21
Buffalo lithia water . . . .   10 - 20
Bunker Hill pickles, honey amber   30 - 40

59

(continued)

Burnham's beef wine and iron ...	6 -	10
Camel saddle, hand-blown	44 -	51
Champagne, magnum, green ...	26 -	34
Geisha Girl, purple	21 -	32
Glover's Imperial mange medicine, amber	6 -	16
H.J. Heinz, patented 1890	14 -	30
Harden's Hand Grenade, star, blue, still full	21 -	34
Horlick's malted milk, tin lid	7 -	12
Hudson's Bay, flat, miniature (rare)	38 -	46
Belt buckle, Civil War	12 -	21

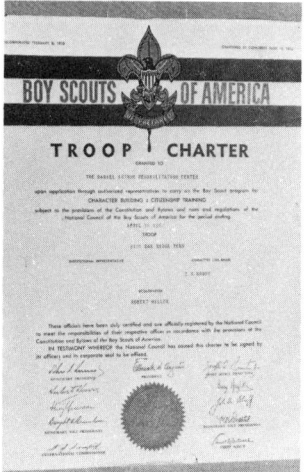

Boy Scout Collectibles

Boy Scout Collectibles

The Boy Scouts of America were incorporated Feb. 8, 1910.

Bugle, brass	$ 35 -	50
Old Scout Manuals, 1920s and 1930s	10 -	22
Scoutmaster pins	8 -	15
Scout and Cub Scout charters (ill.)	5 -	12
Uniform, complete, 1930s	25 -	35

Branding Irons

Used in the West for identifying a rancher's cattle, today they're collectible. Usually twisted iron on a long iron shaft with wooden handle, they were first used in the early 1800s in what is now California. Still being used on cattle and horses today.

Wrought iron, letters "CP" (ill.) . $ 20 - 30
This is an average price, coast-to-coast.

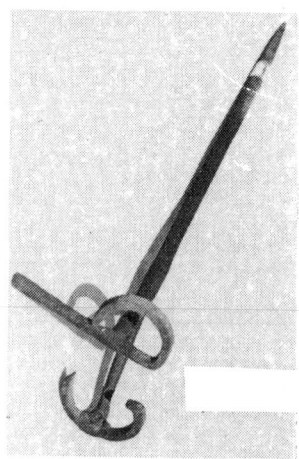

Branding Irons

Brass

Brass

A yellow alloy, usually consisting of copper and zinc, brass is an easily hammered metal which, when polished, takes on a beautiful hue. It's been in use since the days of the early Romans.

Ashtray, 5" diameter, marked India	$ 8 -	15
Ashtray, foliage, marked "India"	9 -	19
Ashtray/match holder, embossed scrolls, dolphins (ill.)	38 -	48
Ashtray shaped like lock (ill.) ...	18 -	23
Bookends, rearing horses, 7" high, pr................	40 -	48
Bowl, 6" diameter, footed, marked India	16 -	27
Bowl, 8" dia., marked "China," dragon motif	50 -	63
Bullet mold, hinged	48 -	58
Candlesticks, English, marked "Storrar's, Chester," 10" high .	76 -	90
Candlesticks, turned stem, 8" high, pr., ...	75 -	90
Candlestick, push-up ejector, 5" high, pr.	78 -	93
Coal hod	120 -	145
Cigarette box, yellow, green, red stones inlaid in lid	25 -	32

Coffeepot, 10" high	40 - 50
Coal bucket, iron bail handle	78 - 90
Dipper, 12½" long	45 - 55
Easel, probably held miniature painting, 4½" high	50 - 65
Jelly kettle, iron bail handle, 2-gallon capacity	74 - 88
Ice tongs, heavy	65 - 80
Incense burner, 2-part, marked China	16 - 27
Incense burner, w/lid, 4" dia., 1890s	18 - 32
Kettles, 6, 8, 10, 12 quarts	70 - 125
Keys, assorted sizes	9 - 20
Letter opener, dragon, marked China, 13" long	13 - 24
Mortar and pestle, pewter-lined, Russian, eagle mark	140 - 150
Pails, 4, 8 quarts	95 - 150
Paperweight, lion and cubs, 6" dia.	40 - 50
Scales, grocery, counter type . . .	75 - 95
Sewing bird—see Sewing Accessories	
Sewing dog—see Sewing Accessories	
Candlesticks, mid-1800s, 10" high, pr.	86 - 98
Sundial, on 3' high marble base . .	175 - 250
Trivet, pierced fretwork, ball feet, 1920s	16 - 30
Tea kettle, 6½" high	75 - 90
Tray, flower motif, 7½" dia.	48 - 55
Umbrella stand, "flower" ring handles	80 - 95
Whistle, factory, 16" high	130 - 160

Bread Plates

Bread Plates and Trays

Usually popularizing people, places and things from the mid-1800s on, they were made of glass, china and metal. The U.S. coin plates are considered scarce.

Bread Is the Staff of Life, clear glass	$ 40 - 50
Philadelphia Centennial, 1876, clear glass	46 - 57
Barley, clear glass	38 - 47
Bible	48 - 58
Bunker Hill Monument	60 - 70
Grant Memorial, clear glass	60 - 65
Liberty Bell, blue glass	63 - 73
Coin, U.S., dollar decoration, clear glass	280 - 320
Coin, Columbian, gold gilt, clear glass	110 - 130
Constitution	85 - 100
Dancing Bears	55 - 65
Faith, Hope and Charity, clear glass	70 - 80
Give Us This Day Our Daily Bread (ill.)	35 - 43
Gladstone	35 - 45
McKinley Memorial, "It Is God's Way," bread platter	55 - 65
Shell and Tassel, oblong, small . .	60 - 70
Teddy Roosevelt	90 - 110
Pacific Fleet	385 - 410
Washington, "First in War"	140 - 160
Constitution	85 - 98
Three Graces	67 - 78
Cupid & Venus	40 - 50
Dog Cart	50 - 60
Sheaf of Wheat	48 - 58
Eureka	44 - 54
Frosted Stork	53 - 60
Theodore Roosevelt, clear, frosted	93 - 110
Garden of Eden	38 - 50
Garfield Drape	60 - 70
Gladstone	35 - 46
Heroes of Bunker Hill	64 - 74
Independence Hall	94 - 110
It Is Pleasant to Labor	52 - 62
Liberty Bell, 7" × 11"	130 - 140
Little Miss Muffet	52 - 62
Nellie Bly (She went around the world in 80 days!)	170 - 180
Little Red Riding Hood	50 - 60
Old Statehouse	72 - 82
Queen Victoria	52 - 62
Last Supper	30 - 40
Rock of Ages	66 - 76
Niagara Falls, frosted	135 - 150
Virginia Dare (1st white baby born in the Virginia Colonies) .	60 - 70
Shield, star border	82 - 92
Waste Not, Want Not	50 - 60

(continued)

Brewery Collectibles

Brewery Collectibles

Brewery Collectibles

Anything to do with breweries, beer halls, the like is collectible today.

Beer bottle labels, any brand before 1940 (lots of repros here!) . .	50¢ -	1
Beer keg paper sign, "Cobb & Co's Margate Ale", 8" dia.	6 -	9
Calendar plate, "Horlacher Beer, 1909," 8¼" dia. (ill.)	55 -	65
Cardboard sign, "Haas Beer," 7" x 18"	8 -	12
Cardboard sign, "Cooks Beer," 10" x 14"	10 -	14
Cardboard sign, bottle-shaped, "Schmidt's Beer," 6" x 16"	4 -	8
Cardboard coasters, most brands, pre-World War II	25¢ -	50¢ each

Poster, Silver Springs Brewery, round, 14" dia., 1910	10 -	13
Tin sign, "Cook's Goldblum Beer," 14" x 28"	30 -	35
Tin sign, "F.W. Cook Co."	25 -	30
Tray, metal, Ballantine's Beer, blue/yellow, 12" dia. (ill.)	5 -	10
Tray, metal, Schmidt's Beer, white/gold/red, 13" dia. (ill.)	5 -	10

Brides' Baskets

These one-of-a-kind novelties, popular as wedding presents during the mid-1800s until the early 1900s, were made in American and European glass factories. A great many came in a silver or silver-plated basket frame.

Amberina, quilted diamond, twisted handle, silver frame . . .	$ 450+

Brides' Baskets

Cased pink and white, EPNS
  holder, mid-1800s . . . .   92 - 115
Clear to threaded, jewels, green,
  amber, silver basket . . . .   120 - 140
Cranberry, opalescent, hobnail,
  gold flecked, EPNS holder . . . .   150 - 165
Crimped amber, ribbon edge, wild
  rose color, floral . . . .   125 - 145
Cut, insert, diamond, strawberry
  and fan, frame . . . .   165 - 175
Hobnail, blue/white, silver-
  plated holder . . . .   230 - 255
Opaque cream color, apple
  blossoms, amber . . . .   300 - 325
Pink, multicolor, ruffled, clear
  applied border . . . .   120 - 140
Pink, camphor, overlay, footed,
  handled, Satin glass . . . .   165 - 185
Satin glass, blue, flowers,
  EPNS holder . . . .   210 - 235
Tiffany, signed, sterling silver
  frame, footed . . . .   850+
Vasa Murrhina, brown, gold
  flecks . . . .   220 - 240
White overlay, pink, amber
  edged, silver frame . . . .   170 - 210
Yellow-to-pink, blue enameled
  florals, sterling silver frame . . .   200 - 240

Bridle Rosettes

Bridle Rosettes

Made of glass, those small buttons were used to decorate the horse's bridle. They're being reproduced. The originals are beautiful when made into pins.

Blue/gray ground, floral, brass . . $ 15 - 23
Double heart, brass background .   17 - 22
Ducks, grass background (ill.) . . .   20 - 25
Eagle and flag, blue background,
  brass . . . .   15 - 22
Flowers, blue/green, birds, brass .   20 - 30
Heart design, initials, brass
  background . . . .   19 - 27
Shield and 13 stars, brass
  background . . . .   22 - 31

U.S. Cavalry, brass, pr. . . . .   18 - 26
Water birds, floral, brass
  background . . . .   19 - 28

Bristol Glass

Bristol Glass

Bristol, England, became a glass center in the mid-1700s. Many of the glass vases attributed to the Amelung Glass Company and other companies in the U.S. were actually made at Bristol. One way to identify them is to hold them to the light—they should look like an orange forest fire.

Apothecary jar, white, green/
  white, enameled, cover . . . . . . $ 90 - 100
Bottle, dresser, green/gold, blue
  enamel trim . . . .   50 - 60
Bowl, cased blue over white,
  scalloped, floral, enameled . . . .   110 - 125
Box, powder, round, dome,
  hinged, children and birds,
  1840 . . . .   78 - 88
Cookie jar, satin finish, floral
  and fauna designs . . . .   85 - 95
Epergne, twin tulips, cranberry,
  fluted edges . . . .   290 - 325
Hand vase, ruffled top, pink/
  clambroth, gilded, frosted (ill.) .   70 - 80
Lamp, blue, enameled yellow,
  blue, lilies, green leaves . . . . . .   120 - 130
Lamp, hanging, white, red/yellow
  color, floral, brass chain . . . . .   115 - 125
Mug, blue, "Love You" . . . .   38 - 48
Platter, raspberry color, bird-of-
  paradise color, matching dish .   37 - 47
Rose bowl, blue, frosted, ruffled
  lip . . . .   85 - 95
Smokebell, white, applied green
  band, crimped rim . . . .   24 - 34
Toothpick, blue, rectangular
  panels . . . .   24 - 34
Tumbler, white, blue/yellow
  enameled flowers . . . .   22 - 30

(continued)

Vase, blue/green, enameled birds
and flowers .... 65 - 75
Vase, brown thistle, white satin,
floral enameled decor .... 75 - 90
Vase, enameled, blue/yellow,
birds, flowers .... 72 - 86
Vase, insects, flowers, enameled
decor, ruffled lip .... 160 - 180
Vases, pair, "Little Girl," fluted
lips, flower outline .... 145 - 160 pr.
Vases, pair, blue opalescent,
enameled flowers, pair,
10″ high (ill.) .... 110 - 125

Britannia
Ware

Britannia Ware

In the simplest language, pewter is cast;
Britannia is spun. Also, they don't look alike,
though the chemical makeup is about the
same. If anything it's better than pewter.
Usually identified by the small catalog
numbers stamped on it. Lots of it has also
the maker's name. When mass production
was started around 1825, the spinning
process used less metal and made it harder.
Unfortunately, it also brought about poorer
designing and less individuality. Consequently, pewter brings higher prices.

Basically, Britannia Ware today brings
about 70% of what pewter pieces bring,
possibly a little less. See PEWTER.

British Patent Office
Registration Marks

From 1842 until 1883 the wares of many
British manufacturers were marked with the
following "diamond-mark," which was an
indication that the design was registered
with the British Patent Office. The topmost
section of the mark indicated the Class (in
this case IV indicates earthenware and
glass). This gave copyright protection for
three years. Unfortunately, the manufacturers didn't take too much time incising or
imprinting the "mark," and today a lot of
pieces are unreadable.

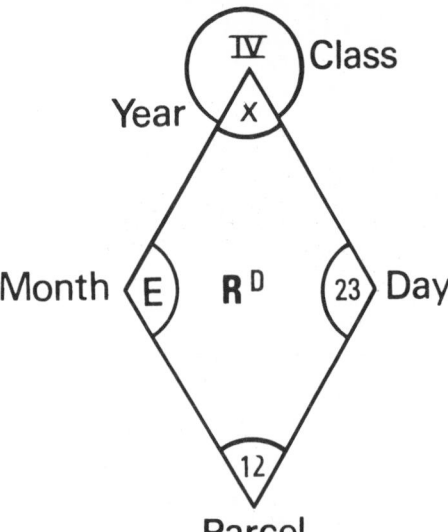

Example of earthenware design registered
on May 23, 1842.

Below is index to letters for each year and
month from 1842 to 1867:

YEARS

1842 X, 1843 H, 1844 C, 1845 A, 1846 I,
1847 F, 1848 U, 1849 S, 1850 V, 1851 P,
1852 D, 1853 Y, 1854 J, 1855 E, 1856 L,
1857 K, 1858 B, 1859 M, 1860 Z, 1861 R,
1862 O, 1863 G, 1864 N, 1865 W, 1866 O,
1867 T,

MONTHS

January C, February G, March W, April H, May E,
June M, July I, August R, September D, October
B, November K, December A.

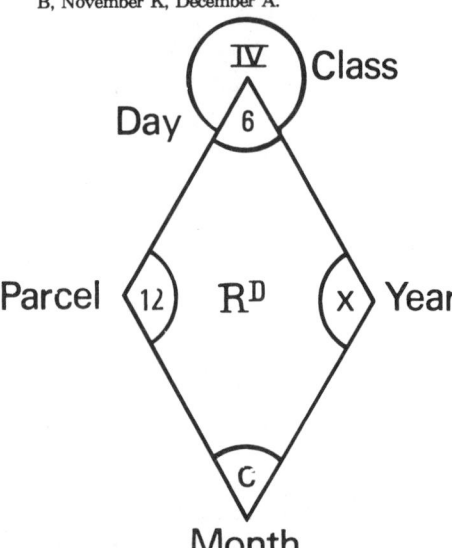

Example of earthenware design registered
on January 6, 1868·

Below is index to letters for each year and month from 1868 to 1883:

YEARS

MONTHS

January C, February G, March W, April H, May E, June M, July I, August R, September D, October B, November K, December A.

Bronze Figures

Bronze Figures

There are bronze figures and there are "bronze" figures. There are too many "pot metal" fakes around, so know your bronzes, and your dealer. A signed figure is worth more than an unsigned. Don't worry about finding any Frederic Remingtons!

Arab on camel, Austria, 6" high .	$110 - 125
Bird, signed Pautrot . . . .).	475 - 525
Bull, Charolais from Burgundy, signed Rosa Bonheur, 7" high (ill.)	800 - 900
Cossack and girl on horseback, Russia, 11" high, signed Bonoguy	750 - 850
Cow, 6" long, signed R. Bonheur .	400 - 500
Dachshund, 5" high, self-base . . .	85 - 100
Deer in forest	70 - 80
Elephant, 7" high, signed Fratin .	500 - 575
Greyhound, signed Mene	725 - 800
Leopard stalking, 5" high, 12" long	125 - 175
Lion roaring, 5" high, 8" long, signed Barye	240 - 250
Panther, 7¾" long, signed Bayre	625 - 700
Panther crouching, 17" long, signed L. Bureau	155 - 200
Pheasant, 7" long, signed Mene .	550 - 625

Polar bear stalking seal, Austria, 4" high, 5" long	140 - 175
Retriever, signed Mene	750 - 825
Running elephant, 5" high, 7½" long, signed Barye	500 - 575
Tiger on marble base, 6" high, 7" long	160 - 220
World War I Doughboy, signed Roman Bronze Works (same firm that cast the Frederic Remington bronzes)	95 - 120

Keep in mind that if you do find a Frederic Remington bronze (usually a Western scene—bucking horse, Indian shooting buffalo, etc.), don't sell it! One sold recently for $66,000!

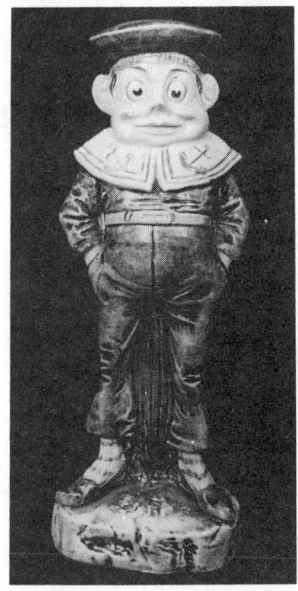

Brownie Collectibles

Brownie Collectibles

Created by Palmer Cox, an artist-author, in 1888, these creatures of fantasy were popular during that period. During the early 1900s they were copied by other artists.

Book, *The Brownies*, Cox . . . . . $	28 - 40
Book, *The Brownies, More Nights*	30 - 40
Candlestick, Brownie, German, 7½" high, blue/brown/green (ill.)	28 - 33
Cup/saucer, American Belleek . . .	42 - 52
Mug, child's enameled Brownie figures, silver-plate	29 - 39
Soda bottle, embossed, patented .	21 - 35
Tile, Brownies, German-made . . .	24 - 38

65

Buffalo Pottery

Dish, pottery, sauce, abino ware, 1912	128 - 140
Jug, pottery, George Washington on horseback, Mt. Vernon, blue/white	125 - 150
Pitcher, willow, blue on white, 1908	38 - 48
Plate, blue willow, 1915	29 - 38
Plate, Grant's Tomb, 7½" dia.	33 - 43
Plate, The Gunner, 9" dia.	64 - 75
Plate, U.S. Capitol, Washington, D.C., 10½", 1911	62 - 72
Platter, deer and doe at stream, signed R.K. Beck, 15" long	48 - 58
Powder jar w/lid	39 - 50
Sugar bowl	45 - 55
Tiles, handles, Ye Lion Inn, signed L. Streissel, 7"	85 - 98

Buffalo Pottery

Established in 1901 in Buffalo, N.Y., the firm supplied pottery for the Larkin Company, which was in the soap business and later developed into a mail order firm specializing in premiums which helped sell its goods. Best known and the most sought-after is the Deldare ware, first made in 1908. The firm continued until the 1940s. Most Deldare is done in old English tavern scenes and hunting scenes.

Bowl, floral, 6" dia.	$ 33 - 40
Chamber pot, green, chrysanthemum decor	$ 34 - 45
Cinderella pitcher	360 - 400
Cup/saucer, Deldare, "Ye Olden Days," signed E. Hacker (ill.)	130 - 140
Creamer, Deldare, village scenes, 1909	75 - 85
Bowl, Deldare, English cricket matches, 1910	62 - 72
Bowl, punch, Deldare, Fallowfield Hunt, signed J.I. Streusel	310 - 370
Candlestick, Deldare, village scenes, 9½" high, pair	150 - 170
Jug, George Washington, 7½" high	300 - 375
Jug, Wild Duck 6¾" high	175 - 225
Mug, shaving, "Wildroot"	73 - 83
Pitcher, Deldare, "Their manner of telling stories," 6" high	168 - 180

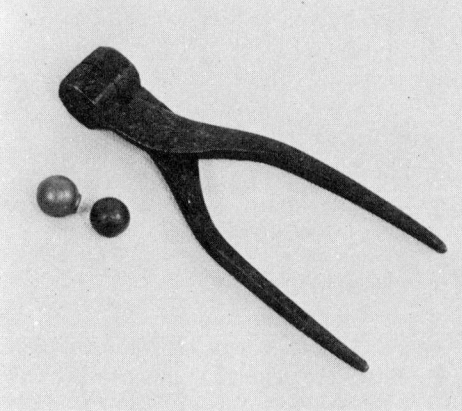

Bullet Molds

Bullet Molds

During the days of the muzzle-loading rifle, hunters, soldiers, frontiersmen molded their own bullets from melted-down lead.

Brass, single, spattered iron, 3" long	$ 47 - 57
Brass, holds 12, 10" long	52 - 62
Iron, single, 2" long	29 - 40
Iron, single, 4½" long (ill.)	40 - 48
Brass, .41 caliber, holds 4, 6" long	53 - 63

Burmese Glass

This translucent, shaded ware, homogeneous in nature, was made at the Mt. Washington Glass Company in the late 1800s. Licensed to produce it in England, Thomas Webb & Sons called it Queen's

Burmese Glass

Buster Brown Collectibles

Buster Brown Collectibles

Dick Outcault created a comic strip in 1902 that was eventually syndicated. Buster Brown and his dog, Tige, appeared on the American market in the form of dolls and other objects, the most famous, of course, being shoes, which are still being sold under that name today.

Buster and Tige bank, cast iron, 5" high	$120 - 135
Buster "to call dog" whistle	10 - 20
Button pin, Buster and Tige	17 - 26
Cup/saucer, Buster, girl (ill.)	21 - 30
Fork and spoon, silver metal	38 - 48
Knife, pocket	70 - 80
Mug, 3" high, gold trim, china	58 - 68
Plate, 5" diameter	42 - 49
Shoe horn, advertises shoes	10 - 16
Silverware set, three pieces, child's	36 - 46
Toy, dog cart, Tige	140 - 155

Burmese. Burmese was a soft canary yellow shading to flesh pink. Unfortunately it's being reproduced today, skillfully enough to fool too many new collectors.

Bell, Ivy motif, pink interior . $	425 -	500
Biscuit jar, Pairpoint silver frame	875 -	975
Bowl, triangular, ruffled top .	490 -	560
Bride's basket, silver holder, 9" diameter	800 -	900
Condiment set, three pieces ..	460 -	500
Epergne, signed Webb	1,800 -	2,200
Fairy lamp, brass, Clarke holder	725 -	800
Glass, juice, satin finish, 4" ..	140 -	160
Paperweight, egg shape	525 -	625
Rose bowl, 4¼" diameter	460 -	490
Pitcher, bright pink-to-yellow, acid, 7" high	1,600 -	1,800
Queen's Burmese, lamp, pyramid shape, salmon-to-yellow, 3¾" high	390 -	450
Queen's Burmese, lamp, same as above, 5¼" high	425 -	475
Salt/pepper shakers, pair, ribbed	525 -	600
Toothpick, decorated, signed Webb, 3¾" high (ill.)	475 -	500
Toothpick, 4-sided, floral design	400 -	500
Toothpick, glossy, 5-sided top	235 -	270
Tumbler	425 -	475
Vase, lemon-to-pink, 8½" high	325 -	350
Vase, flared top, petal style, pair	600 -	700
Vase, Mt. Washington, acid finish, 8" high (ill.)	550 -	625
Vase, satin, pink, yellow, 24" high, pair, signed Webb	2,500 -	2,700

Busts

Busts

Obviously, marble is worth more than plaster, but all are collectible.

"Diane," gilded, tinted plaster, signed, 15½" high (ill.)	$ 60 -	80
"Venus," plaster, on marble base, 6" high	$ 48 -	58

Butter Molds and Prints

Butter Molds and Prints

Normally associated with the Pennsylvania Dutch, they were used all over the country in dairying areas. Familiar designs are cow, eagle, heart, dove, swan, star, pineapple, tulip. Glass molds are rare.

MOLDS:

Acorn and leaf, wood, round	$ 58 - 68
Cherries, wood, round	36 - 46
Cow design, maple (ill.)	160 - 180
Cow design, wood, round	42 - 52
Cow design, glass, round (rare) . .	80 - 90
Eagle, round, maple (ill.)	170 - 190
Fern design, wood, round	33 - 42
Fleur-de-lis, wood	38 - 48
Floral, maple	40 - 50
Swan, wood, round, miniature . . .	39 - 49
Shield, flowers, miniature	40 - 48
Swan, wood, round 3½" diameter	67 - 77
Wheat sheaf, wood, round	42 - 50
Eagle, wood, round	135 - 160
Flower design, 4-petal, wood, round	42 - 60
Pineapple, box-type, maple (ill.) . .	70 - 90
Pineapple, wood, round	47 - 62
Shamrock, wood, round	53 - 63
Tulip design, wood, round	135 - 160
Daisies w/leaves, wood, round . . .	44 - 53
Wood, rectangular	19 - 27

PRINTS:

Acorn and leaves, wood, round . .	47 - 53
Eagle and shield, wood, round . . .	115 - 130
Clover design, wood, round	18 - 28
Cow design, wood, round	110 - 125
Cow design, wood, octagonal . . .	88 - 93
Dove, wood, round	75 - 85
Sheaf of wheat, cherry	62 - 72
Swan, maple	72 - 84
Tulip design, wood, round	96 - 110
Wheat pattern, wood, octagonal .	99 - 117

Button Hooks

What a chore that must have been, putting on and taking off. The gadget they used came in many types: silver, gold, platinum or just plain "hook." Prices paid will depend on whether or not it's marked "Sterling," "14k gold" or no mark at all.

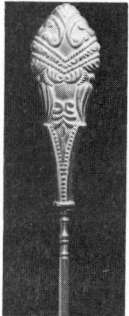

Button Hooks

Buttons

Buttons

In every shape, in every size, in every material, buttons have been around for thousands of years. Those collectible today are from the mid-Victorian period to the early 1900s.

Carved jade, China . . . . $	12 -	17
Cinnabar, carved	7 -	10
Kate Greenaway, children	11 -	20
Ivory, carved rose, flowers	8 -	12
Lady's head, sterling silver	7 -	10
Vermont, military, brass, four . . .	6 -	9
Madonna and Child, coin silver . .	11 -	15
Touring car, brass, 1904	9 -	12
White/gold, cloisonne	6 -	8

There are millions of styles.

1920, Victory decor, merchant . .	20 -	30
1922, fruit, flowers, Newark, N.J.	15 -	25
1923 Grant's Tomb	32 -	50
1925, horse race, merchant	22 -	32
1926 Kentucky Derby, "Winner!"	40 -	48
1927, merchant, Reading, Pennsylvania	18 -	27
1928, rose, trees, merchant	16 -	26
1929, car, flags, "Indy forever!" .	55 -	65
1966, God Bless Our House	15 -	20

Calendar Plates

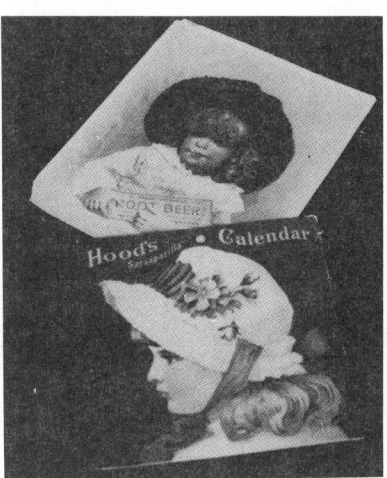

Calendars

Calendar Plates

Originating in England in the 1880s, they were made in the U.S. from 1905 until the late 1920s. Usually a cheap porcelain, some were made of tin and were intended as a giveaway to advertise a merchant's store or product.

1906, girl, tin . . . . $	26 -	38
1908, Santa & Holly . . . . $	55 -	65
1909, Omaha, Nebraska . . . .·	20 -	30
1911, clothing store, Kansas	15 -	22
1912, Heavy Brobst, Nuremberg, Pennsylvania (ill.)	22 -	32
1913, flowers, Santa	42 -	51
1913, portrait, flowers	16 -	26
1916, four-leaf clover, merchant .	15 -	25
1917, Sleigh, "Chicago greets Santa"	48 -	56
1918, doughboy, Uncle Sam	25 -	35
1919, Betsy Ross & flag	29 -	39

Calendars

Calendars

The use of calendars goes back to the days of the Romans—probably even beyond. The Gregorian calendar is used by the western world as well as by the Republic of China, South Vietnam, etc. What you find today in

(continued)

shops are from the late 1800s on. Year and condition dictate the price.

1876 Centennial Home Insurance Company, 12 months (ill.)	$ 13 -	19
1896 Root Beer	2 -	4
1897 John Hancock	35 -	45
1897 Prudential Insurance Co.	6 -	10
1896 Hartford Fire Insurance Co.	5 -	10
1899 Ayer's Cherry Pectoral	4 -	8
1903 Hood's Sarsaparilla (ill.)	24 -	34
1904 Dr. Pierce's Cure	35 -	45
1904 Nehi	38 -	48
1907 Old Forester Whiskey	5 -	9
1908 Clarence Brooks & Co.	5 -	9
1910 Coca-Cola	115 -	130
1912 Firestone Tires	28 -	35
1914 Coca-Cola	140 -	160
1915 Ruppert Breweries	25 -	35
1916 Coca-Cola	135 -	150
1920 Coca-Cola	135 -	145
1932 FDR — Our Man!	31 -	41
1934 Coca-Cola	60 -	70
1939 Coca-Cola	48 -	58
1939 Standard Oil	15 -	20

Eagle, executed by J.M. Schaeffer, Farmersville, Pennsylvania, c. late 1880s	160 - 180
Deer, executed by William Mills, Watertown, New York, c. 1880s	130 - 170
Rooster, executed by Nathanial Borden, Ellenville, New York, c. 1850s	150 - 175
Tiger, executed by Brisbane Wakefield, Portland, Connecticut, c. 1870	140 - 150
Whale, executed by Charles Stich, Roxbury, New York, c. 1850s	135 - 165

Calligraphy

Calling Cards

Calligraphy

Originally called "English Round Hand," this ornamental pen drawing is derived from the "Carolingian miniscule," developed in the late 14th century by Italian scholars intent upon developing a more legible handwriting for manuscripts. It is also called "flourishing."

Bird with plumage, executed by C.P. Zaner, Forks, Pennsylvania, c. late 1800s (ill.) ...... $140 - 160

Calling Cards

Not too many years ago, when it was considered fashionable and polite for a gentleman to rise when a lady entered the room, gentlemen had personalized calling cards which were presented to the maid or butler when they called. Today, it's a bit difficult to distinguish one sex from the other (if there is a difference), and said calling cards are collectible, inexpensive and available in most shops.

Average price, in good condition . 50c - 75c

70

Cambridge Art Pottery

Made in Cambridge, Ohio, c. 1895 until WWI. It was a brown glazed decorated ware, using a variety of marks such as an acorn, the words "Cambridge," "Oakwood" on the bottom. Vases, when found, bring $135 to $160.

Cambridge Glass

Cambridge Glass

Made in Cambridge, Ohio by the Cambridge Glass Company, c. 1902, this pressed glass was marked with a C in a triangle; after 1906, the words "near-cut" were used.

APPLE BLOSSOM
Amber 3-pc. console set . . . . $ 42 - 52 all
CAPRICE CLEAR
Ruffled bowl, 4 feet, 12" dia. . . . . 19 - 25
Alpine torte plate, 4 feet, 14" dia. 17 - 27
Sugar bowl, 2½" high . . . . 10 - 15
Scalloped bowl, Silver Deposit,
   4 feet, 11" dia. . . . . 24 - 36
CAPRICE BLUE
Bowl, 4 feet, 13" dia. . . . . 37 - 50
Handled dish, collar foot,
   9½" dia. . . . . 21 - 36
Ruffled bowl, 10" dia. . . . . 29 - 38
Flared bowl, 10½" dia. . . . . 26 - 38
Relish, 3-part, 7½" dia. . . . . 19 - 32
Ashtray, 3-part, 6" wide . . . . 17 - 27
CAPRICE PINK
Oval bowl, 4-feet, 11" dia. . . . . . . 16 - 28
Candy dish, covered, 3 feet . . . . . 16 - 24
CAPRICE AMBER
Salt, 3 feet . . . . 6 - 11
CHINTZ CLEAR
Sandwich server, handled, 10½"
   dia. . . . . 15 - 26

CROWN TUSCAN
Relish, 3-part, 8" dia. . . . . 23 - 32
DECAGON COBALT
Ice bucket, scalloped rim, handle 36 - 47
DECAGON AMBER
Bowl, handle, 6", signed
   "near-cut" . . . . 12 - 22
Centerpiece bowl, 12" dia., 3½"
   deep . . . . 18 - 29
DECAGON BLACK
Dish, handle, 6" dia. . . . . 10 - 18
2-handled plate, hand-painted
   flowers, 11" dia. . . . . 17 - 27
FARBER CHROME AMETHYST
Compote, 5½" high . . . . 16 - 29
Sugar bowl, 3" high . . . . 8 - 14
Creamer, 4" high . . . . 8 - 14
FARBER CHROME FOREST GREEN
Liquer goblet, 4" high . . . . 7 - 16
Stemmed compote, 5½" high . . . 15 - 27
LIGHTENING EBONY
Creamer/sugar set, footed . . . . . . 15 - 28
Swau, clear glass bowl, cobalt
   head, 10" high (ill.) . . . . 28 - 38

Cameo Glass

Generally speaking, this was a thin shell of glass with another shell blown into it. Then a design was cut through the outer layer, leaving the inner layer exposed. It also is called cased glass and today is highly collectible. See specific types of cameo glass listed alphabetically in this Guide. LaGras and LeMans are two items being reproduced. Careful, beginners!

Cameos

A small carving in relief on glass, lava, stone, shell, or any other hard substance; usually done on agate or shell because these materials have layers of different colors, necessary to the cameoist's work. Cameos were in vogue between 1840 and 1875. Too many repros on the market today.

Bracelet, seven cameos, classic
   figures, silver links . . . . $110 - 125
Brooch, orange-white, lady's
   head, gold frame . . . . 95 - 120
Brooch, pink-white, lady's head,
   gold frame . . . . 115 - 125
Brooch, black-white, church, gold
   frame . . . . 95 - 115
Pin, black-white, woman's profile,
   14k gold . . . . 160 - 180

71

(continued)

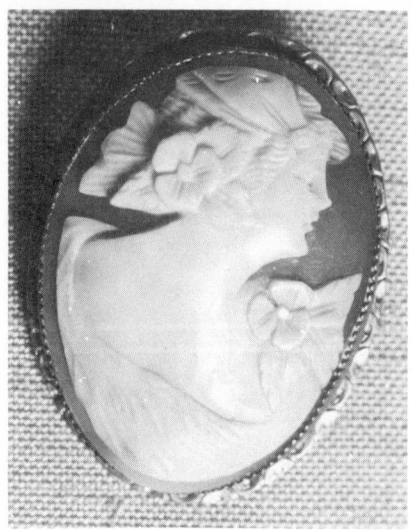

Cameos

Pin, brown-white, woman and
child, 14 karat gold . . . . 160 - 180
Ring, girl, pink-white, 14 karat
mounting . . . . 58 - 69
Tie pin, man's profile, 14 karat
gold . . . . 35 - 45

Campaign Items

Campaign Items

Since the 1840s, politicians at all levels
have "advertised" themselves with kerchiefs,
mugs, plaques, banners, and, especially, buttons. All are sought after today.

Bandanna, Teddy Roosevelt's
Campaign Flag, 1912 . . . . $110 - 125

Mug, "A New Deal With FDR,"
1932, pottery . . . . 25 - 35
Poster, Hoover's "A Chicken in
Every Pot!", 1928 . . . . 40 - 48
Song sheet, Harrison's campaign,
1888 . . . . 22 - 32
Stickpin, McKinley's head,
gold-colored, 1896 . . . . 26 - 38
CAMPAIGN BUTTONS:
McKinley-Roosevelt, "A Full
Dinner Pail" . . . . 65 - 75
"Our War Pres. Wm. McKinley" 12 - 20
Gold bug stickpin, McKinley . . . 16 - 26
"Bryan & Sewall, Victory 1896" . 28 - 36
Delegate's button/badge,
National Democratic Convention, Denver, 1908 . . . . 82 - 92
"The Choice of the People,
Wm. J. Bryan" . . . . 21 - 35
"Down With The Beef Trust"
(Bryan's campaign) . . . . 10 - 18
Roosevelt-Fairbanks, G.O.P.,
1904 . . . . 21 - 32
"My Hat Is In The Ring—T.R." . 15 - 24
Taft and Sherman, flags . . . . . . 22 - 32
"First Voters Taft Club" . . . . . . 8 - 14
"The Man of the Hour—
Woodrow Wilson" . . . . 108 - 119
Wilson—"Stand By the
President" . . . . 28 - 36
"Harding For President" . . . . . . 41 - 52
"Harding and Coolidge" . . . . 21 - 32
"Support The Coolidge
Administration" . . . . 46 - 58
"Home Town Coolidge Club
Plymouth Vermont" . . . . 42 - 54
"John William Davis For
President" . . . . 90 - 110
Davis and Bryan (black-and-
white) . . . . 50 - 56
"OK, America! Play Safe With
Hoover" . . . . 39 - 49
"Hoo But Hoover" . . . . 48 - 59
Al Smith For President . . . . 22 - 28
"Smith and Robinson" . . . . 16 - 27
"Re-Elect Roosevelt" . . . . 12 - 21
"Labor's Choice—Roosevelt" . . . 14 - 26
"Missouri's Minute Men For
Roosevelt" . . . . 27 - 38
"Watch Willkie Wilt" . . . . 6 - 9
"I Am A Democrat For Willkie" . 4 - 7
"Dewey-Bricker—NY Young
Republicans" . . . . 4 - 7

Thousands of these buttons around!

Camphor Glass

A cloudy white appearance identifies this
glass. After being blown or pressed, it was
treated with hydrofluoric acid vapor. Blue

Camphor Glass

camphor glass, attributed to the Sandwich Glass Company, of Cape Cod, is extremely rare today.

Art glass basket, yellow flowers, green leaves . . . . $	90 - 110
Ashtray, raised flowers	14 - 21
Bowl, raised flowers	21 - 32
Bowl, rose color, crimped top, 4″ high	27 - 38
Box, powder, Cocker Spaniel on lid	15 - 22
Cologne bottle, gold gilt, original stopper	28 - 40
Compote, open, 6″ tall	40 - 52
Compote, yellow, 7½″ tall	29 - 38
Creamer, white, flower motif	20 - 25
Dish, blue, Sandwich glass (authenticated)	210 - 250
Jar, powder, pink, silver lid	31 - 45
Lamp, miniature, raised flowers .	62 - 78

Match holder, pipe shape, souvenir, 1906	27 - 40
Plate, 3 kittens	20 - 28
Salt/Pepper, "Three Face," 2¾″ high (ill.) pr.	70 - 75
Toothpick holder, shoe shape . . .	28 - 39
Tray, oval scalloped border, flowers in relief, 11″ long	25 - 36
Vase, raised flowers in silver-plated stand	24 - 36
Vase, light blue, floral motif, 9″ high	30 - 40
Vase, loop handles, 6½″ high (ill.)	10 - 20

Canary Lustreware

Generally attributed to the Staffordshire District, England, early 1880s, the 2 jugs shown are "American"—that is, made to attract the American market. Rare today!

Jug, "Faith and Hope," large $	975 - 1,100
Jug, "Faith and Hope," small	775 - 950
Large jug (ill.), bright canary-yellow ground, American Eagle, edged and divided into 3 cartouches with silver lustre lines. On each side, large American Eagle, names of 11 states, "Peace, Plenty and Independence"	1,000 - 1,250
Mug, "Thrift is spending wisely," 2½″ high	350 - 450
Small jug (ill.), basically same as large jug, "Success to the United States"	975 - 1,200

Canary Lustreware

Candelabras

Candelabras

Candlesticks with arms is one way to describe them. The more ornate ones are called candelabrums, usually attached to a vase. Silver, both sterling and plate, brass, base metal, all were used to make the candelabras. Popular in the French and English palaces as far back as the mid-1600s. What you usually find today are early 19th century.

Brass, alabaster urn and base, pair (ill.)	$ 450 - 525
Brass, 12″ high, 8-light, pair	90 - 115

Gilt metal, George III-type, cut glass, prisms, pair . .	575 - 650
Empire ormolu, 12-light, pair	1,500 - 1,700 pr.
French ormolu figural, 5-light, early 19th century, pair	500 - 600
Sterling silver, mid-1800s, 7-light, pair	575 - 650
Sheffield silver (plate), English, early 19th century, pair	450 - 550

Candle Molds

An early American laborsaving device, they were usually made of tin, sheet iron or, on occasion, pewter, in connected groups of slender, tapered tubes. Melted wax was poured into each tube. Twisted thread acted as the wick. When wax was cooled or hardened, the mold was dipped in hot water to release the candles.

CANDLE MOLD:	
Tin, 4 hole	$ 55 - 70
Tin, 8 hole	68 - 78
Tin, 12 hole (ill.)	88 - 110
Tin, 18 hole (ill.)	110 - 130
Pewter, same sizes as above, 50 percent higher.	
Sheet iron—same prices as tin.	

Candlesticks

Shape is important, age-wise. The earliest were made from solid cast brass or wrought iron. Hollowstems with the sliding knob to

Candle Molds

74

Candlesticks

raise or lower the candle were in use in the early 1700s. The sheet-iron type, early 1800s. 19th century types were larger and more ornate.

Beehive, push-up type, bur-
nished, 9", 10", 11", pair ..... $130 - 160
Brass, 1840s, 11" high, pr. ..... 110 - 130
Brass, altar type, 22" high ..... 48 - 60
Brass, twisted stem, 8" high .... 38 - 48
Brass, India, 11" high (ill.), pr.... 38 - 50
Bull and beehive design, push-up
type, 7" .... 50 - 60
Crucifix, pair, Sandwich-type ... 125 - 150
Glass, dolphin, Sandwich-type .. 75 - 90
Heisey glass, glass prisms,
11½" high, pr. .... 125 - 140
Hog scraper, push-up type, base
metal, 6" high .... 95 - 110
Porcelain, flower motif, pair,
10" high .... 90 - 110
Saucer-type; push-up snuffer
included .... 55 - 65
Winged-dragon type, 8½" high,
pr. .... 52 - 62
Wood, turned cherry, 8½" high . 20 - 28
Wood, turned oak, 8" high ..... 18 - 25

Candy Containers

These were used for holding tiny pellets of candy and came in the shape of guns, ships, fire engines, cars, boats, etc. Popular at the turn of the century, today they're much sought after. A metal screw cap kept the candy in, though a cork was used on the earlier ones. The Liberty Bell is popular to-day.

Airplane, tin wings ....$ 24 - 33
Auto, "Pierce Arrow" .... 38 - 47
Battleship .... 27 - 35
Bear .... 19 - 27
Betty Boop .... 27 - 36
Bus, Greyhound .... 35 - 44
Carpet sweeper .... 28 - 37
Chicken-on-nest............. 14 - 20
Dog...................... 12 - 18
Donkey pulling barrel .... 34 - 44
Duck, sitting .... 24 - 33
Gun, 4" long .... 22 - 31
House .... 28 - 37
Jeep .... 14 - 24
Lantern, tin top............ 30 - 40
Lantern, bail, original cap ..... 30 - 40
Liberty Bell, blue, tin cap ..... 50 - 63
Locomotive .... 40 - 50
Motorboat (ill.) .... 11 - 19
Moon Mullins .... 37 - 47
Peter Rabbit .... 22 - 34
Radio..................... 27 - 36
Revolver, clear .... 31 - 44
Scottie dogs, J. Crosetti Co., pr. . 48 - 58
Submarine................. 28 - 36
Suitcase .... 25 - 37
Tank .... 16 - 24
Telephone .... 24 - 35
Train .... 27 - 37
Turkey .... 27 - 37
Van (ill.) .... 10 - 18
Victory bus .... 32 - 42
Wheelbarrow............... 31 - 41
Whistle .... 9 - 17

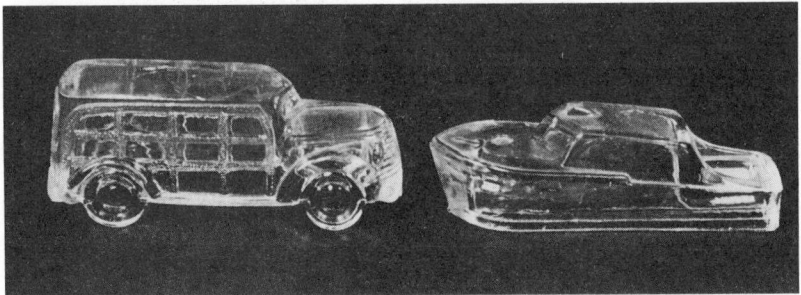

Candy Containers

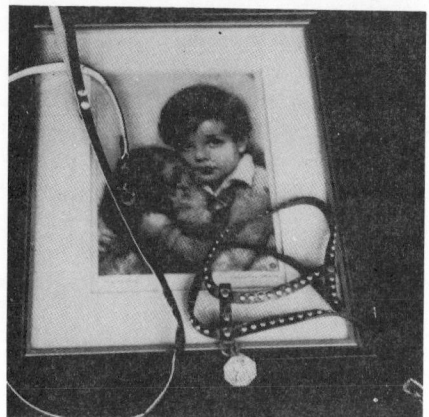

Canine Collectibles

Canine Collectibles

Paintings, lithos, etchings, statuettes—just about anything to do with Fido—is becoming collectible.

Lithograph "Sympathy" (ill.) personally signed by the artist, J. Knowles Hare	$ 45 - 55
Red Cross harness worn by dogs in the A.E.F. during World War I	29 - 42
Lithograph "Grace" copyright 1920, USA, printed in England	22 - 33
Bronze wolfhound, 5″ high, no signature	38 - 50
19th C. pastel, "Dog-with-Tassel"	175 - 220

Cans and Containers

Cans and Containers

Biscuit can, English, "Old Rover"	$ 9 - 12
Biscuit can, Huntley & Palmer, "Churchill"	30 - 38
Biscuit can, Huntley & Palmer, "George V"	35 - 40
Candy box, round, w/lid, decorated (ill.)	5 - 8
Cocoa can, Baker's Chocolate, early 1900s	10 - 15
Dan Patch Cut Plug, late 1800s	19 - 28
Gunpowder can, Winchester Repeating Arms Co., late 1800s	11 - 16
Gunpowder can, American Powder Mills, late 1800s	33 - 42
Hairpin container, Lockford Ltd., early 1900s	11 - 16
Kitchen cannisters, hand-painted, tole type, late 1800s, 6 pcs.	61 - 71
Lard can, Decker & Sons, Snow Brand, late 1800s	15 - 24
Milk/cream can, tole type painting, late 1800s	35 - 45
Sparkplug box, blue, Benford's (ill.)	5 - 7
Syrup can, Log Cabin, small type, early 1900s	15 - 25
Syrup can, Log Cabin, large type, early 1900s	24 - 33
Tea container, Lipton's sailing yacht label, late 1800s	12 - 19
Tea container, Boswell Ltd., japanned finish, late 1800s	20 - 30
Wax can, antique car label, polish for 1910 autos	8 - 17
Yeast can, Fleischmann's, early 1900s	8 - 16

Canton China

A product of Canton, China for over 2 centuries, it was an inexpensive blue-and-white, hand-decorated ware, made primarily for export to England and Europe. Those wares made in the late 1700s and early 1800s are more collectible than the 20th century ware.

Bowl, rice, early 1800s	$ 70- 80
Butter patty, blue	18- 27
Charger, temple scene	100-125
Cup/saucer, blue/white, no handle	33- 42
Dish, shrimp, fish scene	70- 80
Fish bowl, blue/white, on stand, 14″ high	375-450
Fish dish, fish shape, blue/white	37- 47
Ginger jar, blue/white, double ring, 6″ high	39- 48
Lamp, blue/white, shade not original	55- 65
Leaf, 7″ wide (ill.)	69- 80
Milk pitcher, blue/white, mid-1880s	110-120
Plate, 8″	65- 80
Plate, 9″	70- 85
Plate, blue/white, open lattice edge, 8¼″ diameter	70- 80

Canton China

Platter, blue/white, cut corners, late 1700s	175-200
Platter, octagonal, blue/white, temple scene	160-185
Rose bowl, white poppy blossoms, cover	36- 50
Soup, blue/white, 8½" diameter	44- 49
Teapot, blue/white, straight spout, late	60- 65
Tile, 5" square, animal figures	48- 62
Tureen and stand, covered, blue/white	90- 98
Warming dish, octagonal, 9" wide (ill.)	260-310

Capo-di-Monte

Originally made in the factory of the same name in Italy in 1736, since then this ware has been reproduced many times. The N beneath a crown is the usual mark. That made by King Charles of Naples in 1743 is of museum quality and rare. The Doccia factory at Florence has made many reproductions. It's good and fools a lot of people. Just keep in mind that most of the originals are in museums.

Bell, "N/Crown" mark	$ 72- 82
Box, garden scene, 2½" x 3" x 6½"	130-150
Dinner bell, cherubs, blue crown mark	95-125
Figurine, couple carrying water bucket, crown mark	135-155

Capo-di-Monte

Figurine, boy and girl with cow, "N/Crown" mark	160-175
Lamp, swirled green/pink ribbing, usual cherubs	240-280
Plaque, classical figures, 8" x 15" "N/Crown" mark	390-500
Plaque, figures in relief depict civilization, 20" dia. (ill.)	750-875
Stein, drinking scene, blue, crown, mark, 12" high	590-640
Tea set, teapot, creamer, sugar, unsigned	150-175
Urn, compote type, cherubs, blue, crown mark	260-295
Urn, 15" high, cherubs playing, "N/Crown" mark	180-210
Vase, classical figures, "N/Crown" mark, 8½" high	160-190

Card Cases

These were used to hold gentlemen's cards when they went calling during the 17th and 18th centuries. Usually ornate, they were made of gold, silver, ivory, sometimes inlaid with precious stones. (See also SILVER.)

Ivory, carved, ornate	$ 40- 50
Mother-of-pearl	17- 30
Rosewood, carved, initials	20- 30
Sterling silver, initialed	35- 50
Tortoiseshell	20- 35
14 karat gold, tiny rubies	150-200

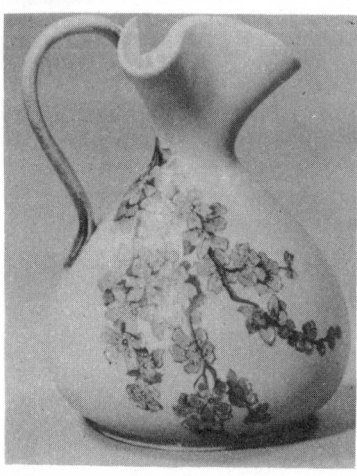

Carlsbad

Carlsbad

Wares from Carlsbad were exported to the U.S. in the 19th and 20th Centuries. Later, when this area was a part of Czechoslovakia after World War I, some pieces were marked "Karlsbad." Wares marked "Victoria" were made especially for Lazarus and Rosenfeldt, a firm in the U.S. that imported from this European country.

Cracker jar, white luster, pink/ green flowers, marked Victoria	$ 38- 50
Pitcher, country scene, twisted snake handle, Karlsbad	70- 80
Plate, cupids, floral border, gold decor, 10″ diameter	35- 45
Plate, pink/green flowers, swirl and flute border, Victoria	35- 45
Platter, apple blossoms in pink, green flower border, Victoria	65- 78
Platter, poppies, birds around border, 12 matching soups, Karlsbad	110-135
Tea set, flowers, birds, fluted border on saucers (set consists	

of teapot, creamer, sugar, waste pot)	100-150
Tureen, blue/pink roses, floral edge, covered Karlsbad	45- 58

Carnival Glass (Taffeta)

This originally low priced, iridized glass was made to compete with the expensive Art Glass (Tiffany, Steuben, Durand, Kew Blas, Quezel, etc.) of the early 1900s. It was originally called Taffeta glass and got its present name during the 1920s when circuses and carnivals gave it away as prizes. Grocery stores also gave it away with food purchases. It was iridized by spraying the glass with hydrofluoric acid; later, it was dipped in vinegar to iridize it. When the sun came into contact with this "vinegar" glass, it left the glass looking as if it had the measles. Color of individual pieces determines value. Prices range upward from Peach (lowest), to Marigold to Blue, Green, or Purple, to Pastels (any color), to Genuine OLD Red Carnival, the most valuable. Being reproduced.

BANANA BOAT	
Floral	$ 38- 50
Grape and Cable, green	155-175
Grape and Cable, marigold	140-150
Peach and Pear, marigold	65- 80
Thistle	78- 88
Wreathed Cherry, purple	125-150
Wreathed Cherry, red	295-325
Wreathed Cherry, white	165-185
BANK	
Bell, marigold	25- 35
Owl, marigold	45- 60
BASKET	
Basketweave, marigold	53- 65
Stippled Rays, 2 handles, purple	35- 45
Tree of Life, marigold	28- 38
BERRY SET	
Beaded Shell, 6 pcs., purple	240-260
Imperial's Grape, 7 pcs., green	120-135
Three Fruits, N mark, 6 pcs., purple	168-185
BONBON	
Persian Medallion, blue	58- 68
Pond Lily, blue	57- 67
Three Fruits, Basketweave, marigold	45- 55
BOTTLES	
Barber, marigold	48- 58
Horn of Plenty	45- 60
Raised Grape, purple	200-225

Carnival Glass

Toilet Water, marigold 45- 55
Whiskey, Golden Wedding,
  marigold 35- 45
Wine, New England Wine Co.
  marigold 38- 48
BOWL
Acorn pattern, marigold 42- 52
Apple Blossoms, 5½" dia., purple 50- 60
Berry, Acorn pattern, 7½" dia.,
  blue 38- 50
Berry, Butterfly and Berry,
  marigold 46- 56
Berry, Lacy Edge, red 130-150
Berry, Peacock at the Fountain,
  amethyst 128-140
Berry, Vintage Grape, 5½" dia.,
  purple 35- 48
Berry, Waterlily and Cattails,
  marigold 42- 52
Blackberry Wreath, 9" dia. 52- 62
Bouquet and Lattice, 6½" dia.,
  cereal 22- 30
Candy, Fine Cut and Roses, N
  mark, purple 58- 69
Captive Rose, 8¾" dia., green ... 50- 60
Chrysanthemum, footed, 10"
  dia., blue 72- 82
Dogwood Sprays, marigold 50- 70
Dragon and Lotus, 8" dia. 50- 70
Embossed Grapes, 9½" dia.,
  marigold 52- 65
Embossed Scroll, 8" dia., green .. 58- 68
Good Luck, 7¼" dia., blue 110-125
Grape and Cable, green 80- 90
Grape and Cable, 6½" dia.,
  marigold 38- 48
Grape and Cable, 7½" dia.,
  purple 50- 60

Grape and Gothic Arches,
  marigold 30- 40
Heart and Vine, blue 50- 60
Heart and Vine, 8" dia., green ... 59- 70
Holly, 9" dia., blue 53- 63
Horse's Head Medallion, 6½"
  dia., marigold 50- 60
Imperial's Cherries, footed, 10"
  dia., marigold .... 50 -60
Imperial's Grape, 8¾" dia. 35- 45
Little Flowers, 10½" dia. 60- 70
Lea pattern, 5½" dia., marigold . 35- 45
Louisa, 8¼" dia., amethyst 38- 48
Millersburg's Cherry, marigold .. 49- 60
Millersburg's Cherry, 7" dia.,
  green 40- 50
Millersburg's Primrose, 9¼" dia. 63- 80
Millersburg's Whirling Leaves,
  9½" dia. 70- 82
Pansy Spray, amber 41- 51
Peacock and Dahlia, 7½" dia.,
  marigold 42- 53
Peacock and Grape, 7½" dia.,
  3" high 40- 50
Peacock and Grape, 9" dia. 135-195
Peacock at the Fountain, 8" dia. . 80-185
Persian Medallions, 9" dia.,
  marigold 42- 60
Roses and Ruffles, 8" dia.,
  marigold 40- 50
Stag and Holly, 10" dia., blue ... 115-135
Stag and Holly, 10" dia.,
  marigold 80- 90
Star and File, 6½" dia., marigold 19- 29
Stork and Rushes, 10" dia.,
  marigold 50- 60
Thistle, footed, 8" dia., marigold . 35- 45
Thunderbird, 5½" dia., marigold 78- 88

79

(continued)

Wild Daisy and Lotus, footed . . .	32- 45
Wild Rose, 6″ dia., green	38- 50

BOWL, CENTERPIECE

Double Scroll and Oval	58- 68

BOWL, FRUIT

Butterfly and Tulip, marigold . . .	200-275
Fenton's Grape	125-150
Imperial Jewels, red	120-150
Ski Star, 5½″ dia., peach	55- 65

BOWL, NUT

Grape, 6-footed, purple	62- 70
Louisa, footed, purple	50- 60
Louisa, footed, red	52- 62
Vintage, red, 7″	165-185

BOWL, PUNCH

Grape and Cable, 2 pcs., 6 cups, purple	500-600
Imperial's Hobstar, 2 pcs., 12 cups	225-265
Memphis, green	245-290
Orange Tree, purple	240-270
Trees, 6 cups, blue and orange . .	245-275

BOWL, ROSE

Butterscotch, blue-green	54- 65
Daisy and Plume, footed	69- 89
Fine Cut and Roses, marigold . . .	65- 75
Grape and Leaf, 6-footed	78- 90
Grape, purple	69- 79
Leaf and Beads, footed, green . . .	81- 91
Leaf and Beads, footed, marigold	54- 65
Leaf and Beads, footed, white . . .	110-140
Louisa, green	49- 60
Star and File, marigold	40- 50
Vintage, purple	70- 85
Wreath of Roses, marigold	178-195

BOWL, SUGAR

Peacock at the Fountain, cover, marigold	60- 75
Stippled Rays, footed, marigold .	22- 32
Strutting Peacock, cover, marigold	58- 68

Carnival, Pony

BUTTER DISH

Acorn Burrs, cover, purple	220-245
Arabic, 2 handles, 8″ dia., blue . .	32- 42
Basketweave	38- 50
Butterflies, marigold	70- 85
Cable and Thumbprint, N mark, blue	175-200
Flute, N mark, blue	128-162
Gold/green, signed Northwood . .	68- 82
Grape and Cable, N Mark, purple	220-265
Grape and Cable, Thumbprint, green	205-228
Maple Leaf, purple	138-163
Question Mark, 2 handles	49- 72
Water Lily and Cattails, marigold	128-142
Wide Panel, marigold	42- 60

CAKE STAND

Butterfly and Berry, marigold . .	92-115
Fine Cut and Roses, green	110-132

CANDLESTICK

Cornucopia, white, pr.	128-142
Double Scroll, 8½″ high, marigold, pr	46- 62
Grape, N mark, 5½″ high, purple, pr.	210-225
White, domed foot, 7¾″ high, pr.	59- 75
Wide panel, 6½″ high, marigold, pr.	64- 75

CARAFE

Grape, purple	130-165

CHAMPAGNE

Masonic, white, 1912	69- 82

COLOGNE

Grape and Cable, stopper, marigold	128-155

COMPOTE

Basketweave, N Mark, 7″ dia., purple	54- 68
Beaded Panel, marigold	32- 45
Blackberry Spray, 6½″ high, green	42- 56
Cathedral, marigold	82- 91
Fenton's Peacock and Urn, marigold	62- 80
Imperial Arcs, 4″ high, marigold .	32- 42
Imperial Jewels, green	50- 62
Mikado, blue	225-265
Northwood's Petals, amethyst . .	72- 82
Octagon, 7¾″ dia., marigold	50- 60
Propellor, marigold	50- 62
Scotch Thistle, blue	69- 82
Smooth Rays, clear stem, marigold	26- 42
Thumbprint, 5″ high, purple	41- 60
Wreath of Roses, 6″ dia., purple .	56- 66

CREAMER AND SUGAR

Grape and Cable, green	225-245
Green/gold trim, signed Northwood	115-145
Millersburg's Cherry, marigold . .	62- 80

Orange Tree, open 81- 96
Pansy Spray, marigold 52- 65
Peacock at the Fountain,
   amethyst 143-165
Pineapple, dome foot, marigold . . 118-150
Singing Birds, marigold 118-140
Stippled Rays, green 52- 65
CUP AND SAUCER
Bouquet and Lattice, marigold . . 18- 28
Many Carnival glass patterns,
   average 19- 28
CUP, PUNCH
Acorn Burrs, N mark 36- 47
Buzz Star, marigold 25- 40
Grape and Cable, blue 42- 60
Grape and Cable, N mark, purple 39- 61
Imperial's Grape, set of 6,
   marigold 58- 69
Memphis, amethyst 41- 61
Vintage, marigold 28- 39
CUSPIDOR
Orange Tree 61- 71
DECANTER
Golden Harvest, marigold 88- 98
Grape Clusters, stopper,
   marigold 60- 70
Imperial's Grape, green 130-140
Imperial's Grape, marigold 72- 82
Octagon, stopper, marigold 78- 91
DISH
Berry, Grape and Cable, N mark . 32- 42
Berry, Octagon, marigold 31- 41
Berry, Peacock and Urn, purple . . 46- 56
Berry, Three Fruits, N mark,
   amethyst 42- 59
Candy, Blackberry, 6″ dia., red . . 119-151
Candy, Fine Cut and Roses,
   8″ dia. 62- 80
Candy, Lacy Rim, blue 32- 50
Candy, Millersburg's Holly,
   green 62- 78
Candy, Persian Medallion,
   marigold 36- 45
Candy, Stippled Rays, marigold . 34- 50
Candy, Wreath of Roses, green . . 45- 60
Celery, Grape and Cable, purple . 81- 95
Celery, Pansy Spray, amber 60- 70
Dessert, Fluted Paneled Rays, N
   mark 39- 59
Ice Cream, Beaded Cable, footed,
   7½″ dia. 34- 50
Ice Cream, Peacock and Urn, N
   mark, blue . . . . :. 110-125
Pickle, Beaded Cable, fluted,
   footed, 7¾″ dia. 49- 61
Pickle, Imperial's Pansy,
   marigold 35- 45
Pickle, Windmills, green 52- 63
Relish, Grape and Cable, purple . 68- 80
Relish, Pansy, marigold 39- 60
Sauce, Acorn Burrs, N mark,
   marigold 26- 36

Sauce, Acorn Burrs, purple 40- 52
Sauce, Butterfly and Berry,
   marigold 24- 38
Sauce, Fenton's Cherry 28- 39
Sauce, Grape and Gothic Arches,
   blue 35- 50
Sauce, Grape and Thumbprint,
   N mark, purple 32- 48
Sauce, Lustre Rose, marigold . . . 22- 38
Sauce, Northwood Flute, purple . 41- 60
Sauce, Panther, ball and claw,
   marigold 48- 63
Sauce, Panther, footed, 6″ dia.,
   purple 56- 69
Sauce, Peacock at the Founatin . 33- 43
Sauce, Star Medallion 29- 40
Sauce, Stippled Rays, purple . . . 41- 60
Sauce, Thistle and Thorn,
   marigold 40- 55
Sundae, Northwood's clear stem,
   marigold 41- 60
Vegetable, Bouquet and Lattice,
   marigold 18- 30
DOUGHNUT STAND
Question Mark, white 62- 72
EPERGNE
Four Lilies, marigold 410-500
Grape pattern, purple 135-170
Vintage, purple 141-165
FERNERY
Grape Variant, footed, green 49- 60
Lustre Rose, green 58- 70
Vintage Grape, footed green 53- 65
GOBLET
Imperial Grape, 6″ high,
   marigold 55- 68
Wine, Flute, blue . . . . 50 -60
Wine, Orange Tree, blue 52- 70
HAT
Blackberry, banded 35- 45
Blackberry, blue 39- 60
Blackberry, 5″, red 128-162
French Knots 38- 50

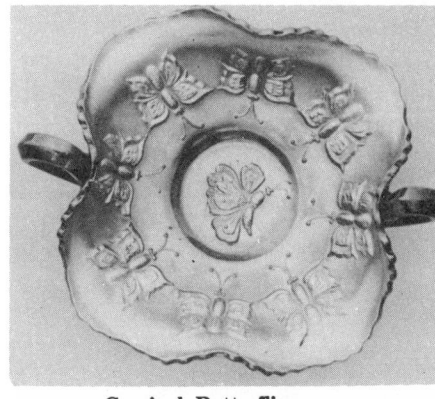

Carnival, Butterflies

(continued)

HATPIN
Bumblebee, purple 45- 56
Butterfly 62- 72
Flying Bat 45- 70
Plum and Stem 38- 50
HATPIN HOLDER
Grape and Cable, N mark   135-160
Grape, purple 71- 81
Orange Tree, marigold   88-110
INSULATOR
Corning Pyrex, marigold 35- 52
Marigold 34- 50
Marigold, large   85-110
JAR
Candy, cover, 8″ high, marigold .   25- 32
Candy, crinkled lid, marigold . . .   50- 60
Cookie, Grape with Thumbprint,
   cover, N mark, white . . . .   750+
Cookie, Hourglass and Daisy,
   cover, marigold 59- 72
Cracker, Grape and Cable, purple   365-400
Cracker, Inverted Feather and
   Hobstar, green   210-240
Pickle, Golden Flowers, marigold   30- 40
Powder, Bambi, marigold 22- 35
Powder, Orange Tree, cover,
   marigold 59- 69
Powder, Vintage cover, marigold   60- 70
Powder, Wreathed Cherries, blue   78- 90
Tobacco, Illinois Daisy, marigold   80- 92
LAMP
Metal holder, marigold 64- 81
Zipper and Loop, 2-burner, 7″
   high, marigold   185-210
MUG
Fish and Cattail, purple 84- 95
Orange Tree, blue 50- 65
Robin Red Breast, marigold 47- 57
Singing Birds, marigold 52- 62
Singing Birds, N mark, marigold   60- 70
Singing Birds, purple 68- 78
Stork and Rushes, marigold 44- 54
Vintage, marigold 39- 70
NAPPIE
Grape and Cable, green   85-100
Leaf Rays, marigold 42- 60
Northwood's Butterfly 50- 62
Question Mark, marigold 28- 38
Stippled Rays, N mark 43- 60
PITCHER
Butterfly and Berry, marigold . .   125-152
Diamond Lace, 6 tumblers,
   purple   430-470
Floral and Grape, 6 tumblers,
   marigold   220-250
Grape, N mark, 6 tumblers,
   purple . . . .   595+
Grape and Gothic Arches,
   marigold   120-140
Imperial's Grape, blue   160-192
Imperial's Grape, 6 tumblers,
   purple   220-260

Millersburg's Diamond, green . . .   130-150
Nesting Peacock   125-145
Northwood's Maple Leaf, 6
   tumblers, marigold   255-285
Peacock at the Fountain, white . .   460-580
Poinsettia, marigold 56- 66
Rose pattern, 8 tumblers   130-155
Singing Birds, marigold   190-240
Star Medallion, small, marigold .   42- 60
PLATE
Grape and Cable, footed, green . .   128-140
Homestead, signed Nu Art,
   marigold . . . .   500+
Honeycomb, purple 54- 64
Imperial Jewels, white 62- 73
Peacock and Urn, white   210-230
Peacock on the Fence, green   175-195
Strawberry, N mark, green   130-160
Three Fruits, marigold 60- 72
Three Fruits, white   154-170
Vintage, green 80- 90
Wild Strawberry, N mark, green .   145-160
SAUCEBOAT
Fan pattern, purple 74- 85
SHADE
Gas, Mayflower, marigold, pr . . .   51- 70
Light, signed Nu Art, marigold,
   pr 55- 67
Light, quilted, white, pr 34- 44
Light, white 26- 42
SHERBET
Bouquet and Lattice, pedestal,
   set of 6, marigold 41- 60
Flute, N mark, green 37- 48
Holly, marigold 30- 40
Iris and Herringbone, marigold .   29- 41
Orange Tree, stemmed, marigold   30- 40
SPOONHOLDER
Acorn Burrs   100-125
Butterfly and Berry, marigold . .   44- 62
Hobstar, marigold 38- 50
Kittens, small, marigold 81- 91
Lustre Rose, green 40- 57

Carnival, Ragged Robin

Peacock at the Fountain	85-140

SUGAR

Grape and Cable, cover, purple ..	80- 90
Lustre Flute, handle	46- 60
Lustre Flute, N mark, purple ...	49- 62
Millersburg's Cherry	74- 85
Star and File	40- 50

SWAN

Millersburg, purple	162-182
Pastel blue	51- 61
Pastel green	56- 66

TRAY

Butterfly, footed, white........	128-148
Grape, center handles, marigold .	60- 70
Pin tray, Grape and Cable, scalloped, marigold	125-145

TUMBLER

Apple Tree, marigold	38- 48
Blueberry, white	52- 62
Butterfly, purple	42- 52
Dandelion, N mark, green	61- 71
Enameled Cherry, blue	35- 45
Grape and Cable, purple	55- 65
Grape and Lattice, white.......	66- 75
Grapes, Maple Leaves, N mark, marigold	42- 52
Lattice and Grape, blue........	35- 45
Maple Leaf, set of 6, purple	220-240
Millersburg's Diamond Band, marigold	28- 39
Oriental Poppy, white	115-135
Peacock at the Fountain, blue ...	48- 60
Peacock, N mark, purple	60- 70
Rambler Rose, marigold	29- 42
Singing Birds, N mark, green ...	57- 67
Star Medallion, set of 6, marigold	143-163
Stork and Rushes, blue	49- 60
Vineyard, set of 6, marigold	130-150
Water lily and Cattails, N mark .	52- 65

VASE

Beaded Bull's-Eye, 11" high, marigold	50- 61
Corn, N mark, green	225-245
Corn, N mark, marigold	285-400
Cornucopia, marigold	51- 6S
Diamond Point, N mark, 8" high, purple	44- 54
Feather, green	34- 50
Fine Rib, N mark, marigold.....	40- 51
Grape, N mark, 16" high, blue...	58- 69
Knotted Beads, 11" high, red ...	138-160
Northwood's Drapery, 8¼" high, amethyst	42- 58
Ripple, 17" high, marigold	40- 50
Rose Column, green	250-288

WATER SET

Butterfly and Berry, blue	550-700
God and Home, blue (rare)......	3,000+
Grape and Cable, 7 pcs., purple ..	420-510
Peacock at the Fountain, N mark, blue	595+

WINE

Grape, marigold	35- 45
Iris, set of 6, marigold	42- 52
Octagon, 7 pcs., marigold	235-245
Orange Tree, green	65- 75
Sailboats, frosted stem, marigold	38- 52

Carousel!

A German, Michael Dentzel, introduced the first carousel to America in 1867. We know the "carousel" in this country as the merry-go-round, a delightful ride for children of all ages, with a chance of grabbing the brass ring. An American, C.W. Parker, was known as the "Amusement King" in the late 1880s. Carousel animals that go up and down are known as "jumpers" and Mr. Parker invented and built them. His horses were a thing of beauty.

"Jumper" dog, 59" long, made by Spillman	$1,600-1,850
"Jumper" dog head, on front of saddle, jewels, 56" long, Parker	900-1,000
"Jumper" horse, lion hide saddle, jewels, made by Parker, 59" long	1,000-1,300
"Jumper" Trojan horse, 60" long, made by Spillman	900-1,200
"Jumper" zebra, 58" long, made by Spillman	1,200-1,350

Castor Sets

Dating from the early 1700s, castor sets you find in shops today are of the Victorian era — 3 to 7 condiment bottles in a metal frame, usually Quadruple Plate or pewter. PICKLE CASTOR: see under that listing.

4-bottle, green/clear cut glass, Quadruple Plate holder, 7½" high (ill.)	$325-350
4-bottle, Quadruple Plate frame, clear glass	140-165
4-bottle, Sheffield Silver frame, Waterford glass, clear	175-200
5-bottle, Quadruple Plate frame etched flowers, clear glass	95-120
5-bottle, Quadruple Plate frame, amber Daisy and Button	140-160
6-bottle, Quadruple Plate frame, clear glass	65- 75

(continued)

Castor Set

6-bottle, Quadruple Plate frame,
   miniature, clear glass 80- 95
6-bottle Quadruple Plate frame,
   Cranberry thumbprint   195-210
6-bottle, Quadruple Plate frame,
   clear glass, Patented 1857   150-170
7-bottle, Sterling Silver frame,
   Amberina-type   475-550
8-bottle, clear glass, Sterling
   Silver caps   250-300
8-bottle, cut glass, Sterling
   Silver caps   350-475

Catalogs

Catalogs

Every company that could afford to issued a catalog extolling their product. The most collectible today are those that deal with the early automobile industry, jewelry and furniture makers and, of course, the now-expensive original Sears, Roebuck catalog from the early 1900s. Montgomery Ward also brings brisk prices.

Franklin auto catalog, Syracuse,
   N.Y. 1907 . . . . $ 45- 55
Montgomery Ward catalog, early
   1900s   150-175
Noritake China catalog, 1964
   (ill.) 1- 2
Sears, Roebuck catalog, early
   1900s   150-175
Singer sewing machine, parts
   catalog, 1920s 8- 15
Spode China catalog, 1964 (ill.) . .   1- 2

Cauldon China

Cauldon China

This firm didn't make porcelain until the early 1900s. It's very collectible today. English.

Bonbon dish, floral decorations . . $ 25- 35
Cup and saucer, Indian Tree
   pattern 37- 45
Egg cup 16- 26
Ewer, Indian Tree design 35- 50
Flower, "frog," floral decor, 10
   holes 20- 30
Plate, hunting scene 10½"
   diameter 28- 40
Plate, floral decor, roses-in-
   wreath, 10½" diameter 30- 40
Vase, round form, roses (ill.) 32- 42
Vase, Indian Tree pattern 40- 50

Ceiling Fans

Ceiling fans

Used in homes and stores after electricity was invented. Being collected today by decorators and others.

Average price, good condition . . . $165-225
Reproductions available—higher
   priced.

Celadon

Celadon

This is a rare type of highly-fired porcelain from the Sung Dynasty. It's scarce and is only mentioned here because some of it has been brought in from Red China in recent years. It features a glaze that meanders from greens through tones of gray-blue, gray-white, etc. It was also made in Japan and Korea, and undoubtedly military personnel brought home original pieces without knowing its value.

Bowl, diamond shape panels, 11½" diameter, Sung Dynasty	$1,800+
Bowl, flower leaves, 6¼" dia., late	65- 75
Creamer, blue/white chrysanthemum leaves, late	75- 80
Dish (used as planters), blue/white floral, early 19th c.	250-300
Jar, birds in relief, 19th century	175-210
Pitcher, green, flower, decor, "bamboo" handle	300-350
Planter, birds in relief, 19th century	210-240
Plate, scalloped rose pattern, birds, butterflies, enameled	150-170
Teapot, floral motif, 6" high	85-100
Vase, on rosewood stand, bamboo motif, 19th century	350-425
Vase, grayish green, blue handles and figures, 16½" high (ill.)	325-350
Vase, blue/gray, dragon motif, 9½" high	185-195

Celluloid ("French Ivory")

Invented by John Hyatt around 1868, it

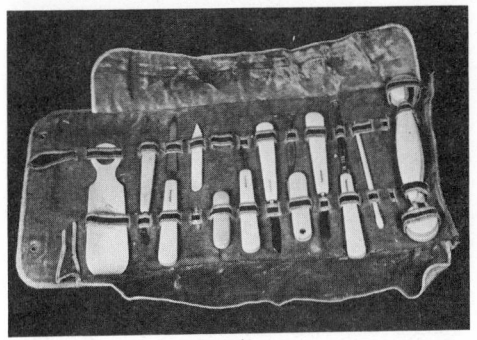

Celluloid

was considered a boon to men who had to wear collars. It was also used for hairbrush backs, combs, etc. It fell from style in the mid-1900s.

Collar box, velvet lined	$ 40- 50
Comb, lady's	12- 18
Cream jar w/cover, glass lining, 3" dia.	17- 27
Dresser set, tray, comb, mirror, hair receiver, powder box, etc.	68- 78
Dresser tray, 11¼" long	9- 18
Frame, 6" x 9"	23- 31
Glove box, woman on lid	31- 41
Hair receiver and covered powder box	7- 12
Handled cuticle tool	6- 12
Lady's travel kit	27- 37
Manicure set, pink velvet case (ill.)	28- 38
Napkin ring	7- 12
Opener, letter	12- 17
Pansy vase, 6" high	15- 27
Powder box w/lid 4½" dia.	14- 19
Nail buffer, chamois covered, 6" long	6- 14
Rattle, baby's	12- 17
Shoehorn	6- 13

Centennial Plates

Centennial plates obviously celebrate the 100th anniversary of cities, states, institutions.

Plate, Baltimore & Ohio, 1827-1927, 10" dia.	$ 32- 42
Plate, Civil War, "North-South United," crossed flags, 10½" dia.	26- 36
Plate, Philadelphia, Declaration of Independence, 1776-1876, 8" dia.	37- 47
Plate, War of 1812, 9" dia.	36- 45

Chain Gang Collectibles

Chain Gang Collectibles

In some states these items are still used. Today, collectors are adding them to their collections.

"Arkansas toothpick" leg		
manacle (ill.)	$ 48-	60
Ball and chain with lock (ill.)	65-	75
Handcuffs, with key (ill.)	48-	56
Leg cuffs (manacles)	50-	60

Chalkware

Contrary to popular belief, this was not made by the Dutch Germans in Pennsylvania in the mid-1800s. Italian immigrants in this country, 1820s to the Civil War, made the best; simply, plaster-of-paris decorated with water colors.

Bank, dog, black, glass eyes	$ 42-	55
Bank, rearing horse	16-	27
Bank, turkey, natural colors	45-	60
Betty Boop, 14½" high	170-190	
Bookends, boy and girl reading		
(ill.) pr.	40-	48
Bookends, pirates, painted, pair .	42-	53
Cat, glass eyes	35-	45

Dog, 11½" high, early	72-	85
Dove, green/blue wings	180-190	
Figurine, bust of Indian	70-	80
Figurine, cat sleeping	55-	62
Owl, 12" high	160-170	
Pigeon, green leaves, red berries		
(ill.)	120-140	
Sailor boy, 9" high	15-	19
Snow White, 12½" high	30-	40
Squirrel	150-175	
Stag, on rectangular plinth	200-220	

Chelsea

This fine English china was made to compete with Dresden in the 1740s. At least 4 different marks were used and in the 1920s, the Spode-Copeland Works in England reproduced many pieces from the original molds. Rooster figurines are collectible today.

Candlesticks, Anchor mark,
   flower motif, 11" high, pr. . . . $1,300-1,400

Chelsea

Chalkware

Dish, Kakiemon decoration, Red Anchor, 1750s	375- 425
Dish, oval, scalloped edge, same mark as above	95- 140
Jardiniere, blue decor, Red Anchor mark, 12½" high	1,300-1,400
Jug, blue decor, gray stoneware, 1920s	55- 68
Lamb figurine, oval base, Gold Anchor mark, 1760s	150- 200
Pitcher, Moses at the Well, 8" high, late	58- 68
Plate, floral decor, Gold Anchor mark, 7½" dia.	385- 400
Plate, hand-painted birds, Gold Anchor mark, 1760s	450- 500
Scent bottle, 2½" high, Red Anchor mark, 1750s	1,400-1,500
Scent bottle, fruit decor, 3½" high, Gold Anchor mark, 1760s	375- 425

Children's Mugs

Children's Mugs

These 19th century items were usually given to children as gifts or as a reward for being good. Leeds, Ironstone, Gaudy Dutch, Liverpool, Bristol; just a few of the many types made. Highly collectible today.

"A present for a good boy" Canary Ware	$150-175
"A new carriage for Ann" Canary Ware	140-155
Boy with farm animals, Ironstone	85- 95
Ding Dong Bell, silver plated	30- 38
"Long may we live" Canary Ware	145-170
Franklin maxim, "The way to wealth"	78- 88
"The house that Jack built"	65- 85

Chocolate Glass

Often referred to as caramel slag, it was made by the Indiana Tumbler and Goblet Company, Greentown, Indiana. Popular patterns were Cactus and Leaf Bracket.

Berry bowl, Cactus, 4" dia.	$ 40- 50
Berry set, Leaf Bracket, 6 pieces	440-500
Compote, jelly, Cactus	120-135
Cracker jar, Cactus	195-220
Creamer, Austrian	83- 93

Chocolate Glass

Dish, butter, covered, Leaf Bracket	115-135
Lamp, 7 panel, fancy base and framework	195-225
Mug, Serenade	75- 87
Nappie, handled (ill.)	67- 78
Sugar, Leaf Bracket	75- 90
Tumbler, Sawtooth	48- 60
Tumbler, 4¾" high (ill.)	45- 55
Tumbler, Cactus	39- 58

Chocolate Pot Sets

Chocolate Pot Sets

Just about every porcelain factory in Europe made these sets, popular in the 18th and 19th centuries. See also specific firms elsewhere in the Guide for prices.

Cream flowers, gold decor with 6 cups (ill.)	$125-150
Lily decor, signed Germany, 6 cups/saucers	130-160
Oriental decor, Chinese garden scene, pot and 6 cups/saucers	130-155
Rose decor, flower trim, signed Germany, 6 cups/saucers	125-145
Roses, cream ground, gold decor, 4 cups/saucers	110-130

Christmas Cards

Louis Prang (Prang and Company, Boston), a contemporary of Currier and Ives, produced what were known as chromolithographic prints. This art was considered finer

(continued)

Christmas Cards

than the cheaper lithographs. Prang is best known for his Christmas, Valentine, Easter, New Year's and birthday cards. During the 1870s, Prang's catalog advertised all items reflecting that period of American life.

Average price for
Christmas card in
good conditon . . . . . . $ 1- 3 each

Christmas Collectibles/Ornaments

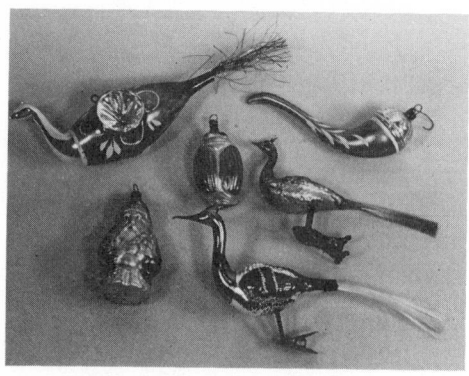

Christmas Collectibles/Ornaments

Christmas Collectibles/Ornaments

Old-fashioned Christmases are a thing of the past in this country. No stringing of popcorn to drape on the tree, no hiking through the snow to cut down a favorite tree. Whoever said, "Let's put Christ back in Christmas!" has my vote! Anyway, the older Christmas items are now eagerly sought after. Please — if you find old electric Christmas tree lights, *please* be careful; old wire can cause a fire in a matter of seconds.

Bulbs, electric:

Basket of fruit, green/red	$ 6-	9
Bluebird, milk glass	6-	9
Gingerbread man, brown	7-	12
Man-in-the-moon, milk glass	6-	9
Santa Claus, red/white	11-	16

Ornaments:

Bettle (ill.)	10-	25
Crane, clip feet (ill.)	10-	25
Peacock (ill.)	10-	25
Pipe (ill.)	10-	25
Santa Claus (ill.)	10-	25
Swan (ill.)	10-	25
Santa Claus, heavy pressed paper, tinted, 9½" high (ill.) . . .	47-	12
Santa Claus, open bag (holds candy), pressed paper, 10" high (ill.)	9-	16

Christmas Plates

Bing and Grondahl and the Royal Copenhagen factories in Copenhagen, Denmark, make the best-known Christmas plates. Many American firms are now producing a plate.

YEAR	B&G	RC
1895	$ 3,700+	
1902	310-350	
1903	200-225	
1904	130-145	
1905	125-155	
1906	100-120	
1907	130-150	
1908	80- 90	$ 1,800+
1909	105-130	135-150
1910	92-102	115-140
1911	90-100	140-150
1912	87-100	120-135
1913	92-105	135-150
1914	75- 85	120-135
1915	130-150	110-125
1916	95-110	110-130
1917-'36	70- 80	85-120
1937	100-115	140-150
1938	115-135	250-275
1939	165-185	240-260
1940	160-180	425-475
1941	300-325	340-360
1942	155-175	410-455
1943	158-168	450-500
1944	94-110	195-225
1945	145-170	370-400
1946	72- 82	190-240
1947	90-110	240-260
1948	55- 65	130-160
1949	60- 70	140-155
1950	93-103	140-165
1951	82- 92	280-310
1952	65- 75	110-140
1953	86- 92	92-110
1954	72- 82	135-150
1955	88-100	250-270
1956	110-120	150-160
1957	140-160	110-125
1958	120-130	130-140
1959	155-175	133-143
1960	140-160	135-160

1961	240-260	133-143
1962	68- 78	185-210
1963	100-115	50- 60
1964	78- 88	40- 50
1965	60- 70	40- 50
1966	55- 65 (ill.)	55- 60
1967	52- 62	24- 34
1968	42- 52 (ill.)	18- 29
1969-79	30- 42	20- 30

YEAR	FRANKOMA	BAYREUTHER
1965	185-210	
1966	80- 95	
1967	62- 72	90-110
1968	21- 30	30- 40
1970-'79	25- 30	35- 55

Christmas Plates

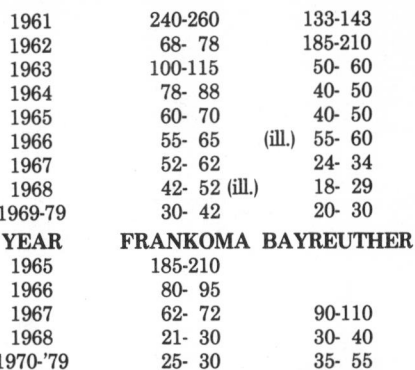

HAPPY FELIX

Cigar Box Labels

Cigar Box Labels

They are being collected and some of the older labels are bringing good prices. An average price would be 50¢ to $1. each.

Cigar Cutters, Pocket

When gentlemen wore vests and watch chains, the pocket-type cigar cutter was one

Christmas Plates

89

(continued)

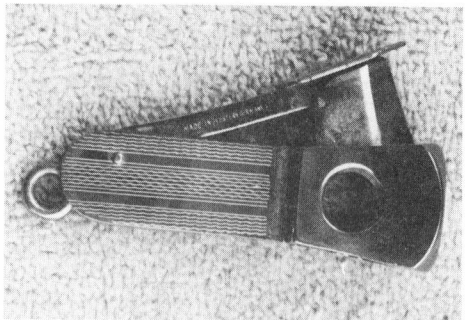

Cigar Cutters, Pocket

of the attachments. Most were utilitarian but 14 karat gold and sterling silver models were much in vogue. A quality cigar always has to have the tip snipped off; a 5¢ stinker comes with the hole.

Combination cutter and knife blade, 10 k gold	$ 40- 50
Combination cutter and watch fob, 10 k gold	40- 50
Combination cutter and small scissors, stainless steel	28- 38
Cutter, stainless steel, Germany (ill.)	12- 18
Cutter, embossed, 14 k gold	125-150
(Note: It *isn't* the cutter, it's the price of the gold)	
Cutter, initialed, sterling silver . .	50- 60

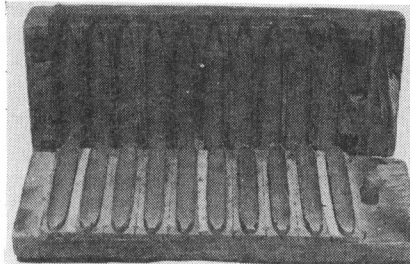

Cigar Molds

Cigar Molds

Used to shape the cigar in the early days, today they make pleasant items to hang in the kitchen or on a den wall.

Cigar molds, wood, 2 pieces (ill.) .	$ 30- 40
Cigar molds, base metal, 2 pieces	28- 40
Cigar molds, wood, carved "Havana's Best" on top lid . . .	40- 48

Cigar Store Figures

Used in America during the 19th century, almost life-size effigies of Indian braves and squaws were popular decorations outside

Cigar Store Figures

tobacco shops. Other figures were also used. The practice comes from the Dutch who used this type figure to advertise tobacco in the 1600s. Also used in England in the 1600s.

Indian, 72" high	$6,400-6,900
Indian chief, wood painted, 6½" high (R. ill.)	7,500-8,000
Indian chief, small	5,400-6,200
Indian chief, wood, painted 4' high (L. ill.)	6,300-6,600
Indian chief, painted, 5' high . .	5,500-6,000
Indian maiden, 5' high	5,200-5,500
Indian squaw, wood, painted, half size	5,000-5,700
Turk, wood, painted	6,400-6,800

Cigarette Pictures

Cigarette Pictures

Pictures of actors, athletes and others were

enclosed in packages of cigarettes in 1880s to the 1900s. Strollers Cigarettes was one of the companies that put one of these cards on each pack. Remember Ruth Roland, Renee Adoree, Gertrude Olmsted, Alice Terry, Ann Forrest, Hope Hampton? If you do, you're older than I!

Depending on celebrity ...... $ 1- 2 each

Cinnabar

Cinnabar

Red lacquer built up slowly with layer after layer is called Cinnabar, the best coming from China in the late 17th century. It's made today any place in the Orient.

Bowl, red-brown, carved	$ 78- 88
Box, red, carving on cover and sides, 4" x 5"	60- 70
Button, lotus flower design 4/5" diameter	23- 32
Plaque, red, carved, black and gold frame, 6" x 7½"	40- 45
Snuff bottle, lacquer, floral, birds	125-140
Snuff bottle, red, white, jade top .	175-190
Vase, brass rim, top and bottom, pr	180-190
Vase, trees, mountains, carved, 8" high	105-115
Vase, carved overall floral and foliage design	122-134
Vase, carved flowers on teakwood base, 8½" high, pair, (ill.)	325-360

Civil War Collectibles

Also known as the "War Between the States," depending which side you were on. "C.S.A." means "Confederate States of America" and "G.A.R." means "Grand Army of the Republic"; and, the "Blue" was

Civil War Collectibles

the North and the "Gray" was the South. "Rebs" were Southerners, those who rebelled and joined Jeff Davis; "Blue Bellies" were Union troops, so named because the dye in their blue uniforms stained their bellies blue.

Album, regimental photos, 8" x 11"	$250-300
Bayonet w/scabbard, CSA	50- 58
Belt buckle, CSA, brass	33- 45
Bowie-knife, bone handle, w/scabbard, marked "I*XL"	425-475
Bowie knife, ivory handle, w/scabbard, no marking	325-365
Box, cartridges, leather, "CSA" imprint	28- 42
Canteen, cloth-over-wood	75- 80
Cap badge, GAR, enlisted man's	40- 50
Cartridge pouch, GAR, leather	74- 84
Colt revolver, Navy model, ivory grips	1,450-1,600
Diary, private's account, 150th Regiment	125-140
Discharge paper from 1st Ohio Volunteers, dated June 15, 1863	55- 65
Holster w/belt, Dragoon imprint	160-185
Horses bit	22- 32
Knapsack, GAR...........	40- 45
Leather belt, brass buckle, GAR	45- 49
Naval cutlass, Confederate navy, 26" serrated edges	165-180
Naval sword, dress, US Navy, 35" long	190-220
Photograph, Major Joseph O.V.S. Archambault, taken in Philadelphia, July, 1865, in walnut frame (ill.)	185-210
Poster, asking recruits to join Glennon's Brigade, GAR ...	52- 60
Poster offering reward for GAR deserters	51- 63

(continued)

Saddle bags, CSA, Virginia 1st Cavalry, pr.	225-250
Saddle, McClellan-type, w/saddle bags	200-250
Slave document, 1846, purchase of Becky from Christopher Hutchins to I.W. Rawlings	55- 65
Spurs, CSA, officer's	150-170
Telescope, US Navy	190-210

Clambroth Glass

Clambroth Glass

Its gray color, semi-opaque, supplies its name. Popular during the Victorian era.

Barber bottle, Bay Rum, stopper	$ 38- 48
Candlestick, Sandwich glass, 1850s, 10" high (ill.)	250-275
Cruet, applied blue twisted handle	58- 68
Dish, footed, 8" diameter	22- 31
Egg cup, Diamond Point w/panels	115-125
Goblet, souvenir of Philadelphia, 7" high	25- 35
Toothpick holder, souvenir-type .	16- 27
Tumbler, souvenir-type	27- 37
Tumbler, whiskey	175-200
Vase, fluted top, 8½" high	68- 80

Clevenger Glass

Clevenger Glass

During the depression years of the 1930s this glass was "freehand blown" — sugar bowls, vases, pitchers; in the 1940s it was "mold blown." The Clevenger brothers, Tom, Lorenzo, and Allie, remained in business until the early 1960s. A few years later the shop was reopened and is still in business in Clayton, New Jersey. Early pieces are sought after by serious collectors.

Creamer, amethyst, swirl pattern, 3½" high (ill.)	$ 85- 95
Pitcher, aqua, expanded diamond pattern	90-110
Sugar bowl, amethyst, ribbed, 3¾" dia. (ill.)	80- 90

Clews, Ralph and James

Established in Cobridge, England, in 1814, this pottery operated until around 1835 when it was taken over by Wood and Brownfield. Dr. Syntax and the Valentine were two of the most popular subjects. Probably the most popular series was the States.

Creamer, 5½", eagle on urn	$100-125
Cups/saucers, dark blue, landing of Lafayette	110-132
Gravy boat with tray, "Landing of General Lafayette at Castle Gardens, N.Y., August 16, 1824"	240-260
Pitcher, dark blue, 13 original states, series, 8" high	295-300
Plates: 9" dia., dark blue, states series	170-195
7¼" dia., dark blue, Dr. Syntax Turned Nurse	200-240
10" dia., dark blue, Dr. Syntax and the Bees	210-235
10½" dia., black, Pittsburgh Pennsylvania . . . . '. .	160-180
9" dia., "Dr. Syntax Reading His Tour"	220-250

Clocks

For a history of clocks, their current prices and a glossary of terms, see CLOCK GUIDE, Identification with Prices, Volumes I & II, Wallace-Homestead Book Co., Des Moines, Iowa, $8.95 each.

American-made, 30-hour, lever escapement, metal cased clock, time and strike	$120-150
American-made, desk calendar clock with alarm, metal case .	62- 90
American-made electric table clock, carved wood case, 1920s, time only	45- 60

American-made iron front shelf clock, possibly Seth Thomas — 160-185

American-made kitchen wall clock, 8-day, time only — 60-75

American-made, metal cased clock, time and alarm — 50-60

American-made, miniature cottage clock, time and alarm — 130-160

American-made, Mission-type wall clock, green/white glass behind pendulum, time only — 110-140

American-made sterling silver bedside clock, 8-day, time and strike — 65-80

Ansonia Clock Co., Brooklyn, N.Y., "Chrystal Palace" clock, walnut base, mirrored sides, 8-day, time and strike — 500-600

Ansonia Clock Co, Crystal Regulator, 8-day, time and strike, mercury pendulum, open escapement — 310-360

Ansonia Clock Co., Brooklyn, N.Y., marble mantel clock, matching candle stands on either side — 325-450

Ansonia Clock Co., Regulator wall clock, time and strike, mahogany veneer — 375-475

Ansonia Brass & Copper Co., Ansonia, Conn., rosewood case, sharp Gothic, 8-day, time and strike, 1851-1878 — 260-295

Ansonia Clock Co., bronze figure mantel clock, "Mercury," metal case, open escapement, time and strike — 525-625

Ansonia Clock Co., Brooklyn, N.Y., round top table clock, time and strike — 100-150

Ansonia Clock Co., statue clock, cast metal case, 8-day, time and strike — 270-355

Ansonia Clock Co., walnut shelf clock, "King," 8-day, time and strike — 550-675

Ansonia Clock Co., brass table clock, 8-day, Pat. 1892 — 165-195

Atkins Clock Co., Bristol, Conn., miniature Empire shelf clock, rosewood case, stenciled tablet, 8-day brass movement, time, strike and alarm, 1859-1879 — 485-575

Birge, Mallory & Co., Bristol, Conn., shelf clock, 8-day, roller pinion, weight driven, time and strike — 550-650

Brewster & Ingraham, Bristol, Conn. walnut Gallery clock, time only — 325-450

J. C. Brown (Forestville Mfg. Co.), Bristol, Conn., steeple fusee, mahogany veneer with painted tablet, 8-day, time and strike — 300-400

L. F. & W. W. Carter, Bristol, Conn., walnut mantel clock, 8-day spring movement with B. B. Lewis Patented calendar. 1862, time and strike — 1,600-1,850

Chelsea Clock Co., Chelsea, Mass., wardroom clock, "U.S. Marine Corps" on dial, time only — 200-250

Darch Electric Clock Co., Chicago, Ill., flashlight and alarm clock, 30-hour, battery operated, Pat. 1910 — 80-95

Davis Clock Co., Columbus, Miss., column flat top shelf calendar, rosewood, (movement made by Gilbert), 8-day, time and strike — 1,200-1,400

Dutch, porcelain hanging wall clock, time only — 60-75

English carriage clock, brass case, time and alarm — 250-350

English carriage clock, brass case, time and strike — 210-240

English watchman's clock, punch-type, fusee movement, walnut case — 280-295

Esberger Bros., Jeweler, Cincinnati, alarm clock made for their customers — 55-70

European case, American movement wall clock, walnut case, time and strike — 195-255

Chas. W. Fleichtinger, Sinking Spring, Pa., oak case, Victorian kitchen, shelf calendar clock, 8-day, time and strike — 1,400-1,600

French carriage clock, silver case, repeater with alarm — 220-270

French desk clock, brass case with finials, 8-day, time and strike — 250-295

French Statue clock, brass/marble, time and strike — 295-400

French Statue clock, bronze figure, porcelain inserts in cast brass base, time and strike — 450-575

French Statue clock, bronze, on marble base, time and strike — 500-650

German "game" clock, cast metal, time only — 70-95

German mantel clock, time and strike — 90-110

German 3-piece mantel set, bisque, time only — 140-170

(continued)

German miniature carriage
clock, time and strike 120-165
German shelf clock, time and
strike 150-175
German wall clock, time only . . 130-150
Gilbert L. Gilbert Clock Co.,
Winsted, Conn., kitchenette
model, light stenciling, 8-day,
time only 95-130
Wm. L. Gilbert Clock Co.,
Winsted, Conn., metal cased,
bronzed, mercury pendulum,
8-day, time and strike 290-350
Wm. L. Gilbert Clock Co.,
Winsted, Conn., miniature
shelf clock, octagon top,
rosewood case, 1866-1871,
time only 150-195
Wm. L. Gilbert Clock Co.,
Winsted, Conn., oak wall
clock, 8-day, time, strike and
alarm "Elipse" 400-475
Gilbert Mfg. Co., rosewood
case, steeple, 30-hour, time
and strike, dated 1868 190-260
Elisha Hotchkiss, Jr., Burlington, Conn., mantel clock,
wooden movement, 30-hour,
weight driven, time and
strike 390-490
Robert H. Ingersoll & Bros.,
Waterbury, Conn., and
Trenton, N.J., alarm clock . . 49- 70
E. Ingraham & Co., Bristol,
Conn., "Doric" rosewood
mantel clock, 8-day, time and
strike, Pat. 1871 300-400
E. Ingraham & Co.,
Bristol, Conn., night and day
alarm clock 70- 90
Ingraham Clock Co., Bristol,
Conn., oak shelf clock, 8-day,
time and strike 150-185
E. Ingraham & Co., Bristol,
Pa., walnut kitchen clock,
time and strike, 1890-1910 . . 290-320
International Time Recording
Co. (later became part of
IBM) time clock 180-245
Ithaca Calendar Clock Co.,
Ithaca, N.Y., No. 3½ walnut
parlor calendar clock, black
dials, etched glass pendulum
bob, time and strike 4,000-4,800
Ithaca Calendar Clock Co.,
Ithaca, N.Y., No. 4½",
"Favorite" calendar clock,
walnut case, gold letters,
time and strike 2,400-2,800
Ithaca Calendar Clock Co.,
Emerald #5, walnut case,
open carving, time and strike 2,600-2,900

Clocks

1. French Statue clock, ormolu,
gilt . . . . $ 420- 495
2. Seth Thomas, Thomaston,
Conn. chronometer lever
(ship's type) clock, nickel-
plated, 15-day 465- 615
3. Sangamo Electric Co.,
Springfield, Ill., Sangamo
electric clock, mahogany
case, with 11-jewel Illinois
watch movement, 1926-28 175- 190
4. Chauncey Ives, Bristol,
Conn., Pillar and Scroll
clock, wooden movement,
mahogany veneer case,
painted tablet 2,200-2,750
5. American-made, novelty
tape measure" clock,
30-hour 75- 95
6. E.N. Welch Mfg. Co., Bristol
Conn., small cast iron
"valise" clock, 30-hour . . . 60- 95
7. Western Clock Co., La Salle,
Ill., Westclox alarm,
30-hour 35- 45
8. E.N. Welch, Bristol, Conn.,
paperweight clock, octagon
lever, duplex movement,
emerald green glass case,
30-hour 300- 375
9. Seth Thomas Clock Co.,
Fashion calendar clock,
Model #5, long pendulum,
made for Dixie Calendar
Clock Co. 2,800-3,100

94

Ithaca Calendar Clock Co., No.
5 round top, rosewood case,
30-day, time only 1,700-1,950
Ithaca Calendar Clock Co.,
Ithaca, N.Y., No. 11 octagon,
black walnut calendar clock,
8-day, time, strike and alarm 1,600-1,850
Ithaca Calendar Clock Co., No.
9 shelf-cottage clock, perpetual calendar, time and
strike 1,700-1,975
Ithaca Calendar Clock Co. #10
Farmer's model, perpetual
calendar, time and strike ... 750-975
Ithaca Calendar Clock Co.,
Bellgrade model, walnut
case, wooden pendulum
hangs in front of calendar
movement, time and strike .. 1,850-2,250

Clocks

1. Forestville Clock Manu-
   facotry, Bristol, Conn. (one
   of J. C. Brown's trade
   names), triple-decker, carved
   top, walnut case, painted
   tablets, 8-day brass movement, 1849-53 900-1,150
2. Bradley & Hubbard Mfg.
   Co., Meriden, Conn., cast
   iron case, stenciling with
   mother-of-pearl inlay, clock
   movement by Ansonia, 1854-
   1890 .... 275- 385
3. French shelf clock, gold gilt
   with porcelain dial and cap,
   1860-70 .... 365- 475

Ithaca Calendar Clock Co.,
large Index model, walnut
case, "Index" letters in gold,
made for Lynch Brothers,
8-day, time and strike 2,600-2,900
Ithaca Calendar Clock Co.,
small Index model, walnut
case, "Index" letters in gold,
made for Lynch Brothers,
8-day time and strike 2,475-2,750
Ithaca Calendar Clock Co.,
Ithaca, N.Y., walnut shelf
steeple calendar clock, fretwork under dials, 8-day, time
and strike, 1870s 2,500-3,000
F. W. Jansen, Chicago, Ill.,
"Nitelite" alarm clock 70- 85
C. Jerome, Bristol, Conn.,
miniature cottage clock,
mahogany veneer, time and
alarm 160-195
"Jerome & Co." (trade name
used by New Haven Clock
Co.) "Christmas Tree"
kitchen clock, time and
strike 250-300
Jerome Mfg. Co., New Haven,
Conn., mahogany miniature
steeple, 30-hour, time and
alarm, 1845-1850s 175-225
F. Kroeber Clock Co., New
York City, miniature time-
piece 110-150
R. Lalique (French) table clock,
pressed glass case, cut glass
dial, battery operated, signed
"R. Lalique," 1890s 185-225
Lux Clock Mfg. Co., Waterbury, Conn., "Cupid" novelty
clock, time and strike 130-170
Lux Clock Mfg. Co.,
Waterbury, Conn., Show
Boat alarm clock; paddle
wheel on steamboat revolved
with balance wheel, animated
dial 60- 90
Galusha Maranville, Winsted,
Conn., octagon drop wall,
calendar, rosewood, time and
strike, Pat. March 5, 1861 .. 1,200-1,400
Mission wall clock, oak case,
time only 90-115
Mission wall clock, time and
strike 95-110
Nicholas Muller's Sons, New
York City, flat top black
marble mantel clock, outside
escapement, time and strike . 125-175
National Watch Co., Elgin, Ill.,
8-day car clock 75-115

(continued)

New Haven Clock Co., bronze figure mantel clock, 8-day, time and strike 375-425

New Haven Clock Co., chime mantel clock 140-195

New Haven Clock Co., New Haven, Conn., small Gothic, mahogany veneer, 30-hour, time and alarm 165-195

New Haven Clock Co., oak kitchen clock, time, strike and alarm 170-210

New Haven Clock Co., statue clock, cast metal case, black wood base, open escapement, time and strike 400-500

New Haven Clock Co., New Haven, Conn., statue-type clock, 8-day, gold dipped, time and strike 160-190

New Haven Clock Co., walnut shelf clock, 8-day, time and strike 165-198

New Haven Clock Co., walnut shelf clock, "Etna," turned columns, time and strike . . . 350-425

New Haven Clock Co., wood base, brass case, time and intermittent alarm 75- 98

Perry & Shaw, New York City, shelf clock, wooden dial, 30-hour, weight driven, time and strike 225-275

Daniel Pratt & Co., Reading, Mass., mahogany Beehive, 8-day, time and strike, 1832-46 350-425

Sandoz-Wullie, Swiss, 8-day car clock 65- 92

Sangamo Corp., Springfield, Ill. (Subsidiary jointly owned by Hamilton Watch Co. and Sangamo Electric Co.), "Sangamo" electric clock . . . 172-196

Sessions Clock Co., Forestville, Conn., mantel "advertising" clock, calendar-type, originally had "Calumet Baking Co." on front 400-475

Sessions Clock Co., Forestville, Conn., iron front case, brass trim, 8-day, time and strike . 128-192

Sessions Clock Co. (Forestville), Bristol, Conn., oak kitchen clock, "Hiawatha," 8-day, time and strike 199-245

Seth Thomas Clock Co., Thomaston, Conn., column gold leaf and gilt columns, painted tablets, Empire style, 8-day brass movement, Pat. 1867, time and strike . . . 700-875

Seth Thomas, parlor #1, calendar clock, model #1, mahogany veneer, 8-day, time and strike 775-1,100

Seth Thomas, black iron front mantel clock, twin marbleized columns on each side, time and strike 195-275

Seth Thomas, "Eclipse" walnut kitchen clock, 8-day, time, strike and alarm 350-475

Seth Thomas, Thomaston, Conn., engine room clock, 8-day, brass, Pat. April 16, 1878, time only 500-600

Seth Thomas electric chime clock 95-160

Seth Thomas, Fashion, model #2, walnut veneer, made for Southern Calendar Clock Co., St. Louis, Mo., 8-day, time and strike 2,700-3,000

Seth Thomas, Fashion, model #4, walnut case, made for Southern Calendar Clock Co., St. Louis, Mo., "Fashion" in gold letters on door, 8-day, time and strike . . . 2,850-3,200

Seth Thomas, Thomaston, Conn., long alarm, metal case, 8-day, time and alarm . 150- 175

Seth Thomas, oak wall clock, Regulator, No. 1, weight driven, time only 1,100-1,400

Seth Thomas, oak case, chimes and strikes on bells, 8-day, 1918 . . . . 150- 195

Seth Thomas Clock Co., reproduction Pillar and Scroll, walnut case, brass 8-day movement, 1929-1934, time and strike 175- 220

Seth Thomas, cottage clock, rosewood case, 8-day, strike and alarm 275- 320

Seth Thomas Clock Co., Plymouth Hollow, Conn., rosewood case, hexagon columns, stenciled tablets, 8-day weight movement, time and strike 450- 550

Seth Thomas, round top shelf clock with full pillars, 8-day, time, strike and alarm 275- 310

Seth Thomas Clock Co., Plymouth Hollow, Conn., shelf clock, calendar, rosewood case, hexagon columns, stenciled tablet, 8-day weight movement time and strike . . 2,300-2,650

Seth Thomas Standard OG,
mahogany veneer, 30-hour,
time and strike 385- 500
Seth Thomas Clock Co., walnut
calendar clock, parlor No. 5,
8-day, time and strike 1,600-1,800
Seth Thomas and Sons,
Thomaston, Conn. walnut
shelf clock, with fretwork,
time, strike and alarm 285- 450
United Electric Co. Brooklyn,
N.Y., FDR— The Man of the
Hour clock, plain dial, 30-
hour, time and alarm 110- 145
United Electric Co., Brooklyn,
N.Y., FDR—The Man of the
Hour clock, animated dial,
bartender's arm "shakes"
drink, 30-hour, time and
alarm 150- 165
Vienna Regulator wall clock,
baby 2-weight, time and
strike 550- 625
Waltham Watch & Clock Co.,
Waltham, Mass., 8-day car
clock   78-   96
Waterbury Clock Co., Water-
bury, Conn., calendar No. 43,
walnut clock, 8-day, 1860s,
time and strike 1,550-1,800
Waterbury Clock Co., carriage
clock, 8-day, strike and
repeat 220- 265
Waterbury Clock Co., metal
cased, bronze figure mantel
clock, time and strike 255- 295
Waterbury Clock Co., metal
cased mantel clock, outside
escapement, time and strike .   150- 198
Waterbury Clock Co., Water-
bury, Conn., miniature OG,
mahogany veneer, gold-
leafed inner frame, 30-hour,
time and strike 220- 275
Waterbury Clock Co., minia-
ture schoolhouse clock,
time only 175- 250
Waterbury Clock Co., oak
kitchen clock with barometer
and thermometer, time and
strike 250- 325
Waterbury Clock Co., walnut
shelf clock, 8-day, time and
strike, mercury pendulum . .   250- 300
Waterbury Clock Co., walnut
shelf clock, 8-day, time and
strike 225- 285
Waterbury Clock Co., Water-
bury, Conn., shelf clock,
walnut case, 8-day, time and
strike 190- 270

Waterbury Clock Co., Waterbury Conn., shelf clock, open
pendulum, time and strike . .   150- 170
Waterbury Clock Co., walnut
shelf clock, time and strike . .   180- 250
Waterbury Clock Co., Water-
bury,Conn., walnut kitchen
clock, time, strike and alarm .   220- 250
E. N. Welch, chestnut shelf
clock, "Coghland," time,
strike and alarm, 1864-1903 .   275- 350
E. N. Welch (Forestville),
Bristol, Conn., "La Reine,"
1-day desk clock, lever
escapement, brass plated,
Pat. Sept. 17, Oct. 11, 1878 . .   140- 185
E. N. Welch, pressed oak
shelf clock, "Robert E. Lee,"
time and strike, 1864-1903 . .   400- 475
E. N. Welch, shelf clock,
mahogany veneer, painted
tablet, 8-day, time and strike   160- 250
E. N. Welch Mfg. Co., Forest-
ville, Conn., walnut kitchen
clock, time and strike, 1864-
1903 . . . .   240- 290
E. N. Welch, Bristol, Conn.,
walnut shelf clock, full, open
columns, time and strike . . .   415- 515
Welch, Spring & Co., Bristol,
Conn., "Lucca" shelf clock,
rosewood case, 8-day, time
and strike 320- 327
Welch, Spring & Co., Bristol,
Conn., Patti movement, rose-
wood case, 8-day, time and
strike, 1870 . . . .   525- 650
Welch, Spring & Co., Bristol,
Conn., wall clock, rosewood
case, painted tablet, time
only 400- 450
Western Clock Mfg. Co.,
Westclox alarm clock   40-   50
Western Clock Co., Westclox,
"Baby Ben" alarm   28-   38
Western Clock Co., Westclox,
"Big Ben" alarm   40-   52
Western Clock Mfg. Co., Inter-
mediate "Big" Ben alarm
clock   29-   38
Western Clock Co., Westclox
miniature alarm   27-   38
Western Clock Mfg. Co.,
LaSalle, Ill., Waralarm, made
during World War II   54-   63
Western Clock Mfg. Co., War-
alarm clock   27-   38
Western Clock Co., La Salle,
Ill., Westclox ironclad alarm
clock   27-   38

NOTE: All these clocks and many, many more can be seen in CLOCK GUIDE, Identification with Prices, Volumes I & II, Wallace-Homestead Book Co., Des Moines, Iowa 50305, $8.95 each.

Cloisonne Enamel

Cloisonne Enamel

Developed during the 19th century, glass enamel was applied between small ribbon-like pieces of metal on a metal base. Supposedly from Japan, most of what is found in shops today is European and brought into the U.S. between 1870 and 1900.

Ashtray, dragon motif, "China," 3½" dia. .... $	20-	25
Ashtray, enameled, matchbox holder attached	28-	38
Bowl, brown ground, multi-colored floral design	74-	85
Bowl, green/red, "China," 4" dia.	35-	45
Box, black ground, yellow/green/red, dragon, 3" square	58-	68
Candlesticks, black, blue/green, dragon motif, 11" high, pr...............	105-	120
Clock w/two yellow urns, other colors include blue, pink, green. Clock, 11" to top of finial (ill.)	2,200-	2,750
Decanter, usual color, pr	75-	90
Desk blotter, blue/green, roll-type	28-	38
Dish, floral design, Oriental motif	36-	46
Dish, Chinese, yellow, dragon motif, 5" dia.	90-	120
Incense burner, Foo Dog, 10" high	95-	115
Ginger jar, blue ground, red flowers, cover	110-	125
Napkin ring, blue/green, birds	38-	48
Pitcher, black ground, butter-flies, birds, floral	180-	200
Plate, Japanese, blue/red/green, 6½" dia..........	70-	80
Plate, blue, flowers, 11" dia...	58-	64
Snuff bottle, blue ground, Buddhist emblems stopper	144-	166
Urn, Japanese, covered bronze finial, floral design, 2½" high, 2¼" dia........	100-	150
Teapot, yellow ground, cane handle	72-	82
Tray, Japanese, morning glory, fruit, bamboo pattern brass rim, 12" dia.	350-	400
Vase, beige ground, turquoise, gold, pr.	162-	172
Vase, blue, butterflies	135-	155
Lamp, pink/blue flowers, 14½" high, (ill.)	200-	250
Teapot, brown ground, flowers 7" high	95-	140

Clothing

Clothing

Old frock tailcoats and dresses of the same period are in demand today. Most of what you find in attics and shops is from the late 1800, early 1900 period. World War I uniforms are much in demand. Nazi uniforms are becoming collectible.

Coat, coonskin, 1920s	$250-	290
Dress, homespun, early 1800s ...	25-	38
Gowns, silk, velvet, lace, puffed sleeves	35-	45
Neckpieces, fox or mink, foot snaps	22-	32
Top hat, black silk, collapsible-type, Brooks Bros (ill.)	40-	50
Swallowtail coat, velvet lapels, early 1900s	60-	70

Coal Hods

Lugging coal from out-of-doors was a pain in the 1800s, but at least the hods were decorative in nature. Usually black with

bright flowers and birds, the coal hod stood
out in every room.

Tin/copper, painted with removable liner, flower motif, 17½"
high . . . . $ 65- 90
Stamped iron, black, removable
liner, flowers/birds, claw feet . . 65- 85
These are average prices.

Coalport

The factory operated at Coalport, England,
from the late 1700s until 1926, since then at
Stoke-on-Trent, making bone china.

Bowl, fruit, blue fluted and
ruffled sides, castle scene . . . . . $ 68- 80
Chocolate pot, Indian Tree, rose/
green foliage, 6 cups and
saucers 168-182
Cup/saucer, Indian Tree 32- 46
Cup/saucer, black/orange
floral on white 22- 32
Dish, floral decor, 1820, 9¼"
square 85- 95
Letter holder, 1820, rose/green . . 145-165
Mug, leaf design, white, 4½" high 70- 80
Plate, Indian Tree, scalloped,
7½", set of 6 . . . . 74- 88
Pitcher, Indian Tree, 5" high 75- 85
Platter, Indian Tree, 13" 50- 60
Salt/pepper, Indian Tree, beehive
shape, pr 38- 50
Tea service, blue banding, gilt,
pink blossoms, approximately
30 pieces 400-475
Trivet, Indian Tree 40- 49
Vase, 6", cobalt, gold trim,
handled 90-120

Coat of Arms

Coats of Arms

Mentioned here because too many firms,
both in America and in Europe "guarantee"
to trace your family's heritage. The New
England Register's "Roll of Arms" is a
reliable firm. Too many firms are not reliable,
in business only to get your money. Many
families can be traced, but it's expensive and
if you're a Miller, Johnson, Smith, Jones,
save your money! If you don't know where
your family came from, read Darwin's
Theory, See GENEALOGY.

Coca-Cola Collectibles

Coca-Cola Collectibles

Anything with "Coke" or "Coca-Cola" on it
is highly sought after today. The prices are
high too.

Blotter, 1930s . . . . $ 5-   9
Calendars, 1909-1915,
complete 440- 495
Calendars, 1891-1897,
complete 950-1,000
Calendars, 1900-1908,
complete 575- 650
Case, miniature, 28
bottles, gold finish . . . 33-   43
Case, wooden, 24
bottles, c. 1920s 8-   12
Cigarette case, 50th
Anniversary, 1936 . . . 128- 155
Key fob, 1900, 1½" dia.,
celluloid 270- 300
Key fob, 1906, oval, 1¾"
x 1¼", celluloid and
metal 240- 270
Key fob, 1925, Bulldogs,
1½" x 1", metal 90- 110
Sign, 1915, 8" dia., glass 85- 115
Sign, 1927, 30" x
7¾", tin, in shape
of arrow 75-   95
Sign, 1904, "Hilda
Clark," 15" x 18½"
tin 1,300-1,500

(continued)

Sheet music, c. 1905:
"Old Folks At Home";
"The Palms"; "Rock
Me To Sleep Mother";
"Juanita"; "My Old
Kentucky Home" ... 120- 140 each
Bookmarks, 1899-1904 . 170- 190
Postcard, "Duster Girl,"
1906 .... 120- 140
Postcard, "The Coca-
Cola Girl," 1909 ..... 110- 160
Postcard, "Gaining"
(racing power boat),
1913 .... 110- 150
Postcard, "Coca-Cola
Delivery Truck," 1915 65- 95
Buddy Lee doll, delivery-
man, 1928, 12½" high 140- 170
Binoculars, 1910 ...... 140- 165
"Megaphone" popcorn
holder, 1940s 32- 52
Playing cards, 1909 to
1927 .... 60- 70 deck
Playing cards, 1930s,
1940s .... 19- 26 deck
Milk glass shade, dome
light, 1920s, 10" dia. . 375- 425
Leaded glass globe,
hanging type, late
1920s 2,950-3,400
Coupons, good for 1 free
bottle of you-know-
what, 1900 .... 110- 120
Coupons, 1920s, same
deal 40- 60
Menus, 1900-1905,
"Hilda Clark" ...... 150- 170 each
Thimble, 1920,
aluminum 32- 39
Pretzel dish, 1936,
"Coke" bottle for legs 47- 58
Needle cases (held
sewing needles), 1920s 40- 50 each
Seltzer bottles, 1900-
1920s .... 52- 62 each
Syrup bottles, 1910-
1920s .... 135- 170 each
Glass, drinking, 1900 .. 170- 185
Glass, drinking, 1921 .. 40- 50
Glass, drinking, 1930s,
pewter 54- 64
Miniature plastic bottle
and case, 1970 ..... 12- 18
Radio, shaped like
"Coke" bottle, 1930,
24" high 270- 290
Radio, shaped like drink
box, 1949 .... 160- 180
"Coke Can" radio, 1971 . 33- 42
Knife, blade and cork-
screw, 1906 .... 168- 192

Knife, switchblade-
type, 1909 .... 70- 90
Toy stove, electrified,
1938 .... 160- 170
Toy drink dispenser,
1960 .... 90- 110
Bingo board, 1930s 12- 18
Frisbee, 1970 (why not!) 17- 19
Dominoes, 1940 ...... 21- 38
Cribbage board, 1930 .. 29- 42
Ashtrays, all sizes, all
years 8- 60
Fans, 1900s-1940s 12- 60
Blotters, 1900s-1920s .. 15- 50
Pencil sharpeners,
1930s-1960s 10- 30
Truck, delivery,
mint, original
box (ill.) 22- 32
Thermometers, 1930s-
1950s 37- 50
Bottle openers, 1910-
1920s 26- 36
Book, *Know Your
War Planes*, 1943 .... 26- 36
Book, *Pause for
Living* 1960s 7- 11
First aid kit, 1940 ..... 24- 34
Comb, "Drink Coca-Cola
5¢," 1940 .... 19- 24
Mechanical pencil, 1930 26- 36
Night light, "Courtesy
of your C-C Bottler,"
1945 .... 9- 17
Place mats, set of 6,
1972 .... 12- 18
Tray, "bottle," 1900,
9¾" dia. 800- 900
Tray, "Hilda Clark,"
1904, oval, 18½" x
15" 875-1,000
Tray, "Vienna Art,"
1905, 10" dia. 155- 170
Tray, "Farm Boy with
Dog," 1931, 10½" x
13¼" 70- 90
Calendar, 1975 (ill.) 2- 3
Take home carton, late
1930s 30- 40
Carrying tray, 1915 (ill.) 70- 90
Tray, girl in yellow
bathing suit
1937 (ill.) 40- 48
Tray, "Elaine," 1917,
8½" x 19" 110- 135
Mirror, "Girl in bonnet,"
1914 .... 125- 165

Thousands of other items; so keep looking!

Coffee Grinders

Coffee Grinders

This product was made for the wall, the lap and the table, of glass, metal, or wood. When ready-made coffee came on the scene in the early 1920s, out went the grinder. The large, wheel-types are in demand today.

Arcade, iron and glass	$ 40- 50
Box type, Stobridge	60- 75
Dovetail, Arcade Manufacturing Company, wood and iron	52- 62
Drawer, wooden base	50- 60
Glass container, iron, Enterprise	25- 38
Iron, early	52- 62
Lap type, cherry box, brass crank (ill.)	65- 80
Lap type, metal 7½" high, 6" wide	52- 62
Lap type, wooden, iron dome top	58- 70
Lap type, handled, cherry (ill.) . . .	75- 85
Iron base, patented July 12, 1898, Enterprise	140-150
Pewter bin, dovetailed, brass knob, signed W. W. Weaver . .	88- 98
Store type, signed Enterprise Manufacturing Company, 1873, 12" high	84- 94
Table model, drawer, iron and wood, 6½" high	180-200
Turn crank, drawer, iron	60- 70
Two wheels, red, Cole Manufacturing Company, Philadelphia .	400-500

Repros all over the place!

Coins, American

You'll notice that we haven't listed prices here as the value of gold and silver has gone absolutely crazy. How can you say that a gold coin is worth $75 on Monday and $500 on Friday! Just be sure you do business with a reliable coin dealer.

TOP ROW
   U.S. $5 Gold Liberty Head . . . .
   U.S. $2½ Gold Indian Head . . . .

Coins, American

   U.S. $1 Gold coin . . . .
   U.S. $5 Indian Head . . . .

MIDDLE ROW
   U.S. $10 Liberty Head . . . .
   U.S. $20 St. Gaudens . . . .
   U.S. $20 Liberty . . . .
   U.S. $10 Indian Head . . . .

BOTTOM ROW
   Silver Morgan Dollar, 1882, uncirculated, CC mark . . . .
   Silver 1922 Peace Dollar, uncirculated, S mark . . . .
   Eisenhower, 1971 copper/nickel $1, uncirculated (not ill.) . . . .
   Eisenhower, 1971-S 40% silver $1, uncirculated (not ill.) . . . .

Coins, Elongated, Rolled Out

Coins, Elongated, Rolled Out

Earlier ones were rolled out or pressed by hand. The Franklin Institute in the 1930s had a machine that, for 10¢, would deliver

(continued)

one. You had your choice of "The Lord's Prayer" or "St. Christopher Protect Us." How many pennies were elongated or rolled out is unknown.

Lord's Prayer on copper penny	$ 5-	9
St. Christopher Protect Us	5-	9

Coins, Foreign

Coins, Foreign

Only a publication for coin collectors could list all the money that's collectible. Consult a reliable coin dealer if you're interested. Generally speaking, copper coins of foreign countries are of no value. Gold coins from foreign countries are a different story.

Coin Spot Glass

Coin Spot Glass

Opalescent spots in the glass that look like coins. Light blue, clear, cranberry, amethyst. Mid-1800s, many firms made it.

Bowl, ruffled edges, 6" dia.	$ 29-	40
Bride's basket, opalescent spots	172-190	
Cruet, light blue	76-	86
Pitcher and 6 glasses, blue and white	200-240	
Shade, light blue, 8¼" high (ill.)	80-	90
Shade, white, ruffled, 6½" high (ill.)	38-	48
Sugar shaker, cranberry, opalescent spots	52-	60

Syrup, cranberry, handled, pewter cap	62-	70
Tumbler, light blue	27-	36
Tumbler, red with opalescent spots	62-	71
Tumbler, amethyst with opalescent spots	61-	71
Vase, amethyst, 7½" high	78-	88
Vase, cranberry with opalescent spots	110-120	

Collectors' Plates

Workmanship, who made it, the artwork itself, how many in the "limited" edition? Those are the important things to know before you buy and/or invest in collectors' plates. Less than 10,000 in a "limited" edition would be a good buy, and always check the hallmark on the underside.

AMERICAN CRYSTAL		
1969—Astronaut	$ 32-	39
1970—Christmas	34-	40
1971—Christmas	27-	32
1971—Mother's Day	26-	37
AMERICAN STERLING		
1971—Christmas Customs	25-	36
1971—Mother's Day	22-	29
1971—12 Days of Christmas	21-	31
ANRI (Italy)		
1971—Birthday	55-	65
1971—Christmas	120-	140
1971—Plaque, carved	45-	55
1972—Father's Day	45-	55
1972—Mother's Day	40-	48
1974—Mothers' Day	60-	68
AUGUST, WENDELL		
1972—Columbus, pewter	70-	85
Sterling silver	350-	375
1972—Kennedy, pewter	55-	65
Sterling silver	270-	300
1972—Pilgrim, pewter	52-	62
Sterling silver	270-	325
BAREUTHER (Bavaria)		
1968—Christmas	35-	40
1969—Christmas	28-	38
1969—Mother's Day	58-	68
1969—Father's Day	58-	68
1970—Christmas	22-	29
1971—Mother's/Father's	19-	26
1972—Mother's/Father's	22-	32
1973—Christmas	28-	38
BELLEEK (Ireland)		
1970—Christmas, "Castle Caldwell"	118-	129
1971—Christmas, "Celtic Cross"	45-	60
1972—Christmas, "Flights of the Earls"	53-	63

Collectors' Plates   Photo courtesy Franklin Mint

BERLIN (Germany)			
1970—Christmas		130-	150
1971—Christmas		28-	38
1971—Christmas stein		33-	43
1971—Father's Day		27-	38
1971—Mother's Day		27-	38
1972—Olympic		24-	34
1974—Christmas		38-	48
BING & GRONDAHL (also see Christmas Plates)			
1969—Poster Plaque	$	16-	26
1969—Mother's Day		330-	365
1970—Jubilee		48-	58
1971—Jubilee		52-	60
1971—Mother's Day		22-	32
1972—Mother's Day		24-	35
BOEHM (U.S.A.)			
1972 Mute Swans		425-	475
1973 Eaglet		225-	295
BURGUES (limited edition)			
Carolina wren w/dogwood		850-1,000	
Chipmunk w/fly amanita		450- 500	
Golden-wing warbler on nest		1,400-1,700	
White throated sparrow		950-1,150	

CARTIER			
1972—Annual Cathedral plate		80-	90
CASTLE			
1970—Fountainbleu		25-	35
1971—Fountainbleu		32-	50
CHURCH			
1968—Christmas		25-	35
1969—Christmas		24-	34
1970—Christmas		18-	27
CYBIS (limited edition)			
Chinese goddess		1,500-1,900	
Clematis w/house wren		1,500-2,100	
Hamlet		1,600-2,100	
Hiawatha		1,500-1,750	
Limnettes—Wonderful Seasons, set of 4		625- 800	
Minnehaha		1,700-1,900	
Nashua		2,700-3,100	
Sacagawea		3,500-4,200	
Stallion		625- 800	
Tranquility Base		1,700-2,200	
CYBIS (non-limited edition)			
Bunny		32- 42	
Buffalo		54- 64	

(continued)

Colts	300-345
Deer mouse	88- 98
Eskimo child's head	180-210
First Flight	54- 64
Heidi	140-160
Madonna 5″	58- 68
Madonna with bird	172-182
Magnolia	220-240
Mushroom	240-270
Owl	40- 50
Pandora	110-125
Pinto colt	170-195
Wood wren w/dogwood	155-165

DALI, SALVADOR

1971—Lincoln Mint	140-160

DAUM (France)

1972—Four Seasons, set of 4	600-675
Bach & Beethoven, pair	110-160

DELFT, BLUE

1969—First Men around Moon	32- 42
1969—First Men on Moon	35- 45
1970—Christmas	16- 26
1970—Mother's Day	12- 22
1970—Pilgrim Fathers	15- 28
1971—Mother's Day	12- 21
1971—Father's Day	17- 27
1972—Father's Day	16- 26

DELFT, ROYAL (Holland)

1971—Mother's Day	60- 72
1972—Commemorative, Apollo 8	24- 34

DONALDO

1968—John F. Kennedy	28- 38

DOUGHTY

1972—Birds	375-425
1973—Birds	360-420

ELLARD

1970—Thanksgiving, first edition	31- 41
1971—Thanksgiving, "Home in the new world"	22- 32

FENTON

1970—Christmas, Little Brown Church	17- 27
1970—Christmas, marble	18- 26
1970—Glass Blower	15- 26
1970—Mother's Day	19- 27
1971—Printer	15- 25
1971—Valentine	22- 34
1972, 1973 Mother's Day	18- 22

FRANKLIN MINT (Sterling Silver)

1970—Rockwell Annual	600- 700
1971—Rockwell Christmas Annual	250- 300
1972—Rockwell Christmas (ill.)	210- 230
1972—Cardinal	175- 195
1973—Easter, "The Resurrection," 22K	4,000+

FRANKOMA

1965—Good Will towards Men	220- 250
1966—Bethlehem Shepherds	72- 82
1967—Gifts for Christ Child	60- 70
1968—Flight into Egypt	18- 28

1969—Laid In a Manger	9- 12
1969—VIP bottle vase	30- 40
1969—Cherokee alphabet plate	8- 12
1969—Oklahoma plate	9- 17
1973—Bicentennial	15- 27

FUERSTENBERG

1971—Christmas, Rabbits	23- 33
1972—Easter, Chicks	19- 29
1972—Mother's Day	22- 32
1973—Mother's Day	19- 27

GORHAM

1971—Rockwell, 4 seasons (4 plates)	150- 160
1972—Rockwell, 4 seasons (4 plates)	92- 102
First Edition—Rockwell, butter girl	85- 95

GRANGET (limited edition)

Bob white quail	3,200-3,800
Canada geese	3,950-4,400
Great blue heron	8,200-8,800
Hairy woodpecker	2,700-3,100
Mallards	2,600-3,000
Mourning doves	1,500-1,900
Pintails	3,200-3,600
Ring-necked pheasants	5,500-5,800
Screech owl	2,900-3,200
Woodcocks	1,300-1,450

GRANGET (non-limited edition)

1972—Christmas, European glaze, finish	50- 60
1973—Spring	82- 90

HAVILAND (France)

Abraham Lincoln	95- 110
Martha Washington	35- 42
1970—Christmas, partridge	115- 125
1971—Dancing angels	22- 34
1971—President Grant	115- 128
1971—Partridge	38- 50
1971—President Lincoln	128- 155
1971—Rutherford B. Hayes	110- 120
1971—Unicorn tapestry	125- 145
1972—Unicorn tapestry	85- 95
1974-5-6—Independence series	60- 70

HUMMEL, BERTA

1971—Christmas, angel	1,300-1,700
1972—Mother's Day, Hooky	115- 140

HUTCHENREUTHER

Dancing girls (white)	160- 175
Geese in flight	320- 355
Peacock	120- 160
Pheasants	160- 180
Song birds of America, set of 2	175- 210
Stag and dog (color)	210- 220

IMPERIAL

1969—America the Beautiful, red Carnival	33- 43
1970—America the Beautiful, green Carnival	35- 45
1970—Christmas, Carnival	17- 27

1961—Christmas, Carnival ...	22-	34
1971—Christmas, Doeskin ...	22-	32
1971—Coin plate, Crystal ...	25-	35

ISPANKY (limited edition)

Morning	525-	650
Jessamy	475-	575
King Arthur	325-	425
Orchids	1,300-1,600	
Owl	775-	800
The Hunt (decorated)	2,400-2,700	

Collectors' Plates

ISPANKY (non-limited edition)

Elizabeth	168-	180
Huck Finn	140-	150
Peter Pan	138-	158
Prudence	140-	160

ISRAEL

1967—Tower of David	22-	32
1967—Wailing Wall	22-	32
1968—Masada	19-	28
1969—Rachel's Tomb	15-	25
1970—Lake of Galilee	17-	28
1973—Acre	16-	29

JENSEN, SVEND

1970—Mother's Day	72-	82
1971—Mother's Day	70-	85

KAISER (Bavaria)

1970—Passion Play	22-	32
1970—Royal Horse Show	26-	36
1970—Christmas, first edition	37-	44
1971—Christmas	19-	29
1971—Mother's Day, first edition	26-	36
1972—Mother's Day	20-	30
1973—Yacht, "Cetonia"	68-	78

KIRK

1972—Thanksgiving	120-	165
1972—Washington	140-	175
1972—Mother's Day	150-	160
1973—Christmas	165-	195

1973—Mother's Day	125-	145

LALIQUE (France)

1965—Crystal	1,550-1,785	
1965—Annual	1,700-2,250	
1967—Annual	160-	175
1968—Annual	100-	125
1969—Annual	95-	110
1970—Annual	80-	90
1971—Annual	65-	75
1972—Annual	66-	80
1973—Annual	68-	78

LINCOLN MINT (Sterling Silver)

1971—Dali, Don Quixote	150-	170
1972—Dali, Dionysos	135-	150
1972—Easter, Dali, gold-on-silver	133-	153
1972—Madonna Della, sterling	160-	175

LINDNER, DORIS (limited edition)

Aberdeen Angus	725-	800
Charolais bull	825-	900
Dairy Shorthorn	925-1,200	
Hereford bull	725-	950
Jersey bull	750-	950
Jersey cow	675-	775
Quarterhorse	825-	975
Shire stallion	1,500-1,900	

LLADRO (Spain)

1971—Christmas	44-	54
1972—Mother's Day	110-	135
1972—Mother's Day	42-	72
1973-74—Mother's Day	68-	80

MARMOT

1970—Christmas, "Polar Bear"	50-	60
1970—Father's Day, "Stag"	24-	34
1970—Stag Plaque	26-	36
1971—Christmas, "Buffalo"	22-	32
1971—Father's Day "Horse"	17-	27
1971—President Washington	32-	42
1972—Mother's Day "Seals"	20-	30
1973—Christmas, "Snowman"	38-	50
1974—Mother's Day	38-	50

MOSER (Czechoslovakia)

1970—Annual	425-	500
1972—Annual	125-	175
1971—Mother's Day, Peacocks	250-	300
1972—Annual	120-	155
1972—Mother's Day, Butterflies	125-	165
1973—Mother's Day, Squirrels	110-	170

NORITAKE

1970—Easter Egg, first edition	35-	45
1971—Easter Egg	22-	36
1972—Easter Egg	18-	32
1973—Valentine Heart, first edition	35-	47

ORREFORS

1970—Notre Dame Cathedral	75-	90
1971—Westminster Abbey	65-	85
1972-1973—Mother's Day	58-	68
1973—Annual	70-	75

(continued)

PICKARD

1971—Game Birds (pair)	400-	500
1972—Truman plate	60-	80
1973—Lincoln	55-	70

PORSGRUND

1968—Christmas, church scene	95-	125
1969—Christmas	25-	40
1970—Castle, Hamlet's	16-	40
1970—Christmas	19-	36
1970—Deluxe Christmas	65-	78
1970—Jubilee..............	25-	40
1970—Mug	16-	27
1971—Christmas	22-	34
1971—Father's Day	16-	27
1971—Mother's Day	16-	27
1972—Easter	16-	27

REED & BARTON

1970—Christmas	300-	375
1971—Christmas	140-	175
1972—Silver & copper annual .	90-	140
Sandpiper, silver & copper		
1972 Audubon plate	145-	185
1973—Russell's "Free		
Trapper"	130-	160

RORSTRAND

1968—Christmas	45-	60
1969—Christmas	18-	29
1970—Christmas	20-	30
1971—Christmas	19-	28
1971—Father's Day	22-	32
1971—Mother's Day	19-	28
1972—Mother's Day	26-	36
1973—Father's Day	18-	38

ROSENTHAL

1967—Christmas	110-	145
1971-3—Winblad Christmas ..	200-	275

ROSKILDE

1968—Church	24-	34
1969—Church	15-	27
1970—Christmas	18-	30
1971-2-3—Church	20-	35

ROYAL COPENHAGEN, RC (See Christmas Plates)

1969—Apollo II	48-	65
1969—Mermaid Summer	35-	50
1971—Mother's Day	110-	140
1971—Statue of Liberty	40-	50
1972—Mother's Day	38-	50
1972—Olympic	42-	70
1973—Mother's Day	30-	40

ROYALE

1971—Mother's Day	22-	32
1971—Father's Day	40-	50
1972—Mother's Day	26-	37
1972—Father's Day	25-	35
1972—Christmas	24-	36
1972—Game plate	220-	260
1972—Crystal annual	320-	365
1973—Christmas	32-	42

ST. AMAND

1970—First edition	22-	40

1971—Second edition	16-	27
1971—Christmas	18-	32

SANTA CLARA

1970—Christmas	18-	29
1971—Mother's Day	24-	28
1972—Christmas	19-	32
1972—Mother's Day	28-	39

SCHUMANN

1970—Beethoven	18-	32
1971—Christmas (Azburg)....	22-	34
1972-73 Christmas	24-	36

SEVEN SEAS

1969—Astronaut	18-	29
1970—Christmas, New World .	22-	33
1970—Mother's Day	18-	27
1970—History	30-	40
1971—Christmas Carol	22-	34
1971—Mother's Day	22-	32
1972-73—Mother's Day	21-	31

SPODE

1970—Christmas	39-	59
1970—Annual	44-	59
1970—Charles Dickens	110-	135
1970—Winston Churchill bust .	138-	168
1971—Christmas	30-	40

STANEK

1968—First Moon Landing ...	1,400-	1,900
1972—Columbus	850-	1,100

TIRSCHENREUTH

1969—Christmas	26-	36
1970—Christmas	24-	34
1971—Christmas	22-	32
1972-3—Christmas	21-	31

VAL ST. LAMBERT

1968—Rembrandt & Rubens,		
pr	88-	98
1969—Pilgrims plate	158-	170
1969—Van Dyck and Van		
Gogh	65-	85
1970—Old Masters (set of 2) ..	58-	75
1970—Pilgrim Fathers	56-	77
1970—Rembrandt Crystal	59-	79
1970—Rubens Crystal	40-	50
1970—Van Dyck Crystal	44-	62
1970—Zodiac	160-	190
1971—Washington	280-	310

VENETO FLAIR

1970—Madonna.............	650-	850
1971—Elephant	275-	350
1971—Three Kings	340-	390
1972—Mother's Day	160-	195
1971-Wildlife, Stag	425-	550
1972—Last Supper, set of 5 ..	1,600-	1,950
1974-Cat	70-	80

VERNONWARE

1971—Christmas, Poppytrail..	40-	55
1972—Christmas, Poppytrail..	38-	53
1973—Christmas	30-	40

WASHINGTON MINT

1972 Mint Picasso	125-	165
1972 Mint Sawyer	138-	168

WEDGWOOD

1969—Astronaut (Apollo II) ..	170-	185
1969—Christmas	160-	175
1970—Christmas	49-	69
1971—Calendar plate	28-	48
1971—Christmas, Picadilly Circus	47-	62
1971—Mother's Day	39-	59
1973—Christmas	52-	62

WYETH, ANDREW

1971—The Kuerner Farm	68-	80
1971—Royal Tettau Pope Paul VI	95-	120
1972—Fourth of July annual ..	170-	210

Combs

Combs

Usually made of tortoiseshell, though some were made of silver, ivory or bone. They go back to the 16th century. Those you find in shops today cost from $5 to $13.

Average price	$ 7-	18
Barette, carved (ill.)	9-	12
Ivory, inlaid, imitation diamonds	12-	27
Sterling silver, ornately carved ..	20-	35
Tortoiseshell, carved (ill.)	11-	16
Tortoiseshell, ornately carved ...	14-	24

Comic Books

Would you believe that a 10¢ comic book from the 1920s may be today worth over $150? Volume I, No. 1 has a lot to do with the value. Big Little Books, early comic pages from newspapers, etc., are all collectible today.

COMIC BOOKS

Adventure into Terror, No. 44, 45	$ 7-	9
Babe Ruth Sports, No. 2 thru 9 ..	8-	11
Bulletman, early	30-	40
Captain Marvel, No. 30 thru 50 ..	19-	29
Joe Palooka, early	8-	14
BIG LITTLE BOOKS (most published by Whitman Publishing in early 1930s)		
Alley Oop series	12-	37
Blondie series	12-	24

Bobby Benson on the H-Bar-O Ranch	9-	20
Buck Rogers series	28-	59
Flash Gordon series	34-	84
Tarzan series	18-110	

Commemorative Glasses

Commemorative Glasses

Any event, such as the 100th anniversary of the Winchester rifle, is likely to be commemorated in glasses, wristwatches, plaques, and the like. Because they're fragile, glasses that last over the years eventually bring high prices.

Winchester-Western glasses, set of 6 (ill.)	$ 15-	25
World's Fair (1939) glasses, set 12	40-	50
"Presidents" glasses, 1930s, set of 12	28-	38

Commemorative Medals

Commemorative Medals

More and more collectors are seeking out commemorative medals, made to celebrate a particular event or individual. They were made of cast metal, sterling silver, 14k gold,

(continued)

and bronze. The illustration here, "The American Doughboy," was made by M. Lordonnois in 1919 and is bronze. Prices vary according to artist and type of metal used.

Commemorative Mugs

Commemorative Mugs

Just about every event is celebrated; a lot of famous buildings, too, such as the one shown in this illustration. It's now the Museum of Yesterday's Toys, 52 St. George Street, St. Augustine, Florida. For a complete look at the toys in this fine museum, purchase PRICE GUIDE TO TOYS, Wallace-Homestead Book Co., Des Moines, Iowa 50305, $9.95 — and visit the toy museum too!

Compasses

Compasses

Instruments for indicating direction; those with a magnetic needle swinging freely on a pivot and pointing to the magnetic north are highly sought after.

Engineer's compass in mahogany box, signed "W. & L.E. Gurley, Troy, N.Y.," "E" and "W" backward (ill.)	$125-185
Boy Scout compass in canvas case, 1920s	13- 22
Ship's compass, in original box, WWI destroyer	275-375

Confederate Provisional Stamps and Envelopes

June 1, 1861, the South stopped using stamps made by the federal government. The Confederacy set up provisional post offices throughout the South. Today, a stamp and/or envelope from one of these offices, dated October 14 or after, which was the first day the proper Confederate stamps were available for use, would be worth a considerable amount. Some stamps from the following "offices" range in value from $1,200 to $16,000. A stamp's value depends on its rarity, condition, etc. Consequently, we give you only the locations of some of the Confederate post offices. If you think you have a rarity, check with a reputable stamp dealer.

Athens, Georgia
Autaugaville, Alabama
Baton Rouge, Louisiana
Beaumont, Texas
Bridgeville, Alabama
Danville, and Emory, Virginia
Franklin, and Lenoir, North Carolina
Goliad, and Gonzales, Texas
Helena, Texas
Knoxville, Tennessee
Macon, Georgia
Spartenburg, South Carolina
Uniontown, Alabama

Not all are mentioned. There are probably 25 more. Any southern stamp dated between June 1, and October 14, 1861, should be checked.

Construction Collectibles

Construction Collectibles

Anything to do with the early days of building is collectible today.

Audels Masons and Builders (set of 4), copyright 1924 (ill.)	$ 8- 12
Early handmade level, late 1800s	19- 27
Blueprints of old buildings	6- 9

Old brass door plates and
doorknobs, each 11- 20

Cook Books

Cook Books

These gourmet's delights, especially those printed in the early 1900s are collectible today. Who can ever forget Fannie Farmer's candies and her cook books? Condition and age establish the price.

Average price, in good con-
dition . . . . $ 3- 9
Common Sense in The House-
hold, 1900, Scribner's (ill.) 3- 6
The Herbalistic Almanac,
1950 (ill.) 3- 6

Cookie Molds

Cookie Molds

Hand-carved, these have been around for centuries. Most European countries export them into the U.S. antiques shops. Those from Holland are particularly collectible. They make great wall decorations!

Depending on age and con-
dition . . . . $ 28- 40

Cooking Items

Cooking Items

Apple roaster, tin, late 18th
century . . . . $ 95-120
Bird roaster, stamped, soldered
tin, 12″ wide, early 19th
century 40- 50
Bread pans, black sheet iron, 4
sizes from 5″ to 12″ wide, all . .   40- 50
Chafing dish, copper, Sterno
burner, 1920s (ill.) 55- 70
Cylinder churn, cedar, galvanized
iron hoops, c. 1895 . . . .   55- 65
Dough mixer/kneader, tin, cast
iron, c. 1880s 30- 40
Egg beater (or mixer), blue glass,
cast iron, tin, crank-type
beater 28- 38
Fish boiler, pieced tin, 20″ wide,
has fish rack and cover,
c. 1890 . . . .   45- 55
Jelly bag strainer, wire, cloth,
fastens on bowl, c. 1930s 20- 28
Omelette pan, polished iron,
c. 1870s 23- 33
Peach parer, cast iron, 10″ long,
crank type 28- 38
Pea sheller, galvanized iron, 9″
long, "Acme Pea Sheller Co" . .   25- 35
Potato slicer, iron, wood, c. 1870s   28- 38
Sausage stuffer, tin, wood, 2
handles, 21″ long, c. 1870s 20- 28

Coors Pottery

In 1910, the Coors Porcelain Company began manufacturing pottery in Golden, Colorado, but what is found in shops today is the pottery and dinnerware made in the 1930s. There were about 35 vase styles and 4 lines of earthenware dishes. The pottery has a satiny texture; most pieces have a matt finish. Some

(continued)

colors are Delft blue, white, yellow, turquoise, brown-beige, peach-beige, pastel aqua and lilac pink.

Ashtray, white, "Coors" in center, raised signature	$ 8- 12
Casserole, white	14- 19
Cookie jar, covered, rosebud pattern, ink stamp "Coors USA"	14- 25
Honey pot, lilac pink, two-handled, ink stamp mark	17- 27
Jug, water, rosebud pattern, turquoise, 7" high, ink stamp mark	25-34
Mortar and pestle, 1¾" and 3" high, ink stamp "Coors Porcelain"	12- 18
Salt/peppers, rosebud pattern, ink stamp mark "Coors USA"	20- 28
Vase, rope-handled, 8" high, turqoise liner, 8" high	22- 31
Vase, white, 6" high, turquoise liner, ink stamp mark	21- 31
Vase, yellow, rope-handled, 12" high, ink stamp mark	26- 34

Copeland - Spode China

Copeland-Spode China

Joseph Spode, 1770, Staffordshire, England, later taken over by W. T. Copeland and Sons who marked their wares "Late Spode." Delft, Salt Glaze and Jasperware were a few of the many items made, including porcelain figurines and fine dinner services. Copeland and Garrett came along later to continue the line.

Chocolate pot, Indian Tree, 6 cups and scalloped saucers	$140-180
Creamer, shell shaped, c. 1860 . . .	92-100
Ewer, heavy beading, leaves, ring handle with mask, 1870 . .	92-110
Gravy boat, heron, palm tree, gilded grape leaves, 1847	52- 62
Jug, Jasper ground, applied grapevine and drinking scene .	142-152

Pickle, pink, embossed hunting scene, silver fork, 1897	52- 62
Pitcher, blue/white, raised figures, cherubs, floral decor	85- 95
Plate, plover, blue/white	47- 54
Plate, bird's nest, butterfly rushes, daisies	30- 40
Sugar bowl, shell-shaped, c. 1860	95-110
Teapot, Jasper ground, grapevine, 6¼" high	125-150
Teapot, white, birds, bamboo in relief, pewter lid, 1875	125-150
Tureen, cream ground, storks, palm trees, ladle and tray	75- 90

Copper

Copper

One of the world's most important metals, it's been used for centuries in every shape, size and object. Wire, cooking utensils, jewelry, weathervanes, you-name-it.

Coal hod, helmet-type, brass handle, 18" to top of handle, old	$ 195-	250	
Basket, Art Nouveau, cherubs in relief, 13" high (ill.)	65-	75	
Basket, double handle, hammered bottom, 1920s, 10" dia.	35-	45	
Chafing dish, complete, 1920s	95-	120	
Dippers, many types, all ages	20-	90	
Funnel, 11" long, late 1800s	44-	52	
Coffee set, French, 4-piece, 1890s	120-	130	all
Desk set, 5-piece: inkwell, blotter holder, letter holder, pen(s) holder, tray, 1920	110-	128	all
Milk pail, iron handle, late 1800s	85-	110	

Cover pan, zinc handles, 1900s	40-	52
Apple butter kettle, dovetail bottom, mid-1800s, 25″ dia...............	400-	475
Candy kettle, mid-1800s, 19″ dia...............	175-	225
Water kettle w/lid, late 1800s	85-	110
Samovar, brass-footed, 15″ high	225-	275
Bed warmer, pierced lid, wooden handle, early 1800s	240-	260
Washboiler w/lid, burnished, early 1900s	125-	175
Weathervane, American eagle, complete, mid-1800s	1,800-2,900	
Weathervane, racing sulky, complete, after Civil War	1,900-2,700	
Brewery mug, 28″ high, brass-lined spout, mid-1800s, European ..	115-	140
Plaque, hand-tooled, "Viking-in-ship," dated "1905," 3″ x 7″	62-	72
Coachman's horn, 38″ long, pewter mouthpiece, mid-1800s	110-	130
Foot warmer, brass bail handle, early 1800s	60-	80
Planters, set of 6, brass handles, footed, pre-WWI	70-	80 all
Umbrella stand, brass bottom, tooled scenes of flowers, 1900s	110-	130
Vase, pewter base, tulip lip, 14″ high, 1900s	50-	60
Vase, silver inlay of butterflies, flowers, 9½″ high, 1900s	92-	112
Water can, brass spout, 8″ high, 1900s	50-	61

Copper Lustre

The use of a copper compound in the glaze resulted in a metallic, copperlike surface. Made in the Staffordshire district, England, in the early 1800s. Most of what you find today was imported into the U.S. between 1835 and the late 1800s. Reproductions since the 1920s have caused this ware to fall from popularity. The new is heavier and much thicker than the old.

Bowl, floral on green bands ..... $ 68- 78

Copper Lustre

Bowl, dark green, raised red roses, 4″ dia.	58-	68
Chalice, beaded border, enameled floral decor, 4½″ high	62-	71
Compote, royal blue band, 3 raised groups, girl, cat, 1820 ..	68-	78
Creamer, 3″ high	23-	33
Flowerpot, beaded border, enameled decor, 4½″ high	190-220	
Goblet, pink and white floral, green leaves	82-	92
Mug, blue band, greyhound, cow in relief, 3″ high	71-	81
Mustache cup and saucer, left-hand, 3 brothers, ship	88-	98
Pitcher, blue band with pink roses, 6″ high	88-110	
Pitcher, bulbous, up-down ridges, Hawkes spout, 6″ high	95-125	
Pitcher, Wedgwood, brown, "Fallow Deer," 4″ high, (ill.) ...	65-	80
Salt, master, blue band, embossed pink roses, footed	38-	47
Sugar bowl, blue band, beaded, raised floral, children, footed	48-	64
Teapot, floral and leaf design, 6½″ high	160-175	
Toby jug, early, high relief on hat and cheeks	260-300	

Coralene

Coralene

Glass with applied glass beading that looks like natural coral. Made at the New England Glass Company, in the late 1800s, it's highly collectible today. Don't be fooled by the

111

(continued)

cheap type sold in stores during the same period. Rub the surface; if the beads come off, it's junk.

Pitcher, birds and leaves	$400-500
Pitcher, ribbed, green opalescent, bird and flowers, 7½" high, signed Webb (ill.)	465-525
Toothpick, satin glass, silvered, cased	335-385
Tumbler, Seaweed pattern on yellow cased glass	235-270
Tumbler, graduated pink, cased, gold branches, 5" high	230-240
Tumbler, white satin, brown oak leaves, Mt. Washington Glass Company	240-260
Vase, blue/white, cream casing, yellow seaweed branches, 8½" high	262-290
Vase, coral branch beading, off-white casing, 4½" high	390-430
Vase, pink overlay, ruffled top . .	362-480
Vase, red beads, garnet gems . . .	370-400
Vase, yellow coral branch beading, white casing, 5½" high . . .	410-450
Poor imitations now available.	
Vase, satin, yellow & white, wheat sheaf, 5" high (ill.)	230-270

Coronation Collectibles

Coronation Collectibles

After a coronation, items in china and glass appeared on the English market. Tin candy and cracker boxes are especially collectible today. Elizabeth II paperweights are considered prizes today by those who seek out coronation items.

Beaker, Edward VII, 1902, Royal Doulton	$ 35- 45
Brandy snifter, King Edward VIII, coat of arms	25- 35
Cup, Garter emblem, 5" high (ill.)	30- 40
Cup/saucer, Elizabeth and George VI	22- 30
Cup, King Edward VII	27- 35
Globe, Edward VIII, porcelain . .	26- 35
Handkerchief, Elizabeth II, 1953	6- 8

Humidor, Queen Elizabeth II, 1953, silver plate	27- 37
Mug, George V and Mary, 1911, portraits, 3" high	34- 50
Paperweight, QE II, 1953, St. Louis	250-275
Plaque, Edward VII, Alexandra, 1902, Royal Doulton	70- 82
Plate, bread, George VI, 1937 . . .	25- 35
Plate, Edward VII, 1902	27- 36
Spoon, George VI, 1911, demitasse	16- 22
Teapot, Elizabeth II, 1953, gold portrait, crest	34- 44
Toby mug, George V, Queen Mary, 1910, hand-painted, 6" .	37- 47
Tray, QE II, 1953	8- 12
Tumbler, Elizabeth II, blue	22- 32

Cosmos Glass
See PATTERN GLASS SECTION.

Coverlets

Coverlets

Made during the 18th and 19th centuries, they were the original "do-it-yourself" item. Women sheared the sheep, carded the wool, dyed it to the desired color, spun it on a wheel, wove it on a loom. There are 4 kinds of coverlets, each popular for a short time only: Double-woven, Jacquard, Summer/winter, oversheet. The jacquard weave coverlet shown here was made by Harry Tyler for Henry T. Alcott and is dated 1860. Prices vary as to condition, location and collector. — See Quilts.

Bedspread, popcorn pattern, crocheted, 90" x 100" . . . . . . $	285- 325
Bedspread, "United We Stand," Alcott (ill.)	975-1,400
Bonnet, hoop, 1790s	230- 285
Carpet, oblong panels, needlework, 175" x 90"	270- 320

Coverlet, blue/white, double-bed size, handloomed, 1840s	190-	210
Dresser scarf, Battenberg, 4½" long, 16" wide	38-	58
Lap robe, sleigh, horse head design, woolen, 50" x 60"	135-	175
Quilt, log cabin pattern, patches, wool and cotton, 75"	135-	165
Robe, blue silk, gold thread, gold birds, China	220-	290
Rug, needlework, England, 85" x 41"	320-	400
Sampler, alphabet, animals, child's age, dated 1828	70-	92
Shawl, black silk, embroidered, Spanish, 5' square	60-	90
Spread, Statue of Liberty, 100" x 85"		365+
Tablecloth, homespun, cream color, crocheted edge, 68" x 64"	58-	78
Jacquard, unsigned, red, eagles at corners	210-	270
Jacquard, signed, red, eagle motif	260-	300

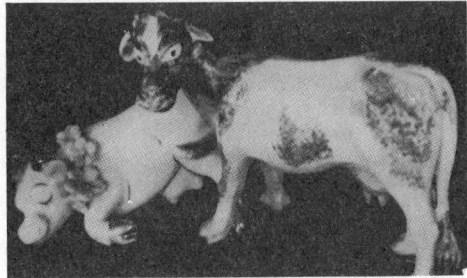

Cows and Bulls

Cows and Bulls

This is a "don't-ask-me-why" category, but for some reason, especially in the dairy regions of Illinois and Wisconsin, collectors are going "ape" for anything that has to do with a cow — and that's no bull!

Staffordshire cow (ill.) 1800s	$ 50-	60
Reclining cow (ill.) not old	6-	12
Oil painting of cow, Sheffield Farms, early 1900s	90-125	
Brass cow marked "Old Nell"	9-	17

Cracker Jars

These are kissin' cousins to the cookie jar. In continuous use for the past 150 years, they come in pottery, wood, glass. Some had silver-plated lids.

Acid finish with enameling, Britannia handle and lid (ill.)	110-120
Bristol glass with enameled flowers/butterflies (ill.)	80- 98

Cracker Jars

China, blue/green, floral decor	50-	65
Limoges, shell design, gold trim	50-	65
Satin glass, frosted, Bead and Grape design (ill.)	185-199	

Crackle (Craquelle) Glass

Crackle (Craquelle) Glass

Invented by the Venetians in the 16th century, it was made by plunging hot glass into cold water, then reheating and reblowing it. This process produced the crackled effect. It's also called "frosted" and "iced" glass, as well as "overshot." Some of the finest was made at Sandwich; also at Hobbs, Brockunier and Company, Wheeling, West Virginia, late 1800s. Being reproduced by Pilgrim Glass Corp.

Bowl, Mt. Washington, gold iridescence, enameled lobster decor (ill.), 5½" high	$100-160
Bowl, blue, white, 8¼" diameter	260-280
Pickle jar, hourglass shaped, silver plated	52- 62
Lemonade set, blue, 8 pieces	60- 70
Pitcher, applied reeded handle, clear	48- 57
Sweetmeat jar, sapphire, blue, red strawberries, amber edge	368-400
Sugar bowl, pink, enamel floral, silver cover	48- 58
Toothpick holder, marine green	32- 39
Toothpick holder, hat, green	34- 44
Vase, applied blue glass buttons, 12½" high	36- 46

(continued)

Vase, Chinese decor, floral,
13½" high 112-140
Vase, iridescent, signed
Imperial 122-130
Vase, cranberry, 6½" high 65- 82

Cranberry Glass

Cranberry Glass

Gold was added to the glass batch, which was then blown or molded. When reheated at a low temperature, the cranberry shade developed. It also was called Ruby glass. In later years, copper was substituted, creating a harsh amber-red tint. There are many Cranberry pieces represented in this Guide. Here are a few. Oh, those repros!

Bottle, barber, green/white
flowers, 8" high . . . . $ 42- 52
Bowl, finger, Inverted Thumb-
print (ITP), 5" dia. 84- 96
Bowl, rose, pleated and fluted
top, 4¾" dia. 84-110
Box, blue decorated flowers,
4½" square 40- 50
Candlesticks, twisted stem, 10¼"
high, pr. 110-116
Compote, clear pedestal base,
6¼" high 90- 97
Creamer, fluted lip, clear
handle, 3½" high 40- 50
Knife rest, ball ends are cut,
3¼" wide 60- 75
Rose bowl, ribbed, applied
clear rigaree, snail
feet, berry prunts,
signed Webb, 5" high
(ill.) 320-370
Wine set, 11" high decanter,
10" wide tray, 6 glasses 140-160

Crazing

This word is included in this Guide because it confuses so many people. It's simply a fine network of cracks or fissures in the glaze caused by the unequal shrinkage of the body and glaze during the cooling. It does not mean the piece is cracked and/or damaged.

Some pottery factories deliberately "crazed" certain pieces. Rookwood Pottery Company was one.

Creamware
See QUEENSWARE.

Crest China

Crest China

An inexpensive "fairing" (small souvenir) china made in England and the U.S. during the late 19th century. Usually found in mugs, toothpick holders, shoes, pin trays.

Creamer, miniature, green crown
emblem, 2¼" high (ill.) $17-24
Figurine, "The first to rise,"
man in bed, nightcap, Germany 38-47
Mug, "Sip slowly," 5½" high . . . 28-38
Powder box, "Love's light never
dims," 1887, Germany 27-32
Toothpick holder, "Take one,"
1890s, Germany 11-16
Pin tray, floral design, 1888,
France 12-17
Shoe, applied flowers 14-22

Cros

Henry Cros revived the 17th century method of molding glass objects from pate-de-verre, "paste of glass." The Egyptians developed the technique hundreds of years before. Cros made large panels in relief from 1840 to 1907, successfully making pate-de-verre in 1884. It's scarce but still found occasionally in Europe and in American shops that specialize in imports.

Crown Derby

An earlier factory of the same name operated in the early 1800s, but what we know as Crown Derby today was made in England in the late 1870s until the late 1880s.

Coffeepot, Oriental decor, brown
floral . . . . $ 77- 86
Creamer, flowers, Oriental-type,
crown mark 24- 33

Crown Derby

Cup/saucer, white/blue, floral
decor 21- 32
Ewer, turquoise ground, raised
gold floral decor, 9" 91-110
Figurine, seated lady, white
ground, 6½" high 75- 90
Plate, dark blue/white, rust
panels, 9" dia. 22- 29
Plate, flower border, 8½" dia. 42- 56
Toothpick, white ground, flowers 31- 42
Vase, red/gold, 6" high 82- 92

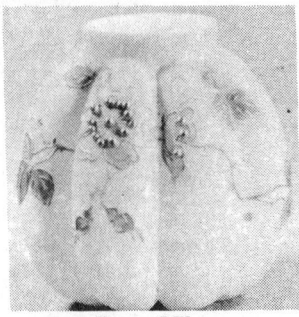

Crown Milano

Crown Milano

This fine glass was made in the late 19th
century by the Mt. Washington Glass Company. It is often decorated with flowers and
leaves overlaid with gold and silver. Quite a
few pieces were marked with the letters C. M.
in the pontil.

Bride's basket, enameled pansy
decor, tricorn, signed $2,000-2,500
Bowl, melon rib, floral decor,
4½" 400- 500
Bowl, tan, flowers, pewter top
and handles 395- 495
Cookie jar, signed 870- 970
Cracker jar, apricot, apple blossom limbs and flowers,
signed 585- 670
Cracker jar, jeweled, mottled
background, applied gold
threading, signed "MT. W.G.
Co.," c. 1890 (ill.) 1,200-1,350

Cracker jar, Quadruple Plate
rim and lid, pansy decor,
signed, c. 1894 (ill.) 625- 780
Cracker jar, pansy, signed 600- 700
Jewel box, original lining, Mt.
Washington Glass Company 490- 590
Humidor, cream ground, pan-
sies, silver-plated lid, signed
M.W. 700- 775
Shade, floral, gold, Burmese
coloring 510- 600
Sugar bowl, covered, melon rib,
floral decor 370- 425
Sugar shaker, Mt. Washington,
pewter top 385- 425
Tumbler, gold decor, signed
Crown 370- 395
Vase, yellow to peach ground,
Mt. Washington Glass
Company 840- 950
Vase, white satin ground, pink
shading, pansies, 6" high ... 860- 925
Vase, cream ground, apple
blossoms, signed, 6½" high . 850- 925

Cruets

Cruets

These came in all sizes and usually were
made of pressed or blown glass. The more
expensive were cut. Every glass company
made them, from the late 1700s on. Reproductions galore!

Amber, clear handle .... $ 44- 54
Beveled Star, amber, clear
stopper 34- 45
Blue, amber stopper and handle,
8" high 68- 82
Bohemian glass, deer scene 28- 40
Cobalt overlay cut to clear, rose
pattern 78- 98
Cranberry, enameled lilies of
the valley (ill.) 70- 98
Cranberry, ITP, clear stopper ... 85-120
Cut glass, signed Hawkes 108-115
Depression glass, American
Sweetheart 22- 31
Emerald green ground, white
enamel lily of the valley 62- 72

115

(continued)

Frosted glass, green enamel decor, 7½" high	38- 48
Green cut to clear (ill.)	88-118
Green ground, white and gold enamel, floral	49- 61
Mary Gregory glass, boy with hoop, blue/white	90-120
Millefiori, canes, yellow/white, blue, cut glass stopper	190-230
Opalescent, "Stars and Stripes" (ill.)	80-115
Panelled Thistle, prism stoppers .	38- 50
Peachblow, Wheeling, yellow, amber handle and stopper	600-710
Pink swirl, blown	65- 75
Rayed Star base, notched handle, cut glass, 7½"	38- 50
Spatter glass, clear stopper	50- 58
Strawberry, Hobnail, clear applied handle and stopper . . .	32- 42
Tiffany, blue, ribbed, signed	295-365
Vasa Murrhina, clear stopper . . .	68- 82
Vaseline to pink, Hobnail, 7" high	49- 60
Venetian glass, blue swirl	52- 60
Waterford, new mark	60- 70
Zipper edge on ribs and handles, 5½" high	28- 39

Cuff Links
Cuff Links

Came the first double cuff on the sleeve of a shirt or blouse, the type where the cuff turned back on itself and was fastened with a link, came the first cuff links. They were made of inexpensive metal on up to platinum, solid gold, sterling silver, inlaid with diamonds and emeralds. The earlier types are collectible today.

"Artist's palette" cuff links, 1900s, pr . . . . $	8- 12
Imitation jewels cuff links, 1900s pr	6- 10
14k gold, inlaid with emeralds, 1930s pr	450-525
Brass, army coat buttons, made into cuff links (ill.) . . .	18- 23 pair

Cup Plates

Cup Plates
During the mid-1800s, gentlemen drank their tea or coffee from the saucer. The plates that held the cup while he was "slurping" are collectible today, both in glass and in china. Sandwich made the most beautiful glass ones. They should ring when plinked. Reproductions were made in glass by Westmoreland Glass Company in the 1930s. They don't ring. Still being made.

Beaded hearts, Midwest, glass . . $	28- 37
Benjamin Franklin, clear glass . .	29- 39
Blue/white, Clews china, 1819 . . .	30- 40
Brown, eagle and floral border, boat center, Clews, 1825	31- 42
Bunker Hill, Sandwich	39- 49
Dark blue, scenic views, Clews, 1822, pr.	50- 60
Heart center, 13 hearts, clear glass	22- 32
Sailing ship, men in rowboat, ship border, brown, Staffordshire . .	22- 32
Henry Clay, clear glass	22- 31
Log cabin, clear glass	125-145
Sandwich, clear glass, 3 5/16" diameter, eagle looking left . . .	55- 65
Sandwich, clear glass, 3½" diameter, Henry Clay, star under bust	44- 54
Sandwich, clear glass, 3 7/16" diameter, U.S. Constitution . . .	52- 62
Valentine, blue	128-165
Wedding Day, 3 weeks after (reverse faces)	20- 30

Currier and Ives
Nathaniel Currier worked for himself in 1834; in 1857, James Ives joined him in the firm that was to become one of the world's greatest producers of inexpensive lithographs. Scenic, political, disaster, nautical,

116

Currier and Ives

sporting scenes, horses, animals, biblical scenes; no subject was ignored. Original C & I prints show up under magnification as a series of short lines; reproductions show up as a series of small dots. C & I prints were made in three sizes: small folio, 7.8" x 12.8"; medium folio, 13" x 20"; large folio, 18" x 27". Do beware of insurance company calendar prints and all those reproductions! C & I went out of business in 1907.

American Farm Scenes, #1 (Spring), large folio	$ 580-	620
American Farm Scenes, #2 (Summer), large folio	420-	510
American Farm Scenes, #3 (Autumn), large folio	430-	520
American Farm Scenes, #4 (Winter), large folio	1,600-1,900	
American Girl, 1871, small folio	80-	125
Arkansas Traveler, 1870 small	95-	135
Autumn Fruits, small, medium	110-	225
The Bad Husband, 1870, small	75-	130
Battle of Gettysburg, Pa., 1863, large	220-	240
Beach Snipe Shooting, 1869, medium	525-	625
Belle of the Winter, medium	275-	360
The Best Horse, small	110-	140
The Bible & Temperance, N. Currier, small	170-	220
Reading the Scriptures, N. Currier, small	58-	68
Savior of the World, N. Currier, small	40-	50
A Black Squall, 1879, small	35-	45
The Boatswain, N. Currier, small	90-	120
Bombardment of Fort Sumter, small	120-	140
Boy and Dog, small	120-	150
Brigham Young, medium	110-	135
California Gold, N. Currier, small	500-	600
Canvasbacks, small	175-	210
A Champion Race, 1889, small	295-	370
Champions of the Union, large	160-	180
The City of Boston, 1873, large	420-	520
City of New York, N. Currier, 1844, small	380-	420
City of New York, N. Currier, 1855, large	1,500-1,700	
Clipper Ship *Flying Cloud,* N. Currier, 1853, large	5,800-6,300	
Dartmouth College, small	1,400-1,600	
The Death Shot, small	150-	170
A Fair Start, small	80-	92
Farmyard Pets, small	120-	140
Feast of Roses, 1873, small	120-	140
Flying Fish, 1879, small	150-	195
The Game Cock, N. Currier, small	190-	228
General Grant, medium, large	70-	140
General Robert E. Lee, small	80-	110
General Tom Thumb's Marriage, 1863, small	100-	120
Going it Blind, N. Currier, small	75-	95
The Beautiful Persian (ill.)	45-	60
The Golden Morning, small,	130-	150
The Grand Drive, Central Park, NY, 1869, large	1,800-2,100	
Grant in Peace, small	85-	95
Great Exhibition of 1860, small	110-	130
Hanover, 1887, small	120-	160
Highland Fling, 1876, medium	110-	140
Horace Greeley, medium	95-	110
The Hunter's Dog, N. Currier, small	190-	220
In the Harbor, small	240-	295
Indian Buffalo Hunt, medium	450-	550
Iroquois, 1882, large	550-	700
The Jockey's Dream, 1880, small	95-	120
Jolly Young Ducks, 1866, small	72-	82
Quail, 1865, small	260-	290
Rail Shooting, small	1,200-1,450	
A Run of Luck, 1871, small	70-	95
Rush for the Pole, 1887, small	120-	150
St. Lawrence, small	125-	155
Santa Claus, 1882, small	110-	140
The Season of Joy, 1872, small	70-	90
The Shoemaker, small	90-	115
Starting Out on His Mettle, 1876, small	120-	145
View on the Rondout, small, medium	160-	195
Warming Up, 1884, small	110-	158
The Water Jump, 1884, small	310-	365
Wood Ducks, small	165-	185
A Wreath of Flowers, small	110-	140

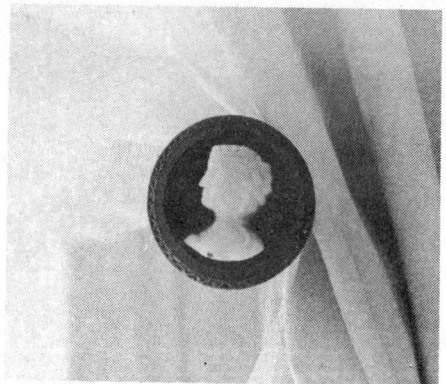

Curtain Tiebacks

Curtain Tiebacks

During the Victorian era, the day of the floor-to-ceiling drapes, usually velvet, these tiebacks were used to hold the drapes open during the day. Sandwich Glass tiebacks are very rare today. Made of brass, cast iron, inlaid with porcelain medallions (illustrated), sometimes just a velvet cord with tassels.

Medallion type, brass framing (ill.), pr.	$ 50- 60
Brass, stamped design, pr.	28- 38
Sandwich Glass (authentic), star-petal design, pr.	90-110
Sandwich-type, blue or other colors, pr.	38- 48
Porcelain-head, iron spike, screw-type, pr.	24- 34

Cuspidors

Cuspidors

Usually made of brass, the early ones were made of pottery, also glass. When it was fashionable to chew tobacco, before cigarettes and cigars, every hotel lobby, barbershop, and beer parlor had at least one. They were also called spittoons.

Brass, 10″ dia.	$ 55- 65
Glass, patent January 8, 1898	58- 70
Rockingham pottery	95-130
Rockwood 11″ dia., 1914	125-165
Silver-plated, hotel-type	45- 65
Porcelainized metal, 2 pieces	18- 28

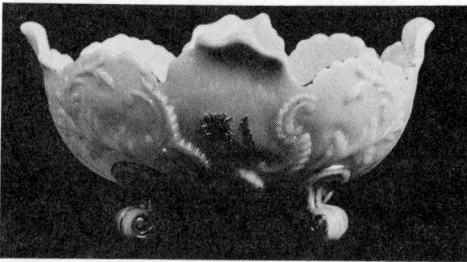

Custard Glass

Custard Glass

See PATTERN GLASS section for specific items and prices. Look out for reproductions!

Banana boat, Louis XV, 5″ high (ill.)	$165-188

Cut Glass

The "brilliant period" of this glass ranges, generally, from 1880 until 1915. How do you tell if it is "cut" or "pressed"? (1) **Ring.** Cut glass will ring like a bell when tapped lightly. (2) **Sparkle.** When held to the light, you can notice the refractions made by the cutting. Pressing destroys this quality. (3) **Sharpness.** If the edges are sharp, the glass is cut; smooth edges denote pressed glass. (4) **Weight.** Cut glass, because of a high lead content, is usually heavy. Cut and engraved glass are done on a wheel; etched glass is not a type of cut glass — it's made by the application of a corroding acid. Cut glass is always hand-blown or blown-molded, never pressed. Since there are thousands of reproduction pieces on the market today, don't assume that (1) through (4) above distinguish the old from the new. Study, learn by feeling, but know from whom you buy! So **many** repros!

BASKETS:

a. 8½″ wide	$ 190- 210
b. Harvard pattern, Intaglio floral, 12″ high	185- 200
c. Pinwheel pattern	155- 175
d. Cornflowers, handled, 13½″ high (ill.)	290- 310

BOWLS:

a. Hobstar; Pinwheel pattern, 8″ dia.	150- 170

b. Etched flowers, signed
Clarke, 9″ dia. 240- 270

c. Russian pattern, panels of
fans 110- 130

d. Flowers, deep cut, signed
"Irving," 8″ dia. (ill.) 150- 175

e. Green cut-to-clear, signed
"Dorflinger," 5″ high (ill.) . . 310- 400

BOXES:

a. Cigarette, signed Hawkes,
late 60- 70

b. Collar, mirror inside for
m'lady, silver bindings 170- 180

c. Dresser, Venetian pattern,
silver trim 120- 130

d. Dresser, silver rim, 5¾″
dia. (ill.) 450- 500

BUTTER DISHES:

a. Hobstar, Strawberry,
Diamond Point and fan,
signed Hawkes 260- 280

b. Rosette flowers, cut knob
finial 95- 110

c. Pinwheel and Fan, cut knob
finial 110- 135

CELERY DISHES:

a. Grecian pattern, signed
Hawkes 180- 190

b. Florence pattern, boat type,
signed Libbey 260- 275

c. Strawberry, Diamond and
Fan, also boat type, Hawkes 160- 185

CHAMPAGNE TUBS:

a. Basketweave 192- 207

b. Chrysanthemum, jug, 2
quart, no stopper, Hawkes 180- 195

CHANDELIERS:

a. Empier Ormolu, 19th
century . . . . 3,500+

b. Gas fixture-type, clear and
frosted glass, mid-1800s . . . 900-1,100

c. Hanging lantern with smoke
bell, early 1,200-1,400

d. Five branch, cut glass
hurricane globes (ill.) . . . . . 2,500+

CHEESE DISHES:

a. Hobstar, 5″ high, cut knob
finial 275- 295

b. Diamonds, fans, sterling
silver dome 240- 260

c. Pinwheel and Star, cut knob
finial 235- 270

d. Mitre star, varied pattern,
7½″ high (ill.) 410- 500

COMPOTES:

a. Strawberry and Diamond
early 1900s 180- 195

b. Isabella, 7″ high, short-
stemmed, square top 165- 190

c. Seashells, 6″ high, short
stem, signed Clark 210- 275

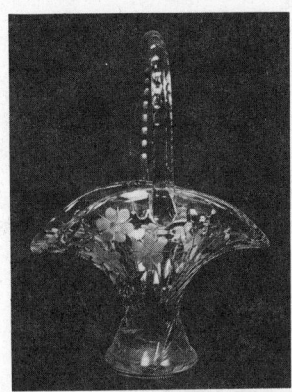

Basket

Bowl

Bowl

Box

119

(continued)

d. Compote, flowers, signed
"Hawkes," 7¼" high (ill.).
Sits on plate of same design,
16½" dia. Both pieces 800- 900

CREAMERS:
  a. Pinwheel 58- 68
  b. Harvard, jug, straight-
    sided, fluted top 66- 75
  c. Hobstar 70- 80
  d. Flower design, 2¾" high
    (ill.) 125- 150

CRUETS:
  a. Harvard, 8-ounce, tall
    signed J. Hoare 155- 170
  b. Prism, 4, 5, 6-ounce, short-
    stemmed, signed Libbey . . 150- 160
  c. Corinthian, 4-ounce oil,
    vinegar to match, both . . . 120- 140

DECANTERS:
  a. Corinthian, pint and quart,
    long necks, some handled . 210- 240
  b. Bull's-Eye, pint, quart,
    1½ quart 200- 220
  c. Pinwheel, usual sizes 160- 190
  d. Diamond Point, 12¼"
    high (ill.) 140- 165
  e. Mitre Star, 10½" high (ill.) 350- 400
  f. 4 sherry glasses to match
    decanter (ill.) ea. 18- 27

EWER:
  a. Victorian cut, 14" high,
    Quadruple Plate "Cherub"
    handle (ill.) 250- 285

FRUIT BOWLS:
  a. Corinthian, 20-point
    Hobstar base 220- 240
  b. Hobstars, ribbon cut 110- 125
  c. Sunburst, prism, cane
    ribbons 110- 130

HUMIDOR:
  a. Deep cut, sterling silver lid,
    6½" (ill.) 325- 365

ICE TUBS:
  a. Florence, 9" dia. 150- 170
  b. Corinthian, 5¾" dia. 140- 150
  c. Hobstar and Diamond cut,
    5½" dia. 140- 155

INKWELLS:
  a. Swirl Rib, brass lid 43- 53
  b. Pinwheel, sterling lid 52- 70

KNIFE RESTS:
  a. Finecut shaft, frosted
    knobs, 3" long 48- 58
  b. Zipper, squared ends, 3"
    long 43- 54
  c. Prism, star cut ends, 6"
    long 67- 77

LAMP:
  a. Box Diamond, 17" high
    (ill.) 450- 485

Chandelier

Cheese Dish

Compote

Mitre Star Decanter

Humidor

Creamer

Sugar Bowl

Ewer

Lamp

121

(continued)

PITCHERS:
- a. Pinwheel, tankard type . . .   210- 230
- b. Florence, miniature, 6″
     high 120- 130
- c. Hobstar, Thumbprint
     handle, 10″ high 210- 240
- d. Brilliant cut, signed
     "Hawkes," 6½″ high (ill.) . .   220- 245

PUNCH BOWL:
- a. Mitre Star, Leaf Fan, 11″
     high, base separate (ill.) . . .   1,350-1,500

SUGAR:
- a. Flower design, 2¾″ high
     (ill.) 125- 150

TOOTHPICK HOLDERS:
- a. Diamond and Fan 52- 65
- b. Fluted sides, prism base . .   57- 67
- c. Pinwheel 51- 61

TUMBLERS:
- a. Block, Star bottom 51- 61
- b. Diamond and Fan 44- 54
- c. Middlesex, signed
     Hawkes, late mark 64- 74

VASES:
- a. Brunswick, V shape,
     signed Hawkes, 12″ high .   280- 295
- b. Harvard, frosted flower
     decor, 13″ high 250- 260
- c. Middlesex, signed
     Hawkes, late mark, 12″
     high 150- 170
- d. Heavy cut, signed
     "Hawkes," 16″ high (ill.) . .   750- 800
- e. Intaglio flowers, signed
     "Sinclair," 14″ high (ill.) . .   450- 500

Punch Bowl

Pitcher

Decanter

Vase

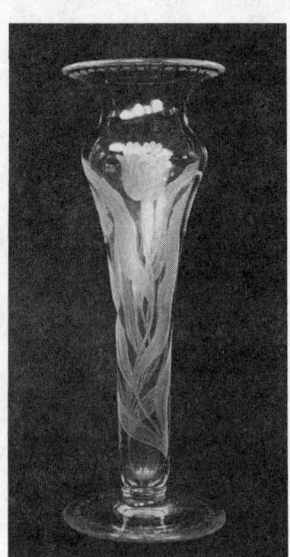

Pitcher

122

Cut Glass Trademarks

Early American Period, 1771-1830
Middle Period, 1830-1880
Brilliant Period, 1880-1905

Most signed cut glass that one finds today is from the Brilliant Period. There were over a thousand cutting shops during this 25-year period. They did not make glass but bought their blanks from firms such as Libbey, Pairpoint, C. Dorflinger & Sons, Gillinder & Sons, T.G. Hawkes Glass Co., United States Glass Co., H.C. Fry Glass Co., and Corning Glass Co. "Signatures" were acid-etched on the bottom, inside the bottom, or on handles. Look carefully — "signed" pieces bring 40%-50% more than unsigned. Here are a few trademarks used during the Brilliant Period.

1. T.B. Clark & Co., Honesdale, Pennsylvania (1886)
2. C. E. Wheelock & Co., Peoria, Illinois (1893)
3. H. P. Sinclaire & Co., Corning, New York (1890s)
4. Tuthill glass Co., Middletown, New York (1890s)
5. H. C. Fry Glass Co., Rochester, Pennsylvania (1900s)
6. C. Dorflinger & Sons, Inc., White Mills, Pennsylvania
7. J.D. Bergen Co., Meriden, Connecticut
8. Lotus Cut Glass Co., Barnesville, Ohio (1911)
9. Richard Murr, San Francisco, California (1905)
10. H. Perilstein, Philadelphia, Pennsylvania (1906)
11. T. B. Clark & Co., Sellyville, Pennsylvania (1898)
12. Phoenix Glass Co., Monaca and Pittsburgh, Pennsylvania (1881)
13. Corning Glass Works, Corning, New York (1904)
14. Corning Glass Works, Corning, New York (1904)
15. Corning Glass Works, Corning, New York (1909)
16. Corona Cut Glass Co., Toledo, Ohio (1906)
17. L. Straus & Sons, New York, New York (1894)
18. Thatcher Bros., Fairhaven, Massachusetts (1894)
19. C. Dorflinger & Sons, White Mills, Pennsylvania (1892)
20. C. Dorflinger & Sons, White Mills, Pennsylvania (1892)
21. O.F. Egginton Co., Corning, New York (1899)
22. T.G. Hawkes & Co., Corning, New York (1890)
23. T.G. Hawkes & Co., Corning, New York (1890)
24. T.G. Hawkes & Co., Corning, New York (1902)
25. J. Hoare & Co., Corning, New York (1895)
26. Libbey Glass Co., Toledo, Ohio (1895)
27. Libbey Glass Co., Toledo, Ohio (1896)
28. Libbey Glass Co., Toledo, Ohio (1901)
29. Libbey Glass Co., Toledo, Ohio (1901)

123

(continued)

16

23

17 STRAUS CUT GLASS

24 GRAVIC

18 DIAMOND FINISH

25 J. HOARE & CO. 1853

19 COLONIAL

26 *Libbey*

20 LORRAINE

27 *Libbey*

21 EC GINTON

28 *Libbey*

22 HAWKES

29

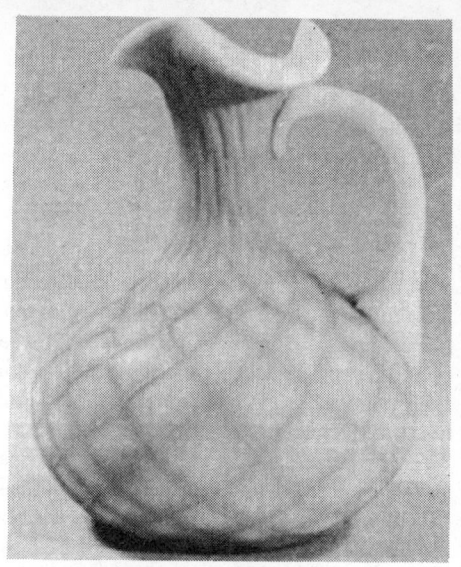

Cut Velvet Glass

Pennsylvania made a great deal of it in the late 1800s. Repros, repros!

Blue, fluted lip, 8″ high	$225-255
Bowl, Diamond Quilt, deep rose, 6″ dia.	220-240
Creamer, fluted top, white lining, ribbed yellow, signed Mt. Washington Glass Company . .	220-250
Diamond Quilt, pink	110-135
Pitcher, deep rose, diamond-quilted, applied handle, Pheonix Glass	155-170
Tumbler, blue, ribbed, glossy, 7″ high	140-165
Tumbler, honeycomb, pink, diamond-quilted, 6½″ high, Phoenix	180-200
Vase, blue, diamond-quilted, 10″ high	210-240
Vase, pink/white casing, slender neck, 7½″ high	225-245
Vase, yellow and white diamond-quilted, 6″ high	160-190

Czechoslovakia

Cut Velvet Glass

Satin glass that shows the design in high relief with the white lining showing where the pattern was cut is called Cut Velvet. It was sometimes found with diamond quilting but usually ribbed. The Mt. Washington Glass Company and the Phoenix Glass Works in

Czechoslovakia

This country claimed its independence from Austria-Hungary after World War I. Most pieces are marked "Czechoslovakia" though some pieces are artist/maker marked, indicating they were made before the country became independent. Most of what you find are in the $8 to $30 range.

Vase, handled, stenciled design
under glaze, signed "Erphila
Art Pottery" on paper label,
7" high (ill.) .... $ 18- 25

Da Latte

Another of the cameo types, it was usually opaque and was made by Andre De Latte in Nancy, France, in the 1920s. Light fixtures were also made there, but De Latte is best remembered for his cameo glass.

Box, 3½" high, 4" square, pink
ground, cut blue flowers,
signed $425-500
Vase, blue ground, purple iris
decor, signed, 9½" high 465-515
Vase, pink with mottled blue
ground, lavender-pink floral,
signed 325-450
Vase, opaque ground, handled,
river scene, 14" high 275-300
Vase, yellow, trees, deer, brown
background, signed, 8½"
high 420-525
Vase, gold/red ground, yellow/
pink floral, signed, 11½" high . 450-525
Vase, aqua grounds, birds,
flowers, blue/green decor,
signed, 8¾" high 465-515

Daguerreotypes

Daguerreotypes

The method is named for the Frenchman who discovered it — Louis Jacques Mande Daguerre — in 1837, who covered a bright copper plate with silver salts, then placed it between 2 pieces of glass to protect it. When exposed to light, the silver compound produced a picture. Civil War scenes are collectible and rare.

Civil War soldier, Union Army .. $ 50- 65
Girl with dog 24- 29
Daguerreotypes without case ... 2- 3
Eagle on American Flag 29- 39
Volunteer fireman, Ambrotype* . 50- 60
Wedding photo (ill.) 22- 29

*Ambrotypes are photographs on glass.

Daguerreotype Cases

Daguerreotype Cases

Littlefield, Parsons and Company patented these on October 14, 1856. When you find them with the daguerreotype missing, they make fine holders for your favorite photo.

Average price .... $ 8- 15

D'argental

Another of the cameo-type glasses produced in the last part of the 19th century, it was named for its originator who lived in France. Somewhat similar to Galle and Lalique. Scarce.

Bowl, yellow matte, red roses,
leaves, carved, 6" high, signed . $375-400
Bowl, red matte, blue/white
flowers, carved cameo, 8½"
high 400-475
Vase, 3-layer, amber-rose ground,
signed, 7" high 470-495
Vase, frosted blue ground, brown
and rust leaves, signed, 6"
high 390-420
Vase, blue morning glories, yellow ground, cameo, 8" high ... 375-425

Darning Eggs

In Grandmother's day, this was a very important item in the sewing basket. They're

(continued)

collectible, especially those with sterling silver and 14k gold handles. What you pay depends on condition, etc.

Darning Eggs

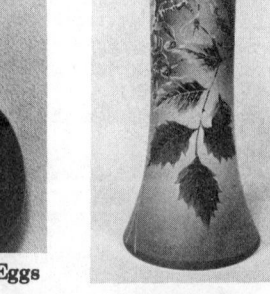

Daum Nancy

Daum Nancy

Auguste and Antonin Daum made and signed this beautiful cameo-type glass in the late 1800s. They also made fine enameled glass. Both are hard to find today.

Bottle, acid cut ground, man and windmill, enameled, stopper	$410-	460
Bowl, blue iris cut through, floral, 8″ high, signed	600-	675
Bowl, fruit decor, blue ground	295-	335
Box, carved blue crocus, blue-green ground, lid, signed	420-	435
Compote, amethyst, footed, 8½″ high, signed	195-	245
Compote, blue and brown ground, sprigs, leaves, footed, 8″	385-	450
Jar, floral scene cut through, acid finish, signed	375-	450
Lamp, enameled leaf decor, mottled floral background, signed	1,100-	1,300
Pitcher, frosted green, floral, 9½″ high, signed	435-	445
Plate, turned up sides, yellow/orange	325-	385
Rose bowl, green, blue cut through, 3½″ high	280-	360
Tumbler, barrel shape, gold ground, flowers, 5″ high	350-	425
Tumbler, white ground, shaded red, blue, green, signed	400-	500
Vase, birds in trees, green/blue/brown/red, 8″ high, signed	625-	710
Vase, enamel, floral, medallion, 4½″ high, signed	410-	450
Vase, mottled orange, yellow, 6½″ high, signed	395-	420
Vase, summer scene, 10″ high, signed	420-	495
Vase, winter scene, 9″ high, signed	415-	495
Vase, serpentine shape, floral, brown/green/blue, 7¼″ high, signed	450-	495
Vase, satin, orange/green, enameled pseudo-cameo technique, 8¾″ high (ill.)	170-	185

Davenport China

Davenport China

Made by John Davenport at Lonport, England, late 1700s, this china is light in weight, cream colored and has a soft, velvety texture. It's marked with the name Davenport above an impressed anchor. The factory closed in the late 1800s.

Cup/saucer, Derby colors, 1810	$ 62-	72
Creamer, bulbous white with deep blue decor	80-	90
Dish in plated holder, Imari colors, 1875	88-	98
Dish, vegetable, berry pattern, impressed signature and anchor	44-	54
Ewer, white, blue marbling, 1815	110-	135
Jug, bright blue decorations, 1800	170-	195
Platter, blue/white Oriental, reticulated border, anchor mark	88-	100
Teapot, pink lustre decorations	220-	245
Tea set (teapot, covered sugar), spring pattern in red/green, anchor	220-	245
Trivet, blue/red decor, no mark	88-	98
Urn, blue/gold on white, 6″ high (ill.)	200-	255

De Vez

This glass was made in Pantin, France, and was similar in style to that made by Marinot, Rousseau, and others. It is another of the cameo-types, late 1800s and scarce today.

De Vez

Atomizer, birds, brown/yellow,
6″ high, signed $380-445
Bowl, 3″ high, 5″ diameter,
flowers/birds 240-260
Bowl, 4″ high, 4½″ diameter,
scenic, blue/green, signed 350-400
Vase, scenic, satin ground,
signed, 8½″ high 485-650
Vase, 7″ high, river scene,
mountains, signed 410-490
Vase, translucent ground, castle
scene, signed, 10″ high 495-650
Vase, 7½″ high, house/trees,
pink, green, signed 375-450
Vase, 11″ high, scenic, blue/red
iridescent, signed 365-475
Vase, acid cut, harbor scene,
8½″ high, signed 625-750
Vase, 14″ high, clouds, blue/
green ground, signed 450-525

DeVilbiss

DeVilbiss

Steuben made both atomizers and cologne
sets for this company. All pieces are signed
"DeVILBISS."

Atmozier, black satin glass,
orange enamel floral, brass
fittings, 5½″ high (ill.) . . . . $ 30- 45
Atomizer, blue opalescent, 6″
high 28- 38
Atomizer, gold/amber, 4¼″ high .   30- 45
Atomizer, orange/gold, brass
fittings, 5½″ high (ill.) 30- 45
Atomizer, white opalescent, 5¾″
high 25- 35

Cologne, orange/gold, brass
fittings, 4½″ high (ill.) 30- 45
Cologne, white opalescent, 5½″
high 25- 35

Decanters

Decanters

Used mainly by taprooms and inns to store
their wines and liquors, they became stylish
in homes in the mid-1700s. The first were
crude in shape and material; later they were
made of cut glass, Amberina, even Tiffany
glass.

Amber, Inverted Thumbprint,
stopper, pedestal foot . . . . $ 53- 60
Brown, blown, fluted sides,
clear stopper, attributed to
Sandwich, 1850s, 14″ high 110-160
Clear, hand-painted eagles,
dated 1779, blown, clear
stoppers, pair 600-700
Clear, 4-part, stoppers, Sand-
wich-type, late 1800s, France,
12½″ high 110-130
Clear, signed Libbey, silver
overlay, Riverboat type 165-195
Cobalt, swirled body, clear
stopper, pontil mark,
mid-1800s 125-150
½ pint, 3-mold (McKearin
G 111-14) 160-185
Pair, engraved glass, floral/
cupid designs in silver base,
6½″ high (ill.) 440-470

Decoy

(continued)

Decoys

Prices for these have gone "sky high." Prices given are for those in good condition, taking age and wear into account.

Goldeneye Drake, by Mason's Decoy Factory, Detroit, Mich., Standard Grade . . . . . $. . 65- 75

Black Duck, by Mason's, Premier Grade 150- 170

Brant, by Mason's, Challenge Grade 170- 190

Coot, by Xavier Bourg, Larose, La. 130- 140

Coot, maker unknown, initials branded in bottom 58- 68

Coot, by Benjamin J. Schmidt, Centerline, Mich. 150- 170

Coot, made of cork, from Central Illinois River area 48- 58

Red-Breasted Merganser Drake, by Hurley Conklin 155- 165

Red-Breasted Merganser Drake, by Frank Dobbins, Jonesport, Me. 82- 92

Scaup Drake, by William Heverin, Charlestown, Md. 73- 83

Canvasback Drake, by Norris E. Pratt, c. 1922 . . . 92- 110

Chesapeake Bay Coot, by Madison R. Mitchell, Havre de Grace, Md. 88- 110

Goldeneyes, pair, Drake and Hen, by Madison R. Mitchell . . . . .275- 325 pair

Ruddy Duck Hen, by L. T. Ward, 1965 . . . . .130- 150

Old Squaw Drake, by Norris E. Pratt 72- 88

Canvasback Drake, made of balsa, by the Ward Brothers, Crisfield, Md. Both Stephen W. (1895-1976 and his brother, Lemuel T., Jr., B. 1896) are world-famous for their birds 510- 575

Canvasbacks, pair, balsa, Drake and Hen, by the Ward Brothers . . . . . . 1,200-1,400 pair

New Jersey Black Duck, hollow-carved by Charles McCoy, Tuckerton, N.J. 80- 91

Scaup Hen, hollow-carved by Capt. Jess Birdsall, Barnegat, N.J. 52- 62

Delaware River Brant, by Gumpy Gilbert, Trenton, N.J. 134- 150

Cape Cod Black Duck 68- 78

Redhead Hen, by H. Keyes Chadwick, c. 1949, when he was 80! . . .240- 270

Red-Breasted Merganser, by Gus Wilson, Casco Bay, Me. 200- 250

Black Duck, by Gus Wilson 135- 155

White-Winged Scoter 85- 95

Old Squaw Drake, by Milton Crowley, South Addison, Me. c. 1920s 70- 80

White-Winged Scoter, by Warren Wass, Cape Split, Me., c. 1905 . . . . 52- 70

Sleeping Canvasback Hen, by J. Corbin ("Corb") Reed, 1962 . . . . .195- 250

Gadwall Drake, by John English; repainted by Robert White 400- 425

Black Duck, by Thomas Fitzpatrick, Delanco, N.J. 135- 155

Mallard Drake, by Harry Fennimore, Bordentown, N.J. 168- 179

Mallard Hen, by the Jester family, Chincoteague, Va. 78- 88

Buffleheads, pair, Drake and Hen, by Doug Jester . . . . .200- 250 pair

Coot, by Singing River Decoy Co., New Orleans, La. pre 1940 . . . . . 57- 67

Scaup Drake, hollow-carved, by Harry V. Shourds 150- 162

Red-Breasted Merganser, by Harry V. Shourds 230- 260

Black Duck, by Wildfowler Decoys, Inc., Old Saybrook, Conn. 65- 95

Life-sized Great Horned Owl, by C. Victor Bracher, c. 1943 . . . . .375- 400

Dedham Pottery

Alexander Robertson founded this company in Chelsea, Massachusetts, in the late 1860s; changed its name from Chelsea Pottery to Chelsea Ceramic Art Works in 1872;

Dedham Pottery

finally to Dedham Pottery around 1894. They specialized in crackleware in blue and high-fired colored pieces. The rabbit motif is what you see the most of on Dedham pottery. Most collectible today.

Bowl and plate, rabbits, signed ..	$115-130
Bowl, mushrooms, Chelsea Pottery mark	68-78
Candlesticks, rabbits, signed, pr.	160-170
Chocolate pot, rabbits, signed ...	155-168
Creamer, elephants, 4½" high ...	148-170
Creamer, rabbit, 3¾" high	110-125
Creamer, rabbit, 6¼" high	130-144
Cup/saucer, rabbits, elephant, polar bear	110-130
Dish, elephants, Chelsea Pottery mark	70- 85
Egg cup, rabbits	140-170
Mayonnaise bowl, rabbits, 6¼" dia.	95-120
Mug, handled, rabbit border, 5½" high	180-250
Mug, handled, water lily, large ..	80- 90
Plate, duck, 10" dia.	120-140
Plate, rabbit, 8"	95-110
Plate, rabbit, 10" (ill.)	68- 80
Plate, turkey, 8"	110-130
Plate, swan, 8½" dia.	160-185
Platter, rabbit border	185-195
Salt/pepper shakers, rabbit pr. ...	140-152
Saucedish, rabbits	60- 68
Saucer, water lily, 4" dia.	53- 64
Sugar bowl, lid, 3"	140-155
Tile, 6" square, horse chestnut ..	80- 90
Tray, elephant border, 7¼" long .	230-275
Vase, blue over green, 4½" high .	450-525
Vase, charcoal gray, raised floral decor, 6" high	85- 95

Dejeuner Set

A porcelain tray, teapot, cream jug, sugar bowl and one or two cups with spoons. A set for one was called Solitaire; for two Tete-a-tete. Usually made of soft paste porcelain, they were popular in the early 1800s until just before the turn of the century.

Deldare
See BUFFALO POTTERY.

Delft

Delft

Earthenware with a blue decoration on a white background. Tin compound was used to produce the glaze and a number of companies made it at Deft, Holland, at the beginning of the 17th century. It was also made in England. Most of what you find in shops today is from the late 1800s until World War I. Now being reproduced.

Ashtray, windmill scene	$ 25- 32
Bottle, blue/white, 9½" high, 1740s	210-230
Bottle, Dutch girl with dogcart, windmill scene	40- 50
Clock, Dutch scene, 8-day German movement	150-170
Coffee grinder, wall type, typical .	85- 97
Cow, 6" long, signed Delft	65- 75
Creamer, sleeping cow, Germany, 1890	40- 50
Creamer, flowers, Holland, 2¾" high (ill.)	13- 18
Cup/saucer, windmill scene	9- 14
Cup/saucer, floral, Holland, 2" high (ill.)	9- 14
Figurine, Dutch, girl and boy, pair	42- 53
Inkwell, stand, metal cap, blue/white, no mark	30- 40
Jar, lid, Dutch boy, 13" high	240-275
Plaque, sailing scene, 18th century, 14½" high	275-295
Plate, blue, Dutch canal in winter, 13½" diameter	40- 50
Stein, drinking scene along canal, dated 1723, 11" high, pewter cap	340-355

129

(continued)

Tray, water scene, blue/white,
12" wide 135-170
Vase, windmill, handled, Holland,
2¼" high (ill.) 8- 18
Vase, blue/white, scrolls, lovers,
16" high, pair 250-270
Wine bottle, Holland, Dutch boy,
7½" high (ill.) 38- 48

Demography
See GENEALOGY

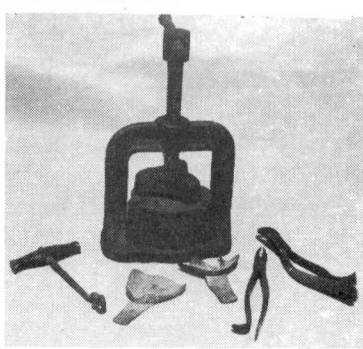
Dental Collectibles

Dental Collectibles

If you think going to the dentist today is
fun, you should note what our grandparents
went through. Old dental tools, tooth pullers,
and the like, are being collected today.

Cast iron mold for making false
teeth, late 1800s (ill.) . . . . $ 40- 45
Dentist's cabinet, glass doors,
wooden drawers, early 1900s . . 70- 85
Dentist's chair, felt covered,
tilt-back type, late 1800s 125-160
Dentist's drill, foot-powered
type, late 1800s 60- 75
Hook-type tooth puller, mid-
1800s (ill.) 18- 23
Plier-type tooth puller, late
1800s (ill.) 16- 28

Depression, Miss America

Depression Glass

The glass is confusing because collectors
and those doing books about it have given
names to patterns otherwise unnamed by the
makers. It was made during the Depression
years of the late 1920s and early 1930s and
was considered inexpensive tableware. Hocking, Westmoreland Glass Company and the
Indiana Glass Company were three of many
firms making it. Pink, green, milk-white,
amber were just a few of the colors.

BOWL
American Sweetheart, cereal,
pink . . . . $ 8- 14
Horseshoe, berry, 9" dia., topaz . 18- 28
Normandie, berry, 8½" dia.,
green 14- 22
Patrician, berry, 8½" dia.,
green 13- 24
Petal Swirl, console, footed,
10½" dia., teal 21- 31
Poppy, vegetable 16- 27
Royal Lace, fruit, 3 legs,
10" dia., green 24- 36
Sandwich, console, 9" dia. 17- 27
Sharon (Cabbage Rose), cereal,
pink 11- 19
Windsor Diamond, berry,
8 3/8" dia., pink 12- 20
BUTTER DISH, COVERED
Cherry Blossom, pink 40- 50
Floral, green 40- 52
Lace Edge (Open Lace), pink 29- 39
Windsor Diamond, green 28- 40
CANDLEHOLDER
Madrid, pink, pr. 17- 30
Petal Swirl, double branch, teal,
pr. 19- 29
CHILD'S SET
Cherry Blossom, 14 pcs.,
Delfite 155-170
Cherry Blossom, 14 pcs., pink . . . 125-155
COOKIE JAR
Cameo 18- 28
Princess, pink 16- 27
Royal Lace, glass cover, cobalt . . 55- 65
CREAMER AND SUGAR
Cameo 14- 24
Madrid, blue 28- 38
Petalware, monax or cremax 12- 22
Princess, topaz 17- 27
CUP AND SAUCER
Adam (Adams) 9- 13
American Sweetheart, monax . . . 12- 17
American Sweetheart, pink 8- 18
Cameo 8- 18
Cherry Blossom 11- 21
Dogwood (Wildrose), thin, pink . . 11- 21
Horseshoe, pink 9- 19
Madrid 9- 18

Mayfair (Open Rose), blue	26-	36
Miss America, pink	12-	23
Moderntone, cobalt	8-	19
Petalware, pink or crystal	7-	18
Princess, topaz	7-	18
Ribbon Candy, crystal	8-	16
Rosemary (Dutch Rose), pink . . .	8-	17
Royal Lace, cobalt	20-	30
Royal Lace, crystal	8-	20

DECANTER

Cameo 10″ high	35-	45
Mayfair, drop stopper	38-	47

PITCHER

Adam, 8″ high	30-	38
Doric and Pansy, footed, 7½″ high, teal	55-	67
Floral, footed cone, 32 oz. 8″ high	18-	29
Horseshoe, footed, ½ gal., green	53-	63
Miss America, 65 oz. 7¾″ high, pink	40-	49
Patrician, 67 oz. 8½″ high, amber	35-	45
Sharon (Cabbage Rose), 80 oz. green	118-152	

PLATE

Adam, cake server	12-	22
Adam, dinner	8-	19
American Sweetheart, dinner, monax	9-	21
American Sweetheart, salad, 8″ dia., cherry red	80-	90
Cameo, dinner	7-	17
Cherry Blossom, dinner	7-	15
Christmas Candy, dinner, teal . . .	7-	17
Cloverleaf, salad, 8″ dia.	7-	18
Cloverleaf, salad, 8″ dia., ebony .	16-	27
Dogwood, dinner, pink	9-	20
Floral, salad, 8″ dia.	7-	19
Florentine, dinner, hexagonal . . .	7-	19
Florentine, dinner, round	7-	19

Lace Edge, salad, 8 3/8″ dia.	7-	19
Madrid, divided grill	7-	18
Mayfair, cake, footed, 10″ dia., green or pink	14-	23
Miss America, salad 8½″ dia., green	8-	19
Moderntone, cake, 10 5/8″ dia., cobalt	12-	23
Normandie, divided grill, 11″ dia., pink	7-	18
Petal Swirl, serving or cake, teal	14-	23
Princess, dinner, topaz	7-	17
Rosemary, dinner, green	8-	19
Sandwich, dinner, 10½″ dia.	8-	19
Sandwich, footed salver	14-	24
Sandwich, dinner, 12″ dia.	8-	19

PLATTER

Cameo	14-	24
Doric, oval, 12″	9-	20
Miss America, oval 12″, crystal .	10-	21
Petalware, oval, 13″, cremax	19-	31

SALT AND PEPPER SHAKERS

Cameo, footed, 4″ high, pr.	29-	40
Cube, pink	15-	25
Miss America, footed, pink, pr. . .	21-	31
Moderntone, footed, 4½″ high, cobalt, pr.	20-	30
Sandwich, pr.	18-	30
Windsor Diamond, pr.	23-	34

TUMBLER

American Sweetheart, table, 9 oz., pink	16-	24
Cameo, footed cone, 9 oz. green . .	9-	20
Cherry Blossom, cone, round foot, 9 oz., Delfite	20-	30
Doric and Pansy, table, 9 oz., teal	14-	23
Floral, footed cone, 7 oz., 4¾″ high	7-	18
Mayfair, 9 oz., pink	7-	19
Patrician, 9 oz.	9-	20
Royal Ruby, table, 9 oz.	7-	18

Depression, American Sweetheart

Desk Set

Desk Sets

Every type, from the lowliest to the most expensive, was in vogue until the invention of the ink-filled pen.

Brass desk set, French, mid-1800s, signed M. Bounel....	$425- 470
Desk set, iron, 2 inkwells, footed, mid-1800s	45- 55
Desk set, brass, cut glass inkwells, early 1900s	85- 92
Paperweight type, pelican, signed "Davesen" (ill.)	64- 80
Tiffany desk set, 5 pieces, signed Tiffany Studios, bronze/glass	775-1,100
Tiffany desk set, 6 pieces, Spider Web, signed and numbered	1,000-1,600

Disneyana Collectibles

Disneyana Collectibles

Mickey Mouse watches are out of sight, price-wise. Anything having to do with the early days of Disney is highly collectible today. Look out for reproductions!

Bugs Bunny mug, plastic	$ 5- 8
Davey Crockett pocket knive ...	14- 23
Donald Duck watch, Ingersoll, 1939, marked "WDP" (ill.)	175-190
Donald Duck bank, plastic	35- 45
Dopey figurine, chalkware, 4" high	18- 27
Dumbo creamer	14- 22
Mickey Mouse alphabet bowl, cereal premium	35- 45
Mickey Mouse clock, Ingersoll, 1930s	325-360
Mickey Mouse dishes, child's service for 6, Japan	85- 95
Mickey and Minnie Mouse figurine, painted	48- 60
Mickey Mouse watch, Ingersoll, metal band, running condition	each 225-260
Pluto mug, Japan	32- 42

Pluto pencil sharpener	6- 9
Snow White and 7 Dwarfs cottage cheese glass, milk company premium, set	95-110 se
Snow White fork	17- 24
Snow White watch, running condition	95- 130

Documents

Old deeds, land grants, marriage certificates, all are collectible and bringing good prices today. A land grant dated later than 1836, isn't too valuable as presidents were given secretaries about that time and said secretary "signed" for the president. Fun to collect — getting more valuable every day.

Average price, common variety	$ 3- 8

Doll Furniture

Doll Furniture and Accessories

Bed, complete with spread, blue finish	$ 25- 35
Birdcage with bird	30- 40
Bookcases, balsa wood	15- 22
Booth table, 3 pieces	16- 23
Candelabra, pot metal, 2" high, pair	17- 23
Chair, ladderback, 3" high.....	12- 21
Chair, wicker rocker, 2½" high ..	15- 19
Cradle, hand-carved, 12" x 16" ..	30- 35
Desk, dropfront, with matching chair	24- 37
Desk, wooden, brass pulls, 6¼" high (ill.)	58- 70
Fireplace tools with stand, 6 pieces	7- 11
Knives and forks, service for 12, complete	27- 37
Living room suite, 6 pieces, complete	40- 50
Stove, 4-burner, 4" high	18- 29
Trunk for doll clothes	58- 68

Brass bed, 4" x 19", springs,
  pad, spread   175-195
Walnut bed, 5" x 21", tester,
  rope springs, hand-carved   250-300
Bird's-eye maple, 4" x 21",
  slats, handmade quilt   190-210
Bedroom set: 5-piece, bed, tin
  washstand, table, 2 chairs,
  oak, 1" scale   120-140
Cradle, hand-carved, walnut,
  13½" high to hood, pre-
  Civil War 85- 95
Parlor set: 7 pieces, 4 chairs,
  upholstered seats, side table,
  lady's chair, gentleman's
  chair, 1" scale   142-157
Wicker porch set: 4 pieces,
  swing, settee, 2 chairs   98-115

Dolls

This category is one of the most popular
and getting more expensive every day. Just
know your dolls or get a book and study.
THE PRICE GUIDE TO DOLLS, Wallace-
Homestead Book Co., Des Moines, Iowa
50305, $9.95, is considered the best Price
Guide by most of the knowledgeable doll collectors and dealers.

All Bisque
American, all painted bisque,
  marked STORY BOOK
  DOLL USA 11; mohair wig,
  painted features, jointed at
  hips and shoulders, 5" tall . .$ 48- 58
American, "Nancy Ann Story
  Book Christening Baby," all
  painted bisque, marked
  STORY BOOK DOLL USA
  2; molded/painted hair and
  features, jointed baby body.
  All original, 3½" tall 50- 65
American, "Nancy Ann Story
  Book Doll," all painted
  bisque, marked STORY
  BOOK DOLL USA; mohair
  wig, molded/painted features,
  shoes and socks, jointed at
  shoulders, 5¼" tall 50- 60
Austria and Germany, all stone
  bisque, marked C.D. Kenny
  Co. (ink stamp); molded/
  painted hair, features, and
  clothes; jointed at hips and
  shoulders, 4" tall 60- 70
French (?), all bisque, socket
  head, marked 2; mohair wig,
  glass sleep eyes, closed
  mouth, jointed at hips and
  shoulders, molded/painted
  shoes and black stockings,
  8" tall 410- 450

French Type, all bisque, swivel
  head, marked 16/0; human
  hair wig, paperweight eyes,
  closed mouth, jointed
  shoulders and hips, molded/
  painted shoes and socks, 7"
  tall 375- 425
French Type, all bisque, clothes
  sewed on; mohair wig, glass
  inset eyes, closed mouth;
  jointed shoulders and hips,
  molded/painted shoes and
  socks. All original, 4" tall . .   335- 365
French Type, all bisque,
  marked 13 on head and body;
  socket head, mohair wig,
  glass inset eyes, closed
  mouth; molded/painted shoes
  with heels and long black
  stockings, 5" tall 228- 260
German, all bisque, swivel
  head, marked 4; mohair wig,
  glass inset eyes, closed
  mouth; jointed shoulders and
  hips, molded/painted shoes
  and socks, 9" tall 395- 470
German, all bisque, unmarked;
  molded/painted hair, features, and clothes; jointed at
  hips and shoulders, 6" tall . .   250- 275
German, all bisque, unmarked;
  molded/painted hair, fea-
  tures, and clothes, 2½" tall .   165- 185
German, all bisque, marked
  Germany; molded/painted
  hair, features, and clothes,
  2¼" tall 175- 210
German, all bisque, marked
  Germany 4325; molded/
  painted hair, features, and
  clothes, 2" and 3" tall, each .   175- 220
German, all bisque, marked
  Germany; molded/painted
  hair, features, and clothes,
  2¼" tall, each 175- 220
German "Rachel," all bisque
  nodder, marked RACHEL
  Germany; molded/painted
  face, features, arms, hat and
  clothes; swivel/nodding
  head, 3½" tall 190- 225
German, "Andy Gump," all
  bisque nodder, marked
  ANDY GUMP Germany;
  molded/painted features, hat
  and clothes; swivel/nodding
  head, 4" tall 250- 325
German "Nodder," all bisque,
  marked Germany; molded/
  painted hair, features, bonnet, purse, clothes, and
  shoes, 3" tall 175- 210

133

(continued)

German, "Nodder," all bisque, marked Germany; molded/ painted hair, features, hat, clothes, shoes and socks; swivel/nodding head, 3" tall . 165- 190

Celluloid Dolls
Buschow & Beck (?), celluloid, swivel head, molded/ painted hair, inset glass eyes, closed mouth; celluloid jointed body marked (a helmet) Minerva. 18½" tall 175- 220

Best & Company, all celluloid, marked BEST U.S.A.; molded hair, features and body, 3" tall 40- 50

Buschow & Beck (?), celluloid shoulder-head, marked (a helmet) Germany To2 8ct; molded/ painted hair, inset glass eyes, closed mouth; cloth body with celluloid hands, 10½" tall 80- 90

Company Unidentified, all celluloid, marked patent NO. 12574 No. 12575; molded/painted features, legs push into body, squeaker, 5" tall 58- 75

Company Unidentified, celluloid shoulder-head, marked Made in France; molded/painted hair, inset celluloid eyes, open/closed mouth; all cloth body, 15½" tall 158- 178

Company Unidentified, all celluloid, jointed at hips and shoulders, molded/ painted features and clothes. Marked JAPAN, 3" tall 28- 40

Company Unidentified, all celluloid baby; jointed at hips and shoulders, molded/painted hair, painted eyes, closed mouth. Body marked CVO (super-imposed in a circle) U.S.A., 7" long . . . 55- 70

Company Unidentified, celluloid head, hands, and feet, molded/painted features; cloth body stuffed with excelsior. Marked JAPAN, 8" tall 48- 59

Rheinsche Gummi, celluloid shoulder head marked turtle in a diamond; human hair wig, inset glass eyes, open mouth, cloth body with celluloid arms. All original Swedish costume, 11" tall, pair 300- 350

Unmarked, "Carnival Doll," all celluloid; molded/ painted hair, features, shoes and socks; jointed at shoulders, 12" tall 58- 78

Unmarked, all celluloid, molded/painted features and clothes, jointed at shoulders, 6" tall 50- 62

China Frozen Charlottes, Frozen Charlies
Charlotte in a Tub, pink china with molded/ painted features in white china tub, 1¼" and 2" 178- 220

Frozen Charlottes; three black Charlottes are unglazed with molded hair and features; white Charlotte is white china with painted hair and features. 1" down to ½" tall . . . . 38- 55 each

Frozen Charlotte, white china, molded/painted hair (1850s type) and features, gold lustre shoes, 2" tall 165- 195

Frozen Charlotte, unglazed, molded hair and features with painted eyebrows, 3" tall 40- 55

Frozen Charlotte, unglazed, mohair wig, painted features, 3¼" tall 115- 140

Frozen Charlotte, white china, mohair wig, painted features, 4" tall . 175- 220

Frozen Charlotte, white china, molded/painted hair (1850s type) and features, 4¼" tall 145- 175

Frozen Charlotte, white china, molded/painted hair (1850s type) and features, 5½" tall 145- 175

Frozen Charlie, flesh tint face; molded/painted boy style hair, molded eyelids, painted features, white china body, 11½" tall . . . 625- 725

Frozen Charlie, all over flesh tint; molded/painted boy style hair, painted features, 14″ tall 625- 700

Frozen Charlie, flesh tint face; molded/painted boy style hair, painted features, white china body, 15½″ tall 850-1,000

Frozen Charlie, flesh tint face; molded/painted boy style hair, painted features, blue tie, white china body, 16½″ tall ... 925-1,200

Frozen Charlie, flesh tint face; molded/painted boy style hair, painted features, white china body, 16½″ tall 1,100-1,400

China Head Dolls

1830s Biedermeier Type, china-shoulder-head; human hair wig, blue painted eyes; cloth body with china arms and legs, 19″ tall 2,400-2,750

1830s Biedermeier Type, china-shoulder-head; human hair wig, blue painted eyes, cloth body with china arms, 24″ tall 2,700-2,950

1830s Biedermeier Type, china-shoulder-head; wig missing, blue painted eyes, cloth body and china arms and legs, 9″ tall, each 1,150-1,375

1830s Biedermerier Type, china-shoulder-head; light creamy tint; mohair wig, blue painted eyes, cloth body with china arms and legs, 18″ tall 2,100-2,400

1830s Biedermeier Type, china-shoulder-head, light flesh tint; human hair wig, blue painted eyes, cloth body with china arms and legs, 15½″ tall 2,300-2,500

1840s Type, china-shoulder-head, pink tint; brown painted eyes, cloth body with kid arms, 27″ tall 2,000-2,400

1840s Type, china-shoulder-head, slight pink tint; blue painted eyes, cloth body with kid arms, 23½″ tall 1,500-1,700

1840s Type, china-shoulder-head, pink tint; blue painted eyes, cloth body with china arms and legs, 17½″ tall 1,350-1,500

1840s Type, china-shoulder-head; brown painted eyes, cloth body with kid arms, individually stitched/wired fingers, 14″ tall 1,400-1,575

1850s Type, Jenny Lind, china-shoulder-head, creamy tint; brown painted eyes, cloth body with kid hands and feet, 16″ tall 2,000-2,350

1840s Type, china-shoulder-head, pink tint; blue painted eyes, cloth body with china arms and legs, 14″ tall 1,500-1,800

1850-60s Type, china-shoulder-head; blue painted eyes, cloth body with china arms and legs, 4¼″ tall 200- 275

1850s-60s Type, china-shoulder-head, flesh tint; brown painted eyes, molded lids, lower lashes, exposed ears, cloth body with china hands on kid arms, 20″ tall 2,700-3,200

1850-60s Type, china-shoulder-head, creamy tint; brown painted eyes, molded lids, lower lashes, smiling mouth, cloth body with kid arms, 27½″ tall 4,000-4,950

1850 to 60s Type, china-shoulder-head, marked 1845 (in black under glaze) on lower part of back left shoulder; light flesh tint, blue painted eyes, cloth body with kid arms and feet, 25½″ tall 2,750-3,200

1850-60s Type, Jenny Lind, china-shoulder-head; blue painted eyes, molded lids; cloth body marked Patd. Dec. 15, 1885; china arms, Philip Goldsmith body, 22″ tall 3,200-3,800

China, Heads Only

Doll Heads, 1850-60s type, creamy china, 3″ tall, $125-150; 2½″ tall 130- 160

Doll Head, 1850-60s type, 2½″ tall 95- 130

Doll Head, 1850-60s type, turned head, 6″ tall.... 240- 280 each

1880s Type, 3″ tall, $125-150, 4″ tall, $125-150, 2½″ tall 110- 135

Doll Head, 1880s type, china-shoulder-head, white china, blue painted eyes, 4½″ tall 140- 170

135

(continued)

Doll Head, 1880s type,
china-shoulder-head,
white china, blue paint-
ed eyes, 3½" tall 130- 162
Doll Head, 1880s type,
china-shoulder-head,
white china, blue paint-
ed eyes, 2" tall 120- 144

Cloth Dolls

Chase, Martha J., Boy, cloth
stockinet head; molded, oil
painted hair and features,
molded ears, early pink
sateen covered cloth body
with oil painted stockinet
arms and legs, 18½" tall. . . .   245- 270
Chase, Martha J., Baby, cloth
stockinet head; molded, oil
painted hair and features,
molded ears, sateen covered
cloth body with oil painted
stockinet arms and legs, 26"
tall 265- 300
Unmarked, molded cloth head
covered with silk stockinet,
mohair wig, painted eyes,
cloth body with mache
hands, 26" tall, pair 425- 525
Kamkins, molded cloth head;
mohair wig, oil painted features, all cloth body, jointed
at hips and shoulders, 21"
tall 230- 260
Chase (?) (similar to Martha
Case except a finer finish),
cloth stockinet head; mohair
wig, molded, oil painted features, molded ears, sateen
body with oil painted stock-
inet arms and legs, 20½" tall   225- 270
Chase, Martha J., Toddler,
cloth stockinet head; molded,
oil painted hair and features,
molded ears, sateen covered
cloth body with oil painted
stockinet arms and legs,
16½" tall 245- 295
Kruger, R. G., Dwarfs, molded
mask face with painted features, velveteen body; tag
reads AUTHENTIC WALT
DISNEY CHARACTER,
exclusive with R. G.
KRUGER New York. 12"
tall, each 95- 135
Lenci, molded felt head, mohair
wig, painted eyes; felt, straw-
stuffed body, jointed at hips
and shoulders. All original.
Boy marked #300J, girl's
tag missing, 18" tall 240- 285

Lenci, all felt, swivel head;
yarn-like hair sewed into felt
in rows, molded/painted
features with side glancing
eyes; body jointed shoulders
and hips. Paper tags on
dress, MODELLO DEPO-
SITATO LENCI TORINO
made in Italy. 19" tall 240- 285
Lenci, molded felt head, mohair
wig, felt, straw-stuffed body,
jointed at hips and shoulders.
All original including tags.
Marked boy #300/10, girl
#300/34, 18" tall each 240- 290
Lenci, Troubadour & Dancer,
all felt, swivel head; molded/
painted hair and features,
body jointed shoulders and
hips, stitched knee. Paper
tag says LENCI di E.
SCAVINI Made in Italy
N 161. All original, 25" tall
each 265- 295
Lenci, Flapper, molded felt
head, painted eyes; felt,
straw-stuffed body, jointed
at hips and shoulders. Orig-
inal costume, 25" tall 270- 310

Steiner, Jules Nicholas, bisque
socket head marked J.
STEINER Bte S.G.D.G.F.I.
re A 13; human hair wig,
paperweight eyes, closed
mouth; mache/wood jointed
body. 20½" tall (ill.) $2,200-2,600

Unmarked, early molded cloth
head, molded/painted hair
(1840s type), painted eyes,
all cloth body, 21" tall 345- 385
Unmarked, German Peasant
Girl, cloth head; molded/oil
painted features, cloth body.
All originals, 12" tall 165- 185
Unmarked, all printed cloth
boy with printed clothes.
Box in hip pocket marked
QUAKER CRACKELS, 15"
tall 120- 140
Unmarked, all printed cloth
doll, 11" tall 65- 85
Unmarked, Orphan Annie, all
cloth doll with painted
features, mohair wig. All
original, 16½" tall 120- 140
Unmarked, all printed cloth doll
with printed clothes. Marked
on body, My Name is Miss
Flaked Rice, 25½" tall. 122- 145

Walker, Izannah, molded cloth
shoulder-head, oil painted
hair and features, all cloth
body with oil painted hands,
16½" tall 1,900-2,200
Wellings, Norah, Jack Tar,
felt head, molded/painted
features, all cloth body;
marked on foot, Made in
England by Norah Wellings,
10½" tall 68- 83

Composition Dolls
Alexander Doll Company,
compo swivel head, marked
MADAME ALEXANDER
SONJA HENIE; mohair wig,
glasslike eyes, open mouth;
compo jointed body, 17½"
tall 135- 165

Jumeau, bisque socket head
marked TETE JUMEAU 8;
human hair wig, paper-
weight eyes, open mouth;
mache/wood jointed body
marked BEBE JUMEAU
Diplome d'Honneur; has
mama-papa pull cords,
walking mechanism. 17"
tall (ill.) $2,800-3,200

Kammer & Reinhart, "Char-
acter," bisque socket head
marked 11 K (star) R SIMON
HALBIG 115/A; mohair wig,
glass sleep eyes, closed
pouty mouth; mache/wood
jointed body 12½" tall (ill.) . $1,400-1,650

(continued)

Alexander Doll Company, compo swivel head, marked PRINCESS ELIZABETH ALEXANDER DOLL CO.; mohair wig, glasslike sleep eyes, open mouth, compo jointed body, 17″ tall 145- 180

Alexander, Madame, "Sonja Henie" all compo, swivel head, marked MADAME ALEXANDER SONJA HENIE; mohair wig, plastic sleep eyes, open mouth, body jointed shoulders and hips, 18″ tall 140- 175

Alexander Doll Company, compo swivel head, marked MADAME ALEXANDER SONJA HENIE; mohair wig, glasslike sleep eyes, open mouth, compo jointed body, 21″ tall 148- 178

Alexander, Madame, all compo, swivel head, marked X (in a circle); human hair wig, plastic sleep eyes, open mouth; body marked 13, jointed shoulders and hips, 13″ tall 120- 155

Alexander, Madame, "Dionne Quints," all compo, swivel head, marked "DIONNE" ALEXANDER; molded/painted hair, plastic sleep eyes, open/closed mouth; jointed baby body marked MADAME ALEXANDER. All original, mint condition, 10″ long, 9½″ head circumference, set 650- 800

Alexander Doll Company, compo flange head, marked MADAME ALEXANDER; molded/painted hair, glasslike sleep eyes, open mouth; cloth body with compo arms and legs. All original, 24″ tall 140- 170

Foreign, in Native Costume
Haiti, Black Woman, all painted wood, jointed at hips and shoulders, 9″ tall 48- 58

Hungary, boy has mache head, molded/painted hair and features; girl has silky, fine, thread-type hair, molded/painted features; both have all cloth bodies with stitched fingers; oilcloth shoes on boy, woolen shoes on girl. All original, 9″ tall, each 33- 47

Ireland, Nu-Art-Dolls, marked Georgene Novelties, Inc., U.S.A.; all cloth, yarn-type hair, molded/painted features. All original, 14″ tall .... 52- 62 pair

India, Dancer; all cloth, thread-type hair, molded/painted features; painted/stitched fingers and toes. All original 12″ tall 48- 60

Italy, Musician; cloth head, silky threadlike hair, molded/painted features, hard plastic unjointed body. Original clothes with paper tag, 6″ tall 32- 42

Italy, cloth head, fine, thread-type hair, molded/painted features; cloth body with plastic hands. All original, 8″ tall 30- 40

Japan, Crawling Baby, mache bobbing head, human hair wig, inset glass eyes, closed mouth; cardboard body with mache arms and legs, 8″ long 70- 90

Japan, Geisha Girl, mache head, human hair wig, inset glass eyes, closed mouth; cloth/cardboard body with mache hands and feet, 8¼″ tall 33- 46

French Bisque, Children
Gaultier (probably), bisque socket head marked F. G. inside scroll; human hair wig, paperweight eyes, closed mouth; mache/wood jointed body 23″ tall 925-1,100

Gaultier & Fils (probably), bisque socket head marked F6G; human hair wig, paperweight eyes, closed mouth; mache/wood jointed body, 15″ tall 690- 770

Gaultier & Fils (?), Bapteme or Christening doll, bisque socket head marked F. G. (in a scroll) 6; human hair wig, paperweight eyes, closed mouth; mache torso and arms jointed at shoulders, bisque hands; mache lower portion container for sweetmeats. "Paul" ink-stamped on bib, 12″ tall 800- 900

Gesland, bisque swivel head marked F 5 G; mohair wig (probably original), paperweight eyes, closed mouth; stockinette covered body, mark stamped on back, (first words or letters not readable). F. GESLAND Brevette S.G.D.G. 5 Rue Berange PARIS; wood shoulderplate, arms and legs jointed, 17″ tall   1,400-1,600

Jullien, Jr., bisque socket head marked JULLIEN 12 human hair wig, paperweight eyes, closed mouth; mache/wood jointed body, 30″ tall . .   1,550-1,900

Jullien, Jr., bisque socket head marked JULLIEN 8 importe; human hair wig, glass sleep eyes, open mouth; mache/wood jointed body marked with paper label, BEBE L'UNIVERSEL INCASSABLE; mama-papa pull cords, 23″ tall 700- 825

Jumeau, bisque socket head marked DEPOSE TETE JUMEAU Bte S.G.D.-G. 15; human hair wig, paperweight eyes, closed mouth, applied pierced ears; mache/wood jointed body marked BEBE JUMEAU Diplome d'Honneur, 33″ tall   1,700-1,950

Jumeau, bisque socket head marked DEPOSE TETE JUMEAU Bte S.G.D.-G. 6 (red check marks); human hair wig, paperweight eyes, closed mouth; mache/wood jointed body marked JUMEAU MEDAILLE D'OR PARIS; mama-papa pull cords, 16″ tall   975-1,200

Jumeau, bisque socket head marked Depose TETE JUMEAU Bte SGDG; human hair wig, inset paperweight eyes, closed mouth; mache/wood jointed body marked JUMEAU MEDAILLE D'OR PARIS, 19½″ tall   925-1,100

Jumeau, bisque socket head marked DEPOSE TETE JUMEAU Bte S.G.D.-G. 6; (red check marks); human hair wig, paperweight eyes, closed mouth; mache/wood jointed body marked BEBE JUMEAU Depose d'honneur, 15″ tall   950-1,200

Jumeau, bisque socket head marked 1907 16; human hair wig, paperweight eyes, open mouth; mache/wood jointed body, 33″ tall   850-1,100

Jumeau, bisque socket head marked Depose TETE JUMEAU Bte SGDG; human hair wig, inset paperweight eyes, closed mouth; mache/wood jointed body marked JUMEAU MEDAILLE D'OR PARIS, 18½″ tall   2,300-2,700

Jumeau, bisque socket head marked DEPOSE TETE JUMEAU Bte S.G.D.-G. 2 H8; human hair wig, paperweight eyes, closed mouth; mache/wood jointed body, 11″ tall, RARE SIZE   950-1,150

Jumeau, Portrait, pale bisque socket head, unmarked; human hair wig, inset paperweight eyes, closed mouth; mache/wood jointed body marked JUMEAU MEDAILLE D'OR PARIS, 16″ tall   1,000-1,300

Steiner, Jules Nicholas, "Phenix," bisque socket head marked five pointed star 92; human hair wig, paperweight eyes, closed mouth; mache/wood jointed body; mama-papa pull cords, 22″ tall   2,400-2,600

Tiburee, Alexandre Celestin, "Bebe Mothereau," bisque socket head marked B.M.; human hair wig, paperweight eyes, closed mouth; mache/wood jointed body, 23″ tall . .   2,200-2,400

Steiner, Jules Nicholas, bisque socket head marked STEINER Bte S.G.D.G. Sie C 3 BOURGOIN Jne; human hair wig, wire handle at crown of head behind ear opens and closes the glass eyes; closed mouth; mache/wood jointed body, 20″ tall . .   2,250-2,550

(continued)

Unmarked, Bru Type, bisque
swivel head on bisque
shoulder plate; mohair wig,
glass sleep eyes, open/closed
mouth with five molded
teeth; kid body with bisque
arms, 19½″ tall 2,300-2,600

French Bisque, Fashion

Gaultier (probably), French
Fashion, bisque swivel head;
mohair wig, paperweight
eyes, closed mouth; bisque
shoulder plate marked F.G.;
kid gusseted adult body with
individually wired and
stitched fingers, 12½″ tall .. 855- 925
Jumeau, bisque socket head
marked X over 7; human hair
wig, paperweight eyes, open
mouth; mache/wood jointed
adult body marked BEBE
JUMEAU Diplome d'Hon-
neur, 22″ tall............. 765- 845
Rohmer, untinted Parian type
bisque swivel head; mohair
wig, paperweight eyes, closed
mouth; bisque shoulder
plate and arms; kid/wood
body and legs, marked on
stomach MME ROHMER
BREVETE S.G.D.G. PARIS
(in an oval); typical two eyelet
holes below the mark, jointed
shoulders and hips, 16″ tall . 3,200-3,650
Unmarked, French Fashion,
bisque socket head; human
hair wig, paperweight eyes,
closed mouth; adult kid
body, fingers individually
wired and stitched, bisque
shoulder plate, 33″ tall 2,700-3,100
Unmarked, French Fashion,
Parian quality bisque
shoulder head; mohair wig,
paperweight eyes, closed
mouth, head bent forward
looking down; kid body,
individually wired and
stitched fingers, 15″ tall 795- 865

German Bisque, Babies

Bahr & Proschild, bisque
socket head marked 604
(over) 5; mohair wig, glass
sleep eyes, open mouth;
mache jointed baby body.
13″ long, 11″ head
circumference 320- 355

Borgfeldt, Geo., & Company,
"Character," bisque socket
head marked G 326 B A 3
M.D.R.G.M. 259; molded/
painted hair, glass sleep
eyes, open mouth; mache
jointed baby body 14″ long,
9½″ head circumference 325- 450
Company Unidentified,
"Character," breather baby,
bisque socket head marked
Made in Germany 100/12;
human hair wig, glass sleep
eyes, open nostrils, open
mouth, oscillating tongue;
mache/wood jointed baby
body. 23″ long, 15″ head
circumference 500- 575
Gans, Otto, bisque socket head
marked OTTO GANS
Germany 975 A. 11. M.;
human hair wig, glass sleep
eyes, open mouth; mache/
wood jointed baby body.
22″ long, 14″ head circumference 395- 455
Heubach, Ernst, bisque socket
head marked Heubach Kop-
plesdorf 300 19/0 Germany;
mohair wig, glass sleep eyes,
open mouth; mache jointed
baby body, 7″ long, 5½″
head circumference 195- 245
Heubach, Ernst, "Character,"
bisque socket head marked
HEUBACH-KOPPELS-
DORF 300 • 3 Germany;
human hair wig, glass sleep
eyes, open mouth; mache/
wood jointed baby body. 18″
long, 13″ head circumference 410- 510
Heubach, Ernst, "Character,"
bisque socket head marked
HEUBACH-KOPPELS-
DORF 300 7/0 Germany;
human hair wig, glass sleep
eyes, open mouth; mache/
wood jointed baby body.
12½″ long, 9½″ head
circumference 310- 410
Kestner, J. D., Jr., Hilda,
"Character," bisque socket
head marked Made in F
Germany 10 237 J D K Jr.
1914 c (in circle) Hilda
Gesgesh N. 1070; mohair
wig, glass sleep eyes, open
mouth; mache/wood jointed
baby body. 12″ long, 10″
head circumference 745- 820

Kestner, J. D., Jr., "Character," bisque socket head marked J. D. K. Made in 17 Germany; molded/painted hair, glass sleep eyes, open mouth; mache/wood jointed baby body. 22″ long, 16″ head circumference 575- 675

Kestner, J. D., Jr., "Character," bisque socket head marked J. D. K. Made in Germany; painted hair, glass sleep eyes, open mouth; mache jointed baby body. 14½″ long, 11″ head circumference 340- 400

Kestner, J. D., Jr., "Character," bisque socket head marked Made in Germany 152 4; mohair wig, glass sleep eyes, open mouth; mache jointed baby body. 12″ long, 10″ head circumference 320- 385

Kley & Hahn, "Character," bisque socket head marked K & H (in a streamer) Germany 167-15; human hair wig, glass sleep eyes, open mouth; mache/wood jointed baby body. 26″ long, 17″ head circumference 625- 700

Marseille, Armand, bisque socket head marked Germany 341/3K. A.M.; painted hair, glass sleep eyes, closed mouth; mache jointed baby body. 9″ long, 7½″ head circumference 260- 325

Marseille, Armand, bisque flange head marked A. M. Germany 347-19; painted hair, glass sleep eyes, closed mouth; cloth body with bisque (replacement) hands. 13″ long, 9″ head circumference 225- 275

Marseille, Armand, brown bisque socket head marked ARMAND MARSEILLE Germany 990 A 7/0 M; human hair wig, glass sleep eyes, open mouth; brown mache/wood jointed baby body. 11″ long, 7½″ head circumference 295- 335

German Bisque, Children

Company Unidentified, "Dollar Princess" bisque socket head marked THE DOLLAR PRINCESS 62 SPECIAL made in Germany; mohair wig, glass sleep eyes, open

mouth; mache/wood jointed body, 25″ tall 240- 260

Goebel, William, bisque socket head marked "W.G." (intertwined) 120 3 Germany (in a rectangle); human hair wig, glass sleep eyes, open mouth; mache/wood jointed body, 16″ tall 225- 300

Handwerk, Heinrich, bisque socket head marked 109-11 Germany Handwerk 2½; mohair wig, glass sleep eyes, open mouth; mache/wood jointed body. Original costume, 21″ tall 300- 375

Handwerck, Heinrich, bisque socket head marked 11½″ 99 DEP HANDWERCK 3; human hair wig, glass sleep eyes, open mouth; mache/wood jointed body, 21″ tall . . 325- 395

Handwerck, Heinrich, bisque shoulder head marked Hch 3/0 H. Germany; human hair wig, glass inset eyes, open mouth; kid body with bisque arms, 19″ tall 230- 265

Handwerck, Max, bisque socket head marked 30 H (K over 3 inside the H); human hair wig, glass inset eyes, open mouth; mache/wood jointed body, 24½″ tall 260- 285

Marseille, Armand, bisque socket head marked ARMAND MARSEILLE Germany 390 A. 6 M.; human hair wig, glass sleep eyes, open mouth; mache/wood jointed body, 23″ tall . . 325- 400

Marseille, Armand, "Floradora," bisque shoulder head marked FLORADORA A.M. -6-DRP made in Germany; mohair wig, glass inset eyes, fur eyebrows inserted in slits in bisque, open mouth; kid body, bisque hands, 24″ tall . 290- 325

Mon Tresor, bisque socket head marked MON TRESOR Germany 10; human hair wig, glass inset eyes, open mouth; mache/wood jointed body, 23″ tall 550- 610

Recknagel, Th., bisque socket head marked R/A DEP 12/0; solid dome, mohair wig, glass inset eyes, open mouth; mache body, jointed shoulders and hips, painted shoes and socks, 8″ tall 200- 250

(continued)

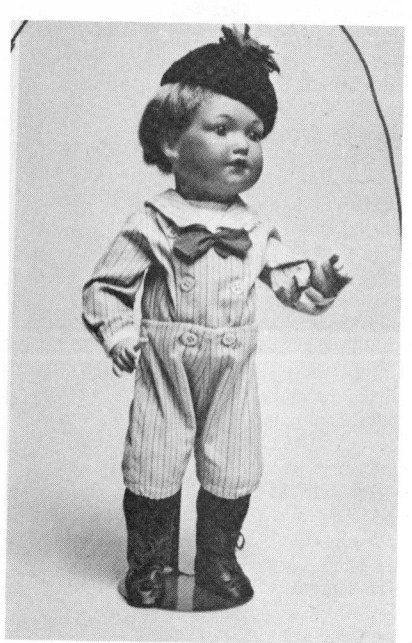

Marseille, Armand,
"Character," bisque socket
head marked ARMAND
MARSEILLE 971 Germany
A 3 M; human hair wig,
glass inset eyes, open mouth;
mache/wood jointed body.
17″ tall (ill.) $1,000-1,250

Heubach Figurine, all bisque,
unmarked; molded/painted
hair, features, and clothes;
intaglio eyes. 12½″ tall (ill.) $1,300-1,650

Recknagel, Th., bisque socket
head marked 1909 D E P R 2
A; mohair wig, glass sleep
eyes, open mouth; cardboard
body with mache arms and
legs. Original costume, 18″
tall 240- 265

Schmidt, Paul, bisque shoulder
head marked Germany P.
Sch 1899 6; human hair wig,
glass inset eyes, open mouth;
kid gusseted body, bisque
hands, 22″ tall 340- 375

Simon & Halbig, bisque socket
head marked S H 1078;
human hair wig, glass sleep
eyes, open mouth; mache/
wood jointed body, 26″ tall .. 445- 495

Simon & Halbig, bisque socket
head marked 12 SH 1039
D E P; human hair wig, glass
sleep eyes, open mouth;
mache/wood jointed body,
24″ tall 460- 550

Simon & Halbig, bisque
shoulder head marked 10 SH
8; human hair wig stationary
glass eyes, open mouth; kid/
cloth body with bisque arms,
17″ tall 410- 485

German Bisque, Naughty Nudies

Bisque Nude Girl, marked 40 V;
mohair wig, molded/painted
features, molded pink
slippers. 3½″ tall 160- 185

Bisque Girl, mohair wig,
molded/painted features,
molded white slippers;
marked 400 L, 5″ long 130- 145

Bisque Girl, mohair wig,
molded/painted features,
molded blue slippers, marked
405 J, 6″ long 175- 198

Bisque Girl with kitten, unmarked; molded/painted hair,
features and clothes, 5″ long   155- 175

Bisque Nude Girl, marked
405R; silk net over mohair
wig, molded/painted features,
molded pink slippers, 4" tall .   162- 192
Bisque Nude Girl, marked
2829 Germany; molded/
painted hair, features, cap
and slippers (rust), 3" long ..   110- 140
Bisque Nude Girl, marked 2829
Germany; molded/painted
hair, features, cap and
slippers (blue), 3" long 90- 115

Mechanical Dolls
Lanternier, A & Cie, walking
doll with spring windup cart;
bisque swivel head marked
MON CHERI PARIS 03 on
bisque shoulder plate; human
hair wig, inset pupil-less
glass eyes, open/closed
mouth with molded teeth;
cloth body with bisque arms
and metal jointed legs, 10½"
tall 2,350-2,750
Limoges Peasant Cart, key
windup boy pulls girl in cart
(she shakes bell on stick); girl
has bisque socket head
marked S & H Germany,
mohair wig, inset glass eyes,
closed mouth, mache body
with bisque arms; boy has
bisque socket head marked
Germany S & H Simon
Halbig. All original, 12" tall   1,950-2,400
Unmarked Mechanical, mache
head, human hair wig, glass
eyes, closed mouth; brass
body with mache arms, legs
and violin; mechanism in
body connected to music box.
When wound, head turns,
eyes roll, arm with bow
moves as if playing; music
box plays three melodies,
18" tall (overall) 1,400-1,750
Wolf, Louis & Company,
"Mechanical," bisque socket
head marked L. W. & CO.
12 11/0; mohair wig, glass
inset eyes, open mouth;
mache body, jointed
shoulders and hips with wind
key; wooden rocker rocked
by flip lever. 10" tall
(overall)................   800-1,000

Metal Dolls
Heller, Alfred, metal shoulder
head marked DIANA DEP
(in a square); molded/painted

hair, painted eyes, closed
mouth; cloth body with
bisque arms, 12½" tall 85- 110
Juno (head only), metal
shoulder head marked
JUNO; molded/painted hair
and features, 6" tall 80- 100
Juno, metal shoulder head
marked JUNO; molded/
painted hair, painted eyes,
closed mouth; kid body with
bisque arms, 16½" tall 110- 140
Juno (head only), metal
shoulder head marked
JUNO; wig missing, glass
sleep eyes, open mouth, 6"
tall 82- 102
Minerva, metal shoulder head
marked MINERVA Ger-
many; molded/painted hair,
painted eyes, closed mouth;
all cloth body, 10" tall......   80- 100

Miscellaneous Materials
Plaster-Bisque, swivel head
marked 463 17/0; mohair
topknot, inset pupil-less,
glass googlie eyes, open
mouth, brass rings in nose
and ears and around neck;
mache body jointed at hips
and shoulders. Original
grass skirt, 7" long 200- 275
Plaster-Bisque, flange head
with molded/painted hair and
features; all cloth body.
Original clothes, 5¼" tall ...   28- 38

Plaster-Bisque, swivel head
with molded/painted hair and
features; body same
material, jointed at hips and
shoulders, 7" tall 62- 75
Plaster, "W.P.A. Project
Dolls," molded plaster heads,
mohair wig, painted features;
cotton wound, wire armature
bodies with plaster arms and
legs. All original, 9½",
15½", 16", group 250- 285
Porcelain "Mickey Mouse," all
porcelain with molded/
painted features and clothes;
paper sticker, C (in circle)
1960 WALT DISNEY
PRODUCTS, INC.........   62- 72

Rawhide, African (?), jointed at
hips and shoulders, molded
asphalt hair, inset bead eyes,
brass ring in nostril. Primi-
tive museum piece, 8" tall ..   260- 270

143

(continued)

Rawhide, "Darrow's Rawhide Head," molded/painted features and hair, 6¼″ tall 260- 295

Rawhide, "Darrow's Rawhide Head," molded/painted features and hair, 4½″ tall 225- 295

Soap, "Shirley Temple," all soap, unmarked; molded/painted hair and features; molded arms, legs and dress, 5½″ tall 22- 33

Terra-Cotta shoulder head, unmarked; molded/painted hair with ribbon and bow, molded/painted features; new cloth body with bisque arms and legs, 13″ tall 170- 210

Pincushion Dolls

China Pincushion marked 6102 Germany; molded/painted hair with ribbon, features, and clothes, 2¾″ tall 70- 80

China Pincushion marked 74500 Made in Germany; molded/painted hair, features, and clothes, 4″ tall ... 77- 87

China Pincushion marked 5230 Germany; molded/painted hair, features, and clothes, 3″ tall 65- 80

China Pincushion, unmarked; molded/painted hair and features, 6″ tall.......... 70- 77

China Pincushion marked Germany; molded/painted spit-curls, features, and collar. 1¾″ tall.......... 82- 92

China Pincushion marked Germany 2352; molded/painted hair, features, bonnet, and clothes, 3¾″ tall 82- 94

China Pincushion marked 5468; molded/painted hair with ribbon/flowers, and features, 2″ tall.......... 71- 81

China Pincushion marked 6233 Germany; molded/painted hair with comb, features, and clothes, 3″ tall 69- 79

Plastic and Vinyl Dolls

Alexander, Madame, "Kathy," all soft vinyl, swivel head marked MME 1958 ALEXANDER; molded/painted hair, plastic sleep eyes, closed mouth, nursing hole; jointed baby body. All original. 16″ long, 11½″ head circumference........ 84- 104

Alexander, Madame, hard plastic swivel head, unmarked; synthetic wig, plastic sleep eyes, closed mouth; hard plastic body, jointed at hips and shoulders, "Walking" legs, turns head, 14½″ tall 80- 95

Alexander, Madame, "Elise," all hard plastic except soft vinyl over-sleeved arms, swivel head marked ALEXANDER; synthetic wig, plastic sleep eyes, closed mouth; body marked MME. ALEXANDER; jointed shoulders, elbows, hips, knees, and ankles. All original, 16″ tall 84- 104

Alexander, Madame, "Cissette," all hard plastic swivel head, synthetic wig, plastic sleep eyes, closed mouth; body marked MME. ALEXANDER; jointed shoulders/hips above knee, 9″ tall 48- 60

Alexander, Madame, "Jacqueline," vinyl swivel head marked ALEXANDER Co. 1961; rooted hair, plastic sleep eyes, closed mouth; vinyl body, jointed at hips and shoulders, 21″ tall 140- 170

Alexander, Madame, "Little Genius," hard plastic swivel head; synthetic wig, plastic sleep eyes, open mouth/nurser; soft vinyl jointed baby body. All original with paper tag and dress label— LITTLE GENIUS by Madame Alexander, 7″ long . 55- 78

Alexander, Madame, "Little Granny," soft vinyl swivel head marked ALEXANDER 1965; synthetic rooted hair, plastic sleep eyes, closed mouth; soft vinyl arms, hard vinyl torso and legs, jointed shoulders and hips. All original, 13″ tall 60- 73

Alexander, Madame, "Little Mary Sunshine," soft vinyl swivel head marked ALEXANDER 1961; synthetic rooted hair, plastic sleep eyes, open/closed mouth; soft vinyl arms, hard vinyl torso and legs, jointed shoulders and hips. All original, 14″ tall 75- 95

Alexander, Madame, "Madame Doll," soft vinyl swivel head marked ALEXANDER 1965; rooted synthetic hair, plastic sleep eyes, closed mouth; hard vinyl body, jointed shoulders, hips and knees. All original, 14″ tall . 74- 93

American Character Doll Company, "Tiny Tears," hard plastic swivel head marked AMERICAN CHARACTER DOLL PAT. NO. 2.675.644; synthetic hair rooted in skull cap, plastic sleep eyes, open/closed mouth with nursing hole; all rubber jointed baby body. 15½″ long, 13″ head circumference 85- 105

Company Unidentified, all latex compo, swivel head marked STEHA (in an elongated diamond) DRP 839466; synthetic wig, "flirting" sleep eyes, closed mouth; jointed body and voice box, 21″ tall 61- 74

Company Unidentified, all hollow rubber with molded/painted hair, features, and clothes. Marked Made in France (in a circle), 9½″ tall . 18- 28

Seiberling Latex, "Dopey," all latex marked "DOPEY" (on hat) c (in circle) WALT DISNEY SEIBERLING LATEX MADE IN AKRON, O. U.S.A. (marked on back), 5½″ tall 28- 38

Sun Rubber Company, all hollow rubber with molded/painted hair, features, and clothes. Marked Ruth E. Newton The Sun Rubber Co., 8½″ tall 14- 24

Unmarked, Early American Rubber Doll (possibly gutta percha mixture), rubber shoulder head; molded/painted hair, painted eyes, closed mouth; cloth body with leather arms, 18″ tall . . 265- 300

Wax Dolls
Unmarked, solid wax shoulder head and arms (head and arms molded in one piece); mohair wig, inset pupil-less eyes, closed mouth; cloth body with solid wax legs. All original, 9″ long 168- 190

Unmarked, Novelty Doll-Candy Container, poured wax head; inset glass eyes, birdlike fur body with metal feet; head comes off to open container, 5″ tall 115- 140

Unmarked, French Novelty, poured wax baby head, arms, and legs, painted features; mache egg. All original, 5¼″ tall 400- 475

Unmarked, wax-over-mache head; mohair wig inserted in slot in head, inset pupil-less glass eyes, closed mouth; cloth, straw-stuffed body with kid arms, 15″ tall 250- 310

Unmarked, wax-over-mache head; molded hair and ribbon, inset pupil-less glass eyes, closed mouth; cloth, straw-stuffed body with mache arms, 15″ tall 245- 260

Unmarked, wax-over-mache head; molded hair and ribbon, inset pupil-less glass eyes, closed mouth; cloth, straw-stuffed body with mache arms, molded/painted mache legs, 17½″ tall 245- 255

Unmarked, wax-over-mache head; mohair wig in original setting, glass sleep eyes, closed mouth, pierced ears; cloth, straw-stuffed body with wax-over-mache arms; mache legs with molded/painted shoes. Mint condition, 17½″ tall 240- 270

Wooden Dolls
Schoenhut, Albert, wood swivel head; mohair wig, decal eyes, open/closed mouth; wood body with metal spring joints marked SCHOENHUT DOLL Pat. Jan. 17'11 U.S.A. and Foreign Countries, boy, 19½″ tall 450- 575

Schoenhut, Albert, wood swivel head; mohair wig, decal eyes, open/closed mouth; wood body with metal spring joints; marked SCHOENHUT DOLL Pat. Jan. 17'11, U.S.A. and Foreign Countries, girl, 19½″ tall 450- 550

Schoenhut, Albert, wood swivel head; mohair wig, painted intaglio eyes, closed mouth; wood body with

145

(continued)

metal spring joints marked SCHOENHUT DOLL Pat. Jan. 17'11, U.S.A. and Foreign Countries, boy, 19" tall 345- 415

Schoenhut, Albert, wood swivel head; mohair wig, painted eyes, open/closed mouth; wood body with metal spring joints marked SCHOEN-HUT DOLL Pat. Jan. 17'11, U.S.A. and Foreign Countries, girl, 16" tall 425- 475

Schoenhut, Albert, "Character Toddler," wood swivel head; mohair wig, painted eyes, closed mouth; wood body with metal spring joints marked SCHOENHUT DOLL Pat. Jan. 17'11, U.S.A. and Foreign Countries, 16½" tall 350- 415

Unmarked Early Peg-Wooden, all wood; gesso/painted hair and features with tuck comb; peg-jointed at hips, shoulders, elbows, and knees, 2¼" tall 220- 266

Unmarked, Chinese Man, wooden head; carved/painted features, painted black hair with human hair pigtail in back, cloth body. All original, 8½" tall............ 85- 110

Unmarked, Early Peg-Wooden, all wood, gesso/painted hair and features with tuck comb; peg-jointed at hips, shoulders, elbows, and knees, 3" tall 295- 325

Door Knockers

Door Knockers

These have been around for hundreds of years and are made of wood, metal, even glass. Iron and brass were the most popular types, in animal heads, other forms.

Brass, American Eagle, 1800s (ill.)	$265-300
Brass, dog's head, 7" high, old .	55- 67
Brass, fox head, 8" high	50- 60
Brass, hand holding ball	60- 70
Brass, horse's head, flowing mane, dated 1845	130-150
Brass, jaguar growling, 8" high	55- 67
Brass, lion with ring in mouth, French, 1800s	128-150
Iron, cat's head, smiling, 4" high	24- 34
Iron, gloved hand	40- 48
Iron, hand, fist-shaped, 8" high, old	28- 38
Iron, hammer	35- 45
Iron, horseshoe	28- 38
Iron, spur hits metal block on wooden board	39- 50
Grecian bust, head only, bronze, 4½" high	60- 78
Iron, horseshoe hitting hammer head, 1930s	33- 43
Pewter (?), hand holding ball, 1920s	24- 36
Spur	33- 50

Doorstops

Doorstops

Made of many materials. Metal stops in the shapes of animals, buildings, were used for propping open doors. Particularly popular in the 1920s.

Cottage, iron, 5¾" high	$ 22- 32
Dogs: Airedale, Bulldog, Chow, German Shepherd, etc.	38- 45
"Fala," FDR on side, 10" high .	38- 43
Flower basket, cast iron (ill.) ...	18- 27
Flowerpot, cast iron, enameled, 7¼" high (ill.)	19- 29
Frog, iron, webbed feet, 15" high	27- 37
Horse pulling cart, iron, 6½" high	27- 35

Horse, rearing, lead base, 1930s	25-	35
Lady, cast iron, enameled (ill.)	14-	23
Lion, painted, 15″ high	30-	38
Parrot, red/yellow/green, 10″ high	33-	43
Polo player on horse, 9″ high	26-	35
Rabbit, iron, 11″ high	37-	46
Ship, Mayflower, cast iron	37-	47
Sunbonnet girl, 6½″ high	30-	35
Squirrel, iron 11″ high	37-	47
Wagon train, horse, 10″ high	38-	45
Wolf, on leash, iron	32-	42

Dorflinger Glass

Dorflinger Glass

Christian Dorflinger founded his first factory at White Mills, Pennsylvania, in 1865, having come from Alsace, France, in 1846 to learn the American glass trade. He also operated a factory in Brooklyn, New York, from 1852 until the late 1880s when J. S. Hibbler took over all the firm's interests. The "Kalana Lily" pattern shown here is but one of the many fine examples of glass made by one of the greatest glassmakers in the world. It's of interest to know that Mr. Dorflinger brought the great Nicholas Lutz to America in 1860.

Doulton Pottery

Doulton Pottery

In the mid-1850s Henry Doulton's partner, John Watts, retired and Mr. Doulton continued the firm as Doulton and Company. From the 1850s until just before 1900, his wares were marked Doulton Lambeth. After 1901, Royal was added to the firm's name, without the Lambeth. See ROYAL DOULTON in this Guide. Salt-glazed stoneware was just one of the many fine types of pottery made at Doulton.

Biscuit, jar, 1880s	$150-170
Bowl, flowers, gold trim, artist-signed	87- 97
Ewer, blue scrolling, floral decor, 9″ high	49- 59
Ink bottle, slipware finish	27- 37
Mug, probably for ale, tan/ brown, artist Hannah Barlow	62- 73
Mustard pot, blues, brown, 1883	72- 82
Pitcher, hunting scenes, tan/ brown	68- 78
Pitcher, (ill.), Columbian Exposition, 1893	110-125
Plate, Dickensware, Tom Pinch	58- 68
Plate, Melrose, 9″ dia.	38- 45
Plate, varicolored flowers, 1884, 10″ diameter	32- 43
Plate, tavern scene, artist M. Aitken, 9″ diameter	50- 60
Tray, Dickensware, signed Noke	92-107
Vase, multicolored, 8″ high	63- 74
Vase, hunting scene, 1870s	65- 75
Whiskey jug, marked JRD and Fine Old Scotch Whiskey	145-155

Dresden China

In the early 1700s Johann Bottger invented the first porcelain in Europe that was considered quality. His factory was at the Royal Saxon Porcelain Works at Meissen, Germany. His work was finely decorated in exquisite shapes, often with raised enamel flowers. The famous crossed swords in blue are known throughout the world. Unfortunately the factory is now behind the Iron Curtain. Most of the Dresden in the U.S. was brought in by importers in the late 19th century.

Basket, floral decor, twisted handle, 7″ high	$ 95-	140
Bowl, flowers, hand-painted, gold trim, 10″	88-	110

147

(continued)

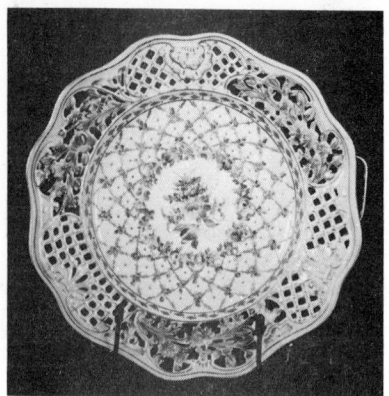

Dresden China

Box, open latticework, silver mounts	345- 400
Candelabra, 6-candle, 22" high, boy/girl, blue ground, flowers, pair	950-1,250
Candleholder, pink-applied roses, 14" high	88- 98
Chocolate pot, cobalt, gold border, miniature roses	235-250
Compote, reticulated, 11" high, pair	445-475
Cup/saucer, floral designs overall	82- 100
Figurine, cupids, flowers, 8¼" high, pair	290-340
Lamp, applied flowers, square base, early	350- 475
Plate, pink floral decor, 9" dia., reticulated border (ill.)	40- 50
Plate, reticulated border, cherubs	64- 74
Plate, deep, ribbed, blue/yellow decor, signed Villeroy and Boch	70- 90
Tea caddy, flowers/roses, gold, blue Crown under glaze	85- 115
Teapot, roses with thorns, leaves, gold, blue Crown	145- 175
Urn, battle scene, 16" high, pair, old mark	130- 150
Vase, floral decor, white ground, 8"	190- 250
Vase, painted birds, signed, 6" high	150-175
Vase, portrait of gentleman, overlay gold decor, 10" high	180-220

Durand Art Glass

Resembling Tiffany in some respects, Durand was made by the Vineland Flint Glass Works in Vineland, New Jersey, around 1924. Victor Durand, founder, put

Durand Art Glass

paper labels on some pieces while others were signed with a V in the pontil. Victor Durand, Jr., ran the factory until his untimely death in 1931. Factory then taken over by Kimble. See Kimble Glass.

Bowl, blue, label, signed	$360-410
Bowl, gold iridescent, signed "V"	190-240
Candleholders, gold lustre, opal and gold, 6" high, signed	215-235
Compote, blue feather pattern, amber base, 7" high	420-460
Decanter, blue, iridescent, signed, 8" high	355-375
Lamp, green, pulled feather design, gold threading, bronze cherub base, electrified (ill.)	240-275
Perfume bottle, orange iridescent, signed DeVilbiss	120-140
Plate, cobalt, peacock feather pattern, cut flowers, 8" diameter	285-295
Rose bowl, green/gold, original paper label	150-165
Shade, gas, white ground, gold/green, calcite interior	115-135
Vase, blue, white, swirls from top to bottom, 9" high	265-300
Vase, peach iridescent, beehive shape, 7½" high	490-575
Vase, green, gold, rose iridescent threading, signed	315-345
Vase, orange, iridescent, blue highlights, 8½" high	350-400
Vase, blue iridescent, orange trim, 8½" high	335-380
Wine glass, blue, white loops, vaseline stem	135-155

Dye Cabinets

These were found in country stores in the

148

Dye Cabinets

late 1800s. They held the many colors of powdered dyes (to be mixed with water) the housewife needed to dye her cloth for dresses, tablecloths, etc.

Dye cabinet, cherry, good portrait on front	$275-350
Dye cabinet, poplar, family scene on front	250-285
Dye cabinet, walnut, hand-painted flowers	275-325

Easter Eggs

Easter Eggs

Usually of blown glass, they were favorites with the children in the mid-1800s. The same type is used to attract hens to a nest. The older types were hand painted, professionally or otherwise.

Easter egg (ill.) 4″ high, hand-blown	$ 30- 40
Easter egg, Russian, 19th century, religious subject	85-100
Easter egg, Polish eagle, dated 1809, flowers	125-150

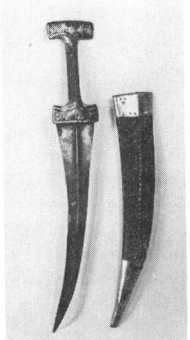

Edged Weapons

Edged Weapons

"On guard!" Two words that brought fear to more than one man. Any and all are collectible and going up in price every day.

Bayonets, W.W. I, ea	$ 45-	55
French officer's small sword, c. 1750, brass hilt, 31″ long . . .	230-	260
British Artillery short sword, c. 1810, brass hilt, 22″ long . . .	228-	255
Knights of Columbus Ceremonial sword, made by Pettis & Ranken, Troy, NY, c. 1925, 29″ long	80-	90
Union Army officer's sword, Civil War	235-	249
British General Officer's sword, silver hilt, c. 1825	875-1,200	
Italian cup hilt rapier, 17th century, 34″ long, double edge blade	230-	270
"Khyber" knife and sheath, pearl handled, 11″ long	140-	185
Balinese kris, 18th century, 16″ meteorite steel blade . . .	240-	260
Deep-sea diver's knife, marked "Siebe Gorman & Co."	72-	92
Australian knuckle-duster fighting knife, WWII, 6½″ long	140-	150
British trench knife, WWI, marked "Robbins-Dudley," 4¼″ long	175-	195
Austrian officer's sword w/sheath, WWI, 29″ single edge blade	158-	172
British prison guard's sword, c. 1850, 22″ curved single edge blade	100-	120
British naval officer's sword, c. 1790, 30″ straight s.e. blade	230-	250
Turkish sword, brass/leather sheath, gilded iron handle, c. 1780 (ill.), 19½″ long	150-	175

(continued)

Indo-Persian fighting knife, c. 1820, 9″ d.e. reverse curved blades	78-	88	
British naval boarding ax, c. 1840-1860, 21″ handle, 10″ iron head	275-	285	
Arabian chieftain's "Jambiya" dagger w/sheath, 9½″ d.e. blade	95-	110	
Ghurka knife ("Kukri"), WWII, 9″ incurved blade, has 2 miniature knives in leather-covered wood case	42-	60	
American Indian pipe tomahawk, c. 1780, 19″ overall	850-1,000		
Spike-tomahawk, c. 1830s, 7″ overall	175-	195	
Confederate cavalry saber and scabbard, 36″ curved s.e. blade	400-	450	
US Navy cutlass, 21″ d.e. blade, marked "U.S.N. 1842-Ames-Cabotville"	280-	290	
American Revolution horseman's saber, 36″ s.e. blade	610-	620	
Revolutionary naval cutlass, 28″ straight s.e. blade	310-	325	
Starr contract 1818 U.S. cavalry saber and scabbard, marked	245-	265	
Special Civil War contract cavalry saber and scabbard, marked "Tiffany & Co.", 36″ curved s.e. blade	345-	370	
U.S. Civil War saber bayonet probably for Merrill Navy rifle	145-	155	

Write to N. Flayderman & Co., Inc., New Milford, Connecticut 06776, for their new catalog if you want to see unbelievable items for sale! Mohawk Arms, Utica, NY 13503, also has some great stuff for sale.

End-of-Day Glass

See SPATTER GLASS.

Engravings, Etchings

If horseracing once was considered the "sport of kings," this category is fast becoming a "collectible of millionaires." The prices being realized at the better auctions are staggering. This is a "for reference only" category.

1. Etching, "Entrance to a Mosque," signed proof, Marius A. J. Bauer, contemporary Dutch etcher, born in 1867
2. Line engraving, "Marie Therese, Queen of France," Nicholas Bazin, French engraver, c. 1636-1706
3. Line engraving, "Pierre Mignard," Jacques Firmin Beauvarlet, French engraver, 1731-1797
4. Etching, "The Punter," proof, signed in pencil, Frank W. Benson, American painter and etcher, born Salem, Massachusetts, 1862
5. Etching, "Three Bargers," proof, signed in ink, Arthur Brisco, English marine painter and etcher
6. Etching and aquatint, "La Place Breda," signed in the plate, Felix Buhot, French etcher, born, Valognes, 1847
7. Etching, "Hotel de Sens," proof, signed in pencil, David Young Cameron, painter-etcher, born, Glasgow, Scotland, 1865
8. Etching, "Leo XIII," signed proof on vellum, C. Chartran
9. Line engraving, "St. Catherine of Alexander," proof before all letters, A.G.L. Desnoyers, French engraver, 1779-1857
10. Engraving, "Apollo and Diana," signed in the plate, Albrecht Durer, 1471-1528; one of Germany's greatest artists.
11. Etching, "The Violin Player," signed in the plate, Cornelius Dusart, Dutch painter-etcher, 1660-1704
12. Etching, "Spring Freshets," Kerry Eby, American etcher, 1889
13. Etching, "Lourdes — La Paralytique," proof, signed in pencil, Jean Louis Forain, French painter, etcher, lithographer, 1852-1931
14. Line engraving, "La Madonna Della Seggiola," proof before letters, G. Garavaglia
15. Etching, "Burgos Cathedral: Interior," signed proof, Axel Herman Haig, Swedish etcher, 1835-1921

Engravings, Etchings

"Night in Ely Cathedral"

16. Etching, "Walt Whitman's House," proof, signed in pencil, Childe Hassam, American painter, etcher, born 1859
17. Line engraving, "Damian Hartard," Philipp Kilian, German engraver, 1628-93
18. Etching, "Le Refectoire," proof, in the second state, Alphonse Legros, French etcher, 1837-1911
19. Etching (ill.) "Night in Ely Cathedral," signed in ink, James McBey, 1883-1959
20. Etching, "Portrait of Jan Asselyn," signed in the plate, Rembrandt Van Rijn, Dutch painter and etcher, 1607-1669. The Rembrandt! (ill.)
21. Line engraving, "Louis, Dauphin de France," dated 1684, Pieter Van Schuppen, 1627-1702
22. Etching, "Blizzard Coming," proof, signed in pencil, Levon West

Epergnes

These elaborate table centerpieces, designed to hold sweetmeats, fruits, or with vases to hold flowers, were in vogue in the early and mid-1800s. Many were attributed to the Sandwich Glass Company, Sandwich, Massachusetts, but as many came from Europe and few were signed; it's another case of knowing your dealer.

Blue, crimped top, bowl with trimming	$225-240

Epergnes

Cranberry, crimped top and lower bowl, 3 lily vases, 20" high	255-275
Crystal/blue, opalescent, 4 lilies, 25" high	160-180
Rose/pink, upper and lower edges ruffled, 4 lilies, 27" high	240-260
Ruffled bowl, 3 lilies, silver frame, 12½" high	250-300
Sandwich Glass overshot, mid-1800s (ill.)	590-700
Single lily, sterling silver base, 12" high	325-360
Silver plate, 11" high, 4 lilies . .	140-175
White satin glass, silver-plated standard, 3 glass lilies, 22" high	195-220

European "Art" Glass

European "Art" Glass

The uninformed collector buys this type of glass too often as Tiffany or Steuben on the basis that it's guaranteed. Many producers

(continued)

of good art glass didn't sign their pieces, thus creating more confusion. If the piece isn't signed, you should demand and get a written receipt when you buy. The American market was flooded with European "art" glass in the late 1800s. Just know from whom you're buying!

Vase, green, yellow flowers, 8″ high	$ 22- 38
Vase, blue, pink/blue flowers, 6″ high	29- 40
Vase, orange, castle scene, fluted top, 7½″ high	33- 42
Vase, ruffled lip, fine enameling, pink liner, 6″ high (ill.)	65- 75
Vase, white satin glass, yellow liner, clear frosted feet, 4¾″ high (ill.)	115-135

Faberge

Faberge

The enamel items named for Carl Faberge were made by him in Russia in the mid-1880s. Today his Easter eggs, made for Russian royalty, bring fantastic prices.

Ashtray, art nouveau, silver, 1900	$ 495- 600
Cigarette case, white enamel	3,500-4,500
Clock, gilded silver, gold overlay, translucent enamel, 1914	2,600-2,800
Figure, Atlas, gilded, silver-mounted	3,600-3,900
Icon, Our Lady of the Sign	3,500-4,000

Penholder, silver	1,600-2,000
Push bell, gilded silver and enamel, 1900	1,550-1,950
Shade, candle, silver-mounted, 1900	975-1,350

The illustrated egg would bring around $400,000 today!

Faience

Faience

A tin glaze earthenware, this "soft" pottery achieves its opaqueness by being treated with tin oxide. Delft and Majolica are made by the same process.

Bottle, white ground, flower motif, 7½″ high	$135-155
Dish, blue/white, Oriental, pair	130-145
Inkwell, French, yellow glaze, signed "VP" (Veuve Perrin) (ill.)	135-160
Jar, blue/white, landscape, handles, Italy, 18″ high, pair	180-210
Jug, tulip, roses, tin glaze, enamel, 1780s	118-130
Plate, floral, insects, Armorial, Italy, pair	165-190
Plate, tin glaze, red/blue, French 1765	120-135
Platter, Delft-type, 18″ x 15″	160-165
Teapot, 11″ high, signed	240-250
Tureen, lettuce decor, French, 1770, pair	390-425
Vase, 12″ high, tin glaze, signed	69- 78

Fairy Lamps

Fairy Lamps

Candle-burning night lamps consisting of 2 parts, base and shade, were first made by the

Samuel Clarke Company, England, in the mid 1850s. Phoenix Glass Company, Monaca, Pennsylvania, was granted the exclusive right to make them in the U.S. Came electricity, out went the light in the fairy lamp. Lazarus and Rosenfeld, New York City, imported thousands of them from Bohemia in the 1880s. Made in every type of glass, from cheap to Tiffany and Amberina.

Amber swirl and cut pattern base, acorn shade, signed Clarke	$125-145
Blue base, bulbous shade, raised floral decor, signed Clarke	175-195
Bisque, Cocker	128-143
Camphor top, clear bottom, blown glass wick holder	210-222
Cranberry glass shade, hobnail base, signed Clarke	165-210
Green satin, ribbed, signed Clarke	90-110
Green/white, swirls, thorn decor	92-102
Lithopane, child scene, white porcelain base, signed Clarke	345-375
Millefiori shade, glass base	190-220
Pink quilted satin glass, signed Clarke	115-140
Rose satin top, Diamond pattern, clear base, signed Clarke	168-188
Satin glass, pink/blue	240-265
White, pink stripes	140-160
Yellow satin glass shade, ribbed pattern base, signed Clarke	112-125

Fans

During the Victorian era young ladies had many signals that were given with the fan. One gesture could mean "Leave me alone!" another, "Mother's watching!" They were made of every type of material. Paper and ivory seemed to be the most popular. Who invented the first fan is unknown.

Advertising, Cafe Brightwood, Kingston, New York, 1908, paper	$ 6- 10
Black lace sticks, floral on black satin, opens to 22"	42- 51
Black lacquer, silver flower painting on back, 21"	40- 50
Celluloid frame, white, carved flower, 7" long	26- 36
Engraved and painted, blossoms, butterflies, 22"	29- 39
Floral, vocalist, buildings, flowers, 24"	19- 28
Ivory splats, chiffon, sequins, 9" long	29- 39
Lace, sandlewood, painted, 8"	32- 42
Paper and wood, matadors, bull fight, 18" long (ill.)	12- 18
Silk, black/green, 13" long	42- 52
Tortoiseshell ribs, 9" long ostrich plumes	64- 74
Turkey feathers, hand-painted, 1870s opens to 19"	69- 79
White lacquer, silver-plated handle, opens to 22", 1900s	38- 48

Feather Work

Cut into the shape of flower petals and leaves, usually painted or dyed, this work is usually found in a glass box-in-frame.

Bouquet of blue and green flowers, glass and frame in good condition	$ 34- 37
Pansies, blue, yellow, green glass and frame in good condition	34- 38
Roses, pink, yellow glass and frame in good condition	44- 49

Fiesta Ware

Fiesta Ware

Homer and Shakespear Laughlin founded the Homer Laughlin China Company in East Liverpool, Ohio, in 1871. At one time it was the world's largest single pottery plant. In March of 1937 Fiesta Ware was patented in red, blue, yellow, and green. Fiesta was a

(continued)

first in commercial pottery. Red was the most difficult color to control. A redesign took place in 1969 and the ware was discontinued in 1973. Most pieces are incised "FIESTA." Red pieces bring 45 to 80 percent more than other colors.

Bowls, nested, 11½", 10", 8", 6", green, all	$24-34
Carafe, 3-pint, green	28-42
Casserole, covered, blue	40-55
Casserole, in metal holder, yellow	53-70
Chop plate, 15" dia., green	14-25
Chop plate, 13" dia., yellow	14-25
Coffeepot, regular	38-55
Creamer, stick handle, blue	6- 9
Mustard jar, yellow	18-29
Marmalade jar, blue	25-35
Marmalade jar in metal holder, green	38-48
Plate, 12" dia., yellow (ill.).	9-14
Tea cup, blue	3- 4

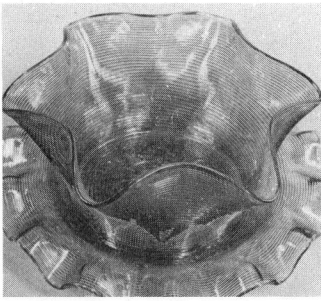

Finger Bowls

Always accompanied by a matching underplate, these small receptacles for cleansing one's fingers after eating were made of a variety of glassware.

Amber, ITP	$ 33-43
Apple green, Depression glass type	12-18
Bohemian glass, blue, deer scene	45-55
Cobalt	38-46
Cranberry, Lutz-type threading (ill.)	70-88
Green, fluted lip	32-42
Moser glass, green/blue	35-45
Pink, Depression glass type	12-18
Threaded, pink/blue	32-41

Fire Fighting Collectibles

Another of the "Americana" series that's now highly sought after. Call it a "fire sale"

Fire Fighting Collectibles

if you will, but the high prices being paid certainly aren't!

Silver-plated engine lamp, "King Neptune"	$1,100-1,300	
Wooden chest, "fire rescue scene" painted on front	1,200-1,400	
Parade belt, lettered "P.R. Abbit"	58-	68
Speaking trumpet, silver plate, dated 1872	250-	325
Fire lantern, Dietz "King," brass	49-	62
Speaking trumpet, brass, engraved names of volun- teers on lip	360-	385
Presentation shield, Tanner- sville, N.Y.	1,200-1,300	
Speaking trumpet, sterling silver, "Boston - 1872"	445-	475
Bell, hand-cranked, East Hampton Bell Factory	120-	135
Helmet, brass eagle finial, English, c. 1870	190-	220
Helmet, leather, Philadelphia, c. 1860s	160-	175
Fire bucket, "Scarsdale's Finest"	250-	270
Fire bucket, "Elmira, Engine 3"	200-	220
Hoze nozzle, brass, 14¾" long, c. 1890	75-	92
Fire bucket, English, "London Fire," paint worn thin	200-	210

Firemarks:
Associated Firemen's Insurance of Baltimore, Maryland, issued in 1848.
Citizen's Fire, Marine and Life Insurance Company, Wheeling, West Virginia, 1856.
City Insurance Company of Cincinnati, Ohio, about 1846.
Clay Fire and Marine Insurance Company, Newport, Kentucky, 1789.

Firemarks

Firemen's Insurance Company
of Pittsburgh, Pennsylvania,
about 1851.
Franklin Insurance Company, St.
Louis, Missouri, 1855 (ill.)
Home Insurance Company, New
Haven, Connecticut, 1859.
Insurance Company of Florida,
Jacksonville, Florida, 1841.
Insurance Company of North
America, extremely rare in
copper, eagle rising from cloud.
Western Mutual Fire and Marine
Insurance Company, St. Louis,
Missouri, 1857.

All these fire marks are worth at least
$200 or more; some as much as $1,600.

Firemen's parade belts, various
sizes and colors .... $ 65- 95

If you're into fire fighting paraphernalia, visit the Home Insurance Company Museum, 15th floor, 59 Maiden Lane, New York City; or the American Museum of Fire Fighting, Fireman's Home; Hudson, N. Y. Other museums, of course, but these two, in particular, are great!

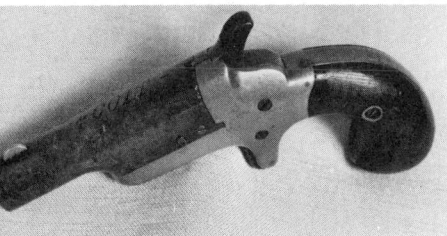

Firearms

Firearms

This is a highly collectible (and expensive!) category. Skillful repros are flooding the market so do business with reliable people, please. Abbreviations used are as follows: cal — caliber; revol — revolver; CW — Civil War; perc — percussion; FL — flintlock; BL — breech-loading; PG — pistol grip; SS — single shot; bbl — barrel; mkd — marked; oct — octagonal; SA — single action; DA — double action. PLEASE NOTE: FEDERAL FIREARMS REGULATIONS: All firearms made

in or before 1898 have been exempted from Federal Firearms regulations which means that unless your state or town has a special law preventing your purchase of such a gun, they can be freely sent and purchased interstate and mail order. On those guns made after 1898, there is a prohibition for sales to anyone except a Federally Licensed Dealer. The federal law does not conflict or cancel any existing state or local laws that might be in effect in your area; hence, although weapons prior to 1898 are exempt under federal law, it is still necessary for you to sign a statement regarding permits or other requirements in your own local area if applicable.

PLEASE READ: don't get cute with the above regulations. You're a candidate for a prison term if you do!

American Hand Guns:

1. Savage .36 cal CW perc ring
   trigger Navy revol .....$ 385- 420
2. H. Aston .54 cal martial
   pistol, 1848 .... 470- 500
3. James Warner 6-shot .31
   cal perc pocket revol.
   2½″ round bbl 250- 300
4. Remington U.S. Navy
   rolling block SS pistol,
   .50 cal 350- 420
5. .31 cal perc pepperbox,
   6-shot, mkd "Allen &
   Thurber, Norwich, Ct."
   3¼″ bbls 470- 500
6. FL martial pistol 900-1,000
7. American perc pocket (or
   belt size) pistol, c.
   1840-50, carved stock,
   silver, gold inlay, 4″ large
   round bbl 1,800-2,000
8. CW Rogers & Spencer .44
   cal perc Army revol 960- 975
9. .35 cal perc pistol, mkd.
   "Bacon & Co., Norwich,
   Ct.," oct/rnd bbl, 4″ long 230- 250
10. Colt .36 cal perc Navy
    revol 920- 500
11. Colt 5-shot .31 cal perc
    revol, 4″ bbl 325- 425
12. Starr SA .44 cal CW perc
    Army revol, 8″ bbl 1,400-1,700
13. Smith & Wesson SA
    "American" revol., .44
    cal, 8″ bbl 600- 700
14. U.S. Navy "Boxlock" perc
    pistol, mkd "Ames-
    Springfield-U.S.N.-1845"
    on lock 650- 750

155

(continued)

15. Remington Beals .36 cal
perc Navy revol 400- 500
16. Cooper .36 cal perc "Navy"
DA revol, 4" oct bbl,
Frankford, Philadelphia
address 700- 850
17. 6-shot perc .31 cal Pepper-
box, 4½" ribbed bbls,
mkd. "S. Bayliss - 1853"
along rib, etc.   2,000-2,600
18. Colt "Open-Top" 7-shot .22
cal spur trigger revol . . .   270- 295
19. Colt 5-shot .31 cal perc
revol, 4" oct bbl, 2-line
N.Y. address 825- 925
20. Manhattan Arms Co. perc
s.s. .31 cal. mkd "Hero,"
14" round bbl 225- 255
21. Deringer pistol, 2¾" fluted
bbl swivels, mkd "Double
Header - E.S. Renwick
Manuf'r — New York —
Pat. June 21, 1864"   4,800-5,400
22. Colt .44 cal perc Army
revol 560- 650
23. Allen & Wheelock 5-shot .31
cal perc DA revol, 4" oct
bbl 400- 500
24. Smith & Wesson Model L 1,
2nd, 3rd Issue 7-shot .22
rim fire revol (called
"Ladysmiths" because
the gay gals in the West
carried them in their
garters). Wesson was
highly religious - when
he learned of this, he
stopped making this
pistol, thus making it
highly collectible today!
Ah, the virtues of man! .   1,100-1,300
25. Merwin & Bray Firearms
Co., N.Y. 5-shot, .30 cal
cup-primed revol, 3½"
cot/ribbed bbl 400- 475
26. .41 cal rim fire deringer,
mkd "XL Derringer,"
spur trigger 220- 250
27. Sharps 4-bbl. .22 cal rim fire
Pepperbox 425- 455
28. Colt .36 cal 5-shot perc
"Pocket Model of Naval
Caliber" 550- 560
29. Cased Colt DA 1878 Fron-
tier Model revol 825- 860
30. Whitney .36 cal CW perc
Navy revol 365- 375
31. Harpers Ferry FL martial
pistol, mkd "Harpers
Ferry-1807"   2,500-2,700
32. Colt #3 Deringer .41 rim fire   500- 550

33. Allen & Thurber 6-shot .31
cal perc pepperbox, mkd
"Young & Smith — New
York — Allen's Patent" .   345- 375
34. Metropolitan .36 cal perc
CW revol, fashioned after
an 1851 Colt   1,400-1,600
35. Colt SA Frontier revol, cal
44/40., mkd on side "Colt
Frontier Six Shooter". . .   780- 880
36. Colt 3rd model .44 cal perc
Dragoon revol, 8" bbl . . .   5,300-5,500
37. Spalding & Fisher dbl bbl
(side-by-side) perc belt
size pistol, .36 cal 5" bbls,
single trigger 350- 425
38. 6-shot .31 cal perc revol,
made by Wm. Marston,
New York, mkd "The
Union Arms Co," known
as 7th model, 5¼" bbl . .   525- 560
39. .22 cal rim fire deringer/
pocket pistol, mkd
"Lombard & Co., Spring-
field, Mass." 365- 385

American Shoulder Guns:
1. Burnside CW perc BL
carbine 425- 455
2. U.S. Springfield "trap-
door" 45/70 rifle, dated
1890 . . . .   380- 395
3. U.S. FL "Common rifle,"
mkd "U.S.-N.Starr-
Midd'n-1926"   1,900-2,300
4. FL Kentucky-style rifle, .54
cal, 36" oct bbl, mkd
"Deringer-Phila"   3,600-3,900
5. CW repeating .50 cal rim-
fire carbine, 30" bbl, mkd
"Triplett & Scott" 520- 600
6. Sharps "New Model 1859,"
.52 cal perc carbine, used
by cavalry in CW 470- 520
7. 1797 State of Pennsylvania
Contract FL musket,
mkd "Miles/CP"   1,800-2,200
8. Henry lever action repeat-
ing .44 rimfire, Ser No.
7055   2,900-3,400
9. U.S. "Mississippi" rifle, .54
cal, mkd "E. Whitney-
U.S.-1848" 550- 625
10. Plains-type rifle, .41 cal, 32"
oct bbl, mkd "J.H.
Johnston-Great Western
Gun Works, Pittsburg,
Pa." 395- 450
11. Kentucky full stock perc
rifle, c. 1830, .38 cal, 41"
oct bbl   2,200-2,500

12. Colonial FL fowling piece, c. 1760, 7' overall, "Tower" mkgs 1,400-1,800
13. Spencer CW 7-shot repeating carbine, .52 cal rimfire, 22" bbl 500- 600
14. FL cavalry carbine, .64 cal, Brown Bess type lock, 20" bbl 550- 650
15. Evans sporting rifle, 30" rnd bbl, .44 cal 600- 650
16. "Colt's Patent-Hartford - 1863" CW .58 cal perc musket 1,300-1,600
17. U.S. FL musket, mkd "Harpers Ferry - 1831" . 1,200-1,450
18. Ballard sporting rifle, combination .44 rimfire & perc, 27½" rnd bbl ... 525- 620
19. Club butt Colonial FL musket, c 1740, 46½" oct/rnd bbl 2,100-2,300
20. Spencer CW cavalry carbine, .50 cal rimfire, 22" bbl 555- 725
21. Winchester Hotchkiss 3rd model, 45/70 cal 1,200-1,500
22. Springfield 1873 rifle, 45/70 cal 385- 425
23. Maine or Massachusetts half stock "Kentucky style" sporting rifle c. 1820, 31½" oct bbl, .64 cal, mkd "Leland" 800- 925
24. Parker DB 10 gauge hammerless shotgun, "D" grade, 29" bbls 265- 295
25. Boy's Cadet size perc military musket, 1840-1860, 45" overall 500- 600
26. "Committee of Safety" FL Revolutionary musket, .41" bbl 1,900-2,200
27. Winchester saddle ring carbine, 38/40 cal, 20" bbl .. 260- 320
28. Confederate-made brass frame Morse BL, made at State Works, Greenville, S.C. 2,400-2,750

Foreign Hand Guns:
1. British naval officer's FL pistol, c. 1790, 9" brass oct bbl .... $ 825- 900
2. Scottish Highland Military style, 18th century, FL belt pistol, type used in Colonial America, .62 cal 885- 975
3. Belgian perc belt pistol, 6½" oct bbl, .52 cal, polygroove bore 440- 550

4. British "Modified Pattern of 1796" FL cavalry pistol, .76 cal, 9" bbl, mkgs of the 17th Light Dragoons 520- 635
5. British cavalry officer's FL pistol, c. 1760-1775, .69 cal 1,500-1,850
6. Miniature blunderbusspistol, FL, mid-Eastern, c. 1750, 11¾" overall, 5½" oct/round blunderbuss bbl 400- 500
7. British perc holster pistol, c. 1830-1840, 8" oct bbl, 14" overall, mkd with American eagle & patriotic motifs 3,800- 4,200
8. Spanish Miquelet belt pistol, c 1810, 5½" oct/round bbl 625- 750
9. English FL Dragoon pistol, Queen Anne period, 18" overall, 11" round bbl, c. 1700-1710 .... 1,900- 2,200
10. European perc pistol, c. 1840, 9" round bbl, 15½" overall, .67 cal 550- 675
11. FL boxlock English pocket pistol, c. 1790, .41 cal, mkd "Brasher-London," 2½" round screw bbl ... 320- 410
12. French boxlock FL holster pistol, c. 1760, .38 cal, 6" overall 260- 330
13. British naval officer's FL holster pistol, c. 1800, .52 cal 710- 795
14. Mid-Eastern FL holster pistol, c. 1750, .60 cal, 19½" overall 4,400- 4,800
15. Miniature FL pistol, c. 1720, 4¾" overall, .28 cal, mkd "Claude Niquet A Liege" 2,600- 2,950

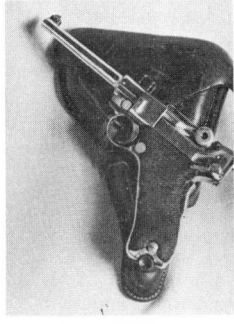

Firearms

157

(continued)

16. English combination FL. pistol and sword, mkd "Clarke-London," .50 cal, 3" round screw bbl, 29½" overall 2,200- 2,450
17. German FL holster pistol, c. 1680, 21" overall, mkd "Herman Ghiot," 13½" round bbl 2,700- 3,150
18. European martial FL pistol, c. 1840, .65 cal, 10" rnd bbl 350 425
19. Dutch over/under pistol, c. 1650, .46 cal, 13¾" oct rnd bbls 9,900-10,400
20. Italian FL holster pistol, c. 1720, 16" overall, 9½" rnd bbl 3,000- 4,200
21. Matched pair, cased English perc dueling pistols, .44 cal, 16" overall, 10" oct bbls, mkd "J. Purdey-Oxford St.-Gun Mfr-London" 7,600,- 9,000

Foreign Shoulder Guns:
1. 2nd model British "Brown Bess" FL musket, 42" bbl, used during French-Indian & Revolutionary Wars 1,800- 2,400
2. British FL swivel blunderbuss, 24" brass bbl, muzzle, 3" dia, 22 lbs., 41" overall 1,300- 1,600
3. French FL musket, mkd "Charlottesville" on lock, American Revolution ... 950- 1,200
4. British officer's FL fusil or or full stock fowling piece, c. 1790, 38# oct/rnd bbl 560 660
5. Dutch FL officer's fusil, 36" bbl, .70 cal 875- 925
6. English perc dbl bbl side-by-side shotgun, c. 1850, 28" bbls, 14 gauge 355- 450
7. British 10 gauge side hammer dbl bbl b. l. shotgun, 30" bbls 250 265
8. French Charleville FL musket, 1763, CP mkgs . 2,300- 2,450
9. French/Belgian DeLvigne .69 cal perc musket, imported for CW use by Union Army, 40" bbl ... 510- 530
10. Japanese pill-lock short hand cannon or carbine, 41" overall, 9 lbs., quite ancient 480- 550
11. CW British Enfield. 577 perc rifled musket,

"Barnett - London," "Tower" mks 425- 485
12. German/Dutch FL musket, 43" bbl, type used in Amer. Revolution 750- 875
13. Dutch FL military rifle, used during Amer. Revolution, 36" oct/rnd bbl, .67 cal, mkd "Thone & Zoon-Amsterdam" 1,500- 1,800
14. Japanese matchlock musket, 40" oct bbl, .57 cal 530- 575
15. Austrian perc .58 cal rifle, issued to U.S. troops at beginning of CW, 37" bbl 500- 600
16. French FL musket, used by Americans in Revolutionary War 1,400- 1,700
17. Ancient matchlock wall gun, India, 8" overall, 18 lbs, early 18th century (or earlier) 450 560
18. Italian FL full stock fowling piece, c. 1750, 5' overall, .67 cal, mkd "P. Bonafino" 2,800- 3,100
19. German FL musket, 17th century, military, 42" oct/rnd bbl, .80 cal, mkd "Leopold I of Wiemer-Neustadt" 2,100- 2,500
20. Japanese matchlock musket, 42" oct bbl, .64 cal 560 575
21. Ancient North African (Berber) Snaphauce camel gun, 5'3" overall, 49" oct/rnd bbl 375- 425
22. Italian Vetterli bolt action rifle 150- 175
23. British Enfield .577 cal perc musket, mkd "1858-Tower" with crown over "VR" 650- 695
24. 1st model, "Brown Bess" musket, 46" bbl, c. 1746 . 1,800- 2,100

Fireglow

Fireglow
When held to a light this glass, attributed

158

to the Mt. Washington Glass Company, shows a fiery opalescence. It was made during the 1890s.

Creamer, ruffled top, pink/blue flowers (ill.)	$ 68- 80
Sugar bowl, ruffled top, pink/blue flowers (ill.)	68- 88
Vase, autumn leaves, 7½" high	100-120
Vase, brown/blue leaves, 7" high	100-120
Vase, Bristol style, child's face, button feet	140-165

Fireplace Accessories

Fireplace Accessories

Our ancestors depended on the fireplace for warmth and a place to cook their food. The tools they used are collectible today. Brass and copper pieces are especially desirable; andirons (fire dogs), coal hods and fenders being among the most desired.

See also ANDIRONS, BELLOWS.

Coal box, English, tooled brass	$100-130
Fenders	
a. Brass, English, mid-1800s	360-425
b. Brass, fan-type (ill.), mid-1800s	540-620
Fire tending tools in rack, brass, mid-1800s, 5 pieces	180-210
Grate, iron, on legs	65- 75
Lighter, Cape Cod (ill.)	23- 30
Screen, hinged type, English	120-130
Screen, solid iron type used in summer to cover fireplace	82- 96
Tools—shovel, poker, brush, in brass stand (ill.)	55- 65

Fischer China

The firm was founded by Moritz Fischer in Herend, Hungary, in 1839. It was still operating in the 20th century just before World War II.

Egg cup, gilt trim	$128-138
Figurine, sitting dog, white	50- 60
Vase, pink/beige/green, 12½" high	275-320
Vase, embossed flowers, reticulated handles, 12" high	290-340
Vase, medallion front and back, yellow scrolls, hunting decor	340-365

Fish Sets

Fish Sets

In vogue during the late Victorian era, they consisted of a large platter and 12 plates. Each piece was decorated with a fish. Haviland, Rosenthal, and most other china companies made these sets.

Hand-painted, embossed gold, sauceboat, 12 plates, blue/green	$155-175
Haviland, green/pink flowers, fish in pond, 16 pieces, in leatherette case	320-340
Limoges, seashells and fish, platter and 6 plates	138-148
Limoges, enameled branches, hand-painted, 23" long (ill.)	350-375
Platter, 12 plates, painted trout, bass, perch, carp, pike	185-195
Porcelain, seashells, lily pads, frogs, signed Germany, 12 pieces	235-260
Roses/vines, hand-painted, Austria, 8 pieces, 1908	165-175

Flags, Pennants

Old Glory! All types are collectible, the older the better. On June 14, 1977, the American Congress resolved that the flag of the thirteen United States be thirteen stripes, alternating red and white; that the Union be thirteen stars, white in a blue field, represent-

(continued)

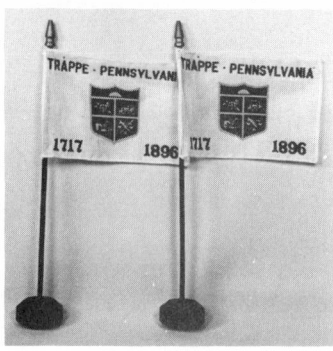

Flags, Pennants

ing a new constellation. Be proud of your nation's flag; a lot of fine people died for it.

Flags, 11" high, commemorate the 179th anniversary of Trappe, Pennsylvania, home of oldest unrestored Lutheran church in America (ill.) $ 20- 25

Flasks

Flasks

"Chestnut," ½ pint, red brown,
c. 1830s $230-245
Cut glass, sterling silver caps . . .   48- 58
Glass, ½ pint, pewter cup fits
over bottom, 1930s (ill.) 27- 37
"Grain," pint, aqua, maker
unknown, c. 1850s   165-200
Hip-type, ½ pint, sterling silver,
1920s 43- 53
"Ribbed," ½ pint, yellow amber,
c. 1840s   170-190
"Success To The Railroad," pint,
olive green, large eagle on
reverse side, made by Kensington
Glass Works, Philadelphia,
c. 1830   275-310
"Violin," ½ pint, aqua, c. 1850s . .   115-125
Walking stick, ¼ pint capacity
glass rod fits inside, silver cap .   122-132
"Washington and Taylor," quart,
aqua   190-210

Florentine Art "Cameo"

Made in Bohemia, this glass has a satin glass body and is heavily decorated with enamel. Some think it's cameo glass but it isn't. Late 18th, 19th century.

Vase, blue satin glass, white
flowers, 8" high . . . . $ 70- 80
Vase, green satin glass, butter-
flies and flowers, 8½" high . . .   66- 76
Whiskey glass, blue satin glass,
castle scene, set of 6   210-250

Flow Blue

Flow Blue

China on which the color ran during the firing is called Flow Blue. Made at Staffordshire and other potteries, it was popular during the early and mid-1800s. Highly collectible today.

Bone dish, Johnson . . . . $ 12- 19
Bone dish, Ormonde (Meakin) . . .   22- 31
Bowl, soup, rose pattern, 8" 12- 20
Butter dish, Gridley 80- 95
Butter pat, bluebirds 13- 19
Cake stand, flower decor, 13"
high   110-125
Chocolate pot, blue/gold, LaBelle   82- 95
Compote, floral decoration,
molded leaf handles, cover 58- 68
Creamer, Alfred Meakin, 4½"
high 49- 58
Creamer, Haddon 49- 58
Cup/saucer, demitasse, Lorne . . .   38- 48
Dish, vegetable, open, 12½"
diameter 44- 54
Gravy boat, boat scene, Ovando .   26- 36
Gravy boat, Paisley 44- 54
Jar, biscuit, barrel shape, elks,
1890 mark 48- 58
Pitcher and bowl, gilt, La Belle . .   126-136
Pitcher, gravy, Lonial 25- 35
Plate, Castro pattern, 14"
diameter 22- 32

160

Plate, flowers/leaves, cobalt, 11″ dia. (ill.)	32- 42
Platter, Blue Danube, oval 10¼″ diameter	41- 51
Platter, Jenny Lind, 11″ long long	73- 82
Platter, scalloped edge, Krona, Wood and Sons	57- 67
Ring tree	26- 36
Sauce, Touraine, Alcock	17- 27
Syrup, dark blue, pewter cap	34- 43
Teapot, Touraine, Alcock	135-160
Tureen, vegetable, Touraine	70- 85

Fluting Irons

Fluting Irons

Made of iron or brass, they rolled pleats in petticoats and cuffs. Early 1800s to early 1900s.

Fluting iron, marked Geneva roller-type (ill.)	$ 50- 60
Iron handled tube, 3-legged stand, early	48- 58

Flytraps

Flytraps

Popular in the mid-1800s, some were crude affairs made of wood or metal. The collectible type are those made of glass. The top was removable so one could put in sugar water to attract the flies.

Blue, Sandwich-type glass, beehive shape, mid-1800s (ill.)	$240-265

Cranberry, other colors, same type as above	160-180
Metal, box-type, late 1800s	50- 60
Wood, box-type, late 1800s	26- 36

Folk Art, American

Folk Art, American

Folk painting is the product of one untrained in art; the effort of the painter to depict or portray scenes, persons or objects of interest to them. A lack of perspective, depth, proportion — are a few of the chief characteristics of folk painting in America. Once again, prices change too quickly to give you an honest cost. A John Brewster, Jr. recently sold for $67,000; a J. Bradley, $43,000; a Nathaniel F. Wales, $12,000. Folk Art, American, is here to stay.

"Brothers," done in crayon, Connecticut, c. 1860, 8″ x 11″
"The Country Church," c. 1855, 7″ x 11″
"Farm in West Cornwall, Connecticut," 1895, 8½″ x 18″
"Farm Scene," signed "J.F. Gilman," dated 1871, charcoal, 19″ x 27″
"Fort Plain, New York," c. 1850, 23″ x 34″
"Home for Thanksgiving," New York State, c. 1850, 25″ x 30″
"Hunters," c. 1870, 14″ x 22″
"Landscape with Sawmill," G. Marston, 1863, 22″ x 30″
"The Mansion," charcoal, c. 1850, 15″ x 23″
"Mississippi Farm by a River," c. 1875, 22″ x 27″
"Morning Chores in New Hampshire," c. 1840, 30″ x 36″
"Train on a Bridge," painted on tin, c. 1840, 10″ x 14″
"The Village Banker's Home in Winter," (ill.) c. 1870, 22″ x 27″

(continued)

Folk Art, American
"Village Lake with Indians," c.
1850, 17" x 23"
"Young Lady on a Balcony," (ill.)
c. 1820, 29" x 36"

Obviously, lots of this type "Americana" around. A lot of fakes around, also, so challenge the auctioneer if you don't think he's right (he probably is), question the antiques dealer, OR, if you're a steady buyer of my books (I thank you!), know from whom you buy!!!

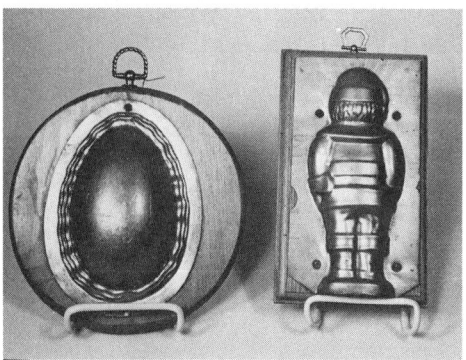

Food, Candy Molds

Food, Candy Molds

Food molds are usually made of ironstone or metal, tin and pewter. Candy molds are usually made of metal.

Bride and Groom	$ 52-	64
Calf's head jelly mold, ironstone, rabbit	35-	45
Candy, Easter egg, mounted on wood (ill.)	12-	18
Candy, Santa Claus, mounted on wood (ill.)	12-	18
Candy, tin, rabbit	33-	43
Candy, pewter, turkey, 4"	29-	40

Gelatine mold, ironstone, boar's head	43-	53
Heart and cupid	39-	51
Hobby horse	42-	58
Pudding mold, ironstone, ear of corn	46-	56
Relish mold, tin	29-	42
Rooster	29-	42

Foot Warmers

Foot Warmers

Some were made of soapstone, some were hollow pieces of pottery into which hot water was poured. Others were crude wood/tin affairs. All had the same purpose.

Glazed blue/white pottery, hollow, marked "Alcove Ohio," 12" wide	$45-	55
Soapstone, 12" x 10", with wire handle	25-	35
Tin, carpet-covered, held charcoal, used in early autos	40-	50
Walnut, 4 pillars, punched tin hearts, 6" high (ill.)	90-	120

Foreign Legion Items

Foreign Legion Items

The French Foreign Legion, based in North Africa, was the most famous of volunteer military units. Now things to do with the Foreign Legion are becoming collectible.

Toothpick holder, paste
  porcelain, late 1800s, (ill.) . . . . . $ 29- 40
Cap badges, French Foreign
  Legion, pre-World War I, each   19- 27
Discharge papers, pre-World
  War II 24- 35

Fostoria Glass

Fostoria Glass

Originally manufactured in Fostoria, Ohio, in 1887, the factory was moved a few years later to Moundsville, Virginia, where they continue, today, to make a quality glassware. Discontinued patterns and those early 20th century pieces are what collectors and dealers look for. Most pieces you find are in the $8, $20, and $65 range. It's lovely glass to collect, and here are a few of the many patterns: American, Baroque, Beverly, Amber and Green; Fairfax Ebony, Green, Pink, Rose, Topaz; Lafayette Clear; Mayfair Amber, Ebony, Green, Pink, Rose, Optic Rose, Pink, Clear — enjoy collecting a lovely glass!

Bowl, pink opalescent $30- 40
Bookends, dog heads, pair 40- 48
Candleholders, Baroque,
  w/prisms, pr. 65- 70
Candleholders, Topaz,
  2-light, pr. 60- 70
Cruet, Optic Rose, 5″ high 24- 33
Figurine, duck, Beverly 21- 31
Mugs, fish-shaped 9- 12
Platter, Ebony, open handles . . .   30- 40
Vase, clear pedestal base, acid
  etched acorns and oak leaves
  (ill.) 60- 70

Frakturs

Frakturs

Simply put, a fraktur is a birth certificate that is ornately decorated. They were popular in the Pennsylvania German area in the early to late 1800s.

Birth certificate, framed, signed
  "W. Grofs, 1861." Printed in
  Allentown, Pennsylvania, 16″
  x 19″, hand-colored birds,
  angels, and an American eagle
  (ill.) . . . . $ 80- 95

Francesware

Francesware

Frosted with stained amber rims or tops, this glass made by Hobbs, Brockunier and Company was both pressed and blown-molded in the 1880s. A real collector's item today. Don't confuse the name with Francis Ware, which was japanned tinware made and decorated by Henry and Tom Francis in Philadelphia around 1830.

Bowl, clear, 7″ square . . . . $ 56- 66
Match holder, frosted, amber
  top 63- 73
Pitcher, blown, 4 mold, amber
  stained top, frosted hobnail
  body, 8″ high (ill.)   235-265
Sauce, 4½″ square, hobnail 24- 33
Tumbler, typical 42- 53
Water set, 6 pieces, frosted,
  amber tops, all   350-400

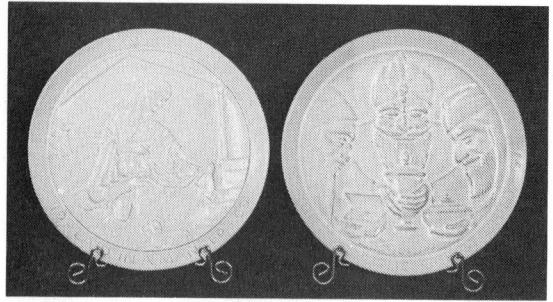

Frankoma Pottery

Fraternal Order Collectibles

Frankoma Pottery

Frankoma Pottery

John Frank began the pottery firm in Sapulpa, Oklahoma, in 1933. He combined his chemical knowledge with the pottery making traditions of the Indians of the Southwest. The mottled lines result from the use of colored earthenware clays. The "pacing leopard" was the original trademark but it was discontinued because of difficulty encountered reproducing it in soft clay. "FRANKOMA" is the mark used today. In 1965 they began making commemorative Christmas plates.

Bowl, 11″ dia., mottled hues of brown and yellow, leopard mark	$45- 60
Cup/saucer, mottled brown and yellow, FRANKOMA mark (ill.)	20- 30
Christmas plate, "Laid in a manger," 1969 (ill.)	24- 35
Christmas plate, "Gifts for the Christ Child," 1967 (ill.)	54- 63
Cookie jar, mottled blue, FRANKOMA mark	35- 43
Vase, 11″ high, brown/green, leopard mark	95-120
Vase, 6″ high, blue/brown, FRANKOMA mark	17- 22

Fraternal Order Collectibles

Elk, Moose, Lion, Eagle, Mason, Odd Fellow — all fraternal organizations. What they wore or carried during the 18th and 19th centuries is collectible today.

BPOE ashtray, Cincinnati, 1904, Rookwood pottery (rare)	$ 50- 60
BPOE handled mug, elk and clock	25- 35
F.O.E., watch fob	19- 28
A.O.F. parasol, 1908 convention	33- 42
Knights of Columbus match safe	23- 33
Masonic jug, Canary Ware, English	265-280
Masonic shaving mug	27- 36
Odd Fellow's jug, pink lustre, English, rare	290-350
Plate, Masonic, 10¼″ dia. (ill.)	12- 18
Shrine goblet, Washington, District of Columbia, 1902, red flashed glass	24- 34
Shrine, Omaha, 1918, mug	24- 33

Freehand Ware

This was made by Imperial Glass Company, Bellaire, Ohio, in the 1920s and is mentioned here because, as a lustred art glass, people are confusing it with late Carnival. They're also confusing it with Imperial's Imperial Jewel, which is an onion-skin type of glass and also being collected as Carnival.

Fruit Jars

In one word — "Mason" — John Landis Mason, that is. A tinsmith by trade, at the age of 26, in his shop in New York City, he designed his now-famous wide-mouth jar, the "Mason's Pat. Nov. 30th 1858." He also invented the tin screw-on lids to fit the jars he farmed out to the various glassmakers in the area. IMPORTANT: this explains why

164

Fruit Jars

...here are so many names on his jars, BUT always with Mason's name, blown into the glass. Many pioneer firms are still in the business, such as Drey, Ball, Kerr, Boyd, to mention a few. Mason's "Black" glass jars are priceless today.

Atlas, Cloverleaf, pint or quart ..	$ 16- 26
Atlas, E-Z Seal, amber, quart ...	28- 39
Ball Ideal, ¼ pint, ½ pint, clear or green	15- 25
Banner, patented February 9, 1864, aqua	34- 39
Clark's Peerless, pint or quart ...	25- 35
Crown emblem, ½ gallon, amber .	36- 43
Eureka, quart, clear	26- 36
Gem, quart, clear...........	12- 20
Globe, pint, amber...........	60- 70
Hazel preserve, Atlas lightning seal, quart, aqua	17- 27
Lightning, quart, amber	38- 48
Mason, Maltese Cross emblem, patented November 30, 1858, ½ gallon, amber	47- 57
Mason's 1872, patented, aqua, quart	26- 36
Smalley self sealer, amethyst, quart	28- 38
Spencer, C.F., patented, quart, aqua..................	22- 31
Victory, quart or ½ gallon, clear .	14- 28
Woodbury, quart, aqua	31- 39
Mason's Pat. Nov. 30th (ill.)	50- 58

Fry Glass

Made by H.C. Fry Company, Rochester, Pennsylvania, 1900 to 1929. Fine cut glass for the first 15 years, then Foval glass was introduced after 1925. Some pieces are marked

Fry Glass

Fry. Gold was used in the batch to make Foval. Collectors are just beginning to appreciate Fry glass. Usually a combination of 2 colors in pastel shades of greens, pinks, blues. Foval is also known as Pearl Art.

Bowl, black, clear bell stem, 6" tall, marked "Fry," dated	$170-185
Candlesticks, blue trim, 13" high, "Foval"	340-370
Cologne bottle, clear, green stopper, signed "Fry"	105-115
Creamer, opalescent, green trim under tray, signed	160-175
Cup and saucer, "Foval," 2½" high (ill.)	70- 80
Custard cup, ovenware, 1919 ...	38- 48
Epergne, intaglio cut, signed	180-195
Foval, barber bottle, milky white, fiery opalescent	62- 72
Foval, candlestick, blue/white, 10" high	180-210
Foval coffeepot, opalescent, white handle, 10" high	260-300
Pitcher, craquelle, applied blue handle (ill.)	95-120
Foval, compote, cream color base, blue standard, 9¼" diameter ..	135-148
Foval, cup/saucer, blue jade handle	75- 90
Foval, pitcher, yellow iridescent, cobalt handle, 6 tumblers	210-250
Pitcher, opalescent blue stripes over blue crystal, 4 tumblers ..	290-310
Sugar bowl, covered	200-225

Fry Glass

(continued)

Toothpick, ruffled, applied blue crystal handles	60- 70
Vase, cream, cobalt handles, 7½" high	160-175
Vase, craquelle, blue application (ill.)	80- 95

Fulper

Fulper

The Fulper Pottery Company in Flemington, N. J., made this pottery in the mid-1880s. It was never the quality of Rookwood or Weller. They also made all-bisque dolls. The firm operates under the name of Stangl Pottery today.

Bookends, dogs, pair, 6½" high .	$ 40- 46
Compote, base is 3 dragons, blue/green	168-179
Jardiniere, multicolor, 8" high . . .	85- 95
Jug, brown, Philadelphia, 1926, 6" high	59- 70
Lamp base, bright blue, reticulated base	83- 96
Lamp, mushroom shade, 17" high	128-140
Vase, blue glaze, 9" high	49- 59
Vase, green matte finish, signed, 6¼" high	52- 62

Vase, tortoiseshell, 13" high, signed	54- 64
Vase, poppies, 12" high	69- 79
Vase, 7" high, brown/blue glaze, "Fulper" (ill.)	73- 83

Funeral Collectibles

Me too, lady! But, like it or not, collectors are avidly seeking things to do with funerals

Embalming tools, early 1900, set of 12	$ 42- 53
2-piece glass coffin, late 1800s (rare)	350-450
Hand-carved walnut coffin 1850s (ill.)	375-425
Horse-drawn hearse, beveled glass windows, original lamps and fixtures	5,500+

Furniture, American

The prices quoted here have to be **very** general in nature as antique furniture prices are climbing steadily, day-by-day. The better auction galleries are getting unbelievable prices for Chippendale, Queen Anne, Hepplewhite — both American and English — and, there's no end in sight. Just know what you're doing and, if not, pay a member of the Appraisers Association of America to assist you.

Furniture, American:
  Pilgrim style, 1650-1690
  William & Mary style, 1690-1720
  Queen Anne style, 1720-1750
  Chippendale style, 1750-1775
  Hepplewhite style, 1785-1800
  Sheraton style, 1800-1820

Funeral Collectibles

American Empire style,
1820-1840
Rococo style, 1840s to 1860s
Louis XVI style, 1865-1875
Gothic style, 1840-1865
Spool-turned style, 1850-1880
Renaissance style, 1860-1875
Eastlake style, 1870-1880
Cottage furniture, 1850-1880
Duncan Phyfe, 1795-1847
Belter furniture, 1844-1863
New England style, 17th to
mid-19th centuries.
Pennsylvania Dutch, 18th,
19th centuries
Shaker, 1776-1900

Furniture, American:
ARMCHAIRS:
Windsor, comb-back, serpen-
tine crest rail $1,700-1,900
Platform type, open arms,
curved wooden frame,
upholstered, c. 1870 . . . .   245- 285
Medallion back, open arms,
oak, upholstered, c. 1890s . . .   140- 170
Ladder-back, Shaker style,
New England, rush seat,
4-slat 445- 485
Bentwood, c. 1860 . . . .   190- 240
Massachusetts, c. 1730s 540- 560
Ladder-back, sausage turned,
old green paint, rush seat . . .   525- 560
Ladder-back, maple, rush seat,
c. 1840 . . . .   420- 450
BEDS:
Cabinet Mantel-type, elm,
beveled mirror, 1890s 285- 295
Brass, double, swell-foot end,
c. 1890s 485- 560
Brass, double, bow-foot end,
c. 1890s 550- 650
Child's iron, white enamel, drop
sides, c. 1890s 205- 225
Walnut, single, molded foot and
head rail, carved crest, c.
1850 . . . .   320- 385
Walnut, single, burl veneer
headboard, applied panels, c.
1860 . . . .   445- 480
Spool, low posts, triangular
headboard, c. 1855 . . . .   565- 585
Rope, high posts, cherry, corn-
shuck mattress, c. 1820 . . . .   795- 850
Oak, double, raised paneling,
foot and headboard, c. 1890 .   225- 268
Oak, twin, carved, head-and
footboard, c. 1895 . . . .   170- 210
Sheraton, canopy, maple, c.
1815 2,200-2,400
Half tester, walnut, recessed
veneer panels, c. 1850 1,800-2,400
"Jenny Lind" spool 375- 425

BENCHES:
Cobbler, complete with all
tools, original condition, c.
1820 . . . .   500- 600
Deacon's spindle back, 8-legs,
Connecticut, c. 1830 . . . .   700- 800
Deacon's, 10' long, original
dark finish, New Hampshire,
c. 1820 . . . .   725- 815
Mammy rocker, removable
guard, stenciled, c. 1840 985-1,100
Mammy rocker, wooden cog to
operate butter churn, etc., c.
1820 1,250-1,400
Church pew, pine, unrestored,
New England, c. 1850s, 10'
long 700- 900
Porch, poplar, heeled through
seat, solid back 110- 115
BOOKCASES:
Globe-Warnake-type, 5-section,
oak, top and base, all 185- 199
Oak, 6 shelves, glass doors,
c. 1880s 175- 275
Oak, 5 adjustable shelves, open
latticework in top, glass door   245- 356
Rosewood, wall-type, 3-shelf, c.
1840 . . . .   220- 230
Library-type, 6' wide, 4 adjust-
able shelves, 3 glass doors,
1890s 450- 525
BUREAUS:
Cottage, 4-drawer, pine 170- 210
Hepplewhite, pine, bracket
feet, 4-drawer 625- 750
Bowfront, maple, carved pulls,
4-drawer, c. 1860 . . . .   510- 615

Furniture, American

167

(continued)

Furniture, American

CHAIRS:

Side, carved cresting, oval back, walnut, needlepoint upholstery	200- 240
Side, Hitchcock type, rush seat, 33″ high (ill.)	140- 195
Side, demi-arms, burl veneer panels, machine lines and carving	195- 225
Side, cane seat, maple, vase back (ill.)	130- 165
Side, molded and pierced back piece supported by turned columns	310- 340
Side, butterfly Windsor, hickory, pine, saddle seat, bamboo turnings, signed "E.P. Rose" (ill.)	200- 250
Comb-back Windsor chair	1,700-1,900
Corner, walnut, burl veneer panels, c. 1850s	300- 345
Eastlake, side, machine lines and carving upholstered, 1875	160- 195
Lady's spoon back, carved crest, upholstered, 1855	340- 400
Lady's, carved crest, balloon back, finger roll, c. 1845	340- 395
Gentleman's, oval back, finger roll, open arms, c. 1860	500- 525
Gentleman's, applied veneer panels, button tufting, c. 1855	460- 500
Arm, open arms, button tufting, walnut, incised lines	260- 300
Arm, Eastlake, open arms, open crested back, 1875	275- 310
Windsor, arrowback, writing arm, unrestored	620- 720
Windsor, lady's birdcage, original black paint	300- 400
Mahogany veneered back, inlaid, c. 1890	125- 200

Furniture, American

Parlor, spring seat, upholstered, oak, mahogany finish, c. 1895	120- 190
Reading, spoke back, birch, open arms, c. 1895	150- 170
Roman, birch, curved seat, open arms, silk damask seat, c. 1895	110- 160
Rocking, lady's parlor, full twist spindles, oak, c. 1890s .	180- 220
Desk/hall, lady's oak, cane seat, 5-spoke back, c. 1890s	125- 160
Student's, oak frame, corduroy upholstery, c. 1890s	115- 175
Morris, reclining, brass rod at back, loose cushions, c. 1890 .	150- 200
Turkish, leather, oak frame, steel springs, moss/hair filled	150- 170
Rocking, large arm, oak, spoke back, silk damask seat, c. 1890s	160- 220
Parlor, made of reed, shellac finish, 1895	170- 225
Parlor, made of rattan, shellac finish, 1895	175- 210
Rocking, rectangular caned back, applied burl veneer, c. 1860	210- 285
Rocking, swan neck arms, caned back and seat, c. 1850 .	200- 275

CHAISE LONGUES:

Cherry frame, fully upholstered, incised lines, Eastlake style	425- 470
Louis XV style (1845-1870), finger roll, tufted back	850-1,000
Oak frame, adjustable back, velvet upholstery, c. 1880s ..	275- 310
Fully upholstered, maple legs, loose cushion, c. 1870s	395- 425

CHESTS:

Blanket, Pennsylvania Dutch, green, dull red trim	1,700-1,900

Furniture, American

Furniture, American

Blanket, cherry, dovetail, rat-
tail hinges, c. 1730s 1,000-1,350
Blanket, pine, strap hinges, 2
drawers in base, c. 1830 . . . .   750- 825
Apothecary, oak, 60-drawer,
porcelain knobs, c. 1840 . . . .   800- 900
Chippendale-type, mahogany,
ogee feet, 6-drawer 512- 593
Dower, Pennsylvania Dutch,
painted green/red w/flowers
on front 3,100-3,400

Dower, Pennsylvania Dutch,
tulip decor, original paint,
c. 1810 3,600-3,900
Chippendale, bowfront, cherry,
6-drawer c. 1760 5,700-6,600
Hepplewhite, pine, 4-drawer,
veneered mahogany front, c.
1790   925-1,100
American Empire, overhang,
veneered mahogany posts,
4-drawer, c. 1825 . . . .   400- 500
Blanket, bracket feet, poplar,
black brush and comb
decoration over red lead,
47″ wide (ill.) 300- 385

CHINA CABINETS:
Corner, swell front, 4 adjust-
able shelves, oak, c. 1890s . . .   400- 500
Oak, glass on 3 sides, mirror
in top, latticework in door,
c. 1890s 310- 400
Mahogany, carved crest,
beveled glass on 3 sides, 5
adjustable shelves 495- 575
Oak, swell-shaped glass in ends,
carved feet, 4 adjustable
shelves, 1890s 575- 650
Oak, spiral fluted pillars,
beveled glass on 3 sides,
c. 1895 . . . .   500- 600

CRADLES:
Rocker type, cutout hearts,
maple (ill.) 325- 375
Round rails, square posts, knob
finials, walnut, c. 1840 . . . . .   260- 280
Rocker type, slat decorated,
cherry, c. 1830 . . . .   310- 350
Hooded, pine, c. 1830 . . . .   295- 325
Open, walnut, spindle construc-
tion, 1850s 300- 320
Hooded, hickory, hand holes,
c. 1820s 400- 425

CUPBOARDS:
Corner, cherry, 2 doors above
and below, 1 drawer, c. 1830 . 2,100-2,600
Corner, poplar, glass doors
above, solid below, original
paint, 1840s 1,400-1,650
Corner, maple, solid doors
above and below, scroll top,
c. 1850 1,600-1,800
Corner, poplar and pine paneled
doors, c. early 1800s, 6′7″
high (ill.) 1,700-1,900
Dutch, cherry, glass doors
above, solid below, cham-
phered corners, solid ends,
wooden knobs, c. 1760s 3,800-3,975
Open, glass doors above, solid
below, 3 drawers in middle,
c. 1850 2,000-2,600

169

(continued)

Open, recessed top, glass doors
above, solid below, carved
pulls, c. 1840 1,100-1,300
Hanging, pine, single glass
door, 3 shelves, c. 1830 . . . . .   450- 475
Linen, Pennsylvania, original
green paint, solid doors, c.
1830 1,400-1,650
Pantry, Pennsylvania Dutch,
red/green, white flower decor,
c. 1740 2,400-2,700
Pie safe, pine, pierced geometric
tin panels (ill.) 475- 575
Pewter, pine, hutch top, 3
shelves, solid doors below 2
drawers, c. 1830 2,000-2,300
Pewter, painted pine, New
England, 6 shelves, solid
doors below, 1750s 2,700-3,000

DESKS:
Butler's, walnut, c. 1850   2,200-2,400
Cylinder front, walnut,
veneered cylinder panel,
machine lines and carving,
spindled gallery, 3 drawers
below, c. 1840s 1,900-2,300
Plantation, glass doors above
lift-top writing surface,
walnut, 1830s 1,700-1,900
Drop front, table type, walnut,
beaded molding, c. 1850s . . .   650- 750
Bureau, fall front secretary
drawer, carved pulls on 3
drawers, 1860s 600- 700
Chippendale style, cherry,
slant-front, Oxbow, Block
and Fan interior, original
pulls, ball/claw feet, c. 1760 . . 9,700-12,000
Hepplewhite, mahogany, slant-
front, original bail handle
pulls, c. 1790 3,400-3,900
Student's, poplar, iron frame,
c. 1890s 80- 150
Lady's, 3 drawers below writ-
ing surface, walnut, c. 1850s .   575- 625
Lady's, pine, 4 drawers below
writing surface, c. 1820 . . . . .   650- 785

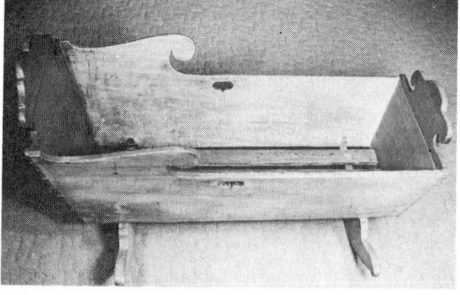

Furniture, American

Furniture, American

Lap, mahogany, brass trim
overall, ink bottles, etc., c.
1840 . . . .   250- 295
Rolltop, oak, c. 1880s 560- 600
Rolltop, walnut, c. 1860s 1,100-1,300
Rolltop, oak, miniature, child's
c. 1880s 400- 480
Schoolmaster's, walnut, turned
legs, single drawer below, c.
1840 . . . .   370- 428
Schoolmaster's, oak, cubby-
holes below gallery rail, c.
1850 . . . .   350- 425
Schoolmaster's, mahogany,
bookcase top, turned legs,
c. 1830s 480- 520

DOUGH TROUGHS:
Poplar, dovetailed box, on box
frame, c. 1830 . . . .   420- 480
Chestnut, lid, turned legs, dove-
tailed box, c. 1860 . . . .   320- 392
Pine, squared tapered legs,
original red paint, c. 1840s . .   512- 587
Pine, turned legs, dovetailed
box, grained finish, c. 1840s .   425- 475

DRESSERS:
Oak, beveled mirror, 4-drawer,
c. 1870 . . . .   190- 255
Pine, 3-drawer, New England,
c. 1790 1,900-2,400
Wooden top, walnut, swing
mirror, 4-drawer, carved
handles, c. 1850 . . . .   600- 850
Wooden top, maple, swing
mirror, 2 hanky boxes,
marble insert, c. 1850 . . . . . .   600- 825

Wooden top, burl veneer panels
on drawers, teardrop pulls,
c. 1855 . . . .   525- 625
Marble top, molded burl veneer
panels on drawers, c. 1840 . .   485- 570
Marble top, swing mirror, 2
boxes, applied molding on
drawers, c. 1840 . . . .   615- 725
Marble top, projecting front,
ring, molding on drawers,
original pulls 550- 575
Dressing case, marble top, burl
veneer on drawers, corner
stiles, mirror frame, applied
molding around lower
drawers, c. 1830 . . . .   725- 775
Oak, German bevel mirror, 2
small, 2 large drawers, c.
1895 (ill.) 175- 200
Oak, lyre frame mirror, 2 small,
2 large drawers, applied
molding on mirror frame and
drawer fronts, brassplated
pulls, c. 1890s 170- 190
Oak, 4-drawer, wooden pulls, c.
1870 . . . .   170- 195
Oak, 6-drawer, spindled gallery
on top, brass pulls, c. 1860s .   200- 240

DRY SINKS:
Pine, single door below, c. 1830   500- 600
Cherry, splashboard back,
single door below, c. 1850 . . .   535- 620
Pine, lift top, 2 drawers below,
c. 1850 . . . .   480- 570
Pine, high back, candle drawer,
single door below, c. 1840 . . .   429- 536

FOOTSTOOLS:
Mahogany frame and legs, up-
holstered, late 1800s 170- 192
Mahogany veneer, cabriole
legs, needlepoint cover, 1870s   200- 280
Scroll type, Louis XV (1845-
1870), velvet upholstery 275- 360
Maple, carved legs, c. 1840 . . . .   170- 192
Walnut, beaded edge, uphol-
stered, bun feet, c. 1860 . . . .   170- 200

HALL TREES:
Oak, French bevel mirror, 6
wooden hat holders, double
umbrella holders, c. 1880 . . .   320- 410
Walnut, burl veneer raised
panels, molded, incised pedi-
ments, double umbrella
holders, pierced back, marble
shelf over drawer, c. 1840 . . .   900-1,100
Walnut, German bevel mirror,
veneer raised panels, brass
double hat hooks, marble
shelf over drawer, carved
applied ornaments, c. 1840 . .   875-1,000
Oak, German bevel mirror, 6

Furniture, American

double hooks, umbrella
holder, seat w/lid, c. 1870s . .   280- 320
HAT RACKS:
Accordion-type, 13 wooden
pegs, porcelain tips, walnut,
c. 1850 . . . .   110- 150
Accordion-type, 7 wooden pegs,
porcelain tips, chestnut, c.
1860 . . . .   115- 175
Walnut, molded frame, 8 wood
pegs, c. 1850 . . . .   160- 185
LOVE SEATS:
Medallion back, walnut frame,
upholstered, Louis XV style .   895-1,000
Serpentine back, walnut frame,
upholstered, c. 1850s 725- 775
Hepplewhite, walnut, carved
mirror back, c. 1790   1,100-1,450
Victorian, mirror back, New
England pineapple uphol-
stery, c. 1850   950-1,100
Wooden framed back, applied
burl veneer panels, incised
lines, c. 1830   900-1,250
MAGAZINE RACKS:
Wall type, walnut, Eastlake
style, c. 1875 . . . .   100- 120
Wall type, reticulated, chest-
nut, c. 1880 . . . .   92- 110
Oak, spindle construction, c.
1890s 70- 92

171

(continued)

Furniture, American

MIRRORS:

Mahogany, scrolled crest, floor-
type, c. 1870 . . . . 260- 350
Courting, walnut, 11″ x 15½″,
c. 1800 . . . . 700- 800
Sheraton, maple frame, carved,
21″ x 29″, c. 1790 . . . . 400- 425
Wall, curly maple, New
England, c. 1830 . . . . 300- 382
Shaving, 2-drawer, walnut, c.
1850 . . . . 261- 296
Wall, Chippendale, carved and
parcel-gilded, walnut . . . 5,400-6,100

SECRETARIES:

American Empire, mahog-
any veneer, bookcase top,
c. 1830 . . . . 950- 1,400
Sheraton, mahogany, orig-
inal pulls, c. 1815 . . . . 2,950- 3,400
Chippendale, Philadelphia,
cherry, slant-front, c. 1765 42,000-49,000
Block front, mahogany,
Massachusetts, all orig-
inal, c. 1750 51,000-59,000
Tambour, mahogany, late
18th century, bureaulike
base, 4 graduated drawers,
French splayed bracket
feet, 2 diamond-glazed
doors above 2,900- 3,700

SIDEBOARDS

Butler's bird's-eye maple,
New England c. 1800 . . . . 2,800- 3,400
Sheraton, mahogany, 4
doors, 3 drawers, c. 1810 . . 4,800- 4,950
American Empire, piecrust
molding, cherry top,
mahogany, c. 1830s 1,600- 1,900
Marble top, circular molding,
carved wooden pulls, 2
doors below, c. 1850 . . . . . 625- 825
Marble top, molded drawers,
veneer panels, chamfered
corner stiles w/applied
molding, projection front,
c. 1840 . . . . 1,700- 1,950
Hepplewhite, breakfront,
butler's mahogany (ill.) . . . 6,400- 7,100

SOFAS:

Mahogany; side, back, seat,
upholstered w/silk
damask, c. 1890s 320- 415
Belter, laminated rosewood,
ornately carved back, c.
1840 10,000-10,800
Serpentine back, walnut
frame, Louis XV style 875- 1,100
Finger roll back, tufted,
walnut frame, 1860 . . . . . . 950- 1,250
Double arch, molded frame,
button tufting, c. 1850 . . . 1,000- 1,400

STANDS:

Wig, mahogany, c. 1830 . . . . 145- 220
Lamp, marble recessed in
molded rim, walnut, tripod
base, c. 1850 . . . . 220- 290

Furniture, American

Lamp, marble recessed in
molded rim, cherry, carved
bird ornament, tripod base,
c. 1840 . . . .   280- 350

Night, maple, curly maple,
2-drawer, turned legs, 28"
high (ill.) 300- 375

Parlor, marble top, squared
corners, incised lines, c.
1855 . . . .   250- 290

Parlor, round wooden top,
walnut, tripod base, c. 1860   170- 250

Parlor, rectangular marble
top, veneer frieze, machine
lines, c. 1850 . . . .   300- 400

Pedestal, mahogany, c. 1850s   200- 300

Night, 2-drawer, porcelain
knobs, turned legs, walnut,
c. 1850 . . . .   195- 420

Sheraton, night, cherry, 2-
drawer, c. 1810 . . . .   420- 485

TABLES:

Banquet, walnut dropleaf,
91" long, c. 1840 . . . .   2,700- 2,900

Card, Hepplewhite, cherry,
1790s 1,100- 1,450

Tilt-top, walnut, tripod base,
c. 1850 . . . .   525- 585

Game, spool legs, walnut, c.
1830 . . . .   750- 825

Dining, rectangular, drop-
leaf, cherry, c. 1840 . . . . . .   625- 745

Dining, round extension w/3
leaves, walnut, turned leg,
c. 1850 . . . .   690- 795

Dining, round extension w/5
leaves, cherry, c. 1830s . . .   2,000- 2,400

Dining, square extension, w/4
leaves, pedestal base, c.
1860 . . . .   650- 675

Butterfly, dropleaf, cherry,
c. 1750s 875- 1,200

Console, maple, lift top, 1
drawer, c. 1820s 750- 875

Kitchen, pine, dropleaf,
drawer at 1 end, c. 1840s . .   510- 520

Kitchen, chestnut, rectangular top, turned legs, c.
1860s 350- 450

Library, lower shelf, 1
drawer, c. 1870s . . . .   ·220- 260

Library, poplar frame, mahogany veneer, rectangu-
lar top, c. 1890 . . . .   150- 180

Tavern, maple, single drawer,
turned legs, c. 1800s 700- 800

Tavern, cherry, round, 1
drawer, c. 1830 . . . .   600- 725

Parlor, oak, half shelf, rectangular top, c. 1895 . . . . .   160- 180

Parlor, mahogany, French
legs, c. 1890s 122- 185

Round, oak, 54" dia., pedestal, square feet, 3 extra
leaves, 1890s 320- 380

Round, oak, 36" dia., round
base, lion's paw feet 365- 420

Hepplewhite, inlaid mahogany, oval top, drop leaves,
single drawer 3,100- 3,400

Chippendale card table,
lunetted corners, c. 1770. .   17,000+

Chippendale, piecrust tilt
top, birdcage, carved base
and claw feet (ill.) 1,400- 1,600

WASHSTANDS:

Walnut, towel bars, 1 drawer,
turned leg, c. 1850 . . . .   250- 320

Walnut, towel bars, wooden
splashboard, c. 1860 . . . . . .   240- 300

Commode, marble top and
splashboard, burl veneer
panels on 3 drawers, molded
pilasters, projection front,
c. 1840 . . . .   510- 570

Commode, marble top and
splashboard, single drawer,
2 doors below, 1850 . . . . . .   415- 525

Maple, 1 drawer, c. 1870 . . . . .   240- 340

Oak, 1 drawer, slop jar com-
partment, brass-plated
handles, c. 1880s 220- 330

Pine, towel bars, opening for
basin, 1 drawer below, c.
1850 . . . .   275- 360

Oak, 3 drawers, slop jar com-
partment, c. 1890s 170- 265

WHATNOTS:

Corner, walnut, 5 graduated
shelves, turned finials, c.
1850 . . . .   480- 590

Corner, on cupboard base, 3
graduated shelves w/fretted
backs, c. 1860 . . . .   420- 485

Side, 5 graduated shelves,
walnut, turned finials, c. 1860   370- 450

Hanging, glass doors above, 2
drawers below, applied
molding at top 275- 375

Hanging, walnut, leaf carved,
4 graduated shelves, c. 1850 .   350- 400

FURNITURE, AMERICAN
OAK:

Bed—combination wardrobe,
desk, bookcase, and folding
bed. Weight, 460 lbs! 430- 480

Bed, folding, mirrored, with
pierced carving trim 220- 260

Bedstead, headboard 6'2",
paneled, applied carving 160- 190

Bookcase, 5'11" by 3'10", combination straight and curved
front, mirror 380- 390

173   (continued)

Bookcase-Desk, adjustable shelves, pidgeonholes in slant-front desk, mirror 350- 450

Cabinet, china, 6″ tall by 4′6″, curved glass sides 570- 625

Chair, pressed-back dining, cane seat 90- 125

Chair, parlor side, upholstered back and seat 92- 152

Chiffonier, 5-drawer, wishbone mirror 138- 178

Desk, rolltop "S" curve, pedestal base, paneled sides/back 575- 655

Desk, slant-top lady's parlor .. 175- 270

Dresser, cheval, bonnet box, applied carvings 240- 260

Hall Tree, oval mirror, 4 hat hooks, umbrella holder, lidded seat 295- 335

Icebox, available in many sizes 470- 565

Rocker, lady's parlor, applied carving, rope spindles 180- 270

Rocker, upholstered seat, armless, rope spindles and posts . 160- 200

Sofa, wooden arms, padded back, spring seat, applied carving on back 170- 198

Stand, small parlor, curved legs, center brace 90- 110

Table, parlor or library, 24″ x 36″, drawer, lower shelf 92- 162

Table, round dining pedestal base 320- 415

Washstand, wishbone, applied carving, brass hardware 180- 195

Wardrobe, 8′ by 4′3″, two drawers, cornice with applied carvings 400- 500

Whatnot, 17″ by 21″, gallery railing, turned spindles 125- 175

FURNITURE, AMERICAN VICTORIAN:

Bedstead, 8′ tall, recessed, veneered panels, molded frame, urn finials, carved, pierced pediment 1,250-1,450

Chair, lady's oval back, finger roll, Louis XV substyle 300- 400

Chair, side, applied burl veneer panels/ornaments, molded cresting, demiarms 175- 280

Chair, side, machine lines, carving, applied burl veneer, Eastlake 165- 250

Chair, side, caned seat, incised carving on slat back, turned legs and stretchers 90- 100

Desk, davenport, sloping lift-top, 2′6″ tall, carved gallery, 4 side drawers 675- 800

Hall tree, 8′1″, carved pediment, burl veneer, marble top over drawer 775- 875

Hat rack, 19″ by 36″, incised lines, porcelain tipped, accordion type 150- 225

Love seat, medallion back, 4′2″, finger roll 725- 825

Mirror, pier, 7′ 10″, machine carving, pilasters, molded, incised pediment, marble top over drawer, Eastlake 450- 550

Rocker, folding fireside, needlepoint upholstery 180- 220

Secretary, slant front, 7′ 40″, molding bands framing front and drawers, applied, carved ornaments 1,900-2,400

Settee, step-back, machine lines and carving, 3′, Eastlake ... 290- 320

Stands, lamp, with or without marble tops, simple to ornate carvings (in demand as plant stands) 250- 285

Table, dining, rectangular extension, 30″ by 42″, incised lines on legs 285- 320

Table, dining, round extension, 48″, applied burl veneers, ornaments on pedastal base . 600- 650

Table, library, 32″ by 53″, burl veneer panels, banding, applied ornaments 590- 650

Table, oval marble top, 24″ by 38″, burl veneer, raised panels on apron/legs, applied ornaments, center urn 400- 480

Table, rectangular marble top, 23″ by 32″, burl veneers on apron/legs, incised lines, Eastlake 450- 495

Wardrobe, 7′ by 3′4″, molded door frames, applied panels on dresser, molded base 510- 620

Washstand, commode, high marble splashback with soap shelves, burl veneers on drawers/doors, teardrop pulls 700- 850

Whatnot, corner, 5′ tall, graduated shelves with fretted backs 280- 385

Furniture, English

The demand for the genuine far exceeds the genuine. The prices are staggering — and going, going h-i-g-h-e-r! The prices listed here are already out-of-date, pricewise.

Furniture, English:
    William & Mary style 1689-1702
    Queen Anne style   1702-1714
    Early Georgian style 1702-1745
    Chippendale style   1745-1765
    Adam style   1765-1790
    Hepplewhite style   1780-1800
    Sheraton style   1790-1810
    Regency style   1793-1820

BEDS:
    Adam style walnut and
        damask bedstead w/round
        fluted pillar legs 1,500-1,800
    Chippendale style carved ma-
        hogany 4-post canopy
        w/acanthus carved flaring
        tester and shaggy claw feet . 5,800-6,400

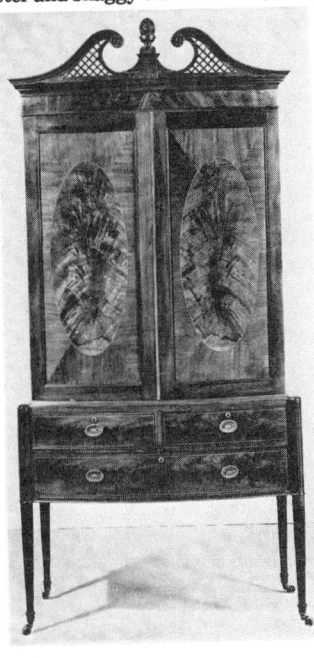

CABINETS:
    Early Georgian breakfront,
        carved and inlaid mahogany,
        plinth base 6,700-7,400
    Regency style breakfast, 4
        glazed doors, cupboard below 5,200-5,800
    Chippendale style book cabinet,
        mahogany, 2 paneled cup-
        board doors, bracket feet . . . 5,700-6,100
    Sheraton style carved and
        inlaid butler's china cabinet
        w/secretary drawer. Double
        doors, single-shelved cup-
        board 6,800-6,950
    Hepplewhite bow-front cabinet-
        on-stand, inlaid mahogany,
        in 2 sections, round tapered
        legs (ill.) 7,200-8,450

CHAIRS:
    Gilded, decorated, inlaid
        M.O.P., papier-mache,
        c. 1860 (ill.)   110-   140
    Queen Anne style corner
        chair, slip seat. Shell-
        carved front legs 3,700- 4,200
    Queen Anne style dining
        chair, solid and burl
        walnut, fiddle-shaped seat,
        leaf-carved cabriole legs . . 2,800- 3,400
    William & Mary style side
        chair, walnut, needlepoint
        seat and back 1,800- 2,200
    Regency style library chair,
        rosewood, leather uphol-
        stery, reeded seat rails,
        incurvate legs 2,700- 2,975
    Sheraton style painted and
        decorated armchair, shield-
        shaped back, square taper-
        ing splayed legs, crewel
        embroidery (ill.) 2,700- 3,600
    Hepplewhite style dining
        chair, leather seat, balloon
        back 2,700- 3,400
    Adam-Hepplewhite arm-
        chair, painted and gilded,
        tapered legs 2,100- 2,900
    Chippendale style wing chair,
        on mahogany molded
        square legs 6,300- 6,800
    Early Georgian chair,
        damask upholstery,
        walnut, pad feet 3,200- 4,100

CHESTS OF DRAWERS:
    William & Mary style, on bun
        feet 3,600- 3,900
    Hepplewhite, inlaid mahog-
        any, serpentine front,
        valanced apron continuing
        to splayed feet 3,750- 4,200
    Hepplewhite, mahogany,
        bowfront, splayed bracket
        feet 3,900- 4,250

175

(continued)

Early Georgian mule type,
mahogany, on ogival
scrolled bracket feet 4,600- 5,400
Queen Anne, inlaid burl elm
and walnut 5,200- 5,600

CHEST-ON-CHESTS:
Chippendale, mahogany,
scrolled bracket feet 19,800-25,000
Queen Anne style, black and
gold, 3 drawers below, 6
above, resting on cabriole
legs, club feet 11,250-12,600

DESKS:
Sheraton style, inlaid mahogany and leather kidney-
shaped pedestal desk,
kneehole style (ill.) 7,800- 9,750
Early Georgian, walnut and
mahogany countinghouse
type 3,400- 3,900
Queen Anne, slant-front,
inlaid walnut, cartouche-
shaped brasses and bail
handles. Molded base
w/bracket feet 6,500- 7,400

LOVE SEATS:
Early Georgian, walnut,
loose seat cushion; on
acanthus-carved cabriole
legs; claw-and-ball feet . . . 5,700- 6,700

SECRETARIES:
Sheraton, bookcase type,
inlaid satinwood; in 2 sections w/2 glazed doors, w/5
graduated long drawers 12,000-14,700
Early Georgian, cabinet type,
inlaid walnut and burl
walnut; 2 mirrored doors;
bracket feet (ill.) 13,700-16,500
Queen Anne, bookcase type,
inlaid burl walnut, slant-
front, double doors above,
bracketed feet 18,500-21,600

SETTEES:
Queen Anne, two-chair-back,
walnut, slipseat, on slight
cabriole legs, pad feet 5,500- 6,400
William & Mary, walnut,
needlepoint covering, loose
seat 5,200- 5,450

SIDEBOARDS:
Regency style pedestal side-
board, inlaid mahogany
and satinwood; valanced
gallery; on quadrangular
pedestals, each w/shallow
drawer and cupboard.
Short saber feet 7,800- 9,600
Sheraton style bowfront,
inlaid mahogany and burl
wood. Bottle drawers, etc.
Square tapering legs inlaid
w/panels of burl wood 8,000- 9,700
Hepplewhite, small bowfront,
inlaid mahogany, tapering
legs w/string lines; spade
feet 7,750-10,100

STOOLS:
Early Georgian, mahogany
and damask fireside type,
cabriole legs, club feet 1,800- 2,400
Queen Anne, w/valanced
frame and cabriole legs,
club feet 2,700- 3,400

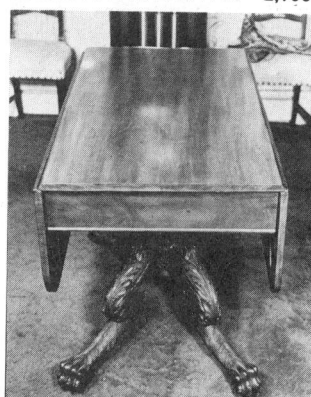

TABLES:
Library, extension, drop leaf,
mahogany, carved base,
claw feet (ill.) 1,200- 1,600
Sheraton style, inlaid satin-
wood sewing, octagonal
top, 2 drawers, sewing
bag, tapered square legs . . 2,400- 2,700
Sheraton style, mahogany
tilting-top breakfast; top
on 4 reeded splayed sup-
ports terminating in con-
forming brass toe caps . . . 2,800- 3,450

Hepplewhite style, card
table, carbriole legs crested
w/shell motifs. Slightly
scrolled toes 2,900- 3,450
Chippendale side table,
mahogany and inlaid satinwood; on square tapered
legs w/ormolu toes 4,200- 5,100
Chippendale mahogany
octagonal tripod table,
tilting top, tilting on a
"birdcage" support.
Whorled feet 3,800- 4,700
Early Georgian three-
pedestal hunt table, ma-
hogany, splayed tripods
ending in snake feet 4,800- 5,700

WINE COOLERS/STANDS:
Regency style, mahogany,
fluted lower border and
square supports 1,800- 2,200
Adam style, mahogany, 2
brass handles, zinc-lined . . 1,600- 1,900
Early Georgian, mahogany,
brass lion mask, loose ring
handles 2,000- 2,600

Furniture French:

Louis XIV style	1643-1715
Regence style	1715-1723
Louis XV style	1715-1774
Louis XVI style	1774-1792
Directoire style	1793-1804
Empire style	1804-1814
French Provincial	(furniture made in the provinces)

BEDS:
Directoire style day bed,
loose cushion and bolster . 2,400- 2,700
Directoire style alcove bed,
carved fluted posts 2,300- 2,600
CHAIRS:
Empire style salon chair 1,250- 1,650
Directoire style armchair,
painted, upholstered loose
cushion 1,600- 1,850
Directoire style ladder-back,
rush seat, fruitwood,
tapered legs 2,000- 2,400
Louis XVI style armchair,
carved and painted, loose
cushion 2,200- 2,750
Louis XV style, wide arm-
chair on cabriole supports.
Sides, back and loose
cushion in floral damask
upholstery 3,100- 3,800
Louis XV style walnut dining
chair, silk damask uphol-
stery, cartouche-shaped
molded back. Cabriole legs 3,200- 3,600
Regence style caned arm-
chair, carved beechwood,
silk damask seat, X-scroll
stretcher, loose cushion 1,900- 2,750
CHAISE LONGUES:
Louis XV style, walnut,
canted back, molded rails,
cabriole legs, upholstered . 4,000- 4,350
CABINETS:
Louis XVI upright cabinet,
inlaid w/tulipwood and
kingwood, marble plateau . 5,400- 5,800
Louis XV style serpentine-
front encoignure, inlaid
tulipwood and kingwood,
marble top, 2 doors,
cabriole feet 7,300- 7,700
Louis XV style inlaid mahog-
any cabinet, inset w/Sevres
porcelain plaques. Oblong
top, cabriole legs w/shelf
stretcher and shaped front 10,600-11,800
CANDLESTANDS:
Louis XVI telescopic,
w/round statuary marble
top; on arched tripod
w/slender shoe feet 2,200- 2,600
CHESTS:
Regence, walnut commode,
marble top, 4 drawers (ill.) . 3,800- 4,200
Louis XVI style commode
w/oblong marble top,
foliated cabriole legs 4,100- 4,400
Regence serpentine com-
mode, inlaid woods, marble
top, 4-drawer 4,400- 4,750

(continued)

DESKS:

Provincial, Louis XV style, slant-front desk, oblong top, whorl feet . . . . 5,000+

Empire style, Bonheur-du-jour (lady's desk), ormolu mounts, mahogany . . . . . . 6,500+

Directoire style fall-front desk, mahogany, 4 long drawers on square tapered supports, plinth feet . . . . . 12,000+

Directoire style boudoir writing desk, mahogany, rectangular 2-tier stand. The rear supports enclose a rising screen, silk 4,000- 4,700

Louis XVI style brass mounted Acajou Bureau a Cylindre, w/marble plateau. Fluted tapering legs. 4,600- 4,900

Louis XV style Bureal Plat, painted and decorated. Serpentine-contoured top, 3 working drawers, the reverse w/mock drawers. Angular cabriole legs . . . . 12,500+

MIRRORS:

Empire style, Cheval glass, mahogany. Frame richly inlaid. Ormolu candel-abras; "urn" mountings . . 3,300- 4,100

Louis XIV style carved and gilded wall mirror. Upright frame w/paneled borders around the mirror. The arched cresting is outlined w/carved leaf scrolls, ... 3,100- 3,850

SECRETARIES:

Louis XVI style brass-mounted Acajou secretary w/marble top, metal gallery, 2 glazed doors; on square tapering feet 5,500- 5,900

SIDEBOARDS:

Provincial, Louis XV style, carved beechwood, in 2 sections. The upper part w/open shelves carved in the front; the projecting lower section having 2 frieze drawers over a pair of cupboard doors; short cabriole legs w/scroll toes . 5,800- 6,600

Louis XV style buffet-verrier. Inlaid fruitwood and ash. Superstructure has 4 open tiers; cabriole legs 5,700- 6,400

Louis XV style buffet base. Carved walnut, oblong top, 2 frieze drawers and 2 fielded cupboard doors, squat cabriole legs 8,500- 9,700

TABLES:

Louis XVI brass-mounted Acajou Bouillotte table, w/drum top and pierced gallery. 2 small drawers; on fluted tapering legs . . . 4,900- 6,200

Louis XVI carved and gilded Petite Console w/marble top. A guilloche-carved elongated S-scroll support 6,100- 6,800

Louis XVI mahogany extension dining table, on square tapering legs 5,900- 6,400

Louis XVI walnut library table, oblong top paneled in leather 4,700- 4,900

Louis XVI yew wood, table, rectangular top. 2 small drawers, on tapering legs . 5,200- 5,800

Louis XV inlaid tulipwood and amaranth tric-trac table w/oblong reversible top. Backgammon well, on angular cabriole legs 7,700- 7,975

Louis XV small writing table, oval top. Tapered angular cabriole legs 7,900- 9,100

Empire style wall table, mahogany, w/marble top, figural supports. Mirror panel 5,200- 5,850

Directoire style mahogany tric-trac table w/removable oblong top on square, tapering legs 4,400- 5,200

178

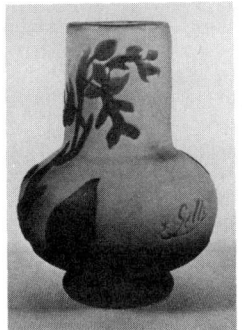
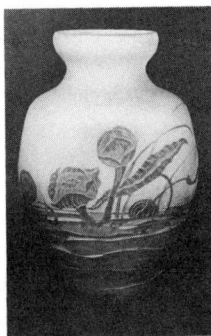

Galle Cameo Glass

Galle Cameo Glass

Establishing his first factory at Nancy, France, in 1883, Emile Galle developed a fine cameo glass. Because so many assistants made Galle glass, it is impossible to know for sure which pieces Emile actually made. After his death in 1904 a star (★) was put in front of "Galle." This was done only for a short time and today, Star Galle is also quite collectible. All pieces were signed.

Atomizer, brown/green, frosted ground	$ 260-	285
Bowl, blue, floral, scenic lake and boats, 6" high, signed	625-	725
Bowl, purple on frost, flowers, 5" signed	710-	900
Box, covered, 6" dia. signed	400-	450
Chandelier, 15" high, floral glass prisms, signed	1,800-2,200	
Cruet, thistles, maroon, beige/pink, applied handle, signed	450-	550
Inkstand, faience, 14" long, signed	460-	560
Jardiniere, yellow/black, acid etched, 8½" high	2,100-2,400	
Lamp, glass, table, 23" high, signed	970-1,100	
Pitcher, 9" high, signed	650-	675
Rose bowl, flowers/birds, Star Galle	675-	850
Toothpick, red/blue/yellow, signed	240-	260
Tray, rose/blue/open handles, 18½" long	750-	950
Tumbler, vaseline color, gold/enamel border, 6" high, signed	295-	310
Urn, cherries/birds, acid etched, Star Galle	2,100-2,400	
Vase, dark green, red ground, Star signature	510-	625
Vase, water lilies, blue/yellow/green, 6½" high, signed	500-	600
Vase, lotus blossoms, yellow/pink/white, 5½" high, signed	500-	600
Vase, apricot/green, acid clear, 7" high (ill.)	385-	450
Vase, "bird" scene, blue/yellow/white, 7¼" high	410-	470
Vase, miniature, frosted, mauve to clear, floral, Star Galle (ill.)	240-	285

Game Plates

Game Plates

Plates decorated with fish, animals or birds fall into this category. They usually came in sets, 12 plates and a serving platter. Popular during the 1800s, most were made in Europe. Globe China Company in Ohio also made them in the late 1800s. Repros!

Bass on fly lure	$ 80-	90
Birds in flight, blue/gold background, France, 8½" dia	42-	52
Buck and doe, forest scene in various colors, 9" dia	37-	47
Deer grazing, Bavaria, 7½" dia	28-	37
Deer, Buffalo Pottery	40-	42
Grouse, gold rim, Germany 11½" dia	46-	56
Mallard duck, gold border, Staffordshire china, 7" dia	46-	56
Pheasant, blue/gold background	54-	64
Pheasants, signed "Crown of Gold" (ill.)	17-	27
Quail, gold rim, pierced for handling (ill.)	51-	61
Turkey, hunter, multicolors, Globe, 8" dia	19-	27
Turkey on platter (ill.)	29-	38
Wild boar in woods, Austria, 8" dia	32-	42

Games

Salem Mass., calls itself the "game capital of the world." The sailors who returned to its port brought home games like parcheesi and chess from the Orient. A form of backgammon goes back to 3,000 B.C. "The

(continued)

Games

games people play" is more than just a song. Oh, those Parker Brothers!

Alley Oop	$ 12-	18
Authors, c. 1912	11-	20
Checkered Game of Life	35-	45
Fibber McGee	18-	27
Fish Pond (ill.)	45-	55
Italian chess board, inlaid with ivory, mid-1880s, all pieces hand-carved	550-675	
Numerica, Parker Bros., 1895	10-	17
Old Maid & Old Bachelor (or Beaux and Belles)	40-	48
Pollyanna	11-	16
Ring My Nose, 1925	19-	27
Sambo Target	29-	38
The United States Game, Parker Bros.	52-	62

Gaudy Dutch

This highly-decorated lightweight china was made around 1825 in the Staffordshire district in England, reputedly for the Pennsylvania Dutch trade in the York, Lancaster, and Philadelphia areas. Today, the general collector confuses it with Gaudy Ironstone. The latter was made at a much later date and was marked. Gaudy Dutch was not.

Bowl, King's Rose, 14" dia	$175-200
Creamer, Dove pattern, 3½" high (ill.)	220-240
Cup/saucer, handleless, signed, 1856	180-200

Gaudy Ironstone

Gaudy Ironstone

This was created in the early 1850s to stimulate more interest in the plain white ironstone. Decorated to some extent in the style of Japanese Imari, it is sometimes confused with Gaudy Dutch. It really looks more like Gaudy Welsh. It never achieved popularity and was discontinued after a few years.

Cup/saucer, cobalt, orange/blue flowers	$158-178
Gravy boat and dish, red/blue/ green, floral decor	52- 70
Pitcher, blue/orange/green, 6" high	145-160
Plate, Pinwheel design, cobalt/burnt orange (ill.)	80-100
Plate, dinner, dark blue, 9¼" dia .	60- 72
Plate, Blackberry/Leaf design, cobalt, impressed "WALLEY" (ill.)	75- 90
Platter, floral, signed Copeland, 10½" dia	158-170

Gaudy Dutch

Gaudy Welsh

Gaudy Welsh

Made after 1850, this type of chinaware is cruder than Gaudy Dutch. Its bluish-purple coloring is one of its characteristics. General collectors confuse it with late Imari.

Cracker jar	$100-120
Creamer, Oyster pattern, signed "Allerton's" (ill.)	53- 62
Creamer, Daisy and Chain pattern	58- 72
Cup/saucer, Tulip pattern (ill.) . . .	70- 80
Cup/saucer, Tulip pattern, no handle	41- 51
Ewer, Tulip pattern, 4" high	58- 68
Mug, handled, Urn or Vase pattern	49- 59
Pitcher, blue/red, reptile handle . .	72- 92
Pitcher, Oyster pattern	72- 82
Plate, Strawberry pattern, 8¼" dia	92-110
Platter, Wagon Wheel pattern . .	96-115
Teapot, Strawberry pattern	180-220
Tea set, complete 24 piece, Tulip pattern	650-725
Sugar bowl, covered, Daisy and Chain pattern	115-140

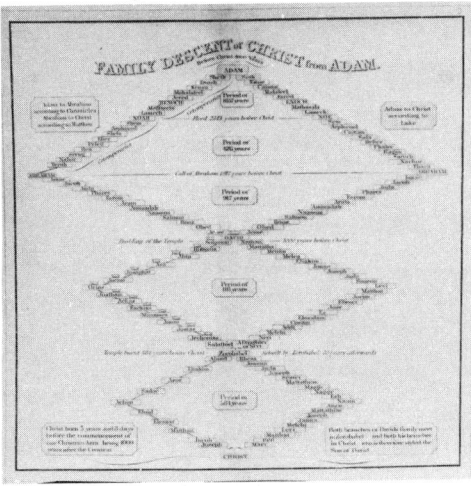

Genealogy

Genealogy

A recorded history from one ancestor to another; demography; the science of vital statistics; paleography; the study of describing or deciphering ancient writings. Look in the "Clubs, Publications" section for places to write, etc. Since our Bicentennial, more and more people are interested in their family backgrounds. The fine book, *Roots* is just one example.

Gibson Girl Plates

Gibson Girl Plates

The eminent American artist, Charles Dana Gibson, produced a series of 24 drawings titled "The Widow and Her Friends." The Royal Doulton Works, Lambeth, England, reproduced the drawings on plates in the early 1900s. A complete set can be seen at the Houston Museum, Chattanooga, Tennessee. Highly collectible today. Most are in the $70-90 range.

Failing to find rest, she returns home	$ 72- 82
Miss Babbles brings a copy (ill.) .	72- 82
Mrs. Diggs is alarmed	72- 82
She finds that exercise . . . (ill.) . . .	72- 82
She goes as Juliet	72- 82
She is disturbed by a vision	72- 82
She looks for relief	72- 82
They all go skating	72- 82

Gillinder Glass

(continued)

Gillinder Glass

You'll find a lot of this fine glass in our Pattern Glass Section. Here are two indicative pieces.

Candlesticks, pair, white milk
glass, crucifixes, 6-sided bases,
9½" high (ill.) .... $ 85- 95
Goblets, pair, 3-part mold, "1876
Centennial," 6½" high (ill.) ... 55- 65

Girandoles

Girandoles

These are mantel garnitures, and a set consists of a centerpiece with a 3-branch candelabra and 2 sidepieces for holding single candles. The bases were usually made of marble or alabaster and the main body cast in brass. Cut prisms, 4 to 6 inches long, hung from the top of the 3 pieces. They were expensive when they were in vogue, early 1800s until mid-1800s.

Gold leaf, marble base, prisms,
girl and boy, birds, 16" high,
pair $365-425
Man and woman in European
attire, double handle, brass,
prisms, pr 410-450
3-piece set, 2-step marble and
brass bases, star-cut prisms .. 425-500
Indian, full figure, spear, 3
branches 525-570
3 ornate brass arms, glass
prisms, girl and boy on marble
base, pr 470-525

Glass Mugs

Also see specific type and make in Pattern Glass section.

Hobnail, blue (ill.) .... $ 12- 17
Little Orphan Annie mug 32- 47
"Mephistopheles", blue
opalescent, 3¼" high (ill.) 43- 53
Mug, lemonade, cranberry (ill.) .. 52- 62
Postum mug, 1930s 26- 36
Shirley Temple, 3¾" high 19- 27
Sterner's Clothing Store mug,
1920s 15- 31
Stump glass mug (ill.) 24- 36

GLASS - TYPES

Cased Glass:

Glass with layers of different colors — one color actually encases another. Usually 2 colors are used, 3 sometimes found. 4 to 5 are rare.

Flashed and Overlay Glass:

A gather of glass of one color is covered while hot with a thin layer of another color. This double gather is achieved by dipping the first quickly into the hot metal of the other. It's then worked out on a metal slab and blown, as if it were one piece; the thin layer being on the outside.

Luster-Stained Glass:

A luster stain is applied much like varnish on the inside or the outside of the glass; after it's "painted," the glass is heated in the kiln to fix the color. Copper luster stains the outside red; green, blue, yellow or purple are also used. This is a cheap imitation of cased glass.

Gold

Too few people know anything about this metal. The weight (karat) of the gold is im-

Glass Mugs

182

portant. 24 karat is pure gold. One karat is one 24th part of pure gold; 20k gold is 20 parts pure gold, 4 parts alloy. Cheap jewelry is usually mounted in 10 or 12k settings; expensive jewelry is usually mounted in at least 18k settings, the other 6 parts being an alloy to harden the setting, as gold is a soft metal. Examples of various types are listed below. Originally, "pure" meant unalloyed metal; "standard," 11/12 fine, or 11 parts pure gold, 1 part alloy. The world's going crazy, goldwise, remember, *always*, that America is the greatest country in the world! When our dollar is down, gold rises; our dollar *will* come back! Buy it if you *like*, but *love* your country!

Gold

Gold Alloys:

English gold: 75% gold, 12½% silver, 12½% copper

Green gold: 60% gold, 40% silver

Roman gold: 10 parts fine gold, 3 parts silver, 7 parts copper, 4 parts guinea alloy

White gold: the basis of all white gold alloys is a fine grade of German silver with a high percentage of nickel. Can be made in any karat weight.

Blue gold: used in place of platinum, 18 parts gold, 6 parts iron.

18k gold for rings, watch cases, etc.: 19½ grains, fine gold, 3 grains, fine copper, 1½ grains, fine silver

Incan God (ill.), 23K gold $750-850

California 25¢ pieces, 14k gold (ill.) 150-200 each

Know what you're doing, especially if you're buying gold outside the United States. **Always** buy from the stores, banks, etc., controlled by the government of that particular nation. Gold-plated lead coins are literally a dime a dozen, valuewise.

Goofus Glass

Goofus Glass

This is pressed glass painted by spraying before firing. What you find today usually has the paint chipped off in places. What Harry Northwood had in mind when he made this product during the late 1800s is lost in the back rivers of time.

Bowl, brown, red flowers, 10″ dia	$ 24- 34
Bowl, Dogwood pattern, 8″ dia . .	26- 37
Compote, red, gold over green, open, 7″ high	17- 27
Dish, ruffled, gold, shaded red, blues, 10″ dia	31- 41
Jar, pickle, flowers, red/gold, 20″ high	26- 36
Lamp base, green, red, gold	32- 42
Plate, cake, red/gold, 8″ dia	7- 11
Plate, ruffled edges, gold/red, 10″ dia. (ill.)	17- 25
Vase, grapes, 8″ high	13- 19
Vase, poppy, opalescent, 8″ high	24- 34
Vase, rose, 7″ high	24- 35

Goss-on-Trent

Considered a "fairing," these ivory-tinted porcelain pieces were made in the 19th century by William Goss at Stoke-on-Trent, England. Other factories imitated his wares.

Elephant	$ 17- 22
Hen-on-nest	16- 21
Cup/saucer, Shakespeare crest . .	12- 22
Pitcher, flowers, 4″ high (ill.)	19- 27
Plate, 4″ and 6″ dia	12- 18
Vase, horseshoe, 3-leaf clover, 4″ high	19- 24

(continued)

Goss-on-Trent

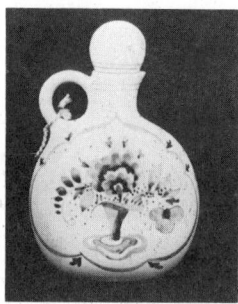

Gouda Pottery

Gouda Pottery

From the land of the cheese, since the early 1700s the area around Gouda, Holland, has been known also as a pottery center. Clay pipes were one of the first products made. Art Nouveau type pottery came in around 1910. What we find today came from the 1910-1920 period.

Bowl, green/blue/yellow	$ 50- 60
Candlesticks, pair, floral pattern, 5½" high	70- 80
Compote, yellow/green, 11" high	65- 70
Decanter, blue decoration on gray, 6" high (ill.)	50- 60
Jug, matt finish, signed "Canada"	90-100
Pitcher, orange/green/black, 6½ high	120-140
Plate, green/yellow pears, striped border, 6½" dia.	30- 40
Tobacco jar, scroll/leaf decor, 7" high	140-150
Vase, multicolored glaze, 8" high, paper label	85- 95

Granite Ware

This is a thick, heavy clay ware that too many people confuse with ironstone. Granite Ware was a product of the 1850s and was mass-produced for the people who couldn't afford anything better. It fell from grace in the late 1880s when the vogue shifted to European porcelains, Haviland in particular.

Graniteware

Graniteware

The speckled glaze that looks like granite gives this metalware its name. Popular in the early 1900s, today it's collectible for decorative purposes. Blue or gray, with mottled backgrounds. Being reproduced.

Cream can, blue/gray	$ 32- 41
Coffeepot gray/blue, 9" high, lid (ill.)	35- 43
Hanging shelf, gray/blue, 16" wide	46- 51
Lunch pail, gray/blue	33- 42
Strainer, brown/white	29- 39
Teapot, blue/gray, lid, 6" high	28- 37
Washbasin, white inside, blue/white outside	39- 47

Greenaway, Kate

Daughter of an artist, she was born in England in 1846. As a young lady she illustrated Christmas cards, later doing many books. English and German potteries used her illustrations of children on their wares.

Buttons, brass, for child's dress, set of 6	$ 78- 90
Coffeepot, children under tree, 5½" high	110-115
Cup/saucer, children playing with dog	34- 44
Fairy lamp, girl, Parian, 6" high	120-150
Matchholder, boy, bisque	61- 71
Mug, pink, children playing	60- 70
Plate, 2 girls playing ball, 5" dia	54- 64

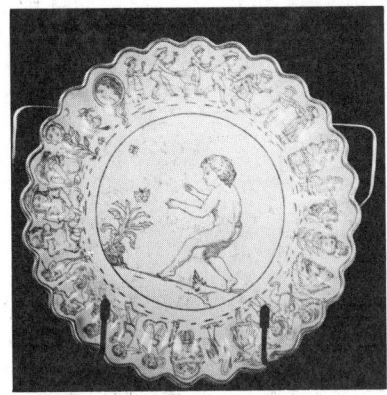

Greenaway, Kate

Plate, Copeland China, 8¼" dia.
(ill.) 65- 75
Salt/pepper, pr. in wicker basket .   79- 89
Teapot, children on cover and
pot, 6" high 50- 60
Tray, boy with hoop, girls
playing, silver frame   134-139

Greentown Glass

Made by the Indiana Tumbler and Goblet
Company, Greentown, Indiana, around 1894,
one of the items sought today is "Fighting
Cocks" on a blue basketweave base. See
specific types in PATTERN GLASS section.

Gunderson Peachblow

Gunderson Peachblow

The Gunderson Glass Company, succes-
sors to the Pairpoint Company, which was
formerly the Mt. Washington Glass Company, all at New Bedford, Massachusetts,
made this "new" Peachblow from 1952 until
1957. It was not as well colored as the earlier
Peachblows and was heavier.

Cup/saucer, reeded, opal handle . $110-135
Decanter   220-265
Goblet   170-198

Pitcher, water   220-275
Toothpick, pink/white, 2½" high
(ill.) 68- 83
Toothpick holder, 1¾" high   110-140
Tumbler   110-160
Vase   220-270

Hair Work

In the late 1850s, *Godey's Lady's Book*
printed directions for hair work, followed in
1864 by *Peterson's Magazine*. The craze
lasted from then until the end of the 1800s.
Brooches, lockets, woven chains, everything
that could be made with human hair (also,
cow's hair, though no one admitted to same),
was produced. Most articles were made by
braiding and interlacing hair over hollow
forms. Hair wreaths, bouquets, and the like
were made and framed for hanging on the
wall. They're being collected today.

Bouquet of flowers, brown/black,
6" high, in open frame . . . . . . $ 20- 32
Wreath, brown/black, 10"
diameter, under glass, in frame   26- 36

Handbags, Ladies'

Some of the late Victorian bags are quite
ornate. Some of the metal frames, clasps, and
chains were 14k gold, others silver plate. Age
and condition dictate price.

Victorian type, blue velvet,
silver plate fixtures . . . . $ 14- 22
Rhinestone covered, silver chain   14- 23

Handel

This firm manufactured lamps, shades,
other items such as tobacco jars, in Meriden,
Connecticut, late 1890s until World War II.

Bowl, cased, brass collar,
signed, 6¼" dia. . . . . $ 85- 100
Box, verde finish, flowers
inside, signed Runge 240- 295
Humidor, brown ground,
Arabic scene, signed 320- 385
Humidor, tobacco, green/red
ground, hunter and dog . . .   290- 340
Jar, cookie, blue/white, flower,
transfer 290- 345
Jar, tobacco, bird dogs, brass
trim, signed 320- 375
Lamp, blue, Arabic scene, 3
lights, 19" high   1,650-1,875
Lamp, desk, green art glass,
gold feather (Quezel?)
overlay, signed 790- 920

(continued)

Lamp, lily pond, frogs, green/ white shade, 3-light, 22″ high	895-1,200
Shade, yellow/opalescent green, floral designs, signed, 13″ diameter	875- 975
Vase, trees, signed and numbered, 8″ high	195- 240

Hatpin Holders

Hand-painted China

Hand-painted China

This is mentioned here because there are so many questionable pieces around today. Haviland specialized in selling white blank pieces to amateur painters, as did other companies. Just because it says Haviland on the back doesn't mean it was painted by their artists.

Plate, floral motif, 8″ dia., signed "Rudolstadt" (ill.)	$ 48- 68
Plate, floral motif, 8½″ dia., signed "Bach and Beyer" (ill.)	48- 68

Hardware

Hardware

Porcelain (ill.) and brass doorknobs, keyhole plates, hinges, doorbells — anything to do with old hardware is being collected today.

Hatpin Holders

Made of every type of material but usually glass, they were plain, decorated, even cut. Popular during the mid-1800s, they make fine flower holders.

Fastened to porcelain tray, ring tree each side, Austria	$ 28- 40
Flowers and birds, gilt, Bavaria	17- 26
Blue/gold, birds, flowers, gilt edge, Austria	27- 36
White ground, blue/green, purple, Iris decor	22- 32
Carnival glass, Marigold, trunk-shaped, N in bottom	47- 57
Sterling silver, initialed, signed Tiffany and Company on side	85- 95
Tiffany glass, probably part of dresser set	110-120

Hatpins

Originally designed to hold m'lady's hat in place, some had a metal shaft of 12 inches long. Usually they had an ornamental "jewel" on the end. They went out of style right after World War I when the gals started wearing smaller hats.

Abalone, 10k shaft, 10″ long	$ 8- 12
Blue/white porcelain button, 11″ shaft	11- 18
Butterfly, rhinestones, 11″ shaft	12- 17
14 karat gold knob, 2 initials, 10½″ shaft	20- 30
Jade button in 14 karat gold setting, 11″ shaft	23- 33
Kitten, 10k shaft 11″ long	10- 15
Porcelain, flowers, 11″ shaft	17- 26
Sterling silver flower, 11″ shaft, Tiffany jewelry, flower-shape	70- 90

Haviland China

Haviland China

This is the most complicated china in the world today. Many people were involved, both here and abroad. Suffice to say, the first factory was started in Limoges, France, in 1842, by David Haviland, an American importer. He called his firm Haviland and Company. If you're a serious collector, you already know these facts. If you're just beginning, buy a book and study.

Bone dish, white	$ 14- 23
Bowl, Marimar pattern, 9" diameter	27- 37
Bowl, salad, strawberries, flowers, gold rim	39- 49
Bowl, berry, blueberries, gold lip .	42- 52
Bone dish, Ranson pattern, set of 6	54- 64
Box, jewel, pink moss roses, blue-velvet lined, hinged lid . . .	40- 50
Butter chip, pink/blue flowers, set of 6	19- 29
Butter dish w/lid, green/yellow roses	70- 80
Cake plate, Clemonceaux pattern, 9" high on standard . .	39- 49
Candlesticks, pair, green/yellow, gold trim, 12½" high	58- 68
Celery vase, purple flowers, gold, open handles	39- 48
Chocolate pot, blue/yellow flowers, gold trim	73- 83
Coffeepot, yellow/roses, signed "C.F.H." (This is Charles Field Haviland china and not made by Theodore or David)	45- 55
Creamer and sugar, lily-of-the-valley motif, blue trim, gold rim	67- 77
Cup/saucer, demitasse, spring flowers, blue/pink ground	27- 37
Decanter, signed "H & Co., Limoges," floral decor	52- 62
Dinner set, service for eight, Autumn Leaf	825-950

Mug, shaving, apple blossoms, initials LBJ	39- 48
Pitcher, grapes on vine, gold handle, signed, 10" high	55- 70
Plate, dinner, 9¾" dia., signed "Theodore Haviland Limoges" (ill.)	20- 28
Plate, bread and butter, autumn leaves, gold rim	24- 33
Plate, oyster, 8½" dia. signed "H & Co. Limoges" (ill.)	22- 32
Platter, pink roses, gold border, blue background	38- 48
Powder box, white/roses, signed "H & Co., Limoges"	53- 63
Toothpick holder, pinched side, Aurene color, 3" high	23- 33
Tray, dresser, floral background, rose/pink border	29- 39
Tureen, vegetable, morning glories, hand-painted, cover . . .	80- 90

Heisey Glass

Heisey Glass

From 1895 until 1954 some of the finest glass in the world was produced by this firm at Newark, Ohio. It was made in clear and in colors. Imperial Glass Company, Bellaire, Ohio, purchased many of the Heisey molds and are reproducing Heisey today sometimes without the Heisey trademark, an "H" inside a diamond. Paper labels were also used. See specific patterns in PATTERN GLASS section.

Bowl, oceanic, clear, 12" dia.	$ 36- 47
Bowl, signed, 9" dia.	32- 40
Crystolite, clear punch cup	7- 11
Diamond Optic, pink, mustard jar w/lid & spoon, 3½" high . . .	17- 26
Express, clear, footed sugar, 3" high	12- 19
Express, pink, dolphin, footed creamer	16- 22
Express, pink, footed sugar	17- 23
Empress, pink, dolphin-footed, 3-handled sugar	16- 19

(continued)

Flat Panel #352, clear, 2-qt. jar, covered, used for tobacco, lid impressed "Benson & Hedges NY Pat Dec 25 03," 6½" dia ..	70- 80
Goblet, Puritan, 4-3/8" high, signed	21- 34
Narrow Flute, clear, footed creamer, 3¼" high	16- 21
Oceanic (Orchid Etch), clear, crimped bowl, 12" dia., unsigned	30- 40
Pillows, clear, footed mint tray, 6½" dia	34- 44
Pitcher, 8" high, signed (ill.)	55- 65
Ridgeleigh, clear, cigarette box w/lid, 4" long	19- 28
Sherbet, Greek Key, clear, 4½ oz.	13- 16
Thumbprint & Panel, clear, ice pitcher	67- 78
Twist, emerald, flared 4-footed bowl, 12" dia	39- 47

Heisey Glass Animals

Some were made in the 1930s but the most famous were designed by Royal Hickman who worked for the Haeger Pottery Company. All were pressed in a mold. Some animals were marked with the Diamond H, some were even marked twice, while others weren't marked at all. Most were made in crystal but some were made in deep amber, honey amber, and cobalt (blue). Some were frosted completely, others only partially frosted. In 1962, Imperial Glass Company, which had purchased Heisey's molds in 1958, reproduced certain animals. Not all the reproductions are marked with the Diamond H. Those listed here have never been reproduced.

Chick, 1" high	$ 42- 52
Rooster, 5 5/8" high	73- 80
Rooster vase, 6½" high	74- 84
Ducklings, floating or standing, 2 1/4" and 2 5/8" high	43- 53
Elephant, 4 1/2" and 5 7/8" high .	70- 80
Fish bookend, 6 5/8" high	82- 92
Tropical fish piece, 12" high	94-105
Gazelle, 11" high	80- 85
Giraffe, 11" high	70- 80

Others were goose (wings down), Clydesdale horses, filly horse (head forward), same (head backward), show horse, horse head bookends, rearing horse bookends, piglets, bunnies, rabbit, cygnet, sparrow. REPRODUCED items, 1962-1968; bull, hen, fighting rooster, dogs (Airedale, Scotty), donkey, ducks (3 mallards), medium elephant, geese (wings up, wings half-way), horses (flying mare, plug horse, ponies) pheasant, pigeon, rabbit and rabbit paperweight, swan.

Hitching Posts

Used for years to keep the horse from wandering while its master visited or shopped. The Jockey is the most famous, also the one being reproduced the most.

Hitching post, Negro boy in jockey's clothing, ring in hand, 27" high	$240-285
Hitching post, black bear on hind legs, ring in paw, 36" high, European	320-390
Hitching block, iron marked "Foundry, Toledo, 1885" (the portable kind you hitched to bridle)	38- 48
Horse's head (ill.)	100-120
Chimney Sweeper, 32" high	120-145

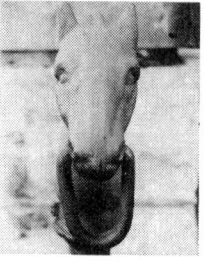 

Hitching Posts   Holly Amber Glass

Holly Amber Glass

See PATTERN GLASS section. Mentioned here because it's so rare, some classify it as art glass. It isn't.

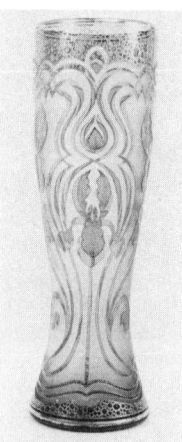

Honesdale Glass

Honesdale Glass

The factory that made this glass was originally established to decorate glass for Christian Dorflinger in White Mill, Pennsyl-

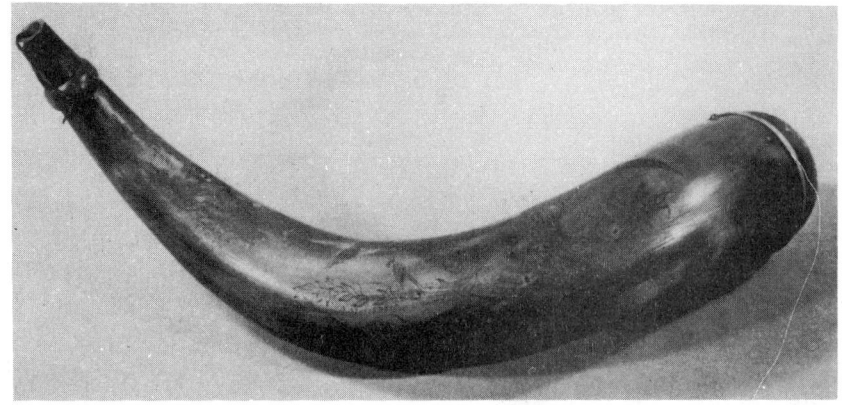

Horn

vania, during the mid-1800s. The factory was purchased in 1916 by C.F. Prosch. He made one of the poorest imitations of cameo glass ever seen.

Cameo vase, frosted iridescent, green/yellow flowers, 12″ high .	$128-158
Cameo vase, blue ground, red/ yellow rose blossoms, 10½″ high, signed	210-270
Cameo vase, clear ground, green grapes, blue base, 12¾″ high, signed	190-225
Vase, iridescent, blue/green enameled flowers, 10″ high . . .	74- 84
Vase, acid cut, blue/gold, frosted, signed, 7″ high	190-240
Vase, Art Nouveau, floral decor, yellow-to-green, 11¼″ high, signed	130-160

Horn

Horns from various animals have been used for centuries to hold liquids, gunpowder, food, you-name-it. Powder horns dating back into the 1800s bring high prices today. To bend the calf's horn, an iron ring was fastened at the base of the skull. No, it didn't hurt! The Texas Longhorn cattle had magnificent horns, some measuring 7 feet across! See also — POWDER HORNS AND FLASKS.

Napkin ring	$ 12- 15
Snuffbox, mid-1800s, American .	31- 40
Texas Longhorns, velvet in center, ready for mounting . . .	92-102
Tumbler	12- 19
Hunting horn (ill.)	58- 70

Hot Plates

Hot Plates

Used to hold hot dishes, plates, etc., just about everyone made them.

Hull Pottery

Hull Pottery

This pottery was made in 1903 by Acme

189

(continued)

Pottery Co. at Crooksville, Ohio. Hull Pottery Co. took over and made art pottery from 1917 until 1950.

Basket, green to blue, handled ..	$ 25- 32
Basket, Ebb Tide, dark red, 15½"	19- 28
Bowl, green to pink, 9" high	18- 25
Candleholder, Blossomflite, handled, rose	9- 17
Pitcher, brown/pink, handled ...	22- 30
Planter, green/pink flowers, 8" high	13- 18
Plate, ovenproof, light green, mottled edge, 10½" dia. (ill.) ..	8- 14
Planter, ducks, green/yellow, 6½" high	11- 18
Planter, dog, cream, paper label, 8" high...................	11- 18
Salt/peppers, Red Riding Hood, 3" high...................	12- 16
Vase, yellow to blue, flowers, 8½" high	18- 26
Vase, tulips, red to blue, 7¼" high	18- 26
Vase, 2 handles, blue/pink, 6½ high	18- 26
Vase, 2 handles, light green, 6" high.................	19- 27

Hummel Items

Sister Maria Innocentia, born Berta Hummel in Massing, Germany, loved children, and her sketches, first sold in the 1930s, attracted the attention of the Goebel porcelain factory in Rodental, a small town near Coburg, in Bavaria. Authentic pieces bear both "M.I. Hummel" and the Goebel mark. Look out for Japanese fakes.

Figurines:		
Apple Tree Boy (Crown)	$190-	225
Apple Tree Girl (Crown)	185-	220
Bird Duet (Crown)	230-	250
Cinderella (TMK-4)	115-	135
Eventide (Crown)	380-	400
Happy Pastime (Crown)	280-	300
Let's Sing (Crown)	250-	275
Letter to Santa (TMK-4)	280-	300
Mail Is Here (TMK-2)	650-	700
She Loves Me (Crown)	240-	260
Ashtrays:		
Happy Pastime (TMK-1)	240-	260
Singing Lesson (TMK-2)	220-	240
Bells:		
Let's Sing (TMK-5)...........	120-	200
Farewell (TMK-5)	50-	80
Thoughtful (TMK-5).........	85-	100
Bookends:		
Bookworm (Crown), pair	660-	680

Candleholders:		
Angel Trio (TMK-1), set	240-	260
Candlelight (TMK-1)	575-	625
Madonnas:		
Flower Madonna, 11½" (TMK-1)	900-	1,100
Madonna with Halo (TMK-3) ...	75-	85
Music Boxes:		
Little Band (TMK-5)	160-	200
Nativity Sets:		
Small (TMK-4)	650-	750
Large (TMK-4)	750-	900
Plaques:		
Ba-Bee Rings (TMK-2), pair	230-	250
Merry Wanderer (TMK-3)	120-	140
Annual Plates:		
1971 Heavenly Angel	800-	1,000
1973 Globetrotter............	150-	220
1974 Goose Girl	75-	120
1975 Ride into Christmas	60-	100
1977 Apple Tree Boy	90-	150
1979 Singing Lesson	90-	150

Hummel Trademarks

TMK-1	TMK-2
Crown Mark	Full Bee Mark

1935-1948	1950*-1959

TMK-3	TMK-4
Stylized Bee Mark	Three Line Mark

© by
W. Goebel
W. Germany

1960*-1965	1966*-1971

TMK-5	TMK-6
VEE/G Mark	G Mark

1972*-1979	1979-

*Dates are approximate — earlier documented examples are known.

190

Icons

Imari

Icons

These are religious mementos, usually paintings with a brass encasement. Dating from the time of Christianity on, what you find in shops today are usually from the mid-1800s on. A triptych is just a 3-panel icon.

Brass, Greek saints, enamel background, 6" x 6½" dia .. $	325-	400
Brass, Orthodox Eastern church scene of Jesus, 5" x 7½"	875-	975
Brass, Greek, on wooden panel, 17th century, 13" x 16"	495-	600
Bronze, Russian Orthodox church scene, 18th century, 14" x 18"	600-	700
Painting on wood, brass encasement missing, 5½" x 7" (ill.) .	140-	185
Triptych, 3-panel, Jesus and Mary scene, 18th century, 15" high	585-	675
Triptych, Cathedral scene, Russian, 17th century, ornate, 16" high	1,400-	1,650

Imari

A gaudy decorated type of chinaware imported into this country mainly from Japan in the last part of the 19th century. The original was made in Japan as early as 1600. During the 19th century imitations were made in England. It's being reproduced today but it shouldn't fool anyone.

Bowl, panels alternating blue and orange, 10" dia. Japanese $	230-	248
Bowl, blue/white, orange flowers, 7", not old	240-	265
Bowl, cobalt, scalloped rim, 6½" dia.	48-	58

Creamer, orange/blue, old, not Japanese	67-	78
Cup/saucer, handles, usual colors, Japanese, 19th century	62-	71
Dish, blue/white, fish shape, 8½" long	77-	86
Jar, ginger, orange/blue, original wood stopper, 6" high, Japanese	130-	160
Jardiniere, plum trees, 14" high	1,400-	1,700
Pitcher, Staffordshire, usual Oriental colors, 1880s, 9" high	160-	180
Plate, green/red/blue, tangerine panels, 8½" dia. (ill.)	67-	80
Platter, blue, red, cobalt design, Oriental signature, old	162-	178
Platter, landscape, dragons, temple, 14" dia., old	155-	180
Teapot, peacocks, prunus, blue/red, w/domed lid	76-	86
Vase, 4 panels, flowers, 7½" high	160-	190

India Brass

Most of what you find in shops today was either brought home by soldiers serving in the China-Burma-India Theater during World War II or brand new. It is usually stamped India on the bottom. It was tooled brass, the items often being made from U.S. Army artillery shells. A form of enamel was rubbed into the tool crevices.

Dinner gong (ill.) $	17-	26
Ewer, handled, 13" high with 6 cups to match	23-	33
Incense burner, hanging type ...	18-	27
Kettle, matching tray	22-	32

(continued)

India Brass

Lamp, hanging-type, electrified	45-	58
Teapot, 11½" high, World War II	19-	29
Vase, 8" high	22-	32
Vase, 14" high on teakwood stand	29-	39

Indian (American) Artifacts

Indian (American) Artifacts

Even with all the fakes flooding the market, this is a H-O-T collectible, nationwide. Just know your Indians!

Arrowheads, common type	75¢-$2.50	
Beaded pouch, Oklahoma Indian	210-	240
Beaded belt, 42" long	110-	125
Necklace, glass beads, bone, seashells, Kiowa	145-	170
Bow, wooden, Plains Indians, 47" long	48-	59
Peace pipe, clay, Sioux	180-	210
Spear, ceremonial, bird point tip	40-	50
Boots, buckskin, coin buttons	92-	106
Tomahawk, original handle and rawhide	65-	75

War club, Comanche	62-	72
Chief's wearing blanket, Three Hills Reservation, gray/white	750-	900
War bonnet, eagle feathers, heavily-beaded, Plains Indians	1,000-1,400	
Low bowl, pottery, Hopi, cream yellow slip, black/orange designs, 8" dia. (ill.)	100-	135
Complete set 18th century bear claw, bead, shell & copper necklace	600-	700
Breechcloth, Navaho, beaded, buckskin	240-	270
Sioux bear claw necklace, c. 1850s, claws about 3½", 21 in all	1,000-1,400	
Moccasins, Arapaho, deerskin, beaded	82-	95
Apache Indian cradle board, c. 1860, 36" overall	430-	480
Necklace, bear claws, beads	90-	125
Eastern Woodlands all beaded cap, possibly Iroquois, c. 1840	395-	450
Pipe, tomahawk, handmade pottery bowl, 9" long	240-	265
Santee Sioux Catlinite pipe-tomahawk, c. 1870s	2,450+	
Purse, Sioux, beaded, deerskin, 4" x 7"	92-	106
Western Plains pipe-tomahawk, c. 1870s, 6½" overall	250-	270
Fighting ax, Mohawk, 8" overall	100-	135
Trade beads, glass, amber, blue	120-	140
Spike-tomahawk, Eastern Woodlands, c. 1750s, 8" overall	360-	385
Vest, buckskin, beaded, tassels, Hopi	550-	650
Halberd type spike-tomahawk, New England, c. 1720s, 7" overall	245-	265
Zia bowl, pottery, white slip, black/red designs, spirals, 8" high (ill.)	225-	265
Hatchet, Western Plains, c. 1870s, 5" overall	110-	150

Indian Tree Pattern

This pattern was popular from the 1850s until just before World War I. It takes its name from an Oriental, not an Indian, shrub. The colors were very soft—blue, pink, green—and it was made by various potters in

Indian Tree Pattern

England; Minton, Cauldon, Maddox, to mention a few. Also see specific firms.

Berry set, Maddox, bowl, 10" dia., 6 sauces, 5" dia.	$135-155
Butter dish, covered, "Burgess & Leigh"	61- 71
Cake stand, Maddox	62- 72
Compote, Copeland, 8" high	34- 44
Creamer	42- 52
Plates, 9", 10", 11" dia., Cauldon	21- 31
Plate, Noritake, 10" dia. (ill.)	18- 22
Salt/pepper shakers, pair, Minton	44- 52
Sugar bowl, covered, Minton	48- 59
Sugar bowl, covered,	49- 60
Teapot, 6 matching cups/saucers	150-160
Vase, Cauldon, 8" high	62- 72
Vegetable dish, 10" dia.	39- 49

Inkwells and Bottles

Inkwells and Bottles

These containers for holding ink usually were made of glass and have been around for centuries. Ink was made from chimney soot, dried berries, dried blood. The ballpoint pen rang the death knell for inkwells.

Blue, iridescent, pewter lid, Steuben-type	$ 40- 50

Brass, glass liner, alabaster base	25- 35
Brass, crab, glass liner	60- 70
Cloisonne, 2 inkwells, on marble base	82- 92
Covered container, 2 lovebirds, footed iron stand, 4" high	32- 44
Cranberry, bronze, marked Germany 1875 on bottom	60- 70
Crystal, two glass-lined, tray, footed	40- 50
Cut, embossed silver hinged top, 3½" high	28- 38
Green alabaster, dome top, square base	36- 46
Horse, 2 inkwells and rack	90-110
Ink stand, French porcelain, blue/green/orange enamels, c. 1910, 3½" high (ill.)	40- 57
Iron inkstand, horse, brass cap, penholder on horse's back	32- 45
Milk glass, two cats, iron base	110-150
Ormolu, cherubs, red/gray marble base, ormolu feet, France	160-185
Pen rack, iron and glass, dated 1877	25- 35
Pewter, holes for quill pens, England, 3" high	30- 40
Porcelain, flowers/cupids, 3 inkwells, on wood base	175-220
Red glass, round base, brass tray, 2 penholders	35- 45
School desk, black bakelite cap	18- 27
Swirl design, star base, brass cover, footed	32- 46

Iowa City Glass

Iowa City Glass

The Iowa City Flint Glass Manufacturing Company was incorporated in April of 1880. Iowa City factory was its general name. It is difficult to positively identify this glass, and the workmanship is on the crude side. Most pieces are quite thick, with mold lines much

(continued)

in evidence. Animal/bird motifs were very popular. Figures were often combined with mottoes such as "BE GENTLE" (with lamb); "BE TRUE" (with dog), etc.

Animal-motto plates, each	$ 30- 45
Compote, etched birds, flowers, 6″ high (ill.)	40- 50
Creamer, Alhambra design	29- 37
Goblet, deer motif	29- 39
Mug, dog motif	35- 45
Platter, beehive motif, oval-and-bar border	50- 60
Platter, Elaine, oval-and-bar border	50- 62
Spooner, open handles	25- 35

Insulators

Insulators

Little did they think that when they strung telephone and telegraph wires from coast to coast, those glass insulators would create such a furor in the antique business today. Books, clubs, magazines, all having to do with the insulator, are in great demand.

Armstrong, dome No. 2	$ 19- 24
B. T. C., Canada, ice blue	22- 30
Barclay, patent spiral groove . . .	16- 19
Brookfield, green, 1865	10- 16
C. C. T. and Company	28- 38
California, baby signal, smoky . .	14- 23
California, signal, gray	16- 26
Diamond pony, olive green	14- 25
Gayner, No. 48-400, aqua	16- 24
Green pottery	18- 28
H. G. Company, aqua, standard signal, double petticoat	14- 25
Hawley, Pennsylvania, aqua, beehive	18- 27
Hemingray, double petticoat beehive, aqua	18- 24
Hemingray, No. 14, vaseline	50- 60
Hemingray, No. 19, cobalt (ill.) . .	42- 53

Hemingray, No. 19, clear	9- 16
Knowles, No. 2, cable, green	17- 26
Locke, No. 21, green	37- 47
Lynchburg, No. 31	9- 13
Maydwell, No. 20, milk glass	17- 23
McLaughlin No. 16, emerald green	7- 12
Muncie, large, with stand	60- 70
No. 63, Carnival glass, Pyrex . . .	27- 37
Opaline, No. E14-B	84- 94
Peru-K. C. G. Company	48- 58
Postal beehive, pink	16- 27
San Francisco, pony, aqua	12- 24
W. E. Manufacturing Company, aqua, Patented December 19, 1871	19- 27
Whitall Tatum Company, No. 1, purple (ill.)	15- 22

Invalid Feeders

Invalid Feeders

During the 18th and 19th centuries many potteries in the Staffordshire district in England made these feeders. Adams, Clews, Jackson, Mayer, Ridgway, Stevenson — those are just a few of the many. Don't confuse with a Scuttle mug.

Invalid feeder (ill.), mid-1800s possibly Clews	$ 82- 92
Invalid feeder, J. and J. Jackson, 1830s	70- 90
Invalid feeder, Ralph Stevenson, early 1800s, marked R. S. W. . .	82- 92

Iron

Without it there would be no United States as we know it today. It rusts if not painted, but it is durable and long-lasting and it helped build our great nation.

Andiron, girl/boy motif, 14″ shank	$ 38- 58
Anvil, blacksmith's size	800-950
Apple peeler	29- 39
Bank, Battleship Oregon (still type)	39- 48
Bookends, horses, pr	19- 27
Bootjack, beetle, 10″	18- 29

194

Iron

Buggy step (makes nice towel holder in kitchen	13- 18
Candle trimmer, Patented 1854 .	39- 40
Cherry pitter	28- 38
Doorstop, flower basket	17- 27
Figurine, boy with flower, garden, 26" high	50- 60
Grinder, for counter or table use .	17- 27
Footscraper, Dachshund, 15" long	30- 40
Harpoon, toggle hook, original . .	155-170
Ice tongs	22- 33
Ladle, long handle, 13"	24- 34
Mold, rabbit, two-part, hinged, for ice cream	37- 47
Nutcracker, dog's tail closes jaw to crack nut	29- 38
Rack, hat, coat, 6 hooks, 28" wide	29- 39
Sadiron	22- 33
Sadiron, French, mid-1800s	30- 40
Stove, potbelly, old, ornate	80- 90
Stove, Sears, miniature, 8½" high (ill.)	24- 34
Tongs, ironworker or blacksmith	28- 38

Irons

Irons

Being reproduced but still collectible. Children's sizes very collectible.

Asbestos "Tourist Iron"	$ 20- 30
Children's flat iron (ill.)	24- 34

Curled handle, original	15- 18
Cross Hatch, original	20- 30
Nickel-plated iron (ill.)	12- 18
Rope handle, old variation	15- 22

Ironstone

Ironstone

Ironstone is an earthenware made from slag from the steel mills, with clay. Durable, it was first patented in 1813 by C. H. Mason. Later, many English firms made it, Meakin being famous for its lightweight ware. Other firms making it were Edwards, Johnson Brothers, Clemenston, Burgess, Podmore and Walker, Meller and Taylor, Wilkinson.

Bone dish, wheat motif	$ 14- 19
Bowl, covered, 6½" high, Meakin	27- 38
Bowl, sugar, floral decor, gold lustre designs, Edwards	32- 42
Coffeepot, Burslem, opaque granite china, 11" high (ill.) . . .	158-190
Dish, relish, oblong, 6" dia. Johnson Brothers	21- 40
Dish, vegetable, covered, Clemenston	28- 42
Jug, red/blue, English, 7½" high .	66- 76
Gravy boat, Cable decoration . . .	14- 22
Mold, pudding, flower designs inside, Wilkinson	32- 42
Pickle dish, flowers/birds, Meakin	19- 27
Pitcher, lustre decorations, Walley	50- 62
Pitcher, white/blue, Meakin, 9½" high	29- 38
Plate, blue/white decor, Podmore and Walker	33- 43
Platter, Oriental pattern, 14" long, Clemenston	30- 40
Shaving mug, white, Alcock	28- 37
Soup tureen w/ladle	68- 79
Sugar bowl, blue/tan, wood	37- 47

195

(continued)

Teapot, lustre decorations, Meakin	61- 74
Vase, red/blue, Mason, 8½" high	47- 57
Vae, Oriental decor, 8" high	50- 60

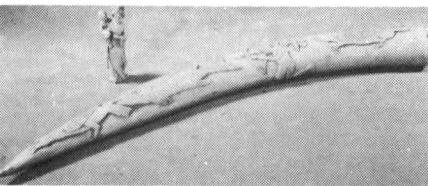

Ivory

Ivory

For centuries the Chinese were experts at carving it, and genuine pieces bring high prices today. Look for the grain; what's being carved today in the Orient is made from the bones of horses and cows. It's easy to "age" new ivory: soak in vinegar, wrap in burlap, bury in the backyard for a few months. Watch out for those netsukes coming in from Japan! And, remember where you buried it!

Bottle, snuff, carved	$ 140- 170
Box, hand-painted miniatures on lid, pink/white, 3" square	95- 120
Chess set, carved from elephant's tusk, Chinese, 18th century	1,200-1,400
Doctor's doll, nude, reclining, Oriental, 9" long	250- 350
(In China until early 1900s, doctors could not touch a female patient — she pointed to the doll to show where she had pain.)	
Figurine, carved, boy playing with dog, 5" high	50- 70
King holding Kuei with both hands, 14" high	450- 485
Letter opener, carved, 9" long	18- 27
Napkin ring, carved, pair	24- 35

Statue, Shou Lao, China, 37" high	1,400-1,800
Tusk, 35" long, carved, 9 figures, dragon, lion, elephant heads	2,200-2,700
Vase, dragons, lotus decor, 7" high	160- 175

Ivory, Miniatures

"The smaller the better!" This was the motto of the skilled ivory carver. A betel nut from India, the size of a small pea, contains no less than 15 perfectly carved elephants. You find these miniatures in shops today and they're fun to collect!

Elephant (ill.) 3" high	$ 65- 70
Mouse, ¾" high	15- 19
Pendant, sun motif, 2½" across (ill.)	35- 42
Ptarmigan, 1½" high (ill.)	45- 52
Rose earrings (ill.)	28- 37

Jackfield Pottery

Sometimes decorated with scrolls and flowers, this red-bodied pottery in relief is covered with a thick black glaze. It differs from Basalt and should confuse no one. Jackfield originated in England in the early 17th century. Most of what you find in shops today was made in the 19th century.

Coffeepot, 9" high	$120-140
Creamer, fluted, gold enameling, 7" high	82- 92
Creamer, cow	94-104
Dogs, black, 10" high, pr	82- 90
Figurine, rooster, black, England, 12" high	88- 98
Jug, green/black, gold leaf, England, 9" high	72- 82
Pitcher, molasses/black ground, 8" high	104-109
Sugar bowl, handleless, enameled birds	70- 87

Ivory, Miniatures

Jackfield Pottery

Syrup, pewter lid, enameled flowers	87- 97
Teapot, black, medallion decor . .	78- 86
Vase, enamel decor, square base, 11" high	90-110

Plate, soup, 10½", City Hall, New York	125-160
Platter, 11", New Haven Connecticut	150-170
Soup tureen, 13" Schenectady on the Mohawk River	155-185

Jack-in-the-Pulpit Vases

Jack-in-the-Pulpit Vases

In vogue around the turn of the century, they were made in all colors and resembled their namesake.

Bowl, rose/amber, paneled glass, applied	$ 62- 72
Vase, Amberina, 8" high	214-262
Vase, blue/pink body, 5" high . . .	30- 47
Vase, Cranberry, clear, star base, 11" high	68- 70
Vase, milk glass, blue, 8½" high .	30- 40
Vase, opalescent, white, 6½" high	72- 81
Vase, Peachblow, Sandwich	325-375
Vase, Quezel, 10" high, signed . .	235-250
Vase, Rubina, Hobnail pattern, 11" high	68- 78
Vase, twisted column, vaseline, 9½" high (ill.)	70- 82
Vase, white/purple slag	34- 44
Vase, vaseline, opalescent, 7½" high	82- 92

Jackson, J and J

Around 1831 this firm made many American views of the states, such as Pennsylvania, Ohio, Connecticut and Massachusetts. Their factory was in Burslem, England, at a pottery formerly owned by the Wedgwoods. The Jacksons closed down around 1843.

Cup plate, 4½", For Conanicut, Rhode Island	$128-158
Plate, 9", Baltimore Monument .	115-160

Jade

Jade

Usually associated with China, this cool, green, semiprecious stone has been around for years. Don't worry about finding any from the Ch'ien Lung dynasty or even finding an Imperial jade ring. But there are lots of interesting pieces in shops today. Know your dealer. It does not mean it's jade just because it feels cool against your face. So does an ice cube! An overrated commodity, much alabaster passing for the "real" thing, know!

Ashtray, 3" dia.	$ 120- 130
Bottle, snuff, black/green, 2¼" high	320- 400
Box, light green-to-white, average color	275- 295
Butterfly, carved, white/green	140- 170
Cordial, green, set of 6	240- 280
Figurine, dragon, trees, brown/green	250- 290
Foo Dog on teakwood base (ill.)	2,800+
Grapes, bunch, 5"	160- 195
Incense burner, Foo Dog, 5½" high	425- 525
Letter opener, 8¼" long	90- 110
Netsuke, dragons, 1¼"	82- 92
Pendant, white/green, 2½" . .	71- 81
Sword ornament, dragon, white/green	120- 145

197

(continued)

Thumb ring	92- 115
Vase, green, carved birds,	
teakwood stand, late 1800s	275- 350
Vase, carved, trees, flowers,	
9½" high	1,200-1,400

Japanese War Items

Japanese War Items

Anything to do with wars is collectible. Japanese military items are no exception. Most are from World War II.

Cigarette pack, "From Island of		
Attu, May 13, 1943" (ill.)	$ 5-	9
Dagger, worn by Japanese		
officer, sharkskin handle	79-	110
Helmet, pith style, cork lined (ill.)	35-	45
Japanese battle flag, white with		
red ball, 14" x 19"	80-	95
Mine detector in mahogany box .	110-	150
Pilot's helmet, name on peak . . .	42-	62
Samurai sword, military issue . . .	110-	150
Samurai sword, name on blade,		
sharkskin hilt	825-1,000	
Wind indicator, used on aircraft		
carrier (ill.)	59-	69

Jasperware

See WEDGWOOD.

Jewel Boxes

Popular in the late 1800s until the early 1900s. They were usually made of pot metal, then quadruple-plated, silver-plated or dipped in a cheap gold solution; they were then stuffed with cotton and velvet covered. Also made of wood, ivory, etc.

Gilded metal, Art Nouveau, pink	
lining (ill.)	$ 38- 50
Gold-plated, blue velvet lining	
(ill.)	22- 32
Quadruple-plate, velvet lined, on	
lid "Where's My"	19- 27

Jewel Boxes

Silver plate, velvet lined, footed .	20- 30
Sterling silver, velvet, initialed	
BHM	58- 70
Velvet ring box, 2" square (ill.) . .	7- 12
Walnut box w/drawer, primitive	
(ill.)	40- 48
Wood, inlaid rosewood, tufted	
velvet lined, lock and key,	
French, mid-1800s	90-105

Jewelry

Jewelry

In a word, antique jewelry is being bought to wear; expensive antique jewelry is being bought as an investment. See — Gold. Always get a receipt and know from whom you purchase. Obviously, you can't get a receipt from the Czar, but Cartier's will oblige if you happen to purchase the Czar Alexander II of Russia necklace, consisting of emeralds and pearls, priced modestly at $1,250,000 or higher. Stop in during your lunch hour. Since the days of the Egyptians, women (and now men) have been fascinated by jewelry of all kinds. The age, content of gold or platinum, karat of the stone, quality — all enter into the price. Careful!

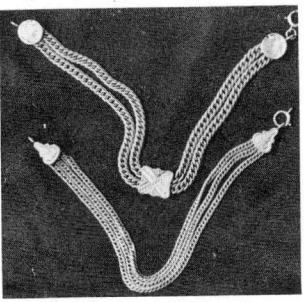

Jewelry

Sterling bar pin, w/11 seed pearls in a row, 1 1/8" long . . . . $	55-	70
18k gold pin in shape of leaf, inset with diamonds and pearls (ill.)	275-	325
Black sapphire ring, 38c stone, 18k gold setting, c. 1850s (ill.)	1,200-1,800	
Amethyst ring, 4 stones, each 2½c, 18k white gold setting (ill.) c. 1830s	480-	590
Watch-chain bracelets, 18k gold, c. 1850s (ill.)	450-	500 ea.
Yellow sapphire ring, 62 carats, 18k gold setting, c. 1880s (ill.)	1,800-2,250	
Rovensky diamond, 46.5 carats	2,500,000!	

L. Black star sapphire, 38k, 18k gold settings, c. 1850s.
R. Amethyst ring, 5 stones, each 2½c, 18k white gold setting, c. 1830s.

Krupp diamond, 33.19 carats	3 million+(!)	
Jonker #4 diamond, 30.70 carats	4,500,000+(!!)	
La Peregrina pearl	950,000+	
(just thought you'd like to see what a few up up, up! items cost today)		
14k child's ring, pearl solitaire	125-	160
18k gentlemen's ring, 4c diamond, marked "Tiffany" inside band	7,800-8,800	
14k bangle bracelet, small emeralds inlaid around entire band . .	650-	675
18k cascading cluster of 36 diamonds, ¼c ea.) .	2,300-2,500	
Garnet bar pin	60-	70
Garnet cross, gold-filled chain	58-	78
Garnet locket, 18k mounting	125-	150
18k bangle bracelet, 5 rubies inset	575-	650
18k stickpin, ½c ruby . .	700-	800
18k stickpin, diamond-studded leaves	650-	750
18k gentlemen's topaz ring, 2¼c	650-	675
18k ring, Australian fire opal, 1½c	1.350-1.600	

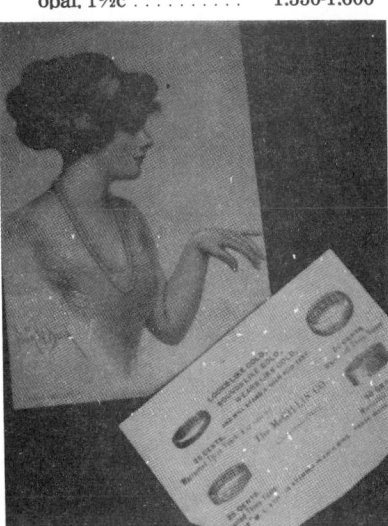

Jewelry Store Collectibles

Jewelry Store Collectibles

By the turn of the century every jewelry store gave away attractive colored cards extolling their products.

Average price, good condition . . . 75¢ - $1.50

199

Jugtown Pottery

Jugtown Pottery

In 1922 this pottery company began operations in Jugtown, North Carolina. Jacques and Juliana Busbee were the founders and Ben Owens worked with them until the early 1960s. Orange was a favorite color with a Chinese blue glaze being a prized color. It was also made in a plain gray salt glaze with dark blue designs and in vibrant colors as described. Most pieces are "Jugtown Ware" impressed.

Bowl, Oriental motif, green/gray glaze, 5" dia. (ill.) . . . . $ 15- 25
Creamer, russet color, clear glaze, 3¾" high (ill.) 18- 22
(these two pieces were made and signed by Ben Owens)
Candleholder, handle loop, orange, 7" dia. 33- 43
Planter, blue/red, mottled, 6" high 38- 48
Pitcher, green/blue, 6½" high . . . 37- 47
Pitcher, orange, 7¾" high 29- 39
Sugar bowl, covered 25- 34
Vase, green/brown, 6" high 24- 34
Vase, orange, 4" high 23- 32
Vase, rose/green, 8" high 37- 47

KPM

KPM

This mark was used at Meissen for two years, circa 1723. Later in the 1830s it was adopted by the Royal Factory in Berlin. Ten years later the Prussian eagle was added to the letters. Other factories adopted the KPM letters in the late 19th century. There is no proof that the factory using KPM was sanctioned by the royal families still ruling in Germany at that time. There's obvious confusion about the late KPM and eagle today. Scarce, but know what you're finding.

Bowl, raised flowers inside, blue, 8" dia. . . . .$	48-	56
Chocolate pot, Silesia, Onion pattern	49-	59
Creamer, sugar, violets, green/ pink ground (each)	48-	60
Cup/saucer, demitasse, white ground, pink roses, 1830s . . .	47-	66
Dish, raised leaves, cover, oval, 10" dia	38-	48
Figurine, boy with goat, 9" high	78-	89
Plaque, cupids, pink/blues, 6" x 8"	1,400-	1,800
Plaque, 5½" x 6¾", musicians .	275-	325
Plate, cake, tulips, reticulated handles, rims, 9" dia	53-	63
Plate, gypsy boy, 10" dia.	68-	78
Picture, porcelain, family scene, 15" x 20"	460-	550
Teapot, creamer, sugar, tray, cups/saucers, flowers/ butterflies	360-	410
Vase, cherries and apples, 9½" high	175-	195

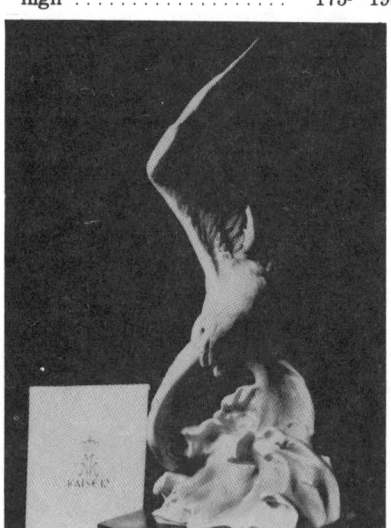

Kaiser Porcelain

Kaiser Porcelain

Bavaria, since 1872. Not antique but highly collectible today. Cybis and Ispanky porcelains are also collectible. Prices listed are for Kaiser.

Flying Heron	$ 69-	79
Goose Girl	120-	140
Humming Bird	130-	168
Kingfisher, limit 2,000	245-	275
Pheasant, limit 1,500	270-	355
Pigeon group, limit 2,000	160-	185
Sea Gull (ill.), limit 1,000	1,700-2,000	

Kelva

See WAVECREST.

Keramo Porcelain

Keramo Porcelain

This was from Karlovy Vary, the world-famous spa in Carlsbad, Czechoslovakia. The illustrated spa glass (porcelain) was filled with the health-giving waters, which were sipped through the top of the handle as illustrated here.

Keramo Spa sipper (ill.)	$ 27- 37
Porcelain bottle to take home a sample for friends	28- 38
Souvenir plate marked Karlovy Vary, 1925	18- 25

Kew Blas Glass

Made at the Union Glass Works, Somerville, Massachusetts, in the 1890s, it was an iridescent glassware contemporary with Tiffany, Durand, Quezel, Steuben, and others. The name is not taken from Walter Blake's last name though he did work at the factory. Sometimes signed Kew Blas on the bottom; otherwise difficult to distinguish from those other glasses named here.

Candlestick, gold swirled, signed 9" high, pr	$425-510
Bowl, rose, gold iridescent/green decor, Zipper pattern	250-290

Creamer, Zipper pattern, 2½" high	190-220	
Plate, iridescent blue, 6½" dia.	225-255	
Tumbler, gold iridescent, 4" high signed	140-185	
Tumbler, blue iridescent, 3½" high, signed	150-190	
Vase, pink/purple iridescent, 8" high, signed	450-550	
Vase, gold iridescent, signed, 5½" high	375-450	
Vase, green/brown iridescent, 9½" high, signed	450-560	
Wine, iridescent gold, 4¾" high	120-140	

Kewpies

Kewpies

Rose O'Neill drew pictures of these pixie-like figures for the *Ladies' Home Journal* in the early 1900s. Around 1911 Kewpie dolls began to appear on the American market. The bisque dolls came from Germany, but the most common were the ones made of celluloid. Being reproduced.

Bank, glass, tin lid	$ 73- 85
Bowl, cereal, 6" dia.	92-110
Candy container, 1915	82- 92
Creamer, Kewpies playing in yard	88- 98
Cup/saucer, Germany, pink lustre trim	79- 91
Dish, feeding	38- 48
Doll, bisque, Japan, 4"	30- 40
Doll, bisque, signed Rose O'Neill	89-109
Doll, dressed, celluloid mark, 2½" high	13- 24
Doll, composition, Rose O'Neill label, 12½"	53- 70
Figurine, seated figure 3" high	163-183
Ice cream mold, hinged, pewter	32- 40
Ice cream tray, signed Rose O'Neill	44- 54
Lamp, chalkware, fringe shade	42- 57
Pitcher, 4 action Kewpies, Royal Rudolstadt	230-255
Plate, Royal Rudolstadt, signed Rose O'Neill	29- 41
Postcard, Christmas, "We love you"	9- 16
Powder jar, signed	83- 93

(continued)

Teapot, creamer, sugar, signed Rose O'Neill, porcelain	110-130
Thimble	9- 15
Toothpick, "Thinker," 5½" high	58- 68
Tray, Kewpies picking berries, signed	238-251
Vase, handled, Kewpies playing, signed	120-135

Keys

Keys

Shown here because there are thousands of different kinds. The old Spanish dungeon keys are quite collectible. Keys are a fun item to collect and decorate with. Too many to give specific prices. Have fun!

Average price	$ 1- 2
Brass, early 1800s	5- 8
Iron, jail type, large	6- 9
Folding type, nickel plated	4- 6

Kimble Glass

Kimble Glass

In the late 1800s, Colonel Ewan Kimble operated a factory at Vineland, New Jersey, for a relatively short time. The factory also operated jointly as "Kimble and Durand." Not too much is known about this glass and it is considered scarce today. After Durand's death in 1931 the factory was taken over by Kimble and today is part of Owens-Illinois. It is **not** spelled Kimball!

Bowl, Cluthra in white, rose, 4" high	$200-240

Candlesticks, blue/green, iridized, 14" high, pair	320-380
Vase, blue, white inside, scalloped, curved top, 7" high	99-115
Vase, Cluthra, blue/gray spirals, yellow iridescent, 6" high	245-270
Vase, Cluthra, orange/white bubbles, dark handles, 11" high, signed "K-20144-11, Dec-7" (ill.)	275-325

King's Rose Pattern

King's Rose Pattern

Produced in the Staffordshire district, England around 1820 to 1830, it's a soft-paste porcelain made especially for the Pennsylvania Dutch trade. The enamel decorations are usually in warm yellows, greens, pinks, and dark reds. Sometimes the colors flake off with use. It was good porcelain.

Cup/saucer	
a. Large size, King's Rose	$220-240
b. Regular size	180-215
Cup/saucer, regular size (ill.)	175-220
Coffeepot, 10¾" high	900-985
Plates	
a. Dinner	175-195
b. Toddy	140-165
Plate, dinner (ill.), divided border, 9" dia.	130-175
Sugar bowl and creamer, Queen's Rose, set	550-600
Teapot, Queen's Rose, 5" high	400-455

Knives

Remember Grandfather's advice, "Always cut away from your thumb!" All kinds of knives are collectible today, especially unusual pocket types.

Barlow, Blue Grass model	$ 68- 78
Barlow, Remington, bone handle	49- 60
Bowie, cased, 15" overall blade, 1860s	185-220

Knives

Case, double X, stag handle, 3-blade	48- 64
Case, double X, wood handle, 4-blade	85- 95
Gurkha, leather case and 2 skinning knives (ill.)	130-175
Hammer & Co., NY, pocket-type, 2-blade	27- 36
Jack, stag handle, 2-blades, old	18- 28
Masonic, 14k gold, ornate enamel and initials	38- 47
Pocket, Hopalong Cassidy, 3-blades	29- 34
Pocket-type, company advertising, fits on key chain, 2" long	22- 31
Remington, Babe Ruth emblem 2-blade, bone handle	87- 97
Remington, R333, Boy Scout insignia, stag handle	112-115
Remington, hunting type, 9" blade, leather case	78- 88
Remington, pocket, 2-blades	32- 42
Sterling silver penknife, 2-blade nail cleaner	36- 46
Winchester, Hawk bill, 1-blade, wood handle	65- 75
Winchester, pocket-type, 3-blade, leather punch	58- 68
Winchester, 2-blades	56- 66

Kutani

Kutani is one of the most famous names in china and pottery in the world, its manufacture dating back to the 1550s. The artists who paint this magnificent ware are referred to in Japan as "human treasures." Most of

Kutani

what you find in shops today is fairly new and varies in price according to size. Usually, each Kutani vase comes in a wooden box with the artist's signature on the outside of the box.

Prices vary between $25 and $200 for the 20th century Kutani.

Vase, 9" high, new (ill.)	$120-150

La Verre Francais Cameo Glass

This was one of the Cameo types exported in bulk from France to New York around the turn of the century. Various stores sold it until it lost popularity around World War I.

Bowl, blue/orange, flowers, signed, 11" dia.	$480-520
Lamp, tortoiseshell color, signed	750-850
Planter, yellow/orange, Art Deco, 7" high	220-245
Vase, blue/orange, berries on yellow ground	330-390
Vase, flying birds, blue/yellow/orange, signed Charder	350-400
Vase, tortoiseshell color, orange/blue, signed	395-450
Vase frosted yellow ground, cut blue/orange, signed	420-450

Lace

There's considerable interest in French crocheted filet, Irish crochet from the 1840s,

203

(continued)

Lace

applique from about 1850. Tatting with small bobbins was popular in the 1870s. Today doll collectors search out the old lace for decorating dresses. European in nature, wherever it's found, today's collector is buying it, by the piece or by the box.

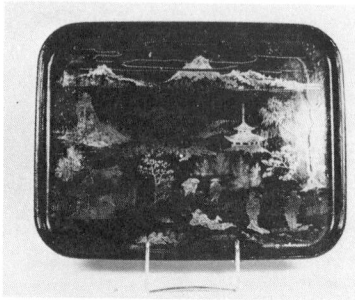

Lacquer

Lacquer (see Cinnabar)

This is an Oriental form of art. Layer upon layer of lacquer was applied to the item being made, then designs were cut into the lacquer layer or painted on in typical Oriental designs.

Bowl, floral designs, painted	$ 48- 57
Box, carved fish designs in red/ black, footed	42- 50
Fireplace screen, carved in litho-pane style	87-100
Jewelry box, 6 drawers, painted designs	98-110
Sewing box, black, gold dragon designs, painted	57- 67
Tea caddy, 2 compartments, pewter lids	93-103
Tray, black, gilded Oriental decor, 12¼" wide (ill.)	35- 44

Lalique Glass

Rene Lalique made this fine art glass in France at the turn of the century. He was an associate of Emile Galle, and their works are similar in many respects. A combination of blowing, pressing, frosting and cutting achieved the excellent effect Lalique gave to

Lalique Glass

his glass. "New" Lalique is being made in France today. All listed pieces signed "R. Lalique".

Bottle, heart-shaped, butterflies, 4½" high (ill.)	$ 88-102
Bottle, perfume, lotus blossom shape, stopper, signed	82- 92
Bottle, perfume, frosted, clear tulips, 6¼" high (ill.)	82-105
Bottle, perfume, plunger type, frosted ladies 14" high (ill.) . . .	110-130
Bowl, fish, shellfish, shell feet, France	275-325
Cup/saucer, leaves, flowers, cut pattern	72- 81
Decanter, clear body, frosted neck, stopper, 9" high	360-375
Clock, frosted lovebirds, cut glass dial, 10" high	280-310
Dish, frosted swan on saucer vase	88- 98
Figurine, lovebirds, frosted base, 7½" high	268-280
Jar, powder, clear/frosted thorns, 4¼" high (ill.)	130-145
Knife rest, crystal center, frosted knobs	67- 77
Vase, frosted pale finish, 11", 10" body	485-585
Vase, raised whirling fish, 4" high	410-435
Covered box, deep gray tone, scarabs in relief, 2½" high, 3½" dia	300-400
Bottle, frosted background, dancing ladies, 6" high	295-365
Perfume bottle, flower motif, 4" high, 1¼" dia	240-275
Plate, annual, 1966, 1967, 1968 . .	330-400
Salt, frosted birds, 2" high	39- 56
Toothpick, frosted cherubs	48- 68
Vase, frosted grape pattern, 10" high	140-160
Vase, frosted, dancing nudes, footed, 10" high	185-220
Vase, lotus blossom, protruding petals, 11" high	165-185

Laminated Glass

Tiffany and Quezal both made this type of glass in the early 1900s. It was a multicolored opaque glass and was hard to make. It's relatively scarce but a real plum when found.

Lamps

Alcohol lamp, glass cover, 4″ high . . . . $	17- 22
Banquet lamp, brass base, procelain shade . .	148- 160
Betty lamp, iron, early 1800s (ill.)	215- 230
Betty lamp, iron, 4″ long, spike hanger (ill.) .	110- 135
Bracket lamp, mercury reflector	38- 50
Bristol glass type, blown olive green font, blue base, 11″ high (ill.)	87- 105
Camphene lamp, double brass burners, pewter base	88- 98
Carriage lamp, bail handle, clamp slot on side, kerosene	50- 60
Chandelier lamp, brass, china shade, pull-down type, 1860s	273- 293
Clear glass lamp, 9″ high	24- 34
Coach lamp, brass, glass, 3 sides, kerosene .	58- 68
Cobalt (blue) lamp, 7½″ high, kerosene	62- 72
Hanging lamp, Tiffany, petal sections, beaded fringe, signed	4,600-4,900
Hanging lamp, brass frame, hand-painted shade, flowers, prisms .	230- 260
Hearse lamp, beveled glass, 3 sides, German silver lining, pair	360- 400
Flint glass lamp, whale oil type, early 1800s . . .	62- 72
Floor lamp, triangular base, green shade, Tiffany-type (not signed) . .	95- 110
Gone with the Wind lamp, brass fittings, cast iron base, 23½″ high (ill.)	340- 370
Gone with the Wind lamp, green ground pink/yellow flowers	240- 270
Hand lamp, Coolidge Drape shade, 9½″ high, clear	85- 110

Fairy lamp—see Kitchen lamp, white shade, brass font, 1880s	65- 75
Log Cabin lamp, clear glass	92- 102
Millefiori, 1880s, 12½″ high, base and shade both millefiori (ill.)	180- 245
Oil lamp, Sandwich Loop pattern, mid-1850s	115- 130
Piano lamp, floor type, marble top, porcelain-painted shade	225- 240
Satin Glass lamp, brass/wood base, ...	195- 220
Pulpit lamp, spring base, copper, 12″ high	62- 72
Student lamp, single, milk white shade, brass	240- 260
Student lamp, double, green shade, brass	575- 650
Table lamp, green/blue ground, flower decor, electrified, 1890s	280- 310
Tiffany floor lamp, shade signed LCT, 6′6″, bronze (See Tiffany)	

Gone with the Wind Lamp

Iron Betty Lamp

 (continued)

Tiffany-type Lamp

Tiffany type table lamp,
caramel slag glass
shade, brass base 450- 485
Tiffany-type table lamp,
tulips/leaves glass,
gilded cast iron finial,
24½" high (ill.) 725- 765
Tiffany table lamp,
green with red flowers,
signed LCT, 16½" high
(See Tiffany)
Tiffany type table lamp,
metal base, caramel slag
glass shade, 16½" high . 300- 350
Wall lamp, tin bonnet . . 58- 68
Wall lamp, iron ring
type, pressed glass
bowl, white shade,
1880s 64- 74

Art Deco lamp,
"reclining" nudes on
base, glass globe, 12"
high 65- 80
Art Deco lamp, clowns
playing, green glass
shade, 14½" high 62- 72
Art Nouveau lamp, ballet
dancer, blue metal
shade, 14" high 210- 250
Auto lamp, brass kero-
sene type 92- 102
Bicycle lamp, carbide, 3"
high, magnifying lens,
4½" high 44- 54
Brass lamp, Rayo-type,
frosted shade, 9" high . 65- 80
Carbide miner's cap lamp,
chrome reflector 32- 42
Gone with the Wind lamp,
red satin shade & base . 235- 285
Gone with the Wind lamp,
hand-painted "cows
grazing," brass base . . . 270- 300

Aladdin: one of the most popular lamps ever
made, the Mantle Lamp Company of America,
Inc. was founded in Chicago in 1908. They are
still being made today in Nashville, Tennessee.
All lamps priced with complete burners and
shades.

Practicus table lamp $200- 220
Model No. 1 table lamp . . 110- 130
Model No. 1 parlor lamp . 220- 240
Model No. 2 table lamp . . 170- 190
Model No. 2 parlor lamp . 215- 235
Model No. 3 table lamp . . 130- 145
Model No. 3 parlor lamp . 235- 265
Model No. 4 table lamp . . 120- 145
Model No. 5 table lamp . . 130- 150
Model No. 10 table lamp . 270- 300
Model No. 1241 varie-
gated (two-tone) Tan
crystal vase lamp, 12"
tall 89- 99
Model No. 1242 Bengal
Red crystal vase lamp,
12" tall 230- 250
Model 1233 blue Venetian
Art-Craft crystal vase
lamp, 10¼" tall 120- 160
Model 1247 Red Venetian
Art-Craft crystal vase
lamp, 10¼" tall 190- 220
Style 99, Venetian, clear,
Model A table lamp,
1932 . . . . 310- 360
Style 101, Venetian,
green, Model A table
lamp, 1932 . . . . 90- 120
Style B-110, Cathedral,
White Moonstone,
Model B table lamp . . . 170- 190
Style B-100, Corinthian,
Clear Crystal, Model B
table lamp 65- 85

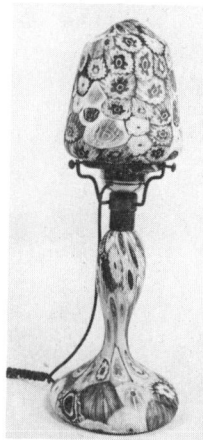

Millefiori Lamp   **Bristol Glass Type Lamp**

Style B-82, Beehive, Amber crystal, light, Model B table lamp . . .	83-	93
Style B-82, Beehive, Amber crystal, dark, Model B table lamp . . .	140-	160
Style B-86, Quilt, Green Moonstone, Model B table lamp	140-	165
Style B-39, Washington Drape (round base), Clear Crystal, Model B .	78-	88
Style B-62, Short Lincoln Drape, Ruby Crystal, Model B table lamp	400-	450
Style B-76, Tall Lincoln Drape, Cobalt Crystal, Model B table lamp (lamps with scallop design on the foot are worth much more)	425-	485
Style B-25, Victoria, decorated china, Model B table lamp	330-	370
Caboose lamp, Model B w/shade	150-	160
Wall bracket lamp, Caboose, Alacite font . .	95-	120
Floor lamp, Model No. 12, w/shade, 1254 series	110-	130
Floor lamp, Model B, brass, w/shade	240-	260
Hanging lamp, Practicus, w/shade	230-	265
Hanging lamp, Model No. 2 w/shade	255-	275
Hanging lamp, Model No. 3, double chandelier . . .	685-	785

Lamps, Miniature

Originally known as night lamps, today we call them miniature lamps. Every company made them in blown, blown-molded, pressed, every color, every price range. Most are collectible today.

Blue glass, Inverted Thumbprint, 6½" high .	$	80-	92
Brass, saucer-type, 4½" high with chimney, patented 1873		47-	57
Brass cabin lamp, 7" high		51-	61
Brass banquet lamp, purple shade, 8" high		78-	88
Bristol glass, pink, chimney-type shade . . .		68-	78
Bristol glass, white, blue decor, 8" high		68-	77
Cased glass, red over milk glass, matching half shade		115-	126
Clear glass, umbrella shade, flower decor		48-	58
Cosmos glass, white shade, 7½" high		290-	328
Cobalt "Little Duchess," 7½" high		51-	66
Cranberry Beaded Swirl, 8" high		90-	110
Cranberry, handled, 5½" high		89-	112
End-of-Day (Spatter Glass), 7" high		86-	96
Milk glass, Columbus bust base (ill.)		150-	160
Milk glass, pink slag, Swan, shade, rare (ill.) . .		825-	870

Lamps, Miniature

207

(continued)

Milk glass, hand-painted, 5½" high	26-	36
Mt. Washington Glass, blue flower decor, 7½" high	245-	268
Satin glass, green 8" high	92-	108
Satin glass, blue, matching ball shade	92-	110
Satin glass, pink, 8" high .	98-	112
Satin glass, red, 6½" high	97-	115
Satin glass, pink with flowers, frosted shade, 7" high (ill.)	99-	115
Satin glass, white/pink diamond quilt, 7" high .	100-	130
Tiffany miniature mushroom lamp with shade, green/ white, original bulb signed Edison Mazda; lamp signed LCT, 8" high (rare)	1,800-2,700	
Tulip lamp, flowers in green, 8½" high	99-	135
Gold Eagle, orange body, gold trim (ill.)	120-	140

Miner's lantern, iron, patented snuffer marked Hailwood	42-	52
Paul Revere-type, pierced tin . . .	69-	79
Police lantern, kerosene, bull's-eye lens, tin, 1880s	48-	58
Porch lantern, electrified	25-	35
Railroad lantern, hooded, inspector's	44-	54
Railroad lantern, red, squat globe, marked Southern RR . .	34-	44
Ship's lantern, red globe, brass frame, 20" high	400-500	
Ship's lantern, captain's, copper reflector	150-225	
Skater's lantern, brass, with wire, kerosene-type (ill.)	59-	77
Skater's lantern, silver-plated, mid-1800s, chain, kerosene . . .	45-	55
Skater's lantern, tin, wire handle (ill.)	44-	55
Whale oil lantern, tapered glass globe, tin, early 1800s	110-140	

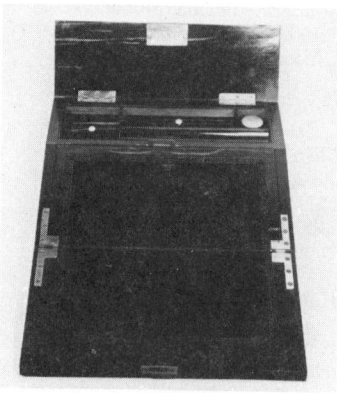

Lap Desk

Lap Desks

When one had to travel in the early days, one took a portable desk along. Usually it was made of wood, contained ink, quills, sealing wax. The ink was usually in a powder form—when mixed with water, it did the trick.

Rosewood, English, 18th century, complete	$155-180
Rosewood veneer box, brass hinges, 4 compartments, 12" across (ill.)	145-165
Walnut, English, hidden compartment under pen tray, 1800s	185-220

Latticinio

Made from an ancient technique lost in

Lanterns

Lanterns

From the earliest pine splints during Colonial times to the first electrical types, 1870 on, lanterns have been made in every size and shape to fit a particular need. Good repros showing up at shows.

Buggy lantern, red bull's-eye reflector	$ 75-	95
Candle lantern, tin and glass, early 1800s	39-	49
Candle lantern, tin, folding type .	50-	60
Candle lantern, tin, 12" high	62-	72
Carriage lanterns, beveled glass, red reflectors, pair	250-325	

Latticinio

time, this glass was produced by various glass houses in the mid-to-late 1800s. Uninformed collectors confuse it with Lutz-type glass. Latticinio's crossed, curved lines beneath the decoration give it a peppermint cane effect. Actually, it's a filigree glassware, first developed in the first or second century, B.C., but don't worry about finding any piece this old. Most of what you find in shops today is in the $55-70 range. If it proves to be old, you've found a bargain; if not, you haven't paid attention when we say, "know your antiques or know your antiques dealer!" Being reproduced — from the island of Murano, near Venice, Italy.

Plates, typical design, twisted
  threads, gold/white (ill.) each $ 55- 65

Lavender Pot

Lavender Pots

The dried flowers, leaves, and stalks of a European flower akin to the mint family, when dried, were used to fill sachets, perfume clothes, linens, etc. The crushed plant was kept in a lavender pot, made by most European porcelain firms during the 1800s and until World War I.

Haviland lavender pot, rose
  petals, pink border, 2 lids . . . . . $ 58- 68
Royal Worcester lavender pot
  (ill.), 2 lids 56- 70

Leather Items

Leather Items

Cowhide has been used for just about everything; postcards, shoes, hats, dresses, pants — you name it! Now collectors are quietly buying things made from cowhide. The bola illustrated here is sitll used by the cowboys in South America. When released, three balls wrap around the legs (or feet) of the cow, horse.

Leeds Ware

Leeds Ware

Begun in Yorkshire, England, about 1758, this was a fine grade of creamware that competed with Wedgwood. A few years later reticulated and punched wares were made, with few pieces ever marked. Extremely rare and collectible today.

Bowl, blue/white, twisted handles . . . . $	49-	69
Cream pitcher, yellow/blue/ green, 4½" high	128-	150
Cup/saucer, handleless, floral decor	79-	89
Jug, creamware, 1780, flowers in red	144-	154
Mug, Chinese decor, early 18th century	98-	110
Pitcher, flower decor, 6" high .	175-	195

(continued)

Plate, creamware, openwork, marked, 9" dia	69-	90
Plate, blue edge, marked, 12" dia	70-	80
Platter, cream, shell pattern, 16½" wide	138-	158
Teapot, red/green, shell pattern in body, 7½" high	200-	235
Tureen, white body, blue decor, 22" high, lid	215-	240
Pitcher, Farmer's Coat-of-Arms (rare) (ill.)	850-1,000	
Sugar bowl w/lid, yellow/green, 4½" high	78-	90

Legal Documents

Legal Documents

Old hand-written deeds and wills, and especially those from England with the magnificent red wax seals and ribbons, all are being sought after today.

Hand-written deed, dated 1878 (ill.)	$ 3-	8
English land deed on heavy parchment with ornate wax seal, early 1800s	40-	50
Framed cemetery plot receipt, "Woodlawn, Bronx, NY," 1892	9-	14
Quitclaim deed, 1849, Hunter, NY, handwritten	10-	16
Aetna fire insurance policy, 1875, $300, on white paper	7-	11
Warranty deed, Westchester County, NY, 1866, "Certificate, Magistracy"	10-	17
Mortgage deed, Norfolk, NY, 1858, hand-written	8-	15

LeGras

This gentleman was known for his unusually imaginative glassware and bottles. He ceased operations just before World War I.

His scenic reproductions, also made at his factory at Saint-Dennis, were considered masterpieces. Being reproduced.

Bowl, beige, brown, green-cased, signed 4½" high	$450-525
Bowl, rose, enameled spring scene, scalloped top, 7½" high .	160-195
Lamp, green, orange, trees, electrified, signed, 7¼" high	365-420
Vase, Art Deco, autumn leaves, 8½" high	310-370
Vase, brown, orange leaves, enameled, 16" high	295-325
Vase, cameo, cut back foliage, green/blue, signed	425-500
Vase, cameo, green, yellow, cobalt, acid cut to clear, 13" . . .	425-625
Vase, cameo white apple blossoms, green background, 8½" high	360-375

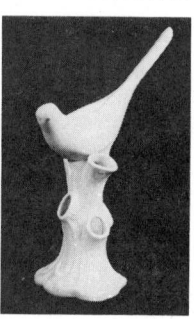

Lenox

Lenox

This firm started business in 1906 in Trenton, New Jersey. Among other wares, they made a good Belleek-type.

Ashtray, shell-shaped	$ 9-	17
Atomizer, perfume, penguin shape, 4" high	36-	46
Bottle, woman's head shape, Hattie Carnegie cosmetics	60-	70
Bowl, oval, cream, gilt edge	52-	65
Candy box, cream, gold edge	62-	71
Coffee service, Ming pattern, pot and bowl, large creamer	72-	80
Cup/saucer, Ming pattern	22-	32
Jar, mustard, green, silver overlay, lid	30-	40
Mug, gold scene, pair (rare)	110-135	
Plate, Ming pattern, 8¼" dia . . .	34-	44
Salt, swan-shape, master and 4 small, set	44-	53
Tray, pin, gold band, 6" dia	24-	28
Vase, bird-shaped flower 10" high (ill.)	38-	49
Vase, Art Nouveau, 6½" high, green, gold gilt	75-	85

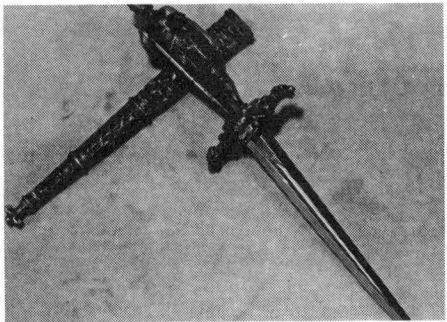

Letter Openers

Letter Openers

Made of bone, ivory, gold, silver, brass, wood, this item has been used for hundreds of years.

Alabaster, carved Chinese designs, 8″ long	$ 16- 22
Brass, ornate case, African figure, late 1800s (ill.)	40- 50
Ivory, carved figures on handle, early 1800s	36- 46
Gold, 14 karat, castle scene, French, dated 1834, 7½″ long	395-475
Silver-plated, souvenir of Philadelphia Centennial, 1876	29- 39
Sterling silver, marked Tiffany, 6½″ long	250-325
Wood, many types, souvenir, etc.	22- 31

License Plates

License Plates

Since the early 1900s these have been collectible. The early plates, porcelain-on-metal, bring brisk prices today. All plates are in demand, from the 1900s until World War II.

Porcelain, on metal, Pennsylvania, 1907	$ 30- 35
Tin, any state, 1900s to 1915	16- 24
Tin, any state, 1920s to 1940s	9- 18
1950s on	1-1.50

Lighter-than-Air

When Count Ferdinand von Zeppelin developed a dirigible airship around 1900, man had another way to "fly" through the

Lighter-than-Air

heavens. Used by our own Navy during the 1930s (see ill.), who can forget that fateful day at the Lakehurst Naval Air station in New Jersey, when the across-the-Atlantic Graf Zeppelin exploded and burned? Menus, air schedules, postcards, sheet music — all collectible today.

Limoges Porcelain

Limoges Porcelain

Limoges, France, is a village, not a maker of porcelain. The uninformed buyer purchases this as a particular brand. Haviland (see HAVILAND) was the most famous maker in this village. Other makers at Limoges were Ahrenfeldt and Son, A. Lanternier, R. Delinieres and Cie., Bernardaud and Cie., P. H. Leonard, Fontanille and Marraud, Raynaud and Cie., Union Limousine. These are but a few and prices are dependent on maker, year, type.

211

(continued)

Atomizer, pearl lustre, hand-painted flowers	$ 28-	38
Bowl, fruit decoration, 9" dia . . .	30-	40
Bowl, orange poppies, 10" dia . . .	28-	38
Box, enamel, farm scene	47-	57
Box, pill, floral scene, hinged 2½" square	46-	56
Butter pat, green floral, gold trim	10-	18
Candlesticks, pair, blue with white violets, 8½" high	60-	70
Chocolate set, pot and 8 cups/saucers, floral background, pink/white	98-115	
Creamer, flowers, pink/green	19-	26
Cup/saucer, daisies, blue border .	19-	27
Cup/saucer, yellow & pink roses, gold trim	20-	30
Dish, bone, floral design, green/pink, set of 6	48-	58
Fish set, yellow platter, different fish on each of 8 plates, set . . .	187-199	
Mug, hand-painted, gold handle, drinking scene, 8" high	58-	68
Pitcher, cider, yellow/green flowers, gold handle, 14" high .	69-	79
Pitcher, tankard, grapes, green background, 12½" high	67-	77
Plate, gold border, gold horse chestnuts, leaves outlined in gold, 9" dia. (ill.)	42-	56
Plate, cake, pink roses, gold border, set of 8	68-	78
Plate, dinner, gold band, roses in center, set of 12	152-172	
Platter, green/blue floral design, gold border, 16" dia	49-	61
Tray, celery, blue and yellow, reticulated border 5½" x 12" . .	52-	59
Tureen, soup, handles, yellow roses inside, pink roses outside, 15" dia	68-	78
Vase, pink poppies, black background, 11" high	59-	69

Lindbergh

Lindbergh

"Lucky Lindy"; "The Spirit of St. Louis" — Capt. Charles Lindbergh left Roosevelt Field on Long Island, N.Y., at 7:52 a.m. (DST), May 20, 1927. With only a tiny kitten to keep him company, he flew nonstop across the Atlantic, arriving in Paris, France, at 5:1 p.m. (DST), on May 21, 1927. One of ou great nation's greatest heroes, his contribu tions to world aviation were many. Anythin to do with "Lindy" is collectible today, ir cluding the tragic kidnapping of his infan son. A great, great man!

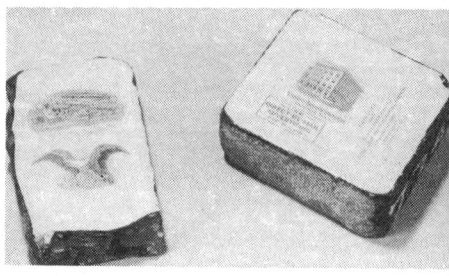

Lithograph Stones

Lithograph Stones

Too many people confuse lithographin, with etching. Lithographs, a form of earl American art, were drawn on blocks of ston with a greasy crayon, then transferred to th paper by pressure of a press. These stone are hard to find but a plum when you fin one.

Lithograph

Lithographs

Currier and Ives made them famous; othe firms also. Most American lithograph: weren't marked with the year and copyrigh words until after 1848. Have fun, there ar lots around. Just know your dealer!

"The Marquis de Sade Suite"
signed twice and dated by
Salvador Dali, 1968, 58/160
(ill.) $425-465

Lithopanes

Lithopanes

Highly translucent porcelains with impressed designs are formed by the difference in the thickness of the plaque. Thin parts let a lot of light through; thicker parts are usually shadows. First made in Berlin, Germany, around 1825, later other factories in France and England also made them. Rarely signed. Terribly fragile. Highly collectible!

Candle shield, 3 scenes, ornate wooden frame	$165-190
Candle shield, woman seated, knitting, metal stand and frame	220-260
Farm family, 5" x 7", metal frame and stand	155-175
Hanging type, boy/girl in doorway, 6¼" x 4½" (ill.)	92-110
Mother, child, puppy, 6" x 5"	158-168
Mug, lithopane bottom, German soldier, WWI, 9½" high	125-145
Plaque, forest scene, 4" x 5"	158-178
Plaque, lovers in boat, village scene, 4" x 5"	140-150
Shade, leaded panels, children scenes, 4" x 4"	275-375
Tea warmer, 4 German scenes, converted burner	210-240

Liverpool Pottery

Liverpool Pottery

Various potteries made this ware from the mid-1700s to the mid-1800s. From about 1788 to 1820 the leading pottery, Sadler and Green, decorated their wares with line drawings, usually in black and white or cream colored. The decorations were often designed for the American colonies with famous people, eagles, and scenes from everyday life. Scarce.

Bowl, covered, blue/white Herculaneum	$152-162
Creamer, white/black transfer, "Temperance"	160-170
Creamer, strawberry lustre	138-148
Cup/saucer, black transfer, castle scene, handleless	99-110
Cup/saucer, 1800, black transfer	98-115
Jug, George Washington, ship, 10" high (ill.)	510-575
Pitcher, large, English farm scene	465-500
Plate, blue Chinese decor, 1780s	112-155
Plate, black, English ship	160-180
Tea set, teapot, sugar and creamer, Queen Anne shape, strawberry lustre	400-500

Lobmeyer Glass

Lobmeyer Glass

Ludwig Lobmeyer opened his factory in Zlatno, Hungary, in the 1870s. He made the first commercial iridescent glass of the 19th century. No two pieces are alike in color. Typical pieces are in fine, clear glass, with transparent enamel washes, and/or flashed with red and yellow.

Cups/saucers, demitasse, transparent washes in floral patterns, flint glass, ground pontils, 2" high (ill.) set	$ 48- 68
Candlesticks, pair, gold rimmed, birds/flowers, pair	55- 65
Vase, gilded, black enameling, chinoiserie decor	175-250

Lockets

These small hinged cases of silver, gold, or other metal, for holding a lock of hair or a

(continued)

photograph of a loved one, usually worn suspended from a necklace, have been collectible for years. The gold ones, often studded with diamonds, that hung from a man's watch chain are especially collectible.

Gold locket, studded with
   diamonds, late 1800s, 14k $350-425
Silver-plated locket, 1930s 12- 19

Locks and Keys

Locks and Keys

Here's a delightful hobby. These have been used to protect everything from a cabin door to the entrance of Louis XIV's castle. They come in all sizes and shapes. Locks with keys bring more than just plain locks. Yale, Sargeant, Keen Kutter—just a few of the famous lockmakers.

Lock, brass, with key, early 1800s $ 48- 60
Lock, brass, with key, late 1800s . 19- 27
Lock, iron, with key, jailhouse
  type 68- 76
Lock, padlock type, late 1800s .. 16- 25
Lock, padlock type, Baltimore &
  Ohio RR 38- 48
Lock, wood, with wood key, early
  1800s 56- 66
Lock, brass, "Quality—Six
  Lever" (ill.) 19- 28
Brass signal lock, N.Y. Central
  Railroad, w/keyhole guard 33- 43

Loetz Glass

Similar in appearance to Tiffany glass and made about the same time, it was made in Austria and was considered a fine quality iridescent glass. The factory was also noted for its fine cameo effects produced on cased glassware. Sometimes marked Loetz in the pontil.

Atomizer, orange, cameo cut,
  5¾" high $185-220

Loetz Glass

Bowl, green shading to gold,
  pinched sides 280-295
Bowl, ribbed with iridescence,
  folded down lip, green iridescent threading, 4½" high (ill.) . 220-245
Inkwell, green, iridescent purple/
  white in base, signed 210-250
Lamp, mushroom shade, tur-
  quoise iridescent, 20" high 285-315
Paperweight, blue, feather
  design, signed 235-275
Rose bowl, Art Deco, amber,
  iridescent, 4½" high 230-255
Tumbler, gold iridescent speck-
  ling, 3" high 82- 96
Vase, blue iridescent, gold/pink
  threads, flower-form, signed .. 250-310
Vase, rose, copper, green 285-325
Vase, iridescent, turquoise, 9½"
  high, signed 300-325

Lotus Ware

Lotus Ware

Knowles, Taylor and Knowles Pottery Company, East Liverpool, Ohio, made this fine and delicate porcelain of warm white and glossy greens in the late 1800s and only for 10 years. First marks were KTK on the bottom; later they put the firm's name in circle enclosing a crescent and star. Scarce.

Berry set, 3 pieces $370-400
Bowl, green/gold, cream ground,
  KTK mark 110-155
Bowl, roses, turquoise medal-
  lions, signed KTK (ill.) 345-390
Creamer, pink flowers, fishscales,
  signed 185-210
Creamer, white, classic shape,
  KTK (ill.) 185-210

Pitcher, fishnet, enameled
  flowers, 4¼" high   395-450
Tea set, green/gold or cream, all .   375-450
Vase, pink/blue floral, gold
  handles, signed KTK   570-620
Vase, roses, fishscales, signed
  8" high   225-265

Lowestoft Porcelain

Lowestoft Porcelain

Made at Suffolk, England, from about 1757 to the early 1800s; it is also claimed that the porcelain pieces were imported from China and only decorated in England. If this is so, it should be designated as Chinese Porcelain.

Basket, blue decoration, floral,
  9" dia. $240-265
Bowl, pink/yellow florals, medal-
  lions front and back, 10" dia . .   330-400
Coffeepot, lighthouse, gold trim,
  initial A   245-260
Cup/saucer, demitasse   88-110
Cup/saucer, Horn-of-Plenty,
  demitasse   92-120
Cup/saucer, rose decor (ill.) 64- 74
Platter, blue decoration, 12" dia .   150-170
Teapot, floral, Famille Rose
  pattern, 6½" high   350-390

Lustre Art Glass

Lustre Art Glass

Conrad Vahlsing made this glass in the 1920s. He was a son-in-law of Martin Bach, Sr., who made the famous Quezal glass.

Vahlsing's glass is most collectible today. Specific prices would be the same as Quezal. See QUEZAL.

Lustres

Lustres

These vaselike vessels with hanging prisms were decorative devices for holding candles and were intended as mantel and tabletop pieces. They were made of every type of glass. Usually the glass was Bristol or Bristol-type, in every color.

Blue/white enamel floral, cut
  glass prisms, 10", pr $295-335
Bohemian glass, one row crystal
  prisms, 1890, 14" tall   320-340
Bristol, blue ground, yellow/green
  decor, 11" high, pair   320-345
Cranberry, gold enameled decor,
  cut glass prisms, 14" high, pr. .   450-500
Enameled decor, gold, ruby,
  single row of prisms   345-365
Green, medallion, flowers, prisms,
  12" high, pr   420-480
White-cut-to-cranberry, prisms,
  pr   410-480

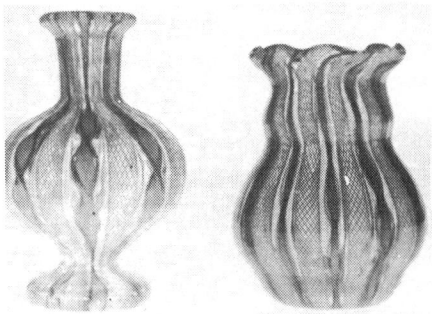

Lutz-type Glass

Lutz-type Glass

Nicholas Lutz came from St. Louis, France,

215

(continued)

in 1860 to work for Dorflinger at White Mills, Pennsylvania. It's really impossible to distinguish his articles of glass from those of other capable glassworkers of the same period. He also worked at Sandwich.

Basket, threaded, ruffled, 6¼" dia.	$ 80- 95
Bowl, berry, threaded, ruffled and crimped	110-130
Bowl, finger, apricot color	130-160
Compote, spiral striped, blue/white, 13½" high	470-520
Cup/saucer, demitasse, Latticino pink/white	150-170
Dish, bonbon, swirled candy cane, red/blue	145-175
Ewer, spiral striped, blue/white, applied pedestal	290-345
Pitcher, blue/gold threading, 13½" high	365-445
Plate, pale blue, gold twisted thread, pink ground	100-145
Tumbler, blue/gold, white striped, flared lip	125-175
Vase, white frosted, embossed cranberry threads, 4" high (ill.)	195-240
Vase, white clear, blue threads, 4" (ill.)	190-210
Vase, white diagonal threads, 7½" high	175-195

Lycett

The Lycett family decorated china for four generations. They came from England to the U.S. in the 19th century. President Lincoln commissioned them to decorate the dinner service for his second inauguration. Their formula for gold decoration was secret and has never been copied.

Maastricht Ware

This is a Dutch product made in Holland from the 1830s until the end of the 19th century. The English taught the Dutch how to make it. Petrus Regout and Company are again making this fine product. The sphinx with the firm's name is on all pieces.

Breakfast set, cup/saucer, plate, dike scene, all	33- 45
Cup/saucer, orange/black, dike scene	39- 47
Dish, blue/orange, deep, 9" dia.	30- 40
Plate, blue, castle scene, signed Regout Company	36- 46
Plate, flow blue, pair, 8½" dia	28- 38
Platter, red/green flowers, yellow ground, 12½" long	38- 47

Maastricht Ware

Tea tile, Oriental scene, Regout Company	24- 34
Tureen, large, white, includes ladle	49- 59
Plate, "Liberation"	48- 58

Magazines

Magazines

The Art Journal of America, 18 issues, 1875-1876, large engraving in each issue	$135-145	all
The Youth's Companion, 1922, 6 issues	35- 45	all
The Delineator, Oct. 1895, illustrations colored w/crayon	4- 7	
Good Housekeeping, 1931-1937	6- 9	all
The Travel Companion, 3 issues	11- 18	all
The Cottage Hearth, February 1883	10- 18	
The Red Book, January, 1906	6- 9	
McClures, November, 1904	6- 10	

Generally, magazines are priced depending on year, condition, etc., $2 to $5. If you're lucky, you'll find a Frank Leslie leather-bound with color fashion plates, $55-70.

Magic Lanterns

These were the forerunners of home movie machines. They operated on kerosene or candles and probably caused more than one fire in their day. Most came from Germany from the late 1800s until the early 1900s.

8-slide candle, reflector, lens .... $ 52- 62
11-slide, kerosene, reflector, lens, tin 70- 84
5-slide, candle, tin, lens 55- 65
24-slide, electrified, 1920s 70- 85
Average price, each slide 2- 5

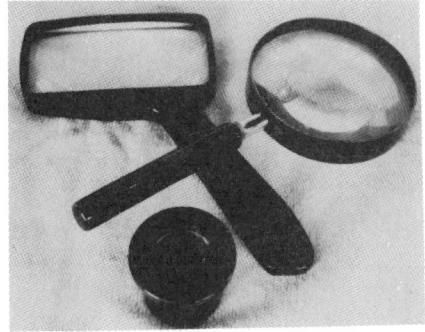

Magnifying Collectibles

Magnifying Collectibles

Old microscopes, magnifying glasses, and the like are all collectible today. If the lens is pre-World War I German, it's even more valuable. Check with a doctor friend or ask the hospitals where they trade their older models for the newer type microscopes.

Majolica

Majolica

This is a soft pottery or faience covered with a glossy coating turned opaque by treating it with tin oxide. It was made as early as the 12th century, later in most European countries. Most of what you find today is from the mid-1800s. Griffin, Smith and Hill made it in the U.S. in the late 1800s and A & P stores gave it away as premiums at that time. They called it Etruscan and it was marked GSH in script on the bottom.

Cake stand, sunflowers, American, GSH 74- 84
Compote, sunflowers, American, GSH 68- 78
Creamer, green/yellow, lovebirds, pink lining 79- 89
Cup/saucer, cobalt/yellow, brown ground, handleless 80- 90
Cuspidor, blue ground, fruit decor, 6½" high 60- 70
Dish, leaf, Etruscan mark, American, GSH 50- 60
Figurine, girl and boy playing, 8" high, pair 92-102
Humidor, Turk, 7" high 80- 90
Jar, tobacco, floral decor, pink/green, pipe on lid, 6" high 68- 78
Jardiniere, flower design, stand, 28" high 98-110
Jug, blue ground, dog, children, pewter lid, 7½" high 48- 58
Match holder, Negro boy, 6½" high 120-140
Pitcher, child with dog, 7" high .. 32- 42
Pitcher, fern pattern 40- 50
Plate, shell/seaweed, "Etruscan Majolica", 7" dia. (ill.) 85-110
Platter, leaf decor, 12" long 56- 62
Spooner, shell/seaweed, pink/green glazes, "Etruscan Majolica" (ill.) 85-110
Sugar, cauliflower cover, Etruscan, GSH, American ... 45- 52
Syrup, pewter top 29- 38

217

(continued)

Teapot, shell/seaweed, pink/
  green glazes, 6" high (ill.) 175-195
Tea set, teapot, sugar, creamer,
  sunflowers, brown ground 180-220
Toothpick, 3-handle, brown/
  green 28- 37
Vase, two monkeys, green
  ground 78- 96

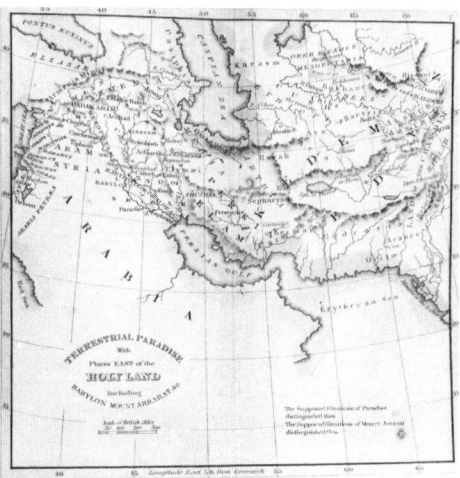

Maps

Maps

The older the better. A lot of guessing
went into making maps many years ago.
Today, examples of these maps are highly
collectible.

Arkansas, double folio, color,
  Bradley's Atlas, 1886,
  22" x 15" ....$ 15- 23
Florida/N. & S. Car./Ala., by
  George F. Cram, Chicago,
  1889 .... 14- 24
State maps of Arizona,
  Wyoming/Idaho, North
  Dakota, Louisiana, Iowa/
  Minnesota, New Jersey, by
  C.S. Hammond & Co., New
  York, 1914, 10½" x13" ... 6- 10 each
Balkan States, L.L. Poates,
  Engraving Co., 1921, 9¼"
  x 11¼" 6- 10
Arctic Regions, same firm,
  measurements as above ... 6- 10
Central America, color,
  Worldwide Encyclopedia,
  10¼" x 7½" 5- 9
Daniel Burges Company,
  New York, 1853, all 9½"
  x 11½":
    Central Europe 22- 33
    North America 29- 44

Indiana, Kentucky, Ohio and
  Tennessee 18- 26
  Africa 27- 42
  Europe 18- 29
Collins and Sons, Glasgow
  France, color, 1873, 8¾" x
  5-5/8" 12- 16
Holland and Belgium,
  color, 9" x 11¾" 12- 17
Holy Land, from Bible Atlas,
  published by Newton Case,
  1832 (ill.) 8- 15

Other fine mapmakers were Edward Cavendish
Drake, London, 1770s; John Cary, early 1800s;
Carry & Lea, 1820s; Emanuel Bowen, 1750s.

Marble

Marble

This is a hard, crystalline or granular meta-
morphic limestone, white or variously colored, sometimes streaked. It will take a high
polish. Don't confuse it with alabaster.

Chinese coolie, contemporary,
  6¾" high (ill.) ....$ 28- 35
Collie dog, 9" long 22- 30
Elephant bookends, 7½" high,
  pair 29- 39
Lion-on-pedestal, 8" high 28- 37
Mother cat with kittens, 7" long . 30- 38
Penguin bookends, 6" high, pair . 27- 35
Rooster, 4½" high 15- 18
Tiger, 8" high 26- 35
Urn, flower motif, 12½" high ... 35- 45
Vase, fluted lip, 11" high 22- 31

Marble Glass

This was an addled or opaque glass. Usually worked on a blower's pipe, it was then
sprinkled with pulverized, colored glass flux.
When reheated, it was finished in the usual
way. It was made by various firms in
England around 1893. Collectible today.

218

Marblehead Pottery

It could be called "therapy" pottery as it was first made by convalescing patients in a sanitarium at Marblehead, Massachusetts, in 1904. About three years later a plant was established, and, although Herbert J. Hall, M.D., is credited with its founding, Arthur E. Baggs should really be given the credit for the actual production. Most pieces are marked with an incised sailing ship and MP, although others have the initials "A.B." incised. Paper labels were also used. Matt-glazed and tin-enameled faience were two of the several finishes used. The plant closed in 1936 and Mr. Baggs took a position at Ohio State University.

Bowl, 3½" dia., blue glaze	$ 30- 44
Tile, blue, sailing ship signature, 4¾" square	140-160
Vase, medium green matt ground, geometric design, 3½" high	58- 72
Vase, mirror blue ground, high glaze, 5½" high, ship signature	63- 80
Vase, bulbous, matt green ground, brown/yellow/black, 7" high	89-125
Vase, matt gray, "tree" design, 12½" high	75- 85

Marbles

Glass companies in Pennsylvania and Ohio made the large glass marbles used by boys at the turn of the century. Some had colored stripes while others had animals inside. The larger are more collectible than the smaller.

Agate, black/white, ½" dia.	$ 16- 22
Agate, brown/white, 7/8" dia.	16- 24
Agate, green/white, ¾" dia.	14- 23
"Kayo" (comic strip), black/white	28- 38
Tigereye, 4/8" dia.	28- 38
Tigereye, 1" dia.	47- 57
Goldstone, 5/8" dia.	25- 35
Limestone, 5/8" dia.	3- 7

Bennington, mottled or fancy, 1¼" dia.	2- 5
China, Bull's-eye, 5/8" dia.	6- 9
China, Bull's-eye, 1 1/8" dia.	14- 18
China, Leaves, ½" dia.	8- 12
China, Leaves, 7/8" dia.	8- 12
Multicolored swirl (ill.)	9- 14
"Sandy" (comic strip) blue/white	28- 38
Sulphide, Baby (all positions)	95-105
Sulphide, Boar	85- 95
Sulphide, Boy on a stump	98-110
Sulphide, Cat, lying down	95-110
Sulphide, Cat, sitting	82- 92
Sulphide, Cow, grazing	89-110
Sulphide, Frog	100-115
Sulphide, Girl and dog	99-109
Sulphide, Goat	72- 81
Sulphide, Lamb (ill.)	68- 78
Sulphide, Owl, wings spread	120-140
Sulphide, Ram	73- 85
Sulphide, Rooster, running	70- 81
Sulphide, Rooster, standing	53- 64

Mary Gregory

Mary Gregory

We know that she did exist and that she did work for the Boston & Sandwich Glass Company on Cape Code. Obviously, she didn't decorate all those pieces attributed to her. She never tinted her figures and/or costumes. They were always white. Look for children, 5 to 12. Tinted figures must be called Mary Gregory-type and were made in Europe in the mid-1880s. No collector should buy this glass as original before talking to an expert. Lots of repros!

Barber bottle, blue, boy playing with kite, all white figure	$160-185
Biscuit jar, girl on swing, all white figure, blue glass	140-150

(continued)

Jewel box, black, girl in tree, all
white figure 140-160
Lamp, black, girl on the tree limb,
all white figure 350-425
Mug, cranberry, girl jumping
rope, all white figure 140-170
Perfume, cranberry, ITP, girl on
swing, all white 133-153
Pitcher, cranberry, boy with
hoop, all white figure 250-295
Pitcher, 6 tumblers, cranberry,
ITP, girl and boy in tree, all
white figure 280-310
Rose bowl, girl, all white figure . . 145-165
Tumble-up (carafe-with-tumbler),
boy, all white figure 245-270
Vase, clear, girl rolling hoop,
all white figure 110-120
Vase, girl on swing, all white
figure 325-375
Vase, green, boy with butterfly
net, all white figure 80- 90
Vase, ruby, boy holding horn,
ITP, 9" high (ill.) 750-850

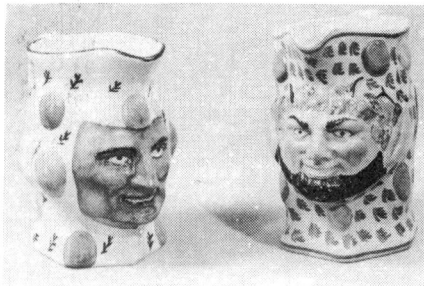

Mask Jugs

Mask Jugs

These are old English Lustre pottery types.
Many firms made them in the late 1700s and
early 1800s, Leeds Pottery, also Thomas
Harley at Longton. They're scarce today.
Though hard to find, a few are still around,
especially in American shops specializing in
English imports.

Masks

Witch doctors and devil's brew! Hand-
carved wooden masks come from every country in the world. Most of the old ones are in
museums, but lately good examples of the art
have been showing up in antiques shops.
Mentioned here because people are beginning
to collect them as antiques. Good Haunting!

Masonic Items

These were commemorative or souvenir

pieces, usually made of red/clear glass
though some were made of metal and/or pottery. Late 1800s until World War I.

Champagne glass, Minneapolis,
Minnesota, 1905 . . . . $ 22- 30
Cup, loving, 3-handle, Solomon's
Lodge, Philadelphia, 1910 . . . . 50- 60
Cup, Syria temple, 1905 . . . . 38- 48
Goblet, clear, Syria Temple,
Lexington, Kentucky, 1908 . . . 19- 27
Goblet, Syria Temple, 1909 . . . . . 49- 58
Jar, tobacco, emblem on lid,
signed, dated, Royal
Bayreuth 112-116
Mold, ice cream 22- 29
Mug, Lulu Temple, 1906 . . . . 31- 41
Plate, Philadelphia, 1911, 9" dia. . 29- 39
Plate, Albany, N.Y., 1914 . . . . . . 28- 38
Spoon, Islam Temple, San
Francisco, 1902 . . . . 16- 25

Mason's Patent Ironstone

Mason's Patent Ironstone

The Mason family first started making
porcelain in 1802. It was 1813 before they
made Ironstone, when Charles J. Mason took
out his famous Ironstone patent. It was in a
"sense" porcelain, as described in the patent.
It was in reality a heavy, hard, opaque earthenware. G.M. and C.J. Mason, 1813-1829,
was the first mark used; then C.J. Mason and
Company, 1829-1844; then C.J. Mason,
1845-1848. The firm went bankrupt in 1848.
Ashworth and Brothers, Hanley, England
produces a Mason-type ware today.

Bowl, red scene, early mark . . . . . $ 45- 55
Butter dish, Chinese decor 60- 80
Creamer, Chinese decor, 1819-
1844 mark, 5½" high 64- 74
Creamer, miniature, red flowers,
blue underglaze (ill.) 2¾" high . 70- 80
Jug, Chinese decor, 6¼" high,
early mark 52- 62

Pickle dish, Oriental pattern	20- 30
Pin tray, Oriental scene, 1829-1844 mark 6″ long	45- 55
Plate, American naval scene, early mark	74- 84
Plate, Oriental pattern, 1829-1844 mark	40- 50
Platter, Japanese scene, 14″ long	48- 62
Teapot, red flowers, blue underglaze, 8½″ high	49- 57
Tureen, red/blue flowers	60- 70

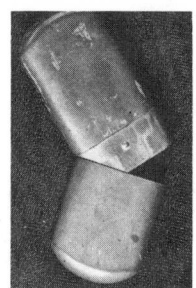

Match Safes

Match Holders

Match Holders

In the days of Lucifers or "house burners" (sulphur-headed matches), match holders were in vogue and were used to hold the matches on the wall or on the table. Mid-1800s until early 1930s. Many repros!

Bird, 4½″ high, iron	$ 29- 40
Boots, china, green/yellow, 4½″ high	26- 34
Bulldog's head, porcelain, Austria	28- 38
Butterfly, milk glass, 5″ high . . .	32- 42
Cast iron, c. 1880s	17- 29
Charlie Chaplin, clear glass (rare)	62- 72
Cricket, brass, hinged lid	34- 45
Dog, stump holds matches, iron .	24- 33
Elephant, clear glass	27- 37
Flower basket, iron	22- 32
Grape leaf, 3″ high, milk glass . .	28- 31
Indian head, 6″ high, hangs on wall, milk glass	40- 50
Jenny Lind, clear glass	56- 66
Man with cane by tree stump, china, Germany	21- 31
"Matches" hangs on wall, tin, 5½″ high (ill.)	18- 24
Rooster, hand-painted, Austria, china	27- 37
Two-compartment w/striker, tin, hanging type, 5″ high (ill.)	12- 18

Match Safes

They did just that—kept the matches safe when in one's pocket. Usually metal with a snap lid or cap, they were inexpensive when purchased. See SILVER.

Brass, bulldog, hinged	$44- 55
Flower/leaves, Germany	9- 17
Papier-mache, painted figures . . .	15- 24
Philadelphia Centennial, silver, 3″ high, hinged	43- 53
Sterling silver, 3″ high, cupids . .	45- 55
Sterling silver, whiskey advertisement, bottle-shaped	27- 37
Tin, many types, average	9- 14

Mayer, T.J. and J. Pottery

Mayer, T.J. and J. Pottery

The year 1829 was the beginning of this fine china company. The coats-of-arms of the 13 original states are especially collectible today. Stoke, Staffordshire, England.

Bowl, scalloped and embossed rim, 10½″, "Arms of Maryland"	$695-770
Cup plate, 4½″, South Carolina .	180-220
Plate, 8¾″, "Arms of Rhode Island"	250-285
Platter, 19″, New Jersey	680-740
Soup plate, 9½″-10″, New York .	135-175
Vegetable dish, 8″, Massachusetts	675-700

McCoy Pottery

McCoy Pottery

This pottery has been made in Roseville, Ohio, since 1910. In 1967 the firm was acquired by the Mt. Clemens (Michigan) Pottery Co. Early pieces are now becoming collectible.

Blossomtime 700 Line
Ivory 6¼" vase, McCoy	$ 8-	12
Yellow 8" vase, concave sides . . .	13-	18
Ivory jardiniere, sq. 4" tall	12-	19
Ivory planter	14-	23

Butterfly Line
Rose 8" planter (leaf relief only), USA	8-	16
Green spoon rest, NM USA	12-	19

Cookie Jars
Bear #22	50-	56
Honey bear	27-	37
Rocking horse	36-	46
Mr. & Mrs. Owl	32-	42
Black antique stove	26-	36
Blue windmill	15-	26
Have A Happy Day (smile)	28-	38

Flowerpots
Green basketweave #2, 3¼"	7-	11
Green long leaves & dots, 3½"d x 3½"t, NM	9-	17
Green long leaves two 3-3¾"d, 2-¾"t,NW	8-	16
Orange Double Beetle Band, 5" .	12-	19
Dark green Double Beetle Band, 5"	11-	18

Springwood Line
Jardiniere pink, 5-3/8", McCoy USA	15-	23
Bowl, 4-ftd pink, 6-5/8" dia., McCoy USA	9-	18
Vase, round bottom, sq. top, 7¼", green, McCoy USA	9-	16

Swirl Line
Orchid Planter, ftd, 7" long, McCoy USA	6-	9
Vase, orchid, ftd, 7" tall, McCoy USA	7-	10

Tea Set Items
Pinecone green creamer	11-	17
Pinecone green teapot & lid	18-	25
Creamer, pink/turquoise, matte, McCoy	6-	8
Tea Set, 3-piece, green/brown . . .	35-	45
Leaf creamer, 2-tone green, #108	8-	16
Teapot lid, as above	8-	14
Pinecone teapot, no lid, light crazing in & out	17-	22
Pinecone green/brown, 3-pc., McCoy	36-	42

Vases
Swan vase, 9", pink, McCoy	15-	23
Cornucopia, 7", cream, light crazing McCoy	14-	22
Handled, ftd vase, 9, turq. Stylized Leaf & Twig	14-	21
Dark green ftd vase 7¼" x 4½", 10-sided, McCoy USA	13-	24
Flowers & Leaf Blades, green, hld 8"	12-	23
Butterfly vase, 7", McCoy	12-	24
S&H/Peppers (ill.) pair	11-	26

McKinley Act, 1894

Required that the name of the country of origin appear on all imports into the U.S.A.

Medals, U.S. and Foreign

Medals, U.S. and Foreign

Ever since the handmade silver medal was given by Congress to the three men responsible for the capture of a British officer connected with Benedict Arnold, the U.S. has been giving out medals for just about everything. The British, French, Italians and Germans are also "medal happy." It should be

…oted that any medal made of sterling silver …as gone up in value, just for the silver con- …ent.

U.S. Army, Medal of Honor, 1862-1904	$700-900
U.S. Navy, Medal of Honor	600-800
U.S. Air Medal	7- 8
U.S. Navy, Byrd Antarctic Expedition	170-195
U.S. Army, Good Conduct	4- 6
U.S. Navy, Civil War	18- 44
British Distinguished Service	92-104
British Burma Star	8- 12
British Korea, 1950-53	13- 19
French Commemorative, WW I, sterling silver (ill.)	175-225
Officer's plate, Devonshire Regiment, 1878	95-115
Officer's plate, 16th Bedfordshire Regiment	425-500
Officer's blue cloth plate, 1870s, 59th Regiment	80- 90
Victoria Cross, English	5,500+
Polish "Independence Cross," WWII	22- 31
Polish Military Service Medal, 1918-21	27- 37
Polish Monte Casion Cross (serial numbered), WWII	18- 26
Italian Fascist Eastern Front Cross, 1941-1942	50- 60
Italian Fascist "10th Legion" Medal, bronze	33- 43
Italian Fascist Ethiopian Campaign Medal	32- 41
Imperial German Iron Cross, 1870, 2nd Class	82- 94

Medical Items

Medical Items

Old instruments, bottles, prescriptions, books—all are of special interest today, especially to one allied with the field of medicine.

Bleeding cup, pewter, handle, 3″ high	$ 35- 50
Bleeding lancet, folding like razor (ill.)	27- 37
Dental cabinet, drawers, on metal legs, old	66- 76
Doctor's bag, most instruments, some original bottles	150-200
Nursing bottle, measure marks on side, clear, old	14- 23
Surgeon's kit, 1850s, in walnut box, all instruments	375-425

Meissen

See DRESDEN.

Meissen, Onion Pattern

Originally known as "bulb pattern," it's more commonly called Onion pattern today. A whiteware with cobalt decorations, it was made in the latter part of the 19th century. Reproductions from Europe are causing havoc with the uninformed collector.

Baby feeder, 6¾″ long (ill.)	$18- 26
Bowl, 6″ dia.	39- 49
Bowls, 7″, 8″ square, pierced edges	54- 64
Breadboard	29- 39
Butter dish, covered	105-120
Candleholders, pair, 4¼″ high (ill.)	50- 55
Cheese dish, covered	122-130
Creamer, individual and porridge, 3½″ to 5½″ high	44- 54
Cups/saucers	
a. Coffee (ill.)	24- 34
b. Demitasse	27- 37
c. Tea	22- 32
Egg cup	18- 26
Plates, 8″ dia.	28- 38
Plates, soup, 9″, dia.	38- 47

Meissen, Onion Pattern

223

(continued)

Plate, chop, 14" long	87- 99
Platter, 12" long	92-107
Rolling pin	42- 54
Salt, master, footed 3¼" dia. . . .	54- 63
Sauce, 4¾" dia.	19- 26
Teapot with matching tile	125-140
Tureen, soup, Crossed Swords . .	162-172
Vase, scroll feet, 6½" high	59- 67
Vegetable dish, covered, 10" square	118-142

Many other pieces made in the onion pattern.

Mercury Glass

Mercury Glass

Silver nitrate was sloshed around inside double-walled objects of glass, then the entrance hole was sealed. As air seeped in, the "mercury" flaked off, leaving an unpleasant-looking object. Made in England and the U.S., late 1800s.

Bowl, 6" dia. . . . . $	45- 55
Bowl, 6" dia., painted flowers, 6" high	58- 67
Bowl, gilt interior, 5" high	44- 54
Candleholder, signed Perdue, 8" high	33- 43
Creamer, clear handle, Quadruple Plate spout, 8½" high (ill.)	74- 90
Dish, sweetmeats, sectioned	16- 24
Ornament, Christmas, grapes, 2½" dia.	7- 12
Pitcher, clear handle, 12½" high .	82- 92
Salt, footed	32- 42
Spooner	52- 62
Sugar shaker, metal cap	52- 62
Tieback, curtain, flower decor, pr	29- 38
Vase, blue/clear, painted flowers on front, 8" high, pr	44- 53
Vase, floral bands, castle scene painted on front, 9½" high, pr.	72- 79
Wig stand, pedestal base, 10" high (ill.)	80- 92

Mettlach

Mettlach

Jean Francois Boch founded the Mettlach pottery in 1809 in an old abbey named Abbey Mediolacum ("Between the Lakes") from which the name "Mettlach" was derived. In 1841, the Nicholas Villeroy family joined the Boch family. V & B developed the technique of "overglaze painting" — firing a particular piece at 2,400 degrees, then low firing other colors at lower temperatures; thus allowing the use of many colors and holding the same true color in stein after stein. V & B developed many other techniques, pioneering the way for many of the world's famous potters. The main factory at Mettlach burned in 1921 and was never rebuilt. All attempts at reproducing this great pottery have failed; what is on the market today should fool absolutely no one. The Black Forest stein is considered the choicest collector's item bringing over $5,000, when found and authenticated. Baskets, beakers, bowls, flagons, jugs, mugs, pitchers, plaques, tumblers, and urns were also made, but the stein made V & B world-famous. Serious Mettlach collectors collect by the number. Stein Collectors International is a great club to join. See — CLUBS TO JOIN.

PLAQUES

#1044 — a large series — most plaques with this number sell . . . . $	255- 300
#1384	750- 850

#1920	620- 650
#2195	675- 725
#2442, 2443, 2445	700- 850 ea.
#3131	175- 240
#3163, 3164	750- 850
#7025, signed "Stahl"	2,500+
#7040, 7041, 7043, 7045 ...	1,800-2,100 ea.
#7066	400- 475

STEINS

#368, ½L (liter-1.0567 liquid quarts)	395- 450
#406, ½ L..............	295- 340
#485, 1 L...............	350- 420
#675, ¼ L..............	160- 195
#675, ½ L..............	240- 290
#1052, ½ L.............	410- 415
#1069	625- 725
#1095, ½ L.............	250- 310
#1100, ¼ L.............	195- 225
#1104, 1½ L	285- 325
#1157, 1 L.............	370- 425
#1164, ½ L.............	385- 450
#1266, ½ L.............	140- 170
#1286, 5½" high (V & B) ..	360- 460
#1498, 5L..............	2,400-2,750
#1526 — a large series # — ½, 1, 3L	190- 400
#1536, ½ L.............	360- 400
#1655, ½ L.............	460- 575
#1786, 1 L.............	925- 995
#1863, ½ L.............	495- 555
#1909, 3/10 L	140- 195
#1932, ½ L.............	500- 585
#1941, 3 L.............	1,600-1,800
#2027, ½ L.............	550- 675
#2035, ½ L.............	500- 700
#2044, ½ L.............	425- 495
#2086, ½ L.............	270- 345
#2089, ½ L.............	450- 580
#2122, 5 L.............	2,450-2,750
#2181, ¼ L.............	190- 225
#2184, 3/10 L	440- 515
#2391, ½ L.............	410- 500
#2479, ½ L.............	685- 795
#2500, ½ L.............	650- 700
#2556, 1 L.............	400- 500
#2582, ½ L.............	400- 500
#2768, ½ L.............	420- 510
#2802, ½ L.............	1,550-1,725
#2878, 1 L.............	550- 675
#2912, ½ L.............	320- 360
#2938, 1 L.............	495- 575
#2950, ½ L.............	520- 610
#2958, 3 L.............	325- 425
#3091, ½ L.............	475- 550
#3099, 5 L.............	4,500-6,500
#3168, ½ L.............	495- 585

Obviously, hundreds and hundreds more. You're mixing with the professionals when you collect Mettlach steins, so read up and save up!

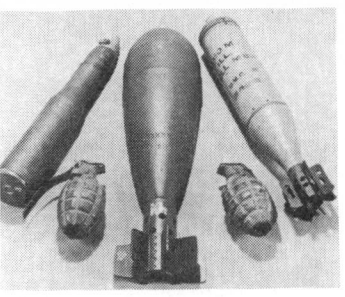

Military Collectibles

Military Collectibles

Items from the Revolutionary War on have been collectible. Nazi items are now collectible, as will be items from the Korean and Vietnam conflicts. Also, see JAPANESE WAR ITEMS AND NAZI WAR ITEMS.

Armband, English firefighter, World War II	$ 14- 24
Bayonet and scabbard for Enfield rifle, World War II ...	38- 50
Bayonet with leather sheath, Civil War, Union Army	42- 52
Belt buckle, brass CSA	29- 39
Canteen, U.S. Cavalry, Civil War	75-100
Canteen, clay (throwaway type), Union Army stamp, brown ...	92-120
Flag, Union Jack, English, World War I, 40" x 28"	40- 50
Helmet, English, World War I ..	25- 35
Helmet, English, World War II .	24- 34
Saddle, McClellan-type, Union Army, Civil War	128-140

Milk Glass

Milk Glass

See PATTERN GLASS section for specific pieces and prices. Prices for a few selected items are given here.

Battleship Maine, white milk glass	$ 95 - 135
Dolphin condiment dish, opalescent, 3¾" high, scroll/ beadwork (ill.)	68- 78
Drum and cannon, covered dish .	78- 88
Hand and dove, covered dish ...	75- 85

(continued)

Hen on nest, covered dish, blue/
white opalescence, 4½" high
(ill.) 69- 79
Uncle Sam, covered dish 90-100
A huge collection of milk glass can be seen at the Houston Museum, Chattanooga, Tennessee. Reproductions have ruined this as a serious collector's item.

Millefiori Glass

Millefiori Glass

This ornamental glass was made by fusing together slender canes or rods of glass then cutting across them in small sections. These sections then were imbedded in the glass object being made. Lots of companies made it, here and abroad, mid-1800s on. General collectors will have a difficult time telling the old from the new. The paperweights are especially hard to distinguish. Watch out! Still being made on the island of Murano, Italy.

Basket, blues/greens, small $165-185
Bowl, 2 handles, 2" high 110-130
Box, covered, 3" high 160-185
Chocolate pot, 9" high, no cups . . 160-170
Creamer, red flower spray,
    striped handle 170-180
Cup/saucer, demitasse 160-170
Cruet, cut glass stopper, 6"
    high 340-350
Inkwell, paperweight base 200-250
Goblet, clear stem 170-190
Globe, lamp, 4" dia. 155-180
Lamp, has matching shade, 14"
    high 220-250
Rose bowl, fluted lip, 6½" high . . 130-150
Salt, open, master, 6 small 295-340
Tumbler, 4" high (ill.) 80- 90
Vase, 4" high 130-160
Vase, 4" high, scalloped top 140-160
Vases, handled (ill.), each 70- 80

Miniatures

In the mid-1800s salesmen carried miniatures of their products; furniture, carriages, anything bulky. Anything miniature is collectible today; dollhouse furniture, pressed glass dollhouse dishes, and other items.

Cowbell, brass, 7/8" $30- 39

Bowl, blue porcelain, 1½"
    diameter 20- 30
Bucket, pressed glass, metal bail
    handle, 2" high 18- 30
Candlestick, brass, 1½" high,
    pair 18- 30
Coal hod, brass 20- 34
Flatiron, on trivet (rare), 2½"
    long 45- 60
Furniture, cabinet, rosewood,
    German, 19th century 92-120
Jug, water, brass, ¾" high 16- 25
Kettle, handle, brass, 1½" high . . 15- 28
Lamp, clear, Thistle Panel, with
    chimney, 3½" high 34- 45

MINTON
YEARLY MARKS

(A chart of Minton yearly marks, a grid of symbols arranged by year from 1842 through 1942.)

Impressed in the clay to show year of manufactur[e]
[18]42—1942 inclusive. The figures 43 etc. have been use[d]
[fo]r 1943 onwards.

"Yearly Marks"

Minton

This factory, established in England around 1793, continues today under the same name. Early pieces were incised with the firm's name and are highly collectible now. Their "Yearly Marks" are shown here.

Bowl and pitcher, blue, leaves,
    flowers, marked $270-295
Bowl, lapis blue, wild vines/
    leaves, 9" dia. 138-155
Butter dish, covered, floral motif   110-135
Chocolate pot, white, etched/gold
    trim, marked 149-163

Minton

Compote, enameled roses, signed, 8″ high	140-170
Cup/saucer, demitasse, blue decor panels in gold rims	80- 92
Egg cup, floral motif	26- 35
Jug, blue/white Jasper, 4½″ high	60- 70
Pitcher, water, grapes, gold decor, 11″ high, marked	150-170
Plate, Tree of Life pattern, 6½″ dia.	44- 53
Teapot, sugar, creamer, white/ gold trim, red roses, marked	115-130
Tile, blue/white, 6″ square	40- 55
Vase, brown/green/turquoise, 10″ high	190-210
Vase, farm scene, blue, 5½″ high, impressed mark	210-225
Vase, birds and flowers, 7½″ high	150-175

Mocha Ware

Mocha Ware

Similar to Leeds ware, Mocha is usually cream colored and decorated with seaweed, worms, or other such "lovely" items, in various colors on bands of blue, tan, red. It was first made in Tunstall, England, in the late 1700s to the early 1800s, by William Adams, later by his son. Apparently it was never marked.

Bowl, tan/blue/white, feather bands, 5″ wide	$260-280
Bowl, seaweed band, blue, 8½″ dia.	380-395
Bowl, earthworm, blue/red, 7″ dia.	210-260
Chamber, pot, creamware, blue/ green, brown bands	270-300
Dish, master salt, green bands, leaf handle	150-170
Jug, seaweed design, 5″ high	190-220
Mug, tree pattern, 5″ high	170-195
Mug, red ground, black/blue/ cream mottling, green-threaded top	170-190
Mug, white ground, blue bands, 5″ high	190-220
Mug, multicolored, 3¾″ high (ill.)	160-185
Mug, large, blue and gray bands, seaweed design, 6″ high (ill.)	175-210
Pitcher, syrup, ferns/leaves, 8½″ high	260-280
Pitcher, water, tan/black/white, 4″ high	245-270
Salt shaker, earthworm design	84- 96
Sugar bowl, trees, green band, 5½″ high	245-265

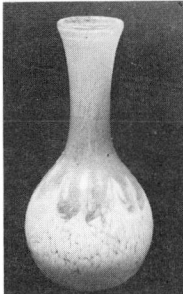

Monart Glass

Monart Glass

This glass was made in Scotland after World War I. Its style is considered Art Deco. Small pieces of embedded colored glass show through the heavy body.

Bowl, 4″ dia., pink/blue/green, dark green swirls	$ 90-110
Vase, 10¾″ high, Cluthra type, green to mottled light blue, ground pontil (ill.)	400-500
Vase, 5½″ high, red to mottled brown, green rim	125-155

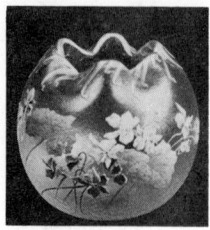

Mont Joy

Moorcroft Pottery

Mont Joy

This is cameo and enameled glass made at Pantin, France, by the same firm that produced De Vez.

Bowl, frosted body with
  enameled flowers, signed,
  3¾" diameter $240-290
Rose bowl, ruffled lip, cameo cut
  back, enameled lavender
  violets, gold leaves, 5" high,
  signed "Mont Joy" (ill.) 160-180
Vase, bud, carved, red poppies,
  purple ground, 20" high 340-400
Vase, flowers, gilded, frosted
  green, signed, 11" high 450-495
Vase, mottled orange/black
  ground, signed, 11½" high . . . 325-400
Vase, enameled iris, buds, gold
  leaves, acid-etched ground,
  6" high 260-325

Moorcroft Pottery

This is a modern English pottery which, for some unexplainable reason, is highly collectible today. Factory established in 1913 by William Moorcroft at Cobridge. Script signature.

Ashtray, red/yellow flowers,
  script signature . . . . $ 28- 38
Basket, metal holder, 6" dia.,
  green flowers 65- 80
Bowl, blue/white decor, fruit 57- 67
Bowl, pewter foot, 6¼" dia., fruit
  decor, lavender/yellow/red/
  green (ill.) 58- 69
Box, covered, orange/maroon,
  4½" dia. 62- 78
Compote, green ground, purple
  flowers, 4½" high 60- 70
Cup/saucer, fruit decor green
  script 50- 60
Inkwell, blue background,
  signed 74- 84
Tea set: pot, sugar bowl,
  creamer, blue ground. All have
  pewter lids 240-280
Vase, bud, light/dark green,
  trees, 8" high, script signature 180-210

Moriage

Not a specific company but a definition that applies to Japanese ceramics that have applied clay (slip) decorations. This type of decoration has been used for more than two hundred years and is quite predominant on export wares produced since the Nippon era (1891-1921). Designs include lacy effects, border trimmings, birds, animals, floral decor, and landscapes. The most popular is the jewel-eyed slip trailed dragon. Workmanship dictates the value.

Cup/saucer, butterflies, Green M
  in Wreath, Nippon . . . . $ 40- 50
Hatpin holder, 6" high, floral
  panels 42- 52
Pitcher, 12½" high, jewel-eyed
  dragon 210-240
Plate, 8" dia., green/yellow
  flowers 55- 65
Teapot, dragon motif, Blue Maple
  Leaf, Nippon 78- 88
Vase, flowers, gold trim, 10½"
  high, Green M in Wreath,
  Nippon 140-165
Vase, peacock, floral decor, 11½"
  high, Double T Diamond mark 185-220
Vase, 14½" high, jewel-eyed
  dragon, Green M in Wreath . . . 240-275

Mortars and Pestles

The Egyptians used a crude form to grind sacred potions. Usually made of brass or a hardwood such as lignum vitae or bird's-eye maple, larger ones served for grinding grain, while smaller ones pulverized salt, spices, drugs.

Brass, early 1800s . . . . $ 75-110
Iron, late 19th century 44- 53
Wood, bird's-eye maple, early
  (ill.) 68- 80
Ironstone bowl (mortar), wooden
  pestle, mid-1800s 59- 70

Moser Glass

This "art nouveau" glass as well as other types, some highly enameled, was made by Ludvig Moser at his factory in Carlsbad, Austria, at the turn of the century. Most collectible today.

Bottle, perfume, blue cut to clear,
  7¼" high, signed $128-148
Bowl, vintage decor, cranberry,
  footed, 7", signed 78- 82

Moser Glass

Candlesticks, Alexandrite, cube type, signed, 10", pr.	245-275
Compote, amethyst, gold border, 7" high	250-265
Compote, cranberry, cut overlay, signed, 9" high	180-210
Cruet, amethyst to clear, mushroom stopper, gold band, 5" high	108-228
Decanter, panel cut, signed	110-120
Dresser set, 2 perfumes, hair holder, tray, jewel box, gold enameled, all pieces signed . . .	425-475
Goblet, cobalt, jeweled/enameled, signed	195-225
Jar, tobacco, panels/florals, leaves, rayed star base	90-110
Toothpick, clear, crystal	60- 70
Vase, opalescent blue and white, enameled leaves and insects, applied red cherries, 6½" high (ill.)	500-550
Vase, amethyst, clear/intaglio cut floral, 11" high	360-380
Vase, clear to yellow, top to bottom decor	120-140
Vase, amber, gold band of Amazon women and centaurs, gold stripes, signed "Moser Karlsbad" (ill.)	225-250

Moss Agate Glass

This is a form of crackled glass and was created by Frederick Carder when he worked for Stevens and Williams in England in the late 1890s. Slightly yellow and very heavy, the orange, yellow, white, and black-colored glass, crushed into a powder and sprinkled on the object while still hot, gave texture to the glass and at the same time recreated the natural color of moss agate. Rare.

Moss Rose Pattern China

Moss Rose Pattern China

In the mid-1800s, the English potters used this garden flower to decorate certain wares. It was used on Ironstone ware for almost 50 years.

Bowl, sugar, cluster, soft-paste porcelain	$ 22- 30
Box, covered, oval, 6¼" long . . .	27- 36
Compote, Wedgwood, Ironstone, 1860	52- 62
Creamer	34- 43
Creamer and sugar, both	72- 78
Cup/saucer, Haviland	27- 37
Bone dish, rose cluster, set of 6 . .	84- 94
Dish, sauce, square, Meakin	27- 37
Pitcher, Wallace and Chetwood, England, 8" high	34- 44
Pitcher, ironstone, 8¼" high	34- 43
Plate, Bavaria	22- 32
Plate, cake, white, 10" dia.	31- 40
Ring tree, hand-painted	24- 34
Saucedish, Johnson and Brothers, England	24- 34
Teapot, Haviland, 7¾" high	56- 66
Teapot, A. Meakin, England, mid-1800s	66- 73
Teapot, 6 cups/saucers	120-130

Motorcycles

The Indian 'cycle once had a self-starter — a Hendee Special; before that, a hand-cranked job. Remember "Cannonball" Baker? He made a fortune in the early days riding motorcycles across the U.S. of A., attempting to set records. In 1911, in England, the front wheel brake was first introduced — a Wilkin-

(continued)

Motorcycles

son. Old motorcycles are highly collectible today.

1908 Hendee (later, Indian), still runs	$2,700-3,200
1909 N.S.U., 7 H.P. ("Horse-power"), poor condition	1,200-1,450
1912 Marvel, good condition	1,400-1,700
1911 Henderson, 4 cylinder, good condition	2,900-3,600
1905 Clement (French), running condition, 4 cylinder	1,300-1,700
1911 Thor, poor condition	1,450-1,650
1910 Excelsior Auto-Cycle, excellent condition	1,800-2,200
1912 Pierce, 4 cylinder, running	1.400-1,900
1914 Harley-Davison, good condition	1,600-2,700
1914 Yale, 2 cylinder, poor running condition	1,350-1,700
1912 Emblem, needs work	1,200-1,400
1913 Merkel, runs	1,300-1,600
1923 Evans Power-Cycle, running	1,200-1,600
1922 Cleveland, modified for racing, good condition	1,400-1,800

Mt. Washington Peachblow

Mt. Washington Peachblow

New Bedford, Massachusetts, 1886. It shades from rose color at top to pale blue in lower portion. Don't buy it if you don't know it! Too many repros!

Biscuit jar, blue florals, flowers, 6" high	$ 220-	260
Box, dresser, blue flowers	245-	285
Cracker jar, melon ribbed, panels of flowers	270-	310
Creamer, Burmese, applied handle	325-	375
Muffineer, peach ground, metal cap	165-	210
Pitcher, decorated with flowers, James Montgomery's poem (ill.)	875-1,000	
Salt/pepper shakers, tomato-shaped, floral decor	325-	390
Tumbler, birds, flowers	180-	240
Vase, bulbous, flower enameled	1,100-1,400	

Movie Photos

Movie Photos

Shirley Mason, Mabel Normand, Gloria Joy, Hale Hamilton. Who remembers them? All movie stars in their own right! Anyway, photos of movie stars are collectible, especially from the early days, the type given away by drugstores, music stores, etc.

Average price	$ 2-	3
If signed (and authenticated)	15-	22
Dedicated to a person	9-	16

Muffineers

Usually made of glass or silver, these containers were used for sifting sugar or cinnamon on muffins. Much larger than a salt

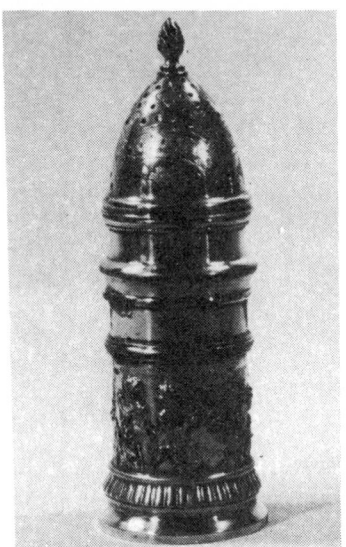

Muffineers

shaker, they were popular in England in the late 1800s.

China, cobalt, floral decor, 5¼″ high	$ 29-	41
China, green/gold, decorated, silver cap	28-	38
Cranberry glass, 5″ high	74-	88
Glass, cut, clear, sterling silver top, 7¼″ high	67-	77
Opalescent, lid, 6″ high	32-	45
Porcelain, silver cap, England, Meakin	28-	36
Spanish Lace, raspberry/satin, plated cap, 6″ high	64-	74
Sterling silver, 6″ high, beaded, 3 curved feet	40-	50

Mugs, Porcelain

Mugs, Porcelain

Used for ale, whisky, tea, every English porcelain firm made them; also other European firms. See specific types for prices.

Mug, pink, red leaves	$ 18-	27

Muller Freres

Muller Freres

The Muller brothers made a fine grade of glass, including cameo, at Luneville and then at Crois Mare, France, from early 1900s until World War II.

Cameo vase, acid cut and enamel scenes in brown/yellow/ lavender, 4″ high, signed	$375-425
Cameo vase, birds, enameled, multicolored, signed	450-525
Lamp, hanging, Art Deco, wrought iron frame	475-550
Lamp, table, 2 hanging shades, cameo cut leaves	785-900
Vase, ringed neck, enameled, flower decor (ill.)	220-270

Music Boxes

The Swiss and Germans were skilled makers of music boxes. Many European countries produced them but the movements usually came from Switzerland. 17th century on.

Artison Disc organ	$1,200-	1,400
Birdcage type, bird moves and sings	500-	650
Bremond, 6″ cylinder	1,700-	1,950
Columbia, 6 selections	750-	900
Coset Calliope, manual, 45 pipes, brass	11,000-16,000	
Dawkins, 6 tunes, 8″ cylinders	2,000-	2,700
Double comb, Polyphon, coin-operated	2,400-	2,800

(continued)

Music Boxes

Lochmann, winding rod,
  gold leaf decor, 21½"
  disc, 42"   2,800-3,300
Mandoline, cylinder, 11",
  No. Co 12 . . . .   1,200- 1,400
Regina, automatic, No. 33,
  12 39" diameter discs,
  metal 5,500- 6,000
Regina, coin-operated, 12
  records 4,500- 5,200
Seeburg, Style K, piano,
  mandolin, xylophone,
  nickelodeon, 62" 5,000- 5,800
Swiss, 9-bell cylinder,
  restored 1,700- 2,200
Swiss, 8-tune cylinder,
  bells, 18" high, circa
  1900 . . . .   2,700- 3,700
Swiss, 10-tune cylinder,
  bells, inlaid wood in lid . .   2,900- 3,600
Swiss, 8-tune cylinder, out-
  side crank, 5½" 1,700- 2,400
Swiss, 12-tune cylinder,
  rose-wood box, inlaid
  top, 5 bells 3,800- 4,400
Swiss, 4 tunes, 5" cylinders   675-   900
Symphonion, double comb,
  5" 1,800- 2,600
Symphonion, single comb,
  7" 1,400- 1,900
Symphonion, 13", with
  bells 4,400- 6,200

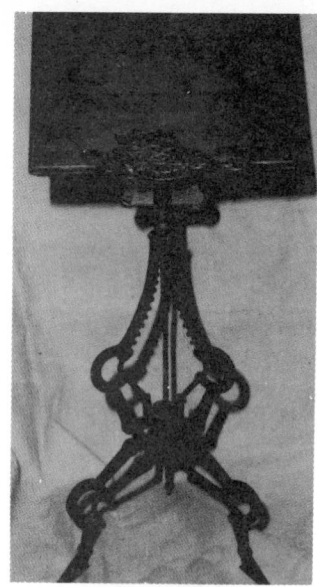

Music Stands

Music Stands

Just that — a rack-on-legs to hold sheet
music. They've been around for years and
collectors use them to hold the family Bible or
dictionary.

Ornate ironwork, cherry board,
  1890s (ill.) . . . . $ 85-120
Ornate ironwork, double board,
  poplar, 1890s   80-100

Musical Instruments

Musical Instruments

Accordion, "Adolphus
  Special" . . . . $ 95- 120
Banjo, 5-string, 1900s 160- 185
Bugle, Boy Scout, brass   35-   47
Bugle, C.S.A., brass 95- 115
Clarinet, w/wooden case   60-   70
Dulcimer, rosewood, 39½"
  long 98- 120
Dulcimer, walnut, all strings,
  w/2 small hammers 120- 140
Glockenspiel, hanging bars
  on carrying racks 175- 220
Lap harp, late 1800s 215- 230
Harp, 4¾" high, complete . . .   910-1,000
Zither, late 1800s 145- 160
Violins-depends on maker.
  Average price 125- 165

Mustache Cups

Mustache Cups

They were popular in the 1800s. The partition in the cup supposedly kept the beverage from running down grandfather's vest. The majority were made in Germany using the transfer method — a method similar to our decals of today. Left-handed cups are rare. Lots of repros here!

Cup, brown matte glaze, left-handed, 1890s	$ 60- 70
Cup, gold band	22- 31
Cup, horses	12- 22
Cup, lavender, flower decor, man's name in gold	47- 59
Cup, "Love the Giver," blue/yellow background	49- 61
Cup, pink/orange, "WJM" in gold	49- 58
Cup, blue floral "Love Is Eternal" in gold	40- 50
Cup, "Papa" in gold	52- 63
Cup/saucer, beaded leaf cluster, gold initials	50- 59
Cup/saucer, blue, white, scrolled medallions, Germany	48- 58
Cup/saucer, bright blue/green, gold initials, 1860s	46- 50
Cup/saucer, floral spray, German inscription, gold letters	44- 52
Cup/saucer, guadruple plate, revised initials, birds	53- 62

Nailsea Glass

This glass was produced at Nailsea, England, beginning in 1788. The loops and swirlings of the colored glass, combined with clear or opal glass, identify it. The more common color combinations are red/white and green/white. More repros!

Atomizer, clear, white loops, 7¼" high	$100-135

Nailsea Glass

Bottle, blue, white looping, blown stopper, 11¼" high with stopper	160-180
Carafe, matching plate, dark blue/white typical looping	120-140
Cookie jar, blue loopings, Britannia lid and bale, 6½" high	135-155
Castor set, 4 bottles, blue/white loopings, cut stoppers	144-153
Cruet, blue, white loops, 6¼" high	165-195
Cruet, dark red, white loopings, blown stopper, 6½" high	62- 72
Cup/saucer, blue swirl, 19th century	53- 64
Epergne, flower base, blue/white loopings around base, brass fittings	210-230
Flask, red swirls, 5½" high, no cap	140-150
Fairy lamp, satin to clear, signed Clarke in base	250-300
Gas shade, white loopings, 3" filter	70- 80
Pitcher, blue, white loops, clear handle, 10½" high	260-280
Rolling pin, cranberry swirl, 16" long	238-278
Rose bowl, blue looping, 4" dia.	160-180
Tumbler, white/blue loops	68- 78
Vase, green satin, fluted top, 19th century	120-145
Vase, white with blue loopings, black handles and base, 9½" high (ill.)	92-115

Nakara

See WAVECREST

Napkin Rings

These were in vogue for less than 50 years, beginning in the late 1870s. They were made of every type of material, including cut glass.

233

(continued)

Napkin Rings

Most common are those from pot metal or "Quadruple Plate."

Cherubs, silver plate, Derby Silver Co.	$ 38- 47
Child's name engraved around chicks scratching, silver	40- 50
Porcelain, hand-painted, flowers and bees, Germany	29- 36
Silver plate, boy fishing on rock	49- 56
Silver plate, large boot	36- 46
Silver plate, cherub, child's initials	30- 40
Silver plate, fireman's helmet, Pairpoint	65- 78
Silver plate, boy with hoop (ill.)	31- 41
Silver plate, cow, (ill.)	30- 39
Silver plate, souvenir, Niagara Falls	37- 46
Silver plate, horseshoe	32- 41
Silver plate, wild boar, barrel type, Pairpoint	62- 72
Sterling silver, dog chasing cat, initialed	165-195
Sterling silver, Georgie, beaded edge	155-185
Sterling silver, owl on branch, child's name	150-220

Nash Glass

Nash Glass

A former employee of the Tiffany Glass Company, Douglas Nash purchased Tiffany's Long Island factory around 1929. His glass was flamboyant in color and most of it was signed Nash on the bottom.

Bowl, gold, stretched edge, 8" dia. signed	$340-375
Candlestick, gold, water base, 5" high	120-140
Decanter, pair, green/shaded gold, 15" high	310-350
Plate, chintz, alternating greens and pinks, signed "Nash," 6¾" dia. (ill.)	125-150
Plate, yellow, orange chintz, signed, 8" dia.	150-170
Vase, flower form, ruffled top, pedestal base, peacock blue, 5½" high (ill.)	400-450
Vase, Tiffany blue, 8" high, signed	360-400
Vase, chintz/orange decor, 7½" high, signed	325-345
Vase, green, fluted top, 8½" high, signed	510-530
Vase, iridescent, gold, impressed veins circling vase, 6" high, signed	520-550

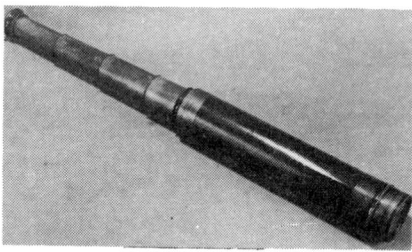

Nautical

Nautical

"Where away?" was the cry from the deck when a sailor in the crow's nest spotted a whale, an enemy ship or land. The English and the Germans made the best telescopes, from the early 1700s on. A real gem when found in original condition.

TELESCOPES:

Ship captain's, 13" when closed; 2 large sections, opened, to 30"	$ 250- 350
Ship captain's, c. 1820, wooden barrel, brass mounts, 35" overall, marked "Gardner & Sons-Glasgow-Day or Night"	260- 320
Ship captain's, 36" overall, original leather covering, c. 1850	265- 400
Ship captain's, made by a woman, Janet Taylor-Minories, London	395- 500
Ship captain's, walnut tube, brass, 26" overall (ill.)	225- 265

OTHER NAUTICAL ITEMS:
Clipper Ship Card, 3½" x 6½",
colorful, used to advertise for
cargo $265- 295
Logbook from the ship *Urchin*,
10½" x 12½", 1838-1839 ... 400- 450
British East Indiaman's
logbook, 9½" x 15",
1799-1802 .... 550- 625
British midshipman's journal,
1929-1932, 8" x 13" 250- 300
Sailing ship's stick-type
barometer, on gimbal mount,
English, 1820 1,200-1,350
Ship captain's telescope, 30"
overall, covered with leather,
twined rope............. 250- 300
Ship's boat horn 16" overall, .. 225- 290
Letter from Commodore Perry
to his wife, hand-written, 4
pages, 1852.............. 295- 345
Copper ship's oil lamp, 18"
high, oil font intact 220- 268
Sailor's valentine, octagon-
shaped, hinged case,
seashells, etc. 420- 450
Notes on torpedo fuses,
by a Lt. Converse, U.S.A.,
1875, published by U.S.
Torpedo Station, Newport,
Rhode Island, 31 pages 65- 78
History of Nantucket by Obed
Macy, Mansfield, Mass.,
1880, 313 pages 45- 60
*The British Mariner's Directory
& Guide to the Trade &
Navigation of the Indian &
China Seas,* by Elmore,
342 pages 400- 500
Ordinance Instructions for the
U.S. Navy, Navy Dept.,
Washington, 1866 .... 78- 88
U.S. Navy ship's
"Battle-rattle,"used to
sound "General Quarters!" . 350- 425
Greener percussion, muzzle-
loading harpoon gun,
English 1,600-1,900
Whaling bomb lance gun, c.
1860s, breech-loading,
American 1,450-1,700
Harpoon for Greener gun, c.
1850, 51" overall, iron shaft . 280- 320
Whale-killing lance, c. 1840s,
59" overall 295- 350
Blubber or "boat" spade, 17"
overall 155- 185
Ship's sextant, brass, 9" wide,
8½" high, 6 swivel filters,
etc. 600- 700

Ship's medicine chest, c. 1830,
mahogany, 8" x 10" x 9",
c. 1840s................. 400- 500
Ship's running lights, pair,
brass, 14" high, 1930s 370- 400
"Lead," used for determining
depth of water, 30" overall,
in pin box 185- 210

Nazi Items

Nazi Items

Hitler may have lost the war but collectors
of his military items are growing every day.
They are so popular, in fact, that reproductions are beginning to appear on the market.

Bayonet, Nazi Police
Eagle's Head, bone-type
grips (ill.) $125-155
Belt buckle, swastika
insignia 70- 90
Eagle, staff car, alloy with
threaded screw for
mounting (ill.) 48- 60
Flag, 4' x 7', swastika
and German Cross 95-110
Helmet, Luftschultz with
wings (ill.) 60- 75
Photograph of Hitler and
friends, signed 150-300
Iron Cross, 2nd Class 45- 65
Afrika Corps Service
Medal 60- 80
Luftwaffe badge, pilot,
marked "Imme" 280-325
Luftwaffe badge, "Gebr.
Schneider A Wien" 350-400
"Kreta" cuff title—awarded
to participants in the
battle for Crete 190-230
Dagger, Army, w/eagle and
swastika cross guard ... 195-240
Dagger, Luftwaffe 1937
model, flying eagle on
cross guard 235-275

235

(continued)

Dagger, carried by the
Brown Shirts, wood grip,
eagle, etc   185-220
Dagger, Hitler Youth,
"Blut Und Ehre" on
blade   260-285
Peaked cap, Army infantry
officer, silver bullion
chin cord   220-245
Peaked cap, Artillery
officer, silver cord,
red piping   220-240
Peaked cap, Luftwaffe,
officer   195-230
Peaked cap, Navy captain,
gold bullion wreath, etc. .   250-285
Helmet, Afrika Corps, tan
camouflage   185-220
Helmet, Nazi Police, chin
strap, etc.   150-170
Helmet, "R.L.B." (Air
Defense League) parade
type   285-310
Pith helmet, Afrika Corps,
green felt body, both
metal badges 80- 95
Uniform, Panzer
Grenadier   210-280
Uniform, medical officer's . .   260-295
Uniform, chaplain's
Reichswehr tunic   310-350
Tunic, Luftwaffe, officer's
summer white, all
complete   470-550
Overcoat, Luftwaffe,
officer's, black leather,
snap-in lining   365-400
Parade dress belt, officer's,
round eagle buckle   110-150
Army mess kit 55- 70

Mountain troops rucksack .   62- 72
Doll, Storm Tropper, 11″
high, painted composition
head   155-188
Armband, H.J. (Hitler
Youth), bevo weave 47- 57
Armband, German Armed
Forces ("Deutsche
Wehrmacht"), black/
yellow 40- 52
Bayonet, police, eagle's
head, etc. (ill.)   95-140
Staff car eagle, alloy with
threaded screw for
mounting (ill.) 60- 80
Helmet, Luftschultz, with
wings (ill.) 60- 98

Needlework

Patterns were first engraved and hand-painted on paper; later they were stamped in color on canvas. If done in wool stitches this was called Berlin work. In addition to personal items, popular patterns were done in the form of bookmarks, mottos, such as "Home Sweet Home," "Welcome," and religious sentiments. Godey's was just one of many magazines that printed patterns for this type of work.

Daily, "God Is Good," early 19th
century . . . . $ 27- 37
Handkerchief flowers, blue/gold,
19th century (frame not
included) 30- 45
Sampler, "Friends Forever,"
early 19th century 52- 70
Scarf, flowers, 36″ long 23- 33

Netsukes

Netsukes

Usually carved of ivory, they're used as fasteners, such as a button for garments. The old are highly collectible and they're being skillfully reproduced in Japan. Careful! It's pronounced "Netski."

Cat	$ 45- 62
Child with dog	62- 72
Dog playing with fish	70- 85
Man holding turtle	62- 72
Man carrying basket of fish	68- 78
Man carrying boat net	62- 72
2-face (smiling, 1 side, frowning, other), 1¾" high	110-140
Sumo wrestlers (reproduction?)	62- 80
(if original and signed Kokusai, ivory, it'd be worth $500!)	
Pearl diver	56- 66
Smiling man with bread, button, ivory	65- 75
Tiger	60- 75
Women talking, 1 holding carp, ivory	62- 72
Boar	65- 75
Crab, stained brown	72- 82
Elephant, two blind men	95-120
Happy/sad face (head revolves)	88- 95
Man carrying donkey	90-110
Hare on turtle's back	60- 70
Houseboat	84- 98
Frogs on lily pad	70- 80
Hare on back of turtle	60- 70
Devil's mask	60- 75
Man carrying bundle of straw	60- 77
Mouse, stained brown	60- 65
Owl	60- 80
Reaper	60- 87
Running boar	60- 75
Apple vendor, woman	60- 90
Kabuki player	60- 70

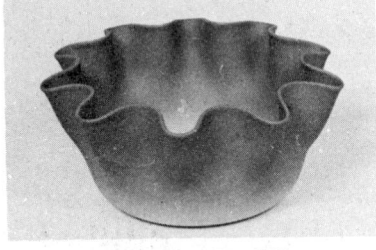

New England Peachblow

New England Peachblow

Also called "Wild Rose," it shades from rose at top to white in lower portion. Edward Libbey patented it in 1886 under the Wild Rose name. Being reproduced.

Bowl, satin finish	$ 675- 700	
Bowl, finger, satin finish, raspberry to white, 5" wide (ill.)	550- 650	
Creamer, 4" high, applied handle, glossy finish	875- 900	
Pitcher, milk		
a. Glossy finish	1,800-2,000	
b. Satin finish	1,800-2,100	
Rose bowl, crimped top, World's Fair, 1893	650- 750	
Vase, acid finish, 8" high	950-1,100	

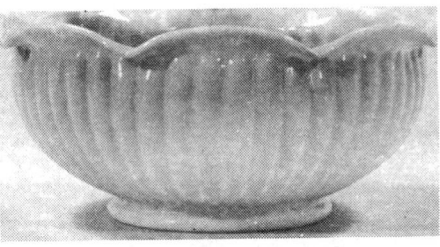

New Martinsville "Peachblow"

New Martinsville "Peachblow"

Its factory name was "Muranese"; made at the New Martinsville, West Virginia, factory in the late 1800s and until 1907, Joseph Webb of the famous Sturbridge, England, family invented it. It got its name "Peachblow" in the early 1940s when antiques dealers tried to unload large amounts of it, following the success story of the famous Wheeling Peachblow — see. It is good glass but doesn't remotely compare to any of the three famous Peachblows — Mt. Washington, New England, and Wheeling

Large berry bowl, "Sunburst"	$165-180
Small berry bowl, "Sunglow"	120-140
Bride's basket w/frame, 10" dia., "Sunburst"	185-220
Bride's basket w/frame, 8" dia., "Sunburst"	180-200
Bride's basket w/frame, 6" dia., "Sunglow"	160-180
Bowl, fluted edges, 8½" dia., "Sunburst"	160-175
Sugar shaker, original cap, "Sunrise"	90-110
Vase, ruffled lip, 7½" high, "Sunray"	140-160
Vase, floral panels, fluted lip, Salmon, 8" high	135-145
Syrup jug, metal cap, 6" high	110-115
Lamp shade, Frosted Salmon, 3½" high	90-115

Newcomb Pottery

Newhall China

Newcomb Pottery

It was opened in 1896 by Ellsworth and William Woodward as a workshop extension of the art school of Sophie Newcomb Memorial College for Women, New Orleans. By 1897 it was producing on a large scale. Most of the pottery was turned on the wheel by Joseph Fortune Meyer. It's highly collectible today.

Bowl 3-7/8" high, blue/green/pink
yellow narcissus motif $185-220
Bowl, plain glaze, undecorated,
2-1/8" high, Newcomb mark . . 120-130
Bowl-vase, 4¾" high, blue/green,
Spanish bayonet motif, matt
glaze, decorator: Julia Michel . 190-210
Bowl, blue/green/pink, tie-vine
motif, matte glaze Newcomb . . 125-135
Inkstand, with liner and lid,
blue/green/brown, glossy
glaze, decorator Joseph Meyer 78- 90
Mug, florals, blue underglaze,
signed Joseph Meyer 700-785
Pot, "Ali Baba" type, plain
green semi-matt, 3 1/8" high . . 85- 95
Vase, green/blue, oak tree motif,
matt glaze, 5¼" high 185-200
Vase, 7¾" high, blue/green con-
ventionalized motif, glossy
glaze 175-195
Vase, misty blue, massed flowers,
blue/yellow 295-340

Newhall China

Some say this was the first true English china. It was made at Newhall in the Staffordshire District, England, around 1781. At first they specialized in hard-paste porcelain, later they produced bone china.

Creamer, enameled flowers, 4"
high (ill.) $120-140
Creamer, Pink Lustre
decorations 85-100
Cup/saucer, Blossom Band
decor 58- 68
Mug, Oriental scene, 3" high 60- 70
Plate, Rose decor, 7¼" dia.,
early 72- 83
Plate, Rose decor, 8" dia. 73- 85
Sugar bowl, Pink Lustre
decorations 120-140
Teapot, creamer, sugar, Oriental
decor 182-192
Teapot, Oriental decor, 7½"
high 190-240

Newspapers

Newspapers

Some are highly sought after, while others are fodder for the recycling machines. Age, condition, information given — all dictate the price.

Harper's Weekly, New York, July 15, 1871 (ill.)	$2-	4
The Stars and Stripes, France, August 9, 1918 (ill.)	2-	4

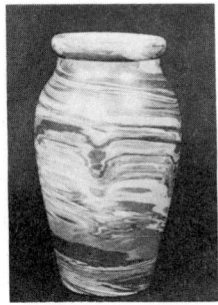

Niloak Pottery

Niloak Pottery

This multicolored pottery was made at Benton, Arkansas, in the late 19th century until 1946. Glazed on the inside, it had a dull finish on the outside. Most desirable colors are rust and chocolate brown. "Niloak" is always stamped in bottom. Beginning to be collectible. Indicative prices are:

Vase, 6½" high, signed	$ 25-	35
Tile, 4½" square	30-	40
Vase, 9" high, signed	42-	52
Chamber stick, 5" high	42-	52
Bud vase, 8" high	42-	51
Bowl with flower frog	50-	60
Wall pocket, 7" high	35-	39
Candlestick, 7½" high, signed . .	40-	50
Jigger, 2¼" high	25-	32
Elephant, 1" high	50-	60
Humidor, 6½" high	72-	82
Cigarette holder, signed	25-	35
Match holder, 1½" high, signed .	26-	36
Vase, brown/tan/yellow, 6½" high, stamped "Niloak" (ill.) . .	28-	38

Nippon

Hand-decorated, generally it's defined as porcelain made in Japan between 1891 and 1921 for export. It was NOT a specific type of porcelain. The name used on the back of each piece denoted the country of origin. After 1891 the U.S. required that imported

Nippon

items from all foreign countries be marked with the name of the exporting country. "Nippon" is the Japanese word for Japan, but in 1921 the U.S.A. stated that the word "Nippon" was no longer acceptable as a country of origin marking. Thus ended the "Nippon" era.

Bowl, handled, gilted flowers, ivory ground (ill.)	$ 18-	24
Candleholders, pair, flowers, Blue Leaf mark, pair	110-130	
Cracker jar, covered, pink roses, hand-painted	73-	83
Humidor, tobacco, green/white, floral decor, Maple Leaf mark .	170-195	
Lemonade set, 8 pieces, violets, leaves, E-OH mark	162-180	
Peanut set, "peanut" decor, 6 matching bowls	160-180	
Plaque, Indian chief, 11" dia. . . .	280-310	
Plate, roses, beaded gold loop, red ground, 10" dia.	34- 44	
Urn, ocean scene, Green Wreath mark, 17" high	310-340	
Vase, blue, flowers, gold trim, 11½" high	85-120	
Vase, iris, blue/yellow, Green Wreath mark	110-135	

Nodding Figures

Sometimes called pagods, they're porcelain figures with heads and hands that are attached to the body with wires. Any movement causes the figure to move up and down. 18th and 19th centuries, considered quite collectible today.

Bird in tree, trunk sways, bisque	$40-	50
Boy holding dog, dog's head moves, porcelain, 18th century	52-	70
Chinese boy in rickshaw, head and hands move, bisque type .	52-	62

239

(continued)

Nodding Figures

Girl and boy kissing, heads nod,
porcelain 28- 38
Farm couple, green/yellow/
orange, 6¾" high (ill.), pair ... 65- 78
Hindu, turbaned, holding basket,
snake moves too, bisque 50- 60
Old lady in chair, sleeping head
nods, bisque 35- 45

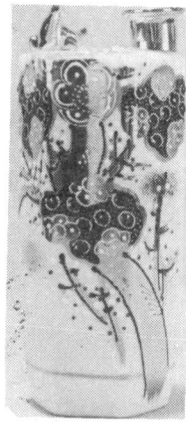

Noritake

Noritake China

Produced by the Nihon Toki Kaisha firm in Nagoya, Japan, after 1904, for export only, "Azalea" is the best-known pattern as it was given away as a premium by the Larkin Tea and Coffee Company in the early 1900s. There is more Noritake on the market than any other mark. Look for "Noritake Nippon," "Noritake M In Wreath Nippon" and "Noritake RC Nippon" marks. They're the earliest. Modern Noritake is marked "Noritake China, Japan" with the familiar "M" in the wreath above.

Basket, Azalea pattern,
5" long .... $ 82- 92
Berry set, 6-piece, floral
scene, Green M in
Wreath mark .... 65- 85 set
Berry set, 7-piece, Azalea
pattern .... 79- 92 all
Bowl, Azalea pattern, 10½"
dia. 27- 37
Cake plate, Azalea pattern,
7" dia. 50- 60
Celery dish, Azalea pattern,
12¼" long 35- 43
Compote, Azalea pattern,
6½" dia. 45- 58
Creamer, Azalea pattern,
4½" high 26- 36
Cup/saucer, Swans, gold
rim, RC mark 14- 18
Cup/saucer, Sedalia pattern,
set of 12, Green M mark . 70- 80 all
Celery dish, crimson roses,
9" long, RC mark 25- 35
Condiment set, Azalea
pattern, 6-pc. 40- 50
Chocolate set; pot, 8 cups,
floral scenes, Green M
mark .... 72- 82 all
Dish, Azalea pattern, sauce
type 7- 12
Dresser set, 7-piece, blue
flowers, gold border,
new mark .... 52- 62 all
Egg cup, Azalea pattern ... 26- 34
Figurine, boy fishing, green/
yellow, RC mark, 6"
high 44- 48
Mayonnaise set, 3-piece,
Azalea pattern 92-115
Plates, Azalea pattern, 7",
8½", 9¾" dia. 8- 17
Platter, Azalea pattern,
14" long 39- 48
Salt/pepper, owl motif,
Green M mark .... 22- 33 pr.
Salt/pepper, Azalea pattern 17- 27 pr.
Shallow bowl, cherry
blossom scene, 3-handled,
Green M mark 32- 42
Tea set, garden scene,
varied colors, RC mark .. 53- 62
Tea set, 17-pieces, floral
scenes, gold rims, Green
M mark .... 110-130 all
Tile, Azalea pattern 25- 35
Tobacco jar, horse's head,
blue/red, Green M mark .. 52- 62
Vase, salmon/pink, 8" high . 33- 43
Vase, floral scenes, 7¼"
high 28- 38
Vase, Azalea pattern, 8¾"
high 72- 85

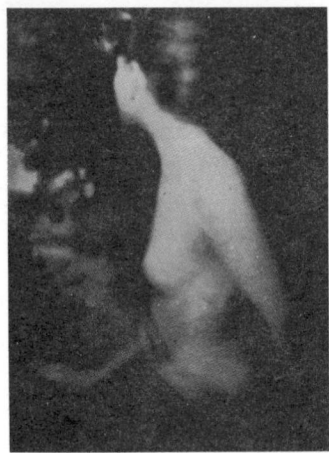

Nudes

Nudes

Those that adorned the walls of the western saloons are priceless today. These 19th century "streakers" are most collectible if and when you can find them. Obviously, an oil painting would be worth more than a lithograph unless the fame of the artist of the nude entered into it.

Nutcrackers

Nutcrackers

Teeth, stones, factory-made devices—they were all used for opening nuts. A popular type in the early 1900s was an animal whose tail opened its mouth, into which the nut was inserted.

Alligator, brass, 13" long	$ 53-	63
Bear's head, wood, 8" long	53-	63
Cat, seated, iron, 11" high, tail opens mouth	26-	36
Dog, iron, 11" long, same operation (ill.)	30-	42
Dragon, brass	49-	58
Squirrel, brass, 8½" long, same operation	37-	45
Tiger, bronze	62-	73

Turtle, iron 8½" long, same operation	26-	37
Wolf's head, iron, marked Renz, 9" high, same operation	34-	51

Occupied Japan Items

Occupied Japan Items

We occupied Japan for 8 years after World War II, and we made the Japanese put "occupied" on everything they exported during those years. When we got out, they removed the word. Today, those items are collectible.

Cup/saucer, floral, signed "Jyoto China" (ill.)	$ 8-	12
Cup/saucer, cherubs, flowers	10-	16
Doll dishes, 12 piece set, floral	15-	20
Figurine, cat at fishpond, pink/green	16-	21
Figurine, football player	12-	18
Flowerpot, miniature, flowers	12-	22
Hanging pot with chains, floral decor	22-	28
Humidor, flowers, covered, lion finial	33-	43
Planter, donkey pulling cart	8-	12
Sugar and creamer, pond scenes	16-	25
Salt/pepper, mountain scenes, 2½" high	22-	28
Tea set, 7 pieces	26-	30
Tea set, 15 pieces, green/blue	33-	42
Tile, flower decor, 4½" square	9-	12
Vase, fishes, blue/yellow, 8½" high	10-	13

Office Equipment

Old adding machines are collectible, as are old typewriters, such as the early Hammond, Blickensderfer. Any mechanical piece of office equipment from the early 1900s on is collectible today.

Adding machine, hand-operated, early 1900s	$ 48-	58

(continued)

Office Equipment

Blickensderfer typewriter, late
1800s 63- 73
Hammond typewriter, wood
case, late 1800s 68- 78
Typewriter, 1910s-1920s, still
works 52- 62

Ohr Pottery

George E. Ohr made his pottery at Biloxi, Mississippi, from 1883 until just after World War I. It was made from local clay and fired at low temperature. An extremely thin pottery, a contorted shape was one of its characteristics as were the many glaze colors Ohr used. Some referred to him as the "mad potter of Biloxi" but few denied his genuis. He signed his pieces "G.E. Ohr, Biloxi" and "Geo. E. Ohr, Biloxi, Mississippi" in block letters or "G.E. Ohr" in script.

Bowl, one side folded halfway
over, mustard glaze, 2¾"
high . . . . $ 58- 70
Bowl, folded lip, dark green/
brown glaze, 2" high 59- 70

Candlestick, dark maroon, rough
texture (ill.) 145-165
Candlestick, handled, mottled
green glaze, 3¾" high 92-120
Mug, handleless, dark brown
glaze, 3¾" high 110-190
Mug, puzzle, green glaze,
decorated handle, pierced
sides, 3½" high 110-190
Pitcher, folded neck, blood red
glaze, 6½" high 285-295
Teapot, applied snake, pink
"raku" glaze, 5¼" high 450-500
Vase, squat, matt pewter finish,
dented side (ill.) 210-235
Vase, 4-petal top, pinched,
pewter/gunmetal bowl (ill.) 220-235
Vase, folded neck, dark lead
glaze, 4¾" high 80-112
Vase, pinched sides, ruffled edge,
3¾" high 165-195
Vase, dark brown glaze, 2½" high 75- 85
Vase, folded waist, green
speckled glaze, 2½" high 92-105

Old Hall Porcelain

Old Hall Porcelain

Originally from Job Meigh and Son, Old Hall Works, Hanley, England, 1790. Name changed to Old Hall Earthenware Company

Ohr Pottery

in 1861; name changed again in 1887 to Old Hall Porcelain Works. The firm ceased production in 1902. It was an opaque earthenware of the Staffordshire-type. Generally, Staffordshire-type earthenware pieces are in the same price range as Old Hall. See specific Staffordshire-types for specific prices. An indicative piece is shown.

Pitcher, cream brown transfer
    leaves & flowers, 4" high,
    signed "Old Hall Earthenware
    Co." (ill.) . . . . $ 30- 45

Old Ivory China

Old Ivory China

The ground color of this ware gives it its name. Made in Silesia, Germany, in the last part of the 1800s, the marked pieces bear the crown Silesia mark, and/or pattern stock numbers.

Berry bowl, numbered . . . . $ 40- 50
Berry set, bowl and 6 small
    bowls 250-285
Celery bowl, Silesia, numbered . . 44- 54
Chocolate pot, peach color/rose,
    numbered 170-190
Comb and brush tray, pattern
    #16, 11½" (ill.) 45- 55
Creamer and sugar, numbered . . 72- 82
Cup/saucer, numbered, orange
    poppies, green leaves 44- 54
Cake plate, 10" dia., numbered . . 68- 79
Cake plate, Silesia, open handles,
    numbered 68- 74
Platter, peach color, numbered . . 110-135
Relish dish, numbered 34- 44
Saucedish, numbered, 5" dia. . . . 28- 37
Teapot, floral, peach, numbered . 165-190
Toothpick, numbered, 2" high . . 62- 72
Tray, numbered, Silesia, 2" 53- 63

Old Paris China

Old Paris China

During the 18th and 19th centuries a number of pottery and porcelain factories were located in Paris. The better products were known as Old Paris, although few pieces were ever marked as such.

Cake plate, white, gold trim . . . . $ 52- 62
Compote, 5¼" high (ill.) 47- 56
Creamer, numbered, white, gold
    trim 38- 48
Cup/saucer, white, gold trim 71- 81
Figurines, children with pets,
    pastel colored, pr. 120-135
Pitcher, water, white, gold trim . . 92-107
Plates, fruit, floral decor, 10"
    dia. 47- 57
Teapot, white with gold trim 88- 98
Tea set, pot, creamer, sugar,
    flower motif, gold trim 300-400
Vases, handled, gold trim, early
    1850s pr. 355-378

Onyx Glass

Onyx Glass

Characterized by its raised, 8 petal and leaf design, this decorative glass was made in 1889 by Dalzell, Gilmore and Leighton Company, Findlay, Ohio. It was only made for 6 months. Colors were silver, amber, orange, raspberry, orchid, and purple. Considered

243

(continued)

scarce today, it was referred to as "Oriental Ware" by the people who made it.

Cream pitcher, silver	$280-300
Lamp, two-post base, silver	650+
Salt shaker, amber	95-125
Sugar bowl, covered	295-375
Syrup, silver floral design, silver plated cap, 6¾" high, applied opalescent handle (ill.)	290-365
Tumbler, raspberry	175-240

Opalescent Glass

Opalescent Glass

Clear or colored with a milky white opalescence, it's usually blown or mold blown. Seldom were pieces made as a set. It was made by Sandwich in their early days. Many other companies also made it, and many other pieces were made. Check various art glass sections and specific companies in Pattern Glass Section, this Price Guide.

Vase, white opalescent-to-clear, tree bark design, 11" high (ill.)	$40- 50
Vase, yellow opalescent with Spanish Lace design, frilled top, 6½" high (ill.)	72- 90

Opaline Glass

This glass looks like the opal when held to a light—milky iridescence with a fiery orange background. Don't confuse it with the cheaper milk glass, also made in the late 1800s. Being reproduced.

Barber bottle, 11" high	$45- 60
Butter pats, rose, beaded, set of 6	33- 42
Bowl, birds, cherries, 10" dia.	32- 43
Box, blue, pink/white flowers, hinged top	50- 60
Inkwell, blue, silver deposit, gold, fluted	57- 67

Lamp, apple green, 13½" high overall, French	82- 92
Match holder, pipe-shaped, souvenir	14- 21
Perfume, opaque white/gold enamel, 1850s England	110-118
Sugar bowl, rose/opaque white, covered, 4" high	66- 76
Tumbler, raised rose/flower pattern	60- 70
Vase, rose, floral, leaves, rose motif, 5½" high	97-107
Vase, blue overlay, pink ground, 6½" high	89- 99
Vase, gray, classic lines, ruffled top, 4½" high	110-115

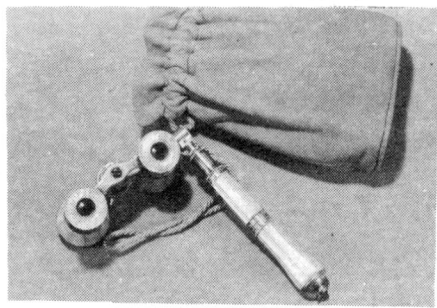

Opera Glasses

Opera Glasses

Simply, these are small binocular telescopes, used at the opera, theater, etc. From the plainest type to the glasses illustrated here, they came in all sizes and shapes. The French and Germans made the best. Some were inlaid with mother-of-pearl (ill.), some inlaid with precious gems. They're turning up in shops today as old estates are emptying their attics and basements.

American, leather covered, in leather case, Bosch and Lomb, 1900s	$ 28- 38
French, mother-of-pearl inlaid, early 1900s, removable handle (ill.)	55- 65
German, polished brass, Zeiss-Ikon lenses, velvet case, early 1900s	48- 58

Optical Items

Optical Items

During the 1800s peddlers traveled from farm to farm selling spectacles. Our ancestors bought the pair they could "see best with," a far cry from the practices in optometry today.

Brass frames, adjustable, in leather case (ill.)	$ 28- 33
Metal frames, no case	14- 18
14 karat gold frames, adjustable, in leather case	58- 68
Metal frames, bifocals pasted on .	27- 37

Organs

Organs

No Victorian parlor was complete without an organ. The cheaper models were made of oak, while cherry and walnut and maple were used in the more expensive models. Most piano tuners can repair the bellows and broken pedal straps. Tuning the pitch keys requires only a musical ear and a wire coat hanger. Type of wood, age, and condition dictate the price.

Oak, swing-out candleholders, display rack, 1880s, working . .	$475-600
Walnut, music rack (ill.) The Grand Sterling, c. 1870s	775-900
Chestnut, complete with adjustable 3-legged stool, c. 1800s . . .	575-700
Home Favorite Piano-Organ, 1903, made by Sears, Roebuck	380-425
Happy Home organ, 1904	275-375
Acme Queen Parlor model, 5 octaves, 11 stops, 2 octave couplers	380-410
Bilhorn Telescope organ, portable	250-280

Oriental Rugs, Others

These beautiful rugs came into vogue in

Oriental Rugs

this country during the late Victorian era. The best were made in Persia (now Iran). Bokhara, Kurd, Cabistan, Sarouk—these are famous names when one discusses the better rugs. Some have over 800 knots per square inch! Some of the new Oriental rugs can fool the less knowledgeable buyer. A little dirt can make them look very old!

Ardebil, 5½' x 3½' . . . . $	975-1,100
Chinese, 4' x 2'	700- 850
Chinese, 5' x 3'	650- 775
Japan, 4½' x 7'	875- 975
Kashan, prayer, 4½' x 7'	2,400+
Kum, 7' x 4½'	2,400-2,800
Kum, mosaic, 7' x 5'	2,300-2,600
Nain, 8' x 5'	4,900-5,600
Sarouk, 13' x 3' (hall runner) . . .	2,800-3,400
Sarouk, Ivory, 13½' x 4'	3,200-3,400
Sarouk, 17' x 3' (hall runner) . . .	3,300-3,600
Aubusson, 6½' x 3'7", c. 1840, scrolling leafage, green/white ground	1,975-2,900
Daghestan prayer rug, c. 1918, 5'11" x 5'3"	2,200-2,600
Ghiordes prayer rug, c. 1840, 4' x 5'8", green mihrab w/stepped arch	2,900-3,600
Kashan prayer rug, silk, c. 1880, 6'5" x 4'1"	2,750-3,400
Kum, mosaic design, 7' x 5', c. 1850	2,400-2,900
Samarkand, sea green field, fawn medallion, pink/fawn borders, 6' x 5'	2,900+
Turkish Bergama prayer rug, 3'10" x 3'6", c. 1800	4,500+
Chinese bird rug, midnight blue ground, peonies, c. Tao Kuang, 7'3" x 4'8"	3,400-3,800
Fachralo Kazak prayer rug, c. 1916, 4'8" x 3'5"	3,700-4,400

245

(continued)

Kashan prayer rug, 4½' x 7',
c. 1830 1,800-2,700
Chinese rug, Ch'ien Lung,
8'11" x 6'1", tawny rose
field, peonies 3,600-3,900
Bessarabian carpet, c. 1860,
10'7" x 9'4", bouquets of
roses, etc. 3,400-3,800
Chinese carpet, Late Ch'ien
Lung, 10'11" square, apricot
fields, birds 3,800-4,200
Hamadan Sehna carpet, 18' x
10', trellised Herati pattern . 3,400-3,800
Bakhshaish Herati carpet, c.
1780, 16'9" x 7'3", rose
leaves, etc. 4,400-4,700
Fereghan carpet, 26' x 19', c.
1730, green/blue field, allover
trellis of blossoms, etc. 4,200-4,700

Overlay Glass

Overlay Glass

Too much of this type of glass is attributed
to the Sandwich Glass Company. Most of
what you find today is from the Stourbridge
district in England, mid-1800s. Reproductions that should fool no one are sold in
this country by a St. Louis, Missouri, firm.

Genuine Sandwich pieces start
at $300-350
Stourbridge-type pieces, slightly
less 250-300
Basket, opalescent, thorn handle,
yellow feet, green leaves,
amethyst stems (ill.) 375-425
Ewer, serrated top, blue to white,
pink/yellow/blue flowers, amber
handle, Mt. Washington (ill.) . . 330-420
Ewer, lavender, white opalescent
design, pink flowers (ill.) 280-310

Owens Pottery

The J.B. Owens Pottery Company pro-

Owens Pottery

duced this pottery in Ohio from the
mid-1800s until 1933. It is comparable to
Roseville and Weller.

Candleholder, Utopian, berry/leaf
decor, brown glaze . . . . $ 57- 68
Letter holder, floral decor, 3½"
high 32- 42
Mug, Utopian, fruit on vine,
5½" high 82-102
Pitcher, orange/brown/yellow
floral leaves, Utopian 91-106
Pitcher, flowers, green leaves,
green ground, 10" high 74- 84
Pitcher, tankard-type, berries/
leaves, artist-signed 72- 82
Vase, green leaves, green-to-pink
flowers, 5½" high 80- 90
Vase, Utopian, orange pansies,
6" high 59- 70
Vase, Utopian, pansy decor,
6½" high 62- 72
Vase, Lincoln, brown, tan,
identical to an earlier Weller
vase 69- 80

Paintings

Oil paintings, water colors, and pastels
from the 17th, 18th, and 19th centuries,
American or European, are highly collectible.
American folk art is especially popular.

"Monastery," signed "Bianci,"
1895, oil. He was the last of
the Borgia family (ill.) . . . . . . $ 425- 500
"Wildflowers," signed
"R. Dayton," 1965,
watercolor 500- 600
Steamer *Lahn,* signed
"Antonio Jacoben," c. 1915
oil 3,400-3,500
"Waterfall Landscape,"
unsigned, Hudson River
School, c. 1870, oil 160- 180

246

Painting

"Seascape Coastline," signed
"George Howde Gay," oil... 170- 190
"Ocean Wave at Twilight,"
signed "A. Eugenie," pastel . 92- 125
"The Cardinal," signed
"E. Nanone," 19th century,
watercolor 220- 240
"Italian Landscape," attrib-
uted to Richard Wilson,
R.A., c. 1750 .... 600- 700
"An Old Courtyard," signed
"Mark Anthony," c. 1855,
oil 750- 900
"Smiling Countryside," signed
"W.H. Hilliard," 19th
century, oil 675- 800
"Seashore in Algiers," signed
"Frederic A. Bridgman,"
1912, oil 600- 750
"A Country Stream," signed
"Henry Pember Smith,"
1875, oil 600- 700
"Coast Scene," unsigned,
possibly Ben Foster, 1890,
oil 450- 500
"Forest Opening," signed
"Roswell Morse Shurtleff,"
1879, oil 575- 625
"Autumn Landscape," signed
"Guy C. Wiggins," 1910, oil . 485- 525
"Crossing the Atlantic,"
unsigned, 19th century, oil . . 600- 700
"Autumn in the Catskills,"
signed "Thomas Cole,"
1827, oil 700- 800
"Fighting Meat," signed "C.M.
Russell" w/skull of buffalo,
watercolor and gouache 3,200-3,700
"The Ambush," signed "F.
Remington," gouache
monotone .... 8,000+

AMERICAN FOLK PAINTINGS:

"Wife of a New England Sea
Captain," signed "William
LaFarge," c. 1860, oil 600- 700
"Village Election," unsigned,
c. 1860, oil 850- 950
"Gentleman at a Fireplace,"
signed "W. Twatman,"
1843, oil 750- 850
"Hunters," unsigned, c. 1870,
watercolor 475- 525
"Civil War Generals," c. 1865,
unsigned, oil 850- 900
"The Dayan Family," signed
"H. Pudor," 1858, oil 700- 850
"Mississippi Farm by a
River," unsigned, c. 1875,
crayon 600- 700
"Young Lady on a Balcony,"
unsigned, c. 1830, oil...... 525- 600
"Thompson's Mill, Bowery
Bay, Astoria," signed "E.
Doolittle," 1877 .... 500- 600
"Landscape with Sawmill,"
signed "G. Marston," 1863,
oil 500- 625
"Mill by a Stream," signed
"Virtue Howard," 1853, oil . . 475- 620

Paintings, Miniature

Paintings, Miniature

These were usually painted on ivory;
children and women in small oval metal or
ivory frames. This type of painting has been
done for centuries.

Court lady, plumes in hair,
signed, in ivory frame $195-275
Duchess of Devonshire, hand-
painted on ivory, ivory frame . 240-290
Gentleman, American, 1860s,
hand-painted, ivory frame 260-280
Lady, pink dress, pearls, signed
Davis, ivory frame 245-300
Man, ivory frame, signed James
Peale, 2" .... 2,600+
Children in garden, hand-painted,
ivory frame, 1800s 150-190
Officer, Continental Army, 1775,
ivory frame 190-240

Pairpoint

Pairpoint

Successor to the Mt. Washington Glass Company, from 1880, these people made silver and silver-plated wares, in addition to good blown glass objects such as candlesticks.

Barber bottle, chased silver, plated, signed .... $	150-170
Bell, cut crystal, 5½" high	44- 60
Box, hinged silver inlay top, cut glass	125-175
Candlesticks, wheel cut, silver leaves base, pair...........	180-220
Castor set in silver frame, handled, 11" high	110-250
Centerpiece, footed bowl, flint, 5¼" high, 12¼" dia. (ill.)	150-175
Compote, Old Colony pattern, 10" high................	190-250
Cracker jar, grape decor, blue, shell feet	220-265
Decanter, orange, ribbed inside, 5" high................	80-100
Lamp, blown red flowers, signed base, 14" high overall	550-625
Mustache cup and saucer	100-150
Paperweight, blue center, bubble design, 3¼" dia............	725-900
Perfume, paperweight base, flower finial on stopper, pair ..	350-375
Pitcher, cut crystal, 11½" high ..	140-160
Plate, flowers/birds, 10" diameter	64- 78
Vase, overlay, cobalt, 6½" high .	60- 70

Paisley Shawls

The Scots at Paisley, Scotland, 1800 to 1860, made a lovely imitation of the Kashmir (India) shawls.

According to condition, average prices today are:	$110-160

Paleography

See GENEALOGY

Paper Money, American

Paper Money, American

Front (obverse); back (reverse); Star Notes COPE, Demand Notes, California Gold Bank Notes. If any of these words confuse you you shouldn't be spending a lot of money for old paper money. Learn before you buy Also, know what "Unc," "Extra Fine," "Very Fine," "Fine," "Good," and "ADP" (average dealer prices) mean in terms of quality, especially if you're buying by mail.

Paper Money, Foreign

Paper Money, Foreign

Seek out a reliable dealer if you don't know what you're doing. It is impossible to list what's collectible except in a publication that specializes in currency.

Paperweights

These small objects of glass were used to hold down paper on desks and tables. The Baccarats, Clichys, Gillilands, and Millefioris bring tremendous prices today when found and authenticated. Scuffing a new one on cement or with sandpaper doesn't mean it's old. Look out! Repros! Repros!

Paperweights

Baccarat, faceted white
Dahlia, 2½" dia. $3,200-3,800
Baccarat, single rose, 2 5/8"
dia. 3,100-3,700
Baccarat, "Liberty Bell,"
contemporary (ill.) 240- 280
Baccarat, flowers — salmon/
pink/white rose, 2½" dia. . . 2,900-3,600
Clichy, Lacy Filigree, scat-
tered fleurettes, 3" dia. 2,600-2,950
St. Louis, Amber Bouquet,
2 5/8" dia. 2,200-2,600
Sandwich, Poinsettia, on
stand, 3" dia. 500- 600
Clichy, Millefiori, marked with
c beneath, 2½" dia. 2,800-3,400
Dorflinger, open flower design
(ill.) 150- 200
New England Sulphide
Portrait, w/portraits of
Victoria and Albert, cameo
profile, 2 5/8" dia. 700- 775
Brooklyn, Millefiori, base cut
in the form of a star, 3½"
dia. 525- 625
St. Louis, Fruits; pears,
cherries, 3 1/8" dia. 1,900-2,200
St. Louis, Faceted Floral, tiny
bouquet of scarlet, blue/
white blossoms, 3 1/8" dia. . . 1,900-2,400
Somerville "Five Little Pigs,"
on a grassy mound, 5" dia. . . 1,600-1,900
Millville, Rose, half-open,
green leaves, 4" dia. 525- 600
Pairpoint, air bubbles, not
signed (ill.) 160- 180
Jersey, Lily, on stand, yellow/
rose flower, 9½" high 725- 800
Bristol, engraved lacy filigree;
5 rosetted clusters, 3¼" dia.   650- 750
Zanesville, Millefiori, 2 5/8"
dia. 650- 800
Baccarat, Millefiori, with four
concentric rings of multi-
color canes, 2½" dia. 3,200-3,600
Pair, Baccarat "flower" door-
knobs, 2½" dia. . . . . 6,700-8,000+
Whitefriars, Millefiori, on
amber gold ground, dated
1848, 2 3/8" dia. 180- 250

Bohemian "Apple," speckled
w/gilded "jewels," 3½" dia.   250- 325
Scottish, Millefiori, by Pierre
Ysart, hexagonal blossoms,
w/maker's initials, 3" dia. . .   425- 525
Scottish, pink flower on
latticinio, by Ysart, 3" dia. .   450- 625
Sandwich, Poinsettia, salmon/
pink petals, green leaves,
2 5/8" dia. 475- 525
Val Saint Lambert, thin
overlay, faceted and cut,
2½" dia. 1,200-1,400
Tiffany, doorstop, "L.C.
Tiffany, Favrile" signature
1900s 1,300-1,600
Baccarat, Periwinkle Bouquet,
3" dia. . . . . 4,200-5,400+

Papier-Mache

Papier-Mache

Chewed paper is a better word for it. Paper
is soaked in water, ground up, molded into
forms, japanned and dried at a high heat,
around 300 degrees. The finished product is
extremely tough and durable. A lot of so-
called Chippendale trays were made by this
method, then decorated.

Basket, MOP inlay, butterflies/
flowers, 11" dia. $120-140
Box, pearl inlay, 4" square 30- 42
Box, snuff, pewter inlay in top,
hinged 26- 37
Inkwell, MOP inlay, 8½" wide . .   52- 70
Easter egg, red, chick and
mama 26- 36
Figurine, bird, glass eyes, 4"
high 27- 37
Pitcher, red, 7" high 38- 43
Inkstand, birds, floral leaves, 3"
square 45- 55
Lap desk, pearl inlay, floral decor,
slant-top cover 60- 72
Lap desk, black, brass fittings,
MOP floral decor 140-160

(continued)

Stationery rack, Oriental gilt, 7" wide	50- 70
Tray, gold Chinese decor	27- 39
Tray, Japanese, embossed and painted, 12" dia., with 6 coasters (ill.)	18- 27
Tray, lacquered, black ground, birds, flowers	160-175
Wine tray, recesses for decanters, pearl inlay	100-110

Pitcher, Calla Lilies and basket-weave design, 10" high (ill.)	270-295
Plaque, Greek goddess, floral border, 11" square	160-180
Sugar bowl, Pond Lily	94-106
Tray, Bennington-type	75- 95
Tumbler, classic figures, 4¼" high	37- 48
Vase, blue/white, Bennington-type	110-130
Vase, corn decor, 6½" high	130-160

Parian Ware

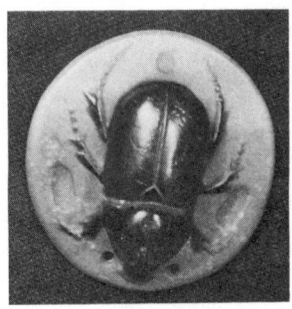

Pate de Verre

Parian Ware

First made by Copeland in England in 1842, Fenton made it at Bennington, Vermont, in 1847, as did the United States Pottery Company, same town, 1853-1858. It was also made by Morrison and Carr, New York City, and by the Southern Porcelain Company, Kaolin, South Carolina. The best American-made is attributed to Fenton and U.S. Pottery Company.

Bowl, lilies, 5" dia.	$ 42- 65
Box, embossed flowers, white, cover, 3½" dia.	66- 80
Bust of Shakespeare, 8" high	90-130
Bust of Dante, 5" high	80- 90
Bust of Dickens, 6¼" high	75- 85
Candleholder, cupid, grapes, tinted leaves, 7" high	96-110
Creamer, miniature, wheat sheafs, blue-tint	70- 80
Cup/saucer, Pond Lily	63- 72
Ewer, ring handle, Copeland, 1850s 8" high	125-155
Figure, bust of Venus, signed, 9" high	90-118
Figure, dog chewing bone	60- 75
Pitcher, hanging game, 10" high, (ill.)	250-275
Pitcher, Niagara Falls design, U.S. Pottery Company	520-620
Pitcher, lavender, white, babes in woods	120-145

Pate de Verre

Translated, Pate de Verre means "paste c glass." This is a molded glass which i formed from ground lead glass. The resultin, powder or crystals are made into a paste by complicated formula. The glass paste is the molded, fired, and carved. As early as 140 B.C. this formula was known and the Frenc seem to have revived it, with the Daur brothers leading the way. It's been di covered as a medium for sculpting by co temporary artists in the past few years.

Atomizer, blue/brown, pine-cones	$725- 780
Bowl, cream/yellow, orange sunflowers, signed "A. Walter, Nancy"	425- 600
Figurine, monkey reading book, signed	875- 925
Lamp, leaves/berries, gold/white, 5" high, signed "A. Walter, Nancy"	850-1,000
Medallion, scarab beetle, sienna coloration, 2¾" dia. (ill.)	300- 375
Pendant, brown/black beetle on gray ground, signed "A. Walter, Nancy"	275- 300

Paté Sur Paté

This means "paste on paste." Its ware were designs in relief, this being achieved b adding layer on layer of thin pottery paste to the design. Solon was the most famous of the Frenchmen making it, but the best known comes from the Minton factory in England. An original, signed M. Solon, would be quite valuable today.

Bowl, cameo center, seraph, green ground, Germany	$170-195
Candy dish, handles, pedestal, signed, 5″ high	800-900
Picture, cherubs, black/blue/ white, velvet mat framed	425-460
Plaque, muse, blue ground, signed, 4″ x 8″	320-380
Plate, blue/white medallions, gold edge, signed, 9″ dia.	260-280
Plate, blue/gold/white, classical figures, 9″ dia.	95-150
Vase, light green ground, white flowers, signed 9″ high	295-310
Vase, white/blue medallions, green floral, signed Birk, 7″ high	450-600

Peanut Collectibles

Peanut Collectibles

When you talk peanuts, you're talking Planters. 1916 saw a schoolboy's drawing create a billion dollar industry. "Mr. Peanut" is as famous as Lincoln, Coca-Cola, and even more famous than that *other* nut from Georgia.

Alarm clock	$ 18-	27
Ashtray, Mr. Peanut, silver metal	48-	58
Bag, burlap, factory, stamped "Mr. Peanut" .	7-	9
Barrel jar, original Planters decal (ill.)	250-	325
Bookmark, Mr. Peanut, World's Fair, 1939	18-	27

Cocktail glass, Mr. Peanut figural stem, red/white/ blue	13-	19
Drink stirrers, Mr. Peanut, set of 6	2-	4 all
Mug, drinking, Mr. Peanut	4-	9
Pen and pencil set, Mr. Peanut, gift boxed	18-	27
Salted peanut scoop, tin, 1.45 ounces (5¢)	60-	70
Scale, Mr. Peanut	900-1,000	
Statue, Mr. Peanut, chalkware	50-	65
Wall clock, Planters	175-	200
Watch, Mr. Peanut	20-	30

Peking Glass

Peking Glass

Chinese cameo glass, 18th and 19th centuries. Scarce today. Some of the finest comes from the Ch'ing Dynasty (Tung Chih period, 1862-1874).

Beaker, bronze-form, painted enamel figures	$ 525-	600
Bowl, blue, blown, 4½″ dia. . . .	1,100-1,300	
Box, green, enamel, lid inlaid with pearl	625-	675
Plate, jade green, 9″ dia.	600-	700
Tumbler, gray/green, 4¼″ high	375-	385
Snuff bottle, amber color, quartz stopper	625-	700
Snuff bottle, black/white	585-	900
Vase, cameo yellow raised floral decor 4½″ high	525-	625
Vase, white ground, carved red flowers, 8½″ high, on box stand	575-	600

Peloton Glass

Peloton Glass

This glass was first made in Bohemia in 1880. Small threads of colored glass were rolled into the surface as the hot glass was removed from the furnace. Sometimes the pieces were dipped in an acid bath to give them a satin finish. Another item being reproduced.

Cracker jar, pink/red, blue ground, silver lid	$ 70- 80
Cruet, multicolors on clear overshot	300-350
Pitcher, pink/blue, enameled decor, white opaque filaments	120-140
Pitcher, pink and blue threads, clear background, pink handle	130-160
Rose bowl, pink/blue, miniature (rare)	220-240
Tumbler, blue filaments, 6" high .	90-120
Vase, yellow, blue red threads clear background, 8" high	160-190
Vase, green, red, yellow threads, ruffled lip, 5" high	150-160
Vase, miniature, pink threads on clear glass, enameled white flowers, 4" high, green leaves (ill.)	160-180

Pennsylvania Dutch Items

Pennsylvania Dutch Items

The Lord's hand helped these gracious people and today many of us are fortunate to know them and to appreciate their work.

Cabbage slicer, 22" long . . . . $	67-	77
Chest, miniature, handmade lock, domed lid, russet background, yellow borders, yellow tulips, 8¼" wide (ill.)	460-	525
Coverlet, blue/green/red/ white, "Mount Joy, Pancaster Co."	1,200-1,400	
Jewel chest, Dutch graining, "Corelia Brunning" on lid .	225-	275
Whatnot, hanging type, green ground, red decorations, 11½" high (ill.)	125-	160

Perfume Bottles

Perfume Bottles

These have been around for centuries in all sizes and shapes. Made of glass, silver, pure gold, carved from jade, inlaid with precious stones, even "Avon calling!"

DeVilbiss (see) atomizer, iridescent, gold trim, flower motif (ill.)	$ 70- 80	
English lavender bottle	7-	9
Tiffany glass, signed LCT Favrile	170-190	
Cut glass, sterling silver cap with applicator attached, early 1900s	80- 90	
Chinese jade, dragon motif, mid-1800s	85-	95
Moser (see) perfume bottle, multicolored enamel, "Czechoslovakia," 6½" high (ill.)	170- 210	

Peters and Reed Pottery

Though established by John Peters and Adam Reed in 1898, it wasn't until 1912, when Moss Aztec was developed, that the first of the art lines was introduced. Other art lines were Pereco, Landsun, Chromal, Persian, and Montene. These finishes were semi-matt in various colors, blended colors, designs, and iridescent variegated finishes.

Frog, Landsun, 4" long	$ 10- 19
Pitcher, wreath design, 11" high .	75- 95
Pitcher, Cavalier design, 7½" high	110-170
Vase, Chromal, Art Deco scene, blue/green, 4¾" high	78- 97
Vase, Moss Aztec, leaf design, 13" high	62- 72
Vase, Pereco, teal blue on Landsun blank, 9½" high	52- 70

Pewter

Pewter

An alloy of tin with lead, brass or copper, Colonial pieces are rare because the early settlers were not permitted to bring much of the raw material with them when they settled in America. Also, many pieces were melted down to make bullets during our Revolution. Pieces marked "Pewter" generally were made after WWI. Older pieces have English or American touchmarks. NEVER polish old pewter!

Mustard holder, footed, blue glass lining . . . . . . $	110- 130
Mug, 1 pint, handled, 7" high	120- 140
Candlesticks, pair, plain with beaded edge, 9" high	200- 250
Candlesticks, pair, fluted base and bobeches, 10" high	240- 270
Cup, American, c. 1840s (ill.)	180- 225

Jug, ½ pint, Irish, touchmark "Austen & Son, Cork," 5" high	160-190
Mug, 1 pint, plain loop handle, made by Lane of Peckham	850- 950
Dinner plates, set of 6, English, 18th century, 9" dia., touchmark of Thomas Swanson	2,900-3,200 all
Syrup pitcher, 5½" high . .	210- 250
Porridge bowl, flat bottom, 6" dia.	240- 270
Peg lamp, American, 4½" high (ill.)	170- 210
Tankard, 6-quart, center rib, handle, 9" high	295- 345
Water pitcher, strainer at spout, 11" high	370- 390
Cake basket on pierced foot, swinging handle, 10" x 3"	280- 380
Hot water pot, bone insulators in handle, 10½" high	290- 350
Teapot, 7½" high	280- 320
Egg cup, blue glass lining, on round foot, 2" x 2" . . .	110- 150
Whale oil lamp w/bull's-eye shade, 8" high touchmark of R. Gleason	1,800-2,200
Queen Anne teapot, 9" high, touchmark of Jas. Dixon	1,100-1,800
Relish holder, 6" high, 5" dia.	450- 550
Wine cooler, English, 18th century, 8" high, reeded rings on the base, 11" dia. at the top	1,800-2,200
Chop platter, 18th century, 11" x 8", indented dragon on bottom	1,250-1,450
Porringer, English, 18th century, touchmark "W.B."	600- 700
Ale cup w/handle, touchmark "D.L."	275- 350
Baptismal bowl, 6" dia. . . .	250- 285
Fruit bowl, pedestal, 9" dia.	90- 115
Candlesticks, American, 12" high, pr.	225- 250
Coffeepot, Dunham, 12" . .	110- 150
Compote, marked Pewter, 5" high	60- 80
Creamer, footed, 5" high . .	90- 120
Creamer, Reed and Barton, 3" high (ill.)	50- 60
Gravy boat	95- 150
Flower holder, D. Barnes . .	50- 80
Inkwell 8" dia.	90- 120

(continued)

Lamp, saucer base, handle,
  4" high 120- 170
Mold, candy, elephant 40- 60
Napkin ring 20- 40
Pitcher, water, Rockford,
  19th century 50- 70
Plate, piecrust edge 175- 200
Tankard, hinged lid, touch-
  marks, dated 1901 . . . . . 100- 125
Teapot, acorn finial,
  Boardman, 8" high 220- 240
Teaspoon, set of 6 . . . . 95- 140
Tray, English touchmarks,
  1880s 8" dia. 150- 160
Tray, hunting scene, 16"
  long 115- 170
Vase, Liberty and
  Company, 7½" high 95- 150

Phoenix Glass

Phoenix Glass

This firm, located in Beaver County, Pennsylvania, made a fabricated Pearl Satin glass in the late 1800s. They also produced other glass, some rather good for the period. Don't confuse it with Lalique!

Basket, dogwood, 5" wide . . . . . . $ 40- 60
Bowl, girl in bathing suit, satin
  finish, pink/green 120-140
Box, covered, green, floral decor,
  6" square 63- 80
Candlestick, blue, swirl stem,
  4½" high 29- 38
Ginger jar, birds, cover, 9½"
  high 70- 80
Lamp, fruit decor, brown leaves,
  vines 110-120
Plate, cherry, 4" diameter 53- 70
Teapot, gold/wine color, 7" high . 40- 50
Vase, pillow, white geese in relief
  on blue ground, 8½" high (ill.) . 95-140
Vase, pinecone decor, purple,
  7" high 72- 84
Vase, pink ground, sculptured
  trumpet vines, original label . . 82- 93
Vase, yellow ground, dancing
  girls, blue/ivory 88-100

Phonograph

Phonographs

Thomas Edison invented it in 1877 and for years it was known as the "talking machine." Many firms manufactured their own versions. Old Edisons are particularly collectible today.

Victor, Gold Medal, 1905, "dog"
  trademark $350-400
Victor, Royal, 1905, "dog" 370-420
Vitanola, 1925 220-250
Sear's Cecelian, 1924 190-215
Columbia Grafonala, 1911,
  "Regent" model 250-270
Columbia Gramaphone, 1886,
  12 cylinders 500-600
Gem Graphophone Talking
  Machine, 1902 165-195
Columbia Grand Graphophone,
  1905 160-210
Grand Peerless Talking Machine,
  24 cylinders 400-500
Graphophone Grand, 1903 240-270
Regina Graphophone, Disc-type,
  1902 220-240
Edison Amberola 260-285
Columbia, keywind 350-450
Columbia, cylinder 390-440
Edison, inside horn, Amberola,
  30 cylinder records 280-320
Edison, Model C, cylinder, 12
  cylinders 425-515
Victor, Model E, horn, table
  model 195-280
Victor, Model VV-IV, oak case,
  1906 250-400

Photography

Mathew B. Brady, best known for his photographs of Lincoln and the Civil War, created the public's interest in photography. Today, millions enjoy this fascinating hobby.

Photography

Photography

Kodak No. 3A, folding pocket camera (ill.)	$ 95-110
Early 1900 photographs, average price (ill.)	3- 7 each
Eastman plate camera, # 4-D, 1901-2	140-180
Conley plate camera (Sear's), 5 x 7, 1908	110-160
Hawkeye Flash	26- 35
Kodak, vest-pocket type, 1918	48- 70
Brownie box camera, Model B, 1916	19- 27
Argus, complete, 1939	52- 62
Bell & Howell movie camera windup type, 1920s	90-110
Leica, 1917, original lens	200-220
Poco, 4 x 5, 1896	140-170
Kodak Petite	92-102
Ansco, # 0	70- 90
Beau Brownie # 2	40- 60
Premo, 1894, Rochester Optical Company	62- 80
Perfection Jr., 1902	54- 65
Seroco magazine type, 1904	50- 72
Delmar 4 x 5, 1905	54- 64
Kenwood 4 x 5 folding type	70- 80
Sears Special Film Camera, 1902	70- 82

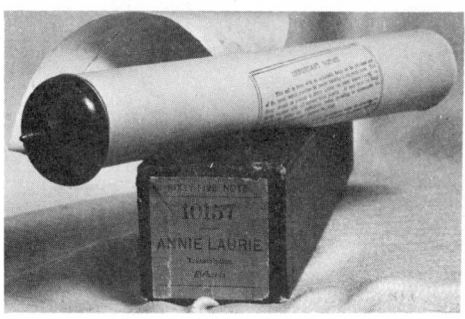

Piano Rolls

Piano Rolls

Now that player pianos are making a comeback, here's a simplified guide to tell you which piano rolls work on which type player piano and/or organ.

Average price, in working
condition . . . . $ 4- 6.50
certain AMPICO rolls bring
$45 or more

PIANO ROLL GUIDE:

A roll—basic coin piano roll of nickelodeon industry.

G roll—later 4X rolls. Keyboard style L, G, KT, KT special.

H roll—Styles J, H and most Seeburg photoplayers.

MSR roll—Styles MO, celeste and most Seeburg photoplayers, interchangeable with H rolls.

HO roll—used on small pipe organs.

XP roll—used on style X expression piano, also style Phono-Grand.

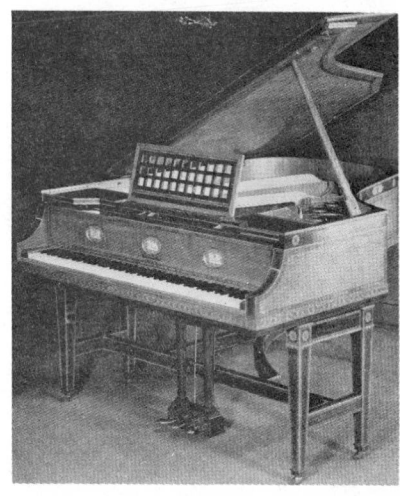

Pianos

255

Pianos

Maker, condition, year made — these dictate price.

American Home upright, maple, full size, 7 1/3 octaves, 1903	$ 290- 450
Oak upright, ivory keys, 1920s	280- 390
Inlaid satinwood/mahogany grand piano w/Wedgwood medallions, Steinway & Sons, New York (ill.)	6,700- 7,900
Cranisch & Bach, rosewood case, handcarved legs, 1890s	4,200- 4,600
Grand piano in Louis XIV style, ornately painted, 1890s	6,600+
Grand piano, 7' rosewood case, Steinway & Sons, 1876	12,500+

Pianos, Seeburg

From 1907 to 1927, J.P. Seeburg's company manufactured thousands of nickelodeon pianos, orchestrions, and other automatic musical devices such as the Phono-Grand, a combination phonograph and compact piano. The Rudolph Wurlitzer Company was Seeburg's chief rival. Most of the rolls for the above instruments were cut by the Clark Orchestra Roll Company, DeKalb, Illinois, or the Automatic Music Roll Company, a Seeburg subsidiary. Other excellent arrangements can be found on Capitol and Columbia rolls.

Pickard

Wilder Pickard founded his company in Illinois around 1894. They're still in business. Once buying their pottery blanks from other firms, they now make their own.

Bowl, flowers and leaves, gold, signed	$ 78- 90
Bowl, fruit, leaves, gold fluted top, 8" high	62- 75
Box, powder, with lid, Art Deco flowers, gold/black/cream, signed	110-185
Candlesticks, etched gold, 4" high, pr.	65- 78
Chocolate pot, pearlized ground, white, orchids, green leaves . . .	210-280
Compote, violet/gold, artist signed, 8" high	175-240

Creamer and sugar, forest scene, gold handles and rim, pr.	90-115
Dish, open handles, 8" dia.	28- 32
Pitcher, cider, gold color, blue trim	58- 70
Plate, gold center, flowers, signed 7" dia.	22- 36
Pitcher, orange poppies, signed "Fuchs"	56- 75
Relish dish, pink/blue, floral, signed	26- 37
Salt/pepper, pair, all gold, 4" high	32- 40
Teapot, gold colors, 5" high, cover	58- 68
Tray, garden scene, signed "E. Challinor"	350-400
Vase, floral, gold, signed, 12" high	67- 77
Vase, scenic, signed "Marke" . . .	80- 92
Vase, peacock, multicolored, paper label, signed "E. Challinor"	525-700

Pickle Castors

Pickle Castors

Consisting of a glass jar sitting in a metal frame, with tongs and/or fork, usually made of quadruple plate, sometimes sterling silver. Considered a novelty of the late 1800s, they were more decorative than functional. Also see Pattern Glass Section for specific patterns.

Amber, cane pattern	$145-165
Amberina, ITP, spoonholder and tongs	375-450
Amethyst, enameled flowers	235-285
Birds/flowers, enameled, blue/ white, silver fork, frame	90-110
Blue/white, Spanish Lace, silver fork, frame	80-100
Blue looping, white threaded glass, silver fork, frame	93-115
Chain and Shield pattern, silver fork, frame	60- 80
Clear, Button and Daisy	70- 80
Cranberry, silver fork, frame	130-140
Cranberry, ITP, silver fork, frame	190-220

Cupid and Psyche, silver fork, frame 110-150

Daisy and Button, amber, silver fork frame 95-118

Dark green glass, thistle pattern down side, silver fork, frame . . 90-110

Fine Cut pattern, clear, silver fork, frame, footed 110-170

Herringbone pattern, green, silver fork, tongs, frame 115-165

Picture Frames

Picture Frames

There are so many composition frames around today that a word of caution is necessary. Never clean gold gilt or gold leaf with water — ALWAYS use alcohol; it won't dissolve the gold and/or plaster-of-paris molding. Use spackle to fill in broken areas, using fingernail cleaning tools to finish the design just before the spackle is hard. Then, regilt. If too shiny, use cigarette ash moistened with water to dull the gold finish.

4-frame, 10" x 12", gold gilt, c. 1870s $110-130

4-frame, 20" x 24", gold leaf, c. 1887 120-140

Walnut cross frame, carved leaf corners, burnished gold liner . . 70- 80

3-frame, 16" x 20", walnut outer frame, gold compo. liner, 1890s 110-135

Black/gold leaf, open network cylinder compo., 18" x 26", 1880s 175-185

Oak, gold liner, 14" x 17", 1860s . 95-110

Tortoise, gold gilt liner, 10" x 12", 1860s 110-130

Simulated wood grain, burnished gold liner, 10" x 14", 1870s . . . 110-135

Toned wood, cylinder compo. 16" x 20", 1860s 140-180

Oak, silver liner, 8" x 10", 1880s . 92-110

Gold leaf, oval liner of wood, 12" x 16", 1870s 125-145

Oval frame, applied compo. pieces, 16" x 20", 1890s 110-140

Oval frame, simulated wood grain, 14" x 18", 1900 92-110

Gold leaf, 9" x 16", 1880s 135-160

Black, gold leaf liner, 16" x 26", 1875 190-220

Oval frame, applied gold compo. pieces, 10" x 12", 1870s (ill.) . . . 110-118

Oval frame, walnut, 9" x 12", 1880s 92-115

Pigeon's Blood Glass

Pigeon's Blood Glass

This red glass was made near the end of the 1800s. Today, some dealers sell any dark red glass as Pigeon's Blood. The original is an orange-red.

Bottle, cologne, 5" high $165-195

Bowl, beaded top, fluted sides, 9" dia. 140-170

Butter dish, covered, 8" wide . . . 170-195

Candy dish, overlay, 8" dia. 62- 72

Candlesticks, footed, twisted stem, 9¼" high, pr 140-180

Castor set, 5-bottle, silver caps . . 195-240

Child's mug, "For a Good Boy," 5½" high, handled 82- 92

Compote, 7" high 180-192

Compote, scalloped edge, 8" high 170-195

Creamer, metal top, clear applied handle 130-160

Pitcher, clear applied handle, 11" high 240-275

Salt, hexagonal, red/orange (ill.) . 19- 30

Syrup jug, metal top 140-170

Tumbler, 4½" high 62- 90

Vase, slender neck, flat base, enameled, 7" high, France 160-180

Vase, pedestal base, scalloped edge, 8½" high 120-140

Vase, pink/white flowers, green leaves, 12½" high 440-485

Pincushions

In every shape, made from every material, they were used for just that — pins; later, they held safety pins. They were popular

257

(continued)

Pincushions

during the 19th century when young ladies stayed home and sewed.

Average price . . . . $ 4- 9

Pink Lustre China

Pink Lustre China

Made in the Staffordshire District, England, in the early 1800s, it gets its name from the pink decorations used on the ware. Houses and fernlike trees were popular decorations. It is comparatively scarce today.

Bowl, houses/trees	$ 80- 90
Butter dish, covered	78- 90
Creamer, copper and floral	66- 76
Cup (handleless)/saucer (ill.)	50- 60
Cup/saucer, demitasse, handleless	50- 62
Mug, child's, pink flowers, trees, gold trim, 1850, 3½" high	73- 83
Pitcher, houses/trees, 9" high . . .	72- 82
Plate, house/trees	48- 58
Plate, pink/burnt orange/green/ blue, 7½" dia. (ill.)	48- 58
Slipper, souvenir, Chicago World's Fair	28- 38
Sugar bowl, house pattern	140-150
Teapot, house/trees pattern	160-170

Pink Slag

This rare glass is surrounded in mystery as to where it was made and by whom. Possibly Challinor, Taylor and Company made some at Tarentum, Pennsylvania. They made the purple (marble) glass. Miniature lamps in the shape of swans bring huge prices today. Also see PATTERN GLASS section.

Berry bowl, 6½" dia	$660- 700
Butter dish, covered, 6" dia	925-1,000
Creamer, 3½" high, handled	560- 600
Lamp, miniature, in shape of swan (one at Houston Museum)	870- 925
Sugar bowl, covered, 4" high	650- 725
Punch cup	475- 500
Tumbler, Inverted Thumbprint or Inverted Feather and Fan, 4" high	430- 440

Pipes

Pipes

Pipe bowls were carved from briar roots, meerschaum, or molded in porcelain and clay. When or who lit up the first one is lost to history.

Briar, carved, sea captain (ill.) . . .	$ 55- 68
Beethoven, briar, carved (ill.)	55- 68
Deer's head carved into bowl, curved 10" stem	85- 97
Elk's head bowl, B.P.O.E. and date, straight 6" stem	58- 68
Face of monk in bowl, curved 7" stem, clay	41- 51
Lion devouring prey, curved stem, 11", briar	68- 78
Meerschaum, deer pursued by dog, 9" curved stem	48- 58
Meerschaum, horse's head, trees, 9½" curved stem	62- 72
Opium pipe, Chinese figures, 14" long, old	67- 87
Porcelain bowl, painted decor . . .	42- 52
Panther's head, glass eyes, 10" straight stem	49- 69
Satyr, briar, carved (ill.)	55- 68

Pisgah Forest Pottery

Walter B. Stephen founded this firm near

258

Pisgah Forest Pottery

Mt. Pisgah, North Carolina, in 1914. With his mother he produced a pate-sur-pate decorating technique, using as themes American scenes such as log cabins, buffalos, and covered wagons. Stephens also developed a high gloss glaze in several colors. He passed away in 1961; the pottery is still in operation. Early pieces would be quite collectible today.

Vase, 5½" high, crackle glaze,
  turquoise color, pink lined (ill.) . $ 30- 40

Pitchers, Glass

Every company made them in every size and shape. The Houston Museum's collection of over 15,000 pitchers is said to be the largest in the world! Any challengers? Also see PATTERN GLASS section.

Amethyst, clear applied handle,
  9" high . . . .$ 50- 60
Blue basketweave, 10" high . . . 55- 65
Clear glass, shades to blue/
  green at top, blown, 11" high 105- 110
Cut, Strawberry and Fan, clear
  applied handle, signed
  Libbey 170- 190
Daisy and Button, V Orna-
  ment, 12½" high 110- 120
End-of-Day (Spatter Glass),
  multicolored, 9½" high 106- 108
Sapphire blue, clear applied
  handle, blown, 8" high 107- 110
Plated Amberina . . . . (see)
Pomona first grind, 7½" high . 600- 675
Royal Vienna, painting of
  church, village background,
  9" high 140- 160

Plated Amberina

This extremely rare art glass was made by the New England Glass Company in 1886. Opalescent glass was plated with a gold-ruby mixture, then reheated to develop a deeper

Plated Amberina

color of certain portions which would then blend into the lighter part of the glass. Being reproduced.

Bowl, 8" dia., 4" high $6,200-6,800
Cup, punch 3,000-3,800
Pitcher, 7" high (ill.) 5,200-5,600
Syrup jug 4,600-5,000
Tumbler 2,800-3,400
Vase, 6½" high in silver holder 6,200-6,400
These and others can be seen at the Houston Museum.

Playing Cards

Playing Cards

The decks you find in shops today are usually from the past 75 years. Index numbers in the corners were used after 1877. The European decks of cards, before 1850, are rare and hard to find.

Advertising-type, 20th Century
  Limited, seal unbroken . . . . . . $ 4- 6
Advertising-type, Louisville and
  Nashville R.R. 4- 7
French, early 1800s (ill.) 18- 27
Russian, early 1800s (ill.) 20- 29

259

(continued)

Marilyn Monroe, different poses,
2 decks in illustrated box 50- 60
Shirley Temple, seal unbroken . .   7- 10
World's Fair, New York, 1939 . . .   9- 12

Pomona Glass

Pomona Glass

Joseph Locke invented it in 1884, first producing it at the New England Glass Company. It's a frosted ground on clear glass and
decorated with mineral stains. Two types
were made — first and second grind. First
grind was etched by acid; second grind, the
cheaper of the two methods, consisted of rolling the glass piece in particles of acid-
resisting materials which were picked up by
it. The piece was then etched. It's always
blown. Don't confuse it with Midwest
Pomona, a pressed glass in which you can see
the mold lines.

Bowl, second ground, amber,
4½" dia. $120-160
Box, cornflower design, first
grind   150-195
Celery vase, amber flashed, first
grind   425-495
Creamer, cornflower motif,
second grind   140-165
Cruet, first grind, applied foot,
cornflower decor, 7" high (ill.)   280-300
Cup, punch, first grind, diamond
quilted, 2¼" high (ill.)   180-220
Cup/saucer, diamond-quilted
pattern, second grind   105-125
Pitcher, blue, floral designs,
pebbled surface, first grind . . .   550-625
Tray, cornflower, first ground,
12" long   260-320
Tumbler, oak leaf, second grind,
4" high   165-195
Vase, amber flashed, second
grind, 3½" high   175-200

Vase, amber flashed, second
grind, 3½" high   175-200

Pontil Mark

So many people ask, "What is a pontil
mark?" It is simply the scar left on the bottom of a piece of blown glass where the pontil
rod has been broken off. The pontil rod was
used to hold the glassware during its manufacture. Pontil marks are either jagged or
ground smooth. Smooth globs of glass on the
bottom sometimes have been put there by
the manufacturers of new glass to make you
think it's old and blown. Careful!

Porcelains, Miniature

Porcelains, Miniature

It was popular in the 18th and 19th centuries to paint faces on tiny pieces of
porcelain which were then put in lockets or inside watches. Church scenes and landscapes
were also popular.

French, church scene, 1" x 1½",
18th century . . . . $ 85-125
French, little boy, 1½" x 2" (ill.) .   90-135
American, 19th century (ill.
far right), Miss Lillian Russell .   130-150

Porto Bello Ware

Made at Portobello Pottery, Midlothian,
Scotland, late 18th century to commemorate
Admiral Vernon's victory over the Spanish at
Puerto Bello, Panama, on November 23,
1739. Usually it is a brownish-red pottery,
glazed, with figures of ships, fortifications or
other scenes. Designs on the first pieces
made were in white. It remained popular until the 1860s and can be found in shops today.

Bowl, 4" dia. $150-200
Jug, 7" high   200-240
Pitcher, large   220-265
Pitcher, small   210-255

Porto Bello Ware

Plate, English coat-of-arms, 7″
dia 145-185
Platter, view of Puerto Bello,
11½″ long 135-170
Tray, octagonal, signed 250-310
Probably many other pieces.

Portrait Plates

Considered fashionable in the late 1800s, these plates featured portraits, usually female, and were produced commercially for several years.

Abraham Lincoln and wife, 10″
dia .... $ 80- 90
Blonde woman, copyright, 1909,
11″ 30- 40
Garfield, 13 stars around border,
10″ dia 36- 46
George/Martha Washington,
reticulated edges, Germany, 8″
dia 58- 68
Girl's head, date 1884, France,
10″ dia 30- 40
His Majesty, Meakin, 11″ dia ... 30- 40
Lady's bust, blue, pink flowers,
8″ dia 34- 44
Louis XV, Sevres, 10″ dia. blue/
gold trim 138-148
Man holding bird, forest scene,
8″ dia 33- 43
Martha Washington, white
ground, pink roses, Germany . 44- 54
Peasant girl in wheatfield, 10″
dia 40- 50
Queen Elizabeth II, Johnson
Brothers, 10½″ dia 40- 55
Three ladies at fountain,
Germany, 11″ dia 30- 40

Postcards

Originating in Austria in 1869, the penny postcard's popularity has grown steadily over the years. Some things to consider when

Postcards

buying postcards for a collection or for resale are: the subject, color and detail, condition; also, has it been cancelled. Cancellation marks are important because of the reproductions flooding the market in recent years. Whether you buy postcards in bulk or individually, collecting them can be a rewarding hobby. Prices range from 10¢ to $50, depending, of course, on value. Average price, 25¢.

Pot Lids

Pot Lids

The Pratt Works at Fenton, England, made most of them. Used for holding shaving soaps, hair oil, etc., they were popular in the mid-to-late 1800s. The designs used were placed under the glaze by a multicolor transfer method similar to our decals of today.

A Pair .... $ 78- 88
Checker game 85- 95
Contrast 85- 96
Garibaldi 84- 94
Hide and seek 85- 95
Lovers on the bridge 84- 96
Low Life 94-110
Racing Scene 94-110
The Shrimpers 74- 84
Village Wedding 84- 95
Warming at the fire 85- 95

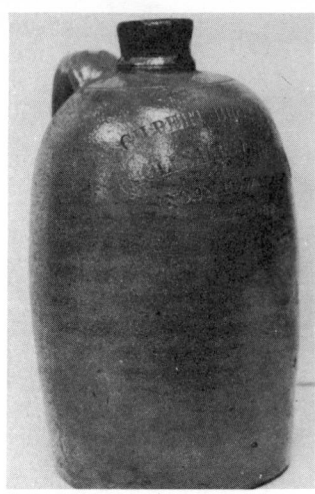

Pottery, Early American

Pottery, Early American

During the 1800s and 1900s, a great deal of homemade pottery was made in this country. What Ma needed in the kitchen, Pa made in his crude kiln.

Bowl, milk, red clay, 10″ dia	$ 37- 47
CROCKS	
2-gallon, gray, blue flowers, no lid	58- 68
3-gallon, Pennsylvania redware, no lid	68- 79
5-gallon, gray, blue lettering, lid .	65- 75
16-gallon, gray, stenciled name, no lid	125-145
Foot Warmer, marked "Logan Cnty., Ohio," blue/gray, with wooden stopper	79- 88
JUGS	
1-gallon, druggist, brown, handled (ill.)	47- 57
2-gallon, for "moonshine," cob stob	40- 50
5-gallon, tan/brown, stenciled name	58- 68
Pitcher, tanware, 5½″-6½″ high .	118-127
Saltbox, hanging type, Logan County, Ohio, blue/gray, wooden lid	38- 48
Tray, red clay, crude handles, dated 1854	58- 68

Powder Horns and Flasks

With the invention of the muzzle-loader rifle and pistol, these items were a necessity. From the crudest type, a cow's horn, to the ornately engraved brass and copper models, all are most collectible today.

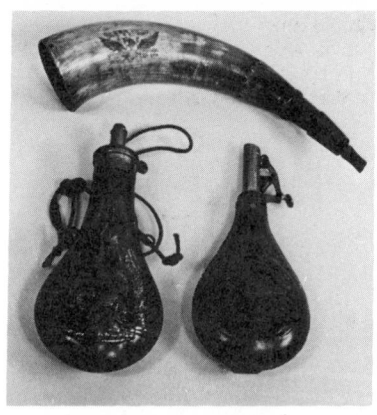

Powder Horns and Flasks

Copper rifle flask, 8″ long, shell design, both sides, c. 1830	$110-128
Brass flask, small, 4½″ long, type found in cased Colts	130-165
Brass, 6″ long, hanging game on both sides (ill.)	75- 90
Cow's horn, 8″ long, brass cap and tip, c. 1845	55- 65
Cow's horn, scrimshaw carved eagle and name, signed "Herman B. Seaborn" (ill.)	160-190
Brass and pewter flask, 8½″ long, c. 1830	90-120
Leather flask, brass trimmings, 9″ long, c. 1845	65- 80
Leather, 6″ long, embossed hunting dog (ill.)	52- 62
Pistol flask, 3½″ long, brass, c. 1835	65- 85
Pistol flask, Colt's Patent, 4½″ long, brass, zinc, c. 1855	115-128
Carved powder horn, New Hampshire, 14″ long, c. 1846 . .	340-380
Persian flask, brass, 10¼″ long, 18th century	110-125
Japanese flask, c. 1750, for matchlock musket, 8″ long . . .	145-180
Japanese wooden priming powder flask, 4″ long, c. 1780 .	97-125
Civil War, pewter, brass cap and tip, 7½″ long, marked "U.S." .	60- 80
Brass, hunter and dog, patent dispenser, 5″ long	150-160
Brass, fluted sides, patent dispenser, early 1800s	140-170
Civil War, CSA, 8″ long, base metal	68- 78
Copper, eagle, dated 1804, 7″ long	145-155
Calf's horn, wooden plug-type, early 1800s, hand-carved	62- 72
Pewter, patent dispenser, English, 1800s	118-127

Tin, "Alamo" crudely scratched
  in one side 56- 73
Zinc, brass dispenser, carved
  "deer" on both sides 76- 89

Pratt Ware

Pratt Ware

The Fenton factory in Staffordshire District, England, made this pottery from 1775 to 1805. Raised figures and decorations highly colored in green, purple, black, and orange are qualities of Pratt. Transfer pictures were also used. See POT LIDS.

Box, green/purple, naval battle,
  covered . . . . $ 72- 82
Candelholder, black/orange, pair
  11" high 70- 80
Compote, church scene, 4" high . 148-168
Creamer, gray/green, cottage
  scene, 4" high (ill.) 134-155
Cup/saucer, scenic transfer 44- 56
Pitcher, Doves of Peace, 5" high,
  purple/orange/green 270-295
Plate, fuchsia/purple/green, 10"
  dia 68- 79
Plate, horserace, blue, gold trim,
  9" dia 72- 82
Pomade jar, signed, 3" high 84-110
Snuff jar, blue/tan/black, animal
  scene 38- 48
Sugar, matches illustrated
  creamer 135-155
Teapot, large, pastoral scenes,
  6" to spout 200-245
Teapot, pastoral scenes, 7" to
  spout 195-225
Urn, hunt scene, 4½" high 79- 89
Vase, red/black, deer in forest,
  8" high 110-135

Pre-Columbian Artifacts

There are so many fakes on the market, it's difficult to give you a fair price. If interested in this type of art, KNOW YOUR DEALER — even that is no guarantee. We mention the

Pre-Columbian Artifacts

subject here because so much of the above is flooding the American and European markets. Watch it, senor! Yes, the illustration is a fake!

Burial figures, male or female,
  solid, from western Mexico,
  3" to 6" tall, each . . . . $ 45- 60
Colima figure, female, 5½" high . 80-100
Clay heads, male or female, from
  Vera Cruz – Huastec culture,
  each 9- 18
Religious figures, Huastec
  (figures were broken as part of
  the religious rite), 2" to 6" tall,
  each 9- 19
Vicus pitcher, dog head, 8½"
  oval 650-850

Presidential Collectibles

Presidential Collectibles

These are items such as autographs, menus from the White House. Matchbooks marked "Stolen from the White House" were presidential favorites. Also photos, lithographs, anything having to do with United States presidents.

Fountain pen marked FDR, used
to sign Congressional bill, 1936 $ 44- 47
Lithograph, Jefferson Davis,
president of Confederate
States (ill.) 37- 46
Matchbooks, presidential seal or
"stolen" type 6- 10
"Peanut" card, Carter campaign,
1976.................... 1- 2
Photo of Harry Truman, signed . 68- 78
Senate restaurant menu, LBJ
scribbled on front 18- 25

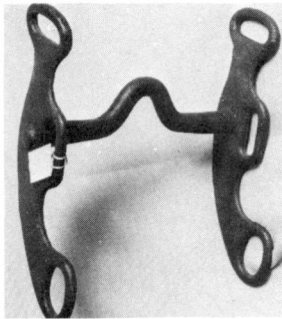

Primitives

Primitives

If you like primitives, buy *American Primitives* by Robert W. Miller; Wallace-Homestead Book Co., Des Moines, Iowa 50305, or from your local bookstore.

Adjustable candleholder, tin,
1840s, 6" high .... $ 58- 68
Andirons, brass, ball-type,
1840s 210-265
Andirons, claw feet, hand-
forged 1840s 128-145
Battling stick, used for
washing clothes, early
1800s 40- 50
Bed warmer, copper, maple
handle, 1830s 224-258
Beeswax mold, used to make
blocks of beeswax, 2-piece,
1820s 92-110
Bellows, wood, leather, crude,
1820s 58- 68
Betty lamp, wrought iron,
twisted rod on hook, 1820s 235-265

Block plane, #4 size, maple,
Kingston, NY, 1840 ..... 50- 60
Branding iron, initials,
"T.Y.", mid-1800s 78- 88
Brass kettle, 6-gallon, w/iron
bail handle, 1840s 310-315
Broad ax, mid-1800s 268-295
Broom press, used to make
crude brooms, early 1800s . 58- 68
Buttress, used for trimming
hooves of oxen, early 1800s 57- 67
Cabbage cutter, 1830s (ill.) .. 36- 44
Cabbage cutter, early 19th
century (ill.) 38- 52
Candle mold, tin, 12-tube,
15" high, 1830s 115-125
Cane or sorghum cutter,
wooden handle, mid-1800s . 85- 97
Cherry pitter, cast iron, 1860s 60- 70
Closed scorp, used to carve
dough bowls, 1820s (ill.) ... 34- 48
Cobbler's clamp, maple,
2-piece, mid-1800s 140-160
Cooper's ax, mid-1800s 222-245
Corn grater, early 1800s 36- 46
Cornhusker, wooden
w/leather thumb holder,
mid-1800s 25- 35
Cowbell, copper, 8" high,
mid-1800s 34- 44
Cowbell, tin, 4" high, 1840s .. 38- 48
Double Cruise (Phoebe lamp),
mid-1700s 190-220
Dough bowl, carved from
buckeye wood, 1820s, 18"
long 84- 94
Fence stretcher, iron,
mid-1800s 68- 78
Flail, used to separate wheat
from chaff, 2-piece, wooden 52- 62
Flambeau or flaming torch,
used to light the way when
checking railroad engines
at night, mid-1800s 90-115
Froe, used to make wooden
shingles, early 1800s 72- 82
Goat yoke, bent hickory,
mid-1800s 77- 87
Grinding stone made from
sandstone, 19" dia., early
1800s 78- 88
Hand adze, early 1800s 70- 80
Hand-carved pulley block,
early 1800s............. 84- 94
Handmade mousetrap,
twisted wire, mid-1800s,
10½" long 52- 62
Hetchel, used to remove flax
husk, early 19th century .. 47- 57
Hitching block, cast iron,
c. 1850s, buggy type 48- 58

Primitives

"Hog scraper" candlestick, 5" high, early 1800s	68- 78
Horse bit, 1830s (ill.)	14- 23
Horse collar made from corn-husks, late 1700s	59- 69
Ice chisel, used to cut ice from frozen lakes and ponds, 1840s	110-130
Ice tongs, iron, late 1800s	78- 90
Kettle, dovetail bottom, iron bail handle, 1830s, 26" dia .	425-525
Maple chopping block, on legs, mid-1800s	320-360
Maple rolling pin, early 1800s	38- 48
Meal scoop, mid-1800s	42- 52
Meal sifter, used to remove lumps from flour, 1840s	50- 60
Meat scale, brass, 1860s	140-160
Nutmeg grater, tin, wall-type, late 1800s	27- 37
Peavey, complete with wooden handle, 1850s	149-163
Pie crimper, double wheel, early 1800s	48- 60
Roll, "devil's wire" (barbed wire), 1860s, per foot	1-$1.50
"Rope key" ("rope jack"), used to tighten ropes on rope bed, 1780	37- 46
School bell, brass, wooden handle, 7" high, original clapper, 1830	110-140
Shoulder yoke, for carrying milk pails, etc., 1840s	92-110
Sled auger, used for boring holes in beams, c. 1820s	55- 65
Sleigh bells, string of 24 on original leather, East Hampton Bell Manufactory, 1840s	240-270
Sleigh bells, string of 30, 1850s	180-190
Spanner wrenches, hand-forged, 1840s	8- 12 each
Spoke shave, mid-1800s	37- 47

Spud, used for peeling bark from trees or logs, early 1800s	66- 76
String holder, iron, "Beehive" type, 1840s	49- 59
Tavern candle chandelier, tin/wood, 1840s	420-470
Three part boot last, hand-carved maple, mid-1800s	88-105
Tin grain scoop, 9½" long, 1830s	32- 42
Tooth puller, hand-forged, early 1800s	30- 40
Turkey feather duster, late 1800s	36- 47
Waffle iron, heart pattern, iron, 2-piece, 1840s	84- 94
Winnowing tray, woven from oak strips, early 1800s	67- 82
Wooden butter churn, complete with lid and dasher	260-310
Wooden mortar and pestle, maple, early 1800s	90-112
Wooden washboard, hand-carved, mid-1800s	25- 35
Wooden lemon squeezer, 2-part, 1820s	21- 32
Wrought iron barn hinges, pair, early 1800s	110-125 pair

Prints

Prints

Signed; signed and numbered; signed, numbered and remarqued; limited edition — all these effect the value, assuming the print has not been altered to fit a frame and is in good condition. "Remarques" are the artist's marks placed on a plate or on the original painting, such as C.M. Russell's buffalo skull.

The Mediator and Alexander, line engraving, colored, Robt. Dodd, published in London, 1783 by John Harris	$ 275- 350

(continued)

Le Serapis et le Bon-Homme-
Richard, line engraving,
without artist's or engraver's
names, framed 150- 200
The Battle of Lake Erie, line
engraving, drawn by Sully,
engraved by Murray, Draper,
Fairman & Co., published in
Philadelphia 340- 400
Chesapeake and Shannan,
colored aquatint, painted by
Robert Dodd, published in
August, 1813 . . . .   195- 240
Fishing along the Seine, pencil,
lithograph, signed "Charles
Mondin" 58- 80
Bonaparte in Trouble, line
engraving, by A. Doolittle . .   158- 192
Battle of New Orleans, print,
aquatint by Debucourt, litho
by Case & Green, 1815 . . . . .   170- 195
Naval Battles of the Civil War,
4 lithographs, C & I   850-1,000
John James Audubon, the
original edition engraved by
Havell & Son called "The
Birds of America"; there
were 435 plates in all:
Plate #6, Hen Turkey   7,300-7,400
Plate #14, Prairie Warbler . .   1,300-1,400
Plate #27 Red-Headed Wood-
pecker   2,700-3,000
Plate #82 Whip-Poor-Will . . .   2,600-3,000
Plate #158 American Swift . .   900- 985

Of the different series — The Havell Prints; The
Brien Edition; The Octavo Edition; The Audubon
Quadrupeds; Audubon Prints on Fabric — the Oc-
tavo Edition is the most valuable.

The Bathers, by Winslow
Homer, 1872, wood engrav-
ing 150- 200
Gathering Berries, by Winslow
Homer, 1874, wood engrav-
ing 125- 160
High Tide, by Winslow Homer,
1871, wood engraving 140- 180

If you're interested in buying and/or selling old
prints, first establish contacts with reputable
dealers who specialize in old prints. Also, read the
periodicals that specialize in this field:
American Artist, 1 Astor Plaza, New York, NY
10036
Art Investment Report, 54 Wall St., New York,
NY 10005
Print Trader, 6762 79 St., Middle Village, NY
11379

The illustrated print, "General Washington," a
mezzotint, was published in 1785 in London. It is
considered excessively rare.

Some other things to remember: if marked "Published According to Act of Parliament," it's
English, after 1735. If marked "Entered According to Act of Congress in the year ____," it's
American, after 1802. The first copyright laws
passed by our government were in May, 1790.

Quartz

Figurine, tiger, green, 7" high,
teakwood base $130-140
Figurine, elephant group, trunks
up, 4" to 7" high   122-145
Figure, Kuan Yin, holding lotus
blossom, 5½" high 49- 59
Snuff bottle, blossoms and
leaves, carved, 3½" high, ivory
stopper 78- 84
Vase, fruit scene, rose-colored,
13" high   128-138
Vase, dragons, birds, fruit motif,
teakwood stand, 8" high   250-275

Queen's Burmese

See BURMESE GLASS.

Queen's Rose

Queen's Rose

English, soft-paste porcelain, maker
unknown, probably early 1800s.
Creamer . . . . $ 68- 80
Cup and saucer 75- 85
Sugar bowl, covered 77- 87
Teapot (ill.)   110-120

Queensware

A cream-colored earthenware developed by
Josiah Wedgwood about 1765. Many potteries have copied it.

Quezal Glass

Quezal Glass

Martin Bach, Sr., made this glass from 1901 to 1920. Formerly associated with Tiffany, Bach somewhat copied his former employer's work. Most pieces are signed Quezal. His son-in-law, Conrad Vahlsing, opened a shop after Bach's death, calling his wares Lustre Art Glass, which is also collectbile today.

Bowl, ruffled top, signed, 4" high	$350- 395
Candlesticks, pair, blue iridescence	750- 940
Compote, blue iridescence, 8½" high	445- 495
Finger bowl, gold iridescent, ribbed, signed, 4" diameter	130- 160
Goblet, footed, iridescent gold, signed, 5½" high	172- 195
Perfume bottle, gold, signed, 8" high	260- 300
Lamp, hanging, 4 iridescent shades, brass fixtures	675- 795
Lampshade, iridescent gold, feather design, signed, 5" high (ill.)	150- 170
Nut dish, blue/rose, iridescent bronze, signed, 2½" diameter	120- 140
Plate, blue iridescent, 11½" dia.	540- 630
Rose bowl, gold, purple/red iridescent, signed	250- 270
Salt, master and 6 individual, ribbed, iridescent gold, all signed	345- 365
Toothpick holder, iridescent gold, feather design, signed 3" high	92- 94
Vase, peacock, blue, signed	720- 745
Vase, feather pattern, white/green/gold, signed, 9" high	900-1,100
Vase, green/gold feathers, white opalescent ground, 8"	850- 975
Vase, feather pattern, red/purple, swirled base, 10" high, signed	850- 900
Vase, silver overlay, iridescent, signed, 9½" high	975-1,450
Vase, trumpet, iridescent gold, signed, 8½" high	400-475

Quilts

Quilts

Most pieced quilts are formed by simple arrangements of diamonds, squares, right-angled triangles, stitched into a geometric design. Many are more than 150 years old. Today, all old quilts are collectible. Crib quilts are especially sought after. Kate and Joel Kopp's "America Hurrah" shop in New York City has one of the better collections of quilts for sale. Some of the more popular patterns are Aeroplane, Basket, Flowerpot, Variable Star, Pansy, Fool's Puzzle, Log Cabin (I & II), Tennessee Tulip — to mention just a few. Be prepared to pay anywhere from $50 to $600, depending on condition and scarcity. See COVERLETS. Does yours need repairs? See "Quilts, repair" in "Repairs, Services. . . ."

Trapezoidal pattern, diamond-quilted, 67" x 82"	$135-145
Sunburst, red on black, 64" x 79"	95-110
Tic-tac-toe squares, white & colors, 70" x 83"	180-200
Double X, 9½" square blocks, 1880s, 70" x 75"	175-195
Double Irish Chain (Shamrock), green on white, 62" x 72"	210-240
Magic Cross, 20 colored, 8 white patches, 65" x 70", 1890s	250-270
Multicolored floral (12 panels) white background, green borders, 76" x 92" (ill.)	173-195
Dragon's Head, 70" x 65", 1890	160-185

Quimper Pottery

Henri Quimper, known as the "peasant's potter," used Breton peasants as subjects for his wares starting in the late 17th century. What you find in shops today dates from the

267

(continued)

Quimper Pottery

early 1900s. It's been reproduced for years.

Ashtray, bone, dish-shaped, Breton figures, 6″ diameter . . .	$ 18-	27
Bowl, signed, 6″ diameter	20-	30
Butter pat, set of 6, peasants in field	33-	43
Cup/saucer, flower and leaf	22-	28
Coffeepot, Breton figures, 11″ high, signed	27-	37
Dish, flower motif, miniature, salesman's sample (ill.)	6-	9
Flower holder, birds, flowers, 7″ high, signed	42-	52
Knife rest, women, flowers, ...	33-	43
Mug	22-	27
Pitcher, milk, signed	41-	51
Plate, flowers, peasant woman, signed Henri Quimper, 8″ dia. (ill.)	23-	27
Platter, peasant man, 12½″ long	58-	68
Porringer, 2 handles, peasants, signed	38-	48
Salt, peasants, oval	20-	23
Salts, flower motif (ill.) each	20-	23
Teapot, 2-cup size, Breton peasants, signed Henri Quimper	75-	88
Tray, man, woman in field, signed, 10″ long	62-	72
Vase, peasant man, flowers, 6½″ high	37-	47

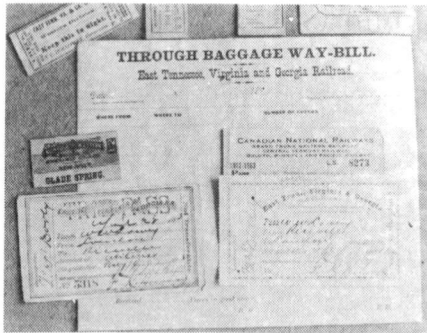

Railroad Collectibles

Railroad Collectibles

Anything to do with the Iron Horse is sought after today. Railroad silver is really just a silver-soldered product — lots of it made by Reed and Barton, is especially collectible.

Hand lantern, red, Southern Pacific	$ 30-	40
Hand lantern, clear, Rock Island Line	34-	44
Cap badges, any railroad, average price, each	19-	27
Cuspidor, porcelainized, Maine Central	18-	28
Railway Express sign, 18″ x 18″, reversible	34-	44
Timetables, most railroads, average price, each	2-	3
Postcards, depicting various R.R. scenes, each	75¢-	1
Attendants and waiters badges, most lines, each	4-	9
Railroad employees' collar insignia, each	4-	9
Breast badges, each	12-	15
Uniform buttons, each	3-	4
Uniform caps, with badges attached	16-	19
Inspector's lantern, Bangor & Aroostock	72-	82
Switch lantern, Missouri Central	53-	61
Caboose lamp	40-	48
Pullman step	52-	62
Journal box oil can, N.Y.N.H. & H	27-	37
Tamping bar, 16 to 25 pounds . . .	10-	18
Track maul, 5 to 10 pounds	12-	15
Conductor's ticket punch, "American" brand	7-	12
Bonds, all railroads issued them, average price	7-	17
Creamer, Southern RR	38-	50
Knife, fork, spoon, napkin holder, Louisville and Southern RR	37-	46
Menu holder, Rock Island Line R.R.	22-	28
Passes: issued to conductors, officers of the company, average price	19-	29
Tickets: Norfolk and Western, E. Tennessee, Virginia and Georgia RR, (ill.) average	14-	18

Razors

For years, Grandfather Pushbutton took his life in hand every time he shaved. Sailors prided themselves on being able to shave with a straight razor while the ship rolled

Razors

from side to side. King Gillette ended it all when he invented the safety razor. The old straight razors are collectible and bringing good prices, depending on age and condition.

Ivory handled, polished Sheffield
 steel, original case (ill.) . . . . $ 28- 36
King razor 9- 17
Others, average price 8- 17
Safety razors, early 1900s,
 average 3- 6

Reading Artistic Glass Works

Reading Artistic Glass Works

Founded by Lewis Kremp in Reading County, Pennsylvania, the firm operated from 1884 to 1886. The usual objects were made, including spittoons and whimsical canes. Opalescent colors included violet, canary, green, pink, white, and sapphire. Flint colors included green, light blue, amber, gold, white. Specialty types had either mottling, overshot or craquelle finishes. Beginning to show up in shops in the Northeast.

Pitcher, 9½" high, pink with
 white mottling, thumbprint
 design, unusual 2-piece opales-
 cent reeded handle (ill.) $240-260
Vase, 14" high, baluster shape,
 black, applied neck ring (ill.) . . . 220-240
Vase, 14" high, baluster shape,
 frilled top, black with white
 mottling (ill.) 248-268

Red Wing Pottery

1878-1967. Produced art pottery in the 1920s; Red Wing, Minnesota. Comparable to Roseville, Weller. Usually marked "Red Wing USA" or "Red Wing Pottery, Inc." or "RW USA."

Bowl, white/brown trim, 8" dia. . . $ 11-21
Candlestick, red maroon, 3" high,
 signed 8- 15
Cookie jar, Dutch scene,
 "RW USA" 24- 33
Bowl, deco relief, 8½" dia.,
 marked "Red/Wing Pottery,
 Inc." 22- 31
Cornucopia vase, ribbed and
 scalloped, 7¾" long, "RW
 USA" 12- 22
Creamer, waffle weave, 5 3/8"
 high, "RW USA" 9- 14
Crock, blue/gray, 7½" high 34- 47
Marmalade jar w/lid, "Red Wing
 USA" 8- 11
Pitcher, ice guard, green swirled
 design, 7" high, marked "Red
 Wing" 30- 40
Vase, leaf-shaped, 9" high, blue/
 pink, "Red Wing USA 1239". . 18- 27
Vase, white, flowers in relief,
 green, RW USA 16- 23
Vase, brown, mottled, "Redwing
 USA" 18- 26
Vase, chartreuse, flowers, bird of
 paradise, "Red Wing USA
 B2000" 21- 31
Vase, white 7½" high, "Red
 Wing, USA Pat Pending" 11- 20

Redware

Redware

This is an unglazed red pottery, often with applied relief motifs, a Staffordshire-type. Few pieces were signed with maker's name.

(continued)

Most of what you find today was made after 1850.

Pudding mold, swirl design	$ 72- 90
Teapot, dragon design (ill.)	84-103
Teapot, Oriental decor	90-110

Religious Items

Religious Items

Bibles, figurines, rosaries — just a few of the many things used for worship. The illustration shows a King James Version Bible, dated 1658. This is at the Houston Museum. The figurines are Staffordshire. On the left is Ira Sankey who was a great song leader and wrote many hymns. The figure on the right is Dwight L. Moody. These figurines are considered scarce and highly sought after today. The plaques are also Staffordshire.

Bible, King James Version	$	4,500+
Bible, leather-covered, brass locks, mid-1800s	72-	90
Cross, ivory, on chain, hand-carved	35-	45
Hymnals, any denomination, good condition	3-	4
Pews from old churches	220-	260
Staffordshire figures, Sankey and Moody (ill.) each	358-	385
Staffordshire plaques (ill.) each	83-	93

See also ICONS and STAINED GLASS WINDOWS.

Remington, Frederic

Remington, Frederic

Lived 1861-1909; painter, sculptor, illustrator; best known for his sketches and bronzes depicting the Wild West as it really was. His bronze statues were cast by the Roman Bronze Works, New York; also Henry-Bonnard Bronze Company, New York. They were marked "Copyright by Frederic Remington." His sketches bring high prices. You can't buy a bronze for under $75,000 today! *The Cheyenne,* 23¾" high, is illustrated here.

Reverse Paintings on Glass

Reverse Paintings on Glass

This type of painting was done on the back of the glass in reverse so the writing could be read. Popular during the early and mid-1800s, some of the English and Scotch paintings are considered rare today. Just about every subject was used; women, children and prominent people being the most popular subjects. Average price $60-160.

White House on the Potomac, gilded frame, 12¼" x 10¾", c. early 1800s (ill.)	$ 54- 67

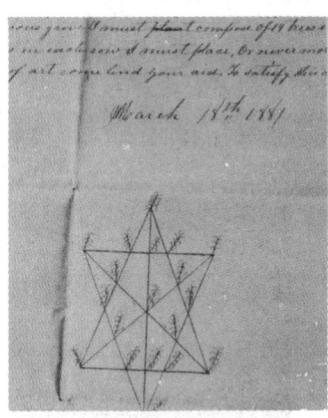

Riddles and Puzzles

270

Riddles and Puzzles

"What has four wheels and flies?" The old riddles and puzzles (see illustration) are finding their way into collectors' hands. The illustrated puzzle was hand-drawn in ink around 1875. They're worth just about what you're willing to pay for them.

Ridgway Pottery

Ridgway Pottery

John and William Ridgway operated their pottery at Hanley, England, from 1814 until 1830. Their "The Beauties of America" series is world-famous. William Ridgway operated at Hanley from 1830 until 1854. Ridgway Potteries, Limited is still in business today. They use scenes and borders of another potter.

Bowl, 10" Capitol, Washington..	$ 90-110
Bowl, 10", Pennsylvania Hospital, Philadelphia	120-140
Bowl, Racing the Mail, 8½" dia. .	56- 67
Gravy, tureen, Bank, Savannah .	130-150
Mug, Eloping, 5" high	36- 46
Plate, 8", Library, Philadelphia . .	165-185
Plate, 6¼", Athenaeum, Boston .	163-173
Platter, Maidenhair Fern, 8½" long	37- 47
Soup tureen tray, Deaf and Dumb Asylum, Hartford	120-145
Vegetable dish, 11", Hospital, Boston	122-142

Ring Trees

Ring Trees

Made of glass, metal, or porcelain, these small, treelike objects held one's rings for safekeeping while one bathed or slept. They were popular during the mid-Victorian era.

Cut glass, clear base, blue stem . .	$44- 56
Parian ware, in shape of upraised hand	50- 60
Porcelain, decorated, American, 2½" high (ill.)	12- 18
Porcelain, 3-branch, Germany . . .	12- 18
Sterling silver in shape of 4-branched tree, 3" high	27- 38

Just about every porcelain maker, here and abroad, made them.

Rockingham-Bennington Pottery

This is sometimes called Bennington ware because it was made there in the mid-1800s. The original was made in the Staffordshire District before 1800. It was heavy, with a brown glaze. Actually, it was made by many potteries in the Ohio River Valley, and theirs was considered as good as that made in Bennington. See BENNINGTON POTTERY.

Bedpan	$ 58- 68
Bottle, monk	125-185
Bowl, chocolate glaze, tan ground, 9" dia	69- 79
Coffeepot, brown glaze, 10" dia . .	56- 68
Compote, blue flower decor	72- 88
Creamer, cow, black, gold, glazed, 6¼" long	80- 90
Cup/saucer, green/gold, flowers . .	52- 63
Cuspidor, brown glaze, flower decor	74- 84
Flask, brown glaze, acorns, leaves, 7½" high	62- 72
Footwarmer	92-120
Inkwell, monk's head, 3" high . . .	86- 96
Pitcher, birds in swamp, 1850s England, brown glaze	128-137
Plate, light brown, 9¼" dia	44- 53
Spill holder, brown glaze	49- 64
Teapot, white, orange, gold, glazed, 7" high	110-135
Toby jug, brown glaze, England, 1850s	128-148
Tureen, covered, brown glaze, acorn finial on cover	198-225
Vase, white, multicolored flowers, 8" high	54- 67

Rogers Statuary

John Rogers, an American born in 1829, studied sculpting in Europe and worked in

271

(continued)

Rogers Statuary

Rookwood

plaster-of-paris to achieve some of his finest works. He put on the market more than 80 different subjects during the mid and late Victorian period, his pieces being reproduced more than 100,000 times! Highly collectible today.

Balcony	$ 520-	570
Bath	500-	540
Henry Ward Beecher	475-	500
Bubbles	515-	575
Bushwacker	450-	475
Campfire	530-	600
Camp Life	530-	545
Charity Patient	555-	580
Checker Players	610-	640
Chess	658-	710
Coming to the Parson	610-	640
Council of War (hands in any of 3 positions)	980-	1,150
Elder's Daughter	480-	520
Favored Scholar	560-	580
Fetching the Doctor	670-	710
First Love	425-	450
Fugitive Story	770-	810
Going for the Cows (ill.)	510-	525
Hide and Seek	660-	680
Home Guard	720-	740
John Alden and Priscilla	650-	670
Mail Day	660-	685
Miles Standish	385-	425
Matter of Opinion	575-	600
Mock Trial	710-	750
One More Shot	620-	665
Referee	600-	655
School Days	710-	740
Taking the Oath—Drawing Rations	710-	725
Traveling Magician	440-	475
Washington	985-	1,150
We Boys (head up or down)	470-	495
Weighing the Baby	720-	780
Wounded Scout	910-	985
Wrestler	1,100-	1,400

Rookwood

Founded in Cincinnati, Ohio, in 1880 by Mrs. Maria Longworth Storer, it was America's first art pottery. "Tiger eye," "Iris," "Vellum," "Ombroso" matte glaze — some of the various glazes used over the 80 year period. The famous reversed R and P, uniformly adopted in 1886, appears on every piece. In 1887 a flame point was placed above the monogram and one point was added each year until 1900. In 1901 Roman numerals showed each ensuing year. Any similarity between the Rookwood produced in Ohio and that produced in Starkville, Mississippi, is purely coincidental. Kataro Shirayamadani, Albert R. Valentien, Matt A. Daly, Laura F. Fry, William Purcell McDonald, Artus Van Briggle — just a few of the many famous artists who worked for Rookwood. "Rookwood" was Mrs. Storer's father's estate cutside Cincinnati, so named because of the many rooks (crows) in the area.

Ashtray, blue "rooks," 4" dia., 1915	$ 38-	48
Ashtray, elk's head, "B.P.O.E.," 6" dia., 1917	54-	63
Ashtray, brown "rooks," 4½" dia., 1912	50-	60
Basket, pink/green matte finish, 11" high, dated 1911	78-	88
Bookends, ships at sea, signed McDonald, dated 1925	170-	190
Bookends, pair, white horses, 7¼" x 6", 1919	120-	130
Bowl, cherry blossoms, 3" high, 1907, Iris Ware	130-	140
Bowl, green matte finish, dated 1920	50-	60
Candleholder, pink, 10" high, dated 1914	76-	86

Candlestick, tulip shape, 8¾"
high, matte glaze, signed C.S. .   140-155
Cigar humidor, Indian head, 9"
high, unsigned, 1932   155-170
Creamer, daisies, initialed C.S.,
1898   165-200
Chocolate pot, water lily motif,
9" high, 1904, initialed M.M. . .   170-190
Electrolier, tulip shape, 14" high,
1905, unsigned, matte glaze . .   250-270
Ewer, brown/tan, flowers,
"Vellum" finish, signed Kataro
Shirayamadani (he was
Japanese, probably
Rookwood's greatest
decorator), dated 1897 . . . .   3,500+
Ewer, Japanese flower, 5½" high,
unsigned, 1904   245-350
Flower frog, green/blue, 1925,
unsigned 60- 70
Jug, handled, grape design, 6"
high, 1905, initialed M.M.   325-375
Lamp, pinecone decoration, "Iris
Ware," 24" high, 1904,
unsigned   350-450
Mug, grape design, 4¾" high,
1905   150-180
Plate, 9½" dia., dragonflies, 1904,
matte glaze, unsigned   140-170
Pitcher, green, floral, signed
Reed, dated 1893   600-700
Sugar bowl, clover design, 4"
high, unsigned, matte glaze . . .   140-170
Tea caddy, poppy design, 5¼"
high, unsigned, "Iris Ware" . .   150-170
Teapot, 7½" high, "Tiger eye"
glaze, initialed O.G.R., 1893 . . .   300-400
Vase, blue, "Vellum" finish,
original store label, signed
LNL, 1918   450-525
Vase, 7" high, brown/tan, ini-
tialed C.S., 1897   485-550
Vase, brown, "Vellum" finish,
signed Carrie Steinle, dated
1901   450-525
Vase, fern fronds, 6½" high,
1893, "Tiger eye" glaze,
unsigned   320-380
Vase, Japanese iris, 10" high,
1907   280-350
Vase, light green, 7" high, 1924,
unsigned   120-165
Vase, matte glaze, green/blue,
1935, 6" high, unsigned (ill.) . . .   65- 80
Vase, night-blooming cereus, 13"
high, initialed S.S.   375-450
Vase, pinecone design, on teak-
wood base, 12" high, 1908   400-500
Vase, green, matte finish, 1932
(ill.) 80- 90
Vase, wild carrot, 6¼" high, 1904   330-450

Rorstrand Faience

Rorstrand Faience

The company was founded in 1726 at Great
Rorstrand, near Stockholm, Sweden. Designs
in the early 1900s took on an art nouveau
style. The firm is still in business. It's mentioned here because it's beginning to show up
in the better shops. It's expensive and you
should know what you're doing if you decide
to collect it. See COLLECTORS' PLATES.

Vase (ill.) $450-575

Rose Bowls

These are crimped and pinched-edge bowls
used for holding dried rose petals. Decorative
only, their rose-scented aroma helped freshen
the air in the parlor or dining room. Mid-1800s,
of every type glass. Being reproduced.

Amerbina, Honeycomb pattern,
6" $290-375
Amethyst glass, enameled
flowers   155-185
Cranberry, white enamel decor . .   89-110
New England Peachblow, acid
finish   675-750
Mt. Washington and Wheeling
Peachblow   580-675
Satin glass, flower decor, gold
trim   170-190
Overshot, fan design   140-190
Bristol glass, enameled flowers . .   110-150
Spanish Lace, blue, 4½" 63- 79
Tiffin glass, black, poppies 52- 65
Vasa Murrhina, pink, red, flecks
of mica   128-138
Vaseline, 3" 74- 84

273   (continued)

Rose Canton

See ROSE MEDALLION CHINA.

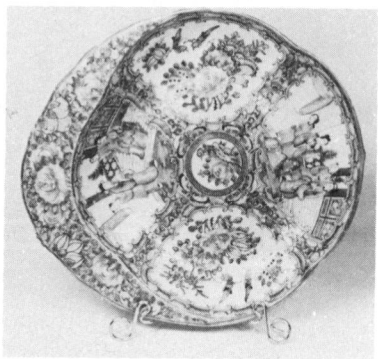

Rose Medallion China

Rose Medallion China

A product of China, it was decorated in Canton and exported to every country in the world. It gets its name from the glazed pieces having figures of people alternating with panels of pink flowers, butterflies, and birds. If all the panels are filled with flowers only, it's called Rose Canton. This ware has been produced and reproduced for hundreds of years. Watch out!

Basket, people, roses, butterflies, 4½" dia.	$ 550-625
Bulb or crocus pot	1,600+
Bowl, people, roses, birds, butterflies	225-275
Box, covered, usual design, 2½" high	110-140
Candleholders, people, flowers, 11½" high, pair	600-700
Canister, set of 3, 3", 4", 5", signed "China"	200-225
Compote, typical design of birds, flowers, etc., 8" high	150-170
Creamer and sugar, covered	145-165
Cup/saucer, thorn handle	82- 92
Cuspidor, typical scenes	440-485
Dish, flowers, figures 10" dia. (ill.)	160-175
Jardinieres, teakwood stand, 8¾" high, pair	800-900
Mug, rose floral band, birds, flowers, etc	150-170
Plate, 7" dia	80- 90
Plate, 12" dia	160-180
Platter, 19th century, typical scenes, 16" dia	320-340
Powder box, roses, people, green ground	95-120
Shaving mug	70- 80

Sugar bowl, berry handles, people and flowers	275-350
Tea set, in lined wicker caddy for traveling, 2 cups	420-500
Teapot, usual scenery, China	250-275
Tea set, teapot, creamer, sugar, all	725-800
Tureen, typical scenes, 11½" long	320-380
Tureen of the early 1800 period, on stand, would be worth $1,600 today.	
Urn, typical decorations, 16" high	375-425
Vase, roses, scenes, people, birds, etc	265-295
Vase, 9¾" high, on teakwood stands, 19th century, pr	340-370
Washstand set, Chinese enameled, mid-1800s, usual design	570-590

Rosenthal China

Rosenthal China

Established in Selb, Bavaria, by P. Rosenthal in the 1880s, the firm specialized in figure groups, dinner sets and other pieces. It was considered a fine hard-paste porcelain, and it's expensive when found today.

Bowl, berry, pink flowers, gold rim, scalloped, footed	$ 68-	78
Box, lady's face on lid, gold border on cover, 5" high	65-	80
Candlesticks, white, gold trim, pair	65-	80
Centerpiece with female figure, white, beige, gray, signed "K. Himmelstoss" and Rosenthal, 17" high (ill.)	1,650-2,100	
Chocolate pot, 6 cups/saucers, pinecones, trees, beige ground	195-	220

Chocolate set, demitasse, blue and gold, service for 6	270-	295
Compote, white ground, flowers, handles, gold trim, 8″ high	50-	60
Creamer/sugar, orchard scene, gold trim	52-	62
Cup/saucer, pink roses, blue ground	53-	66
Figurine, dancer, white and gold, 9″ high	120-	145
Fish set, carp, seaweed edge around plates, 10″ dia	170-	190
Pitcher, white, pink roses, gold trim, 6″ high	42-	56
Plate, blue ground, roses, handpainted artist-signed .	58-	70
Platter, fish scene, 1900, handpainted	72-	82
Sugar, pink and gold	70-	80
Tazza (shallow, ornamental cup or vase, sometimes with pedestal)	77-	87
Tea set, teapot, creamer, sugar, yellow/red roses	77-	89
Vase, pink flowers, gold trim, 8½″ high	78-	88

Roseville Pottery

Roseville Pottery

Roseville, Ohio, 1892, this pottery firm was making stoneware jars, cuspidors and flowerpots. In 1898 the firm moved to Zanesville but didn't make art pottery until 1900. No art pottery was ever made at Roseville. Their first art line was called "Rozane." Some of the marks used were "RPCo."; "Rozane — RPCo" beneath; "Rozane Ware Royal"; "Rozane Ware Mara"; paper "Roseville Pottery Co." labels were also used. This pottery

was comparable to Weller. It never reached the quality level of Rookwood.

Ashtray, red, blue handles, old RV mark	$ 27-	37
Bank, piggy, 4″ high, unsigned	32-	43
Basket, 6½″ high, Bittersweet, "Roseville, U.S.A." in relief	37-	47
Basket, pinecone pattern, script signature	41-	51
Bookends, pinecone pattern, script signature	42-	60 pair
Bowl, Donatello pattern (cherubs), cream color, beige, green	48-	58
Bowl, roses, pansies, blue/green, script signature	44-	52
Candleholder, floral pattern, 10″ high, script signature .	35-	42
Cornucopia, Mock Orange, 5½″ high, "Roseville, U.S.A." in relief	39-	46
Cup, 3½″ high, clover motif, Juvenile line, unsigned	28-	36
Jardiniere, 9″ high, Cameo line, unsigned	59-	69
Jardiniere, pinecone pattern, twig handles, script signature	51-	61
Letter holder, 3½″ high, brown, flowers, "Rozane Ware Royal"	61-	71
Mostique jardiniere, 9½″ high, unsigned	73-	83
Tankard, Della Robbia line, 10½″ high, unsigned	115-140	
Tankard, 11″ high, monk, brown, "Rozane Ware" . . .	151-171	
Tankard, 10½″ high, signed "V. Adams," "Rozane Ware Royal"	158-169	
Teapot, creamer, sugar, flower decor, script signature	60-	75 all
Teapot, 4¼″ high, Mayfair, "Roseville, U.S.A." in relief	30-	35
Urn, 8½″ high, Rosecraft Vintage line, "R" containing small "v"	50-	60
Vase, Aztec, 8″ high	54-	64
Vase, 6¼″ high, Bittersweet, "Roseville, U.S.A." in relief	44-	54
Vase, bud, yellow/green/blue, script signature	52-	62
Vase, double bud, 6″ high, Florentine, "R" containing small "v"	48-	58
Vase, Carnelian line, 10½″ high, blue "R" stamped on bottom	50-	60

(continued)

Vase, 12" high, flowers,
Azurine, no mark (probably
had paper label) 49- 62
Vase, 6" high, Dahlrose line,
unsigned 40- 50
Vase, 13½" high, Della
Robbia line, "Rozane
Ware" 68- 78
Vase, Donatello, 15" high . . . 60- 70
Vase Egypto, 11½" high,
"Rozane Ware Egypto" . . . 72- 82
Vase, 19¼" high, dogs hunt-
ing, "Rozane R.P. Co." . . . 88- 98
Vase, 8" high, Florentine
line, "R" containing small
"v" 43- 54
Vase, 14" high, Indian chief,
brown/red, "Rozane Ware"
inside circle 112-135
Vase, 13" high, metallic
lustre line, "Rozane Ware
Mara" 120-140
Vase, 9" high, Woodland,
"Fujiyama" rubber
stamped on bottom 87- 92
Vase, 11½" high, Woodland
line, floral designs, "Rozane
Ware" 70- 80
Vase, "Rozane Ware," 12"
high (ill.) 120-135
Wall pocket, 10" high, Dona-
tello line 50- 60

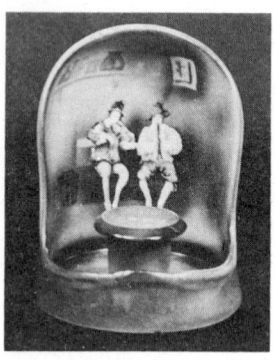

Royal Bayreuth

Royal Bayreuth

This type of novelty ware was made in Germany for many years. The tapestry type
porcelain is collectible today.

Ashtray, clown $110-135
Ashtray, monkeys playing cards,
black mark 68- 78
Berry set, dish, 6 saucers, grapes,
leaves 130-150
Bowl, Little Jack Horner, 5¾"
dia. 51- 63

Bowl, lobster-claw handles, pink/
red/purple 120-140
Box, Jack Be Nimble on lid,
colors 64- 72
Candlesticks, devil playing
cards, pr 85- 95
Chamberstick, green, musicians,
4¾" high (ill.), considered rare . 240-260
Creamer and sugar, fishermen
pattern 72- 82
Creamer, bear 110-130
Creamer, clown 130-160
Creamer, crab 70- 82
Cup/saucer, demitasse, poppy
decor 130-150
Cup, demitasse, devil and dice . . . 60- 70
Dresser dish, pink florals, greens,
7" long 40- 50
Gravy boat, tomato, leaf
underplate 120-160
Hair receiver, Little Bo-Peep,
light blue 66- 76
Humidor, tomato color, lidded,
7" high 88-110
Inkwell, boy in tree, 4" dia. 87- 99
Match holder, clown, black mark 110-130
Mug, Little Miss Muffet, 3¼"
high 89-109
Mustard jar, devil and cards 86- 97
Pin tray, Santa Claus decor 110-140
Pitcher, animal decor, blue mark,
4" high 88-100
Plate, feeding, Sunbonnet Baby . 130-150
Plate, flower basket, pink/blue,
set of 8 110-130
Powder jar, pink/blue 92-115
Salt, open, lobster motif 40- 50
String holder, hanging, poppy
decor 165-182
Sugar/creamer/pitcher, devil and
cards 210-270
Teapot, creamer, sugar, tomato
color 145-170
Tea set, strawberry, 3-piece 260-285
Toothpick holder, deer head 73- 92
Tray, dresser, flower decor,
8" wide 68- 82
Vase, peasants, blue 92-115
Vase, Dutch scene, 6" high 76- 86

Royal Bayreuth Tapestry

This type porcelain, made about 1890, was
created by covering porcelain with a piece of
fabric tightly stretched over the surface. It
was then decorated and glazed. Royal Bayreuth specialized in this in the late 19th century. Prices of this porcelain would be about
75% higher than similar pieces in previously
listed ROYAL BAYREUTH.

Royal Copenhagen Porcelain

Royal Bayreuth Tapestry

Royal Bonn

Established in Bonn, Germany, in the last half of 18th century by Clemers August, most of what you find today is ornately decorated with flowers, sometimes with portraits. It was a fine-paste porcelain. Some pieces were marked with a castle.

Bowl, brown glaze, flowers, 10" dia	$ 58- 68
Celery tray, flower motif	66- 77
Clock, colored flowers, 11½" high	300-400
Cologne bottle, tapestrylike surface, flowers, handled	70- 80
Compote, ships at sea, 8" high	60- 70
Cracker jar, floral, gold trim	140-160
Plate, pink flowers, green ground, 12" dia	60- 70
Plate, guardsman, leaf rim (ill.)	75- 85
Vase, floral, blue ground, handles, 12½" high	82- 92
Vase, Delft blue, white, windmill scene, 8" high	91-107
Vase, green ground, rose/yellow flowers, pair	168-180
Vase, peasant girl, 8" high (ill.)	65- 75

Royal Bonn

Royal Copenhagen Porcelain

Established in 1772, this firm has been in business ever since, manufacturing fine porcelain. Their Christmas plates are world-famous. See CHRISTMAS PLATES.

Bottle wine, castle scene	$ 38- 47
Bowl, sculptured figure of mermaid 6"	88- 98
Coffeepot, blue/white	170-192
Cruet, blue/white, stopper	95-120
Cup/saucer, blue/white, basket-weave, 1924 mark, set of 8	70- 80
Dinner service, six 8-piece place settings	875-950
Figurine, bear, 7" high, deep blue, 1928	88- 98
Inkwell	60- 70
Mug, large, 1968	63- 74
Plate, brown/blue iris pattern	45- 58
Plate, mermaid in wintertime, pair!	42- 60
Platter, blue and white, 10" long	72- 83
Rooster, 1925, 6" high, pair	160-178
Toby jug, John Peel	60- 70
Tray, green and gold, 11" long	45- 55
Vase, bluebirds and flowers	98-120
Vase, flowers, blue/white, dated	95-110
Vase, blue/white, 1934, slender neck	130-145

Royal Doulton Figurines

The Royal Doulton figurines sought by collectors were produced at the Doulton Burslem factory, Staffordshire, England. Early prices date from c. 1909. Figures were produced in both soft- and hard-paste porcelain. Prices will vary according to production numbers on backstamps.

Bather, 7¾" high (ill.)	$475-500
Belle of the Ball, 8" across (ill.)	280-300
Butterfly, 6" high (ill.)	575-600
Pierette (experimental model), 8¼" high (ill.)	775-825

(continued)

Royal Doulton Figurines

Royal Flemish Glass

Vase, cobalt, Arabian heads
form handles, 8½" high ... 90- 110
Vase, mottled blue/pink, birds 62- 72
Vase, dog and horse, blue/
olive/green glazes, 14" high
(ill.) Hannah Barlow
sgraffito decoration 1,900-2,200
Just about all the jugs have been reproduced,
careful!

Royal Doulton Pottery

Royal Doulton Pottery

This is the same DOULTON POTTERY
mentioned earlier in this Guide. After 1901
the word ROYAL was added. Scenes from
daily English life identify this pottery. It's
still being made.

Biscuit jar, horses, white
body, applied flowers,
Lambeth .... $ 400- 475
Bottle, Dewars Scotch 74- 84
Bowl and pitcher, cobalt, gold
trim ...·............. 160- 170
Bowl, Robin Hood 68- 78
Candlestick, castles, Crown
and Lion mark 53- 64
Cheese dish, blue/yellow,
white ground, 6½" high ... 80- 90
Cup/saucer, demitasse 36- 46
Humidor, barrel-headed,
green, fruit decor 68- 78
Jug, grapes, brown glaze,
marked 44- 55
Mug, blue medallions, cobalt . 60- 70
Pitcher, 6" high 45- 55
Plate, Admiral Nelson, fleet at
Spithead 57- 67
Toby mug, 6" high 76- 90
Vase, blue, Dutch Girl, 5"
high 40- 50

Royal Dux

Royal Dux

Made in Bohemia, this porcelain was imported into the U.S. around 1900, mostly for
sale in gift shops. It was considered inexpensive then, not so today.

Basket, blue basketweave
pattern, satin ground, 4½" dia. $120-150
Bowl, girl with long hair, green/
orchid flowers, handles 120-140
Figurine, flapper, white/blue, gold
decoration, 13½" high, c. 1920
(ill.) 490-575
Figurine, hound in lying position
gold matte, 14" long 120-160
Figurine, camel, rider, 17½"
high 415-525
Figurine, lady holding water
jug, Austria, 18" high, pair ... 160-180

Planter, boy playing flute, 7″ high	220-255
Planter, Grecian woman, ivory, on gold base, 11½″ high	190-235
Vase, pink/green, 19½″ high	140-170
Vase, applied flowers, Austria, 15″ high	79-110
Vase, applied flowers, peaches, apples, 12½″ high	190-240
Vase, floral, leaves, pink ground, 17¼″ high	130-152

Royal Flemish Glass

A product of the Mt. Washington Glass Company, 1889, it's identified by the heavy gold enameled lines dividing the surface of the glass into separate sections. Various decorations are found on the matte finish body. The pieces were colored in shades of gold, beige, and brown.

Bowl, tan/pink/light green, mustard panels, alternating w/frosted and gilted, raised coin and rampant lion motifs, 6″ across (ill.)	$1,950-2,200
Cookie jar, gold coin medallions, silver top and handles	1,900-2,400
Rose jar, green medallions, steeple top	1,600-1,800
Pitcher, satin glass finish, russet tan, enameled gold decor	1,900-2,400
Planter, opaque enamel in russet, tan/brown, gold decor, gold lion in medallion	1,400-1,750
Vase, russet, tan and brown, enameled gold decor	1,500-1,900
Vase, stick type, medallion design, 11″ high, initialed R.F. on bottom	1,800-2,400

Royal Rudolstadt

Established in 1720 at Thuringia, Germany. Later the factory was moved to Rudolstadt. Most of what you find in shops today is of the late 19th century. The marks are R for the early years, RW with crown on top for the later years. Pieces marked Germany were made after 1890. It's beautiful china with a Dresden-like coloring, often delicately decorated with flowers, sometimes faces of famous people such as Beethoven.

Basket, floral decor, gold handle, old mark	$ 91-101
Bowl, tiger lilies, footed	135-165

Royal Rudolstadt

Bowl, winter scene, horse, sleigh	135-165
Butter dish, burnt orange/green, covered	135-155
Cheese dish, bridal roses, floral	88- 98
Compote, enameled flowers, gold trim	74- 85
Dish, shell-shaped beige ground, daisies and violets, multi-colored, 8½″ dia. (ill.)	72- 90
Hatpin holder, bluebird decor	70- 80
Nappie, leaf-shaped	52- 70
Pitcher, flower decor, serpentine handle	77- 89
Plate, fruit, gold band, 8½″ dia	58- 70
Plate, green ground, white roses, 8″ dia	69- 79
Tray, pin, oval, pink flowers, 6″ long	22- 32
Vase, multicolor floral, claw feet and handles in gold, 6″ high	130-150
Vase, Psyche, open handles, tan/brown ground, ruby neck	195-240

Royal Vienna

279

Royal Vienna

The factory was founded in 1719 and thrived when taken under royal patronage. This was a Meissen-type ware noted for its brilliant colors and artistic excellence. It was most collectible even in the 1800s. One of its distinguishing marks is the Beehive. What you find in shops today has been produced by other factories, some of which are still making it.

Basket, blue body, handles, applied leaves and fruit .... $	195-	275
Compote, red, cobalt, Beehive mark..................	150-	185
Cracker jar, dancing girls, floral decor	260-	285
Ewer, cream ground, floral sprays, 10" high	128-	142
Jar, lady dancing, cupids, cranberry Beehive mark in red ..	130-	160
Plate, rose, gold, Palette mark, 8" dia	139-	158
Plate, portrait, gold border, signed Wagner, Beehive mark in red	195-	240
Plate, white/black, signed Riener, 1750 mark, set of 12 .	2,400-2,600	
Salt dip, ornate feet, beaded gold, Beehive mark	42-	52
Stein, monk, brown ground, Beehive mark	525-	650
Teapot, white, fruit decor, handpainted, Beehive mark .	110-	135
Tray, green, gold trim	140-	170
Urn, Queen Louise, ormolu finial, 14" high, pair	340-	370
Vase, medallion center, blue, red, Beehive mark, pr	270-	295
Vase, pink ground, painted scene, figure in center, 12" high	350-	400
Vase, handled, Queen Louise, wife of Frederick Wilhelm III, King of Prussia, 13" high (ill.)	1,350-1,700	

Royal Worcester Porcelain

This was a company within a company. See WORCESTER PORCELAIN for details. The Royal Worcester Porcelain Company, Limited, was formed in 1862 and is still in business. Important to know your marks or you'll end up buying new for old.

Basket, beige, green leaves, 6½" dia................... $	130-170
Bone dish, flower decor	40- 50

Royal Worcester Porcelain

Bottle, perfume, roses, flowers ..	78- 89
Cake stand, flowers, gold trim, 8½" high	170-195
Candle snuffer, nun, 6½"	90-110
Cup/saucer, demitasse, floral decor	49- 58
Chocolate mug, floral enameled	36- 46
Chocolate pot, cream background, after 1891	238-258
Creamer, floral decor, large leaf in relief near handle	150-170
Ewer, green/gold lion, 10½" high	189-197
Figurine, Sunday's Child, F. Doughty, 4¾" high	80- 90
Flower holder, horn-shaped, early 1900s	99-140
Mug, blue/white, Dr. Wall, Crescent mark	320-350
Pitcher, 9" high, horn-shaped, cream background	160-180
Plates	
a. 8¼" diameter, floral scene, raised shell edge	68- 78
b. 9" diameter, floral center, leaf border	110-150
Sugar shaker, signed	92-107
Tea caddy, gold/blue spatter	162-172
Tea set (teapot, sugar and creamer), floral decor	390-458
Thimble, flowers, signed	58- 69
Vase, floral decor, applied handles	270-296
Vase, shell design, gilting, 8½" high (ill.)	240-270

RS Germany

This is the same porcelain as RS Prussia. The name Germany was simply substituted for Prussia in 1891. Because of the demand for RS Prussia, especially the red star, dishonest dealers are removing the RS Germany and replacing it with the RS Prussia

Vase, green, pink roses, 6" high . 44- 58
Vase, iris, 5" high 48- 59

RS Germany

...ark. It's a decal, 140 to the sheet, but the ...ettering is too modernistic. If in doubt, ...crape vigorously with your fingernail.

Basket, roses, handles . . . . $ 34- 45	
Bowl, brown/green ground, flowers, 9¼" diameter	57- 67
Bowl, floral decor, 9½" across (ill.)	62- 78
Box, covered, roses, green mark .	29- 48
Candlestick, flared top, green lilies, 6" high	50- 60
Celery vase, pink roses, gold, open handles	47- 60
Cheese dish, flowers, bisque finish	92-110
Chocolate pot, white ground, brown at top, roses, 6 cups . . .	172-196
Creamer and sugar, pink roses . .	80- 90
Cup/saucer, rose decor	50- 60
Dish, yellow, hand-painted, artist signed	40- 50
Hatpin holder, yellow floral, gold, marked	40- 49
Hatpin holder, white lilies	37- 46
Inkwell, covered, hand-painted . .	19- 29
Jam jar, lidded, flowers, green mark	39- 50
Nappie (dish with a handle), beige, apples, green mark	87- 98
Plate, roses, gold edge, 8½" dia.	40- 50
Relish dish, green ground, flowers	14- 26
Salt dip, rose decor, footed, marked	10- 19
Sauce, has tray, apricot roses, gold border, blue mark	37- 49
Sugar, covered, blue/pastel, flower decor	38- 59
Teapot, poppies, gold trim, green mark	30- 42
Toothpick holder, flowers, gold trim	30- 42
Tray, orange poppy, marked, 3¾" dia.	34- 44

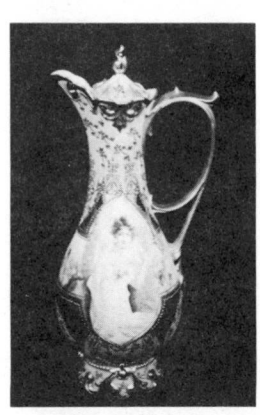

RS Prussia China

RS Prussia China

This porcelain, made by Reinhold Schlegemilch's firm in the Prussian district of Erfurt, Germany, is similar to Haviland. It was made in the last half of the 19th century and is identified by the RS in a wreath and a red (or green) star. Red star is more collectible today. See RS GERMANY. The word Germany was substituted for Prussia in 1891.

Basket, pink/red roses, blue to white bottom $200- 275	
Berry set, 6-piece, water lilies, green/gold trim	450- 495
Bowl, berry, green shading to blue and white, roses, red mark	129- 152
Cake plate, red mark	150- 175
Celery, swans, embossed loop ends, 9½" dia.	115- 170
Chocolate pot, "Autumn," Tiffany coloring, 10" high, red mark	890-1,150
Chocolate pot, 6 cups, floral, roses, white to green	350- 400
Compote, green, roses, gilt handpainted, green mark	160- 170
Creamer and sugar, colored flowers, blended floral decor, red mark	185- 240
Cup/saucer, demitasse, set of 6, red mark	325- 375
Cup/saucer, flower decor, green/ white	57- 67
Dresser set (tray, 2 covered dishes), pink floral, green mark	250- 310

281

(continued)

Hair receiver, castle scene, red mark	92-	110
Hatpin holder, bluebirds	143-	163
Manicure set (tray, buffer holder, jars), red mark	210-	240
Muffineer, white, pink roses on pearlized base, 4" high	160-	185
Mug, shaving, floral, pink, green, red mark	80-	150
Mustard jar, green decor, green sprays	80-	90
Pitcher, milk, garden scene, swans on pool, red mark	260-	340
Plate, tan, green, yellow, floral, red mark	90-	140
Relish, brown decor, gold trim	75-	90

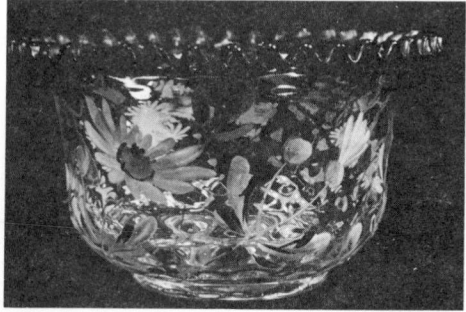

Rubina Verde Glass

Rubina Verde Glass

Hobbs, Brockunier and Company, Wheeling, West Virginia, around 1890. Shading from yellow-green to cranberry, it's now considered Art Glass and brings a good price when found. Alas, being reproduced.

Bowl, crimped top, enameled, ITP pattern, 3" high, c. 1880s (ill.)	$ 90-145
Bowl, vine pattern, applied shell feet	120-130
Cologne bottle, red shading, clear stopper, 4½" high	92-115
Celery, 6¼"	115-118
Creamer, melon-ribbed, 9" high	190-225
Cruet, daisy, fern, opalescent, stopper, clear handle	258-280
Decanter, cut, cranberry, 9" high	160-175
Epergne, clear to opalescent, 2 piece, 12" high	235-255
Perfume, swirl, matching stopper, 6½" high	68- 80
Pitcher, diamond-quilted, reeded handle, 6" high	270-280
Tumbler, ITP, flowers, enameled	97-110
Tumbler, quilted, 4" high	150-170

Vase, double tree trunk, 7" high	60-	78
Vase, hobnail, red shading to green, scalloped top, 7½" high		190-220
Vase, white enamel daisies, gold leaves, pr.		340-365

Ruby Glass

This was a "flashed" glass, usually of the souvenir type. Deep red in color, it was made from the late 1880s until World War II. Some people confuse it with red Carnival.

Berry bowl, Saxon pattern, 12 smaller bowls	$ 49-	59
Butter dish, covered, Button Arches	70-	92
Celery, Dakota (Baby Thumbprint)	44-	56
Cologne bottle, threaded stopper, 8" high	66-	76
Compote, Thumbprint pattern, 7½" high	38-	48
Cordial, Iowa State Fair	32-	48
Creamer, sugar, butter, spoonholder, gold intaglio carnations		92-102
Decanter, clear stopper	34-	44
Goblet, diamond design, set of 12		140-150
Ice bucket, metal bail handle	27-	38
Lamp, signed Glow Lamp, Inc.	28-	38
Mug, souvenir, St. Louis Exposition, 1904, "Saddie"	27-	31
Pitcher, Atlantic City, 1908, To the Fairest	33-	43
Spoonholder, cherubs, 5½" high	36-	42
Toothpick holder, Button Arches	26-	35
Toothpick holder, Bettie	27-	37
Tumbler, Reading, Pa.	22-	32
Tumbler, JHS, King's Crown	28-	37
Tumbler, Thumbprint pattern, 4" high	26-	36
Vase, fluted, disc stem, 8" high	47-	57
Vase, floral sprays, urn shape, 14" high	52-	66

Russell, Charles Marion

Living from 1865 to 1926, he was one of the greatest writers and painters of things having to do with the "Wild West." He always signed his paintings "CM Russell" with a tiny buffalo skull. His works are extremely collectible today. The buffalo skull is called a "remarque" (personal "signature" of the artist). Look for them on many paintings.

282

Sadirons

Sadirons

The old handle types were heated on a stove. They're used as doorstops or bookends today.

Average price	$ 16-	26
Gasoline iron (ill.), early 1900s	14-	25

Salopian Ware

Salopian Ware

Made in England at Salop in 1772, this decorated pottery was by Thomas Turner who took over the works in that year. In 1780 he opened a warehouse in London and marked his wares with an S or Salopian impressed or painted under the glaze. His Willow pattern is highly collectible. After he retired in 1799, the firm was sold and moved across the river by the new owners, John Rose and Company. The factory still operates under a new name, Coalport.

Bowl, blue/white, 11″ dia.	$ 340-	365
Creamer, house pattern	420-	475
Cup/saucer, blue/white, deer pattern, handleless	310-	340
Cup/saucer, early, "cow" pattern (ill.)	320-	360
Cup/saucer, late, "bird" pattern (ill.)	285-	320
Jug, mask spout, 12½″ high	825-	925
Plate, farm scene, 6½″ dia.	320-	345
Saucer, birds, cottage motif, 5″ dia.	160-	180

Saucer, fowl, fishing scene, 5″ dia.	160-	185
Teapot, house pattern	510-	550
Tea set, blue/white, 6 cups and saucers, covered teapot, sugar and creamer, some pieces marked Caughley		1,700+

Salt Glaze

Salt Glaze

Though the Staffordshire District, England, was considered the center of salt glazed pottery, some of the finest was made by the United States Pottery Company, Bennington, Vermont, 1853-1858. See PARIAN WARE.

Butter, covered	$220-265
Creamer, hand thrown, red clay, 5″ high (ill.)	42- 52
Crock, hand thrown, cobalt leaves, signed "R.C.R.–Philadelphia" (ill.)	92-125
Jug, wide-necked, bulbous, pewter lid	170-200
Mug, blue, applied handle, stoneware	70- 85
Pitcher, 4 countries of Great Britain, pewter lid, registry mark	170-195
Pitcher, Niagara Falls design, U.S. Pottery Company	195-220
Platter, white, 8½″ long	115-130
Teapot, wild roses, U.S. Pottery Company	160-170
Tea set, apostle figure, 3-piece, American	825-950

Salts

Open salts, popular from the 18th century on in America, stayed in vogue until the shaker type appeared on the market in the 1860s. Novelties in pressed glass are collectible today, such as those in the shape of birds and animals. You'll find specific prices for specific types listed in this Guide.

(continued)

Salts

Bird salt, pattern glass	$ 14- 19
Bird salt, vaseline glass (ill.)	66- 72
Bird salt, clear glass (ill.)	42- 60
Bird salt, apple green glass (ill.) ..	77- 87
Swan salt, cut glass bowl, sterling silver body and wings (wings fold back when not in use)	68- 78

Samplers

Samplers

Made from the mid-1700s until they fell from style in the early 1900s, samplers were made of cloth, usually, and contained homey messages such as Love Thy Neighbor, the alphabet, etc. Dates are given in listing.

Early 1800s, Jane Foulis Standrews, alphabet, bird/ flowers, blue/green/black (ill.) ..	$140-155
1806 alphabet, 9" x 12", framed .	130-140
1812, Love Thy Neighbor, alphabet around border, frame	180-195
1815, alphabet and numbers, Hannah L. Maywood, framed .	170-185
1818, religious verses, birds in corners, walnut frame	192-220
1819, memorial to W of 1812, child's name, frame	197-250
1847, church, flower border, Ruth Ann Mills, framed	190-225
1866, name of soldier killed at Atlanta, frame	165-295
1869, Home is where the heart is, flowers, etc., no frame	145-170
1873, Child's poem, on linen, birds, flowers, walnut frame ..	150-165

Sandwich Glass

Sandwich Glass

The Boston and Sandwich Glass Company was founded by Deming Jarves in 1825 a Sandwich, Massachusetts, and operated unti around 1888. Many fine types of glass wer made there, including pressed, cut, and blown. See specific pieces listed in PAT TERN GLASS section. Look out for you know-what!

Basket, cranberry, clear handle, 6½" dia..................	$265-285
Candlestick, canary, fluted column, flint, hexagonal base, 8" high	160-180
Cologne, jade green to white, Moorish overlay design, 7" high	140-170
Dish, lacy, "Hearts" design (ill.) .	64- 74
Ewer, pink/white, clear thorn handle, 13" high	310-350
Lamp, amethyst, 9" high	420-485
Lamp, whale oil, Star and Buckle, 8½" high	260-300
Plate, Leaf and Scroll, 6" dia. ...	52- 62
Plate, Beehive, 9¾" dia.	110-135
Pitcher, overshot.............	200-255
Pitcher, icicle, cranberry overlay .	380-425
Pitcher, bladder, (hole in side for ice to cool liquid), frosted cranberry	380-470
Salt, eagle, opalescent	165-175

Sarreguemines China

This factory operated both in Germany and France. It was first established in the 1770s in Germany by Utzchneider and Company later at Degoin, France, where they made chinaware sets, cameoware and other pieces comparable to Wedgwood in quality. Florals

Sarreguemines China

cherubs, and picnic scenes are a few of the many themes used. Usually signed "SARREGUEMINES."

Bowl, fruit, fruit decor, 10" dia...	$ 50- 60
Creamer, green glaze, man's head, 7" high, signed	83- 94
Ewer, butterflies, gold decor	44- 49
Jam jar, covered, dark yellow, molded apple on cover	39- 49
Pitcher, hunting scenes, 10" high	92-110
Pitcher, cream, green/yellow, 5" high marked	65- 75
Pitcher, roses, leaves in relief, green/rose, 8½" high	94-110
Plate, flower decor, reticulated edge, marked, 4½" dia.	28- 39
Toby jug, 6½" high, typical	100-140
Vase, blue, green/yellow geometric designs, 12" high . .	82- 97
Wine jug, cherubs, trees, 11" high	74- 84

Satin Glass

Satin Glass

Frederick Shirley of the Mt. Washington Glass Company was issued the first patent to make this beautiful glass on June 29, 1886.

Seven days later, Joseph Webb of the Phoenix Glass Company was issued his patent on July 6. It would seem both gentlemen had gotten their ideas from one Benjamin Richardson who outlined the method of making Satin Glass in 1858. In any event, this is a satin-finished glass, first blown into a mold, then treated in various ways to achieve the beautiful satin finish. It's been heavily reproduced since World War II, with thousands of pieces flooding the country. Do know your dealer on this glass.

Basket, swirl ribbed, peach/white, thorn handle	$240-270
Bottle, cologne, deep blue, MOP, 6" high.	155-172
Bowl, raised poppies and leaves, blue/black, 5" dia.	155-178
Box, 6" square, pink/blue floral decor	180-210
Candleholder, black/green, quilted base, 9" high	54- 65
Cologne bottle, blue, enamel decor, cut stopper, 7" high. . . .	140-160
Compote, green, MOP, floral decor	340-365
Cracker jar, swirled rose pattern, MOP, 4½" dia.	150-165
Cracker jar, 7½" high, Venetian Swag, Quadruple Plate lid, enameled floral (ill.), signed "M.W."	165-180
Rose bowl, blue and white stripes, Stevens and Williams	210-220
Salt/peppers, enameled floral decor	130-145
Sugar shaker, pink/white	135-148
Tumbler, herringbone pattern, white lining, 4" high	128-140
Tumbler, diamond quilted, raspberry.	120-145
Vase, diamond quilted, white to pink, 7" high	270-295
Vase, tri-cornered, diamond quilted, enameled flowers and leaves, MOP, 6" high (ill.)	235-260

Satsuma Ware

What you find in shops has been made in the past 75 years and cannot be compared to the older Satsuma, originally named for a Japanese warlord who brought the process and technique from Korea in the early 1600s. Oriental in design and motif, it's decorated with red, white, and green flowers and typical Oriental backgrounds.

285

(continued)

Satsuma Ware

Basket, red, green decor, 7" high	$150-160
Bottle, saki, Geisha girls, yellow/ blue, heavy gold	240-265
Cake plate, Showa period, 8" high	130-148
Cookie jar, red/white/green flowers, 5" dia. lid, not metal	110-120
Cup/saucer, demitasse, Oriental forest scene, Showa period	80- 90
Dish, seashells, green/red, white border, 6" dia.	50- 60
Hatpin, marble-sized head, 13" long	55- 70
Incense burner, camel kneeling, reticulated cover, 5" high overall	158-170
Jar, Meiji period, 16" high, Kara shi shi handles, nine-petaled chrysanthemum on upper border	425-465
Jardiniere, figures, Oriental scenes, 8" high, Meiji period	210-240
Pitcher, dragon spout, early and authentic, 12" high, 1830s	400-500
Plate, figural, Edo period, pale hues, Arhats without halos, Nishikide diapers and dragon borders, 9½" dia.	860-910
Saucer, typical Satsuma scenes	42- 52
Teapot, creamer, sugar, 6 cups/ saucers, flowers, green/red	435-470
Vase, early Satsuma markings, 1880s 13" high, pr.	475-525
Vase, bird handles, green/yellow/ pink, 18" high, pr.	330-360
Vase, warrior design, figural dragon handles, 23" high (ill.)	490-520

Scales

They have been used for centuries to weigh anything of value. Brass and iron scales are the most common.

Scales

Apothecary, brass pans, iron base	$118-128
Apothecary, iron, porcelain (ill.)	48- 58
Balance, hand-wrought iron hooks, 24" long	59- 69
Beam, hanging type	130-165
Candy, brass pans	83- 93
Chemist, wood case, glass windows	110-120
Counter, tin basket, hanging, indicator overhead	48- 60
Dayton	29- 38
Drugstore, walnut base, marble top	115-125
Egg weigher, fits in pocket	38- 46
Gold dust, wooden box for traveling, all 9 weights	78- 88
Hanging, 2 pans, brass, 12 weights, marked "pound"	64- 74
Ice, big dial face, brass hand, 30" top to bottom	48- 58
Jeweler, brass pans, drawer	98-110
Platform, iron, 12" x 15"	69- 79
Platform, Fairbanks, Pat'd 1879	125-165
Postal, 6 weights, wood base, American, 1879 date	110-115
Store, goods weighing type, marble base	90-100

Schneider

This is a French glass, identified by its mottled colors and fine craftsmanship Mid-1800s until just before World War I.

Bowl, topaz, acid cut, signed, 14" high	$175-210
Bowl-vase, colors fused in glass, 7" high, signed	195-240
Compote, orange/blue glass, 9½" high, signed	250-320
Finger bowl and plate, Art Deco, smoked glass	158-175
Lamp, wall, red/white shading, 5½" wide signed	160-195
Pitcher, varicolored roses, twisted handle, signed	240-285
Tazza, orange, amethyst, bubble effect, 7" diameter, signed	158-170

Urn, apricot to clear, 10 ribs,
15" high 650-725
Vase, blue/red mottled, 10"
high, signed 240-275
Vase, black blotches, 8"
high, signed, also marked
Ovingtons, France 195-260
Vase, yellow ground, lacy
enamel, pinchbottle shape,
signed 275-350

Schoenhut Toys

Albert Schoenhut established his firm in Philadelphia in 1872 to make toys and pianos. His biggest success was his Humpty-Dumpty Circus, introduced in 1903. His multijointed animals in vivid colors are much sought after today. The firm is still in business.

Alphabet blocks . . . . $	72-	90
Bear, brown, painted eyes	235-	280
Buffalo, glass eyes	240-	265
Bulldog, brown, painted eyes . .	145-	180
Camel, painted eyes	170-	220
Donkey, glass eyes	165-	195
Elephant (ill.)	240-	270
Giraffe (ill.)	230-	255
Hippo	220-	260
Horse, painted eyes	150-	170
Lion	220-	245
Mule	215-	240
Poodle, glass eyes	165-	195
Sheep	172-	179
Tiger, painted eyes	220-	245
Zebra, glass eyes	220-	235
Building blocks, in original box	120-	160
Trinity chimes	140-	175

Humpty Dumpty Circus, The
Toy Wonder—1,001 new
tricks, in original box,
complete with oblong tent,
about 50 pieces 5,500-6,200
Acrobats, lady or man 80-   90
Clown 82-   93
Donkey 220- 250
Goat 140- 165
Lion, small 185- 220
Poodle 158- 172
Bactrian (2-hump) Camel (ill.) . . 700- 825

Sconces

Lighting devices that fastened on the wall, they came in all shapes, usually made of ornate brass and primarily made to hold candles. Many people have them electrified.

Brass, 4-arm, French, flowers in
glass, pr. $340-370
Brass, 2-arm, French, figural
design, pr. 265-295
Brass, 2-arm, eagle design, out-
stretched wings hold candles . . 290-320
Glass, 4-arm, cut, hanging
prisms, American 278-295
Iron, 3-arm, painted, floral
designs 98-120
Tin (Toleware), candle-type, early
1800s, pr. 215-235
Wood and gesso eagle, carved
and gilded, late 18th century,
American (ill.) 700-800

Scrimshaws

These are objects carved from the teeth of whales or the tusks of walrus. This type of carving was a hobby popular with sailors to

Schoenhut Toys

Sconces

(continued)

Scrimshaws

pass the time during the 1800-1900 period. They would rub ink in the carving to make it stand out. Extremely collectible today, they're being reproduced in New England.

Beaver, 4¼″ long (ill.) . . . . $	120-	145
Cane, 38″ high, brass tip at bottom	165-	210
Carpenter's square, teakwood handle, 1850s	210-	270
Corset stays, 8, home scenes, 1840s	160-	190
Bust of man, 3″ high	135-	155
Crochet hook, floral design . . .	34-	44
Mother, child on swing, walrus tusk carved, 11″ long	275-	320
Napkin ring, striped cat	85-	100
Naval battle scenes, square rigged ship, 1840s	650-	750
Naval scene, Union and Rebel flags	250-	375
Powder horn, man's name, date 1793, Boston Harbor	875-	950
Punch, lady's name	45-	55
Sailing ship, cuff links, early 20th century	110-	165
Walrus tusk cribbage board, 1800s, 14″ long	1,500-	1,900
Whale tooth, eagle and flag, 5½″ long	575-	650
Whale tooth, whaling scene, 18th century, 5″	700-	800
Yardstick	100-	125

Scroddled Ware

Manufactured in Bennington, Vermont, at the Fenton Pottery, it was made by varying the amounts of a coloring agent in each batch of clay; then it was all stirred together, this time with a larger amount of the usual cream-colored clay. The finished mixture was then pressed into a mold. After being fired, a clear coat of glaze was applied. Considered rare, you can still find it if you know what to look for.

Cuspidor, Diamond pattern, feldspar glaze, gray/blue	$180-210
Pitcher, Diamond pattern, 11″ high, reddish-brown	270-325

Teapot, brown/tan, feldspar glaze	250-320
Washbowl and pitcher, dark brown, both	470-520

Probably other pieces.

Scuttle Mugs

Scuttle Mugs

This is just another shaving mug, but the shape is so different we thought you'd like to see one. Age group is same as other shaving mugs. Repros!

Cream-colored, floral decor, Germany . . . . $	33-	43
Floral and gold flowers, Thomas in script, Austria	38-	48
Pink roses, Haviland	47-	57
Union, Patent September 20, 1870	35-	45
White ironstone, country scene, Germany	29-	39

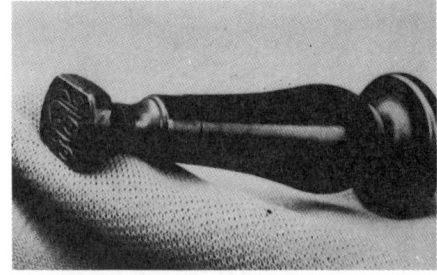

Sealing Wax Seals

Sealing Wax Seals

They've been used for centuries to seal letters, documents, etc. 17th century French seals, solid gold, are especially collectible. Look for signet rings and seals that fastened to gold watch chains.

Gold watch chain-type seal, 1800s . . . . $	58-	70
Hand seal (ill.)	20-	30
Signet ring seal (usually coat-of-arms in 14k gold)	250-300	

Oak Hoosier-type kitchen cabinet, $425–475. Pine slant-top coffee bin, $400–450.

Butternut dry sink, $400–450.

Photographs from *Country Pine Furniture Styles and Prices* by Robert and Harriett Swedberg.

Early Red Wing Stoneware Co. beverage cooler-dispenser with matching mug, $400–600.

Pitcher, Windmill pattern, Red Wing Union Stoneware Co., $225.

Red Wing Union Stoneware "Grey Line" pieces. Small bowl, $75. Orange squeezer, $400.

Photographs from *Clay Giants Book 2* by Lyndon C. Viel.

Left: MR. PEANUT rubber statue, $250. Right: MR. PEANUT pot metal statue, $350.

Left: Planters Salted Peanuts "Mother's Brand" 10-pound can, $300. Right: Planters "Sal-In-Shell" 10-pound can, $300.
Photographs from *Planters Peanuts Advertising & Collectibles* by Richard D. and Barbara Reddock.

Photographs from *Much Ado About Dolls* by R. Lane Herron.

All bisque doll, human hair wig, 2¼" tall, $45-65.

Kammer & Reinhardt "Character," with bisque socket head, marked K star R Simon and Halbig 126 62; human hair wig, flirty eyes, tremble tongue, composition body, 26" tall, $550-650.

GOOD FRIENDS, Hummel 182, $60–85.

GOOSE GIRL, Hummel 47/0, $65–95.

APPLE TREE BOY, Hummel 142/I, $80–120.

BAKER, Hummel 128, $55–75.

Photographs from *Hummel Art II* by John F. Hotchkiss. (Spring, 1981 release.)

Top: Ring box, 2½″, $440–650. Hair receiver, 3¾″, $450–550. Ring box, 2½″, $550–65(
Center: Watch box, 3″, $550–750. Round box, 8″, $1,800–2,000. Watch box, 3″, $450–55(
Bottom: Round box, 3″, $450–650. Round box, 8″, $1,800–2,000. Round box, 3″, $450–55(

Photograph from *Wave Crest Ware* by Elsa H. Grimmer.

Haviland terra-cotta jardiniere, $700–950.

Papillon Bleu miniature tea set, Haviland, $500–750.

Photographs from *Haviland China: Volume One* by Gertrude Tatnall Jacobson.

Mephistopheles humidor pipe rack by Haviland, $750–1,000.

Photograph from *Haviland China: Volume One* by Gertrude Tatnall Jacobson.

Walnut slant-front secretary, $1,300–1,400. Gentleman's chair, carved crest, cabriole legs, rosewood, 41″ high, $325–375.

Photograph from *Victorian Furniture Styles and Prices, Book II* by Robert and Harriett Swedberg.

Row 1: Spooner, $65. Sugar bowl, lid missing, $60. Spooner, $65. Creamer, $65. Syr
pitcher, $35.　　　Row 2: One-cup teapot, $85. Three-pint teapot, $125. Four-pint teap
$125. Coffeepot, eight-cup, $115.　　　Row 3: Bowl and pitcher set, $400. Waste bowl, $5
Row 4: Coffeepot, $150. Covered sugar bowl, $100. Teapot, $125. Coffeepot, $95.

Photograph from *Wallace-Homestead Price Guide to Graniteware* by
Vernagene Vogelzang and Evelyn Welch. (Spring, 1981 release.)

Row 1: Oyster, $60-75, Cambrian Rose, $70-80, Cyclamon, $110-125, Grape IV, $70-80.
Row 2: Wildflower, $50-60, Trumpet, $75-90, Grape V, $110-125, Forget-Me-Not, $85-100.
Row 3: Petunia, $110-125, Begonia, $80-95, Sunflower, $60-70, Grape VI, $135-150.

Photograph from *Gaudy Welsh China* by Howard Y. Williams.

(L to R) Ming Dynasty vase, 15¼" high, $2,500-3,000. Vase, loose-ring handles, 19t century Chinese, 9¼" high, $600-700. Yung Cheng bowl, 9½" dia., $3,800-4,500. Chi'ie Lung pot stand, 6" high, $1,400-1,800. K' ang Hsi covered jar, 18" high, $4,500-5,500.

(L to R) Chinese cloisonne water pipe, implements missing, $125-200. Chinese Openwork vase, $400-650. Chinese cloisonne box, $700-900.

Photographs from *Wallace-Homestead Price Guide to Oriental Antiques* by Sandra Andacht, Nancy Garthe and Robert Mascarelli.

$3 $12 $5 $3

$12.50 $4 $3 $10 $12 $25

$12.50 $3.50 $30 $8 $7.50 $15

$18 $9.50 $11

Photograph from *Depression Glass III* by Sandra McPhee Stout.

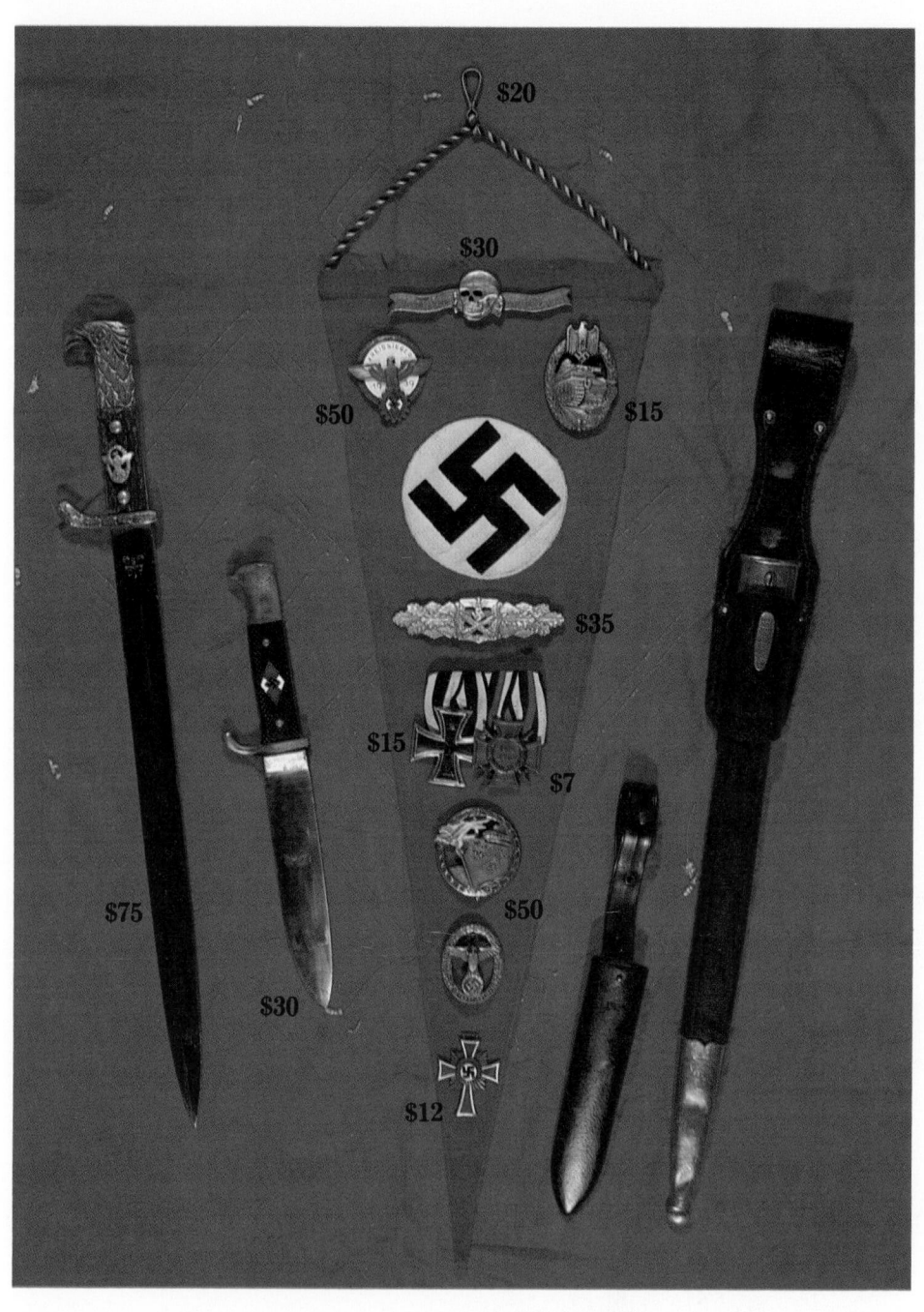

Photograph from *World War II German Collectibles* by John M. Kaduck.

Vase, "Senlis," with bronze mounts, signed "R. Lalique" in block letters, $5,000-$6,000.

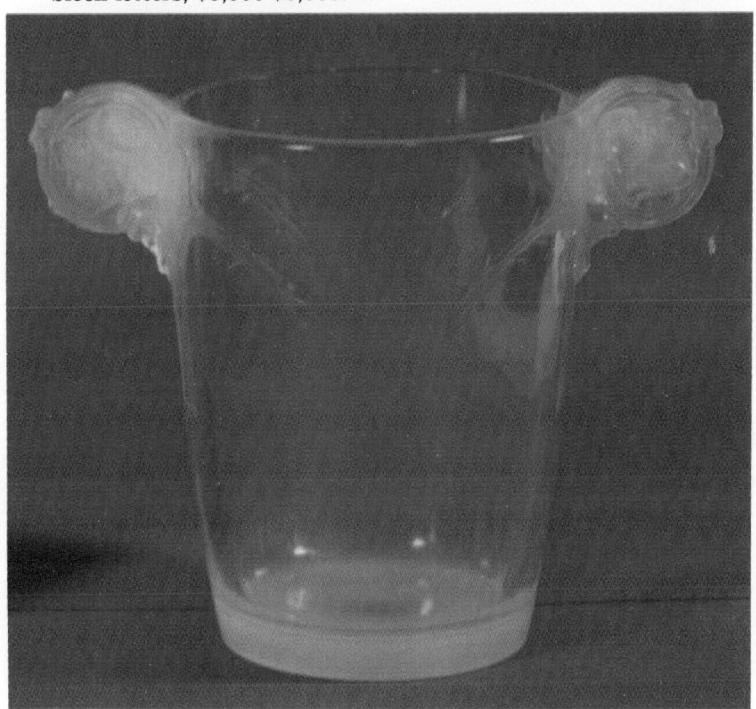

Vase, "Chamarande," signed "R. Lalique France" in block letters, $1,500-1,800.

Photographs from *Introduction to Lalique Glass* by Katharine M. McClinton.

(L to R) Old Daisy and Button, $250. New Daisy and Button, $15. New Star and Panel, $ New amber Plume, $75.

(L to R) New Art, $275. End of Day Glass, $285. Little Beauty, $250. Twinkle, $250.

Photographs from *Evolution of the Night Lamp* by Ann Gilbert McDonald.

Seals

By pressing down on the handle, you could impress the firm's name in the paper. The "seal" was usually made in lead, the holder of cast iron painted black and trimmed in red or green. Much in use in late 19th century and until World War I when notary publics came into popularity. Used today by collectors as paperweights. Illustration is that of the Eckhart Flat Land Co., Frostburg, Md., Incorporated March 24, 1909.

Indicative price, in good
condition . . . . $ 23- 35

Seine Balls

Seine Balls

You find these floating up on the salt water beaches. Used for holding seines (nets), when they break loose they float for thousands of miles. Blown glass balls in green, blue, amber; they're collectible for those decorating a wall or den. They are mentioned here only because you see so many turning up in shops today.

3″ to 5″ dia., colored . . . . $ 32- 40
6″ and larger, colored 38- 49

Service Medals

Service Medals

We're not talking about military but those medals and ribbons that were given to civilians during World Wars I and II for meritorious service. Also lapel pins.

Ribbon, Corps of Engineers,
World War II (ill.) $1.50-2.50
Lapel pin, same as above (ill.) . . . 1.50-2.50

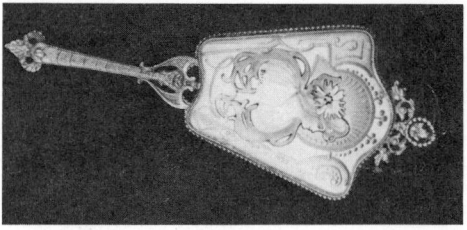

Sevres

Sevres

Madame Pompadour persuaded the factory to move from Vincennes to Sevres, France, around 1750. King Louis XV sanctioned the works, and some of the finest china the world has ever seen was made during that period. Biscuit and soft-paste porcelain were also made. Early pieces are scarce and expensive. Please, know your dealer!

Basket, blue/white, 13½″ oval, signed	$ 875-	975
Bowl, flower decor, ormolu handles and feet, 7½″ high	450-	525
Centerpiece, Art Nouveau, 8″ x 4″	275-	375
Clock, 2 urns to match, signed and dated 1756	2,400-	2,575
Coffee jar and saucer, blue/gold, 18th century	350-	400
Creamer and sugar, yellow/red roses, gold trim, signed Bavaria	150-	225
Cup/saucer, heavily enameled, 19th century	225-	275
Figurine, Bacchus under tree	150-	170
Fruit cooler, roses, flowers, gold, metal liner, 1780s	1,400-	1,650
Lamp, dated 1754, rare (demand receipt when you buy!) pair	2,800-	3,100
Mirror, portrait, plaque of Sarah Bernhardt, brass frame, beveled glass, 6¼″ long (ill.)	120-	140
Pitcher, red rose, gold trim, marked Bavaria	140-	160
Plate, blue, gold trim decor, scalloped edges, 6″ dia.	160-	190
Plate, blue/lavender ground, hand-painted, 1890s	144-	158
Statuette mantlepiece set of 4, bisque, cherub dancers	260-	275
Tea service, 4-piece, dated 1769	520-	560
Teapot, light blue, portrait medallion, gold handle	145-	175
Urn, enameled top, multicolors, 12″ high, pr.	425-	500
Vase, landscape, castle scene, 43″ high, signed	1,200-	1,400

Sewing Accessories

Sewing Accessories

The delicate art of sewing by hand is almost a thing of the past. Those items used in the 18th, 19th, and early 20th centuries are now collectible.

Moroccan leather sewing box, 1730s, brass feet, hinges, pulls (ill.)	$350-450
Chintz sewing bag, c. 1840, complete with needlecase	38- 48
Sewing bird, brass, 1 cushion	46- 56
Sewing bird, brass, 2 cushion	67- 82
Dog-shaped "bird," rare (ill.)	130-140
Sewing bird, iron, 1 cushion	58- 68
Scissors hook; hung from belt, c. 1740	67- 77
Cardboard thread winder, 8-pointed star, c. 1820	27- 37
Leather needle box, c. 1750, "By appointment to her Majesty—"	37- 47
Iron buttonhole cutter, c. 1820	44- 54
Ivory beeswax holder—to wax the thread, c. 1830s	45- 55
Thimble, 14k gold, c. 1850	62- 72
Thimble, Acanthus design, silver, c. 1850	37- 47
Thimble, porcelain, Meissen, hand-painted	92-110
Thimble, ½" tall, Meissen, made by the Herold workshop, early 18th century, sold at auction in London by Christie's in 1969	4,500+
Ivory/cloth tape measure, c. 1750, 3" high, English	55- 70
Ivory fish, 1½" long, for winding thread, c. 1750, English	25- 38

Shades, Glass

Shades, Glass

Banquet lamps, more popularly known as "Gone with the Wind" lamps, produced the first attractive shades. With kerosene, then electricity, glass lampshades really came into their own. A few of the firms who specialized in making glass shades were Dietz, 1874 on; Dithridge, 1896; Douglas, 1871; Bartlett 1871. Today one finds just the shades in many shops. Turned upside-down, they make attractive vases, candleholders, etc. See specific glass companies in this Guide for specific prices.

Iridescent shade (ill.)	$ 20- 30

Shadow Puppets

Shadow Puppets

Their movements cast a shadow behind a light drape, sheet, etc., giving the illusion of moving people, animals. They're beginning to show up in shops.

Dancing girl, Indonesian, carved wood, painted and gilded, arms move, 18" high (ill.)	$ 70- 90
Lancer on horseback, Indonesian, cut and tinted parchment, movable parts (ill.)	60- 80

Shaving Mugs

Shaving Mugs

Popular around the time of the Civil War,
they came into their own when a rash, called
Barber's Itch, swept this country in the late
1800s. After that, men demanded their own
mugs, usually with their name and/or occupa-
tion painted on it. They were made of
porcelain, glass, silver plate. Scuttle mugs
were also a fad of the day. Being reproduced.

FRATERNAL:

A.O.H. (Ancient Order of Hibernians)	$ 60- 70
A.O.U.W. (Ancient Order of United Workmen)	67- 77
B. of L.F. (Brotherhood of Loyal Firemen)	65- 75
B.P.O.E. (Benevolent Protective Order of Elks)	66- 74
F.O.E. (Fraternal Order of Eagles)	63- 73
K. of C. (Knights of Columbus)	68- 78
K. of P. (Knights of Pythias)	62- 72
L.O.O.M. (Loyal Order Of Moose)	55- 65
K.O.L. (Knights of Labor)	57- 67
W.O.W. (Woodmen of the World)—with leaf	54- 64
Masonic, square and compass	65- 75
I.A.S. (Italian-American Society)	62- 72

MISCELLANEOUS:

Deer's Head	42- 52
Automobile, early	165-200
Automobile, 1920s	110-135
Barnyard	42- 52
Bicycle and rider, early	170-190
Birds, any type except American eagle	42- 52
American eagle	75- 88
Horse and buggy	52- 62
Bunch of grapes	36- 47
Chicken	36- 45
Donkey	43- 53
Elephant	50- 60
Flag, sword, and cannon	67- 75
Flag, any nation except USA	39- 48
American flag, early	65- 75

OCCUPATIONAL:

Accordion, initialed	145-162
Anvil and hammer	130-145
Auctioneer's emblem	92-107
Baggage car	140-158
Baker's emblem (2 lions and pretzel)	140-155
Barbershop	130-140
Baseball and bats	138-148
Beer brewer's emblem	92-102
Beer wagon, horses, and driver	160-170
Blacksmith shoeing horse	120-130
Boilermaker at work	129-140
Bookbinder	142-162
Bookkeeper	112-132
Bottle blower at work	140-160
Bricklayer at work	118-146
Brush maker's store	110-135
Buggy maker	142-162
Bull's head and tools	110-120
Butcher dressing a steer	115-119
Butcher chopping meat	115-122
Caboose	98-107
Carpenter at work	110-120
Camera with stand	162-180
Chairmaker at work	115-130
Cigar Store	120-155
Clerk at desk	104-114
Coal miner with tools	130-140
Dentist drawing teeth	210-222
Doctor attending patient	240-260
Druggist working	140-150
Electric streetcar	120-140
Steam engine	125-135
Express wagon, 2 horses	128-138
Fire engine with 2 horses	188-195
Flint glassblowers at work	225-250
Furniture store	115-122
Hardware store	122-148
Harnessmaker at work	150-170
Hatter	148-167
Hearse, horses, and driver	160-170
Hook and ladder, 2 horses	195-220
Horse shoer at work	120-140
Hose cart	133-143
Lager beer wagon	126-136
Letter carrier in uniform	130-140
Locomotive and tender	142-152
Machinist's calipers	110-120
Mail wagon, horse, and driver	118-128
Man shearing sheep	100-107
Marble cutter	127-148
Mattress maker at work	108-118
Miller dressing burr	110-120
Miner with pick and shovel	140-160
Molder at work	110-120
Musicians	110-135
Nailer at work	98-108
Oil derrick and scenery	155-165
Omnibus with horses	140-150
Painter at work	115-125
Paperhanger at work	128-138

(continued)

Sheet Music

The nostalgia boom has renewed the interest in old sheet music. Some of the titles are hilarious. Pre-WWI sheet music is especially sought after. Patriotic, ethnic, ragtime, romance — Irving Berlin, George M., Al Jolson, Rudy Vallee, Frederick V. Bowers (?) — all collectible.

1880s to 1914, average price in
    good condition . . . . $ 5- 13
WWI, patriotic, average price in
    good condition 6- 17
1920 to 1939, average price in
    good condition 3- 9
Obviously, there are exceptions
to these price ranges. If you
like it, buy it!

Shell Work

Shells brought home from the seashore or purchased in kits at stores were used to make these bouquets. Usually found under a glass dome or behind glass in a frame, the work is collectible today.

Shell, bouquet, 8″ high, in glass
    enclosed gilt frame . . . . $ 42- 53
Shell, seashore scene, 16″ x 20″
    in gold frame 47- 57

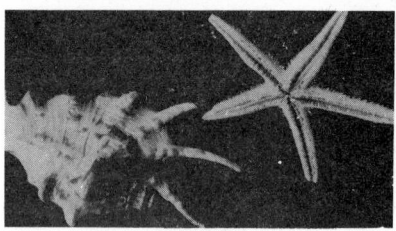
Shells

Shells

Everything else is being collected, so wh not seashells? From the coast of Texas to th Everglades in Florida, people follow the tide and pick up shells. Some are so rare tha they bring upward to $500 each!

Eastern Murex (ill.) . . . . $ 1- 1.50
Starfish (if dried properly) . . . . . . 50¢

Ship Models

Ship Models

Models of ships have been found in th tombs of Egyptian kings. Old models ai highly collectible today, some bringing hug prices.

3-masted schooner, hand-
    carved, 33″ long, dated
    1894 . . . . $ 640- 720
New Bedford whaler, carved
    from ivory, inlaid abalone
    shell, 13″ long, late 1800s . . . 1,900-2,400
Old ironsides, miniature, in
    quart bottle, ivory, 5½″
    long 2,600-3,100
Scale model of French frigate,
    bone, 18th century, all
    original 2,400-2,650
Chinese Junk, bamboo and
    mother-of-pearl, early 19th
    century (ill.) 265- 300

Shoe Buckles

In the 18th and 19th centuries, son buckles were made of solid gold, others platinum and sterling silver. The pair illu trated here are M.O.P. and sterling silver, 1850. A little-known collectible, but a pri when found.

308

Siderolith Ware

Made in Bohemia by many firms, it was earthenware molded in relief and decorated with bright colors. Schiller and Son made it after 1851. Their imitations of Wedgwood confused many people then and still do today. Usually signed S and G. Don't confuse it with Shore and Goulding, England.

Prices 50-60% lower than Wedgwood—see.

Silhouettes

Silhouettes

"Man reduced to his simplest form" is the easiest way to explain them. Supposedly named for an 18th century Frenchman, these are outline pictures. The most famous American ones were cut by Charles Peale, 1800 to 1810. Either cut from black and mounted on white, or white cutouts (Peale) mounted on black. If you find one signed August Edouart, you've found a jewel.

Gentleman in top hat, dated 1897, in walnut frame	$ 95-125
Girl and boy in matching gold leaf/walnut frames, mid-1800s, pr. (ill.)	90-110
Lady in bonnet, in gold leaf frame	110-128
Lincoln (probably done from photograph)	65- 78
Horse-drawn carriage in gold leaf frame	44- 53
Washington, profile, in walnut frame	65- 80

Silver Definitions

COIN

Made from melted American currency, usually before 1860, usually with 800 or 900 parts of silver. Coin silver spoons are fragile, often found in a repaired condition.

PLATED

The base of plated silver is usually Britannia Ware, 10 parts tin, 1 part antimony. After shaping, the article was plated by an electrolytic method which placed a thin coating of silver over the base metal. Less silver was used than in Sheffield silver.

SHEFFIELD PLATE

This is a plated product produced by placing thin sheets of silver on either side of a heavy copper sheet. The basic standard was 8 pounds copper to 2 pounds silver. Dishonest silversmiths used much less silver. There was a heavy penalty if and when they were caught. Pieces you see today that show more copper than silver are examples of this cheaper method.

STERLING SILVER

By law, it must contain 92.5 parts of pure silver, both here and in England. "Sterling" — Irish, after 1720 (rare), or American, after the 1860s.

SILVER PLATE

Silver plate in England is the equal to our sterling in this country. Solid English silver was marked with the familiar hallmarks: Lion Pissant, Leopard's Head, King's (or Queen's) Head, plus maker's touchmark.

EPNS

Electroplate on nickel silver is nickel metal dipped in a silver solution as electricity is run through the piece.

EPWM

Electroplate on white metal—same process as above.

QUADRUPLE PLATE

4-times dipped: **triple plate**, 3-times dipped.

AFRICAN SILVER

English plate after 1850, by Hills, Monke and Company.

BRAZIL SILVER

Globe Nevada Silver Works, Birmingham, England; on a nickel silverware that was not silver plate.

GERMAN SILVER

Silver-colored metal from nickel, copper and zinc.

309

(continued)

OREGON SILVER
Just another trade name used on silver-plated English wares after the 1800s.
SIBERIAN SILVER
Silver on copper, English; Hayman and Company, late 1800s.

Please note: In 1980 the price of 925/1000 (sterling) silver shot to nearly $60 an ounce. That price has since dropped, but the manufacturers of sterling (flatware, holloware) have raised their prices 300 to 500 percent. This does not indicate the intrinsic (antique) value of the silver piece.

Silver
See Definitions for information on specific types.

COIN
Butter dish, engraved floral
  scene, Bailey and
  Company, 1845 . . . . $650-750
Butter knives, scroll/shell
  design, Bailey and
  Company, 1847   150-200
Child's knife, fork, and
  spoon, Gray and Libby,
  Boston, 1847 (all)   250-300
Ladle, mustard, initialed J R,
  marked Pure Coin 37- 44
Ladle, punch, marked Pure
  Coin, 1850   110-130
Spoon, coffin handle,
  Edmond Milne, Phila-
  delphia, 1757 (ill.)   185-200
Spoon, Samuel Williamson,
  Philadelphia, 1794 (ill.) . . .   190-220
Spoon, Wm. Mannerback,
  Reading, Pennsylvania,
  1825 (ill.)   170-200
Spoon, gold washed bowl
  (ill.) 54- 66
Teaspoon, signed Miksch,
  Bethlehem (ill.)   175-225

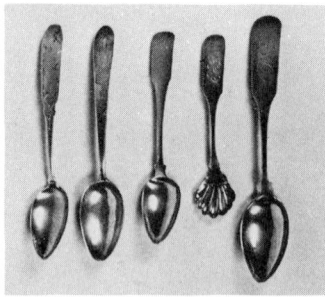

Silver

PLATED EPNS, EPWM, AMERICAN
Basket, 9″ diameter, EPNS,
  1900s 25- 30
Butter dish, EPNS, flower
  pattern, 6″ diameter,
  early 1900s 26- 36
Candlesticks, triple plate,
  Victor Silver Company,
  late 1800s, pair 39- 49
Candlestick, 3-branch, silver
  plate, grape design, 18½″
  high (ill.) 78- 90

Silver

Triple Plate:
CASTOR SETS:
Beefsteak pattern, chased
  caster, 6 bottles, c. 1888 . $104-110
Befitting pattern, plain
  caster, 5 bottles, c. 1888 .   86- 96
Decide pattern, chased
  caster, 5 bottles,
  c. 1889   94-106
Decipher pattern, plain
  caster, 5 bottles, c. 1888 .   88-100
Wince pattern, fancy gilt, 6
  bottles, Derby Silver Co.,
  c. 1885   115-135
Windlass pattern, w/bell
  handle, 6 bottles, Derby
  Silver Co., c. 1885   152-172
ICE PITCHERS:
Grecian pattern, engine
  turned, Meriden Silver
  Plate Co., c. 1887 . . . .   84- 94
Medallion pattern, Meriden
  Silver Plate Co., c. 1885 . .   87- 97
Paneled Chased, Meriden
  Co., c. 1887 . . . .   89- 99
CAKE BASKETS:
Grecian Chased, Meriden
  Silver Plate Company
  c. 1870 . . . .   65- 80
Medallion and Chased,
  engraved, Meriden Silver
  Plate Company, c. 1869 . .   67- 77
Medallion and Chased,
  plain, Meriden Silver
  Plate Company, c. 1868 . .   61- 71

BUTTER DISHES:
  Revolving, Plain, Engine,
  Medallion, Chased or
  Engraved, Meriden Silver
  Plate Company, c. 1868 . .   58- 69
CELERY STANDS:
  Grecian Chased, w/white
  glass, Meriden Silver
  Plate Company, c. 1870 . .   42- 52
  Medallion and Chased,
  w/white glass, Meriden
  Silver Plate Company, c.
  1875 . . . .   44- 54
SYRUP CUPS AND PLATES:
  Damask Chased, with plate,
  Meriden Silver Plate
  Company, c. 1869 . . . . . .   58- 70
  Grecian Chased, without
  plate, Meriden Silver
  Plate Company, c. 1875 . .   52- 62
  Plain, with plate, Meriden
  Silver Plate Company,
  c. 1868 . . . .   47- 57
GOBLETS:
  Engine, Plated or Gilt,
  Meriden Silver Plate
  Company, c. 1874 . . . . . .   33- 43
  Plain, Plated or Gilt,
  Meriden Silver Plate
  Company, c. 1867 . . . . . .   36- 42 each
CUPS:
  Engine, Plated or Gilt,
  Meriden Silver Plate
  Company, c. 1869 . . . . . .   32- 42
  Grecian or Damask,
  engraved or plain,
  Meriden Silver Plate
  Company, c. 1869 . . . . . .   34- 44
TEAPOTS:
  Flowers, signed "Meriden,"
  8½" high (ill.) 83- 98

Silver
Quadruple Plate:
CAKE BASKETS:
  Debris pattern, etched,
  lated 1800s $127-136
  Decade pattern, satin
  chased, c. 1889   110-130

DeCamp, chased, 1880   110-128
SALTS:
  Declivity pattern (owl),
  c. 1889 . . . .   38- 48
  Devotion, cut glass,
  c. 1890 . . . .   30- 40
  Decolor pattern, cut
  glass, c. 1888 . . . .   34- 44
PEPPERS:
  Decorous pattern, c. 1888 . .   22- 32
  Decorum pattern, c. 1892 . .   21- 31
  Decoy, c. 1889 . . . .   18- 28
  Decree, gold lined, c. 1889 . .   28- 38
PICKLE CASTORS:
  Behave pattern, blue, red
  or canary bottle, c.
  1889 . . . .   74- 84
  Deduce pattern, red
  bottle, c. 1890 . . . .   66- 76
  Napkin ring and pepper,
  Defence pattern, c.
  1890 . . . .   80- 92
  Tea caddy, Defaming
  pattern, Satin Bright
  Cut, c. 1889 . . . .   50- 60
NAPKIN RINGS:
  Barefoot boy, 3" high,
  hand-engraved, c. 1900 . .   30- 40
  "Best Wishes," chick
  and wishbone, c. 1880 . . .   32- 39
  Carved man and dog,
  3" high, 1905, satin
  finish, engraved 31- 41
  Deficit pattern,
  hammered and applied
  gilt, c. 1889 . . . .   27- 37
  "Father," hand-engraved,
  3" dia., c. 1890 . . . .   27- 37
CUPS:
  Crumb brush, satin
  engraved, c. 1889 . . . . . .   18- 27
  Crumb tray, satin
  engraved, c. 1889 . . . . . .   31- 41

Silver

311

(continued)

Elfin pattern, hand-
chased, c. 1888 . . . .   40- 50
Florentine pattern, gold-
lined, c. 1887 . . . .   44- 52
Pied Piper of Hamelin,
gold-lined, c. 1889 . . . . . .   44- 53
Rose pattern, engraved
handle, c. 1895 . . . .   37- 47

TEA SERVERS:
Teapot, on warming stand,
3 pieces, 14″ high, signed
"Pairpoint Manufacturing
Company" (ill.) 66- 78

TOOTHPICK HOLDERS:
Boy Riding Turtle,
Umbrella, all plate,
c. 1888 . . . .   71- 90
Card receiver, a non-
tarnishable, c. 1888 . . . . .   41- 51
Deplore pattern,
oxydized boots, c. 1888 . .   29- 39
Jewel casket, "Old
Oaken Bucket," opens
by turning crank, c.
1890 . . . .   80- 90
Manicure set, 7 pieces
in plush case,
hammered old silver,
c. 1889   110-140
Porcupine, plain or gilt,
c. 1889 . . . .   36- 45

VASES:
Bleed pattern, non-
tarnishable, c. 1888 . . . . .   62- 72
Decorated porcelain,
farm scene, c. 1892 . . . . . .   60- 70
Glass container, "Girl
with butterfly net,"
silver and gold, c.
1888 . . . .   88- 92
Valley pattern, Derby
Silver Company, 1883 . . .   82- 92
Value pattern, Derby
Silver Company, 1883 . . .   82- 92

STERLING SILVER, AMERICAN:

Blotter, flowers in repousee, c.
1870s $190-220
Candleholder, embossed roses
and scrolls, "Gorham Sterling,"
1¾″ high   195-220
Desk set, inkwells and calendar,
c. 1880   295-320
Indian Chief, 4″ wide, c. 1910 . . .   250-295
Inkstand, cut glass bottles,
"Cupids," in repousee, c.
1875   300-375
Nude in Pond, 4½″ wide, c.
1890   265-300
Paper knife, Art Nouveau, c.
1895   250-280

Stamp box, "Dog" on top, c.
1880 . . . .   72- 82
Thermometer, repousee frame,
still works, c. 1895   170-200

BOOKMARKS:
Eraser, Indian head in relief,
c. 1890   95-110
Gentleman's cane, mushroom
cap, engraved, c. 1875   125-140
Indian head, 4½″ long, signed
"Tiffany," 1896   110-130
Lobster-shaped, 6″ long, c.
1880   100-115
Penholder, repousee, 8″ long,
c. 1875   110-120
Roman goddess, 4″ long, c.
1885   98-110
Shaving brush, Art Nouveau,
c. 1900   130-160
Shaving mug, "Boxer"
engraved on side, c. 1890   285-325

POCKET FLASKS:
Bar jigger, Imp thumbing nose,
c. 1880   125-130
Button box in shape of collar,
marked "Collar," c. 1875   170-220
Chatelaine, 3-chain, inlaid
diamond, c. 1870   250-300
Cut crystal, Art Nouveau,
"Lady," c. 1895   190-220
Cut crystal, Indian chief in
relief, c. 1890   190-210
Glove cologne, repousee, 3″
long, c. 1870   150-175
Liquor label, "Whiskey," c.
1890   85-110
Nudes in relief, c. 1880   190-225

STERLING SILVER:

STERLING, IRISH
Cup, harp decor, mid-1800s . . .   250- 300
Master salt, footed, with spoon   270- 320
STERLING, ITALIAN
Table bell, late 1800s, coat-of-
arms, 5″ high 185- 220
STERLING, RUSSIAN
Beaker, late 1700s 350- 410
Candlestick, 12″ high, pair 310- 385
Mug, late 1800s 400- 500
Napkin ring, etched flower
decor 160- 195
STERLING, SWEDISH
Creamer, flowers and foilage
decor, early 1800s 310- 450
Tea set (pot, creamer, sugar,
waste bowl, tray) 1800s   4,200-5,100
STERLING, FRENCH
Bonbon dish, gadroon edging,
3½″ high (ill.) 195- 275
Dish, 1810, embossed flowers .   210- 295
Salt cellar, reeded border, set
of 4 . . . .   485- 565

Silver Deposit Glass

Popular since the late 1800s, it's simply silver deposited on the glass, usually by electro-depositing, a method involving electricity, flux, and silver anodes. It's still being made today.

Bonbon dish, footed, 6½″ dia. . . .	$ 55- 67
Bottle, cologne, green, 4″ high . .	42- 62
Bowls:	
a. 7″, 8″, 9″, clear glass	99-110
b. 10″ dia. cobalt	120-140
Bud vase, 6½″ high, marked	
Sterling	190-220
Cologne bottle with stopper, 4″	
high, marked Sterling	250-300
Compote, green, 7½″ high	42- 60
Cruet, 7″ high, cut glass stopper,	
marked Sterling	175-210
Decanter, 9½″ high, cut glass	
stopper, E.P.N.S.	115-130
Mustard jar, 4″ high	47- 53
Perfume bottle, 4″ high, cut glass	
stopper, marked Sterling	195-250
Plate, green, sterling silver	72- 90
Toothpick holders, 2″, 3″ high . .	34- 44
Vase:	
a. 6″, 8″ high	46- 56
b. 9½″ high, marked Sterling .	175-210
Vase, bud, flared top, 8″ high . . .	46- 56

Silver Lustre Ware

Silver Lustre Ware

Produced in large quantities between the early 1800s and 1840, Staffordshire, England, it went out of style in the 1850s when the electroplating of metal items came into vogue.

Bowl, Festoon and shell decor . . .	$ 82-110
Coffeepot, 10½″ high	300-375
Candleholder, ribbed design,	
11½″ high	78- 92
Creamers:	
a. Fine ribbed design (ill.)	
4½″ high to top of handle . .	140-160
b. Dolphin handle	130-150
Footed teapot, 8½″ high	295-310
Goblet, 4″ high	80- 90
Goblet, 5″ high	62- 72

Pitcher, white quilted body,	
silver lustre at top	280-300
Pitcher, "Leaf" pattern, 4½″	
high (ill.)	68- 78
Sugar bowl, ribbed design	120-145
Teapot, 5½″ high	240-265
Toby jug	270-290

Silver Resist Ware

Silver Resist Ware

This ware gets its name from the fact that the drawings or patterns resist the lustering solutions, and when fired in the kiln the entire surface of the piece, except for the pattern, is glazed. Similar to Silver Lustre except the pattern appears on the surface.

Creamer	$158-178
Cup/saucer, berry and leaf	96-108
Jug, 5″ high	150-185
Pitcher, 6¼″ high (ill.)	235-270
Pitcher, canary ground, floral	
motif, 7″ high	240-265
Teapot, 5½″ high	196-206
Teapot, 6″ high (ill.)	198-220

Silveria

Silveria

This glass was produced by Stevens and Williams, Brierly Hills, England, about 1900. Its inventor, John Northwood II, gave it its name, and it was made by sandwiching silver

313

(continued)

foil between two layers of transparent crystal or colored glass. Drippings of transparent glass cover the outer layer of the glass. Two Frenchmen arrived at the formula in the late 1870s but Northwood is generally credited with the manufacturing of the glass. It's interesting to note that Northwood's son came to America and is given credit (?) for creating Taffeta glass, better known, worldwide, as Carnival glass. Some pieces of Silveria are signed "England" while others may have the familiar "S & W" in script, with or without a fleur-de-lis on a ground pontil. Scarce, but a treasure when found.

Vase, applied green handles,
pink/yellow/green drip-
pings, 5" high, c. 1900,
signed "S & W" (ill.) $1,200-1,400

Slag Glass

Slag Glass

See specific items in PATTERN GLASS section.

Bowl, footed, purple, embossed
design, 4" high (ill.) . . . . $ 72- 82
Salt, fish-shaped, purple (ill.) 60- 80

Slavery and Black Items

Of late there has been a demand for paintings, sculptures, advertisting cards, etc., to do with the black race. Also for slavery items, though most of these are in museums.

Advertising cards, average price . $ 1- 2
"Delaware History, Oct. 1863,"
Abolition Society of Del. 4- 9
Freedom papers of black slave,
signed by Lincoln (if
authenticated), rare 370-420

Slides, Chain

These objects helped adjust the length of the watch hanging around the lady's neck. Gold or gold-plated, sometimes ornately set with precious stones, they're hard to find today because so many have been made into bracelets.

Slides, Chain

14 karat gold, inlaid pearl on each
side, late 1800s . . . . $ 49- 60
10 karat gold, imitation diamond   22- 31
18 karat gold, small ruby, initials
on other side, 1800s 54- 64
Keep in mind that 10 karat gold or less was usually used with imitation stones. The same applies to "gold-plated."

Slipware

Slipware

Made in Europe and the U.S. for many years, it's a ceramic decorated by applying slip (clay reduced to a liquid batter) to the surface of the piece being made.

Bowl, gray, 7" dia. . . . . $ 63- 73
Jug, figures in brown, 6" high . . .   68- 78
Pitcher, lustre striping, floral
band, Staffordshire, 13" high .   92-110
Plate, red/brown, Pennsylvania
Dutch motif, 9" dia. 44- 53
Plate brown/cream color, 10"
dia. 132-143
Platter, brown, cream color,
ornate decor, oval, 14" dia. . . . 141-146
Pot, bean, red, glazed inside,
9" high 77- 89

Smallwood and Morton

Probably America's first antique dealers, their shop was located at Roxbury, Massachusetts, in 1850. They also made furniture.

Smith Brothers

Alfred and Harry Smith established the decorating department at the Mt. Washington Glass Company in 1871. They were

nown for their excellence in enameling on
isque or opal glass. They established their
wn firm in 1875 in New Bedford, Massachu-
etts, and made the famous Smith Vase in
he late 1800s until it was cheaply copied and
old in dime stores by the hundreds.

Biscuit jar, daisies, blue shading, silver top, signed	$310-345
Bowl, covered, signed	220-255
Cream bowl, white daisies, beaded top	180-195
Creamer/sugar, blue flowers, silver collar, white	170-190
Cracker jar, Burmese color, gold florals, silver bail	410-425
Plate, Santa Maria, 1880s 10" dia., signed	520-540
Sugar shaker, ribbed, opaque, white, flowers, silver top, 9" high	93-108
Toothpick, flower decor, 3" high, signed	90-110
Vase, bird decor, enameled, signed	220-240
Vase, Burmese pink, yellow, fruits, acid cut	265-285

Smoking Accessories

Smoking Accessories

Box, cigar, mahogany, brass fittings, 14" x 11" (ill.)	$ 60- 70
Box, cigar, inlaid M.O.P. top, rosewood, 12" x 10½"	75- 85
Cutters, cigar — see	
Stand, smoking, brass, 27" high, glass ashtray, matchbox holder	40- 50
Tobacco jars — see	

Snowbirds

These were wrought or cast iron birds,
usually in the shape of eagles, that were set
on roofs in rows to prevent the snow from
sliding off. About 1830 until 1890.

Wrought or cast iron, eagle	$ 68- 78

Snuff Bottles

Snuff Bottles

Usually intricately carved on the outer surface, they were made of glass, porcelain, jade,
coral, etc. They were carried originally by
Orientals in the 18th century. The habit of
taking snuff, thought to be a medical cure-all,
spread to Europe in the mid-1800s, probably,
even earlier. Snuff bottles were usually carried by women.

Agate, carved, woman on bridge, stopper, Ch'ien Lung mark . . .	$490-550
Glass, blue painting on inside, 2¼" high (ill.)	35- 46
Jade, woman in garden, stopper .	220-285
Lapis lazuli, garden scene, coral stopper	170-185
Mother-of-pearl, 19th century . . .	92-102
Opal, fish scene, coral stopper . . .	380-410
Peking enamel, women in garden	175-195
Rock crystal, quartz stopper	178-188

Snuffboxes

Snuffboxes

Made from metal, usually gold or silver, intricately carved, sometimes inlaid with
precious gems, carried by men during the
same period as snuff bottles.

Chinese, gold-on-steel, hinged lid, footed	$210-230
Cloisonne, blue enamel, flowers, with lid	175-190
Glass, green/blue enamel, floral decor	88- 98
Sterling silver, initialed, lid	158-169

 (continued)

Tortoiseshell, primitive figures,
Chinese, early 1800s 300-350
Wood, inlaid silver, 4 leaf clover
on lid (ill.) 50- 58

Soapstone

Soapstone

Call it steatite, if you want to get technical.
Also sometimes called potstone. Usually attributed to China, most of what you find in
shops today was found in the Delaware River
area and New England and was carved there.

Ashtray (ill.) .... $ 16- 19
Bed warmer, wire handle 33- 43
Bookends, brown/black, pr. 36- 45
Candleholder, carved fruit,
brown/white, 3" high 26- 35
Figurine, Chinese woman, 7"
high 40- 48
Figurine, elephant, 3½" high ... 34- 44
Figurines, pair, Chinese couple,
4" high (ill.) 44- 52

Toothpick, fruit decor, 4" high .. 29- 38
Vase, brown/black, carved leaves,
8" high 40- 50
Vase, floral, neutral to black/
brown, 5" high 52- 61

Songbooks

Anyone remember Blind Lemon Jefferson
Ida Cox, the Jubilee singers, or Charli
Jackson? All "greats" in their own right
long, long ago. Songbooks of the blues, fol
songs, hymnals are all collectible today.

The Paramount Book of Blues,
1924 (ill.) .... $ 15- 23
Folk Songs of the American
Negro, 1907 (ill.) 8- 12
Revival Songs, published in
Dallas, Texas, in 1929 (ill.) 3- 5

Souvenir and Commemorative
Plates

Souvenir and Commemorative Plates

Don't confuse these with the better qualit
early Staffordshire plates, popular in th

Songbooks

mid-1800s. The souvenir plates came into vogue about the time of the Philadelphia Centennial in 1876 and stayed popular until the 1930s.

Alaska Yukon Pacific Exposition, 1909	$ 35- 42
Ashbury Park Amusement Park, New Jersey, blue	37- 47
Capital Island Maine, sailing ships, 9" dia.	34- 44
Carolinas, Pinehurst, North Carolina, 9" dia.	31- 41
Faneuil Hall, Boston, 8" dia.	33- 42
Israel, Independence, 7" dia.	33- 43
West Virginia Centennial, red/ blue, 10" dia.	34- 44

Souvenir Ribbons

Everyone brought something home from the Expositions in days-gone-by. The colorful ribbons are highly collectible today. Age, condition, rarity — these establish the price you'll pay.

Souvenir Spoons

Made as mementos for fairs and other events, they enjoyed their greatest popularity in the late 1800s. They covered every conceivable subject and were usually made of a silver-plated material or sterling silver. Reproductions in almost every category.

Actress, Norma Talmadge	$ 20- 30
Atlanta, Georgia, bale of cotton	14- 17
Atlantic City, N.J., Steel Pier, 1904	11- 20
Brooklyn Bridge, 1883	10- 19
Colorado state seal, Denver engraved in bowl of spoon	16- 21
Indianapolis, 1909	10- 16
Louisiana Purchase Exposition, 1903, sterling silver	120-130
Mt. Vernon, Virginia, sterling silver	120-130
Pan American Exposition, 1901	23- 33
Saratoga, New York, demitasse, sterling silver	120-130
William Shakespeare, England	23- 33
World's Fair, 1904	28- 38

Spangle Glass

Mica or other metallic flakes were imbedded between two layers of glass. Many firms made it in the late 1800s. Don't confuse it with Spatter (End-of-Day) Glass. Poor repros being made.

Basket, green/yellow, mica, thorn handle, 7¼" dia.	$145-155

Spangle Glass

Basket, blue/pink, mica, fluted rim, clear handle (ill.)	112-130
Bowl, blue, mica, 7" dia.	78- 88
Bowl, cased pink/yellow, 6½" dia.	74- 84
Cookie jar, usual marking, silver-plated top and holder, 6" high	68- 78
Paperweight, blue flowers, gold mica flakes	135-155
Pitcher, blue, mica, cased, miniature, 4½" high	122-128
Sugar/creamer, green, cased, mica flakes	68- 78
Vase, yellow ground, peach, mica, cased, pair, 6" high	74- 84
Vase, cream lined, white/pink, spangles, 8" high	74- 86
Vase, ruffled, spatter and spangle, 6½" high (ill.)	82- 92
Vase, pink, silver flecks, red cherries, applied clear handle, "Stevens and Williams" (ill.)	88-108

Spanish Lace Glass

The opalescent designs of flowers and foilage identify this glass, popular in the late 1800s.

Barber bottle, cranberry, 9" high	$ 62- 72
Basket, blue/pink, ruffled, scalloped, silver holder	88- 98
Bowl, blue/pink, ruffled lip	120-130
Bride's basket, blue, ruffled	140-160
Finger bowl, opalescent swirls	50- 60
Epergne, cranberry, 14" high	245-275
Lamp, cranberry, Fenton Glass Works	142-152
Pitcher, vaseline, original tin top	138-148
Rose bowl, vaseline glass	65- 75
Salt shaker, opalescent ruby, 4" high	32- 42
Spooner, vaseline	72- 82
Toothpick, blue swirls, 3" high	40- 60
Vase, blue, opalescent, 8½" high	63- 73
Vase, blue opalescent, ruffled top, 6½" high	60- 70

317

Spatter

Spatter

This is not a ware but a type of decoration used by potters worldwide. That made by Staffordshire potters, 1820-1850, interests collectors most. Much of it is Ironstone. Adams made a lot in both the regular Staffordshire, 1830s, and in Ironstone in the 1840s. Most platters are octagonal. Plates are smooth rim or sided. The most popular pattern is Schoolhouse; Peacock is second. The most colorful is called Rainbow. Most popular colors were yellow, green, purple, pink, and blue. G. Adams and Son; Alcock, Cotton and Barlow; Davenport; J and G Heath; Powell and Bishop; Wedgwood (blue rim type); just a few of the many firms who used this type decoration.

Bowl, blue, peacock pattern, 6½" dia.	$192-240
Creamer, blue, Schoolhouse pattern, 6" high	154-180
Cup/saucer, pea fowl (ill.)	220-245
Cup and saucer, blue, peafowl pattern	210-240
Pitcher, red and blue, Schoolhouse pattern, 7" high	255-295
Plate, red, peacock pattern, 9" dia.	270-310
Plate, Star pattern, 8¼" dia.	200-220
Plate, red/green background, Schoolhouse pattern, 9½" dia.	345-375

Spatter Glass

Spatter Glass

It's doubtful that this glass was ever formally called "End-of-Day." Legend has that at nightfall the glassblowers used what was left over to make "whimsies" for friends and family. There's too much of it on the market and though it was commercially made, it never achieved any great popularity when made in the late 1800s by many firms. Being reproduced.

Basket, multicolored, clear handled	$ 68-	78
Bowl, cased, typical spatter colors, rigaree feet	62-	73
Creamer, 4" high	29-	38
Cup/saucer, blue ground, usual colors	31-	41
Ewer, tortoise/opalescent background, 8" high	48-	58
Jug, milk, yellow/blue spatter, 6" high	31-	41
Pitcher, blue/yellow/brown, clear handle, 3" high	58-	68
Pitcher, yellow/red/blue/green, 7½" high (ill.)	85-115	
Slipper (souvenir or whimsey item), green, white/red	31-	41
Toothpick, pink/green/brown, 4" high	33-	43
Tumbler, 5" high	26-	28
Tumbler, diagonal ribbing, 4¾" high (ill.)	53-	68
Tumbler, yellow/brown/green	27-	35
Vase, blue/red/green, 11" high	48-	58
Vase, red/bronze/green, 7½" high	42-	52
Vase, exterior horizontal wale in clear glass (ill.)	40-	49

Spongeware

Spongeware

Similar to Spatter the designs were applied to the ware by daubing the color. Dealers call it Spatterware, or lump the two together. Any knowledgeable person can tell the two apart.

Bowl, green or cream ground, 10" dia. (ill.)	$ 49-	62

Bowl, blue, 8" diameter	52- 68
Bowl and pitcher, American made	245-295
Butter crock, covered, blue, 18" high	130-165
Cup/saucer, multicolored, marked Adams	72- 92
Cuspidor, blue, blue bands	36- 47
Pitcher, blue, New England, 8" high	79- 90
Pitcher, blue decoration on buff ground, 6½" high (ill.)	49- 62
Plate, blue, 8½" diameter	41- 56
Spittoon, blue, 3" high	50- 60
Vegetable dish, blue, 5" diameter	44- 57

Spoons

Spoons

Sterling silver spoons are especially collectible. The maker and year decide the price. Prices given are for sterling only. Spoons are classified by maker, with pattern and type specified. Keep in mind what sterling silver has done in 1980.

DURGIN
Bead, fruit spoon, gold bowl	$160-180
Bead, table or teaspoon, 5½" ...	160-180

GORHAM
Blythe Spirit, sugar spoon	120-140
Cambridge, soup, teaspoon	120-140
Celeste, sugar, teaspoon	115-135
Etruscan, tablespoon	125-155

INTERNATIONAL
Blossom Time, dessert spoon ...	120-130
Charles II, teaspoon	125-140
Edgewood, sugar spoon	128-145
Moonbeam, teaspoon	130-145

REED AND BARTON
Century, iced tea spoon	135-145
Columbia, teaspoon..........	135-145
Majestic, tablespoon	142-152
Tapestry, teaspoon	130-145

TIFFANY
Wave Edge, serving spoon, gold bowl	150-160
Wave Edge, teaspoon	125-130

TOWLE
Contour, sugar spoon	130-140

Lady Diana, dessert, dinner spoon	120-130
Old Colonial, teaspoon	115-125

WALLACE
Dawn Star, teaspoon..........	130-140
Eton, soup spoon	138-142
Rose, ice cream spoon	120-130
Waverly, teaspoon	130-140

Hundreds of other makers and patterns. Find a reliable dealer if you're interested in collecting silver, especially sterling. Also, see SILVER, SOUVENIR SPOONS.

Sports
Photo Courtesy Hake's Americana & Collectibles

Sports Collectibles

The older the better — a few items bringing high prices today are listed below.

Blankets — cloth fabric inserts, found in early 1900 tobacco packages	$ 11-	20
Bowmans — cards issued by the Bowman Gum Co., 1948-1955 .	75¢	2
Caramels cards — trading cards inserted in candy products, 1900-1930	2-	4
Cereal cards — trading cards issued with breakfast food	1-	2
Club-issued postcards — players sent these to fans asking for an autograph	2-	3
Diamond Stars — baseball cards issued by the National Chicle Co., 1934-36	1-	2
Fatimas — Ligget & Myers Tobacco Co. issued these cards in the early 1900s	3-	5
Hot dog cards — issued by meat companies in their weiners	1-1.50	
Gum cards — issued with gum products; Leaf, Topps, Fleers, Gum, Inc	2-	4
Game programs (ill.) "Cubs, Chicago National League Ball Club"	5-	7

(continued)

Old photos (ill.) J.J. Corbett" ... 8- 12
Autographs actually signed by
the player (Autopens — signatures signed by a machine have
little or no value) 6- 9

Staffordshire Figurines

Staffordshire Figurines and Figures

Boy and girl under tree, 5½"
high .... $ 84- 92
Cinderella, marked, 4" high 34- 44
Dog, white lustre, seated, 14"
high 71- 82
Dog, miniature, glazed white,
3" high (ill.) 24- 34
Greyhound chasing rabbit, 11"
high 38- 48
Horse, rider, groom holding
bridle, 11" high, 1785 .... 66- 76
Lover in a bower, 15" high 53- 63
Man and lion, 8" high 72- 78
Old woman and pipe, 4½" high
1770 400-475
Red Riding Hood, wolf, etc.,
7½" high 82- 92
White cow, boy herder, 7" high .. 180-190

Staffordshire Items

Box, boy riding Newfoundland
dog, cover ....$ 40- 50
Cheese dish, blue/white,
Fenton, England 48- 53
Creamer and sugar, stag
pattern, blue, white 39- 49
Cup/saucer, light blue,
Challinor, handleless 36- 46
Hen dish, white bisque top,
colored head, basketweave
base 131- 139
Ice pail, ribbed, lion mask
handles, cylindrical, pair 400- 485
Inkwell, masks on side, claw
feet, cobalt bands 120- 135
Jug, brown/yellow, willow,
Pagoda, Porto Bello, 5" high 80- 90
Match holder, boots, striker, pr. 34- 42
Mug, Bacchus head, beard,
pointed ears, 1800 .... 138- 147

Needle case, enamel, blue/
green, red garlands 120- 135
Pitcher, apple green, 12" high . 52- 62
Plate, Avon cottage, blue, set
of 6, 10" dia 33- 43
Plate, Italian villa, purple, 10"
dia 33- 43
Platter, Lambton Hall, castle
scene, blue 88- 98
Quill holder, tree trunk, 2
white dogs 52- 62
Tea service, strawberry lustre,
1825, 24 pieces 1,100-1,350
Toby jug, black/green, lustre
trim, 10" high 170- 195
Urn, Nottingham stoneware,
1775, 6" high, pr 205- 220
Thousand of reproductions.

Stained Glass Windows

Louis Comfort Tiffany made some of the most beautiful! The more valuable come from Europe, but be on the lookout for old churches, old houses, even old railroad stations being torn down.

Church window, all glass perfect,
3' x 6' $600-700
Railroad station window,
Southern, 2½' x 6' 385-425
Window, green/blue, glass
prisms, beveled glass, 6' x 4' .. 475-525
Windows, each side front door,
Victorian house, late 1800s, pr. 450-525

Stamps

Stamps

There are more common stamps to be found than rare ones. Also, rarity doesn't necessarily mean you will sell it for a lot of money. If no one wants it, rarity is of little value market-wise. Consult a reliable dealer if you think you have a valuable stamp.

Stangl Pottery

J. Martin Stangl was superintendent of the technical division of the Fulper Pottery Company as early as 1911. In 1930, Stangl acquired the Fulper firm. After 1935 emphasis

Stangl Pottery

was shifted from artware to dinnerware, produced under the Stangl name. In late 1955 the corporate title was formally changed to the Stangl Pottery Company. The pottery was made as late as 1972, the year of Stangl's death. "MS" is sometimes found on certain pieces though not all were signed. The Stangl birds are the most collectible.

Bowl, white, flower shape, 8" dia.	$ 10-	15
Bluebird, signed	30-	40
Cardinal on stump	47-	55
Hummingbird, signed "STANGL POTTERY COMPANY" (ill.) .	48-	58
Oriole, signed as above	33-	43
Rooster, signed as above	57-	65

Stationery

Lots more fun than stealing hotel or motel towels or ashtrays. The early writing paper was quite ornate to go with the Spencerian handwriting. Don't throw away those old letterheads, envelopes, postcards. A dealer will always buy old stationery, postcards, etc.

Statuary, Ivory

Statuary, Ivory

Hong Kong ivory, seen more and more in shops today, is actually bone from a horse's leg. Don't be fooled. See IVORY.

Buddha (ill.)	$ 40-	48
Camel (ill.)	40-	45
Elephant (ill.)	66-	74
Man and woman in garden, 11½" high	990-1,150	

Statuary, Porcelain

Statuary, Porcelain

Bisque, porcelain, plaster-of-paris (see ROGERS STATUARY), Parian Ware, Majolica (European and American). See specific categories.

Nude, feeding fawn,
Hutchenreuther, Bavaria,
12" across (ill.) $390-420

Steins

Steins

The Westerwald area of Germany in the 17th century made the finest steins ever made. Mettlach also made fine steins as did Dresden at Meissen, Germany. Also, see METTLACH. Another repro item.

½ liter, green/buff, Liberal Arts Palace, St. Louis Exposition, 1904	$280-295
½ liter, flower motif, forest scene, pewter lid	310-340
½ liter, roses, castle scene, porcelain, pewter lid	295-310
1 liter, etched decor, porcelain lined, pewter lid	340-360
1 liter, musicians, barmaid, drinking scene, pewter lid	340-350
2 liter, blue and buff, pewter cap, 17" high	360-370
3 liter, brewery wagon and horse, advertising item, 1890s	180-195
Bardolph and Falstaff, #614, Germany, 9½" high, pewter cap (ill.) 1½ L	165-188

(continued)

Crystal deer, forest, hunters, 11½" high, pewter cap	270-290
Family crest, pewter lid, dated 1863, Germany	210-230
Geschut, No. 1102, ½ liter	235-265
Hunt scene, wild boars, pewter lid, 3 liter, 16" high	260-275
Lithopane bottom, nude, pewter top, 10" high, Germany, new	90-115
Musterschutz, Bismarck, multi-colored	355-375
Schultz and Dooley, Utica club beer, advertising item, 1900s	92-102
Stoneware, 3 liter, 16" high, pewter cap	160-180
Character steins — plain	150-180
Fraternal — glass or pottery	160-175
Hand-painted, glass	130-150
HR — Etched	180-335
Musterschutz characters	195-295
Occupational porcelains	150-170
Pewter — scene in relief (ill.)	185-195
Pottery — scene in relief	98-135
Etched and Art Glass	190-210
Plain crystal	120-155

Stereoscopes and Cards

Stereoscopes and Cards

These viewers came into use in the U.S. around 1850. They were invented in England a few years before. The picture is taken with a dual lens camera, then reproduced as 2 pictures. Seen through the viewer, the pictures blend into one 3-dimensional view. Every subject known to man was put on the cards.

Stereoscope and 12 cards	$ 95-130
Stereoscope and 300 cards	195-325
Stereoscope card, Philadelphia actress (ill.)	1.50- 2
Stereoscope, hand viewer, brass-mounted, 1896, 24 cards	130-150
Stereoscope, sliding adjuster, wooden, 36 cards	125-145
Stereoscope, sliding adjuster, 75 cards in box, Civil War Scenes	275-325
Stereoscope, table model, walnut stand, Saturnscope, 1892, 12 cards	170-190

Single cards, any subject, average $1.50 to $30.

Steuben Glass

Steuben Glass

Frederick Carder founded the firm in Corning, New York, in 1903. In the field of Decorative Arts few men contributed more. In 1918 the huge Corning Glass Works assumed control of the Steuben Glass Company. Mr. Carder stayed with Steuben until 1933, acting as art director. He continued working in his own laboratory until he closed it in 1953 at the age of 90. He passed away in 1963 at the age of 100. Few men of his genius will pass this way again.

ACID CUT-BACK

Rosaline and alabaster vase, 4½" high	$ 640-	670
Black and alabaster vase, 7" high	775-	820
Black and amethyst, 12" high	700-	800

AURENE

Bowl, blue, signed Aurene under glaze, 8" dia	385-	410
Candlesticks, twisted stem, gold, 10" high, pr	390-	420
Compote, gold, Aurene under glaze, 6" high	350-	380
Decanter with tray and 6 liquor glasses, signed	700-	800
Goblet, gold, red-gold interior, signed Steuben on bottom	195-	240
Gold Aurene and alabaster vase, 8½" high	1,350-1,450	
Perfume, blue, Aurene under-glaze, numbered, pr	250-	280
Salt, gold, Aurene underglaze, pedestal-type, 1½" high	160-	180
Vase, blue, ribbed, Aurene underglaze, 5½" high	240-	250
Vase, blue, acid cut, 12" high	725-	765
Vase, red (rare)	2,800+	
Vase, blue, iridescent, 9" high in silver holder	230-	250

CALCITE

Candlesticks, gold Aurene, pr .	260-	275
Compote, gold Aurene	240-	270
Sherbet with plate, blue Aurene (rare in some colors)	330-	360
Vase, footed, blue Aurene (rare in some colors)	540-	560

DIATRETA
Is not shown, as it is extremely rare and seldom found.

IVORY

Vase, 7″ high, paper label	238-	265
Vase, 6½″ high, paper label . . .	198-	245

IVRENE

Vase, 12″ high, lightly incised script Steuben signature . . .	800-	900
Vase, 5″ high, paper label	500-	600

JADE

Bowl, yellow, 3″ high Steuben signature	365-	385
Perfume, blue, 6″ high, script Steuben	340-	360
Candlesticks, blue jade and alabaster, 12″ high, pair	745-	785
Vase, blue, not signed	280-	295

ROSALINE

Bowl, finger, with plate, paper label	360-	400
Perfume, alabaster foot, stopper, paper label	300-	400
Sherbet with plate, paper label .	210-	240
Vase, alabaster disc foot, 7½″ high, no signature or label . .	128-	165

TOPAZ

Carbon yellow bowl, 11″ diameter, paper label	150-	195
Topaz yellow vase, 6½″ high, no label	140-	160

VERRE DE SOIE

Basket, paper label	195-	220
Bowl, rose, paper label	185-	240
Compote	260-	280
Perfume, cut flowers and leaves, sterling cap (ill.)	135-	150
Perfume, cut floral design, plunger type, brass fixtures, 4½″ high, pedestal base (ill.) .	140-	160
Vase, Jack-in-the-Pulpit, 6″ high, paper label	160-	190
Vase, bud, 6″ high, paper label .	180-	210

Stevengraphs

Thomas Stevens established his firm in 1854 at Coventry, England. He produced his first bookmarks in 1862, his first Stevengraph in 1874. He originated the name "Stevengraph"; his bookmarks should be called "Stevens Bookmarks." The bookmarks were originally sold pinned to a paper

Stevengraphs

backing bearing his name and trademark. Longer than wide, they are mitered at one end and finished with a tassel (see illustration). His Stevengraphs are miniature silk pictures and matted. His name was never woven into the Stevengraph. His name is woven into the bookmarks at a mitered corner.

BOOKMARKS:

Many Happy Returns of the Day	$ 88- 93
Birthday Blessings	72- 84
Centennial, George Washington .	150-160
Home Sweet Home	140-170
The Lady Godiva Procession . . .	150-160

STEVENGRAPHS:

Madonna and Child, Stg. 87	670-710
The Old Tyne Bridge, Stg. 144 . .	770-820
Clifton Suspension Bridge, Stg. 140	385-410
Iroquois, Stg. 162	520-600
The Lady Godiva Procession, Stg. 150	260-281
The Death of Nelson, Stg. 152 . . .	270-285
The Last Lap, Stg. 176	260-277
Triump (ill.) 1879	95-135

Stevens and Williams

Their factory has been at Brierley, Hill, Staffordshire, England, for years. Some of the world's finest glass has been made by this firm.

Basket, clear to green, floral, crystal motif, 6″ dia	$250-300
Bowl, swirls, camphor to cranberry, metal holder	375-450
Ewer, blue satin, enameled bird, coralene stem	250-325
Jam dishes, Rubina, pair set in footed silver holder	225-260
Rose bowl, cranberry threading, blue interior, footed	360-400
Tazza, Rosaline baluster stem, 9″ across	400-475
Vase, enameled iris, acid-cut green ground, cameo-type, 9″ high	425-475

(continued)

Vase, peach color, enameled
floral, blown 290-350
Vase, white satin, enamel floral,
rainbow lining, 9" high 370-410

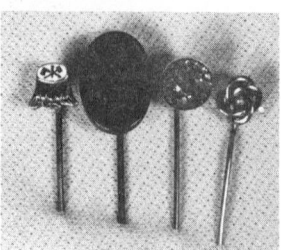

Stickpins

Stickpins

Today they're collectible because scarf pins
are back in style. Diamond Jim Brady wore
one that was $5,000 worth of diamonds. Most
of what you find in shops today are in the $6
to $10 range. One exception is the Tennessee
River pearl, worth about $50 to $500. See
TENNESSEE RIVER PEARLS. Of course,
if it's marked 14 karat or 18 karat, it's worth
much more. Generally, $6 to $10 for gold
filled, $20 to $25 for 14 karat, with authenticated diamonds, rubies, etc., much more.
"Get it in writing!" Also, see JEWELRY.

Indicative types: anthracite
diamond (ill.) . . . . $ 17- 22
Brass plated (ill.) 9- 12
Gold with seed pearl 17- 26
Silver plated (ill.) 9- 12

Stiegel-type Glass

Stiegel-type Glass

"Baron" Henry Stiegel made what is referred to as Stiegel glass at the American
Flint Glass Works, Manheim, Pennsylvania,
around 1765. Few authorities will positively
identify it.

Case bottled, etched designs, pr . $360-420
Flip glass, painted decorations . . 215-245
Ink bottles, clear, etched designs,
pewter cap 155-175

Glass, 2 etched birds in sunburst
(ill.) 135-160
Glass, 2 lovebirds and a heart
(ill.) 360-560
Glass, fluted sides (ill.) 130-155
Mug, strap handle, etched tulip,
6½" high (ill.) 160-178
Tumbler, floral designs 130-140
Wine, etched designs, 4½" high . 120-140

Stoneware

Stoneware

For centuries potteries worldwide have
made items to hold fluids, herbs, and the like.
Though usually crude earthenware, some
have been made of salt-glazed ware, basalt,
and other formulations.

Bottle, Pennsylvania, early 1800s $ 38- 48
Bowls, every size 52- 62
Canteen, round, to be carried over
arm in field, European (ill.) 82-122
Churn, lug handles, blue stencil,
"Hamilton & Jones," 19" high 80- 98
Crocks, every size, those
inscribed worth more 70-140
Jar, blue stencil "H & J, Greens-
boro, Pa.," 12¼" high 58- 70
Jug, sorghum, whiskey, syrup,
water 40- 50
Milk pitcher, 8" high, mid-1800s . 53- 63
Mug, impressed and blued band
top, blue band bottom, 5¼"
high 48- 64
Pudding mold, flower design
inside 40- 50
Stein, blue/gray, figures,
Germany 50- 60

Store Items

Spool cabinet, 2-drawer (ill.) $255-275
Adding machine, American,
1900s 33- 42
Can, Arbuckle Tea, painted tin . . 21- 29
Card, advertising Hood's Pills . . 5- 8
Cash register, hand-crank,
National, 1900 600-775

Cheese cutter, counter-type	75- 85
Chewing gum machine, coin- operated	265-280
Cigar box, dated 1885	6- 9
Cigar cutter	44- 54
Cigarette slot machine, penny . . .	215-226
Cracker box, square, tin, 7″	6- 9
Dispenser, wrapping paper	22- 27
High-button shoe sign, iron, hung over cobbler's shop	140-160
Ice tongs, store	63- 73
Lunch box, Union Leader tobacco, tin	8- 10
Machine for dispensing gum, 1¢ each with Fortune card, 1900s .	278-325
Sausage stuffer	40- 50
Spool cabinet, J. and P. Coats, 5 drawers, brass, knobs O.N.T.*	410-440

*O.N.T. Means "Our New Thread"

Stoves (Ranges)

When electricity arrived a lot of coal and wood stoves went out of style. And a lot of old stoves were melted down at the beginning of World War I. Those that have survived are being collected today. Bussey & McLeon made a lot, as did Elmwood. The ornate iron-work on some of the European stoves is ab-solutely beautiful!

"Stradivarious" Violins

No you do not own a Stradivarius! — Ac-cording to authorities, there are few unlisted violins made by this genius, Antonio Stradivari, Italian, 1644-1737. Fakes? Thousands! Over 2,000 in East Tennessee alone. Most fakes were made in the late 1800s. Some labeled, some not, all "guar-anteed." There are few genuine Strads for sale.

Good fakes, with or without labels, bring any-where from $125-$175.

Stretch Glass

An iridescent glass whose surface looks like onionskin. Unknowing collectors buy it for Steuben's Verre De Soie or Tiffany! Made in the 1930s by Imperial.

Ashtray, blue iridescence, Imperial	$ 32- 40
Bowl, reticulated 9¼″ dia., pedestal base, light green (ill.) .	38- 49
Bowl, 8½″ dia., light blue	39- 52

Stretch Glass

Candlesticks, pair, amethyst, 9½″ high	46- 56
Compote, 7½″ dia., pedestal type, blue	40- 50
Plate, 9″ dia., white	27- 37
Vase, peacock blue, 8¼″ high . . .	36- 46

Being reproduced.

String Holders

String Holders

The hanging type and the beehive type were the most common. Used in grocery stores and homes, 1800s to 1900s. Near-perfect reproductions on the market today.

Counter type, pyramid cone	$ 25- 30
Glass beehive (scarce)	150-165
Iron beehive (ill.)	38- 48
Iron, hanging-type, 4½″ high . . .	36- 46
Pottery, many shapes, cone- shaped	26- 36
Sandwich Glass, overlay, red/ white	92-102

Sugar Shakers

Sugar Shakers

Pressed, blown, in every kind of glass, from the cheapest pressed glass to the most expensive blown glass. Used for sprinkling sugar on toast, cookies, they've been around for years. See specific types of glass for specific prices. Being reproduced in every size and shape.

Challinor's "Forget-Me-Not,"
4½" high (ill.) . . . . $ 68- 78

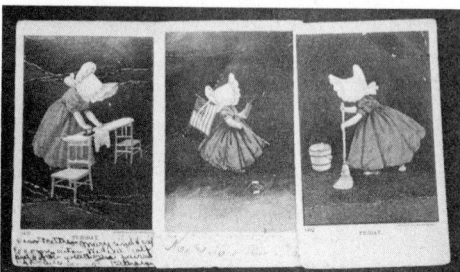

Sunbonnet Baby Collectibles

Sunbonnet Baby Collectibles

These cute figures were originated by Bertha Corbett in the early 1900s. Cards, prints, and porcelain were decorated with the Sunbonnet figures. Royal Bayreuth China Company made many items in children's dishes.

Card, Tuesday (ill.)	$ 13- 21
Card, Fourth of July (ill.)	13- 21
Card, Friday, (ill.)	13- 21
Card, Saturday, Ullman's	13- 21
Creamer, babies cleaning house, Royal Bayreuth	158-175
Mug, babies sweeping floor, Royal Bayreuth	112-130
Nappy, "Washing," 5" dia.	180-220
Pitcher, 5" high, babies eating supper, Royal Bayreuth	155-165
Picture, babies sewing, framed . .	80- 90
Picture, babies gardening, framed	82- 92
Plate, "Ironing," signed "R.B.", 7 5/8" dia.	145-165
Platter, signed KT & K, 7¼" . . .	72- 82
Postcard, set of 7, doing something different on each	60- 70
Sugar bowl, babies setting table, Royal Bayreuth	155-165
Tea tile, babies serving guests, Royal Bayreuth	140-150
Tray, "Washing," 7¼" x 10", signed "R.B."	210-265
Vase, babies playing in yard, Royal Bayreuth	150-160
Vase, "Mending," 6¼" high	270-315

Sunderland Lustre

Sunderland Lustre

Marbled or spotted decorations shading from pink to purple describes this fine ware. Gold compound applied over a white body created many shades of pink lustering. Many potteries made it, the better known firms being Wedgwood, Enoch Wood, and Adams.

Bowl, "Sailor's Departure," 10" dia.	$375-460
Box, black transfer, Old English scene, unattached lid	115-130
Button jar, purple lustre, pincushion on lid, 1820s	128-138
Cake plate, cottage scene	150-170
Creamer, raised floral figures . . .	120-130
Cup/saucer, circa 1880	95-110
Jug, coat-of-arms, scenic, 6" high	240-260
Mug, bridge over river, late 1700s	140-170
Pitcher, ship scene, ocean, 5½" high	245-275
Plaque, "Prepare to Meet Thy God," 9" x 8"	140-160
Plaque, "For man dieth," 6½" x 8" (ill.)	130-140
Shaving mug, soldiers in barracks, late 1800s	140-150
Salt shaker, 4" high	88- 98
Teapot, black/pink, 6¼" high . . .	220-265

Sundials

By the position of the shadow of a pointer (gnomon), cast by the sun on the face of a dial marked in hours, one could tell the time of day. Pocket-size sundials were also used in the late 1700s and early 1800s. Full-sized sundials were popular in gardens in the 1920s. Look for one at an old home being torn down. The early ones are collectible today.

Brass, unmarked	$150-170
Pewter, unmarked	155-180
Pocket, ivory, 18th century	160-175
Pocket, silver dial, silver engraved case	120-130

Swansea Porcelain

This pottery/porcelain was made at Swansea, Glamorganshire, Wales, about 1764, until the late 1800s. The wicker-bordered Swansea plates — birds, flowers, landscapes — are especially collectible today. The most reliable mark is an impressed SWANSEA, with or without crossed tridents. Know your dealer, please!

Cup and saucer, Willow pattern .	$ 70- 88
Plate, wicker bordered, 8″	115-135
Platter, Willow pattern, 22″	138-170
Saucer, Willow pattern, 3½″	80- 90

Syrup Jugs

Some were blown, others pressed; some had pewter lids, others were of base metal. They were popular in the mid-1800s until just before World War I.

Taffeta

See CARNIVAL GLASS

Tape Measures

Look for these in Grandma's sewing box, old sewing machine drawers. When you're cleaning out that attic or basement, don't ever throw away a box without looking through it carefully. Tape measures were made of tin, ivory, bone, wood. The older types were silk with hand-lettered numbers.

Bone, thimble-shaped, 24″, late 1800s	$ 12- 18
Ivory, in shape of ship, late 1800s	22- 32
Porcelain, hand-painted, Germany, late 1800s	14- 23
Wood, 18″, primitive, mid-1800s .	10- 15

Tapestries

There are tapestries and there are "tapestries." Some hanging in the Louvre, the ancient royal palace now converted into a museum in Paris, France, are worth a king's ransom. Most of what you find in shops today are late 18th or mid-19th century. A great many dealers are stripping "tapestry" drapes; that is, removing lining and selling them as genuine tapestries. Watch out! Expensive!

Court of Louis XIV, France . . . $	270- 295
Court scene, French, 4′ x 6′ . . .	238- 260
English court, pastoral scene, 3′ x 3½′	185- 250

Tapestries

Castle scene, pond, fish, birds, French, 80″ x 90″	1,400-1,600
Deer and birds, scarlet on ivory, c. 1910 (ill.)	45- 55
Troubadour serenading ladies .	68- 80
Ladies on horseback, gentlemen companions, French, 3′ x 6′	225- 255
Shepherd, shepherdess, sheep, original, France, 70″ x 95″ . .	2,700-3,100+

Taxidermy

Taxidermy

Stuffed animals, birds, some good, some bad, are collectible today. The pileated woodpecker, illustrated here, is a fair example. Any, in good condition, make nice items to decorate a den.

Average price, birds, animals, in good condition	$ 60- 70

Tea Leaf Lustre

This inexpensive type of lustre was produced both in England and America, using gold lustre decorations on late Ironstone china. Sometimes called "Lustre Band with Sprig."

Bone dish	$ 20- 30
Bowls, vegetable, 16″ dia	52- 62
Butter dish, covered	58- 68
Butter pat, Wedgwood	8- 11
Cake plate, Meakin	44- 54
Coffeepot, Wedgwood, 9″ high . .	75- 93

(continued)

Tea Leaf Lustre

Creamer	38- 48
Cup/saucers, coffee, handleless	33- 43
Pitchers, milk, water	56- 66
Plates, 8″, 9″, 9″ soup, 10″	22- 32
Platters, 12″, 13″, 14″, 16″, 16½″ long	44- 56
Sauce	42- 52
Soap dish, removable insert	48- 58
Sugar bowl	56- 66
Teapot, small	52- 62
Tea service, pot, creamer, sugar, 6 cups, 6 plates, all	275-300
Tureen, soup, Wedgwood	185-220
Washbowl and pitcher, Meakin, Royal	180-195

Tea Sets

Tea Sets

Usually a teapot, creamer, sugar and 6 cups/saucers; sometimes with a tray to match. Made by the earliest pottery factories in Europe; price is dependent on maker, date, and condition of set; how many pieces. See specific types and prices elsewhere in this Guide.

Flowers on cream ground, Limoges, France, teapot, covered sugar, creamer, 6 cups, 6 luncheon plates (ill.)	$250-275
Grasshopper with bamboo handles pattern, English, mid-1800s	240-260

Telephone

Telephones

The first one was patented in 1876 b**y** Alexander Graham Bell. The wood case wa**ll** type is the most common. European type**s,** Dutch, and French, are more expensive. Goo**d** reproductions are on the market today.

Desk-type, dial, American, 1930s	$ 45- 50
Dutch, cradle-type, ivory mouthpiece	130-140
French, cradle-type, lacquered box	144-150
German, cradle-type, 8″ high, marked "Kjabhavend Telefon-Aktieselskab" (ill.)	150-160
Wall-type, American, oak box, crank, mouthpiece	180-190

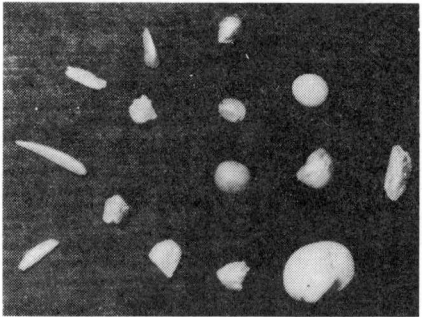

Tennessee River Pearls

Tennessee River Pearls

This is a member of the mussel family. I**n** the late 1800s they were found in mussels "farmed" from the rivers. The shell of th**e** mussel was used for "pearl" buttons. O**n** occasion an odd-shaped pearl was found**.** Worthless then, today they bring high prices**.** Some bring upwards of $500! Found primari**-** ly in Southern shops.

Teplitz

This porcelain was mass-produced in th**e** late 1800s in Germany, usually in vase form**.**

Originally priced in shops from 25¢ to $3; prices have soared.

Basket, floral decor, twisted handle, 6½" high	$110-125
Bowl, 5-legged pedestal, black/ green mottling	80- 90
Ewer, cream background, gilded Art Nouveau lizard handle, gold sunrise, bird, raised gold feathers (ill.)	95-120
Jardiniere, 4-handled, cream/ maroon banding	165-185
Mug, Indian chief, blue background, 4½" high	60- 72
Vases, all types and colors, typical price	88- 98
Wall plaque	235-265

Teplitz   **Theater**

Theater

Old programs, autographs, photos, costumes, just about anything to do with the theater of old is collectible today. Strollers Cigarettes card with such stars as Ruth Roland, Alice Terry — most collectible. The illustrated cover of THE PLAYBILL shows the cast of "On the Town," September, 1945. The cutie in the lower right-hand corner is Nancy Walker, star of "Blansky's Beauties," amongst others.

What you'll pay for a particular item depends on quality, age, and demand.

Thermometers

These instruments for measuring temperature consist of three principal types: (1) **Fahrenheit,** in which the freezing point of water is 32 degrees and the boiling point 212 degrees. (2) **Centigrade,** in which the freezing point is 0 degrees and the boiling point 100 degrees. (3) **Reaumur,** in which the freezing point is 0 degrees and the boiling point 80 degres. Now you know! The earlier types are being collected and bring brisk prices.

Thimbles

Thimbles

The Greeks, the Egyptians, from the earliest times, used this sewing tool. Tailor's thimbles, open thimbles, some say the word is derived from "thumbpbell." Whatever, these tiny objects are collectible and come in every material from stone to gold to glass to porcelain to aluminum to plastic. What you'll pay for a specific type depends on the material, scarcity, demand.

Threaded Glass

Threaded Glass

Supposedly made at Sandwich, the glass threading around the object was put on by hand, later by machine. Attributed to Nicholus Lutz, probably more than one person made it to keep up with the demand in the mid-1800s. All colors were used, including cranberry. Another repro item.

Atomizer, red/blue	$ 58- 68
Basket	92-120
Biscuit jar, cranberry/clear	125-160
Bowl, 5" high, applied white feet	150-170
Decanter, blue on clear, 11½" high	74- 84
Jam jar, silver-plated lid and bail	98-120
Pitcher, 12" high, cranberry, floral decor, clear handle (ill.)	160-180
Tumbler, cranberry	85- 95
Vase, cranberry, green shading	95-140

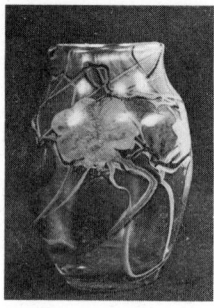

Tiffany Glass

Tiffany Glass

Louis Comfort Tiffany was an artist, an interior decorator, and a genius at making glass. His stained glass windows were beautiful creations and are today world-famous. He usually marked his glass L.C.T., sometimes with the word Favrile and a number. Metal lamps bases were stamped with the firm's name. He also marked certain pieces L. C. Tiffany. Unfortunately, he marked a great many pieces with paper labels only. If you're seriously interested in collecting genuine Tiffany, know the source and know your dealer. Keep in mind that some people buy "to hedge inflation." The piece may not be worth it but they're paying it. Grossly *overrated!*

Table lamp, Daffodil pattern, 20" dia., fully signed	$23,000-25,000
Table lamp, Arrowroot pattern, 20" dia., fully signed	16,500-17,800
Floor lamp, Dragonfly pattern, 22" dia, fully signed	26,000-32,000
Floor lamp, 12-light "Lily" pattern, fully signed	18,500-23,000
Floor lamp, green Turtleback design, 22" dia., fully signed	12,300-12,700
Chalices, gold iridescent, pink highlights, 5½" high, signed "L.C.T. Favrile" (ill.) each	260- 280
Vase, green stemmed, signed "L.C.T."	700- 800
Master salt, gold, signed	260- 275
Sherbet, blue, opalescent, "L.C.T."	295- 325
Tumbler, gold, "twist" pattern signed	430- 465
Bowl, finger, and underplate, gold iridescent, signed "L.C.T.," plate, 6¼" dia.	288- 345

Vase, gold, blue/green decoration, 8½" high, paper label	950- 1,100
Vase, blue, iridescent, signed, 7¼" high	900- 1,200
Vase, green iridescent, "threaded" pattern, 7" high, signed	1,350- 1,600
Vase, green, alabaster base, fluted lip, 6¼" high	1,450- 1,700
Basket, flowers on handle, sterling silver, 5" dia. LCT	450- 600
Bowl, gold, Favrile glass, 6" dia., LCT	1,100- 1,700
Bowl, ribbed, blue, ruffled edge, signed LCT Favrile	1,000- 1,400
Champagne, gold, 7" high, hollow stem, signed	475- 700
Compote, pedestaled, gold, 8" high, signed LCT Favrile	975- 1,300
Inkwell, beige mottled panels, signed Tiffany Studios	575- 725
Lamp, table, Favrile and bronze, Peony Wisteria shade	64,000+(!)
Pitcher, etched grapes, blue, 5½" high, signed LCT, etc	1,500- 1,700
Pitcher, blue, 3" high, signed LCT	2,000- 2,300
Plate, gold, 8" dia., signed	375- 500
Plate, pastel blue and yellow, signed LCT Favrile and number	650- 700
Toothpick, gold, Favrile, signed	375- 450
Vase, amber, peacock feathers, 13" high, signed	1,600- 1,800
Vase, flower form, signed	2,600- 2,900
Vase, dark green, gold and blue feathering, signed	1,400- 1,500
Vase, paperweight base, floral/cream/orange/green, signed "L.C. Tiffany Favrile 375 T," original paper label (ill.)	4,850- 5,650+
Vase, trumpet, gold irides-cent, 19", signed, in metal holder	395- 525

Tiffin Glass

One of the prettiest wares made by the Tiffin Glass Company, Tiffin, Ohio, was their Black Satin glass. It was also made by the U.S. Glass Company, Pittsburgh, late 1800s. All prices listed are for Black Satin.

Basket, 10" high	$ 54- 66
Bottle, perfume, brass plunger	33- 42
Bowl, 4" high, 7" dia. at top	34- 44

Tiffin Glass

Compote, crystal stem, 7" high . .	38- 47
Tumbler	12- 19
Urn, 5½" high	42- 48
Vase, 6½" high, gold decoration	
around top	49- 60
Vase, 7" high, flower decor in	
gold trim	49- 62
Wine set, 6 wines and decanter,	
all	88- 97

Tiles

Tiles

Decorative tiles have been used for floors, benches, fireplaces, for centuries; table tiles for the same length of time. Made in every country in the world.

Blue/gold, flower decor, Austria .	$ 12- 19
Delft, sailing scene, in frame	19- 28
Fireplace type, floral decor,	
6" x 6"	16- 24
Mercer tile, Moravian Pottery	
& Tile Works, Doylestown,	
Pennsylvania, octagonal,	
brown glaze (ill.)	18- 22
Mercer tile, octagonal, "Rain,"	
terra-cotta, 6½" high (ill.)	44- 54
Mercer tile, octagonal, blue	
glaze, cutout grape design (ill.) .	18- 22
Rookwood, blue/green, dated	
XVII	62- 70
Roseville, flowers, multicolored . .	29- 36
Spanish dancers (ill.)	11- 15

Tinsel Pictures

Colored tinsel was used by children and housewives to make decorative plaques, usually depicting birds, flowers, Bible scenes.

It's a form of primitive art, popular from early 1800s until late 1800s.

Average price, in wood frame . . . $ 50- 60

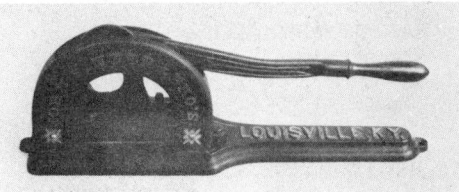

Tobacco Cutters

Tobacco Cutters

Before the advent of cigarettes, plug tobacco and snuff were the thing along with foul-smelling cigars. Plug tobacco came in bars and had to be cut. The cutter was used for this purpose.

Black Beauty	$ 40- 48
Brown Mule, iron	38- 48
Climax Plug	33- 43
Imp Thumbing Nose, iron	69- 79
John Finzer & Bro's., Louisville,	
Ky., iron, gilded letters (ill.) . . .	38- 48
Ordinary types, iron	30- 40
R.J.R.T. Company (R. J.	
Reynolds Tobacco Company),	
iron	42- 52

Tobacco Jars, Containers

Tobacco Jars, Containers

Usually made of porcelain, wood, or metal with a lid, they were used as humidors for cigars or pipe tobacco. In vogue in the mid-1800s.

Bulldog, Bristol glass	$ 72- 82
Black boy, straw hat	98-110
Dutch scene, glazed pottery, pipe	
finial on lid (ill.)	70- 85
Elephant toe, ivory handle on	
lid, 10" high (ill.)	60- 80
Kitten holding friends, porcelain .	97-115
Pig with broom	105-110
Indian Chief, Majolica	110-150
Pirate, Staffordshire	120-160

331

(continued)

Human skull, white, black bones .	93-104
Lion's head, 7" high	54- 63
Monkey's head, Majolica	92-103
Owl, Majolica, 7½" high	58- 68
Rookwood, brown, tan, 1909	150-170
Royal Bayreuth, tapestry ware, pasture scene	120-140
Sea captain, Majolica, pipe in mouth	130-150
Mayo's "Roly Poly," litho-on-tin, fat man w/pipe	270-290

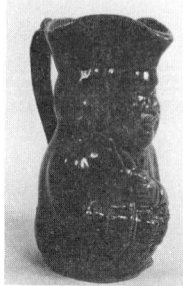

Toby Jugs

Toby Jugs

Supposedly taken from Sterne's *Tristam Shandy,* Uncle Toby was a popular shape for ale mugs in the early 1800s. The better ones came from England, in every color. Hundreds of fakes on the market, especially from Japan.

Cat, 9" high	$142-143
Creamer, Delft type, blue/white .	180-220
Creamer, Rockingham type glaze, man with tricornered hat, 6" high (ill.)	120-145
Jug, Staffordshire, 1850s, old gentleman holding jug	390-425
Jug, Staffordshire, 1850s, squat, embossed figure	420-460
Jug, Napoleon, 10" high	250-285
Jug, Ralph Wood, seated man with tricorn hat	395-440
Jug, identical to above, except marked "Japan"	59- 68
Jug, George Washington head, American-made (New Jersey), probably Trenton	520-540
Jug, Santa Claus, 8" high	90-110
Jug, Toby Philpot, Pratt ware, 11" high	720-780

Tokens, Hotel and Others

Hotel, streetcar, political, commemoratives — all these tokens are collectible today. Prices range from 50¢ to $3 depending on rarity and availability.

Toleware (Tin)

Toleware (Tin)

This is a misnomer as "tole" originally meant items made of sheet iron and then decorated. Popular use has caused "tole" to be known as decorated tin items, especially those coming from the Pennsylvania Dutch country in the mid-1800s. Scarce today because so much was thrown away when it became dented. Being reproduced.

Document box, handled black, gold floral stenciling, red/ yellow striping, 3" x 3¼" (ill.) .	$ 90-120
Document box, handled, stenciled	248-270
Tea canister, red/green, 6" high . .	120-130
Coffeepot, blue/yellow, flowers .	210-270
Syrup pitcher, green/black, red flowers, 5½" high	150-180
Muffineer, fruit/flowers, 4¼" high	125-145
Jug, typical colors, 5" high	420-475
Food warmer, stenciled flowers . .	140-160
Pitcher, red/yellow, hinged lid, 7" high	165-195
Candle box with loop for hanging	185-225
Coffeepot, black, orange, red, green decor, 12" high	240-270
Creamer, 6" high, initialed M.B. .	200-240
Deed box, original stenciling, black, green, red decor	280-330
Lantern, processional type, cross on staff, original stenciling . . .	200-250
Tray, black, gold stenciled flowers, leaves and borders, red/green/yellow (ill.)	80- 95
Tray, red, pink, white flowers, original paint	260-280

Toothpick Holders

In the 1800s it was considered polite to pick one's teeth after eating. The holders were made of every type of material, usually glass or a pot metal, silver-plated, with the toothpicks being made from wood slivers or shaved quills from birds' feathers. Wealthy

Toothpick Holders

Tortoiseshell Glass

gentlemen carried gold toothpicks, usually attached to their watch chains.

Baby's bootie, clear glass	$ 19- 31
Boot, star on heel, blue glass	24- 34
Butterfly, glass	25- 33
Canoe, green glass	22- 32
Carnival Glass, marigold, kittens	48- 58
Chick-in-egg	57- 67
Chicks eating grain, wicker basket pattern, clear glass	46- 56
Chicken on wishbone, quadruple plate No. 346	22- 32
Dog with hat, light blue glass	31- 41
Glass, flint (ill.)	12- 17
Glass, Diamond Fau, 2″ high (ill.)	10- 14
Horse and cart, clear glass	31- 41
Lizard holding container on back, clear glass	44- 52
Monkey on log, blue	27- 37
Ribbed, opal glass	30- 40
Saddle on barrel, frosted base, glass	40- 48
Seashell, amber glass	27- 38
Souvenir-type, red/clear, 1910, glass	16- 24
Uncle Sam's hat, painted milk glass	53- 63

Tortoiseshell

In the Orient this unusual shell is made into boxes, hair combs, dresser sets, jewelry. Popular in the mid-1800s, it went out of style around World War I. See COMBS.

Tortoiseshell Glass

A German chemist developed this glassware in imitation of tortoiseshell. The process involved blowing several bulbs of different shades of brown glass. These were broken into fragments, etc., then rolled among fragments of brown glass. It's a scarce glass and was made by the Sandwich Glass Company and a few firms in Germany.

Basket, gold enamel rim	$175-185
Bowl, 8″ dia.	60- 70
Box, jewelry, three-tiered	190-220
Finger bowl, ruffled, metallic flecks throughout, 6″ dia., Sandwich (ill.)	95-110
Rose bowl, enameled flowers	72- 82
Vase, silver rim, 9″ high	60- 70

Touraine Pattern China

The Alcock family made this semivitreous paste porcelain in England in the mid-1800s, using dark blue decorations and a faint gold band around the border.

Butter dish, covered	$ 24- 34
Cheese dish, covered	37- 44
Creamer	26- 37
Cup/saucer	28- 38
Pitcher, milk	38- 47
Plates, 6½″, 8¼″, 10″, 11½″ dia.	26- 39
Platter, 12″ long	38- 47
Teapot, 6 cups/saucers	150-170

Toys

Carved from wood, stone, cast from iron, machine-pressed, soldered, the very old, and the not-so-old — all highly collectible today. (See BANKS — MECHANICAL and STILL.)

Airplane, by Marx, tin mechanical windup, 1940s	$ 28- 40
Amos 'n' Andy Fresh Air Taxicab, tin mechanical windup, 1930s	310- 390
Amos 'n' Andy radio script, "Amos' Wedding," 1935	92- 110
Amos walking toy, tin mechanical windup, 1930s	110- 140
Andy walking toy, tin mechanical windup, 1930s	120- 140

(continued)

**Tin Mechanical Windup
(Balky Mule)**

Animated Cow, 1920s.
  Moving the tail made
  it "moo." 38- 48
Are-E-Go-Round, tin
  mechanical windup,
  Reeves, Milford, Con-
  necticut, early 1900s,
  patent applied for 178- 240
Baby Carriage, GoCart
  Sleeper, sateen parasol,
  wire wheels, 1900s 118- 132
Baby carriage, tin, cloth
  top 2½' long, 1920s . . .   65- 80
Baby Grand piano,
  Schoenhut, tin, 1900s .   230- 260
Balky Mule, tin mechan-
  ical windup, 1920s, by
  Lehmann, (ill.) 62- 78
Bear-on-a-ball, composi-
  tion, mechanical wind-
  up, 1940s 42- 52
Bellringers, cast iron and
  brass, 7" long, 1892 . . .   92- 102
Blocks, lithograph-on-
  cardboard, alphabet,
  mid 1800s . . . .   55- 70 set
Boat, tin, steam-operated,
  1900 . . . .   525- 625
Brake, four seat, iron,
  Pratt & Litchford, Con-
  necticut 28" long, 1906,
  iron . . . .   7,500-8,400 (and,
                                              climbing!)
Buckboard, cast iron,
  Wilkens, 1895, 14" long   220- 260
Bus, cast iron, Arcade
  Mfg. Co., 1920s 165- 190
Buster-Brown-in-Cart,
  7½" long, 1900s 165- 185
"Busy-Bee" see-saw, tin
  mechanical, sand oper-
  ated, litho, 1920s 50- 60
Cab, No. 662, iron,
  Hubley, late 1800s, 9¾"
  long 128- 143
Calliope, cast iron,
  Hubley, 1920s, 16" long   195- 240
Cannon, wooden, 1900s . .   34- 44

Cannon, "Big Bang" type,
  3" barrel, 1930s, carbide
  type 44- 56
Car, VW, cast iron, 1950s.   28- 39
Carousel, tin mechanical
  windup, bisque-headed
  dolls, 1880s   2,100-2,450
Casey Jones rider-type,
  metal, late 1930s 178- 192
Cash register, tin, "Benja-
  min Franklin," by
  Kamkap, 1930s 60- 70
Cat-with-ball, tin mechani-
  cal windup, U.S. Zone,
  Germany, 1940s 19- 36
Chalkware "hearth" cat,
  early 1900s 53- 62
Charlie Chaplin "squeeze"
  toy, Germany, 1920s . .   225- 295
Chicken-in-a-Basket, tin
  mechanical windup,
  5½" high, 1920s 60- 80
Chimes, wooden
  "Trinity," lithograph on
  wood, 8 buttons, late
  1800s 110- 130
Clown-and-Monkey, cellu-
  loid/tin mechanical
  windup, 1930s 56- 70
"Columbia" tin pull toy
  steamboat, late 1800s. .   320- 380
Crapshooter, by Cragston,
  tin windup, 1930s 48- 59
Dog-and-cat-fight, bell
  toy, cast iron, 1890s,
  9" long 140- 152
Double-decker, friction
  toy, 1930, 13" long 110- 125
Drum, lithograph-
  decorated, w/sticks,
  early 1900s 44- 49
Figure-on-horse, wooden,
  clockwork mechanism,
  1900s 88- 98
Galloping horse and
  buggy, tin mechanical
  clockwork, 1882, 18"
  long 250- 300
Girl-with-doll-on-sled bell
  toy, cast iron, Daisy,
  1893, 9" long 110- 120
Greyhound bus, cast iron,
  1930s, 9" long 60- 80
Gyroscope, pot metal,
  complete with instruc-
  tions, 1930s 32- 46
Hanson, No. 661, iron,
  Hubley, late 1800s, 9¼"
  long 128- 138
Harmonica, "Original
  Emmet Richter,"
  tin/wood, 1920s 22- 40

**Soldier, Speedboy,
San Francisco Streetcar**

Horse-in-hoop, Merriam
Mfg. Co., Durham, Con-
necticut, 1870s 320- 345
Horse, wooden, pull toy,
1900s 260- 275
Hose Reel, cast iron,
Hubley, 20″ long, 1900s 390- 410
Ice skates, wood/iron,
hand-forged, 1880s 55- 62
Irish Mail velocipede,
1910 .... 525- 650
Jumbo-on-wheels,
stuffed, 1882, 9″ long .. 320- 370
Kid Sampson, tin
mechanical windup,
"B & R" trademark,
1921 .... 220- 260
"Little Daisy" sweeper,
made by Bissell for give-
aways, 28½″ long,
1920s 54- 67
Magic Lantern Kit, com-
plete — tickets, brass
lantern, 12 slides, in
original box, late 1800s . 138- 160
Mansion of Happiness
game, Parker Bros.,
1885 .... 50- 62
Matchbox fighter planes,
6 in set, 1940s .... 4- 7 each
Mercedes, tin mechanical
windup, early 1900s 375- 450
Merry-go-round, clock-
work toy, Althof Berg-
man, New York, late
1800s 650- 750
Merry-go-round ring, cast
iron, 1890s .... 19- 24 each
Monkey, tin mechanical
windup, mohair coat,
Japan, 1920s 38- 50
Monkey Cage, revolving,
iron, Hubley, 21½″ long 220- 265
Moody's New Racer, by
Moody & Co., Chicago,
1870, child-size veloci-
pede 480- 525

Moon Mullins (and Kayo)
"Railroad Handcar,"
by Marx, deluxe model . 510- 650
Moon Mullins (and Kayo)
"Railroad Handcar,"
by Marx, regular model 280- 335
Motorboat, tin mechanical
windup, 1920s 62- 72
Motorcycle, cast iron, 6″
long, 1920s 45- 65
Naughty Boy, tin
mechanical windup by
Lehmann, 1910 ...... 280- 295
Noah's Ark animals, hand-
carved, 2″ to 3″ high,
late 1800s .... 14- 19 each
Noah's Ark, wooden pull
toy, lithographed paper
on wood, early 1900s .. 82- 92
"Oh Boy" bus, No. 105,
1920s 68- 78
Overland Circus, animals
in cage, iron, 1920 ..... 220- 250
Pail, wood handle, litho-
graph-on-tin, 1920s 15- 20
Phaeton, cast iron, 1901,
11″ long, pony type ... 170- 190
Piano, upright,
Schoenhut, wood,
w/stool, 1900s 230- 260
Plate, "Alphabet,"
ceramic, 2½″ dia.,
Germany, late 1800s .. 64- 80
Plate, "Buster Brown,"
ceramic, 2½″ dia., Ger-
many, 1900s 34- 45
Popeye and the Parrot
Cages, Marx, tin
mechanical windup,
1930s 125- 150
Projector, hand-operated,
concave mirror at rear,
6″ high, 1920s 82- 92
Roller skates, hard rubber
wheels, child's, 1950s .. 19- 27
San Francisco Streetcar
No. 41, tin, 1900s 240- 275
Sewing Machine, child's
size, early 1900s 45- 62
Singing bird, tin mechan-
ical windup, 4″ high,
Germany, 1950s 42- 52
Sled, wood/metal, child's,
handpainted, 1920s,
33″ long 54- 64
Soldier, tin mechanical
windup, 1910 .... 130- 160
Speedboy 4, tin mechan-
ical windup, 1920s 72- 85
Steam engine, horizontal,
heated electrically, by
Weeden, early 1900s... 260- 285

(continued)

Steamroller, tin, Buddy L, "rider" type, 1930s, 12½" high 85- 110

Stereoptican (stereoscope), Buckeye Stereoptican Co., Cleveland, 1900s 84- 94

Streetcar, tin, friction, doors open and close c. 1920s (ill.) 150- 200

Stove, Hubley, No. 893S, 4¾" high, cast iron, 1900s 74- 92

Sulky, cast iron, Hubley-type pull toy, 8½" long, early 1900s 200- 245

Superman Fighting Airplane, tin mechanical windup, litho, Marx, 1940 . . . . 235- 265

Tally-Ho, iron, 1893, 18" long 480- 560

Taxi, cast iron, by Arcade, painted, 5" long, 1928 170- 190

Teddy Bear, miniature, by Steiff, 1920s, 2½" high 62- 82

Temple toy, India, brass mid-19th century, Bankura bronze 140- 160

Tin Lizzie, 1920s, friction type 120- 140

Toonerville Trolley, tin mechanical windup, made by Nifty, 1922, 6¾" high 450- 550

Toy solider, friction type, 1920s (ill.) 52- 62

"Traffic B" squad car, tin mechanical windup, Marx, 1930s 120- 140

"Train," cardboard puzzle, Milton-Bradley, early 1900s 43- 53

Train, lithograph-on-wood, 3-piece, 1850s 200- 240

Train, miniature, tin, lithographed, 6½" long, 4-piece, late 1800s 260- 280

Train, tin, lithographed, mid-1800s, 7" long 210- 240

Truck, metal Buddy "L", 1920s 150- 175

Truck, tin, Metalcraft Corp., St. Louis, 1930 140- 160

Tricycle, "Tom Thumb," metal, wooden hubs, spokes, 1910 . . . . 220- 270

Tut Tut, tin mechanical windup by Lehmann, 1904 . . . . 285- 350

Walking-on-Hands-Clown, by Chien, 1920s 50- 62

Waterloo game, Parker Bros., 1895 . . . . 39- 48

"Wells Fargo" stagecoach, Tootsietoy, 1920s 35- 60

Wheelbarrow, tin, 29" long, 1920s 49- 60

Wheelbarrow, wooden, 1920s, 18" long 12- 19

Tramp Art

Tramp Art

Supposedly, the tramps (hoboes), durin, the depression years carved boxes, birdcage: chests, etc., to "pass the time." The art wa known before the 1930s and is still bein, practiced.

Birdcage, green trim $250-275
Box, porcelain knobs, hinged lid . 90-120
Magazine rack, wall-type, 24" high 110-125
Rack, wall type, inlaid wood designs, 11" high (ill.) 75- 95

Travel Folders

Years ago it was considered fashionable to travel to Niagara Falls, Devil's Kitchen (in the Catskill Mts.) and health spas such a Saratoga Springs, N.Y., and Warm Springs W. Va., where the service was high and the rates low. Folders describing these places are becoming collectible.

Average price . . . . 50¢- $1.00

Trays

Those that advertise a soft drink or "harder" beverage are highly collectible (se Coca-Cola Items) today. Age and conditio dictate the price. They're reproducing Col trays; the illustrated tray is a repro, so watc yourself!

Trays

"Falstaff," new (ill.) .... $ 42- 52
Rockwell's "Butter Girl" 43- 50
Rockwell's "Christmas" 62- 72

Trevais Glass

Trevais Glass

In 1907 the Boston and Sandwich Glass Factory was reopened by the Alton Manufacturing Company. One of the items they made was Trevais ware, a glass to compete with Tiffany. It was quite good but the life of the company was short-lived. This glass is occasionally found on Cape Cod and is expensive when found. Mentioned only because it was associated with one of the world's great glass manufacturers.

Vase, gourd shape, green with
silver pearlized effect, orange
liner, silver floral and leaf
overlay, 9″ high (ill.) $1,100-1,300
Most pieces are in the $1,000 to $1,600 range.

Trivets

Old wrought-iron types of the 1830s were equipped with tall legs for use over a fire or

Trivets

with a ring to hold a pot. A 3-legged trivet was called a spider; 6-legged, a cat. Those with short legs were used to hold hot dishes. What you find in shops today are cast iron and were used to hold a sadiron (flat iron). Beware of reproductions flooding the market.

Crisscross .... $ 16- 27
Diamond T, iron 19- 27
Eastern Star 24- 33
Fox and Grapes, brass 42- 60
George Washington, iron (brass
  100% higher), (ill.) 28- 36
Harp, iron 20- 28
Horseshoe shape, Good Luck,
  iron 28- 37
Jenny Lind, iron (ill.) 32- 42
Order of the Cincinnatus, iron (ill.) 31- 41
Order of Odd Fellows, iron 26- 35
Snake and Eagle Head, iron 22- 32
Sunflower 15- 22
Turtle, iron 32- 42

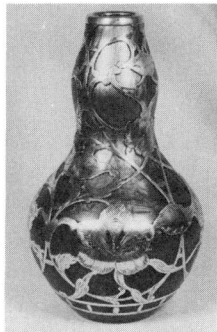

Tucker China

Tucker China

Made only from 1825 to 1838 in Philadelphia, this rare china is believed to be the first porcelain made commercially in America. It is similar to Sevres. William Tucker made the first. In 1828, Thomas Hulne joined the firm. Judge Joseph Hemphill and William's brother, Joseph, took over the firm in 1832

337

(continued)

when William died. In 1837 the judge withdrew from the firm, and Joseph Tucker continued for one more year. All pieces were hand-decorated and rare.

Bowl, delicate florals, 3″ high
(ill.) . . . . $ 125- 150
Cup/saucer, tea, no handle,
floral pattern 330- 375
Dish:
  a. Oval, covered 700- 775
  b. Round, covered. 560- 600
Plate:
  a. 6¾ dia. landscapes of
    Philadelphia, set of 6 1,100-1,400
  b. 7¼″, 8¼″ dia., set of 6 . . . 425- 450
Pitcher, floral pattern 475- 525
Platter, floral pattern 950-1,300
Urn:
  a. 3½″ high, floral pattern,
    gold decoration on base,
    pr 1,400-2,000
  b. 10¼″ high, floral pattern,
    gold painted base,
    handled, pr 2,300-2,600

Val St. Lambert

Bowl, crystal/cranberry, 11½″
dia. 165-195
Box, blue/rose poppies, 4″
square, signed 260-280
Cologne bottle, blue/red flowers,
frosted ground, signed 215-240
Dish, blue, clear ground, 5″ dia.,
signed 220-235
Jewelry box, pink flowers, frosted
ground, hinged lid, signed 295-360
Plate, game bird, 8″ dia., signed . 116-128
Tray, dresser, etched crystal,
clear/green, 6″ long 95-140
Vase, blue/purple, frosted
ground, signed (ill.) 400-450
Vase, red-to-clear, signed 320-370

Tumblers

Tumblers

Cobalt, pressed (ill.) . . . . $ 26- 36
Cut, 3¾″ high (ill.) 32- 40
Cranberry, ITP (ill.) 42- 52
Herringbone Satin glass 130-150
New England Peachblow 450-470
Geneva pattern custard glass . . . 52- 70
European Mary Gregory 22- 32
Hobnail-in-Square 32- 42
Decorated cranberry 42- 52
  Lots of repros around!

Val St. Lambert

Founded in the late 1700s, this Belgian firm made a cameo glass which featured cased glass bodies lavishly cut with the lapidary wheel and acid-engraved. They also made other types of glass.

Biscuit jar, blue/green floral,
silver cover, signed $420-500
Bottle, perfume, frosted crystal
cut to yellow, silver stopper,
6½″ high 250-320

Valentines

Valentines

In early Christian times and based on pagan feast called Lupercalia, church[e] adopted February 14, the day of the marty[r] dom of Bishop Valentine in 270 A.D., [a] Valentine's Day. The first written valentin[e] in America date back to the late 1600s, b[u] they really didn't get started until t[h] mid-1700s. Lithographed valentines da[te] from the 1840s. The lace-paper type [is] credited to Esther Howland, 1840s. Fun [to] collect today.

Assortment, 1920s-1930s (ill.) . . . $ 1- 2
Lacy type, mid-1800s 3- 7
What you're willing to pay is about wh[at]
they're worth!

Vallerystahl Glass

This French/German glass has been ma[de] for years at Vallerystahl, Lorraine, Fran[ce]

338

After the Franco-Prussian War the area became part of Germany. Returned to France in 1918, the factory was destroyed by Allied bombers in World War II. What you find in shops today is from the mid-1800s to 1915 era.

Bottle, perfume, blue, swirl ribbed, gold star decor	$ 97-110
Box, covered, blue milk glass, 3½" x 4"	64- 74
Candlestick, carved frosted glass	110-125
Compote, fluted top, milk glass	82- 94
Covered dish, swan, milk glass	90-110
Dish, covered, cow motif	72- 82
Jam jar, Grape and Leaf	62- 72
Plate, Thistle pattern, 6" dia. signed	70- 80
Goblet, footed, blue, signed	48- 59
Salt dip, Ram's Head, white	42- 52
Tumbler, cobalt, 4" high	44- 53

Van Briggle Pottery

Artus Van Briggle worked at Rookwood Pottery in the late 1800s, then moved to Colorado Springs for his health. The company is still in business. Van Briggle's work at Rookwood was far superior to anything he ver made in Colorado. He died in 1904.

Bookends, maroon/green, pair	$ 84-120
Bowl, blue, 1924, paper label	42- 52
Candleholder, red/brown	49- 57
Creamer, blue, Grecian key	42- 52
Pitcher, maroon, 5" high, 1932	59- 67
Planter, oval shape, green/blue, incised signature	44- 54
Plaque, Indian maiden, blue, signed	68- 78
Vase, plum color, handled, incised signature, 1934	45- 60
Vase, floral decor, Colorado Springs mark	50- 58
Vase, red/green, Greek Key, 6" high (ill.)	42- 48

Van Briggle Pottery

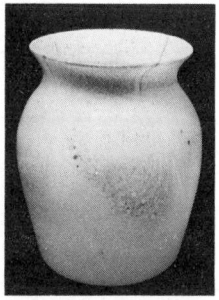
Vasart Glass

Bowl, Persian Rose, dated "1918" in bottom, 3" dia	46- 53
Figurine, Indian maiden, Turquoise	110-145
Vase, turquoise, 2½" high, scalloped rim, signed	32- 42
Candlesticks, Persian Rose, 3¾" high, Pat. #733, signed	40- 48
Lamp, Deco style, figural lady, Oriental, 10½" high, monogram mark	62- 70
Tulip bowl, turquoise, 8½" long, 3" high, signed	41- 49
Tulip flower frog, 20 holes, signed	23- 33
Vase, turquoise, daffodils, 9½" high, signed	74- 85

Vasa Murrhina Glass

Vasa Murrhina Glass

Made by the Vasa Murrhina Art Glass Company, Sandwich, Massachusetts, in 1884, this was a glass in which the body was transparent, showing imbedded pieces of colored glass and mica flakes. Another repro item.

Art Glass basket, pink and white swirls, silver mica, clear handle	$120-140
Bowl, multicolored, mica flecks	130-150
Bride's basket, tan/gold flecks, white casing	195-220
Creamer, rainbow, cased, 5" high	72- 82
Decanter, cranberry, gold flecks, ribbed handle	166-177
Fairy lamp, green/blue mottling	230-260
Lamp, amber, mica flakes, 9" high	170-180
Tumbler, blue/white, silver mica flecks	92-105
Vase, pink/blue, silver flecks, 8" high	120-130
Vase, blue/pink, silver flecks, ruffled, 8" high	120-130
Vase, clear, red and silver flecks, 3¾" high (ill.)	62- 77

Vasart Glass

Made in Scotland by the Streathearn Glass Company, this is a fairly new art glass. "Vasart" is usually engraved on the base.

339

(continued)

Basket, blue/yellow, loop handle, 6" high, signed	$ 75- 85
Bowl, yellow on base, speckled at top, 4" dia., signed	67- 77
Mug, handled, green/blue, signed	48- 58
Tumbler, blue/white, striped, signed	46- 60
Vase, Cluthra-type, apricot to clam broth, 9" high (ill.), signed	270-280

Vaseline Glass

A greenish-yellow glass that looks like petroleum jelly. A product of the 1870s, it's still being made today.

Basket, 5" high	$ 29- 39
Berry set, Wildflower, clear, 7-piece	72- 82
Bowl, embossed flowers, footed	40- 50
Butter dish, covered, Diamond Quilted	48- 57
Cake stand, opaline swirl	56- 62
Candleholder, twisted stem, 11" high	29- 38
Compote, dolphin stem, opalescent rim	74- 79
Cruet, Argonaut, original stopper	140-170
Dish, candy, covered	17- 28
Mug, kitten pattern	26- 34
Perfume bottle with stopper	32- 40
Pitcher, Maple Leaf	72- 82
Salt/pepper, Diamond Quilted, pr	24- 34
Spooner, Alaska	70- 83
Teaberry gum stand	50- 60
Toothpick holder, flower decor, ribbed, footed	22- 32
Tumbler, Wreath and Shell pattern, opalescent	58- 68
Vase, swirl, 6" high	42- 52
Wine, clear stem and foot	22- 32

Venetian Glass

A lot of people confuse it with Carnival because of its iridescence. It isn't and was first made 700 years before Carnival on an island near Venice, Italy. The factory wa government-owned and continued until th early 1900s. It was usually colored, fragil and very thin.

Basket, swirled blue/pink threads, handled	$ 40- 50
Bowl, ruffled edge, blue/gold threads, 4" dia	34- 44
Candlesticks, pair, yellow with cobalt edging, applied pink and white violets, green leaves, 10½" high (ill.)	83- 94
Candy dish, typical Venetian, 6" dia	40- 50
Compote, Dolphin, early 1800s	170-180
Cup/saucer, pink, lacy	44- 54
Epergne, pink/blue opalescent, 23" high	130-150
Goblet, blue/gold threads, 8" high, clear stem	34- 44
Paperweight, twisted red/blue threads	70- 80
Vase, blue swirl design, 7½" high, fluted top	72- 82

Verlys Glass

Verlys Glass

This is a French glass, made there in th 1930s. It is also made in America. It's eithe blown or molded, the American glass signe with a diamond-point-scratched name. Th French has a molded signature. Bringir brisk prices today.

Ashtray, doves, French signature	$ 32- 42
Bowl, blue acorns, signed, French	120-135
Bowl, daisy pattern, 6-sided, American	78- 88
Box, hinged, flower decor, American	64- 74
Plate, fish swimming, clear and frosted, 5" dia. (ill.)	44- 54
Tray, child with animal in relief, American	78- 88
Vase, frosted lovebirds, 5" high, French	99-112
Vase, flowers in relief, 7" high, American	75- 90
Vase, lovebirds, flowers	88- 97

Vaseline Glass   Venetian Glass

340

Villeroy and Boch

Villeroy and Boch
This firm of potters began in Luxembourg around 1875. Later known as Boch and Buschmann, besides making the world-famous Mettlach steins, (see METTLACH) the firm also made plaques, cider sets, breadboards and garden tiles.

Bowl, punch, floral decor	$ 92-107
Butter dish, covered, design in heavy relief	73- 83
Compote, creamware, 9″ high	62- 72
Cup/saucer, Dresden pattern	22- 42
Mug, advertising Detroit beer company, 5″ high	22- 32
Pitcher, gravy, tray attached, flower decor	32- 42
Plaque, ocean liner at sea, 11″ dia	67- 77
Plate, 9½″ dia., windmill, cows in field	32- 42
Plate, 10″ dia., Dresden pattern	50- 62
Stein, American eagle, pewter top, 9″ high (ill.)	475-500
Teapot with 6 cups/saucers, flower decor	92-102
Vase, 8″ high, garden scene	49- 60
Vase, 11½″ high, ancient German castle	58- 68

Walking Sticks (Canes)
They were considered stylish in Europe during the late 17th century. Usually they were made of rattan; later some had concealed guns, swords, liquor flasks. In the 1800s wealthy gentlemen had canes with 14 karat gold heads, some inlaid with diamonds.

Gold-headed, insert tube for ¼ pint whiskey	$170-220
Silver-plated head, Malacca type	40- 48
Sterling silver head, Malacca type	79-110
Sword concealed in handle, Malacca type, English, 18th century	285-375

Two-shot pistol concealed in handle, Malacca type	750-850
Walking stick, carved burl head, thorn wood	28- 38

Warwick China

Warwick China
Made in Wheeling, West Virginia, 1887. It's comparable to Weller and Roseville pottery, same price range.

Indicative piece, plate, 12¼″ dia., signed "Laport" (ill.)	$ 15- 21

Washboards
They are mentioned here because those from the early 1900s made of wood, brass or glass are being collected for use in the kitchen and den as bulletin boards.

Average price, in good condition	$9- 19+

Wash Sets

Wash Sets
A water pitcher and large bowl, usually with toothbrush holder, soap holder and a smaller pitcher for hot water, were called a "wash set." They were used before the days of indoor plumbing. Some were run-of-the-

(continued)

mill, some were ironstone, others were made by Haviland. Highly collectible today. Many "new" sets on market today.

Ironstone, Mason's Patent, bowl and pitcher, smaller pitcher . . .	$170-210
Meakin, floral decor, bowl and pitcher	180-225
Haviland, complete 7 piece set, yellow/pink flowers, signed . . .	290-350
Pink lustre bowl and pitcher, Sailor's Farewell, 1840s (ill.) . . .	475-550
Weller pottery bowl, pitcher, toothbrush holder, soap dish . .	195-230

Watch Chains and Fobs

Some are very ornate; all had the same purpose.

Baseball player, leather strap . . .	$ 18- 27
14 karat gold, double strand, locket inset with diamonds, pen/pencil holder, c. 1875 (ill.) . .	700-800
Caterpillar Tractor Company, leather strap	20- 30
10 karat gold, single strand, 10" long	65- 80
14 karat gold, single strand, 12" long	575-650
Silk vest chain, gold-filled mountings, 12" long	38- 50
Curb chain, 3-strand, gold-filled, hand engraved slide	35- 46
Rope chain, 2-strand, gold-filled, 11" long	32- 42
Sailing ship, leather strap	20- 25
State of New York seal, enameled	19- 28
Woven hair vest guard, gold-filled mountings, 8½" long . . .	25- 35
Onyx charm chain, 8" long, gold-filled	20- 30
W.O.W. (Woodsman-of-the-World), strap	14- 21

Watches

Watches

The Europeans were far ahead of us when it came to making watches. We got around to making them in the 1830s. Until then every one we used was imported from Europe. Keyless watches came into being around 1700; with a second hand, around 1780; radium dials, around 1898; the wristwatch, around World War I. Any Elgin, Hamilton, or Waltham, numbered under 1,000 is collectible today.

Bugs Bunny . . . . $	170-	180
Dick Tracy	262-	282
English, silver hunting case, key wind, 1820	150-	185
Lady's hunting case, stem wind, 14k, Waltham, signed "Missy"	550-	600
Pocket, open face, stem wind 14k, Waltham	475-	525
Man's silver open face, French, c. 1895, stem wind, second hand	185-	220
Calendar watch, 8-day, hunting case, silver, c. 1910	268-	300
Minute repeater, 14k, hunting case, c. 1890, repeat button in band	1,750-2,000	
Elgin, hunting case, 14k, 17 jewel movement (ill.)	300-	350
Waltham, hunting case, 14k, lever-set gilt movement	785-	875
Keywind, gold and enamel, Swiss, c. 1830, engraved gilt Lepine caliber movement, enameled "courting scene" on back, gold hands	2,200-2,400	
South Bend, 14k, 17 jewels	350-	450
Hunting case watch, gold, c. 1890, signed Joseph Penlington, Liverpool	800-	900
New York Standard, gold filled, 15 jewel (ill.)	140-	160
Repousee verge watch, gold, white enamel dial, gold hands, c. 1780	1,500-1,800	
Longine 900, silver Niello enamel (won 4 grand prizes at Paris-Milan Exposition)	220-	250
Art Deco minute repeating dress watch, platinum, signed Cartier, Paris, repeat mechanism activated by rotating the front bezel	5,800-6,200	
Hunting case, gold inlay, dog, gun, deer, Swiss	170-	185
Key wind, silver, 1865, type carried by Union Army officers	220-	240
Lady's hunting case, lake scenery, Waltham, 14k gold .	270-	285
Man's hunting case, stem wind, 14k gold, Elgin	285-	375

342

Open face, cylinder movement, engraved, silver	82-	92
Pocket, hunting case, 14k gold, Swiss	310-	340
Pocket, open face, key wind, 14k gold	350-	400
Waltham, hunting case, size 14, 1880s	375-	425

Waterford Glass

Waterford Glass

This fine glass was first made in Ireland in 1729. The chandeliers are world-famous. A flint-type glass, it was dark in color before the 1830s, then the formula was improved and the color became whiter and more brilliant. They shut down in 1852 and didn't reopen for 100 years. Now back in production, the glass they're making today is marvelous.

Celery, Diamond Point Fan	$ 39- 52
Cracker jar, etched, silver lid	110-130
Cruet, cut stopper, 11½" high, old mark, pr	170-225
Goblet, large	135-175
Knife rest, signed Waterford	95-145
Lustres, 13" high, cut prisms, pr.	550-625
Mustard jar, contemporary, 3½" high (ill.)	22- 28
Pitcher, ornate silver lid, 11" high	170-220
Salt, new (ill.)	12- 17
Souvenir-type wines, Queen Elizabeth II Coronation, each (ill.)	35- 45
Toothpick (ill.)	12- 16
Tumbler, cut	56- 70
Urn, cut, square base, 10" high	292-315
Vase, Diamond cut, square base	180-225

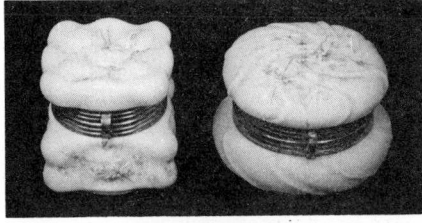

Wave Crest Ware

Wave Crest Ware

The C.F. Monroe Company, Meriden, Connecticut, bought their blanks abroad and also from the Pairpoint Manufacturing Company, New Bedford, Massachusetts, in the late 1890s. All pieces were formed from opaque white glass, blown into shape in full-size molds. Reminiscent of Crown Milano, the pieces were decorated at Meriden. Kelva and Nakara were two of their registered marks. The firm discontinued business during World War I. The marks are Wave Crest with company initials, and Nakara with company initials.

Basket, swirls, ornate handle	$140-165
Biscuit jar, enameled pink/yellow roses, decorated lid	180-200
Bowl, floral decor, brass collar, signed Nakara, 4" dia	140-160
Box, letter, pale green and white swirl, 5" long	245-285
Cracker jar, floral designs, embossed scroll pattern, lid	285-320
Jewel box, pink/blue daisies, hinged lid, signed Kelva	210-240
Jewel box, decorated, ormolu collar, 3¼" high (ill.)	170-185
Jewel box, enameled flowers, ormolu collar, 4" high (ill.)	198-240
Pin box, blue/white floral decor, brass collar, no lid	130-150
Planter, 6-sided, brick red, floral decor, signed, 7½" dia	345-370
Powder box, blue/pink, hinged lid, signed Nakara	220-240
Stationery holder, pink roses, scrolled design, Kelva	165-195
Syrup jug	180-220
Vase, blue, enameled scroll, 8" high	380-420

Wax Work

This type of "work" was revived around 1850. Instead of the earlier portraits and figures, wax flowers and fruit designs were made. Molds were available for larger objects such as animals and birds. The fruit was usually arranged in a plaster-of-paris basket and framed or placed under a glass dome. This was considered an important art form during the 1850s.

Typical piece, fruit basket under glass dome, late 1800s	$ 72- 82

Weather Vanes

They were usually in the shape of birds, animals, racing sulkies, ships. Scarce today, the old ones are being stolen in New England from atop old barns and homes.

Angel Gabriel, remounted on
iron bracket . . . . $ 16,000+
Automobile, early, brass, on
orb 1,800-2,200
Deer running, hollow copper,
N.E.S.W. on orb, directional
arrow 950-1,100
Eagle, spread wings, hollow
copper, N.E.S.W. on orb,
arrow 1,500-1,900
Fish, on orb, brass, 3' long 875- 975
Hog, tin, on orb 650- 750
Indian, with bow and arrow,
"Mashamoquet" . . . . 25,000!
Rooster on milk glass ball,
usual N.E.S.W. directional
arrow 875- 995
Sulky driver, complete with
horse 1,500-2,000
Cow, copper, made by J.W.
Fiske, 1893 1,200-1,400
Fish, 30" long, made by J.W.
Fiske, 1898 900-1,100
Peacock, copper, on ball 9,700-10,400
Rooster and arrow, Fiske, 1895,
copper, gilded with gold
leaf 650- 850
Horse over hurdle, 30" long,
J.W. Fiske, 1893 1,600-1,800

Webb Glass

Thomas Webb and Sons operated their factory at Stourbridge, England, and made some of the finest glass the world has ever known. Poor imitations being made.

Bottle, probably perfume,
white with red, green, gold
palm leaves . . . . $ 250- 295
Bowl, cameo, cranberry, white
carving, signed Thomas
Webb 1,200-1,400
Jam jar, 4" high, cranberry,
white roses, silver bail and
cover 950-1,200
Lamp, 14" high, as usual,
signed 1,300-1,600
Punch bowl, red and white,
signed Thomas Webb and
Sons 3,600-4,000

Wedgwood

Josiah Wedgwood founded the first pottery at Burslem, England, around 1759. Jas-

Wedgwood

perware is the best known product. Basalt, Creamware and Terra-Cotta are other well-known types. Jasperware was made in over 25 colors; blue and white being the most popular over the years. Wedgwood's history is equally as confusing as that of Haviland.

Bowl, Basalt, early $275-350
Box, hinged, blue Jasperware . . . 195-230
Candlestick, terra-cotta decor,
impressed Wedgwood, pair . . . 260-290
Clock, green Jasperware, 5½"
high 220-250
Creamer, green, classical figures
in white, grape and leaf, 3¾"
high (ill.) 110-125
Creamer, blue Jasperware,
impressed Wedgwood 150-170
Cruet, blue Jasperware, 4 piece
on silver-plated stand 165-195
Plaque, pink Jasperware,
cherubs, birds, 5" dia 145-180
Cheese dish, blue Jasperware . . 370-400
Pitcher, green, white figures,
grape border, 5½" high . . . 138-158
Plate, white ground, flowered
border 240-260
Tea set (pot, creamer, sugar),
blue Jasperware (all) (ill.) 395-475
Tankard, pink Jasperware,
tavern scene 395-465
Vase, blue/white, birds and
dogs, impressed Wedgwood, 5"
high 150-190

Weller Pottery

344

Weights

The kind used on grocers' and apothecaries' scales make fine paperweights, decorative background for planters, etc. They're not expensive by today's standards.

Grocer's type, set of 8, ¼ oz. to 2 lb., iron	$ 14- 24
Druggist's set of 12, brass, in mahogany box	26- 40
Grain scale type, slot in side, 1 lb. to 5 lb., set of 6	35- 48

Weller Pottery

In 1872 Sam Weller made Bluebird pottery on his Fultonham, Ohio, farm; in 1882 he moved to Zanesville. In 1890 he produced glazed ware, cuspidors, umbrella stands and jardinieres. In 1895 he organized the Lonhuda Faience Company with William A. Long. Pieces made were marked with an "L" and "F" and an impressed shield. Weller got rid of Long in 1896, changing the name of the pottery to "Louwelsa," a combination of letters from his and his daughter's name. Many kinds of pottery were made by Weller including Sicard, Thurada, Eosian, Floretta. Aurelian Dickens Ware, and LaSa. Weller competed with Roseville and Rookwood. His quality matched Roseville's, but other than Sicard and LaSa, he never matched the Rookwood quality. The factory closed in 1949.

Basket, hanging, fruit decor, 9" dia.	$ 66- 78
Bowl, flowers, blue/pink, artist-signed	62- 72
Candlestick, Louwelsa mark, brown/green, 9" high	82- 92
Clock case, flowers, green leaves, Louwelsa, 7" high (clockworks, Seth Thomas, 1870s)	350- 400
Decanter, handled, flower decor, 10" high	72- 82
Mug, Etna, blue/red decor	62- 72
Pitcher, ivory ground, multi-colored panels, kingfisher decor, 8" high (ill.)	24- 36
Spittoon, floral decor on brown glaze	65- 95
Tankard, Dickens Ware, handled, 6½" high	190-220
Umbrella stand, Louwelsa, brown/flowers, 19" high	260-360
Vase, blue/pink flowers, signed McLaughlin, 11½" high	92-102
Vase, lavender flowers, white background, 10" high	72- 90

Vase, dogwood flowers, pink/ blue, incised Weller	58- 68
Vase, 6" high, signed Sicard	425-480
Vase, 7" high, signed Weller, LaSa (ill.)	140-160

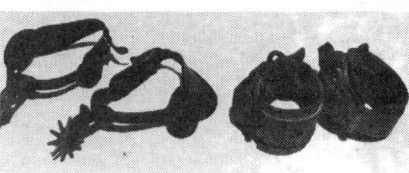

Western Frontier Items

Western Frontier Items

For less than 40 years the Wild West was really wild. Anything to do with this period of American history is collectible today.

Branding irons — see Buckles:		
a. Brass, stagecoach, stamped Tiffany, old	$ 29-	42
b. Silver, copper initials	19-	30
Also see Belt Buckles		
Colt revolver, Wells Fargo, marked WF and Company, 5-shot	475-	500
Hobbles (leg tethers)	32-	42
Knife, Bowie-type, with leather scabbard, 1860s	410-	480
Lariat made from woven horsehair	62-	72
Saddle, silver inlaid, tooled leather, rodeo prize, 1926	1,800-3,000	
Spurs, rowel-type, probably Mexican silver	56-	66
Spurs, rowel-type, Mexican, cast iron (ill.)	35-	45

Wheeling Peachblow

Wheeling Peachblow

Hobbs, Brockunier and Company, Wheeling, West Virginia, made this fine ware, simulating the coloring of the original Morgan Peach Blow vase which was supposedly sold at auction (the original from the collection of a Chinese gentleman named Wang Ye) for some $18,000 in the late 1800s. The Wheel-

345

(continued)

ing-type is red-rose at the top, shading to a bright yellow at the bottom. The rare vases, glossy or acid finish, on a gargoyle stand, are priceless today. Being reproduced.

Butter dish	$1,400-1,600
Cruet, glossy, with stopper, 6¾" high	950-1,000
Pitcher, acid finish	1,650-1,750
Pitcher, rose to yellow, white liner, 5" high (ill.)	770- 850
"Morgan" vase on gargoyle stand, glossy finish 15½"	1,700-2,000
Rose bowl	650- 725
Tumbler, glossy finish, rose to yellow, 3½" high (ill.)	300- 325
Water set, glossy finish, pitcher/6 tumblers	3,750-4,400

Whieldon

Whieldon

Thomas Whieldon started his first factory at Fenton Low in 1719. Josiah Wedgwood was in business with him from 1754 until 1759. Whieldon made agateware, a deep cream-colored earthenware of the Astbury type, decorated with a mottled lead glaze stained brown, blue and yellow, green, grayish-black. Whieldon stayed in business until 1795. His pieces are highly collectible today.

Creamer, flower pattern, lid attached by metal chain, 1750s	$440-520
Mug, flower pattern, 1760s (ill.)	290-360
Plate, Tortoiseshell ware, 18th century	230-260
Plate, mottled browns, 1750s	100-155
Pitcher, flower patterns, 1760s (ill.)	435-525

Whimsies

These were not production items. The workers at the glass factories in the 1800s made them for family and friends, usually with the glass batch left over at the end of the day's work. Free-blown or blown in molds,

Whimsies

usually miniature, the whimsey had no purpose except to please the maker and delight whomever he gave it to.

Bull, glass, 7" high (ill.)	$ 50- 60
Pear	42- 51
Pepper	42- 51

Whiskey Sample Glasses

Whiskey Sample Glasses

In the late 1800s and early 1900s, salesmen, drummers, carried these little shot glasses to impress the customer that their product was best.

Big 6 Gin shot glass, 1 ounce	$ 16- 26
Calvert, 2¼" high (ill.)	7- 9
Dilley's No. 5 Pure Rye shot glass, 2 ounce	13- 22
Habanero "Piza" Tabasco, ½ ounce	7- 16
Hanover Rye, Cincinnati, Ohio, shot glass, 2 ounce	15- 25
Hayner Distilling Company, Dayton, Ohio and St. Louis, 3 ounce	14- 22
Vino Chinato bitters/wine shot glass, 1 ounce	9- 11

Wicker Furniture

Staging a big comeback after years of neglect — that old "porch" furniture is very "in" again. Particularly popular are birdcages and ferneries. Prices of all pieces will vary considerably depending on condition, materials used, and whether wicker is hand-

346

Wicker Furniture

woven or machine-loomed. New pieces are flooding market, so watch out!

Baby carriage, hand-woven willow	$220-260
Birdcage with stand, hand-woven	135-165
Child's highchair, hand-woven willow	155-175
Chair, c. 1880s (ill.)	140-165
Chair, large fireside, hand-woven cane	250-280
Chair, large fireside, loomed, man-made fibers	135-165
Chair, rocker, loomed, man-made fibers	130-145
Desk and chair, loomed, man-made fibers	280-320
Fernery, depending on materials, condition, etc	150-170
Lamp, floor, 72″ high	225-255
Love seat, photographer's prop, 40″ across (ill.)	325-375
Phonograph cabinet, floor, hand-woven willow	340-365
Settee, depending on materials, condition, etc	210-275
Sofa, 76″ wide	365-410
Table, round top, 36″ dia.	175-195

Willow Ware

This was first made in England in 1772, in America about 1880. It was made in every quality, from Spode and Minton to the 5¢ and 10¢ store variety. Chinese legend says two escaping lovers were turned into doves. Found in light and dark blue, also in pink and green. Red is rare. Lots of scenes other than the "dove" bit were used. Maker, year and quality dictate prices here.

Butter dish, covered, Ridgway	$ 58- 68
Butter pat	6- 9
Butter tray, 6″ dia	11- 19
Cereal bowl, Meakin	15- 23
Cup/saucer, Allertons	22- 32

Willow Ware

Egg cup, Buffalo Pottery	16- 24
Pitcher, red, Ridgway	70- 80
Plates, 8″, 8½″, 10″ dia., made in Ohio, each (ill.)	19- 29
Platter, 12½″	42- 60
Sugar bowl, covered, Ridgway	52- 62
Teapot, Doulton	92-102
Tureen, gravy, covered	165-190

Window Glass

The "bubbly" glass found in old houses, and that glass turned purple by the sun, is collectible today.

Witch Ball

From the early 1820s until the late 1890s these glass globes, usually placed in a stand or hung in the window, were supposed to prevent disease or ward off evil spirits. Wiping daily removed whatever evil was lurking in the neighborhood. Highly collectible today. Don't confuse them with the heavier glass balls used to float fishing nets.

Witch ball	$ 55- 70

Witch Canes

Doubtful if these served the same purpose as Witch Balls — see. Probably the product of the whimsy maker — see Whimsies. Whatever, they're beautifully made and fragile. Valuable when found.

Glass, twisted thread, crook handle, 5½″ long	$375-450
Glass, Latticinio type, bulb on end, 5″ long	385-465

Wood Carvings

Wood Carvings

Carrying on probably the oldest form of art, whittlers have been around since the days of the Romans. European woodcarvers, especially the German and French, decorated many of the finest palaces in the world. What we find today usually was carved in the mid-1800s.

Buddha, lacquered, late 18th century	$125-	160
Angel heads (probably from a church), early 1800s, pair	260-	290
Drunk under lampost, 10" high. Removable head is a bottle opener; lamp is a corkscrew	15-	26
Duck, outspread wings, hand-painted, late 1800s	170-	190
Eagle, outstretched wings over flag shield, mid-1800s	500-	525
"Sinister" eagle (looking to left), stern shield for ship	975-	1,100
Hunter with dog, European, early 19th century	220-	245
Sailing ship in oval walnut frame, New England, mid-1800s	195-	225
Swiss couple, early 20th century, pair, 5" high (ill.)	40-	50

Wood, Enoch and Sons

About 1784 Enoch Wood established his factory at Burslem, England. Later his sons joined him and they exported a large quantity of ceramics to the U.S. From 1819 until the 1840s the firm produced more marked American historical views than any other Staffordshire firm.

Jug, Sunderland Lustre, impressed mark (ill.)	$380-	400
Plate, 7½" dia., dark blue, Pass in the Catskill Mountains	160-	180
Plate, 8¾" dia., dark blue, The Capitol, Washington	155-	170
Plate, soup, dark blue, City of Albany, 10" dia	140-	160

Wood, Enoch and Sons

Platter, dark blue, Military Academy, West Point, 9¼" x 12"	550-	600
Platter, dark blue, 15" long, Niagara from the American side	350-	375
Platter, dark blue, Highlands, Hudson River	450-	500

Woodenware

Woodenware

These wooden items used in the home in the last half of the 19th century are collectible today. Dough bowls are scarce.

Bootjack, cherry, dated 1830	$ 79-	90
Bowl, maple burl, 4" dia	44-	52
Breadboard, maple, 11" dia	52-	62
Breadboard, pine	48-	57
Broom, 1-piece, oak splint	59-	63
Bucket, oak, for well	28-	38
Butter molds — see Butter paddle	29-	39
Calf yoke, with bow	145-	160
Candle box, pine, sliding top, 16" long	68-	78
Candy scoop, poplar, 5" long	22-	32
Canteen, round	92-	102
Cheese ladder, cherry	50-	60
Churn, barrel, with crank	68-	78
Churn, bucket-type	77-	88
Churn, complete with dasher and lid	170-	185
Cider funnel, poplar, 5½" long	24-	34
Cookie board, carved daisy pattern, 6" x 8", walnut	48-	58
Cranberry picker, maple, child's size	92-	110
Cream skimmer, pine, handled	46-	52
Cup, burl walnut, handled	62-	72

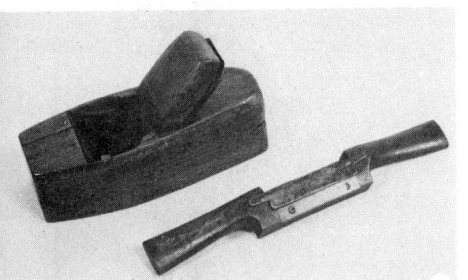

Woodenware

Cutting board, walnut	24- 34
Darning knob, 8" long, maple . . .	25- 33
Dough bowl, maple, hand-carved	81- 92
Egg carrier, 1 dozen, wooden dividers	40- 50
Flour scoop	35- 46
Knife tray, 2-compartment w/handle, cherry	52- 62
Ladle, 14" long	40- 50
Lemon squeezer (ill.)	25- 35
Letter box, cherry, hinged lid . . .	78- 88
Oak keg, staved and hooped with hickory bands	80- 90
Ox yoke, large, with bows	210-230
Pickle bucket, original lid	60- 70
Pie crimper, walnut wheel	52- 62
Piggin, staved and hooped	68- 78
Plane, maple, 7" long, signed "L. Cook" (ill.)	35- 42
Potato masher, pine, 9" long	15- 24
Rolling pin, pine, 15" long, solid .	18- 28
Sap bucket, hickory bands	46- 53
Scriber, maple, 5½" long (ill.) . . .	18- 24
Shoulder yoke, pine	92-102
Spoke shaver, maple, brass insert and handle (ill.)	32- 43
Spoon rack, pine, 8 carved slots, 16" high	175-195
Spoon rack, walnut, 6 carved slots, hanging type	180-200
Stirrup, pine (great for holding paper napkins)	18- 24
Sugar bucket	48- 58
Towel rack, cherry, removable roll	47- 57
Vise, used for holding leather, wood, etc.	92-102
Wooden box, Shaker type, "T.F." initials in top	170-190
Wooden grain or gunpowder shovel	220-250
Yarn winder, maple	85- 92

Worcester Porcelain

This was Tonquin, originally titled in 1751 Worcester Tonquin Manufacture. Dr. John Wall (and partners) founded the firm at Worcester, England. The Dr. Wall or "First Period" ended in 1783; then Thomas Flight purchased all assets. In 1793, Martin Barr came in as a partner. Flight and Barr changed in 1807 to Flight, Barr and Barr. Name changed again in 1813. In 1840 Chamberlin and Company consolidated with the parent company. This firm sold in 1852 to Kerr and Binn which is still in existence. What you find of the early Worcester is from the 1870-1900 period, with Royal Worcester entering the picture in 1862. It's confusing so if you don't know what you're about, learn, find a reliable dealer, or collect something else. Reproductions of the Dr. Wall period are in shops today, having been reproduced over 60 years ago. No one agrees on what Worcester porcelain should or will bring. The well-known price guides are from $200 to $500 apart on the SAME item! Let me say that experience only will teach the "new" collector. The experienced collector will spend little time reading my remarks. I can't even say, "Know your dealer!" as few dealers can honestly tell you the real from the unreal.

World's Expositions, Fairs

The first Exhibition opened at the Crystal Palace in London in 1851. The first World's Fair opened at the Crystal Palace in New York City in 1853. The first Exposition opened in Philadelphia in 1876. Mementos of these great events are highly collectible today, the older the better. What you find in shops is from the late 1800s in the form of spoons, glass mugs, toothpick holders, in metal or glass. These items stayed in vogue until the Sesquicentennial Exposition in Philadelphia, 1926.

Bottle, milk glass, New York World's Fair, 1939	$ 17- 29
Creamer, Chicago Exposition, 1893	20- 28
Match holder, New York World's Fair, 1939	12- 17
Plate, St. Louis Exposition, 1904	16- 26
Spoon, Chicago Exposition, 1893	19- 27
Stein, Chicago Exposition, 1893 .	18- 32
Umbrella, paper, New York World's Fair, 1939	15- 24
Engraved pass, picture of Columbus, Lincoln, Washington, etc, each	12- 18
Arlington Mills woven advertising display, 12″ x 18″, Columbus	85- 95
Handkerchief, panorama of Fairgrounds	12- 20
Photo album, red velvet cover, color pages of buildings	56- 66
Discovery of America medal	20- 30
Elongated (rolled-out) dime	21- 31
Elongated (rolled-out) penny	7- 9
Santa Maria medal	11- 22
Holy Bible, souvenir of Exposition	27- 37

Writing Accessories

Writing Accessories

The pieces illustrated are all sterling silver — see. Many writing sets were made of plated materials, metal-over-glass — see TIFFANY. As a complete set or individually, these accessories are collectible today, especially when one finds a piece stamped "Tiffany Studios, New York."

Letter opener, Art Nouveau lady, brass, 10″ (ill.)	$ 41- 52
Letter opener, Eskimo, 6¾″ long (ill.)	75- 90
Letter opener, sterling silver, 6¼″ long (ill.)	40- 50

Stamp box, Japan, bronze/brass, 1¾″ high (ill.)	60- 70

Zanesville Art Pottery

Zanesville Art Pottery

David Schmidt organized the Zanesville Roofing Tile Company in 1896 and changed the name to the Zanesville Art Pottery Company in 1900. Cobalt blue jardinieres were produced and also a line of utensils for baking and cooking purposes. Around 1904, art pottery, a luster type, was introduced. Their most famous pottery was called La Moro; it looks like Weller's Louwelsa. They also produced a matt-ground ware. In 1920, after a series of fires, the firm was sold to Sam Weller of Weller pottery fame.

Bowl, brown-and-white lined, 6″ dia., early	$ 68- 80
Bowl, enameled flowers on a crackled ground, 10″ dia.	130-160
Casserole, brown-and-white lined, 9½″ dia., early	95-110
Coffeepot, pink floral, early	80- 90
Jardiniere, brown and gold glazes, 9″ high (ill.)	118-135
Vase, 9 1/2″ high, floral decor on dark brown, La Moro	135-148
Vase, 6″ high, wild rose decor, La Moro	85- 95
Vase, 7″ high, flowers, high glaze, La Moro	165-190

Zsolnay Porcelain

In the 1850s the factory was established at Funfkirchen, Hungary by Vilmos Zsolnay to make soft-paste porcelains, usually enameled in many colors and highly glazed.

Bowl, harbor, blue, gold, signed	$160-185
Dish, castle, gold, green, iridized, 4½″ dia	82- 92
Pitcher, floral decor, multicolored, 7″ high, signed	140-150
Tea set (teapot, creamer, sugar, 6 cups/saucers) signed	170-190
Vase, blue, green, gold, reticulated at top, 6½″ high, signed	245-275
Vase, enameled, 10″ high, signed	220-262

Guide to Pattern Glass
with Duplicate Names

Acme—see Butterfly with Spray
Acorn—see Willow Oak
Alexis—see Priscilla
Amberette—see Klondike
Arched Fans—see Caprice
Arctic—see Polar Bear
Ashland—see Snowdrop
Atlanta—see Clear Lion's Head
Austrian—see Fine Cut Medallion

Baby Thumbprint—see Dakota
Ball—see Notched Bar
Banded Prism Bar—see Doyle's 400
Beaded Bull's Eye and Drape—see Alabama
Berkley—see Blocked Arches
Beaded Mirror—see Beaded Medallion
Bearded Man—see Queen Anne
Bearded Prophet—see Bearded Head
Bean—see Egg in Sand
Beatty Rib—see Ribbed Opal
Big Block—see Henrietta
Blazing Pinwheels—see Shoshone
Blazing Star—see Pinwheels
Block and Pleat—see Persian
Block with Stars—see Hanover
Blockade—see Diamond Block with Fans
Bluebird—see Bird and Strawberry
Boswell—see Seashell
Bosworth—see Star Band
Brilliant—see Stars and Stripes
Broughton—see Pattee Cross
Bryce—see Ribbon Candy
Bullet—see Atlas
Buttressed Loop—see Buttressed Arch

Cable with Ring and Star—see Cable
    with Ring
California—see Beaded Grape
Cameo—see Classic Medallion, also see Ceres
Candlewick—see Banded Raindrop
Cannonball—see Atlas
Centennial—see Liberty Bell
Centennial Shield—see American Shield
Chain Lightning—see Lightning
Challinor's No. 313—see Challinor's Tree
    of Life
Challinor's Thumbprint—see Barrelled
    Thumbprint

Clear Lily—see Daisy and Button with
    Narcissus
Clear Panels with Cord Band—see Rope
    Bands
Colossus—see Lacy Spiral
Columbia—see Heart with Thumbprint
Columbian—see Coin
Column Block—see Panel and Star
Coral—see Fishscale
Crescent and Fan—see Starred Scroll
Cross Roads—see Ashman
Crow-Foot—see Yale
Crown Jewels—see Chandelier
Crystal Anniversary—see Crystal Wedding
Crystal Ball—see Atlas
Cut Log—see Cat's Eye and Block, also
    see Ethol

Daisy—see Thousand Eye
Daisy in Oval Panels—see Bull's Eye and Fan
Daisy in Panel—see Two Panel
Daisy in Square—see Two Panel
Deer and Doe—see Deer and Pine Tree
Derby—see Pleat and Panel
Dewey—see Spanish American
Diamond (Lippman)—see Flat Diamond
Diamond and Concave—see Diamond
    Thumbprint
Diamond Bar—see Lattice
Dinner Bell—see Cottage
Diamond Horseshoe—see Aurora
Dogwood—see Art Novo
Doll's Eye—see Memphis
Double Arch—see Interlocking Crescents
Double Loop—see Ribbon Candy
Double Pear—see Gypsy
Double Red Block—see Hexagon Block
Draped Top—see Victoria
Duquesne—see Wheat and Barley
Dynast—see Radiant

Egyptian—see Parthenon
Elite—see Pillow and Sunburst
English Hobnail Cross—see Klondike
Enigma—see Wyoming
Excelsior—see Ruby Thumbprint, also see
    Giant Bull's Eye

Fancy Diamonds—see Three-in-One
Figure Eight—see Ribbon Candy
Fine Cut Bar—see Panama
Finecut and Blazing Star—see Pinwheels
Finecut and Feather—see Cottage
Finger Print—see Almond Thumbprint
Fisheye—see Torpedo
Flamingo—see Frosted Stork
Flat Panel—see Pleating
Flora—see Opposing Pyramids
Floral Diamonds—see Shoshone
Florida—see Herringbone, also see Emerald
    Green Herringbone
Flower Flange—see Dewey
Flowered Scroll—see Duncan 2000
Fluted Diamond Point—see Panelled
    Sawtooth
Flying Robin—see Hummingbird
Forest Ware—see Ivy-in-Snow
45 Colonis—see Colonis
Frosted Banded Portland—see Barred Oval
Frosted Fleur-de-Lis—see Stippled
    Fleur-de-Lis
Frosted Flower—see Twinkle Star
Frosted Magnolia—see Water Lily
Frosted Waffle—see Hidalgo

Galloway—see Virginia
Gem—see Nailhead
Georgia—see Peacock Feather
Gloria—see Pattee Cross
Goddess of Liberty—see Ceres, also see Act
Golden Agate—see Holly Amber
Good Luck—see Horseshoe
Guardian Angel—see Cupid and Venus

Hand—see Pennsylvania
Hartley—see Paneled Diamond Cut and Fan
Hearts and Spades—see Medallion
Hinoto—see Diamond Point with Panels
Honeycomb—see New York
Hops and Barley—see Wheat and Barley
Hops Band—see Maple

Iceberg—see Polar Bear
Ida—see Sheraton
Indiana—see Cord Drapery
Indiana Swirl—see Feather
Indian Tree—see Barley
Inverted Prism—see Masonic
Inverted Thumbprint with Daisy Band—see
    Honeycomb with Flower Rim
Irish Column—see Broken Column

Japanese—see Grace
Jersey Swirl—see Swirl
Jewel Band—see Scalloped Tape
Job's Tears—see Art

Kamomi—see Balder
Kansas—see Jewel with Dewdrop
King's Crown—see Ruby Thumbprint

Lace—see Drapery
Lacy Medallion—see Princess Feather
Large Thumbprint—Ashburton
Late Sawtooth—see Cobb
Lawrence—see Bull's Eye
Leaf—see Maple Leaf
Lily—see Sunflower
Lippman—see Flat Diamond
Lion's Leg—see Alaska
Locust—see Grasshopper with Insect
London—see Picket
Long Spear—see Grasshopper with Insect
Loop—see Pillar
Loop and Jewel—see New England Pineapple,
    also see Jewel and Festoon
Loop with Pillar—see Michigan
Loop with Stippled Panels—see Texas
Looped Cord—see Beaded Chain

Magic—see Rosette
Maltese—see Jacob's Ladder
Maple—see Panelled Grape
Maryland Pear—see Gypsy
Mikado—see Daisy and Thumbprint,
    Cross Bar
Mitred Diamond Points—see Mitred Bars
Moon and Star with Waffle—see Jeweled
    Moon and Star

N.P.L.—see Pressed Leaf
Nautilus—see Argonaut Shell
Neptune—see Queen Anne
New Century—see Delaware
New Grand—see Grand
New Jersey—see Loops and Drops
North Pole—see Polar Bear
Notched Rib—see Broken Column
No. 11—see Thousand Eye

Oaken Bucket—see Pail
Oak Leaf—see Willow Oak
Oats and Barley—see Wheat and Barley
O'Hara—see Loop
Old Acorn—see Chestnut Oak

352

Washboard—see Adonis
Water Lily—see Frosted Magnolia, also see
  Rose Point Band
Winged Scroll—see Ivorina Verde, also see
  Louis XV

Winona—see Barred Hobnail
Wisconsin—see Beaded Dewdrop
Wreath—see Willow Oak

Zipper—see Cobb

Section of Pattern Glass
Alphabetical by Pattern Name

The discovery of a mechanical means for producing press-molded glass articles was probably the most significant contribution made by American craftsmen to the glass industry's development in the 19th century. That it would prove to be of great national importance is now an accepted fact from an historical point of view.

The unfortunate fire of December 17, 1836, which destroyed much of the Patent Office and its records, left the patent records for the first half of the 19th century somewhat incomplete; therefore the controversy of who was first, in Pattern Glass, and with what, still rages.

Generally, Joseph Magouun's patent for a manually operated glass press (December 6, 1845); Frederick McKee and Charles Ballinger's patent for a steam-operated glass press (March 29, 1864); William King's patent for a revolving block-type press and Henry Leasure's patent for an air-cooled glass press (March 5, 1872) — these are usually accepted as milestones in the industry. Certainly, there were others, such as Hiram Dillaway's patent for a glass mold (August 21, 1841) in which ten glass stoppers for decanters or cruets could be pressed in one operation. Equally important was Daniel Ripley's patent (October 20, 1868) for a mold that pressed two or more articles of glass in one operation.

There are three methods of pressing glass: (1) Block Molding, the simplest; (2) Split Molding, where the mold is made up of two or more parts; and (3) Font Molding whereby each article is made absolutely identical in form and dimension.

For those who could not afford expensive, hand-cut pieces, pressed glass, which gave way to Pattern Glass with a clear, rather than a stippled background, conferred a great benefit of beauty and utility. This inexpensive glass for everybody revolutionized the glass industry in America.

Aberdeen

Maker unknown, c. early 1870s, clear, non-flint.

Butter dish, covered $34-44
Compote, open 18-23
Creamer 27-38
Egg cup 14-25
Goblet (ill.) 16-28
Pitcher, water................ 40-50
Sauce, flat 11-16
Sugar bowl, open, covered 24-52

Aberdeen

Acanthus Scroll

Maker and date unknown, clear, possibly color, possibly engraved.

Butter dish, covered $24-36
Cake stand 18-29
Creamer 26-35
Goblet 17-27
Pitcher...................... 30-42
Spoonholder 15-26
Sugar bowl, covered 24-37

If color, if engraved, 50% higher than clear prices listed.

Acorn

Maker and date unknown, probably c.

1870s. Don't confuse it with Hobbs' opaque colors, c. 1890, or Beaumont's crystal colors, c. late 1890s.

Butter dish, covered, acorn finial $33-45
Celery 26-37
Egg cup 24-34
Compote
  a. Covered, acorn finial 55-68
  b. Open 45-59
Creamer 40-52
Goblet 32-42
Pitcher...................... 58-72
Sugar bowl
  a. Covered, acorn finial 44-55
  b. Open 33-44

Probably other pieces. Goblet being reproduced.

Actress

(Theatrical; Goddess of Liberty): La Belle Glass Company, Bridgeport, Ohio, about 1872; probably Crystal Glass Company, same town, 1879. Clear; clear and frosted prices given. 20% less for clear.

Bowl, footed, 6" ....$ 42- 53
Butter dish, covered 65- 78
Cake stand 92-125
Candlesticks, pr. 170-195
Celery "Pinafore" 150-170
Cheese dish, covered, scene from
  "The Lone Fisherman" 170-198
Compote
  a. Covered, clear, 8" high
    standard 115-160
  b. Covered, low standard.... 110-140
Creamer 68- 78
Goblet, clear, footed 74- 85
Honey dish, covered 68- 78
Marmalade jar, w/cover 62- 72
Pickle dish, "Love's Request" .. 42- 52
Pitcher
  a. Milk (ill.) 162-180
  b. Water 170-182
Platter
  a. Scene from "Pinafore".... 118-152
  b. "Miss Nielson" 92-128
Relish dish 33- 43
Sauce
  a. Flat 18- 27
  b. Footed 26- 36
Salt/Pepper, pr. 57- 69
Spoonholder, clear or frosted .. 58- 72

 (continued)

Sugar bowl 74- 88
Tray, bread, "Give Us This
Day" 65- 88
Pickle jar is being reproduced; possibly other pieces.

Actress

Adonis

McKee & Bros., Pittsburgh, 1897. Crystal, canary, blue, others.

Celery
  a. Oval $19-32
  b. Tall 22-34
Compote, stemmed
  a. Covered 55-65
  b. Open 37-46
Dish, round
  a. 1½" 9-12
  b. 4" 14-22
  c. 8" 30-40
Jelly, footed, 4½" high 27-34
Molasses can, pewter top 37-48
Pitcher
  a. 1 quart (ill.) 44-55
  b. 1 gallon 62-74
Plate, 10" 10-15
Tumbler 19-30

Alabama

(Beaded Bull's Eye and Drape): U.S. Glass Company, Pittsburgh, 1898. First

Adonis

Alabama

of the extensive "States" series made by above company. Clear, probably in colors with gilt trim.

Butter dish, covered $37-48
Cake stand 44-55
Celery 22-32
Compote
  a. Covered 28-42
  b. Open, 5" 28-36
Creamer 24-35
Goblet 24-36
Honey dish, covered 9-13
Nappie, handled 17-20
Pitcher
  a. Milk (ill.) 59-69
  b. Syrup 36-47
  c. Water 47-60
Relish dish, oblong 9-12
Spoonholder 26-36
Sugar bowl, covered 44-54
Tumbler 18-27

Alaska

356

Alaska

(Lion's Leg): Northwood Glass Company, 1897. Opalescent, pearl blue, pearl yellow, pearl flint, green.

Berry set
- a. Bowl, berry, op. blue .... $ 74- 84
- b. Bowl, berry, vaseline 36- 47

Butter dish, covered, op. blue 78- 86
Creamer, green (ill.) 54- 65
Sugar, creamer, square, pr., pearl
   blue 145-160
Jewel tray 33- 46
Pitcher, water, decorated 235-265
Rose bowl, op. blue, vaseline,
   or emerald on stand, round
   pedestal foot................. 62- 72
Spoonholder 52- 76

Probably other pieces.

Alligator Scales

Alligator Scales

Maker unknown, c. 1870s, clear, flint.

Goblet (ill.) $27-45
Other pieces?

Almond

Maker and date unknown, clear, nonflint.

Decanter $17-29
Goblet (ill.) 16-27
Salt, footed 11-17
Wine 10-16

Probably other pieces

Almond

Almond Thumbprint

(Pointed Thumbprint; Finger Print): Bryce Bros., Pittsburgh, 1890. Clear, colors.

Butter dish, covered, cable
   edge $81- 92
Celery vase 62- 74
Creamer 61- 73
Compote, covered
- a. High standard, 4¾", 7",
   10" 64- 82
- b. Low standard........... 50- 60

Egg cup 18- 31
Goblet, several styles 22- 39
Pitcher, water (ill.) 100-120
Sugar bowl 52- 65
Tumbler 32- 47

Probably other pieces. Color, 150 percent higher than clear prices listed.

Almond Thumbprint

Amazon

(Sawtooth Band): Bryce Brothers, Pittsburgh, Pennsylvania, c. 1890, crystal, plain and engraved. Reissued by U.S. Glass Company after 1891. Set consisted of 65 pieces!

Bowl, waste	$24-34
Butter dish, covered	36-47
Cake stand	36-48
Compote, 6¾" high	40-50
Creamer	27-38
Goblet (ill.)	23-35
Pitcher, water, milk	48-58
Salt/Pepper, pr.	27-42
Sugar bowl, open, covered	32-42
Wine	18-27

Amazon

American Shield

(Centennial Shield): Maker unknown, probably made for 1876 Centennial. Clear, non-flint.

Butter dish, covered	$150-180
Creamer	100-138
Spoonholder	99-127
Sugar bowl, covered	150-172

Only known pieces.

Angora

Maker unknown, c. late 1880s, clear, non-flint.

Butter dish, covered	$32-47
Creamer	22-32
Goblet	26-36
Spoonholder	19-27
Sugar bowl, covered	26-37

Probably other pieces.

Anheuser Busch

"A" ale glass possibly LaBelle Glass Company, Bridgeport, Ohio, c. 1880, clear, non-flint.

Ale glass	$22-36

Anthemion

Model Flint Glass Company, Findlay, Ohio, 1890. Crystal glass only; possibly emerald green, others.

Bowl, berry, 7"	$27-39
Butter dish	43-54
Cake plate, high standard, 9¼" high	35-44
Celery	22-33
Creamer	28-37
Marmalade jar	19-28
Pitcher	
a. Milk (ill.)	61-71
b. Water	63-73
Plate, 10"	24-35
Relish dish	18-26
Sauce, flat	15-22
Spoonholder	40-50
Sugar bowl	42-52
Tumbler	27-38

Anthemion

Anvil

Toothpick (or match holder, anvil-shaped), Windsor Glass Company, Pittsburgh, Pennsylvania, c. 1887.

Clear	$38-50
Canary	40-50
Amber	58-70
Blue	48-59

Apollo

Adams & Company, Pittsburgh, 1875; also, McKee Bros., same city, 1894. Etched and frosted. Prices are for Plain. Etched, 20% more.

Bowl, 9½" d., etched	$22-32
Butter dish, covered	37-47
Cake stand	35-44
Celery, etched	34-42
Cheese dish	24-34
Compote	
a. Covered, high standard	56-72
b. Open, low standard	40-49
Creamer	36-48
Egg cup	15-21
Goblet	32-42
Pickle	12-22
Pitcher, water, etched	44-55
Pitcher, syrup (ill.)	28-38
Sauce	
a. Flat	12-17
b. Footed	15-19
Spoonholder	24-36
Sugar bowl, open and covered	37-50
Tray, water	38-47
Tumbler	19-27
Wine	15-24

Apollo

Apple Blossom

Northwood Glass Company, Indiana, Pennsylvania, c. 1896, decorated milk glass.

Butter dish, covered	$65- 79
Cake stand	53- 64
Compote	58- 69
Creamer	40- 50
Goblet	37- 45
Pitcher, syrup	88-110
Sugar bowl, covered	78- 89
Sugar shaker	65- 79
Tumbler	46- 56
Probably other pieces.	

Aquarium

Aquarium

Maker and date unknown. The water pitcher is occasionally seen. Probably tumbler to match.

Water pitcher (ill.)	$130-162
Tumbler	24- 36
Probably other pieces.	

Arabesque

Arabesque

Bakewell, Pears & Company, Pittsburgh, before 1864. Clear.

Butter dish	$45-55
Celery	26-37
Compote	
a. Covered, 6" and 8", high standard	48-59
b. Covered, 6" and 8", low standard	37-50

359

(continued)

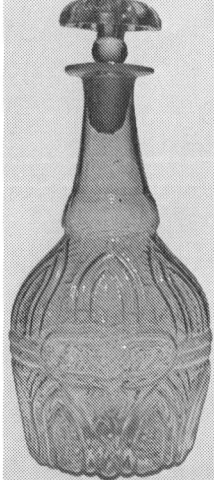

Arch and Fern
with Snake Medallion

Arch and Fern
with Snake Medallion

Sandwich Glass, mid-1800s. This is NOT Pressed Glass. It is blown 3-mold; just that, blown into a mold, not plunger-pressed. It is shown as a comparison only.

Arch and Forget-Me-Not Bands

Arch and Forget-Me-Not Band

Maker unknown, 1880s.

Berry bowl $19-28
Butter dish, covered 32-40
Creamer 22-39
Pitcher, water (ill.) 38-49
Saucedish 8-15
Spoonholder 18-28
Sugar bowl, covered 33-46
Tumbler 19-27

Probably other pieces.

Arched Grape

Arched Grape

Sandwich Glass, 1870s. Clear glass.

Butter dish, covered $46-58
Celery vase 39-48
Compote
   a. Covered, high standard 52-65
   b. Covered, low standard 46-56
Cordial 22-32
Creamer 40-50
Goblet 30-40
Pitcher, water (ill.) 57-66
Saucedish, 4″ 15-19
Spoonholder 18-29
Sugar bowls
   a. Covered 47-58
   b. Open 22-34

Probably other pieces.

Arched Leaf

Arched Leaf

Maker unknown, c. 1870s, clear, flint, non-flint.

Goblet	$32-40
Plate	27-38
Salt, footed	17-28
Sugar bowl (base ill.)	37-48

Flint, 50% higher than non-flint prices listed.

Arched Ovals

United States Glass Company, c. 1900, clear, flashed with red; cranberry-flashed ("rose"), emerald green.

Goblet	$44-54
Toothpick holder	27-38
Tumbler	38-49
Wine	34-42

"Rose" and emerald green, 25% higher than clear, flashed with red prices listed. Probably other pieces.

Argonaut Shell (Nautilus)

Argonaut Shell (Nautilus)

Northwood Glass Company, about 1900. Custard, colors, clear, opalescent. Custard decorated in dark green and gold.

Berry set	Custard	Color
a. Large bowl	$140-150	$ 92-102
b. Small bowl	49- 67	30- 42
Compote	110-135	72- 80
Salt/Pepper, pr.	158-162	84- 92
Butter dish, covered	185-200	81- 91
Sugar bowl, covered	285+	72- 82
Pitcher, water	350+	140-160
Tumbler	82- 92	40- 48

Probably other pieces. Custard bowl being reproduced.

Argus

Argus

(Thumbprint): Bakewell, Pears & Company, 1870. Crystal, colors (rare).

Ale glass, 7½"	$126-145
Butter dish	67- 77
Celery vase, 2 types	65- 79
Champagne	50- 62
Cordial	19- 32
Creamer, applied handle	58- 67
Decanter, pint, quart	64- 74
Goblet	43- 53
Mug, applied handle (scarce)	73- 82
Sauce	27- 37
Spoonholder	34- 45
Sugar bowl, covered	69- 82
Tumbler, footed jelly, water	42- 52
Tumbler, whiskey, handled	44- 54
Wine	42- 47

Arrowhead in Oval

Arrowhead in Oval

Higbee Glass Company, c. 1890, clear, non-flint; all pieces marked with "bee" trademark.

Cup, punch .... $ 8-15
Goblet (ill.) 19-32
Wine 15-27

Undoubtedly other pieces.

Art

Art

(Job's Tears, Teardrops and Diamond Block): Adams & Company, Pittsburgh, 1870s. Clear.

Basket, fruit $48- 57
Bowl, berry, 8″ 28- 38
Butter dish, covered 45- 57
Cake stand, 10″ 39- 54
Compote
  a. Covered, footed, 7″ 53- 60
  b. Open, footed, 7½″ 42- 54
Cracker jar 31- 39
Creamer 40- 52
Cruet 22- 34
Dish, banana 92-108
Goblet 48- 59
Mug 18- 26
Pitcher, water (ill.) 68- 78
Relish 17- 29
Sauce, footed, flat 18- 25
Spoonholder 27- 37
Sugar bowl, covered and open .. 40- 50
Tumbler 19- 32
Wine 20- 28

Art Novo

Art Novo

(Dogwood): Co-Operative Flint Glass Company, Beaver Falls, Pennsylvania, 1905. Clear.

Butter dish $25-36
Creamer 19-28
Lamp, miniature (ill.) 30-40
Spoonholder 19-27
Sugar bowl 26-36

Probably other pieces.

Artichoke

Artichoke

Probably Dalzell, Gillmore and Leighton, Findlay, Ohio, 1890s. Crystal, opaque white, also with the figure work in satin finish, colors.

Bowls $10-14
Butter dish 46-53
Cake stand 47-57
Compotes
  a. Covered, high standard 47-56
  b. Open, high standard 19-32
Creamer 23-35
Cruet 15-19

362

Goblet 18-24
Pitcher (ill.).................. 48-59
Sauces 12-28
Spoonholder 42-52
Sugar bowl, covered 50-60

Probably other pieces. Opaque white, colors, 50 percent higher than clear prices listed.

Ashburton

Ashburton

(Large Thumbprint): New England Glass Company, Cambridge, Massachusetts, 1855. Clear. Also made at Sandwich; also McKee Bros., 1850s.

Ale glass, 5″ high, flint ......$ 48- 62
Bitters bottle 50- 62
Butter dish 120-155
Celery	
a. Plain top 68- 79
b. Scalloped top 172-192
Cordial, 4½″ high 62- 80
Creamer, (rare) 168-190
Decanters, 7 types 46- 82
Egg cups, 2 types, flint 30- 42
Goblet	
a. Flaring sides, flint, barrel (ill.) 74- 85

b. Straight sides, lady's 54- 65
Lamp 74- 82
Lemonade glass 44- 58
Mugs, 2 types 50- 60
Sauce, 2 sizes 19- 29
Spoonholder 34- 44
Sugar bowl, covered 110-122
Toddy jar, covered, 2 sizes
(rare)..................... 230-250
Tumbler
a. Jelly.................... 27- 39
b. Water 37- 49
c. Whiskey, handled........ 130-152
Wine bottle, with tumble-up .. 140-162
Wine, straight stem or barrel .. 36- 48

Cordial, goblet (flaring sides), quart jug, lemonade glass, sugar bowl, wine being reproduced. Possibly other pieces.

Ashburton with Grape Band

Ashburton with Grape Band

Maker and date unknown.

Tumbler (ill.) $29-39

No other pieces known to this writer.

Ashman

Maker unknown, c. mid-1880s, clear, etched.

Butter dish, covered $36-46
Cake stand 32-42
Celery 33-47
Compote	
a. Covered, 6″ to 12″ 44-63
b. Open, 6″ to 12″ 22-38
Creamer 27-36
Goblet 27-37
Pitcher 39-52
Spoonholder 15-29
Sugar bowl, covered 29-40

Probably other pieces.

Assassination Mug

Assassination Mug

(Also called "The Martyrs' Mug"): Garfield on one side, Lincoln on other. Obviously made after 1881, the year Garfield was assassinated. By whom this mug was made is not known. Clear glass.

Mug, 2¼" high (ill.) $52-68

Atlas

Atlas

(Cannon Ball, Bullet): Adams & Company, Pittsburgh, 1889. Clear, vari-colors, ruby flashed.

Bowls, open $15-29
Butter dish, covered 29-41
Cake stand, 10" high, clear 40-49
Creamer, covered, applied handle. 28-41
Goblet 27-37
Pitcher, water................. 32-42
Sauce, footed 15-22

Spoonholder 17-24
Sugar bowl, covered 29-42
Wine......................... 33-42
Probably other pieces.

Atlas

Atlas

(Cannon Ball; Bullet): Bryce Bros., Mt. Pleasant, Pennsylvania. 1889. Clear; sometimes flashed with red, gold.

Bowls, covered, flat, clear $44-55
Butter dish, covered, ruby,
   flashed 68-81
Creamer, ruby, flashed,
   gold trim 52-62
Cake stand, 10" high, clear 42-52
Goblet (scarce) 33-47
Sauce, footed 12-19
Pitcher, water, 2 types 53-62
Spoonholder, flat or footed base .. 24-37
Sugar bowl, covered 27-36
Wine, clear 28-38

Probably no other pieces. Red, gold, 30% more than clear prices listed.

Aurora

(Diamond Horseshoe): The Brilliant Glass Works, Brilliant, Ohio, c. 1888, clear, panels sometimes engraved. Pattern produced by Greensburg Glass Company, c. 1889, when Brilliant got into financial difficulties.

Butter dish, covered $36-44
Cake stand 29-42

Compote
  a. Covered 33-42
  b. Open 17-28
Cordial 16-26
Creamer 25-37
Goblet 26-38
Pitcher, water................. 36-49
Salt/Pepper, pr. 17-30
Spoonholder 17-32
Sugar bowl, open 24-38

Prices are Greensburg. Many other prices.

Bakewell Block

Bakewell, Pears & Company, Pittsburgh, c. early 1850s, clear, flint.

Butter dish, covered $170-190
Celery 84- 94
Champagne.................. 88- 98
Creamer 160-180
Decanter 120-140
Goblet 97-115
Spoonholder 59- 69
Sugar bowl, covered 75- 88
Tumbler, bar, whiskey 76- 89

Probably other pieces.

Balder

Balder

(Kamoni; Pennsylvania): U.S. Glass Company, Pittsburgh, through early 1900s. Clear, colored or gilt tops.

Bowl, gilt trim $40-51
Butter dish, covered 39-49
Creamer, small, gold trim 15-27
Goblet 19-29
Pitcher, syrup (ill.) 32-40
Spoonholder, w/ruby flashed top.. 25-30
Sugar bowl, covered 31-44

Tumbler, water or whiskey 19-29
Wine......................... 27-30
Probably other pieces.

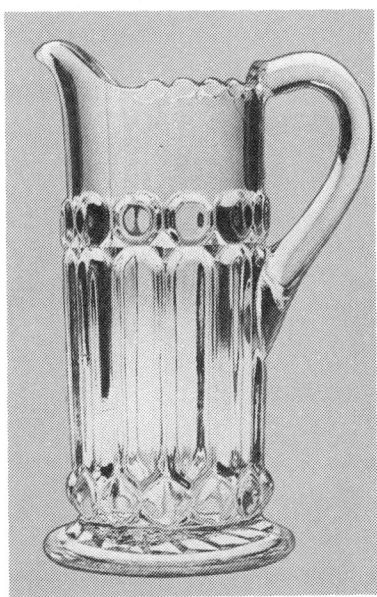

Ball and Bar

Ball and Bar

Westmoreland Glass Company, Grapeville, Pennsylvania, 1896. Clear.

Butter dish $34-44
Creamer 29-36
Pitcher (ill.)................... 52-63
Spoonholder 27-37
Sugar bowl 34-44

Probably other pieces.

Balloon

365

(continued)

Balloon

Made in lower Ohio Valley in early 1850s. Clear.

Creamer $155-195
Goblet 60- 70
Pitcher (ill.) 258-288
Sugar bowl 170-195

Probably a few other pieces but considered extremely rare today.

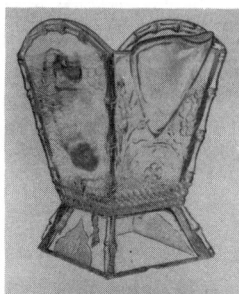

Bamboo

Bamboo

La Belle Glass Company, Bridgeport, Ohio, 1883. Plain and engraved crystal glass.

Butter dish $39-52
Celery 32-50
Compotes, 7″, 8″, 9″, covered 46-59
Creamer 25-32
Dish, 7″, 8″, 9″, oblong 17-26
Pitcher, water................. 37-50
Sauce, 4″ 9-18
Salt/Pepper, pr. 27-36
Spoonholder (ill.) 18-32
Sugar bowl, covered 36-48
Tumbler 17-28

Banded Buckle

Sandwich glass, mid-1850s; other factories, Pittsburgh, 1870s. Clear glass.

Bowls, open $12-19
Butter dish 38-48
Compote
  a. Open, low standard 39-48
  b. Covered, low standard 32-42
Cordial 23-36
Creamer...................... 32-37
Egg cup 19-29
Goblet (ill.) 21-33
Pitcher, water................. 44-55

Banded Buckle

Salt, footed 8-14
Spoonholder 15-27
Sugar bowl 33-47
Tumbler 19-28

Probably other pieces.

Banded Fleur-de-Lis

Banded Fleur-de-Lis

Imperial Glass Company, Bellaire, Ohio, 1890s. Clear.

Butter dish $29-40
Creamer 19-29
Pitcher (ill.).................... 35-44
Spoonholder 18-29
Sugar bowl 26-38

Probably many other pieces.

Banded Icicle

Bakewell, Pears & Company, 1870s. Clear.

Butter dish $35-45
Compote
  a. Covered, 6″, 8″, high
    standard 44-56
  b. Open, 8″, low standard...... 28-40

Banded Icicle

Creamer	29-42
Goblet	19-27
Pitcher (ill.)	52-70
Sauce	12-26
Spoonholder	18-32
Sugar bowl	38-48

Probably other pieces.

Banded Portland (Virginia)

Banded Portland (Virginia)

U.S. Glass Company, 1901. Crystal and rose flashed.

Bottle, water	$33-42
Butter dish, covered	19-32
Celery	18-29
Compote	
a. Covered	28-42
b. Covered, jelly	22-32
Cruets	12-18
Dish, sardine	15-21
Jar, jam	19-28
Pitcher, syrup (ill.)	32-50
Relish boat	12-16

Salt/Pepper, pr.	17-29
Sugar	
a. Bowl, covered	22-37
b. Shaker	25-36
Toothpick holder	19-29
Tumbler	16-25
Wine	28-30

Probably other pieces. 50 percent higher for colors than for clear prices listed.

Banded Raindrops

Banded Raindrops

(Candlewick): Clear, rare in amber, opalescent blue and milk glass. These pieces 100 percent more than clear pieces listed.

Butter dish	$36-44
Celery	19-44
Compote, 7", covered	28-39
Creamer	18-26
Cup and saucer	15-27
Goblet	18-32
Pitcher, water (ill.)	39-49
Plates, 7½" and 8¾"	15-24
Relish	10-18
Sauce	8-16
Spoonholder	15-27
Sugar bowl	32-42
Wine	22-40

Banner Butter Dish

Probable Bryce, Walker and Company, made for Centennial, 1876. Clear, blue and amber. A rare pattern!

Butter dish (ill.)	
a. Clear	$110-165
b. Blue	150-220
c. Amber	250-450

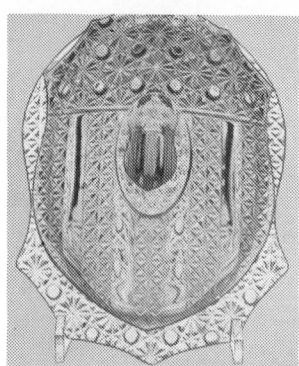

Banner Butter Dish

Barberry

Barley

Barley

(Sprig; Indian Tree): Late 1870s. Clear, any piece in color, rare; 50 percent more than clear.

Butter dish, covered	$35-47
Cake stand, 9″, 9¼″, 9½″, 9⅝″	36-46
Celery	33-42
Compote, covered and open	46-56
Cordial	26-32
Creamer	32-40
Dish, oval	19-28
Goblet	28-40
Jam jar, with lid	36-46
Pickle	19-27
Pitcher, water, 2 types	44-52
Plate, 6″	31-42
Platter, oval	38-47
Sauces, footed, 4″, 5″	18-27
Spoonholder	36-46
Sugar bowl, covered and open	40-50
Wine	27-37

Barberry

Boston & Sandwich Glass Company, Sandwich, Massachusetts, 1860s. Later reproduced by several companies in Pittsburgh area, 1880s. Clear and colors; amber and blue, 50 percent and 70 percent more.

Bowl, covered, 8″	$32-42
Butter dish	51-61
Cake plate	39-49
Celery	32-42
Compote, covered, high and low standard	56-66
Cordial	38-47
Creamer	48-55
Egg cup, oval berries	34-50
Goblet, oval berries	29-33
Pickle	12-21
Pitcher, water, applied handle (ill.)	68-80
Plate, 6″ deep	32-42
Salt, footed, 6″	26-36
Sauce, flat and footed	20-30
Spoonholder	52-62
Sugar bowl, covered	62-72
Syrup jug, pewter top	68-80
Wine	17-26

Barred Forget-Me-Not

Barred Forget-Me-Not

Canton Glass Company, Canton, Ohio, 1883. Clear, canary, vaseline amber, blue, apple green.

Butter dish	36-46
Cake plates	
a. 9″, closed handles	39-49
b. Extra large, on stand	42-56
Compote	
a. Covered, on high foot	37-45
b. Covered, low foot, 8″	48-59
c. Open, small, on high foot	39-47
Cordial	12-16
Creamer	27-38
Goblet	27-37

Pickle dish, square handles...... 15-27
Pitcher (ill.).................... 39-48
Spoonholder 34-46
Sugar bowl, square handles 40-50
Wine........................ 19-28

Probably other pieces. Canary, 30 percent, blue, 60 percent, apple green, 100 percent higher than clear prices listed.

Barred Hobnail

Barred Hobnail

(Winona): Brilliant Glass Works, Brilliant, Ohio, 1888. Clear, opalescent, varicolored.

Bowls $11-21
Butter dish, covered 27-36
Creamer 19-29
Goblet 20-32
Pitcher, water, ½ gallon (ill.) 35-44
Salt shaker 9-19
Sauce, flat 10-22
Spoonholder 10-26
Sugar bowl, covered 27-36

Probably other pieces.

Barred Oval

Barred Oval

(Frosted Banded Portland): George Duncan & Sons, Pittsburgh, Pennsylvania, c. 1890, clear, frosted or color flashed. Reissued after 1891 by U.S. Glass Company.

Bottle, water $27-36
Butter dish, covered 28-36
Celery 22-29
Compote, open 19-28
Creamer 19-27
Goblet 19-32
Pitcher, water................. 40-50
Plate, small.................. 19-27
Sugar bowl, covered (ill.) 38-44

Frosted or color flashed, 50% higher than clear prices listed.

Barred Star

(Spartan): Gillinder & Company, Pittsburgh, c. early 1880s, clear, non-flint.

Butter dish, covered $26-38
Cake stand 27-39
Celery 19-32
Compote, covered 22-36
Creamer 29-40
Pitcher...................... 30-42
Salt/Pepper, pr. 10-19
Spoonholder 15-29
Sugar bowl, covered 26-35

Probably other pieces.

Barrel Excelsior

Sandwich, early; later, McKee Bros. Pittsburgh, 1850s and 1860s. Clear.

Ale glass ....$ 32- 46
Butter dish, covered, early 78- 92
Celery
  a. Plain top............... 42- 54
  b. Scalloped top 69- 82
Decanters, pint, quart, 3 pints,
  early 67- 83
Goblets, flaring and
  straight sides 32- 44
Lamp, early................. 95-115
Mug 38- 52

(continued)

Barrel Excelsior

Spoonholder (ill.) 37- 46
Sugar bowl, covered, early 140-172
Tumbler, water, whiskey 32- 51
Wine bottle, with tumble-up,
   early 128-172
Probably other pieces.

Barrelled Thumbprint

Barrelled Thumbprint
(Challinor's Thumbprint)

Challinor, Taylor, Ltd., Tarentum,
Pennsylvania, 1880s.

Butter dish $39-48
Celery 29-37
Creamer 35-48
Goblet 40-50
Pitcher (ill.).................. 54-63
Spoonholder 27-35
Sugar bowl 36-42
Wine....................... 24-33
Probably other pieces.

Basket Weave

Basket Weave

Mid-1880s. Clear, amber, blue, canary,
milk white, apple green.

Bowl
   a. Berry ....$ 31- 41
   b. Covered, flat 26- 35
   c. Large, finger 19- 27
Butter dish 34- 46
Cake plate................... 27- 48
Compote, covered............. 42- 49
Cordial 25- 35
Creamer..................... 32- 42
Cup and saucer 29- 34
Egg cups, double 18- 27
Goblet...................... 20- 30
Lamp 24- 34
Mug 22- 32
Pickle 15- 21
Pitcher
   a. Syrup, metal top, clear 37- 49
   b. Water (ill.) 40- 50
Plate, sheaf or wheat handles .. 110-140
Salt........................ 10- 18
Sauce, round, flat........... 12- 18
Salt/Pepper, pr. 27- 39
Spoonholder 19- 32
Sugar bowl 34- 46
Tray, round, 12″ dia. 37- 52

Probably other pieces. Goblet and water
pitcher being reproduced. Color pieces
50 to 100 percent higher than clear
pieces listed.

Basket Weave with Frosted Le:

A design of the 1880s, it was made by
many companies in many patterns. Clear,
canary, yellow, blue, green.

Basket Weave with Frosted Leaf

Bowl, berry	$15-20
Cake plate	32-41
Compote, covered	29-39
Cordial	12-16
Egg cup, double	15-19
Cups/saucers	12-19
Goblet	15-19
Pitcher, water (ill.)	43-53
Saucedish, round, flat	8-15
Syrup, metal top	19-27
Tray, water	22-28

Prices are for clear. Canary, yellow, green, 40 percent more; blue, 100 percent more. Probably other pieces.

Bead and Scroll

Bead and Scroll

Maker and date unknown.

Berry bowl, 8"	$15-20
Butter dish, covered	22-31

Compote, jelly	18-27
Creamer	26-36
Goblet	14-21
Pitcher, water (ill.)	29-39
Saucedish, flat	9-19
Spoonholder	21-32
Sugar bowl, covered	28-37
Tumbler	17-26

Probably other pieces.

Bead Column

Bead Column

Maker and date unknown.

Butter dish, covered	$22-34
Creamer	15-27
Pitcher (ill.)	27-38
Spoonholder	15-27
Sugar bowl	18-29

Possibly other pieces were made.

Beaded Acorn Medallion

The Boston Silver-Glass Company, East Cambridge, Massachusetts, c. 1869, clear, non-flint.

Butter dish, covered	$42-58
Creamer	54-64
Goblet	34-46
Pitcher	52-62
Spoonholder	39-47
Sugar bowl, covered	44-53
Wine	19-28

Probably other pieces.

Beaded Arch Panels

Maker and date unknown.

Goblet	$17-29
Mug, handled (ill.)	22-36

Probably other pieces.

371

Beaded Arch Panels

Celery	26-38
Creamer	34-42
Goblet	27-34
Pitcher, water	39-49
Plate, 6″	24-36
Sauce, flat	12-18
Spoonholder	22-36
Sugar bowl, covered	34-39

Probably other pieces.

Beaded Dart Band

Beaded Band

Beaded Band

Maker unknown, c. 1884, clear, color (rare).

Butter dish, covered	$18-32
Compote, open	19-34
Creamer	17-32
Jug, syrup	33-48
Pitcher, water	34-44
Spoonholder	14-27
Sugar bowl, open, covered (base ill.)	16-30
Wine	19-29

If color, 100% higher than clear prices listed.

Beaded Chain

(Looped Cord): Maker unknown, c. 1870s, clear, non-flint.

Butter dish, covered	$40-50

Beaded Dart Band

Possibly McKee Bros., Pittsburgh, 1880s. Clear, colors.

Butter dish	$29-40
Celery holder	14-21
Compote	27-39
Creamer	24-38
Goblet	16-28
Pickle castor with fork (ill.)	52-70
Spoonholder	12-21
Sugar bowl, covered	27-39

Probably other pieces.

Beaded Dewdrop

(Wisconsin): U.S. Glass Company, Gas City, Indiana, 1898.

Bottles, oil, vinegar	$12-18
Bowl	
a. Covered, oblong, 6″, 8″	20-30
b. Covered, round, 7″, 8″	27-37
Butter dish, large, small, covered	52-60
Celery vase	50-62
Celery tray	39-50
Compote	
a. Covered, 6″, 7″, 8″	52-60
b. Open, 8½″, 9½″, 10½″	42-52

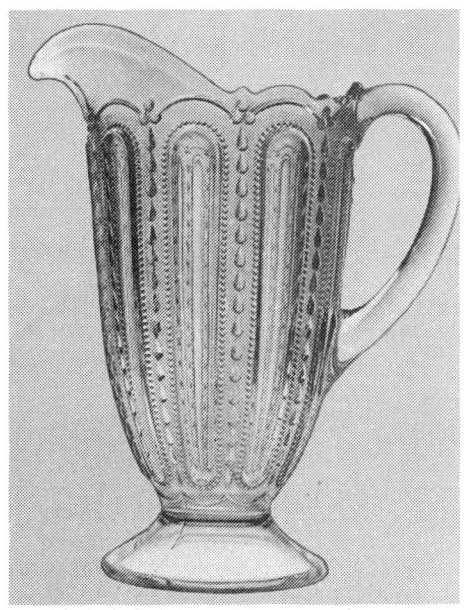

Beaded Dewdrop

Condiment set, 4-piece in holder .. 60-70
Creamer, individual and large .. 49-60
Cruet 21-32
Dish
  a. Candy 21-32
  b. Oval, handled, covered, 6" .. 50-60
  c. Oval, handled, open, 6" 18-28
  d. Sweetmeat 27-30
Goblet 50-60
Mug, large 42-52
Pitcher
  a. 3 pints 66-76
  b. 1 quart (ill.) 62-78
Sauce, flat and handled 9-17
Salt/Pepper, short, tall, pr. 21-32
Spoonholder 19-27
Sugar bowl, large and small,
  covered 54-64
Syrup jug, with cover 52-68
Toothpick holder 33-43
Tumbler 42-52
Wine........................ 39-47

Beaded Ellipse

Cambridge Glass Company, Cambridge, Ohio, late 1890s. After 1906, all products permanently marked "Near-Cut" on inside base. Clear.

Butter dish $32-42
Creamer 18-28

Beaded Ellipse

Compotes..................... 34-44
Goblet 19-27
Pitcher
  a. Milk.................... 28-38
  b. Water (ill.) 33-46
Spoonholder 14-21
Sugar bowl 28-40
Wine........................ 12-21

Probably other pieces.

Beaded Fan

Beaded Fan

Maker unknown, 1875-1880. Clear.

Butter dish $32-43
Celery vase 19-27
Compote 28-38
Creamer 27-39
Pitcher (ill.)................... 26-38
Spoonholder 19-26
Sugar bowl
  a. Covered 34-46
  b. Open 15-22

Probably other pieces.

Beaded Fine-Cut   Beaded Flange

Beaded Fine-Cut

Maker and date unknown. Clear, possibly in colors.

Butter dish $21-30
Creamer 19-30
Goblet 20-32
Pitcher (ill.) 31-41
Spoonholder 16-27
Sugar bowl 22-31
Probably other pieces.

Beaded Flange

Fostoria Glass Company, 1891. Crystal and colors.

Butter dish $19-32
Creamer 25-37
Goblet 19-26
Pickle dish 15-24
Spoonholder 18-27
Sugar bowl 27-38

Probably other pieces. Colors, 50 percent higher than clear prices listed.

Beaded Grape

Beaded Grape

(California): U.S. Glass Company, Pittsburgh, 1880s. Clear and emerald green.

Bowl, rectangular $16-28
Butter dish, covered 52-68
Cake plate on stand 51-61
Celery tray, oblong 40-50
Compote
  a. High foot, 7", 8", 9" 68-70
  b. Small, 4" high (rare) 77-82
  c. Shallow, on standard 52-62
Cordial 41-51
Creamer (ill.) 52-60
Cruet 44-54
Dish
  a. Oblong, deep 38-48
  b. Square, 5¼", 6¼", 7¼", 8¼".. 42-52
Goblet 52-63
Pickle 21-32
Pitcher, water
  a. Round, several sizes 43-63
  b. Square, several sizes 44-60
Platter, oblong (rare) 62-91
Plate, square, 8½" 28-38
Sauce, 3½", 4", 4½" 15-27
Salt/Pepper, metal tops, pr....... 39-52
Spoonholder 39-56
Sugar bowl, covered 50-60
Toothpick holder 22-30
Tumbler, water 29-42
Vase, 6" 27-41

Probably other pieces. Green pieces 50 percent higher than clear prices listed. Almost EVERY piece being reproduced!

Beaded Grape Medallion

Boston Silver-Glass Company, East Cambridge, Massachusetts, late 1860s. Clear.

Butter dish .... $ 58- 68
Celery vase 60- 70
Compote, covered, high, low, oval . 66- 82
Creamer, applied handle 90-110
Egg cup 40- 50
Goblet 40- 50
Pitcher, water (ill.) 110-140
Salt, footed, oval and round, flat .. 22- 32
Spoonholder 40- 50
Sugar bowl 60- 70

Probably other pieces.

Beaded Grape Medallion

Cordial	18-29
Creamer	29-39
Dish, oval, 7½", 9½", 10½"	12-16
Goblet	29-38
Mug, handled	21-31
Pickle dish, boat shape	22-32
Pitcher	
a. Milk (ill.)	39-49
b. Syrup	32-42
c. Water, ½ gallon	40-44
Saucedishes, 2 types	18-27
Shakers	
a. Salt/Pepper, pr.	31-41
b. Sugar	32-42
Spoonholder, footed and flat	44-54
Sugar bowl	
a. Covered	32-50
b. Open	39-49
Tray, bread	38-52
Tumbler	37-44
Vase, toothpick holder	27-38
Wine	36-42

Beaded Loop

Beaded Loop

(Oregon): U.S. Glass Company, 1906-08.
Clear, ruby-flashed.

Bowl, berry, covered	$32-41
Butter dish, 2 types	32-42
Cake stand, 6", 9½"	44-54
Celery	48-58
Compote	
a. Large, covered	42-52
b. Open, jelly	30-40

Beaded Medallion

Beaded Medallion

(Beaded Mirror): Sandwich Glass, late
1860s, or early 1870s. Clear only.

Butter dish, covered	$58-69
Compote, covered	44-53
Creamer	48-58
Egg cup	32-47
Goblet	36-46
Pitcher (ill.)	72-82
Relish dish	22-32
Salt dish, footed	27-38
Sauce, flat and footed	12-19
Spoonholder	32-42
Sugar bowl, covered	35-45

Probably other pieces.

Beaded Oval and Scroll

Beaded Oval and Scroll

(Dot): Bryce Bros., Pittsburgh, late 1870s. Clear.

Bowl, 6½"..................... $26-37
Butter dish, covered 42-52
Cake stand 30-40
Compote
  a. High standard, covered 38-50
  b. High standard, open........ 36-46
Cordial 15-27
Creamer 28-38
Dish, oval.................... 17-26
Goblet 32-46
Pickle dish 26-36
Pitcher, water (ill.) 52-60
Sauce 12-19
Salt/Pepper, pr. 22-36
Spoonholder 40-50
Sugar bowl
  a. Covered 52-62
  b. Open 37-49

Beaded Panels

Beaded Panels

Crystal Glass Company, Pittsburgh, Pennsylvania, 1877. Crystal.

Butter dish $27-36
Compote 32-41
Creamer 24-34
Egg cup 18-29
Goblet 17-27
Honey dish 12-19
Pitcher, water (ill.) 30-40
Salt/Pepper, pr. 18-29
Sauce 12-19
Spoonholder 19-27
Sugar bowl 34-44
Tumbler 22-32
Wine....................... 15-28

Probably other pieces.

Beaded Panels

Beaded Panels

Maker unknown, late 1880s. Clear.

Goblet $26-36
Spoonholder 19-29

Undoubtedly other pieces.

Beaded Swirl and Disc

Beaded Swirl and Disc

Maker and date unknown.

Butter dish, covered $32-42
Cake stand 29-36
Celery 19-27

Compote, covered	34-52
Creamer, covered	32-47
Cruet	15-19
Pitcher	
a. Milk (ill.)	40-50
b. Syrup	32-47
c. Water	50-62
Salt/Pepper, pr.	21-32
Sugar bowl, covered	34-48

Probably other pieces, possibly in colors.

Beaded Tulip

Beaded Tulip

McKee Brothers, Pittsburgh, c. 1894, clear, non-flint; possibly, blue.

Bowl, oblong	$36-46
Butter dish, covered	44-58
Cake stand, 9" high	33-46
Creamer	29-39
Goblet (ill.)	40-50
Pickle, oval	27-36
Pitcher, water, milk	44-54
Spoonholder	24-34
Sugar bowl, covered	36-46
Tray, water	38-62
Wine	33-52

Tray, water, blue, 100% higher than tray, water, clear, listed.

Bearded Head

(Viking; Bearded Prophet; Old Man of The Mountain): Hobbs, Brockunier & Company, Wheeling, West Virginia, 1876. Clear. The bearded head is that of a Roman Warrior, NOT a Viking.

Bearded Head

Bowl, covered, large	$56-72
Butter dish, covered	62-74
Celery	42-52
Compote, covered, 7", 8"	52-63
Creamer, 3 heads	44-54
Pickle dish	24-34
Pitcher, water (ill.)	58-68
Platter	45-55
Relish, footed	34-47
Salt	26-36
Sauce	29-38
Spoonholder	44-57
Sugar bowl, covered	50-62

Goblets and tumblers were not made. This pattern apparently was reproduced before World War II. In what pieces it is not known. Careful!

Bellflower

Bellflower

(Ribbed Leaf): Sandwich Glass Company, 1840s; McKee Bros., Pittsburgh, 1868; others. Clear, cobalt blue, amber, opaque. Amber considered rarest. Blue next. One could write an entire book on Bellflower. There are many qualities and types—this must be taken into consideration when giving a price on a particular piece. A silvery-looking "lace glass" would probably be Sandwich; the dull-looking glass, some of it with worn designs, would be the lesser glass, probably made after the Civil War. Prices given here are for what one generally finds in shops today. If you can authenticate a piece as being genuine Sandwich, it's worth at least 150 percent more than the prices given here. Know your dealer, please!

Bowl
  a. Berry, flat, scalloped $110-140
  b. Round, 6", 8" edge 105-130
  c. Deep, oval 92-120
  d. Flat, scallop and point
    edge 118-130
Butter dish, covered
  a. Beaded edge 78- 96
  b. Rayed edge 80- 90
  c. Scalloped edge 92-102
Cake stand (rare), if found .... 1,400+
Castor sets, 5 bottles (rare) .... 450+
Celery vase (rare) .... 275+
Compotes, any and all, 6 types.. 130-190
Creamer, Double or Single
  Vine 130-150
Decanter, 3 types (rare) 140-160
Egg cup (rare in colors) 38- 48
Goblets, 6 types 44- 54
Honey dish, 3", 3¼", 2½" 32- 42
Lamps, 3 types, quarts and
  pints 150-170
Mug, handled, small (rare) 132-150
Pitcher
  a. Milk, Double Vine (rare) .. 750+
  b. Syrup, 10-sided (rare) .... 900+
  c. Water, 2 sizes 172-196
Plate, 6" (rare) 82- 92
Salt
  a. Covered, footed (rare) 150-170
  b. Open, footed 40- 60

Sauce 22- 32
Spoonholder
  a. Double Vine 58- 68
  b. Single Vine 47- 59
Sugar bowl
  a. Double Vine, covered 96-108
  b. Single Vine, covered 84-105
  c. Octagonal (rare)......... 450+
Tumbler, footed, fine rib 72- 82
Whiskey — small tumbler
  (rare) .... 275+
Wine, Single Vine 62- 72

Belted Worchester

Belted Worchester

Maker unknown, c. late 1850s, clear, flint.

Champagne...................$42-56
Cordial 32-42
Goblet (ill.) 33-41
Sugar bowl, covered 49-60
Whiskey, handled,............. 32-41
Wine........................ 31-41

Another member of the "Worchester" family. Probably other pieces.

Berlin

Adams & Company, Pittsburgh, 1874, Clear.

Butter dish $29-38
Compote
  a. Covered 44-52
  b. Open 32-42
Creamer 22-36
Dish, oval.................... 14-21

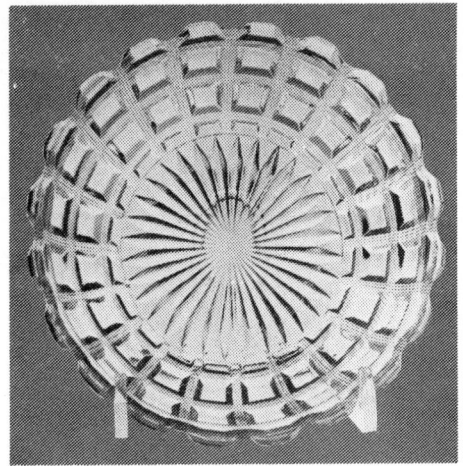

Berlin

Egg cup 17-27
Honey dish 15-24
Pickle dish 13-22
Pitcher
  a. Milk 51-61
  b. Water 52-62
Plate (ill.), 7″ deep 20-32
Salt/Pepper, pr. 22-32
Sauce 14-27
Spoonholder 18-29
Sugar bowl 33-39
Tumbler 27-37
Wine 26-36

Berry Cluster

Berry Cluster

Maker unknown, 1880s. Clear.

Butter dish $44-52
Celery vase 17-29
Creamer 34-48

Goblet 18-29
Pitcher, water (ill.) 48-59
Spoonholder 17-27
Sugar bowl
  a. Covered 38-49
  b. Open 17-28
Probably other pieces.

Bethlehem Star

Bethlehem Star

Maker unknown, 1880s, clear.

Butter dish $27-36
Celery 17-27
Creamer 19-28
Goblet 24-37
Pitcher (ill.) 34-44
Sauce 10-18
Spoonholder 15-27
Sugar bowl 19-26

Probably other pieces.

Beveled Diagonal Block

(continued)

Beveled Diagonal Block

Challinor, Taylor & Company, 1880s.
Clear. Also by Bryce Bros., 1888.

Butter dish	$32-42
Compote	31-40
Creamer	33-41
Cake stand	36-46
Celery vase	27-37
Cordial	10-18
Goblet	20-27
Marmalade jar	16-29
Pitcher, water	28-38
Plate	12-21
Salt/Pepper, pr.	16-26
Spoonholder (ill.)	19-27
Sugar bowl	31-41
Tumbler	20-30
Wine	22-42

Probably other pieces.

Beveled Star

Beveled Star

(Pride): Model Flint Glass Company, Findlay, Ohio, 1890, called this pattern PRIDE. Clear, emerald green, cobalt, amber.

Butter dish, covered	$42-52
Celery	19-27
Compote, covered, high standard	48-56
Creamer	27-37
Goblet	28-39
Pitcher, water (ill.)	50-60
Salt/Pepper, pr.	27-37
Spoonholder, emerald	34-46
Sugar bowl	28-38

Probably other pieces. Emerald green,

cobalt, 50 percent higher; amber, 100 percent higher than clear prices listed.

Bicycle Girl

Bicycle Girl

Dalzell, Gilmore and Leighton, Findlay, Ohio, 1880s; later by National Glass Company, Greentown, Indiana.

Pitcher, water, clear (ill.)	$340-380
Possibly tumbler to match	138-165

Bigler

Bigler

Boston & Sandwich Glass Company, Sandwich, Massachusetts, c. 1850s, clear, flint.

Bowl	$62- 72
Celery	72- 84
Champagne	92-102
Cordial	80- 90
Decanter, bar type	58- 67
Goblet, (ill.)	54- 63
Mug, handled	57- 66

Tumbler 49- 57
Wine 42- 52
Possibly creamer and sugar bowl (rare).

Birch Leaf

Birch Leaf

Maker unknown, c. 1870s, clear, milk glass, flint.

Butter dish, covered, on pedestal
(ill.) $58-71
Creamer 27-38
Egg cup 15-27
Goblet 18-30
Salt, master, footed 12-21
Spoonholder 16-27
Sugar bowl, covered 58-60

Milk glass, 100% higher than clear prices listed. Probably other pieces.

Bird and Strawberry

Bird and Strawberry

(Bluebird): 1890s, berries, birds, leaves, colored, clear.

Bowl, footed, berry, round $60- 70
Butter dish, covered 50- 72
Cake stand, 9" diameter 54- 63
Compote, open, 2 sizes 88-110
Creamer, w/color 52- 66
Goblet 29- 38
Pitcher (ill.) 54- 64
Relish, heart-shaped 22- 28
Sauce, clear 15- 27
Spoonholder 27- 38
Sugar bowl, covered 40- 50
Tumbler 19- 27
Wine 38- 60

Probably other pieces.

Bird Napkin Ring

Bird Napkin Ring

With salt (in bird's back) and pepper. Sandwich Glass; considered scarce. There is a pair of these at the Houston Museum, Chattanooga, Tennessee.

Bird napkin ring w/Salt/Pepper,
pr. (ill.) .... $375+

Bird on Nest Mug

Challinor & Taylor, Ltd., Tarentum, Pennsylvania, 1880s.

Mug $56-66

Bird on Nest Mug

Birds and Harp Mug

Birds and Harp Mug

A novelty drinking mug for children in the late 1800s.

Mug $35-52

Birds at Fountain

Birds at Fountain

Early 1880s. Clear, opaque.

Bowl	$19-27
Butter dish	38-47
Cake stand	39-47
Compote	28-38
Creamer	29-39
Goblet	39-42
Mug (ill.)	19-27
Spoonholder	19-30
Sugar bowl, covered	26-40

Probably other pieces.

Blackberry

Blackberry

William Leighton, Jr., Wheeling, West Virginia, 1870. Clear, milk, white.

Butter dish, covered	$ 60- 70
Celery vase (rare)	62- 72
Champagne	44- 56
Compote	
a. Covered, high foot........	84- 94
b. Covered, low foot	73- 97
Creamer	66- 80
Dish, oval, 8¼" x 5½" (rare) ..	60- 70
Egg cup, double and single	48- 60
Goblet, (rare)	49- 58
Honey dish	22- 32
Pitcher, water (rare) (ill.)	170-185
Salt, footed, 2 styles	33- 43
Sauce, flat	17- 27
Spoonholder	54- 64
Sugar bowl, open	72- 90
Syrup	40- 50
Tumbler	30- 40

Milk glass, 50-60 percent higher than clear prices listed. Being reproduced in butter dish, celery vase, creamer, egg cup (single), goblet, water pitcher, sugar bowl. Possibly others. Careful!

Blaze

New England Glass Company, East Cambridge, Massachusetts, c. 1869, clear, flint.

Butter dish, covered	$62-71
Celery	69-80
Compote, covered, low standard,	
7", 8"	70-81
Creamer	80-92
Goblet	45-55
Plate, 6", 7"	27-37
Sauce, 4", 5"..................	19-28

Spoonholder 37-47
Sugar bowl, covered 62-74
Tumbler 40-40
Wine 55-72
Possibly other pieces.

Bleeding Heart

Block and Circle

Block and Circle

Maker and date unknown. Clear.

Goblet $24-36
Lamp, miniature 24-33
Pitcher, water (ill.) 48-60
Tumblers to match 19-28
Possibly other pieces.

Bleeding Heart

Sandwich Glass Company, 1860-1875, other companies later. Clear, opaque.

Bowl, waste $32-42
Butter dish 47-57
Cake plate on stand, 9½″ high ... 52-62
Compote
  a. Covered, high foot 61-71
  b. Covered, low foot 48-58
  c. Oval, covered 52-60
Cordial 28-37
Creamer, applied handle 42-53
Dish, oval, large 29-39
Egg cups
  a. Barrel shape 30-40
  b. Straight side 27-37
Goblet
  a. Plain and knob stem 32-42
  b. Thin, design low on bowl
    (ill.) 36-47
Mug, handled 29-36
Pickle dish, oval 26-33
Pitcher, water, 2 sizes (ill.) 84-94
Plates (rare) 67-77
Platter, oval 66-76
Salt, oval and round, footed 29-39
Sauces, 3 types 16-26
Spoonholder 48-58
Sugar bowl 52-62
Tumbler
  a. Footed 41-51
  b. Water 36-46
Wine 39-48

Block and Fan

Block and Fan

(Romeo): Richards & Hartley Glass Company, Tarentum, Pennsylvania, 1880s. Clear, clear with red flashing.

Bowl, berry, 8″ dia. $23-34
Butter dish 38-49
Cake stand, 10″ dia. 47-52
Celery 30-40
Compote 58-67
Cordial 22-34
Creamer 33-43
Cruets, large and small 27-37
Goblet 30-40
Lamp 32-42
Jam jar 26-36
Pitcher, water, pedestal base 33-44
Plate, large 27-37
Sauce, flat and footed 15-19
Salt/Pepper, pr. 28-39
Spoonholder 26-36

383

(continued)

Sugar, covered and open 39-44
Tumbler 18-27
Wine......................... 29-40

Block and Honeycomb

Block and Honeycomb

McKee & Bros., Pittsburgh, 1874. Clear.

Butter bowl....................$36-48
Goblet 26-36
Pitcher (ill.).................... 62-70
Sugar bowl 40-50

Probably other pieces.

Block and Palm

Probably Beaver Falls Co-Operative Glass Company, Beaver Falls, Pennsylvania, c. 1890, clear, milk glass, non-flint.

Butter dish, covered $38-48
Cake stand 36-45
Celery 27-36
Creamer 41-52
Goblet 28-37
Pitcher, water................. 41-50
Salt/Pepper, pr. 28-38
Sauce, flat 9-17
Spoonholder 22-32
Sugar bowl, covered 37-48

Milk glass, 100% higher than clear prices listed. Probably other pieces.

Block and Rib

Block and Rib

Maker and date unknown. Chalk white glass, also clear.

Butter dish, covered $30-40
Celery holder 18-29
Creamer 16-27
Goblet 18-28
Pitcher, water (ill.) 32-38
Spoonholder 19-26
Sugar bowl, covered 28-38

Probably other pieces.

Block and Star

Block and Star

(Valencia Waffle): 1885-1895. Clear, canary, blue, amber.

Butter dish, covered $21-32
Celery 24-33
Compote
  a. Covered 31-36
  b. Open 21-30

384

Creamer 18-27
Goblet (ill.) 19-25
Sauce
  a. Flat 12-19
  b. Footed 13-21
Spoonholder 20-30
Sugar
  a. Covered 26-37
  b. Open 19-27
Relish 12-18
Wine 19-27

Probably other pieces. Color, 60 percent more than clear prices listed.

Block and Sunburst

Block and Sunburst

George Duncan and Sons, Pittsburgh, 1880. Clear, ruby flashed.

Butter dish $44-52
Compote 41-51
Cream tankard 36-46
Goblet 18-27
Mug 22-32
Pitcher, water (ill.) 63-73
Sauce 14-19
Spoonholder 24-33
Sugar bowl 34-46
Tumbler 27-37
Wine 19-27

Probably other pieces.

Block and Thumbprint

Possibly Union Glass Company, Somerville, Massachusetts, c. 1860s, clear, flint and non-flint.

Butter dish, covered $36-46
Celery (ill.) 28-37
Compote, covered 36-48
Creamer 33-40

Block and Thumbprint

Spoonholder 27-28
Sugar bowl, covered 32-42
Tumbler, footed 34-43

Flint, 40% higher than non-flint prices listed. Probably other pieces.

Blockade

Blockade

Challinor, Taylor, Ltd., Tarentum, Pennsylvania, 1885, clear only.

Butter dish, covered (stemmed) ..$22-30
Celery (stemmed) 24-33
Compotes, covered, 6″, 7″, 8″, 9″,
  flared or straight 19-36
Creamer (stemmed) 15-27
Goblet (ill.) 23-33
Pitcher, qt., ½ gal. 42-52
Sugar bowl, covered (stemmed) .. 34-47
Tumbler 19-26

Many other pieces. Lower half of stem is hollow.

Blocked Arches

Blocked Arches

(Berkley): U.S. Glass Company, c. 1893, clear, non-flint, possibly stained ruby.

Bowl, finger	$22-34
Creamer	38-48
Cup/saucer	22-42
Goblet	27-36
Jug, syrup	40-50
Shaker, salt	12-20
Spoonholder	10-21
Sugar bowl (base ill.)	33-44
Tumbler	19-26
Wine	24-27

If stained ruby, 50% higher than clear prices listed. Other pieces.

Bosc Pear

Bosc Pear

Maker unknown, 1920s. Clear, flashed purple pears, gold flashed leaves.

Butter dish, covered	$34-44

Celery	23-34
Creamer	40-50
Pitcher, water (ill.)	42-49
Spoonholder	29-42
Sugar bowl	34-44
Tumbler	19-27

Probably other pieces.

Bow-Tie

The Thompson Glass Company, Uniontown, Pennsylvania, c. 1886, clear, non-flint.

Bowl, fruit, 10"	$56-66
Butter dish, covered	72-79
Creamer	53-63
Goblet	51-62
Pitcher	81-90
Spoonholder	27-36
Sugar bowl, covered	68-79

Firm only in business for three years. Possibly other pieces.

Boxed Star

Boxed Star

Maker unknown, 1890s, clear.

Butter dish	$24-32
Creamer	16-26
Pitcher, water (ill.)	32-42
Spoonholder	21-29
Sugar bowl	25-34
Tumbler	22-32

Probably other pieces.

Bradford Grape

Bradford Grape

Maker unknown, c. 1850s or 1860s, clear, flint.

Butter dish, covered ....$ 86-110
Champagne................. 62- 72
Cordial.................... 62- 71
Creamer 90-110
Goblet (ill.) 68- 80
Pitcher, water 172-185
Spoonholder 45- 70
Sugar bowl, covered 88- 98
Tumbler (rare) 99-110
Wine...................... 68- 78
Possibly other pieces.

Branched Tree

Branched Tree

Probably National Glass Company, Greentown, Indiana, 1890s.

Butter dish $42-52
Celery 22-32
Compote, covered, high, low
   standard 40-50
Creamer 28-38

Goblet 27-37
Pitcher, water (ill.) 68-80
Spoonholder 24-34
Sugar bowl 36-48
Probably others.

Brickwork

Brickwork

Probably National Glass Company Greentown, Indiana, around 1900. Clear and caramel slag.

Butter dish $34-44
Celery 18-27
Creamer 24-34
Goblet 33-43
Pitcher, water (ill.) 39-48
Salt/Pepper, pr. 19-32
Spoonholder 21-29
Sugar bowl, covered 32-42

Brilliant

Brilliant

Possibly McKee Brothers, Pittsburgh, c. 1870s, clear, flint.

Goblet (ill.) $49-62
There should be other pieces.

387

Bringing Home the Cows

Bringing Home the Cows

Dalzell, Gilmore and Leighton Company, 1870s. Clear.

Butter dish, covered $160-185
Creamer 120-148
Pitcher, milk (ill.) 270-300
Spoonholder 88-110
Sugar bowl, covered 150-172
Probably other pieces.

Britannic

Britannic

McKee Bros., Pittsburgh, 1893. Clear crystal with ruby stain. Popular after Columbian Exposition of 1893.

Butter dish, covered $33-42
Compote
a. Covered 50-60
b. Open 42-52
Cake stand, small, large 40-50
Creamer 28-38
Cruet 22-32
Cups, custard 11-15
Goblet 19-28
Pitcher (ill.) 37-47
Salt/Pepper, pr. 19-28
Spoonholder 24-34
Sugar bowl, covered 42-52
Tumbler 32-42
Wine 22-34

Red flashing, 65 percent higher; amber flashing, 45 percent higher than clear prices listed.

Broken Column

Broken Column

(Irish Column, Notched Rib): U.S. Glass Company, 1892, before that by Columbia Glass Company, Findlay, Ohio, 1891. Clear, clear with ruby-stained depressions.

Banana dish $52- 62
Basket, handled 98-110
Bowl
a. 8½″ diameter 41- 50
b. Covered, various sizes 28- 43
Butter dish, covered 38- 49
Cake stand, large 39- 47
Celery 34- 45
Compote
a. Covered, high standard 52- 62
b. Open, high standard 42- 52
Celery tray 40- 50
Creamer 37- 47
Cruet 32- 42
Custard cup.................. 21- 31
Finger bowl.................. 18- 28
Goblet, lady's 40- 50
Pickle castor, complete 72- 82
Pitcher, water (ill.) 44- 54
Plate, 7″ (rare) 42- 52
Sauce, flat 12- 19
Salt/Pepper, pr. 28- 40
Spoonholder 19- 27
Sugar
a. Bowl, open 38- 52
b. Shaker (rare)............. 34- 48
Syrup jug.................... 34- 45
Tumbler, plain 26- 37
Water bottle 38- 50
Wine....................... 20- 30
Goblet is being reproduced. Ruby-stained depression pieces 200 percent higher than clear prices listed.

Brooklyn

Brooklyn

Maker unknown, c. late 1860s, early 1870s, clear, flint. Possibly a Bakewell, Pears product.

Compote
  a. Covered $60-72
  b. Open 32-42
Creamer 48-62
Decanter 44-53
Goblet (ill.) 48-58
Pitcher, water 62-72
Sugar bowl, covered 66-73
Probably other pieces.

Buck and Doe

Maker and date unknown.
Goblet .... $130-165+

Buckingham

Buckingham

U.S. Glass Company, 1906. Clear, cranberry and green.

Bowl, 8¼" dia. (ill.) $52-73
Butter dish, covered 44-60
Celery 22-34
Compote
  a. Covered 40-50
  b. Open 42-52
Creamer 40-50
Goblet 32-42
Pitcher, water 56-66
Spoonholder 22-32
Sugar bowl, covered 44-54
Tumbler 19-28
Probably other pieces. Color, 25 percent higher than clear prices listed.

Buckle

Buckle

Sandwich Glass, early 1870s; also Gillinder & Sons, Philadelphia, same period. Clear, sapphire blue (rare).

Bowl, wire basket container .. $ 62- 80
Butter dish, covered, flat 78- 93
Champagne.................. 42- 56
Compote, open, low standard .. 62- 74
Cordial..................... 66- 76
Creamer, applied handles,
  pedestal foot 92-110
Egg cup 50- 60
Goblets, 2 types 52- 65
Pickle dish, large, oval 42- 52
Pitcher, water 120-140
Salt dip
  a. Footed 28- 38
  b. Oval, flat (rare) 39- 49
Sauce dish, 4" 17- 26
Spoonholder, scalloped rim 50- 60
Sugar bowl, covered, flint 62- 72
Tumbler 55- 64
Color, 80 percent more than clear prices listed.

Buckle with Diamond Band

Maker unknown, c. 1880s, clear, non-flint.

Butter dish, covered $40-50
Creamer 33-42
Goblet 38-47
Pitcher, water................ 35-45
Spoonholder 27-38
Sugar bowl, covered 42-52
Probably other pieces.

Buckle with Star

Buckle with Star

(Orient): Bryce, Walker & Company, Pittsburgh, Pennsylvania, c. 1875, clear, non-flint.

Bowls, oval, round $17-27
Butter dish, covered 40-50
Celery 41-48
Compote, covered 52-62
Creamer (ill.) 33-40
Goblet 40-50
Pitcher...................... 42-53
Relish, oval 18-29
Sauce, flat 6-12
Spoonholder 16-29
Sugar bowl, covered 34-48
Wine........................ 29-39
Probably other pieces.

Bulldog with Hat Toothpick

A scarce novelty from Sandwich. Supposedly clear only, but the Houston Museum, Chattanooga, Tennessee, has one in amber and one in blue! Being reproduced in all colors.

Bulldog with Hat Toothpick

Clear ....$ 72- 92
Amber 130-160
Blue 140-155
Also made by Belmont Glass Co., Bellaire, Ohio, c. 1885.

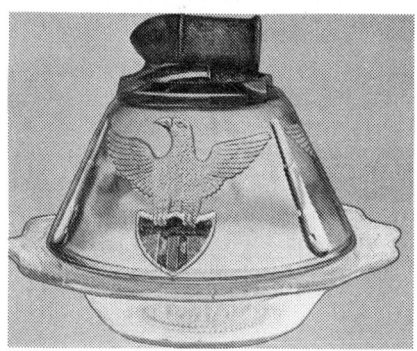

Bullet Emblem

Bullet Emblem

(Shield in Red, White and Blue): Clear, Spanish-American War souvenir, made in 1898.

Butter, covered (ill.) $240-280
Creamer 160-182
Spoonholder 120-145
Sugar bowl, covered 190-240
Possibly other pieces.

Bull's Eye

Bull's Eye and Daisy

Bull's Eye

(Lawrence): New England Glass Company; also Sandwich. Clear, milk-white, other colors (rare).

Bitters bottle	$92-125
Butter dish	95-110
Castor bottle	28- 40
Celery vase	64- 80
Champagne	74- 82
Cologne bottle	63- 73
Compote	
a. Open, large, high standard	88-110
b. Open, low standard	74- 92
Cordials, 2 styles	40- 50
Creamer	79- 92
Cruet	50- 60
Decanter	
a. Bar lip, pint and quart	54- 64
b. Usual type, pint and quart	48- 58
Egg cup, covered (rare)	47- 59
Goblet, knob and plain stem	42- 52
Jar, covered, small	60- 70
Lamp	68- 78
Pickle dish, oval	39- 49
Salt	
a. Footed	19- 27
b. Footed, oblong, covered (rare)	40- 50
Spoonholder (ill.)	42- 50
Sugar bowl	97-110
Tumbler, water	55-120
Water bottle with tumble-up	60- 70

Colored pieces, 50 percent higher than clear prices listed.

Bull's Eye and Daisy

Maker unknown, c. 1890s, clear, clear with bull's eyes in red, purple, green, gilt rims.

Butter dish, covered	$41-52
Creamer	38-48
Goblet	27-36
Pitcher, water	40-50
Salt shaker	15-27
Spoonholder	19-29
Sugar bowl, handled (ill.)	21-32
Tumbler	15-28
Wine	14-26

Colors, 80-100% higher than clear prices listed.

Bull's Eye and Fan

Bull's Eye and Fan

(Daisies in Oval Panels): Mid-1890s. Clear; sometimes combined with color.

Bowl	$ 7-11
Butter dish, covered	15-22
Creamer	19-22
Goblet	15-27
Pitcher, water (ill.)	36-46
Sauce, flat	12-22
Spoonholder	12-20
Sugar	
a. Covered	22-31
b. Open	14-27

Probably other pieces. Pieces with colored dots in eyes, 20 percent higher than clear prices listed.

Bull's Eye and Prism

Bull's Eye and Prism

Maker unknown, c. late 1840s, early 1850s, clear, flint.

Goblet (ill.) $72-91
Other pieces unknown.

Bull's Eye and Spear Head

Bull's Eye and Spear Head

Dalzell, Gilmore & Leighton, Findlay, Ohio, c. late 1870s, clear, non-flint.

Bottle, castor $19-30
Butter dish, covered 46-56
Compote
  a. Covered 18-29
  b. Open 50-60
Creamer 33-47
Decanter (ill.) 35-55
Goblet 35-60
Lamp, night 27-39
Spoonholder 28-39
Sugar bowl, covered 52-62
Wine (ill.)..................... 32-51
Probably other pieces.

Bull's Eye with Fleur-de-Lis

Bull's Eye with Fleur-de-Lis

Boston & Sandwich Glass Company, mid-1800s; probably Union Glass Company, Somerville, Massachusetts, 1860s. Clear and amber.

Ale glass (rare) $125-150
Butter dish, covered 94-110
Celery 98-120
Compote
  a. Open, high standard 100-130
  b. Open, low standard 92-105
Creamer 120-132
Decanter
  a. Pint 72- 82
  b. Quart 92-110
Goblet 62- 92
Lamp
  a. Glass only 60- 70
  b. Glass bowl, brass stem,
    marble base 120-130
Pitcher, water (rare) (ill.) 195-198
Salt, footed 40- 60
Sugar bowl 92-120

Butterfly

392

Butterfly

Bakewell, Pears & Company, Pittsburgh, 1895-1905. Clear or clear with frosted handles.

Butter dish, covered	$42-52
Celery	19-27
Creamer	30-40
Mustard, covered, handled	15-22
Pickle dish	14-27
Pitcher, water (ill.)	52-62
Relish dish, oval	16-27
Salt/Pepper, pr.	19-27
Sugar bowl, covered	50-60

Probably other pieces.

Butterfly and Grape

Butterfly and Grape

Fenton Art Glass Company, Williamstown, West Virginia, early 1920s, "Golden Iridescent" only.

Bowl, berry	$52-62
Butter dish, covered	50-60
Creamer	40-49
Pitcher, water, jug, not footed	48-58
Spoonholder	27-29
Sugar bowl, covered, footed	50-60
Tumbler	19-27

Butterfly with Spray

Butterfly with Spray

(Acme): Bryce, Higbee and Company, Pittsburgh, early 1800s. Clear.

Butter dish, covered	$42-52
Celery	17-27
Compote, covered, high, low standard	29-37
Creamer	24-33
Goblet	29-33
Mug (ill.)	26-37
Pitcher, water	42-56
Spoonholder	32-42
Sugar bowl, covered	40-50
Tumbler	19-29

Probably many other pieces

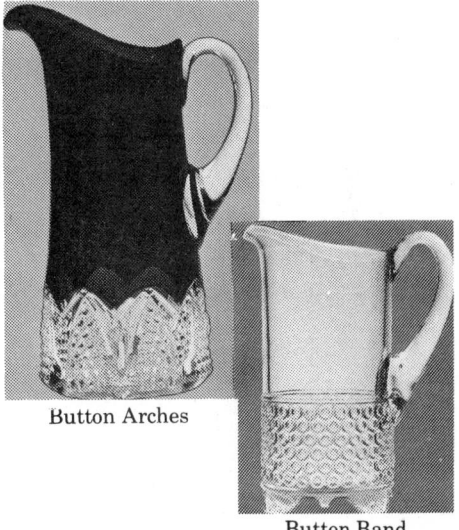

Button Arches

Button Band

Button Arches

(Scalloped Daisy, Red Top): Duncan & Miller Glass Company, Washington, Pennsylvania, 1897. Clear, clear with red top.

Bowl, 8"	$28-37
Cake stand	37-42
Compote, jelly	19-27
Creamer	30-40
Cruet	29-39
Goblet	32-42
Mug	32-40
Pitcher, water (ill.)	42-50
Salt/Pepper, pr.	33-42
Spoonholder	29-48

 (continued)

Sugar bowl, covered 42-52
Toothpick holder 36-46
Tumbler 42-52
Wine....................... 29-58
Probably other pieces. "Red top" pieces
35 percent more than clear prices listed.
Reproduced in butter dish, wine,
creamer and goblet.

Button Band

Early 1880s. Clear.

Bowl $22-32
Butter dish 32-42
Cake stand 50-60
Compote, open 42-52
Creamer 32-42
Goblet 27-32
Pitcher, water (ill.) 36-47
Sugar bowl, covered 38-47
Tumbler 28-38
Wine....................... 27-37
Probably other pieces.

Buttressed Arch

Buttressed Arch

(Buttressed Loop): Possibly Adams
Glass Company, Pittsburgh, mid-1880s.
Clear.

Butter dish, covered $33-43
Celery vase 25-35
Creamer 27-37
Goblet 22-32
Pitcher, water (ill.) 48-58
Sauce 12-15
Spoonholder 16-27
Sugar bowl, covered 32-42
Probably other pieces.

Cabbage Leaf

Cabbage Leaf

Maker unknown, 1870s and 1880s.
Clear amber, heavily stippled and frosted, opalescent.

Butter dish, covered $64-78
Celery 65-80
Compote, covered, high standard   77-88
Creamer 52-62
Pickle dish, large leaf shape 24-33
Pitcher, water (ill.) 74-84
Plate, rabbit head in center 46-66
Spoonholder 40-52
Sugar bowl, covered 72-90
Stippled and frosted pieces 10 percent
more; amber 50 percent more than clear
prices listed. Tumbler not known but
probably made. BEWARE! Every pat-
tern has been reproduced in almost
every color — even goblets!

Cabbage Rose

Cabbage Rose

Central Glass Company, Wheeling,
West Virginia, 1880s; possibly at Sandwich earlier. Clear.

394

Butter dish ....$ 68- 78
Cake plate on standard, 11" .. 75- 90
Celery 48- 60
Compotes, 6", 7", 8", 9" 62- 78
Cordial...................... 42- 47
Creamer 63- 72
Egg cup 28- 38
Goblet 49- 58
Pickle dish 22- 33
Pitcher
  a. Quart (ill.) 64- 72
  b. Three pints (rare)........ 115-142
Salt, footed 22- 32
Sauce dish, 4", 5" 17- 27
Spoonholder 48- 59
Sugar bowl, open 62- 72
Sugar bowl, with lid 62- 72
Tumbler, water 48- 58
Wine (rare) 50- 60
Goblet being reproduced.

Cable

Cable

Possibly Sandwich Glass of the 1850s, clear, flint; rare in opaque, blue opaque, green opaque, silver-stained panels.

Butter dish, covered $105-120
Compote, open 59- 72
Creamer (rare) 410-420
Egg cup 31- 41
Goblet 50- 60
Lamp, marble base 98-115
Pitcher, water (rare).......... 675+
Spoonholder (ill.) 42- 52
Sugar bowl, covered 98-115
Tumbler, footed 190-250
Colors, 120-140% higher than clear prices listed.

Cable with Ring

Cable with Ring

Sandwich Glass Company, 1860s. Clear only.

Butter dish ....$ 78- 88
Compote, open, 8¼" 72- 90
Creamer..................... 72- 85
Honey dish 27- 37
Lamp 96-106
Pitcher (ill.) 115-125
Sauce, flat 25- 35
Sugar bowl, covered 88- 98
No goblet or tumbler known.

Cactus

Cactus

(Panelled Agave): Indiana Tumbler & Goblet (National) Company, 1903. Crystal, chocolate (caramel slag).

Berry bowl ....$ 88- 98
Butter dish 120-135
Butter dish, stemmed 220-245
Celery tray 50- 60
Compote
  a. Large 167-185
  b. Medium 130-140
  c. Small 92-109
Cracker jar 118-128
Creamer 78- 88
Cruet 95-110
Mug 60- 70
Mustard jar.................. 120-140
Pitcher, water (ill.) 180-190

(continued)

Relish dish 72- 82
Salt/Pepper, pr. 62- 72
Spoonholder 68- 78
Sugar bowl 82- 92
Syrup, Dewey or metal lid 79- 94
Toothpick 47- 56
Tumbler, water and lemonade 60- 70

Prices listed are for chocolate. Being reproduced — careful!

Canadian

Canadian

Burlington Glass Works, Canada, 1870s. Clear.

Butter dish, covered $56-68
Celery 42-52
Compote
  a. Covered, 6", 7", 8" 60-70
  b. Open, high and low
    standard 42-52
Cordial 30-40
Creamer 46-56
Goblet 39-58
Jam jar, covered............... 34-44
Pitcher, milk and water
  a. Large (ill.) 66-76
  b. Small 52-62
Plate, 6", 8", 10" 34-45
Sauce, flat and footed, 4" 12-19
Spoonholder 42-52
Sugar bowl covered 52-62
Wine........................ 29-39

Cane

Cane

Sandwich Glass Company, 1875-1885. Also Gillinder Glass Company and McKee Glass Company, same period. Clear, amber, apple green, blue, yellow.

Bowl, berry, 3-panel, footed $33-46
Bowl, finger................... 29-42
Butter dish 42-58
Creamer 23-43
Goblet 29-40
Jam jar...................... 39-42
Pickle dish, oval............... 17-24
Pitcher, water (ill.) 36-46
Sauce
  a. Covered 15-30
  b. Flat 19-27
Salt/Pepper, pr. 30-40
Spoonholder 35-50
Sugar bowl 42-52
Toddy plate 24-37
Tray, water 29-44
Tumbler, water 28-39
Green, common. Amber and blue, 60 percent higher than clear prices listed.

Cane Column

Mid-1800s. Clear, canary, amber, blue.

Butter dish, covered $31-40
Creamer 32-41
Goblet 32-43
Pitcher (ill.).................. 39-47
Sauce, flat 22-38
Spoonholder 28-38
Sugar bowl
  a. Covered 32-42
  b. Open 19-27
Wine....................... 28-38

Cane Column

Probably other pieces. Color pieces, 80 to 100 percent higher than clear prices listed.

Cane Insert

Cane Insert

Tarentum Glass Company, Tarentum, Pennsylvania, 1898-1906, clear, clear with gold gilt, emerald green with gold gilt, pink with gold gilt, custard, pea green custard.

Butter dish, covered $37-48
Cake stand 35-42
Compote 27-39
Creamer (ill.) 22-40
Goblet 26-36
Pitcher, water................. 49-62
Sugar bowl, covered 28-37
Made in a full line of ware. Gold gilt, custard, 75% higher than clear prices listed.

Cane Medallion

Cane Medallion

Westmoreland Glass Company, Grapeville, Pennsylvania, 1896. Clear, opaque.

Bowl, berry, oblong, oval $18-29
Butter dish 29-39
Creamer (ill.) 31-42
Pickle 14-21
Pitcher, water................. 42-52
Spoonholder 21-29
Sugar bowl, covered 31-41
Toothpick..................... 24-38
Tumbler 22-34
Probably other pieces.

Cape Cod

Probably Sandwich, c. 1870s, clear, non-flint.

Bowl, handled.................. $32-42
Butter dish, covered 60-70
Celery 38-48
Compote
  a. Covered, 6″, 7″, 8″ 58-68
  b. Open, 6″, 7″, 8″ 38-48
Creamer 50-60
Goblet 50-60
Jar, jam 58-68
Pitcher, water................. 63-78
Spoonholder 27-39
Sugar bowl, covered 61-78
Wine........................ 39-49
Probably other pieces.

Capitol Building

Souvenir glass of the 1920s. Different buildings on different pieces.

Dessert plate $34-45
Goblet (ill.) 48-58
Sherbet...................... 32-46
Tumbler 40-50

Capitol Building

Caprice

Caprice

(Arched Fans): Possibly Cambridge Glass Company, Cambridge, Massachusetts, c. early 1900s, clear, frosted, blue, gold, non-flint.

Goblet (ill.)	$24-35
Plate, 14½"	42-52
Salt dip	12-17
Sauce	8-16
Wine	14-22

Colors, 80% higher. Clear, frosted, 20% higher than clear prices listed. Probably other pieces.

Caramel Strigil

Caramel Strigil

Probably Indiana Tumbler and Goblet Company, before 1903, when the factory burned. McKee Bros. made an identical pattern in 1897, calling it "Nelly," only in clear glass. In 1900, both firms joined National Glass Company, so either firm could have made this pattern.

Tankard, cream (ill.) .... $130-160+
Probably other pieces made.

Cardinal Bird

Cardinal Bird

Probably Ohio Flint Glass Company, Lancaster, late 1870s. This company was the ancestor of the Anchor-Hocking Glass Company. Clear.

Butter dish, covered $48-62
Creamer 34-52

Goblet 28-37
Pitcher, water 60-70
Sauce
  a. Flat, round 18-27
  b. Footed, 4", 5½" 19-27
Spoonholder (ill.) 22-32
Sugar bowl, covered 48-59
Possibly other pieces were made.

Carmen

(Panelled Diamond and Fine-Cut): Fostoria Glass Company, Moundsville, West Virginia, c. 1896, clear, clear flashed with yellow, non-flint.

Bowls, berry, 7", 8" $12-22
Butter dish, covered 30-42
Cake stand 28-40
Celery 15-22
Compote
  a. High standard, 7", 8" 29-42
  b. Low standard 17-27
Creamer 26-40
Cruet, oil 17-28
Goblet 19-29
Pitcher, water, tankard 27-39
Spoonholder 16-29
Sugar bowl, open 19-32
Wine 16-29
Yellow flashing, 20% higher than clear prices listed.

Cat on a Hamper

Cat on a Hamper

Indiana Tumbler & Goblet (National) Company, Greentown, Indiana, before 1903. Chocolate, amber, blue, green, clear. Two types made, short and tall. Prices listed, same for both.

Chocolate $150-175
Amber 125-142
Blue 170-180
Green 120-140
Clear 92-102

Extremely rare when top of hamper is in red, as shown in photo. It is believed no museum except the Houston has this type hamper.

Catawba Grape

Catawba Grape

Fairly new glass. Clear, also colors. Lots of it around.

Goblet $14-21
Wine (ill.) 12-20

Cathedral

Cathedral

(Orion): Bryce Bros., Pittsburgh, late 1880s. Crystal, amber, vaseline, blue amethyst.

Bowl, berry, 5", 6", 7", 8" $32-42
Butter dish 50-60
Cake plate on stand 52-62
Compote
  a. Covered, large, high
    standard 70-80
  b. Open, low standard 42-52
Creamer 48-58
Dish, round, footed 22-38
Egg cup 29-42
Goblet 39-47
Pitcher, water, 3 quart 62-69
Saucedish
  a. Flat, 4" 19-27
  b. Footed, 4", 4½" 22-32
Spoonholder 35-45
Sugar bowl, covered 50-60
Tumbler, water 28-38
Wine glass 34-44
Vaseline and amber, 45 percent; blue, 90 percent; amethyst, 125 percent higher than clear.

Cat's Eye and Block

(Cut Log): Westmoreland Specialty Company, c. 1896, clear, sometimes in camphor glass.

Butter dish, covered $56-66
Cake stand 60-72
Celery 50-60
Creamer, 3", 5" 16-27
Goblet 25-29
Pitcher, water 40-50
Sugar bowl, covered 48-58
Tumbler 22-31
Wine 32-50
Camphor, 50% higher than clear prices listed.

Celtic Cross

Duncan, Miller Glass Company, Pittsburgh, Pennsylvania, c. 1888, clear, etched, non-flint.

Butter dish, covered $39-50
Compote, covered 31-52

Creamer 29-37
Goblet 30-40
Spoonholder 28-38
Sugar bowl, covered 35-49
Etched, same price. Probably other pieces.

Centennial Beer Mug

Centennial Beer Mug

This was made by M. Daniel Connolly, or designed by him.

Beer mug $42-52

Centennial Beer Mug

Centennial Beer Mug

Hobbs, Brockunier & Company, designed for Philadelphia Centennial, 1876.

Butter dish $62-72
Centennial mug (ill.) 34-42

400

Ceres

Ceres

(Cameo, Goddess of Liberty): Possibly Indiana Tumbler & Goblet Company, 1898-1900. Crystal, opaque white, opaque turquoise, clear, amber, purple-black opaque.

Butter dish $60-70
Candy jar, covered 29-40
Compote, open, low standard 40-50
Creamer 32-52
Mug, handled 32-39
Pitcher, water 52-60
Spoonholder (ill.) 24-34
Sugar bowl, covered 42-52
Probably other pieces. Colored pieces, 50 percent higher than clear prices listed.

Chain

Chain

Maker unknown, c. early 1880s, clear, non-flint.

Butter dish, covered $27-38
Compote, covered 33-44
Cordial 18-27
Creamer 18-28
Goblet 18-31
Spoonholder 17-26
Sugar bowl (base ill.) 27-38
Wine 16-23
Probably other pieces.

Chain

Chain

Possibly Sandwich, early. The creamer shown here is almost identical with one made by R. B. Curling & Sons, Fort Pitt. This glassworks was located in Pittsburgh.

Butter dish $48-58
Creamer, cheaper version 38-47
Goblet, cheaper version 22-31
Pitcher, water (ill.) 37-47
Platter 23-34
Spoonholder 32-41
Sugar bowl 44-54
Wine 25-37

Chain and Shield

Late 1870s. Clear.

Butter, covered $29-41
Creamer 26-37
Goblet 18-31
Pitcher (ill.).................. 27-39
Platter, oval 25-38

401 (continued)

Chain and Shield

Sauce, flat	10-17
Spoonholder	16-27
Sugar, covered	27-38

Undoubtedly other pieces.

Chain with Star

Chain with Star

Possibly A. J. Beatty & Company, Steubenville, Ohio, 1880s. Clear.

Bowl, footed, small and large	$18-30
Butter dish, covered	39-52
Cake stand	26-38
Compote, covered, high and low standard	35-47
Creamer	42-51
Dish, oval	20-32
Goblet	23-35
Pickle dish	16-25
Pitcher, water (ill.)	42-60
Plate, 7", 9", 10", 12"	21-40
Plate, bread, handled	31-50

Sauce, flat and footed	18-29
Salt/Pepper, pr.	22-33
Spoonholder	35-47
Sugar bowl	44-56
Wine	19-29

Challinor Thumbprint

(Tall Baby Thumbprint): Challinor, Taylor & Company, Ltd., Tarentum, Pennsylvania, c. 1880s, clear, non-flint.

Bottle, water	$29-40
Bowl	26-41
Butter dish, covered	32-44
Creamer	32-42
Goblet	27-38
Spoonholder	24-34
Sugar bowl, covered	34-44
Tumbler	22-32

Other pieces.

Challinor's Tree of Life

Challinor's Tree of Life

(Challinor's No. 313): Challinor, Taylor, Ltd., Tarentum, Pennsylvania, 1885-1893, opal, olive green, roseblush pink, turquoise blue, yellow. Pieces were plain or hand-decorated in colors.

Butter dish, covered	$40-50
Can, molasses	16-27
Creamer	18-30
Dish, diamond-shaped	12-22
Jar, cracker (ill.)	40-52
Salt/Pepper, pr.	20-33
Spoonholder	21-36
Sugar bowl, covered	39-54

Hand-decorated pieces, 75% higher than plain prices listed.

Chandelier

Chandelier

(Crown Jewels): O'Hara Glass Company, Ltd., 1880s.

Bowl, finger.	$18-29
Celery	27-36
Compote	
a. Covered	42-52
b. Open	28-44
Creamer, clear or etched	25-39
Pitcher, water (ill.)	37-49
Salt, footed	18-29
Sauce, flat	15-27
Spoonholder	24-36
Sugar	
a. Covered	43-54
b. Open	22-32

Probably other pieces.

Checkerboard

Westmoreland Glass Company, Grapeville, Pennsylvania, c. 1900, clear, nonflint.

Bowls	
a. Large	$28-41
b. Small	18-29
Butter dish, covered	29-42
Celery	14-28
Cheese dish	16-29
Creamer	21-32
Cruet	22-38
Goblet	16-27
Pitcher, milk	26-38
Salt/Pepper, pr.	18-29
Spoonholder	20-34
Sugar bowl, covered	27-38
Tumbler, iced tea	10-16
Wine	15-26

Kemple Glass Company, East Palestine, Ohio, reproducing some pieces in milk glass.

Cherry

Cherry

Bakewell, Pears & Company, Pittsburgh, Pennsylvania, c. 1870, clear, opal, flint.

Butter dish, covered	$38-54
Compote	
a. Covered, high standard	46-57
b. Open, high and low standard	29-44
Creamer	38-54
Goblet (ill.)	32-46
Sauce	15-26
Spoonholder	18-29
Sugar bowl, covered	34-47
Wine	16-27

Opal, 50 percent higher than clear prices listed. Being reproduced in most pieces. Know the original or leave it alone!

Cherry and Fig

Possibly Sandwich, 1880s. Clear. Usual pieces; prices could be compared with those of Circled Scroll.

Cherry Lattice

Northwood Glass Company, 1890s, 1900s. Clear.

Berry set	
a. Large bowl	$52-64
b. Small bowl	16-27
Butter dish, covered	51-62
Compote	42-56
Creamer (ill.)	44-58
Spoonholder	43-59
Sugar bowl, covered	45-58

Possibly other patterns.

Cherry and Fig

Cherry Lattice

Chestnut Oak

Chestnut Oak

(Old Acorn): Possibly Sandwich, early 1870s. Clear.

Butter, covered	$28-39
Celery	14-22
Compote	
a. Covered	31-42
b. Open	21-33
Egg cup	12-17
Goblet	16-27
Pitcher, water	32-42
Sauce, flat	14-22
Spoonholder	16-25
Sugar	
a. Covered	39-50
b. Open	18-32

Chrysanthemum Sprig

Chrysanthemum Sprig

Northwood Glass Company, 1890s. Custard.

Banana boat	$142-162
Berry set	
a. Large bowl	130-159
b. Small bowl	55- 67
Butter dish, covered (ill.)	147-167
Creamer	72- 91
Salt/Pepper, pr.	95-118
Pitcher, water	160-172
Spoonholder	68- 80
Sugar bowl, covered	92-118
Tumbler, water (rare in blue)	48- 62

Probably others. Rare in blue. 100 percent higher than Custard prices listed.

Church Windows

(Tulip Petals): U.S. Glass Company, c. 1903, clear, non-flint. They called it "No. 15,082." Previous maker is not known, nor is date known.

Butter dish, covered	$43-56
Cake stand	19-32
Celery	17-28
Compote, jelly, covered	34-50
Creamer	20-35
Dish, sardine	22-36
Goblet	24-38
Pitcher, ½ gal.	37-49
Spoonholder	17-28
Sugar bowl	
a. Covered	41-54
b. Open	29-44

Many other pieces.

Circled Scroll

Circled Scroll

1880s, 1890s. Clear, canary, green, blue, with opalescent edge and trim.

Bowl, berry	
a. Covered	$28-40
b. Open	17-31
Creamer	37-49
Pitcher, water (ill.)	60-76
Sauce, clear	13-24
Sugar	
a. Covered	40-54
b. Open	22-37
Tumbler	26-38

Probably other pieces. Colored pieces, 50 percent higher than clear prices listed.

Circular Saw

Circular Saw

Maker and date unknown. Clear, some have gilt trim.

Bowl	
a. Berry	$15-26
b. Punch	42-54
Butter dish, covered	26-38
Cracker jar	16-28
Creamer (ill.)	26-39
Saucedish	12-26
Spoonholder	18-29
Sugar bowl, covered	26-38
Tumbler	16-28

Probably other pieces.

Classic

Classic

Gillinder & Sons, 1880s, open and closed feet. Clear, frosted.

Bowl, footed 6¼" dia.	$ 37- 49
Butter dish, covered, log feet	122-152
Celery vase, 6 log feet	82- 97
Compote	
a. Covered, open feet	178-199
b. Open, 6" standard	82- 97
Creamer	132-147
Goblet	180-192

(continued)

Pitcher
- a. Collared base........... 288-320
- b. Open, log feet (ill.) 315-362

Plate
- a. President Cleveland...... 90-105
- b. Blaine, Hendricks, Logan . 88-101
- c. Warrior 96-110

Sauce, open, log feet 40- 49
Spoonholder, open, log feet 112-136
Sugar bowl, covered, very
large 135-162

Footed type brings 25 percent more than collared base type.

Classic
Medallion

Classic Medallion

(Cameo): Another good clear, non-flint glass of the 1880s.

Butter dish, covered $28-38
Celery vase 18-33
Compote
- a. Covered 37-44
- b. Open 27-39
Creamer 21-28
Pitcher, water (ill.) 37-49
Spoonholder 21-34
Sugar bowl
- a. Covered 27-36
- b. Open 18-29

Probably other pieces.

Clear Diagonal Band

Late 1880s. Clear.

Butter dish $39-54
Celery vase 19-29
Compote
- a. Covered, high standard 44-61
- b. Covered, low standard 27-39

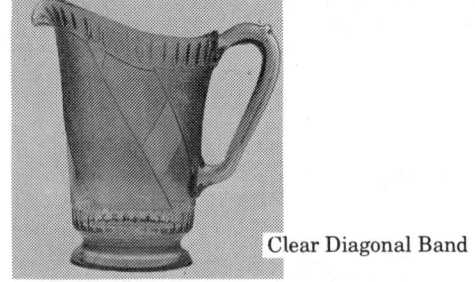

Clear Diagonal Band

Cordial 14-22
Creamer 22-34
Goblet 18-29
Marmalade jar, covered 18-32
Pitcher, water (ill.) 24-38
Platter, "Excelsior" 20-34
Sauces, flat and footed 12-26
Salt/Pepper, pr. 17-32
Spoonholder 16-29
Sugar bowl
- a. Covered 39-54
- b. Open 18-29
Wine........................ 28-39

Probably other pieces.

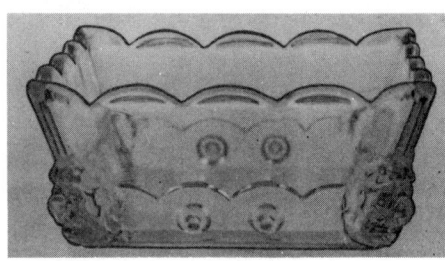

Clear Lion's Head

Clear Lion's Head

(Atlanta): Fostoria Glass Company, Moundsville, West Virginia, 1895. Plain, etched and engraved.

Bowl, berry (ill.)............... $27-37
Butter dish, covered 42-60
Cake stand, large, square 42-57
Compote
- a. Covered, 5", square stem.... 44-54
- b. Open, 5", square stem 24-33
Creamer 38-44
Goblet 28-44
Jam jar....................... 16-24
Pickle dish 18-26
Salt 14-28
Sauce, flat 12-27

Spoonholder 18-34
Sugar bowl, covered 45-58
Sugar bowl, open 33-41
Toothpick holder 18-32

Clear Stork

Clear Stork

Possibly Mosaic Glass Company, Fostoria, Ohio, 1890-91.

Butter dish $52-64
Compote 63-81
Creamer 48-59
Goblet 47-62
Pitcher, water (ill.) 66-84
Spoonholder, ... 28-42
Sugar bowl, covered 48-59
Tumbler 23-38

Probably other pieces. Frosted Stork prices 50 percent higher than clear prices listed.

Clio

Clio

Challinor, Taylor, Ltd., Tarentum, Pennsylvania, 1885-1891, clear, amber, blue.

Butter dish, covered $29-39
Celery 14-27
Compote, covered (ill.) 18-32
Goblet 16-29
Pitcher, qt., ½ gal. 34-54
Spoonholder 14-29
Sugar bowl, covered 27-42

Probably other pieces.

Coach Bowl

Coach Bowl

McKee & Bros., 1886. Crystal, amber, canary, blue (draft tongue in photo broken off). Also being reproduced in milk glass, amber, purple, blue, other colors.

Coach Bowl (ill.) $130-165

In colors, 50 percent higher.

Coarse Cut and Block

Coarse Cut and Block

Model Flint Glass Company, Findlay, Ohio, 1880s. Clear.

Butter dish $18-28

(continued)

Celery	16-32

Compote
a. Covered, high standard 29-41
b. Open, low standard 16-25
Creamer 20-30
Goblet 16-19
Pitcher, water (ill.) 28-42
Spoonholder 16-25
Sugar bowl, covered 31-44

Probably other pieces.

Cobb

Cobb

(Late Sawtooth; Zipper): Richards & Hartley, Tarentum, Pennsylvania, 1888. Clear.

Butter dish, covered $32-46
Compote, covered 44-57
Creamer
a. High..................... 23-39
b. Low 26-39
Goblet 18-28
Pitcher(ill.) 35-47
Salt/Pepper, pr. 14-20
Spoonholder 22-40
Sugar bowl 31-42
Tumbler 16-28

Probably other pieces.

Coin

Coin

(Columbian; Spanish, Coin): Made by one of the factories mentioned in Coin, U.S., where they used Spanish coins and possibly some English coins, same date, 1892. Spanish coins are bronzed. Never as collectible as U.S. coins.

Bowl
a. Berry, 10" $101-122
b. Finger 60- 85
Butter dish, covered (ill.) 128-143
Cake stand 100-120
Compote
a. Covered, 6", 7", 8" 170-195
b. Open, 7", 8", 10" 140-168
Creamer 100-118
Goblet 90-107
Pitcher, water 162-182
Salt/Pepper, pr. 110-128
Sugar bowl, covered 122-142
Toothpick holder 72- 89
Tumbler 84- 94

Being reproduced. Know your seller!

Coin

(U.S.): Central Glass Company and Hobbs, Brockunier, Wheeling, West Virginia, for a few months in 1892. Space doesn't allow us to tell all about this glass. Because real coins were used, the Treasury Department made the company stop after only a few months' production. Terribly scarce today. 5¢ piece, 10¢, 25¢, 50¢ and the silver dollar. Clear, frosted, sometimes silvered or gilded. Prices given for indicative pieces. Being skillfully reproduced. Careful! Demand a receipt!

Bowl, berry
a. 25¢ $240-260
b. $1.00 285-320
Bread platter, frosted coins.... 275-310
Butter dish
a. $1.00 550-610
b. 50¢ 490-565
Cake stand
a. $1.00, frosted 450-490
b. 50¢ 420-445
Celery, 50¢ 320-365
Celery, 25¢ 240-270
Compote, covered
a. 50¢, 8″ dia. 550-600
b. 25¢ (ill.) 465-525
c. $1.00, frosted, final 600-650
Creamer, 25¢ 355-385
Goblet
a. $1.00 355-420
b. 10¢ 320-360
Mug, $1.00 220-260
Pitcher
a. Milk, 50¢............... 450-510
b. Water, $1.00 560-580
Sugar bowl
a. Covered, 50¢, final 545-585
b. Covered, 25¢, final 475-540
Toothpick holder, $1.00 145-188
Tumbler
a. $1.00 on base (rare) 240-275
b. 10¢ 220-245
Wine, one-half dime (rare) 320-385

The toothpick holder was reproduced in Indiana a few years ago before the government stopped it. A few reached the market. Now, bread tray (50¢) and tumbler ($1.00 on base) are being reproduced.

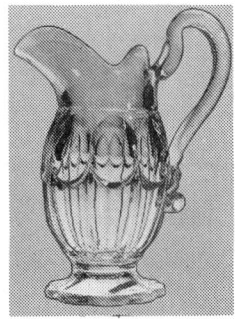
Colonial

Colonial

Sandwich Glass, 1850-1860. Clear, opal or other colors, rare.

Ale glass, tall, footed...........$54-66
Celery glass 57-72
Champagne................... 71-84
Egg cup 18-29
Goblet, knob stem 50-60
Pitcher (ill.)................... 62-80
Spill holder 35-47
Sugar bowl 57-69

Possibly other pieces. Colors, 150 percent higher than clear prices listed.

Colonis

Colonis

(45 Colonis): U.S. Glass Company, 1913. Clear.

Butter dish $25-36
Cake stand, 8″ 24-38
Celery vase 18-29
Compote
a. Covered, high standard 28-42
b. Open, low standard 24-36
Cordial 16-27
Creamer 20-32
Dish, oval.................... 12-19
Egg cup 14-26
Goblet 18-32
Pitcher
a. Milk (ill.) 34-50
b. Water 34-48
Sauce 12-22
Spoonholder 15-27
Sugar bowl, covered 34-46
Tray 22-32
Tumbler 18-29

Colorado

Colorado

U.S. Glass Company, 1897, another of their "States" series. Crystal glass, both plain, engraved, and crystal with ruby stain. Also green and deep blue with gold decorations. Also amethyst — rare in this color.

Banana bowl	$54-68
Bowl, berry, 6 pc. set	34-48
Butter dish, covered	50-62
Cheese dish, low, footed	42-52
Creamer, individual and large	28-38
Dish	
a. Crimped edge, 4″, 8″	18-32
b. Flared edge, 4″, 8″	18-32
Pitcher, water (ill.)	62-80
Salt/Pepper, pr.	22-40
Spoonholder	24-38
Sugar bowl	
a. Individual	28-39
b. Large, covered	50-64
Toothpick holder	18-32
Tumbler	20-35

Ruby, 20 percent; blue, 55 percent; green, 100 percent; amethyst, 200 percent higher than clear prices listed.

Columbia

U. S. Glass Company, 1907. Clear. Probably others earlier.

Bowl, 7″, 8″, 9″, 10″	$18-29
Butter dish, covered	24-37
Celery tray	15-29
Creamer (ill.)	19-32
Custard cup	14-23
Dish	12-23
a. Olive	15-26
b. Sundae	24-35

Columbia

Pitcher, water	28-39
Relish bowl	12-22
Salt/Pepper, pr.	16-26
Spoonholder	16-32
Sugar bowl, covered	22-32
Tumbler	14-27

At least 125 different pieces were made in this pattern.

Comet

Comet

Sandwich Glass, c. late 1840s, clear, flint. Don't confuse this rare glass with McKee Brothers' glass of the same name, c. 1887.

Goblet (ill.)	$ 72- 86
Pitcher, water	390-445
Tumbler, whiskey, water	135-165

Possibly other pieces.

Concaved Almond

Concaved Almond

Maker unknown, used for souvenir purposes in 1890s, a style created at the Chicago Exposition in 1893. Emerald green, ruby stain.

Goblet $22-36
Pitcher, water (ill.) 42-54
Toothpick..................... 25-40

Probably other pieces. Colors, 50 percent higher than clear prices listed.

Connecticut

U.S. Glass Company, c. 1898, clear, non-flint.

Bowls, 4", 6", 8" $15-28
Butter dish, covered 22-36
Cake stand, 10" 22-40
Celery tray 15-27
Creamer 22-35
Pitcher, tankard, 3 types 26-38
Salt/Pepper, pr. 16-24
Tumbler 14-24
Wine........................ 18-29

Many other pieces.

Continental

A. H. Heisey Company, Newark, Ohio, 1903. Not all pieces marked with "Diamond H."

Butter dish
a. Covered $42-49
b. Covered, footed 52-62
Creamer
a. Flat 38-48
b. Footed 36-45

Continental

Pitcher, water (ill.) 75-83
Spoonholder
a. Flat 28-37
b. Footed 34-42
Sugar bowl
a. Covered 46-55
b. Covered, footed 54-68

Prices are for signed pieces.

Continental Bread Tray

Continental Bread Tray

Another in the series of historical plates sold at the Philadelphia Exposition in 1876. Clear only. Atterbury and Company, Pittsburgh.

Plate, 13" by 9" (ill.) $98-125

Coolidge Drape

Coolidge Drape

Maker unknown, 1880. Clear and cobalt (blue) in several sizes. Lamp famous because this was pattern of lamp in room in which Coolidge took presidential oath after Harding's sudden death.

Any size in clear .... $ 88-107
Any size in cobalt 150-192

Cord and Tassel

Cord and Tassel

Central Glass Company, 1872. Clear.

Bowl, oval	$15-27
Butter dish, covered	36-49
Cake stand, high standard	34-47
Celery	34-48
Compote, high standard	39-52
Cordial	27-38
Creamer, applied handle	42-49
Egg cup	17-24
Goblet	27-40
Lamp, applied handle	36-48
Mug	16-21
Pitcher, water (ill.)	52-64
Sauce	18-24
Spoonholder	34-47
Sugar bowl, covered	42-55
Wine	20-32

Probably other pieces.

Cord Drapery

Cord Drapery

(Indiana): Indiana Tumbler & Goblet (National) Company, Greentown, Indiana, 1900. Clear, amber, blue, green, chocolate, opal.

Berry bowl	$18-25
Butter dish, clear	22-34
Cake plate	24-34
Compote	
a. Stemmed, large	50-60
b. Stemmed, covered, jelly	34-44
c. Stemmed, fluted	52-62

Creamer	17-26
Goblet	17-32
Pitcher, water (ill.)	32-44
Spoonholder	15-22
Salt/Pepper, pr.	12-19
Tumbler	14-21

Chocolate, 400 percent higher; other colors, 300 percent higher than clear prices listed.

Cordova

Cordova

O'Hara Glass Company, Pittsburgh, 1890. Clear.

Bowl	
a. Covered	$16-27
b. Finger	12-18
c. Open	15-27
Butter dish	24-36
Cake stand	27-39
Celery	34-48
Compote, covered and open,	
high standard	25-39
Creamer	22-34
Cruet	22-32
Inkwell (rare)	62-95
Pitcher	
a. Syrup (ill.)	27-42
b. Water	36-47
Spoonholder	18-26
Sugar bowl	26-35
Tumbler	18-28

Probably made in other pieces.

Coreopsis

Possibly, Dalzell, Gilmore & Leighton Company, Findlay, Ohio, c. 1888, white opaque.

Butter dish, covered	$82-97
Creamer	67-82
Spoonholder	48-62
Sugar bowl, covered	82-94

Probably other pieces.

Cornucopia

Cornucopia

Maker unknown, 1885-1890. Clear, fine fruit group on reverse side.

Butter dish, covered $29-46
Celery 16-27
Compote, covered 32-39
Creamer 16-27
Goblet 14-24
Pitcher, water (ill.) 43-60
Spoonholder 14-24
Sugar bowl, covered 29-42

Probably other pieces.

Cosmos

Cosmos

(Stemless Daisy): Probably Dithridge & Son, New Brighton, Pennsylvania, 1900. Opaque.

Butter dish, open and covered
  (ill.) $198-235
Castor set; salt/pepper,
  mustard 220-260
Creamer 140-175
Lamps
  a. Large, round with shade .. 185-220
  b. Miniature with shade 140-165
  c. Miniature, base only 92-134
Lemonade pitcher with 6 mugs . 440-500
Pitcher, water, 8¾" high 230-280

Salt/Pepper, pr. 120-160
Spoonholder 95-126
Sugar bowl, covered 210-240
Tumbler 90-115
Probably other pieces.

Cottage

Cottage

(Dinner Bell; Fine Cut Band): Adams & Company, Pittsburgh, 1874. Clear, dark green (rare), amber.

Butter dish, covered $29-45
Cake stand, 9" high 28-40
Celery vase 22-35
Compote, covered and open,
  high standard 28-42
Creamer 21-32
Cruet, w/stopper.............. 19-33
Fruit bowl, high standard 29-42
Goblet 18-32
Pitcher, pint, quart, half
  gallon, amber 24-38
Plate, 6", 7", 8", 9" 14-20
Salt/Pepper, pr. 16-28
Spoonholder 18-32
Sugar bowl, covered 29-37
Tray, water 22-31
Tumbler 16-27
Wine........................ 14-28

Probably other pieces made. Colors 70 percent higher than clear prices listed.

Cow

Maker unknown, c. 1870s, clear, non-flint.

Butter dish, covered, 6" long $70-80

413

Cradled Prisms

Probably Challinor, Taylor, Ltd., c. late 1880s, clear, non-flint.

Butter dish, covered $28-39
Creamer, footed 22-40
Spoonholder 16-32
Sugar bowl, covered 24-37

Probably other pieces.

Croesus

Croesus

Riverside Glass Works, Wellsville, West Virginia, 1897. Crystal, emerald, royal purple (amethyst), gold trim.

Bowl, berry $52- 70
Butter dish 72- 84
Celery...................... 54- 68
Creamer..................... 52- 65
Cruet 54- 69
Pickle dish 29- 42
Pitcher, water (ill.) 97-118
Salt/Pepper, pr. 40- 50
Spoonholder 42- 54
Sugar bowl 88-110
Toothpick holder 31- 43
Tumbler..................... 30- 41

Emerald green, 125 percent; amethyst, 250 percent higher than clear prices listed. Entire table set being reproduced in Japan.

Crossed Block

Possibly Hartley & Richards, late 1800s. Clear.

Butter dish, covered $38-52
Creamer (ill.) 26-36

Crossed Block

Spoonholder 18-27
Sugar bowl, covered 38-52

Probably other pieces.

Crossed Fern

Atterbury & Company, Pittsburgh, Pennsylvania, c. 1876, clear, opal, turquoise, non-flint.

Bowl, collared $12-20
Butter dish, covered 26-38
Compote, covered 27-39
Creamer 11-22
Pitcher..................... 27-38
Spoonholder 15-28
Sugar bowl, covered 18-32
Tumbler 14-24

Opal, turquoise, 40% higher than clear prices listed.

Crossed Ferns with Ball and Claw

Atterbury & Company, c. 1876, clear, opal, turquoise, non-flint. Same prices as "Crossed Fern" — see.

Crossed Shield

414

(continued)

Crossed Shield

Fostoria Glass Company's No. 1303, late 1890s. Clear.

Butter dish, covered	$28-42
Creamer	32-39
Compotes, several sizes	30-47
Cordial	16-28
Decanter	47-62
Egg cup	14-26
Goblet	17-22
Pitcher, water, lemonade (ill.)	44-55
Spoonholder	18-29
Sugar bowl, covered	26-40
Tumbler	18-32

Probably other pieces.

Crystal

McKee Brothers, Pittsburgh, c. 1859, clear, flint.

Ale glass	$23-40
Bowl, covered	42-60
Celery	22-34
Compote, covered, high standard	44-58
Creamer	42-60
Decanter	33-47
Egg cup	33-47
Goblet	28-39
Pitcher, water	62-80
Spoonholder	22-35
Sugar bowl, covered	44-56

Other pieces.

Crystal Wedding

Crystal Wedding

(Crystal Anniversary): Adams Glass Company, early 1880s. Clear, amber, canary, blue.

Banana stand	$48-60
Butter dish, covered	40-56

Cake stand, high standard	50-62
Celery	34-50
Compote	
a. Open, low standard	34-45
b. Covered, high standard (ill.)	62-74
c. Covered, low standard	48-61
Creamer, clear	33-47
Goblet	33-50
Pitcher	49-62
Salt/Pepper, pr.	24-36
Spoonholder	30-42
Sugar bowl, covered	19-29
Tumbler	21-34

Probably other pieces. Goblet and compote being reproduced. Colors 100 percent more than clear prices listed.

Cube with Fan

U.S. Glass Company, c. 1900, clear, non-flint.

Bowl, finger	$19-30
Celery	22-35
Dish, jelly	18-29
Goblet	18-32
Plates, 5", 7½"	15-27
Sugar bowl, covered	29-42
Tumbler	16-29

Many other pieces.

Cupid and Venus

Cupid and Venus

(Guardian Angel): Richard & Hartley Glass Company, Pittsburgh (Birmingham), Pennsylvania, 1875-1884. Clear, yellow, amber.

(continued)

Butter dish $74-86
Cake plate, 11" 52-64
Celery 47-61
Champagne 44-54
Compote
  a. Covered, high and low
    standard 58-68
  b. Open, high standard 44-54
Creamer, footed 50-62
Jam jar, covered (ill.) 44-52
Mug, 2", 2½", 3½" 24-48
Pickle castor 62-75
Pitcher, large and small 55-69
Plate, bread, 10½" 40-54
Plate, bread, handles 38-49
Sauce
  a. Flat, round 18-24
  b. Footed, 3½", 4", 5" 16-27
Spoonholder 50-60
Sugar bowl, covered 62-74

Probably other pieces. Color, 40 percent higher than clear prices listed.

Currant

Currant

Sandwich glass, 1870s. Later, Campbell, Jones & Company, Pittsburgh, 1870s. Crystal.

Butter dish $61-69
Cake plate on stand, 2 types 64-75
Celery vase 46-58
Compote
  a. Covered 8", high foot 54-66
  b. Covered, 8", 9", low foot 55-68
Cordial 40-52
Creamer 52-68
Dish, oval, 6" x 9", 5" x 7" 29-42
Egg cup 28-39
Goblets, 5½", 6" 34-44
Pitcher, water (ill.) 64-74
Spoonholder 44-60
Sugar bowl, covered 54-65

Tumbler, footed 35-49
Wine 38-49
Probably other pieces.

Currier and Ives

Currier and Ives

Bellaire Goblet Company, Findlay, Ohio, 1880s. Clear, rare in colors — amber, blue.

Butter dish, covered $45-58
Cordial 22-34
Creamer 28-42
Cup and saucer 34-49
Goblet ....
Lamp, No. 2, complete w/burner
  and chimney 27-42
Pitcher, large and small 34-52
Salt/Pepper, pr. 22-40
Spoonholder 19-32
Sugar bowl, covered 37-52
Tray, "Balky Mule on RR
  Tracks" 77-90
Wine 17-27

Probably other pieces. Color, 250 percent higher than clear prices listed.

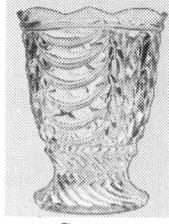
Curtain

Curtain

(Sultan): Bryce Bros., Pittsburgh, 1875-1885. Clear.

Bowl, covered, 6", 7", 8" $19-32
Bowl, open, 6", 7", 8" 16-27

Butter dish 42-54
Cake plate on stand 28-42
Celery boat 34-49
Compote
  a. Covered, high standard,
    6″, 7″, 8″ 43-56
  b. Open, high standard,
    7″, 8″, 10″ 38-47
Creamer 39-48
Goblet 29-41
Mug, large 22-34
Pitcher, quart, half gallon 49-65
Salt/Pepper, pr. 26-36
Spoonholder (ill.) 32-48
Sugar bowl 44-55
Tumbler 27-38

Probably other pieces.

Curtain Tieback

Maker unknown, c. mid-1880s, clear, non-flint. Two types of feet.

Bowl, berry, 7″ square $15-28
Butter dish, covered 29-42
Celery 16-27
Creamer 19-32
Goblet 24-34
Pitcher, water 38-50
Spoonholder 16-27
Sugar bowl, open 18-29
Tumbler 16-29
Wine 15-33

Other pieces.

Dahlia

Dahlia

Canton Glass Company, Canton, Ohio, 1880s. Clear, amber, vaseline, blue, green. Amber and yellow are scarce.

Butter dish $54-66
Cake plate on stand 36-49
Champagne 42-56
Compote, large, covered, high
  standard 64-79
Cordial 36-44
Creamer 49-64
Egg cup, double (rare) 53-66
Goblet, etched (scarce) 44-56
Mug, handled, 2 sizes 29-56
Pitcher, water, milk (ill.) 47-62
Platter, grape handles, oval 48-59
Spoonholder 36-47
Sugar bowl, open 42-49
Wine 38-47

Colors 30-50 percent higher than clear prices listed.

Daisy and Button

Daisy and Button

Gillinder and Sons, Philadelphia, 1876, in time for the Centennial; also, Hobbs, Brockunier and Company, Wheeling, West Virginia. Souvenir items were extremely popular at the Fair. This D & B wheelbarrow with metal wheel is rare today. It can be seen at the Houston Museum.

No single glass pattern has been or is being reproduced more than Daisy and Button in all its variations. Collect it if you like it but not because you think you're getting a bargain. KNOW YOUR DEALER!

Daisy and Button

Daisy and Button

This is a rare blue creamer with clear handle. Probably Hobbs, Brockunier and Company. We're showing you four different D & B pieces to show you how many, many different pieces were made. Enjoy looking. But save your money!

Daisy and Button

One of the rarest pieces ever made is this "Helmet" covered butter dish. Don't look for it in shops. You can see this one at the Houston Museum in Chattanooga.

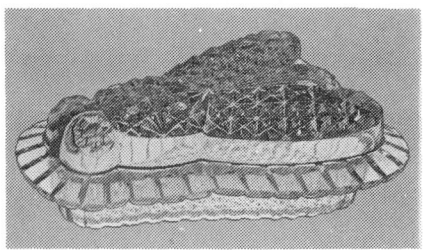

Daisy and Button

Daisy and Button

Another rarity in the D & B pattern is the "Bee" covered dish. I honestly believe that every original D & B pattern is being reproduced today. Be so terribly careful when you buy. Make sure your dealer is an authority before you buy! This "Bee" is at the Houston Museum.

Daisy and Button

Daisy and Button,
Oval Medallion

Daisy and Button, Oval Medallion

One of the most popular patterns ever produced in this country.

Usual D & B prices. But, do be careful!

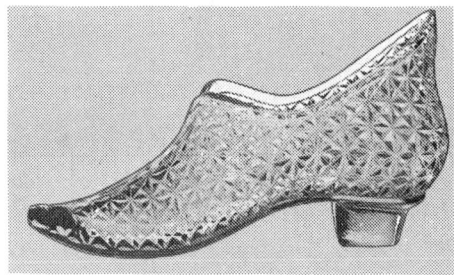

Daisy and Button, Oxford

Daisy and Button, Oxford

Sandwich, early. Clear and colored.

Clear	$42-56
Amber, canary	42-56
Blue	57-69

What one sees today in shops are reproductions. Watch it!

Daisy and Button, Panelled

Here again another of the D & B patterns. Too many reproductions to take a chance on this or any other D & B pat-

Daisy and Button, Panelled

tern. This pattern is rare in two colors —
amber and clear — but don't worry about
finding it outside of in a museum such as
the Houston Museum in Chattanooga,
Tennessee. Save your money.

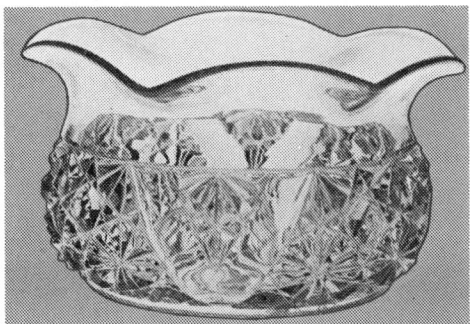

Daisy and Button "V"

Daisy and Button "V"

A. J. Beatty & Company, 1886-1887,
Clear.

Just as many patterns reproduced in
this "V" as in D & B. Not worth discuss-
ing. You're buying new unless you're
an expert.

Daisy and Button
with Narcissus

(Clear Lily): Another D & B, maker unknown, late 1880s. Clear. Sometimes
flashed with gold.

Butter dish	$28-40
Celery	22-32
Compote, open	27-39
Creamer	22-34
Decanter	42-51
Goblet	16-32

Daisy and Button with Narcissus

Pickle dish	12-22
Pitcher, water (ill.)	34-46
Sauce, 4″	14-27
Salt/Pepper, pr.	15-22
Spoonholder	16-26
Sugar bowl, covered	24-34
Tumbler	19-28
Wine	15-26

Probably other pieces. Wine being
reproduced, also bowls and vases.

Daisy and Button with Prisms

Daisy and Button
with Prisms

It sounds like a broken record but save
your breath on these D & B patterns with
variations such as below. Just about
every genuine piece has been reproduced
and they're good. Buy it for what it is —
new — and enjoy it as such. But don't put
your money into it unless you know it
yourself. Few dealers can tell you
whether it's old.

Daisy and Thumbprint Cross-Bar

Daisy and Thumbprint Cross-Bar

(Mikado): Richards and Hartley Fliŋt Glass Company, 1888. Clear, yellow, amber, light and dark, blue.

Bowl, flat, 6″, 8″	$17-25
Butter dish, flat, footed	37-49
Catsup bottle	22-34
Compote	
a. Covered, 7″, 8″	38-54
b. Open, 7″, 8″	24-34
Creamer, individual, regular	22-31
Cruet	20-34
Goblet	24-36
Lamps, 4 sizes	27-52
Pitcher, quart, half gallon	37-49
Salt/Pepper, pr.	21-40
Spoonholder	19-28
Sugar bowl, covered	32-42
Tumbler	19-38
Wine	18-26

Probably other pieces. Amber, yellow, 40 percent higher; blue, 100 percent higher than clear prices listed.

Daisy in Diamond

O'Hara Glass Company, Pittsburgh, 1886. Crystal, amber, rose, blue

Butter dish, covered	$27-36
Celery	18-27
Creamer	22-29
Egg cup	14-27
Goblet	16-32
Pitcher, water (ill.)	29-46
Spoonholder	17-28
Sugar bowl, covered	24-36
Tumbler	17-28

Probably other pieces. Colors, 100-125 percent higher than clear prices listed.

Daisy in Diamo

Daisy Medallion

Daisy Medallion

(Sunburst Medallion): Maker unknown, 1880s. Clear.

Butter dish, covered	$22-32
Cake stand	19-29
Compote	19-31
Creamer	17-32
Pitcher	24-34
Spoonholder (ill.)	16-28
Sugar bowl, covered	22-34

Probably other pieces.

Daisy Whorl

Maker unknown, 1870s. Clear, also in colors.

Butter dish, covered	$27-42
Compote	
a. Covered	28-36
b. Open	19-29

Daisy Whorl

Goblet 18-32
Pitcher, water (ill.) 39-50
Spoonholder 14-22
Sugar bowl
   a. Covered 32-44
   b. Open 20-30

Probably other pieces. Colors 50-75 percent higher than clear prices listed.

Dakota

Dakota
(Baby Thumbprint; Thumbprint Band): Doyle & Company, Pittsburgh, 1890s. Clear, red-flashed.

Bowl, berry $28-38
Butter dish, covered, etched 48-57
Cake stand, 10″ 44-55
Celery, flat base 40-49
Compote, covered, 5″, 6″, 7″, 8″ .. 44-58
Creamer, pedestal base 32-42
Goblet, etched 33-42
Pitcher, water, etched (ill.) 75-84
Salt/Pepper, pr. 27-36
Spoonholder 33-42
Sugar bowl, covered, etched 44-56
Tray, water, 13″ 48-59
Tumbler 40-50
Wine 28-38
Probably other pieces. Red-flashed, 50 percent higher than clear.

Dancing Goat

Possibly, LaBelle Glass Company, Bridgeport, Ohio, c. 1878, clear, non-flint.

Ale glass $49-58

Dart

Maker unknown, c. 1880, clear, non-flint.

Butter dish, covered $24-36
Creamer 23-35
Goblet 14-28
Sauce 9-17
Spoonholder 14-24
Sugar bowl, covered 25-35

Other pieces.

Deer and Oak Tree

Deer and Oak Tree

Dalzell, Gilmore & Leighton, Findlay, Ohio; also, Indiana Tumbler & Goblet (National) Company, Greentown, Indiana. National took over both factories in 1889.

Pitcher, water (ill.) $135-162

Chocolate color, 150 percent higher than clear price listed.

Deer and Pine Tree

(Deer and Doe): Sandwich glass, 1860s. Clear, blue, amber, green, yellow.

Bowl, waste, green............. $62-80
Butter dish, covered, clear 64-82
Cake plate on standard, clear.... 73-84
Celery, clear 58-66

(continued)

Deer and Pine Tree

Compote, covered, oblong, large	89-99
Creamer, clear	50-60
Goblet, clear	47-59
Jam jar	44-58
Pickle dish, oblong, deep	22-31
Pitcher, large and small, clear	58-67
Plate, bread, amber	48-58
Plate, bread, clear	42-53
Plate, bread, green	50-60
Platter, 13¼" x 8", clear	49-60
Sauce, flat and footed	19-26
Spoonholder, clear	49-60
Sugar bowl, covered, clear	62-72
Tray, large, 11" x 15", handled, yellow	74-85

Probably other pieces.

Delaware

Delaware

(New Century): U.S. Glass Company, 1899. Crystal glass with rose stain and gilt trim; also, green glass with gilt trim; amethyst (rare).

Bowl, round, fluted, boat-shaped, banana	$32-42
Butter dish	38-50
Celery	27-39
Creamer	29-40
Cruet	27-40
Pitcher, water (ill.)	40-52
Spoonholder	22-38

Sugar bowl	37-62
Toothpick holder	18-27
Tumbler	19-29

Probably other pieces. Colors, 100 to 150 percent higher than clear prices listed. Amethyst, rare, 400 percent higher.

Dewdrop and Flowers

Dewdrop and Flowers

Probably originated at Sandwich; late 1870s, early 1880s. Clear.

Butter dish, covered	$29-38
Compote	
a. Covered	35-47
b. Open	24-38
Creamer	24-39
Goblet	18-28
Pitcher, milk or water (ill.)	34-42
Spoonholder	12-18
Sugar bowl	
a. Covered	27-40
b. Open	21-32
Wine	16-24

Dewdrop and Raindrop

Dewdrop and Raindrop

Kokomo Glass Manufacturing Company, Kokomo, Indiana, 1900-1905. Clear, clear/gilded, clear/ruby.

Bowl, berry $44-56
Butter dish 59-72
Cordial, set of 6, each 44-56
Creamer 54-66
Cup, sherbet 29-40
Goblet 49-62
Pitcher, water (ill.) 69-79
Sauce 18-27
Salt/Pepper, pr. 48-59
Spoonholder 44-58
Sugar bowl 64-74
Tumbler 38-50
Wine 44-54
Cordial, goblet, sherbet cup and wine
being reproduced.

Dewdrop in Points

Dewdrop in Points

Greensburg Glass Company, Greensburg, Pennsylvania, probably 1875-1885.
Clear.

Butter, covered $27-37
Cake stand, large 32-40
Compote
  a. Covered 32-40
  b. Open 19-28
Creamer, covered 26-39
Goblet 29-42
Pickle dish, oval 12-28
Pitcher (ill.) 32-47
Plate, bread 20-32
Sauce, footed 12-22
Spoonholder 18-32
Sugar bowl, covered 22-40
Probably other pieces.

Dewdrop with Star

Dewdrop with Star

Campbell, Jones & Company, Pittsburgh, 1877. Clear.

Butter dish, covered, star base . . $68-82
Cake plate on standard 74-84
Celery, star in base 60-70
Compote
  a. Covered, high and low
    standard 66-78
  b. Covered, footed, 6", 7",
    star base 58-72
Creamer, star base 60-74
Goblet 44-56
Pickle dish 20-32
Pitcher, water (ill.) 74-88
Plates, 4½" thru 11" 22-37
Sauce, flat and footed 15-24
Spoonholder 49-62
Sugar bowl, covered, star base . . 64-76
Tumbler 29-44

Probably other pieces. The 7¼" plate
and salt and probably footed sauces are
being reproduced.

Dewey

Dewey

(Flower Flange): Indiana Tumbler &
Goblet Company, 1898. Crystal, canary,
green, amber, blue, chocolate.

Bowl, berry $15-24
Butter dish, covered (ill.) 28-38

(continued)

Creamer	24-39
Cruet	32-44
Mug	27-38
Pitcher, water, 9½" high	42-56
Salt/Pepper, pr.	29-44
Serpentine tray	27-36
Spoonholder	28-39
Sugar bowl	32-42
Tumbler	22-34

Other pieces were made. Chocolate, 300 percent higher; other colors, 70 percent higher than clear prices listed.

Diagonal Band

Diagonal Band

A pattern of the 1800s; clear. Apple green, scarce.

Prices almost identical with Diagonal Band with Fan, except apple green 100 percent higher than clear prices listed.

Diagonal Band with Fan

Diagonal Band with Fan

Maker unknown. Clear, 1880s.

Butter dish	$37-49
Celery vase	36-48
Compote, high and low foot	37-52
Cordial	14-28
Creamer	29-40
Goblet	26-39
Pitcher, milk, 8" (ill.)	35-47
Plate, 6", 7", 8"	18-29
Sauce, footed, 4", 4½"	12-21
Salt/Pepper, pr.	22-31
Spoonholder	26-39
Sugar bowl	38-52
Wine	16-31

Probably other pieces.

Diamond and Sunburst

Diamond and Sunburst

Maker unknown, late 1860s. Clear.

Butter dish, covered	$23-38
Cake stand	22-37
Celery vase	18-29
Compote	
a. Covered	28-39
b. Open	14-26
Creamer, applied handle	22-32
Decanter	27-39
Egg cup	12-22
Goblet	16-30
Pitcher, water (ill.)	37-49
Spoonholder	19-33
Sugar bowl, covered	32-44
Tumbler	19-29

Probably other pieces.

Diamond Band

(Prism and Diamond Band): Central Glass Company, Wheeling, West Virginia, c. 1870, clear, non-flint.

Butter dish, covered	$40-48
Celery	18-27
Compote, small, footed	37-47
Creamer	32-43
Dish, shallow	9-16
Goblet	19-29
Pitcher, water	32-43
Spoonholder	17-28
Sugar bowl, covered	38-50
Wine	18-29

Other pieces.

Diamond Point

Diamond Block with Fans

(Blockade): Challinor, Taylor, Ltd., c. 1880s, clear, non-flint. It was their "No. 309." The pattern may have been continued by U.S. Glass Company after 1891.

Bowl, waste	$17-25
Butter dish, covered	36-48
Celery	18-29
Creamer	22-33
Goblet	19-32
Pitcher, water	34-46
Spoonholder	18-27
Sugar bowl, covered	36-49

Many other pieces.

Diamond Point

Sandwich glass, 1830; Bryce, Richards & Co., Pittsburgh, c. 1854; others, c. 1880s. Clear, rare in colors, flint.

Ale glass	$39-47
Butter dish	74-88
Celery, flint	62-80
Compote	
a. Covered, 6″, 7″, 8″, high and low standard	70-84
b. Open, 6″, 7″, 8″, high and low standard	54-66
Creamer, footed, scalloped	62-81
Egg cup (rare in color), flint	34-43
Goblet, large and small	48-57
Pitcher, half pint, pint, quart	58-75
Plates, 3″ thru 8″	16-42
Spoonholder	49-70
Sugar bowl, covered	66-76
Tumbler, jelly, water, whiskey	32-45

Probably other pieces.

Diamond Mirror

Diamond Mirror

Maker unknown, late 1880s. Clear.

Butter dish, covered	$24-36
Celery	18-29
Creamer	18-32
Spoonholder (ill.)	17-28
Sugar bowl	
a. Covered	24-34
b. Open	19-32

Probably other pieces.

Diamond Point Discs

(continued)

Diamond Point Discs

Probably made at Findlay, Ohio, late 1880s. Clear.

Butter dish, covered	$33-47
Cake stand	32-46
Celery	18-27
Compote	
a. Covered, 7″, 8″, high standard	34-44
b. Covered, 7″, 9″, colored base	38-52
Creamer	22-34
Goblet	20-28
Pitcher	48-59
Salt/Pepper, pr.	14-24
Spoonholder	20-34
Sugar bowl, covered	32-42

Probably other pieces.

Diamond Quilted

Butter dish, covered	$23-36
Creamer	24-36
Goblet	17-29
Pitcher, water	30-40
Sauce, footed (ill.)	8-12
Spoonholder	16-28
Sugar bowl, covered	24-38
Tray, water	22-37
Tumbler	12-24

Canary, 100 percent; light blue, 150 percent; light, dark amethyst, 200 percent higher than clear prices listed. Probably many other pieces.

Diamond Point with Panels

Diamond Point with Panels

(Hinoto): Boston and Sandwich Glass Company, 1850s. Clear, flint.

Celery	$100-120
Champagne	62- 75
Goblet	78- 90
Pitcher (ill.)	130-155
Salt, footed	42- 60
Spoonholder	49- 62
Sugar bowl	78- 89

Diamond Quilted

Maker unknown, c. 1880s, clear, many colors, non-flint.

Diamond Rosettes

Diamond Rosettes

Several Pittsburgh factories, 1870s until early 1900s. Clear, sometimes found in color — yellow, blue, light green.

Butter dish, covered	$27-42
Bowl	14-24
Celery holder	16-28
Compote	30-50
Compote, covered	42-60
Creamer	24-35
Goblet (ill.)	18-30
Pitcher, water	37-49
Spoonholder	16-19
Sugar bowl	
a. Covered	27-34
b. Open	12-16
Tumbler	14-26

Probably many other pieces. Color, 50 percent higher than clear prices listed.

Diamond Sunburst

(Plain Sunburst): Bryce, Walker & Company, Pittsburgh, c. 1860s, clear, non-flint.

Butter dish, covered	$37-48
Cake stand	27-40
Celery	26-38
Compote, covered, high standard	44-56
Creamer	28-40
Goblet	27-39
Lamp	28-42
Pitcher, milk	29-42
Spoonholder	19-32
Sugar bowl, covered	39-52
Tumbler	18-32
Wine	16-27

Probably other pieces.

Diamond Thumbprint

Diamond Thumbprint

(Diamond and Concave): Sandwich glass; McKee & Bros., 1850s. Clear, green-tinted, amethyst (due to improper mixing of metal), and yellow (rare), flint.

Bowl, waste	$ 92-125
Butter dish, covered	160-175
Cake stand, 2 sizes	235-265
Celery, flint	220-262
Champagne	190-240
Decanter, original stopper	120-145
Goblet (rare)	280-300
Pitcher, milk and water (ill.)	310-355
Spoonholder	65- 84
Sugar bowl, 2 styles	182-220
Wine jug, places for holding glasses, set	450-525

This glass is extremely rare.

Diapered Flower

Diapered Flower

Probably Westmoreland Glass Company, 1890s. Opaque blue. Sandwich made it earlier. It was a container for mustard or other condiments.

Mustard jar (ill.)	$48-60

Probably other pieces.

Dickinson

Dickinson

Sandwich glass, 1860s. Clear.

Butter dish, covered	$37- 49
Compote	
a. Covered	60- 72
b. Open (ill.)	40- 50
Creamer	92-110
Goblet	38- 52
Sauce, flat	12- 20
Spoonholder	21- 34
Sugar	
a. Covered	40- 50
b. Open	22- 30
Pitcher, water	52- 68
Wine	22- 32

Possibly other pieces.

427

Divided Block with Sunburst

Divided Block with Sunburst

(Variant): U.S. Glass Company, after 1891. Crystal, plain and with ruby stain.

Butter dish, covered	$34-42
Celery vase	15-29
Compote, covered, high or low standard	27-42
Creamer	19-32
Goblet	16-29
Pitcher, water (ill.)	35-48
Salt/Pepper, pr.	14-24
Spoonholder	17-29
Sugar bowl, covered	30-43
Tumbler	17-26

Probably other pieces.

Divided Hearts

Boston & Sandwich Glass Company, c. early 1860s, clear, flint.

Butter dish, covered	$120-140
Compote	
a. Covered	110-140
b. Open	92-120
Creamer	110-140
Egg cup	68- 82
Goblet	82- 97
Lamp, marble base	92-110
Sugar bowl, covered	120-145

Possibly other pieces.

Dog

Possibly, Sandwich, c. 1870s, clear, non-flint.

Compote, covered, low	$68-90
Compote, covered, high	82-92

"Dog and Child" Mug

"Dog and Child" Mug

Indiana Tumbler & Goblet Company, (National), Greentown, Indiana, 1902. Chocolate, Nile green.

Chocolate	$210-245
Nile green	220-245

Rare!

Dog Hunting

Dog Hunting

One of a series of animal designs put out by National Glass Company, Greentown, Indiana, before the plant was destroyed by fire in 1903.

Pitcher, water (ill.)	$180-220
Probably tumbler to match	72- 81

428

Dolphin

Dolphin

Sandwich, 1850s; McKee Bros., 1868; Bakewell, Pears & Company, 1868. Clear. Don't confuse it with Greentown's Dolphin covered dish.

Butter dish, covered	$100-160
Compote, high standard	78- 92
Creamer	85- 98
Goblet	66- 74
Pitcher, water (ill.)	130-145
Spoonholder	39- 50
Sugar bowl, covered	110-125

Possibly other pieces.

"Dolphin"

"Dolphin"

Covered dish, Indiana Tumbler & Goblet Company, 1899. Clear, chocolate, blue.

Clear	$115-140
Blue	245-270
Chocolate	170-190

Double Beetle Band

Double Beetle Band

(Smocking Bands): Columbia Glass Company, Findlay, Ohio, 1880s. Clear, yellow, amber, blue.

Butter dish, covered	$27-39
Creamer	22-31
Goblet	18-27
Pitcher (ill.)	38-54
Sauce, footed, flat	12-19
Spoonholder	13-21
Sugar bowl	
a. Covered	26-39
b. Open	18-27

Probably other pieces. Yellow, 50 percent higher; amber and blue, 100 percent higher than clear prices listed.

Double Dahlia and Lens

Possibly an early Northwood or Fenton pattern of the late 1880s or early 1890s. The background is stippled on each panel, the flowers are stained purple, foliage green, on crystal background. Scrolls at top and over lip are in bright gold. At least in table set and probably other pieces.

429

(continued)

Double Dahlia and Lens

Butter dish, covered $44-54
Creamer (ill.) 34-43
Spoonholder 27-38
Sugar bowl, covered 39-49

Double Donut

Double Donut

Findlay, Ohio, 1880s. Clear.

Butter dish $22-32
Cake stand 22-34
Celery 18-27
Compote, open, low standard 34-48
Creamer 19-32
Goblet 19-31
Pitcher (ill.).................... 36-49
Salt/Pepper, pr. 16-25
Spoonholder 18-32
Sugar bowl 22-36

Probably other pieces.

Double Greek Key

This is Canadian glass, made by the Burlington Glass Works, Hamilton,

Double Greek Key

Ontario, 1880s. Clear, stippled, opaque white, blue.

Butter dish, covered $92-110
Compote, covered 58- 70
Creamer 34- 50
Pitcher (ill.).................... 75- 90
Spoonholder 28- 42
Sugar bowl, covered 52- 72
Tassi (small compote), 6" 40- 60
Tumbler 36- 48

Probably other pieces. Don't overlook Canadian glass. Most of it is well made and most collectible. Color 50 percent more than clear prices listed.

Double Ribbon

Double Ribbon

Made by many factories in the 1870s. Frosted and clear.

Butter dish $42-56
Compote
  a. Covered, high foot.......... 50-62
  b. Open, high foot 40-52
Creamer 42-56

Egg cup	28-39
Goblet	37-50
Pickle dish	19-27
Pitcher (ill.)	34-48
Platter, bread, frosted	37-49
Sauce, footed, 4½"	12-20
Spoonholder	36-47
Sugar bowl	38-52

Probably other pieces.

Double Spear

Double Spear

Maker unknown, 1880s. Clear.

Butter dish, covered	$32-42
Celery	38-49
Compote, covered, high standard .	46-58
Creamer	42-56
Dish, oval, deep	23-37
Goblet	35-49
Pickle dish	15-32
Pitcher, water (ill.)	52-64
Sauce	16-28
Spoonholder	38-49
Sugar bowl	48-62

Probably other pieces.

Draped Fan

Doyle & Company, Pittsburgh, c. 1880s, clear, non-flint; pattern reissued by U.S. Glass Company in 1890s.

Butter dish, covered	$32-46
Cake stand	32-48
Celery	17-28
Compote	
a. Covered	28-40
b. Open	18-32
Creamer	26-42
Goblet	20-33

Pitcher, water	32-48
Spoonholder	22-34
Sugar bowl, covered	32-44

Many other pieces.

Drapery

Drapery

(Lace): Sandwich, early and later; Doyle & Company, Pittsburgh, 1870. Clear.

Butter dish, covered	$52-64
Compote, covered	47-59
Creamer	40-54
Dish, oval	20-33
Goblet	34-46
Pitcher (ill.)	37-52
Plate, 6"	25-35
Saucedish, flat, 4"	16-28
Spoonholder	35-49
Sugar bowl, covered	42-54

Probably other pieces.

Drapery

Drapery

Northwood & Company, late 1890s.

	Marigold	Vivid	Pastel
Pitcher (ill.)	$88-100	$130-160	$175-195
Rose bowl	39- 50	52- 70	67- 79
Vase, 4", 5",			
10" high			
flared top	19- 28	29- 39	38- 52

Drinking Scene on Mug

Drinking Scene on Mug

Indiana Tumbler & Goblet (National) Company, late 1890s.

Chocolate	$60- 65
White milk	28- 33
Blue milk	35- 45
Nile green	40- 47
Clear	44- 51
Amber	95-110

With lip, regular size, 100 percent higher; large steins, 350 to 400 percent higher.

Drum

Drum

Bryce, Higbee & Company, Pittsburgh, 1880s. Clear, and milk glass. Finials are tiny cannon.

Butter dish, covered, cannon finial	$55-69
Creamer	48-60
Mustard jar, covered, cannon finial	60-70
Spoonholder	52-64
Sugar bowl, covered, cannon finial	58-70

Possibly a few other pieces.

Duncan 2000

(Flowered Scroll): George Duncan's Sons & Company, Washington, Pennsylvania, c. 1893, clear; sometimes flowered scroll is colored amber.

Butter dish, covered	$28-40
Creamer	30-42
Pitcher, milk	29-42
Spoonholder	12-20
Sugar bowl, covered	28-39
Tumbler	15-27

Amber flowered scroll, 50% higher than clear prices listed. Possibly other pieces.

E Pluribus Unum

E Pluribus Unum

Gillinder & Sons, Philadelphia, Pennsylvania, mid-1800s. Clear.

Mug, handled	$69- 82
Pickle dish	40- 52
Platter (ill.)	81-110

Ear of Corn

Ear of Corn

Challinor, Taylor & Company, Tarentum, Pennsylvania, c. 1885. Clear, colored, opal.

Butter dish, covered	$48-58
Creamer, souvenir-type, green, "corn" in burnished gold	69-80

Creamer, standard size, clear,
colored, opal 48-60
Vase, clear-to-opal, 7" high (ill.).. 67-82
Probably other table pieces.

Early Moon and Star

Early Moon and Star

New England Glass Company, 1840s.
Clear, canary, probably other colors.

Creamer $152-178
Lamp, whale oil 163-220
Spoonholder (ill.) 72- 90
Sugar bowl, covered 168-188
Possibly other pieces. This is an extremely rare pattern.

Early Panelled Grape Band

Early Panelled Grape Band

Maker unknown, 1870s. Clear.

Butter dish, covered $28-46
Celery 19-33

Creamer 24-32
Egg cup 17-25
Goblet (ill.) 32-47
Pitcher, water 42-52
Spoonholder 19-33
Sugar bowl, (ill.)............... 29-44
Probably other pieces.

Effulgent Star

Effulgent Star

(Star Galaxy): Central Glass Company,
Wheeling, West Virginia, 1880. Crystal
and colored glass.

Butter dish, covered $46-60
Cake stand 48-62
Celery 23-29
Creamer 32-41
Goblet 39-52
Pitcher, water (ill.) 62-73
Spoonholder 21-32
Sugar bowl, covered 39-48
Tumbler 15-23
Probably other pieces.

Egg in Sand

Egg in Sand

(Bean): Maker unknown, 1880s. Clear
and amber.

433   (continued)

Butter dish $48-62
Cake stand 42-52
Compote 44-54
Cordial 18-24
Creamer 27-36
Goblet 27-38
Pitcher, water (ill.) 34-42
Sauce 12-22
Salt/Pepper, pr. 18-30
Spoonholder 19-29
Sugar bowl 27-37
Tray, bread 22-32
Tumbler 38-50
Wine 19-32

Probably other pieces. Amber is 80 percent higher than clear prices listed.

Ellipse

Richards & Hartley Flint Glass Company, Pittsburgh; later, Tarentum, Pennsylvania, 1875-1893. Clear only. Standard pieces made. Only goblet made after 1888.

Butter dish, covered $29-42
Celery 18-29
Creamer 16-30
Goblet (ill). 17-30
Pitcher, water 40-50
Salt/Pepper, pr. 12-22
Spoonholder 15-24
Sugar bowl, covered 28-39
Tumbler 16-27

Elk Medallion

Elk Medallion

Maker and date unknown. The elk is shown in three different panels; the piece is acid etched.

Goblet (ill.) $28-42

Ellipse

Emerald Green Herringbone

Emerald Green Herringbone

(Florida): U.S. Glass Company, 1880s. Clear, emerald green.

Bowl, berry, large, deep $39-48
Butter dish 38-52
Celery 38-52
Compote, open, high foot 44-60
Creamer (ill.) 33-48
Goblet 28-40
Pitcher, water 52-66
Plates, square, 7¼", 9¼" 29-40
Salt/Pepper, pr. 32-42
Spoonholder 33-44
Sugar bowl 34-46
Tumbler, water 19-29
Wine 19-32

Probably other pieces. Emerald green, 100 percent higher than clear prices listed. Goblet is being reproduced, especially in green. Probably in clear, amber, and blue. Watch it!

English

Etched Grape

Etched Grape

U.S. Glass Company, 1900-1905. Clear, emerald green, with and without acid-etch, with vineyard design.

Butter dish	$22-32
Celery vase	15-28
Creamer	17-27
Goblet	22-33
Pitcher, water (ill.)	38-60
Tumbler	16-25

Probably other pieces. Emerald green is 50 percent higher than clear prices listed.

English

Westmoreland Glass Company, 1896. Clear, opal ware.

Butter dish	$28-37
Celery	19-30
Compote	22-32
Creamer	19-30
Goblet	19-32
Pitcher, water (ill.)	34-44
Salt/Pepper, pr.	16-27
Spoonholder	18-29
Sugar bowl, covered	25-40
Tumbler	19-26

Probably other pieces. Opal ware is 50 percent higher than clear prices listed.

Esther

(Tooth and Claw): Riverside Glass Company, Wellsburgh, West Virginia, c. 1896, clear, emerald green, non-flint.

Compote		
a. Covered		$34-48
b. Open		18-30
Creamer		22-39
Cruet		47-62
Goblet		32-48
Relish		17-29
Spoonholder		16-29
Sugar bowl		
a. Covered		35-52
b. Open		16-32
Toothpick holder		22-34

Emerald green, 50% higher than clear prices listed. Other pieces.

Ethol

Ethol

(Cat's Eye and Block; Cut Log): Greensburg Glass Company, Greensburg, Pennsylvania, c. 1885, clear, non-flint.

Bowls, round, oblong	$22-34
Butter dish, covered	38-50
Creamer	29-44
Goblet (ill.) '	32-44
Pitcher, milk	36-49

(continued)

Sugar bowl, covered 33-44
Tumbler 16-29
Wine 33-46

Probably other pieces. Don't confuse this pattern with that made by Westmoreland Specialty Company.

Etruscan

Bakewell, Pears & Company, Pittsburgh, c. 1874, clear, flint.

Butter dish, covered $64- 78
Cake stand 82- 94
Compote
  a. Covered, high standard 94-120
  b. Covered, low standard 68- 82
Creamer 59- 71
Egg cup 33- 44
Goblet 48- 58
Sauce 14- 28
Spoonholder 47- 58
Sugar bowl, covered 63- 75
Tumbler 31- 42

Eugenie

McKee & Brothers, Pittsburgh, c. 1850s, clear, flint.

Butter dish, covered .... $ 73- 94
Celery 69- 83
Compote, covered, on standard . 94-115
Creamer (rare) 190-245
Egg cup 40- 53
Goblet 60- 74
Spoonholder 72- 83
Sugar bowl, covered, dolphin
  finial (rare) 265-310
Tumbler 70- 80
Wine 69- 81

Probably other pieces.

Excelsior

Sandwich, 1850s; McKee Bros., 1868; C. Ihmsen and Company, 1851; others. Clear.

Ale glass .... $ 62- 82
Bitters bottle 45- 62
Butter dish 65- 84
Candlesticks, pr. 105-125
Compote
  a. Covered, low foot 115-130
  b. Open, high foot 95-120
Creamer, 2 styles 90-115
Decanter, small, pint, quart .. 60- 70

Excelsior

Egg cup, double and single 42- 56
Goblet, barrel, Maltese Cross .. 52- 60
Pitcher
  a. Milk (rare), Sandwich 182-196
  b. Syrup 90-110
  c. Water (rare) (ill.),
    Sandwich 190-220
Spoonholder 40- 52
Sugar bowl, 2 styles 138-150
Tumbler, footed, jelly, water .. 52- 66
Whale oil lamp w/Maltese
  Cross, Sandwich 120-144
Wine 59- 72

Excelsior Variant

Excelsior Variant

(Excelsior with Double Ringed Stem): Probably McKee and Bros., 1868. Clear.

Butter dish $38-50

Celery
  a. Plain top 32-47
  b. Scalloped top 48-60
Cordial 21-32
Creamer (scarce) 88-99
Goblet 26-34
Spoonholder (ill.) 30-41
Sugar bowl, covered 44-55
Probably other pieces.

Eye-Winker

(Crystal Ball): Maker unknown, c. 1889, clear; possibly made by one of several factories in Findlay, Ohio. This pattern is not "Diamond Point Discs."

Butter dish, covered $42-52
Cake stand 58-72
Compote, open, scalloped edge .. 30-42
Creamer 32-48
Dish, banana 50-60
Lamp 42-62
Pitcher, syrup 42-49
Plate, scalloped edge, 8½" 22-32
Sauce, flat 16-25
Spoonholder 18-29
Sugar bowl
  a. Covered 39-50
  b. Open 18-29

Butter dish, creamer, lamp, pitcher, sauce, covered sugar bowl, toothpick holder and tumbler being reproduced.

Faceted Flower

Faceted Flower

Maker unknown, probably Midwest, late 1800s. Clear.

Butter dish, covered $32-41
Celery 17-28
Creamer 16-25
Goblet 18-28
Pitcher, water (ill.) 26-38
Spoonholder 18-30

Sugar bowl, covered 25-32
Tray, water 19-32
Probably other pieces.

Fairfax Strawberry

Fairfax Strawberry

(Strawberry): Clear and milk glass, late 1860s, some made at Sandwich. Also made at Bryce, Walker and Company, 1870.

Butter dish $100-120
Compote, covered, 8", high, low 135-165
Creamer 93-108
Egg cup 45- 58
Goblet (ill.) 70- 80
Honey dish 35- 45
Pitcher
  a. Syrup 72- 82
  b. Water 138-150
Sauce 32- 42
Spoonholder 62- 71
Sugar bowl 82- 96

Probably other pieces. Prices listed are for milk glass. Clear, 50 percent less. Egg cup, goblet, probably other pieces being reproduced, both in clear and milk glass. Careful!

Falling Leaves

Maker and date unknown. Otherwise ordinary glass, this pattern is unusual because the leaves are embossed on the **inside** of the body. So far, no mold-maker has figured out how it was done. Can anyone tell us? Apparently the usual pieces were made.

Berry bowl (ill.) $27-36
Butter dish, covered 38-44
Creamer 26-34
Spoonholder 22-31
Sugar bowl, covered 31-42
Probably other pieces.

437

(continued)

Falling Leaves

Fan

Fan

Northwood Glass Company, late 1880s. Blue with opalescent trim; made in Custard glass and Carnival glass.

	Custard	Carnival Colors Marigold
Berry set		
a. Large bowl	....$115-130	
b. Small bowl	.... 33- 42	$32-42
Butter dish, covered	78- 90	
Creamer (ill.)	...... 60- 70	
Spoonholder	.... 52- 62	
Sugar bowl, covered	68- 83	

Probably other occasional pieces made in Marigold, Vivid, Pastel.

Fan and Star

Challinor, Taylor, Ltd., c. 1880s, clear, opaque white, decorated with enamelled flowers in different colors, non-flint.

Bowl	$12-18
Butter dish, covered	23-32
Celery	19-27
Compote, covered	21-32
Goblet	19-32
Pitcher, water.................	20-34
Sauce	9-17

Spoonholder	10-18
Sugar bowl, covered	22-40

Opaque white, 100% higher than clear prices listed.

Fancy Diamonds

Fancy Diamonds

Maker unknown, late 1880s, early 1890s. Clear.

Bowl	$17-29
Butter dish, covered	32-42
Creamer	29-40
Goblet	22-34
Pitcher (ill.)...................	44-56
Spoonholder	17-29
Sugar bowl, covered	32-48
Wine	16-28

Probably other pieces.

Fan with Diamond

Fan with Diamond

Maker unknown, late 1870s. Clear.

Butter dish	$40-50
Compote	
a. Covered, high foot	42-53
b. Covered, low foot	42-51
Cordial	14-27
Creamer	22-34
Dish, oval, 9" x 6¾"	12-22
Egg cup	15-29
Goblet (ill.)	32-42
Pickle dish	12-24
Pitcher, water	42-52
Sauce, flat, 4"	12-21
Spoonholder	18-32
Sugar bowl, open	19-32

Probably other pieces.

Feather

Feather

(Finecut and Feather; Indiana Swirl): McKee Glass Co., 1890s. Clear and green, rare in amber, red, chocolate.

Bowl, 7½", 8½"	$20-27
Butter dish, covered	33-43
Cake stand, 8½", 11" (rare)	34-44
Celery	32-42
Compote, high standard	39-46
Cordial	16-24
Creamer	28-40
Cruet	29-40
Goblet	32-42
Pitcher, water (ill.)	32-43
Plate, 10"	28-39
Spoonholder	18-29
Sugar bowl	27-38
Toothpick holder	27-39
Tumbler	38-48
Wine	25-34

Probably other pieces. Green, amber, 85 percent higher than clear prices listed.

Feather Duster

Feather Duster

U.S. Glass Company, 1880s. Clear and emerald green.

Bowl, berry	$26-36
Butter dish	39-47
Compote, covered, 6" high	42-52
Creamer	26-34
Egg cup	19-29
Goblet	26-38
Pitcher, water (ill.)	38-48
Spoonholder	19-29
Sugar bowl	38-52
Tumbler	19-29

Probably other pieces. Emerald green, 80 percent higher than clear prices listed.

Feather with Quatrefoil Center

Feather with Quatrefoil Center

Sandwich Glass Company, probably c. 1850s or 1860s, clear, flint.

Center plate, 9¼" (ill.)	$112-137

Fern Garland

McKee Glass Company, Jeannette, Pennsylvania, c. 1894, clear, non-flint, pieces marked "Pres-Cut."

439

(continued)

Butter dish, covered $26-37
Celery 15-29
Compote
  a. High standard 28-39
  b. Low standard 17-29
Creamer 20-31
Goblet 22-34
Pitcher 38-50
Spoonholder 19-28
Sugar bowl, covered 26-36
Tray, celery 17-28
Vase, violets 18-33

Probably other pieces.

Fern Sprig

Bellaire Goblet Company, Bellaire, Ohio, and Findlay, Ohio, c. 1800s, clear, non-flint. Pattern reissued after 1891 by U.S. Glass Company.

Butter dish, covered $39-48
Creamer 40-50
Goblet 27-38
Spoonholder 19-29
Sugar bowl, covered 38-48

Should be many more pieces.

Festoon

Festoon

Portland Glass Co., Portland, Maine, 1860s.

Bowl, berry, 9″, 10″, finger $34-44
Butter dish, covered 39-47
Cake plate on stand, 9″, 10″, dia. .. 38-50
Celery 27-37
Compote, high foot 39-47
Creamer 26-39
Pickle jar 40-50
Pitcher, water (ill.) 58-68
Plate, 7″, 8″, 9″ 34-50
Spoonholder 38-48

Sugar bowl, covered 40-50
Tumbler 29-39
Wine 22-37

Probably other pieces.

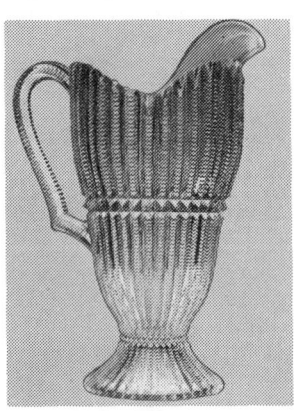

File

File

Columbia Glass Company, Findlay, Ohio, 1890-1907. Clear.

Butter dish $30-40
Celery 17-29
Creamer 28-40
Goblet 24-32
Lamp, tall 39-48
Pitcher (ill.) 46-53
Spoonholder 29-40
Sugar bowl 39-47
Tumbler 19-28

Probably other pieces.

Fine Cut

Fine Cut

Bryce Bros., Pittsburgh, 1870s. Crystal, blue, amber, yellow.

Bowl, finger, small $22-29
Butter dish, covered 40-50
Compote, covered 44-58

Creamer 27-36
Dish, oblong, deep 19-29
Goblet 22-31
Pitcher, water (ill.) 26-35
Plates, 6¼″, 7¼″, 10¼″ 19-28
Saucedish 9-18
Spoonholder 17-26
Sugar bowl, covered 25-35
Toothpick holder 15-25
Tray, bread, water 23-32

Probably other pieces. Colors are 85 percent higher than clear prices listed.

Fine Cut and Block

Fine Cut and Block

King Glass Company, Pittsburgh, 1880s. Clear, amber, sapphire blue, clear with color blocks.

Butter dish, covered $34-44
Cake stand
   a. Large 32-47
   b. Small 19-28
Compote, jelly 20-30
Creamer 27-37
Goblet, buttermilk 28-39
Lamp, handled, flat 22-31
Pitcher, water (ill.) 36-45
Spoonholder 28-38
Sugar bowl 30-40
Tumbler 20-30

Probably other pieces. Colors, 60 percent higher; colored blocks, 125 percent higher than clear prices listed.

Fine Cut and Panel

Probably Bryce Bros., Pittsburgh, 1880s; reissued by U.S. Glass Company in early 1890s. Clear and color.

Butter dish, covered $43-53
Celery 40-50
Compote, open, high standard .. 37-49

Fine Cut and Panel

Creamer 34-43
Goblet 29-38
Pitcher (ill.) 40-50
Sauce 34-44
Salt/Pepper, pr. 16-32
Spoonholder 34-44
Sugar bowl 38-50
Tumbler 28-39
Wine 26-32

Probably other pieces. Amber, yellow, and blue are 100 percent higher than clear prices listed.

Fine Cut and Rib

Fine Cut and Rib

Maker unknown, late 1880s. Clear.

Butter dish, covered $28-38
Celery vase 19-27
Creamer 26-34
Goblet 19-30
Pitcher, water (ill.) 36-47
Spoonholder 20-32
Sugar bowl, covered 24-36
Tumbler 18-30

Fine Cut Medallion

Fine Cut Medallion

(Austrian): Indiana Tumbler and Goblet Company, Greentown, Indiana, 1897-1898. Clear, canary, chocolate, green.

Banana dish	$63-72
Bowl, berry	28-39
Butter dish	60-73
Compote	
a. Jelly	32-40
b. Open, large	38-49
Creamer	26-36
Goblet	29-40
Pitcher, water (ill.)	60-72
Punch cup	15-30
Rectangular bowl	50-62
Rose bowl	
a. Large	55-65
b. Small	48-52
Spoonholder	32-42
Tumbler	33-44

The miniatures in chocolate are rare and expensive. Chocolate, 350 to 450 percent higher than clear; other colors are 300 percent higher than clear.

Fishscale

Fishscale

(Coral): Bryce Bros., Pittsburgh, 1880s. Clear.

Bowl, 6", 7", 8", open	$30-40

Butter dish	46-56
Cake plate on stand, 9", 10", 11"	34-48
Celery vase	47-58
Compote	
a. Covered, high standard, 6", 7", 8"	54-70
b. Open, high standard, 4", 7", 8", 9", 10"	38-52
Creamer	40-52
Goblet	38-50
Pickle dish	29-39
Pitcher, quart and half gallon	40-50
Plate, round, 7", 8"	27-37
Sauce, flared, footed, 4"	15-24
Spoonholder	39-50
Sugar bowl	42-60
Tumbler	26-38

Probably other pieces.

Flared Top Hairpin

Same prices as "Hairpin" — see .

Flared Top Belted Worchester

Maker unknown, c. 1850s, clear, flint.

Cordial	$34-46
Goblet	27-40
Sugar bowl, covered	40-52
Tumbler	22-40
Whiskey, handled	32-50
Wine	28-37

Possibly other pieces.

Flat Diamond

Flat Diamond

(Diamond, Lippman): Richards & Hartley Glass Company, Tarentum, Pennsylvania, 1885-1893, clear only.

Butter dish, covered	$36-46
Creamer	16-29
Goblet (ill.)	18-29
Spoonholder	15-24
Sugar bowl, covered	30-40
Tumbler	17-28

Should be other pieces.

Flattened Diamond and Sunburst

Flattened Diamond and Sunburst

Maker unknown, 1800s. Clear, colors.

Butter dish, miniature	$27-38
Celery	16-29
Creamer, miniature	26-39
Goblet	18-29
Pitcher (ill.)	38-50
Saucedish, 4", 5"	14-23
Spoonholder	22-32
Sugar bowl, covered	26-38

Probably other pieces. Color is 50 percent higher than clear prices listed.

Flattened Sawtooth

George Duncan & Sons, Pittsburgh, c. 1880, clear, flint.

Bowl

a. Finger	$34-43
b. Flat, 10"	64-72
Celery	52-62
Compote, covered	54-65
Creamer	38-49
Goblet	39-49
Pitcher	77-92

Spoonholder	48-63
Sugar bowl, covered	50-60
Wine	22-32

Probably other pieces.

Fleur-de-Lis and Tassel

U.S. Glass Company, c. 1892, clear, opal, green with gilt decoration, non-flint.

Bottle, water	$28-39
Butter dish, covered	32-41
Cake stand	22-31
Celery	18-27
Compote, covered	32-50
Creamer	28-39
Pitcher, milk	50-60
Pot, mustard	19-32
Spoonholder	16-29
Sugar bowl, covered	29-39
Tumbler	16-32
Wine	16-28

Colors, 40% higher than clear prices listed.

Flickering Flame

Flickering Flame

Westmoreland Glass Company, 1896. Clear, some stained with ruby color.

Creamer, covered (ill.)	$26-35
Sugar, covered	28-40

Possibly others in this pattern.

Floral Oval

Maker and date unknown.

Plate, 7¼" square	$29-42
Pitcher (ill.)	47-58

Probably usual pieces.

(continued)

Floral Oval

Flower and Quill

Florida Palm

(Tidal): Greensburg Glass Company, Greensburg, Pennsylvania, c. early 1900s, clear, non-flint.

Bowls, berry, 7", 8", 9" $16-27
Cake stand 22-32
Celery 22-32
Creamer 33-45
Goblet 26-34
Spoonholder 19-24
Sugar bowl, covered 34-44

Probably other pieces.

Flower and Quill

(Pretty Band): Possibly McKee Bros., 1880s. Clear.

Butter dish, covered $42-52
Celery, footed 28-40
Creamer 28-40
Nappy, flange handle, 4" 16-29
Pickle castor 52-63
Pitcher, water (ill.) 42-53
Plate, large, square 28-40
Spoonholder 27-42
Sugar bowl, covered 39-50

Probably other pieces.

Flower Band

Maker unknown, c. 1870s, clear, non-flint; possibly frosted.

Butter dish, covered $62-73
Celery 32-42
Compote, covered 59-72
Creamer 38-50
Goblet 52-63
Pitcher, milk 70-82
Spoonholder 34-44
Sugar bowl
  a. Open 42-53
  b. Covered 70-80

If it was made in frosted, 40% higher than clear prices listed.

Flower Pot

Flower Pot

(Potted Plant): Possibly Adams Glass Company, 1800s. Clear.

Butter dish, covered $52-62

444

Cake stand, 10½" dia. 57-67
Compote, open 50-60
Creamer 40-50
Goblet 39-60
Pitcher, milk (ill.) 50-60
Sauce, open, on standard 20-30
Spoonholder 50-60
Sugar bowl, covered 50-61
Tray, bread 49-62
Tumbler 19-30

Flower with Cane

Flower with Cane

Maker unknown, 1895-1905, flower stained pea-green with gilt center. Upper part also gilded. Ruby probably also used; flower also in other than green.

Creamer $34-52
Pitcher (ill.) 44-58
Sugar bowl, covered 28-42

Probably other pieces. Colors don't affect prices listed.

Flute

Flute

Many factories made this clear glass, 1850s and 1860s. It went by many names: Bessimer Flute; Sexton Flute; Reed Stem Flute; Sandwich Flute; Duchess Flute. Prices listed are basic prices and not specific to any one pattern.

Ale glass $28-38
Bitters bottle (6 and 8 flute) 30-40
Bowl, scalloped 28-42
Candlesticks, pr. (6 flute,
　no sockets) .... 52-63 pr.
Creamer 34-44
Decanter, quart size 58-70
Goblet 29-39
Lamp 48-62
Mug 29-37
Tumbler, half pint, jelly, one
　gill, half gill (toy), each 32-39
Wine....................... 34-44

Probably other pieces.

Flute and Cane

Flute and Cane

Maker unknown, late 1870s. Clear.

Butter dish $32-42
Celery vase 17-28
Creamer 22-32
Goblet 18-28
Pitcher
　a. Milk 29-39
　b. Tankard (ill.) 34-45
Spoonholder 17-27
Sugar bowl, covered 24-36
Tumbler 18-28

Probably other pieces.

Fluted Scrolls

Fluted Scrolls

Northwood Glass Company, late 1880s.
Clear, amber, sapphire blue, custard.

Bowl, footed.................... $27-36
Creamer 29-40
Epergne 54-64
Pitcher, water (ill.) 52-61
Sugar bowl, covered 41-52
Tumbler 30-40

Possibly other table pieces to match.
Amber, sapphire, custard, 100 percent
higher than clear prices listed.

Flying Birds

Maker unknown, c. 1870, clear, non-flint.

Goblet $50-62

There should be other pieces.

Flying Swan

Flying Swan

By Westmoreland Specialty Company,
Grapeville, Pennsylvania, 1890s. Clear,
slag.

Butter dish ....$ 48- 60
Celery....................... 22- 31
Creamer..................... 25- 35
Pitcher (ill.), slag.............. 120-140
Spoonholder 22- 32
Sugar bowl, covered 40- 50
Toothpick holder 22- 32
Vase 34- 46

Probably other pieces. Colors, 75 percent
higher than clear prices listed.

Forget-Me-Not-in-Scroll

Forget-Me-Not-in-Scroll

Maker unknown, c. 1870s, clear, non-flint.

Butter dish, covered $28-40
Creamer 34-42
Goblet (ill.) 27-42
Pitcher 36-48
Spoonholder 18-30
Sugar bowl, covered 29-38

Probably other pieces.

Fostoria's Number 952

Fostoria Glass Company, Fostoria,
Ohio, late 1800s. Clear.

Pitcher, water................. $32-44
Tumbler to match 19-32

Probably other pieces, including four-piece table set.

Fostoria's Number 952

Framed Blocks

Four Petal

Four Petal

Bryce, McKee & Company or McKee &
Brothers, c. 1850s, clear, blue, flint.

Compote, open, 6" high ....$ 69- 82
Creamer 110-138
Sugar bowl, open (ill.)......... 72- 93

Only known pieces. Should be others.
Blue, 50% higher than clear prices
listed.

Framed Circles

Framed Circles

Maker unknown, c. 1840s, clear, flint.

Goblet $52-62
Wine (ill.)..................... 48-58

Probably other pieces.

Framed Blocks

A member of the "Block-and-Thumb-
print" family, c. 1870s, clear, flint, non-
flint.

Goblet $48-60
Wine (ill.).................... 44-54

Flint, 40% higher than clear prices listed. Should be other pieces.

Framed Ovals

447

(continued)

Framed Ovals

Possibly Sandwich, c. 1840s, clear, gilt trimmed, flint. Could also be New England Glass Company, same era.

Brandy (or Pony Ale),
footed (ill.) $110-135

Frost Crystal

Frost Crystal

Tarentum Glass Company, Tarentum, Pennsylvania, 1906. Clear.

Butter dish	$34-45
Celery boat	19-29
Creamer	17-26
Custard cup..................	15-30
Plate (ill.)...................	22-31
Spoonholder	24-33
Sugar bowl, open	38-48

Probably other pieces.

Frosted Block

Frosted Block

Indiana Glass Company, Dunkirk, Indiana, 1913. Clear, amber, yellow, blue, green, pink; also, vaseline with opalescent border. This is a "new" glass. It compares to "Oatmeal glass." It comes in many pieces. If you like it, buy it.

Berry bowl	$10-18
Butter dish, covered	26-36
Celery	14-26
Compote, jelly.................	22-32
Creamer	19-27
Pitcher, water (ill.)	28-40
Salt/Pepper, pr.	15-22
Spoonholder	17-22
Sugar bowl, covered	22-32

Other pieces.

Frosted Circle

Frosted Circle

Bryce Bros., 1870s, U.S. Glass Company, after 1891. Clear.

Bowl, covered and open, 7", 8"	.. $34-44
Butter dish, covered	60-70
Cake stand, 8", 9", 10",	
(10½" with pedestal)	80-90
Celery	58-70
Compote, covered, open, 7", 8"....	62-75
Creamer	52-70
Goblet	53-63
Pickle jar	63-73
Pitcher, water (ill.)	75-85
Plates, 4", 5", 7", 9"	28-38
Salt/Pepper, pr.	55-68
Spoonholder	50-62
Sugar bowl	52-67
Tumblers, 2 types	38-50
Wine........................	46-57

Probably other pieces. Goblet being reproduced.

448

Frosted Fruits

Frosted Fruits

Maker unknown, 1880-1890s. Clear and frosted.

Butter dish	$62-71
Celery	28-40
Creamer	40-50
Goblet	36-46
Pitcher, water (ill.)	82-92
Sauce	18-24
Sugar bowl	52-63
Tumbler	34-47

Probably other pieces. Frosted is 40 percent higher than clear prices listed.

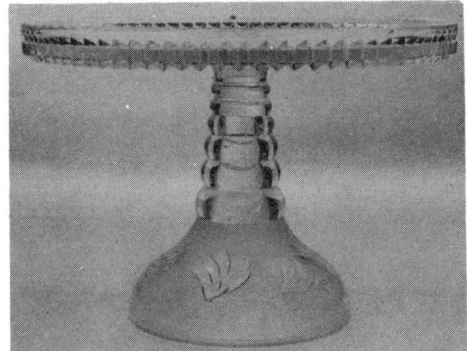
Frosted Magnolia

Frosted Magnolia

(Water Lily): Dalzell, Gilmore & Leighton, West Virginia factory, or Findley, Ohio, late 1800s. Frosted and clear.

Butter dish, covered	$42-56
Cake stand (ill.)	52-70
Creamer	52-62
Goblet	60-70
Sauce, flat, deep, large	19-28

Sugar bowl, covered	43-58
Syrup jug	52-62

Probably other pieces.

Frosted Medallion

Frosted Medallion

(Sunburst Rosette): Maker unknown, late 1880s. Clear.

Bowl, oval	$16-27
Butter bowl, covered	28-40
Creamer	22-29
Compote	
a. Covered	35-47
b. Open	19-28
Goblet	22-32
Pitcher, water, syrup (ill.)	32-39
Spoonholder	19-28
Sugar bowl, covered	29-38
Tumbler	19-27

Probably other pieces.

Frosted Ribbon

Frosted Ribbon

Bakewell, Pears and Company; also George Duncan and Sons, 1878s. Frosted.

Ale glass	$ 29- 39
Bitters bottle	34- 44
Bowl, waste	50- 60
Butter dish	48- 58
Celery	59- 69

449

(continued)

Compote
  a. Covered, high standard.... 62- 72
  b. Covered, low standard 50- 60
  c. Open, Dolphin standard .. 110-130
Creamer...................... 83- 94
Egg cup 33- 44
Goblet....................... 44- 54
Pitcher, water, quart, and
  ½ gallon 56- 66
Spoonholder 58- 68
Sugar bowl 90-110
Tumbler..................... 29- 39
Wine 32- 42

Probably other pieces. Goblet being reproduced.

Frosted Stork

Frosted Stork

(Flamingo): Crystal Glass Company, Bridgeport, Ohio, 1879. Frosted.
Bowl, waste....................$48- 58
Butter dish 66- 79
Creamer 72- 84
Goblet 64- 74
Jam jar....................... 48- 60
Pitcher, water (ill.) 92-102
Plate, 9″ 44- 60
Sauce 22- 32
Spoonholder 62- 70
Sugar bowl, covered, with finial.. 81- 90
Tray, large 78- 92

Probably other pieces. This is a rare pattern.

Fuchsia

Sandwich, early; possibly Hobbs, Brockunier & Company, 1865. Clear.
Butter dish, covered $50-60
Cake stand 39-50

Fuchsia

Celery vase 38-48
Compote, open 58-68
Creamer 42-52
Goblet 40-50
Pitcher (ill.).................. 56-66
Plate, 8″, 10″ 42-52
Spoonholder 32-41
Sugar bowl 58-70
Tumbler 31-41

Possibly other pieces.

Gaelic

Gaelic

Maker and date unknown, possibly 1890-1905 period. Undoubtedly, one of the glass companies absorbed by the giant U.S. Glass Company. This water pitcher has a gold band at top and green leaves.
Bowl, oval, 9″ $28-40
Pitcher, water (ill.) 60-72
Punch cup 14-23

450

Relish dish, 7¼" 13-24
Probably tumbler to match 29-39

Garden of Eden

Garden of Eden

(Lotus): Probably McKee & Bros., 1865.
Clear.

Butter dish, covered $62-71
Cake stand 49-62
Creamer 34-42
Goblet, plain, and serpent head .. 55-70
Mug, handled 32-42
Pickle dish, oval............... 19-24
Pitcher (ill.).................. 52-64
Platter 38-49
Platter, bread 30-40
Sugar bowl, covered 32-42
Tray, bread 19-28

Probably other pieces.

Garfield Drape

Garfield Drape

Adams & Company, Pittsburgh, 1880s.
Clear. One of the Garfield Memorial
plates was produced by Campbell, Jones
& Company, in 1881. Clear.

Bowl $33-43
Butter dish 56-66
Cake plate on stand 59-70
Celery 42-52

Compote, covered, high and
    low standard 57-67
Creamer 62-74
Goblet 33-44
Honey dish 16-26
Pickle dish, oval............... 28-38
Pitcher, water, milk 44-53
Plate
    a. "We Mourn Our Nation's
        Loss" (ill.) 88-100
    b. "Memorial," 11"........... 70- 82
Sauce, footed and round 12- 19
Spoonholder 38- 48
Sugar bowl, covered 50- 60

Probably other pieces.

Garland of Roses

Garland of Roses

Maker unknown, 1880. Clear, vaseline.

Butter dish $22-32
Celery 14-22
Creamer (ill.) 16-27
Egg cup 14-28
Salt, open footed............... 15-26
Spoonholder 18-29
Sugar bowl, covered 26-40

Probably other pieces. Vaseline, 40 percent higher than clear prices listed.

Garter Band

Maker unknown, c. late 1880s, clear,
non-flint.

Butter dish, covered $26-36
Celery 19-27
Goblet 14-28
Sugar bowl, covered 26-35
Wine....................... 13-22

Probably other pieces.

Geneva

Geneva

(Shell and Scroll): Northwood Glass Company, 1900. Clear, custard, with ruby or green decorations.

Bowls, 3 scroll feet	$39-52
Butter dish, covered	42-58
Creamer, covered	42-52
Pitcher, syrup	50-60
Salt/Pepper, pr.	48-58
Spoonholder	29-34
Sugar bowl, open, covered	47-57
Tumbler, footed, plain (ill.)	29-38

Probably other pieces. Custard, 150 percent higher than clear prices listed.

George Peabody

George Peabody

A hero in the War of 1812, a great philanthropist, honored both in England and America. (1795-1869).

Mug, English registry mark	$72-92
Bowl, English registry mark	78-93
Creamer, English registry mark (ill.)	62-80

Considered rare today.

Giant Bull's Eye

Giant Bull's Eye

(Excelsior): Belmont Glass Company, Bellaire, Ohio, 1880s. Clear.

Butter dish, covered	$43-54
Celery	26-32
Creamer	29-40
Goblet	33-46
Pitcher, water (ill.)	62-73
Spoonholder	28-38
Sugar bowl, covered	29-38

Probably other pieces. Possibly in color.

Giant Sawtooth

Maker unknown, 1830. Clear.

Goblet	$ 78- 88
Lamp, whale oil (ill.)	175-220
Spill holder	42- 54
Tumbler	48- 63

Probably other pieces.

452

Giant Sawtooth

Gibson Girl

Gibson Girl

Maker unknown, early 1900s. Clear.

Butter dish $54-63
Creamer 55-65
Pitcher, water (ill.) 62-75
Plate, 10" 38-49
Spoonholder 47-62
Sugar bowl, covered 54-63
Tumbler 28-38

Possibly other pieces.

Girl with Flower

Maker unknown, 1870s. Clear, green, blue.

Girl with Flower

Plate, 6", blue (ill.) $33-44
Sauce, clear 26-37

Probably other pieces. Colors, 50 percent higher than clear.

Gladstone "For the Million"

Gladstone "For the Million"

This pattern honors William Ewart Gladstone, four times Prime Minister of England; (1809-1898).

Bowl, 8½" dia. .... $ 52- 61
Creamer (ill.) 220-260
Mug, amethyst 60- 70
Plate, aqua 50- 60

Of English make, fairly rare, but found on occasion. This is an unusual piece as the words are reversed — backwards. Possibly the only one in the world! Houston Museum.

453

Goat's Head

Hobbs, Brockunier & Company, Wheeling, West Virginia, c. 1878, clear, non-flint.

Butter dish, covered $44-54
Celery 38-49
Creamer 42-52
Compote, 6" 62-72
Sugar bowl
  a. Open 33-44
  b. Covered 36-46

Probably other pieces.

Gooseberry

Gooseberry

Sandwich glass, 1870s. Clear, opaque white.

Butter dish, covered $39-52
Cake stand, 9½" dia. 44-60
Compote
  a. Covered, high foot, large 56-66
  b. Covered, high foot, 6" 44-55
Creamer 33-48
Goblet 45-60
Honey dish 16-27
Lemonade glass 30-42
Pickle dish 12-19
Pitcher, water, syrup 52-63
Saucedish 18-27
Spoonholder 32-42
Sugar bowl 42-52
Tumbler, applied handle 17-27

Probably other pieces. Goblet being reproduced.

Gothic

McKee & Brothers, 1850s. Clear.

Butter dish .... $ 75- 90
Cake stand 52- 62

Gothic

Castor bottle, each 19- 29
Champagne (rare) 93-110
Compote
  a. Covered, on standard 160-170
  b. Open, footed 80- 90
Cordial 62- 72
Creamer 93-103
Egg cup 34- 44
Goblets, 2 styles 62- 72
Pitcher (ill.) 69- 78
Plate (rare) 47- 57
Sauce 30- 40
Spoonholder 54- 64
Sugar bowl 92-107
Tumbler 65- 78
Wine (rare) 95-120

Probably other pieces.

Gothic Arch and Panels

Gothic Arch and Panels

Make and date unknown, clear, flint.

Butter dish, covered $52-62
Jar, horseradish 34-44
Paperweight 30-40
Sauce, footed 19-29
Spoonholder 34-44
Sugar bowl (base ill.) 50-62

Should be other pieces.

Grace

Grand

(New Grand): Bryce, Higbee & Company, 1885. Clear.

Butter dish, covered	$32-42
Cake stand	30-40
Celery	19-25
Compote	40-50
Creamer	20-32
Goblet	19-27
Pitcher, water	32-42
Sauce	15-29
Spoonholder (ill.)	18-32
Sugar bowl, covered	33-42
Tumbler	27-36
Wine	27-38

Probably other pieces.

Grace

(Japanese): Richards & Hartley Flint Glass Company, Pittsburgh, Pennsylvania, 1870s. Pattern was discontinued prior to the company's removal to Tarentum in 1884. Scene is different on each individual table piece, though top and bottom horizontal borders are the same.

Butter dish, covered	$40-50
Compote	25-34
Creamer	19-28
Goblet	26-36
Spoonholder	18-28
Sugar bowl, covered	40-50

Possibly other pieces.

Grape and Festoon

Sandwich, early; they probably produced the clear leaf. Doyle & Company, Pittsburgh, 1870s, stippled leaf; probably other factories.

Butter dish	$80-90
Celery	62-73
Compote, covered, high and low standard	72-82
Cordial	44-54
Creamer, 2 styles	63-74
Egg cup, 2 styles	19-26
Goblet, 2 styles	44-56
Pickle dish, oval	23-32
Pitcher, water (ill.)	73-84
Plate, 6″	32-42
Saucedish, flat, 4″	19-27
Spoonholder	43-53
Sugar bowl, acorn knob	52-63
Wine	22-29

Probably other pieces.

Grape and Festoon with Shield

Possibly produced by Doyle & Company, 1860s. Clear, blue, other colors.

Butter dish	$36-45
Celery	25-37
Compote, covered, high and low standard	54-63
Creamer	32-42

Grand

Grape and Festoon

Grape and Festoon with Shield

Egg cup 16-28
Goblet 29-41
Mug, blue..................... 20-31
Pitcher, water (ill.) 54-64
Saucedish, flat, 4", 6" 13-26
Spoonholder 23-32
Sugar bowl 38-47

Probably other pieces.

Grape Band

Grape Band

Bryce, Walker & Company, Pittsburgh, Pennsylvania, c. 1869, clear, non-flint.

Butter dish, covered $34-46
Compote 40-49
Creamer 35-45
Goblet (ill.) 21-31
Pitcher, water................. 52-63

Spoonholder 18-28
Sugar bowl, covered 40-50
Wine......................... 22-34

Possibly made in flint at an earlier date. If so, 50% higher than non-flint prices listed.

Grape Bunch

Grape Bunch

Sandwich, c. 1870s, clear, non-flint.

Butter dish, covered $40-52
Compote 38-50
Creamer 33-42
Egg cup 27-36
Goblet (ill.) 22-40
Pitcher, water................. 42-52
Spoonholder 27-39
Sugar bowl, covered 34-46

Probably other pieces.

Grape Jug

This is one of the late fruit patterns, made in the late 1890s and early 1900s and should not be considered as Early American glass. Nevertheless, it's collectible today. Clear.

Grape jug (ill.) $27-38

Brings higher price because collectors buy it as a pitcher.

Grape Jug

Grape with Thumbprint

Grape with Thumbprint

Maker unknown, 1890s. Clear.

Butter dish	$59-72
Celery vase	42-54
Creamer	62-72
Goblet	39-50
Pitcher, water (ill.)	70-80
Spoonholder	47-57
Sugar bowl, covered	58-69
Syrup jug, several sizes	44-53
Tumbler	29-38

Probably other pieces.

Grape with Overlapping Foliage

Grape with Vine

Grape with Overlapping Foliage

Probably Sandwich, early. Later, other factories in Pittsburgh area, 1880s. Clear and milk-white.

Butter dish	$33-42
Celery vase	20-30
Creamer	28-40
Goblet	26-36
Pitcher	29-40
Spoonholder	20-32
Sugar bowl	27-37

Probably other pieces. Milk-white, 50 percent higher than clear prices listed.

Grape with Vine

Maker unknown, 1890s. Original pieces, red paint and gilt.

Butter dish	$34-47
Celery	24-34
Creamer	27-36
Goblet	32-42
Honey dish	18-27
Pitcher, water (ill.)	39-50
Spoonholder	22-29
Sugar bowl	34-43

Probably other pieces.

Grasshopper with Insect

Grasshopper with Insect

(Locust: Long Spear): Possibly Belmont Glass Works, Bellaire, Ohio, early 1880s. Clear and color.

Butter dish	$63-72
Celery vase	33-42
Compote, covered	67-75
Creamer	40-50
Goblet	70-80
Pickle dish, oval	20-32
Pitcher, water (ill.)	73-83
Sauce	18-27
Spoonholder	70-80
Sugar bowl, covered	72-82

Probably other pieces. Goblet being reproduced.

Grasshopper, with or without Insect

Grasshopper, with or without Insect

When grasshopper is present, he's climbing up side, directly above floral motif. With insect, 100 percent higher in price. Clear.

Bowl, covered	$22-32
Butter, covered	28-39
Compote, covered	30-40
Pitcher (ill.)	38-48
Plate, large	20-30
Sauce, flat	18-24
Spoonholder	19-27
Sugar, covered	28-34

Probably other pieces. Goblet being reproduced.

Greensburg's 130

Greensburg's 130

Greensburg Glass Company, Greensburg, Pennsylvania, late 1880s. Plain and engraved crystal.

Butter dish	$34-44
Celery dish	19-27
Creamer	29-37
Goblet	28-38
Honey dish	19-28
Pitcher, water, milk (ill.)	35-44
Sauce	17-26
Spoonholder	19-27
Sugar bowl, covered	35-45

Other pieces. Engraved crystal, 25 percent higher than plain prices listed.

Gridley Pitcher

A. J. Beatty & Sons, Dunkirk, Indiana, 1898. Clear.

Gridley pitcher	$122-132

Highly collectible today.

Gridley Pitcher

(Wm.) Haley's Glass Basket

(Wm.) Haley's Glass Basket

Two dates appear in the bottom: July 21, 1874, and April 5, 1881. Where it was made is not known.

Basket $68-83
Wine.......................... 49-63

Other pieces.

Hamilton

Hairpin

(Sandwich Loop): Sandwich, c. 1850s, clear, milk glass, flint.

Celery $64- 74
Champagne.................... 36- 46
Compote, covered, low standard .. 54- 68
Egg cup 38- 50
Goblet 39- 49
Pitcher 82-102
Spoonholder 37- 48
Sugar bowl
  a. Open 38- 49
  b. Covered 68- 78
Tumbler 52- 72

Milk glass, 90% higher than clear prices listed.

Hairpin with Rayed Base

Same prices as "Hairpin" — see.

Hamilton

Sandwich, early 1860s. Clear.

Butter dish, covered .... $ 73- 84
Castor set, in standard........ 128-149
Celery 64- 75
Compote, open and covered.... 75- 90
Creamer, applied or pressed
  handle 86- 98
Decanter, w/stopper 73- 90
Egg cup 40- 50
Goblet (ill.) 42- 52
Pitcher
  a. Syrup, metal top 68- 78
  b. Water 130-145
Saucedish, 4″, 5″ 26- 36
Spoonholder, 2 styles 39- 48

459

(continued)

Sugar bowl, covered 77- 85
Tumbler, water, whiskey 66- 76
Wine 66- 77

Probably other pieces.

Hamilton with Leaf

Hamilton with Leaf

Sandwich, 1870s. Clear and frosted. Other factories, 1890s on. Sandwich prices shown.

Butter dish $110-128
Celery vase 110-120
Compote, open, high and
 low standard 84- 98
Cordial 88-105
Creamer 74- 84
Egg cup 37- 47
Goblet 60- 70
Lamp, two sizes 90-125
Pitcher (ill.) 98-129
Salt, footed 52- 62
Spoonholder 62- 72
Sugar bowl 80- 90
Tumbler, water 60- 70
Wine 32- 42

Possibly other pieces.

Hand

(Pennsylvania): O'Hara Glass Company, Ltd., 1880. Clear.

Bowl, 7″, 8″, 9″, 10″ $37-47
Butter dish 52-62
Cake plate on stand, 10″ 46-56
Celery vase 47-53
Compote
 a. Covered, high foot 62-72
 b. Open 42-52

Hand

Creamer 42-52
Goblet 44-53
Honey dish 19-28
Jam jar 34-46
Pickle dish 20-28
Pitcher, water (ill.) 60-70
Platter, 8″ x 10½″ 43-53
Saucedish, flat, 4″ 14-24
Spoonholder 42-52
Sugar bowl 50-58

Probably other pieces.

Hand Vase

Hand Vase

Gillinder and Sons, Philadelphia, Pa., for Centennial 1876. Clear and frosted.

Hand vase (ill.) $72-94

Highly collectible by "Hand" collectors.

Hanging Basket

Possibly Mosaic Glass Company, Fostoria, Ohio, 1890s. Clear, colors.

Butter dish $52- 70
Compote 48- 68

Hanging Basket

Creamer	36- 47
Goblet	27- 38
Pitcher (ill.)	110-125
Spoonholder	40- 50
Sugar bowl, covered	47- 60
Tumbler	32- 42

Colors, 50 percent higher than clear prices listed.

Harp

Lamps, whale oil
a. Handled, double wick with snuffers	140-170
b. Larger, on glass standard	120-130
Saucedish	40- 50
Spill holder (ill.)	58- 70
Spoonholder	62- 80

Possibly other pieces.

Hanover

(Block with Stars): Richards & Hartley Glass Company, Tarentum, Pennsylvania, c. 1888, clear, non-flint.

Butter dish, covered	$38-50
Cake stand	38-49
Celery	40-49
Compote	
a. Open	26-38
b. Covered	39-47
Creamer	27-36
Goblet	22-32
Pitcher, water	36-47
Spoonholder	19-24
Sugar bowl, covered	42-52
Tumbler	27-37
Wine	32-42

Probably other pieces.

Harp

Bryce Bros., Pittsburgh, 1840s or 1850s. Clear, green, other colors.

Butter dish, two sizes	$115-140
Compote, covered, low standard	162-180
Dish, covered, low foot	110-130
Goblet (rare)	
a. Flared sides	300-350
b. Straight sides	270-310

Hartford

Hartford

Fostoria Glass Company, 1900s. Clear, yellow, amber, possibly green.

Bowl, 4½", 5½", 6", 7", 8", 9"	$22-33
Butter dish, covered	34-41
Celery vase	24-32
Creamer (ill.)	23-33
Sauce, 4½"	18-27
Salt/Pepper, pr.	19-30
Spoonholder	18-28
Sugar bowl, covered, footed, plain base	30-40
Syrup jug	20-31
Tumbler	18-26

Possibly other pieces.

Heart and Waffle

Probably Sandwich, mid-1850. Clear.
Lamp (ill.) $170-220

Harvard

Harvard

(Quixote): Tarentum Glass Company, Tarentum, Pennsylvania, 1898-1912, clear, custard, emerald green, pea green, ruby-stained.

Bowl, finger	$ 9-17
Butter dish, covered	28-40
Compote	22-32
Cup, punch	8-14
Goblet	18-28
Pitcher, water	41-60
Plate, 10½"	15-28
Sugar bowl, covered	27-40
Wine (ill.)	17-26

Many other pieces. Colors 100% higher than clear prices listed.

Heart Band

Heart Band

McKee Glass Company, 1897. Crystal glass with ruby stain.

Butter dish, covered	$38-50
Celery	26-36
Compote	40-50
Creamer	27-37
Goblet	29-40
Pitcher, water (ill.)	52-61
Spoonholder	28-42
Sugar bowl, covered	35-46
Tumbler	19-32

Probably other pieces.

Heart   Heart and Waffle

Heart

Sandwich, very early. Clear. One of many Sandwich pieces at the Houston Museum, Chattanooga. It's shown here because it's Pressed Glass and still around.

Heart Stem

462

Heart Stem

Maker unknown, late 1880s or 1890s. Clear.

Butter dish	$37-47
Celery	23-33
Compote, covered, 7" high	42-52
Creamer (ill.)	38-48
Goblet	26-35
Pitcher	42-60
Spoonholder	22-31
Sugar bowl	36-46
Tumbler	18-28

Probably other pieces.

Heart with Thumbprint

Heart with Thumbprint

(Columbia): Sandwich, early; Tarentum Glass Company, 1898. Crystal, sometimes gold rims. Natural and green custard.

Bowl, berry, 9"	$31-48
Butter dish, covered	52-62
Celery vase	49-60
Creamer, individual, regular	54-63
Cruet with stopper	52-62
Goblet	42-57
Pitcher	51-60
Salt, master (ill.)	29-37
Sauce	18-27
Spoonholder	30-40
Sugar bowl	
a. Covered	49-60
b. Individual	32-43
Tumbler	38-48
Vases, 10", pr.	47-57
Wine	34-44

Probably other pieces.

Heavy Drape

Fostoria Glass Company, 1904. Clear.

Bowl, berry, flat and footed	$16-27
Butter dish, covered	29-41
Celery	27-33
Compote, covered and open	36-46
Creamer	20-30
Egg cup	18-29

Heavy Drape

Goblet	23-32
Pitcher, milk, water (ill.)	49-57
Salt/Pepper, pr.	19-28
Spoonholder	22-32
Sugar bowl, covered	28-39
Tumbler	26-36
Wine	22-31

Probably other pieces as there were some 50 pieces comprising the set.

Heavy Gothic

Heavy Gothic

U.S. Glass Company, 1892. Clear, clear stained with ruby.

Butter dish	$40-52
Compote	44-53
Creamer	28-37
Egg cup	18-29
Goblet	26-34
Pitcher (ill.)	50-60
Spoonholder	27-34
Sugar bowl, two types	37-47
Tumbler	28-40
Wine	28-39

Probably other pieces. Ruby stained has no effect on prices listed.

Heavy Jewel

Heavy Jewel

Fostoria Glass Company, 1900s. Clear.

Butter dish	$39-50
Celery	30-40
Compote, covered and open	42-52
Creamer	27-34
Goblet	27-33
Pitcher (ill.)	39-49
Spoonholder	27-37
Sugar bowl	
a. Covered	33-42
b. Open	27-37
Tumbler	22-32

Henrietta

Henrietta

(Big Block): Adams and Company, 1874. Also Columbia Glass Company, 1889. Clear, blocks flashed in red.

Bowl, berry	$16-28
Butter dish	32-45
Celery	27-37

Compote	29-38
Creamer	23-33
Goblet	26-34
Pitcher, water (ill.)	39-48
Spoonholder	27-36
Sugar bowl	28-34
Tumbler	22-29

Probably other pieces. Red flashing, 60 percent higher than clear prices listed.

Heron

Heron

Another of the animal (and bird) series put out by Indiana Tumbler & Goblet (National) Company, late 1890s. Clear and chocolate.

Pitcher, water	
a. Chocolate	$240-270
b. Clear (ill.)	110-128

Probably tumblers to match.

Herringbone

Herringbone

Indiana Tumbler & Goblet (National) Company, late 1890s.

	Amber	Green	Clear
Butter dish, covered		$62-72	$37-47
Cake stand		52-62	32-42
Cordial	$72-82	58-68	29-38
Creamer		38-48	19-29
Pitcher (ill.)		77-87	42-52
Salt/Pepper, pr.		40-50	19-29
Spoonholder		34-44	27-34
Sugar bowl		46-56	28-37
Wine	62-72	42-52	27-37

Chocolate

Mug (ill.) $52-61

Probably other pieces.

Herringbone

Herringbone

(Florida): U.S. Glass Company, 1890s. Clear and colors.

Berry set, 5 pc.	$58-70
Bowl, 7½", 9" dia.	15-27
Butter dish	49-59
Compote	46-54
Creamer	39-47
Goblet (ill.)	27-34
Pickle dish	17-24
Pitcher, water.................	47-52
Sauce	15-20
Salt/Pepper, pr.	27-39
Spoonholder	29-40
Sugar bowl, covered	41-52

Probably other pieces. Color 50 percent more than clear prices listed.

Hexagon Block

Hexagon Block

(Double Red Block): Maker unknown, early 1890s. Clear, clear flashed in color; possibly amber.

Butter dish, covered	$43-52
Celery vase	28-39
Creamer	28-34
Pitcher (ill.)....................	54-65
Sauce	15-22
Spoonholder	23-32
Sugar	
a. Covered	42-53
b. Open	23-29
Tumbler	22-33
Wine........................	20-31

Probably other pieces. Flashed colors, 40 percent higher than clear prices listed.

Hidalgo

Hidalgo

(Frosted Waffle): Adams & Company, Pittsburgh, 1880. Crystal, plain and engraved; also frosted.

Bowl, large, small	$19-28
Butter dish	34-42
Celery	28-33
Compote, covered, open, high or low standard	38-49
Cup and saucer	15-23
Goblet	24-32
Pitcher, milk, syrup (ill.)	39-49

(continued)

Sauce, flat and footed 14-22
Salt/Pepper, pr. 19-26
Spoonholder 23-32
Sugar bowl, covered 42-53
Tumbler 22-30

Probably other pieces. Frosted, 15 percent higher than clear prices listed.

Hobbs Diamond and Sunburst

Hobbs Diamond and Sunburst

Hobbs, Brockunier & Company, 1880s. Clear.

Butter dish, covered $32-41
Cake stand 35-44
Compote
  a. Covered 39-48
  b. Open 34-44
Creamer, applied handle 28-37
Egg cup 17-25
Goblet 24-32
Pitcher (ill.)................. 47-56
Sauce, flat 13-18
Spoonholder 22-32
Sugar bowl, covered 41-51
Tumbler 22-30

Probably other pieces.

Hobnail

Hobnail

So many companies made a "Hobnail" pattern, including New Brighton Glass Company, A. J. Beatty Company, McKee & Brothers, Gillinder Brothers, others. It came in clear and colors and is heavily reproduced today in just about every color.

Some of the **many** pieces made were berry bowls, perfume bottles, creamers, celerys, cordials, bone dishes, mugs, pitchers, salts (ill.), glass shades, spoonholders, sugar bowls, toothpick holders, trays, tumblers, vases, wines.

Hobnail Band

Hobnail Band

One of the Hobnail group, around 1890. Clear.

Butter dish $33-42
Creamer 24-34
Goblet 20-30
Pitcher, water (ill.) 49-54
Spoonholder 22-30
Sugar bowl 36-47
Tumbler 18-27

Probably other pieces.

Hobnail in Big Diamonds

Challinor, Taylor & Company, 1888. Clear.

Butter dish, covered $41-50
Creamer 28-34
Pitcher (ill.)................... 42-51

Hobnail in Big Diamonds

Spoonholder 25-32
Sugar
  a. Covered 37-49
  b. Open 28-33
Probably other pieces. Hobnail in Diamond same, except hobs are confined inside bars and do not cover the pieces.

Holly

Holly

Sandwich glass, late 1860s, early 1870s. Clear. Others made this pattern in custard.

Butter dish $59-69
Cake stand 48-57
Compote, covered, high or
  low standard 69-83
Creamer 62-68
Egg cup 44-52
Goblet (rare) (ill.) 63-72
Pitcher, water 72-82
Sauce 19-27
Spoonholder 35-46
Sugar bowl 58-68

Tumbler, footed 40-50
Wine 44-53
Probably other pieces.

Holly Amber

Holly Amber

(Golden Agate): Indiana Tumbler & Goblet (National) Company, January to June, 1903 only. Holly amber and clear.

Butter dish (ill.) $1,450-1,800
Candy dish, covered 475- 550
Compote
  a. Covered, large 1,600-1,700
  b. Covered, small 1,150-1,350
Cruet 1,000-1,200
Parfait 625- 665
Pitcher, water 2,350-2,550
Salt/Pepper, pr. 920-1,100
Spoonholder 650- 750
Sugar bowl 675- 725
Tumbler 550- 625

Other pieces made. Clear, 20 to 50 percent of the amber prices listed. Butter dish, covered compote, jelly compote, cruet, 7½″ plate, toothpick, and tumbler being reproduced. A **highly overrated** glass!

Holly-Band

467

(continued)

Holly-Band

Maker unknown, 1870s. Clear.

Butter dish	$36-42
Celery	22-31
.Compote	29-39
Creamer	27-36
,Pitcher, applied handle	68-78
Spoonholder (ill.)	27-37
Sugar bowl	35-43
Tumbler	23-32

Probably other pieces.

Home

Home

Pioneer Glass Company, Pittsburgh, late 1880s; later reproduced by McKee Bros. in 1894. Clear, upper and lower bands sometimes decorated in ruby color.

Butter dish, covered	$34-41
Celery	20-28
Creamer	19-29
Goblet	22-33
Pitcher, water (ill.)	39-47
Spoonholder	20-31
Sugar bowl, covered	28-34
Tumbler	19-29

Probably other pieces. Ruby color has little or no effect on clear prices listed.

Honeycomb with Flower Rim

Honeycomb with Flower Rim

(Inverted Thumbprint with Daisy Band): Greentown, Indiana, around 1903. Clear, blue, green, custard.

Butter, covered	$32-41
Celery	18-27
Compote	
a. Covered	40-52
b. Open	27-37
Creamer	24-33
Pitcher (ill.)	44-55
Sauce, footed	10-15
Sugar bowl	
a. Covered	38-48
b. Open	29-34
Tumbler	18-29

Other pieces. Blue and custard, 90 percent; amber, 65 percent; others, 20 percent higher than clear prices listed.

Horn of Plenty

Horn of Plenty

Sandwich glass, early 1830s; Bryce, McKee, Pittsburgh, 1850s. Opalescent white, canary, clear, flint.

Butter dish	
a. Conventional knob, 6″ dia.	$142-160
b. Washington's head (rare)	525-625
Celery	122-132
Compote	
a. Covered, oblong, on standard	215-230
b. Open, low standard	110-120
c. Oval, on standard	310-328
Creamer, large, small	170-190
Decanter, pint, quart, ½ gallon	128-135

Egg cup	48- 57
Goblet (being reproduced)	71- 82
Lamp, all glass, marble base	120-140
Mug, applied handle, 3″	90-110
Pitcher, water, milk (ill.)	280-320
Spoonholder	58- 68
Sugar bowl, 2 types	138-148
Tumbler, whiskey	110-128
Wine	88-101

Probably other pieces. Canary, amber, blue, 85 percent higher than clear prices listed. Amber tumbler being reproduced.

Horsehead's Medallion

Horsehead's Medallion

Portland Glass Company, Portland, 1870s. Clear; rare in milk-white.

Celery	$ 73- 84
Compote	
a. Covered	110-118
b. Open	90-110
Creamer	70- 90
Spoonholder (ill.)	42- 50
Sugar bowl	
a. Covered	74- 84
b. Open	60- 70

Probably other pieces. Milk-white, 100 percent higher than clear prices listed.

Horseshoe Stem

Maker unknown, 1880s. Clear.

Cake stand	$53- 63
Compote	
a. Covered	50- 58
b. Open	44- 54

Horseshoe Stem

Creamer	35- 41
Goblet	37- 47
Pitcher (ill.)	110-120
Sauce	24- 33
Sugar	
a. Covered	52- 62
b. Open	34- 44
Tumbler	33- 43

Probably other pieces.

Hour Glass

Maker unknown, c. 1880s, clear, yellow, amber, blue, non-flint.

Butter dish, covered	$30-40
Creamer	27-37
Dish, sauce, large	18-24
Goblet	26-36
Pitcher, water	27-37
Spoonholder	19-26
Sugar bowl, covered	24-34

Yellow, 65%; amber, blue, 100% higher than clear prices listed.

Huber

Huber

Several firms made this pattern — Sandwich, New England Glass Company, also Bakewell, Pears & Company, probably others, 1860s, and earlier. Clear.

(continued)

Sandwich prices listed.

Bitters bottle	$44-54
Bowl, covered, 6″, 7″	34-42
Butter dish	52-62
Celery (ill.)	42-52
Compote, covered, high and low standard, 7″, 10″	73-83
Creamer, scalloped rim	52-61
Decanter	
a. Bar lip, pint, quart	50-60
b. With stopper, pint, quart . .	58-67
Egg cup, handled	18-21
Goblet, hotel, large, small	44-48
Jug, quart, 3 pints	38-47
Mug, beer, pony beer	32-44
Pitcher, water, 2 styles	67-77
Plate, 6″, 7″	21-33
Salt, celery dip, footed	14-27
Spoonholder	24-34
Sugar bowl, covered	52-70
Tumbler, gill, one-half pint, large and small, taper bar	29-31
Wine	22-35

Hummingbird

Hummingbird

(Flying Robin): Maker unknown, late 1880s. Clear, canary, amber, blue.

Butter dish	$54-63
Celery	39-47
Creamer, footed	39-46
Goblet	28-34
Pickle dish	12-17
Pitcher, milk, water, 8″ high (ill.)	59-69
Sauce	17-27
Spoonholder	26-36
Sugar bowl	39-49
Tray, water	28-34
Tumbler	28-39

Canary, 40 percent; amber and blue, 75 percent higher than clear prices listed.

Hundred Leaved Rose

Hundred Leaved Rose

Possibly Model Flint Glass Company, Findlay, Ohio, 1890s. Clear, frosted, stippled.

Bowl	$16-28
Butter dish, covered	34-44
Creamer	28-38
Pitcher (ill.)	39-47
Sauce, flat	12-17
Spoonholder	22-32
Sugar bowl	
a. Covered	42-52
b. Open	26-34

Probably others. Frosted and stippled, 40 percent higher than clear prices listed.

Imperial

Imperial Glass Company, Bellaire, Ohio, c. 1901, clear, non-flint.

Butter dish, covered	$37-47
Cake stand	28-37
Celery tray	14-21
Compote	26-35
Creamer	36-46
Goblet	28-38
Pitcher, milk, water	40-50
Salt/Pepper, pr.	22-28
Spoonholder	17-28
Sugar bowl, covered	29-39
Tumbler	27-36
Wine	26-35

Probably other pieces.

In Remembrance Platter

A memorial platter issued after Garfield's assassination in 1881. Garfield

In Remembrance Platter
shares a place with Lincoln and Washington. Clear only.

Platter (ill.) $122-136

Intaglio

Intaglio

Northwood Glass Company, 1910. Clear, custard, colors.

Berry set	Color	Custard
a. Large bowl	$60-72	$115-132
b. Small bowl	24-32	55- 65
Compote, jelly		138-150
Cruet		125-137
Butter, covered	58-64	168-177
Sugar, covered	64-73	92-110
Creamer	51-61	72- 82
Pitcher (ill.)	70-77	210-220
Spoonholder	53-63	70- 80
Pitcher, water	82-92	168-178
Salt/Pepper, pr.		150-160
Tumbler, water	37-47	77- 88

Interlocked Hearts

Interlocked Hearts

Possibly Northwood Glass Company, Indiana, Pennsylvania, late 1890s, early 1900s.

Creamer	$29-38
Goblet	24-32
Pitcher, water (ill.)	42-50
Tumbler	18-26
Wine	22-29

Probably other pieces.

Interlocking Crescents

(Double Arch): The King Glass Company, Pittsburgh, Pennsylvania, c. late 1880s, clear, non-flint.

Butter dish, covered	$29-36
Creamer	30-40
Goblet	27-36
Spoonholder	19-28
Sugar bowl, covered	30-42

Only known pieces.

Iron Kettle

Adams & Company, 1874; Challinor Taylor & Company, 1885. Clear, colors.

Butter dish, covered	$37-47
Creamer (ill.)	26-36

471   (continued)

Iron Kettle

Spoonholder 31-40
Sugar bowl, covered 37-46
Probably other pieces. Colors 60 percent higher than clear prices listed.

Ivorina Verde

Ivorina Verde

A. H. Heisey Company, Newark, Ohio, 1899. Opaque white with green trim (custard).

Butter dish, covered	$127-142
Bowls	94-107
Celery	72- 82
Creamer	82- 92
Cruet	72- 82
Pitcher, water	115-130
Spoonholder	62- 72
Sugar bowl, covered (ill.)	94-104

Probably other pieces.

Ivy-in-Snow

(Forest Ware): Cooperative Flint Glass Company, Beaver Falls, Pennsylvania, late 1880s. Clear, foliage stained red, gold leaf.

Butter dish, flat $49-56

Ivy-in-Snow

Cake stand, square	37-47
Celery	38-48
Compote, covered, small, medium, large, high standard	59-69
Creamer	30-40
Cup and saucer	18-27
Goblet	26-36
Jam jar......................	25-35
Pitcher, water (ill.)	48-58
Sauce, flat, round, 4", 6"	17-27
Spoonholder	47-54
Sugar bowl	40-50
Tumbler	27-36
Wine.......................	28-34

Probably other pieces. Butter dish, cake stand, celery, creamer, goblet, pitcher, sugar bowl being reproduced.

Jacob's Coat

Jacob's Coat

Maker unknown, 1800s. Clear, amber.

Bowl, berry	$28-38
Butter dish, covered	40-47
Celery	42-48
Creamer	42-50
Goblet	37-46
Pickle dish	22-32
Pitcher (ill.)..................	52-62
Saucedish	17-28
Spoonholder	34-47
Sugar bowl, covered	50-60

Probably other pieces. Amber, 50 percent higher than clear prices listed.

Jacob's Ladder

Jacob's Ladder

(Maltese): Bryce Bros., Pittsburgh, 1870s. Clear, amber, yellow; colors scarce.

Bowl, 6″ dia. ....$	33- 42
Butter dish, covered, Maltese	
Cross finial	58- 68
Cake plate on stand	39- 47
Celery	50- 58
Compote, covered, open, large	
standard	53- 63
Creamer, footed	51- 62
Cruet, Maltese Cross stopper ..	60- 70
Dish, oval	17- 27
Dolphin compote (rare)	248-262
Goblet, knob stem	48- 58
Mug	34- 43
Pitcher, water, syrup (ill.)	50- 75
Sauce	
a. Flat, round, footed, 3½″	
4″, 5″	20- 32
b. Footed, 4½″	19- 29
Spoonholder	48- 55
Sugar bowl, covered, Maltese	
Cross finial	62- 68
Tumbler, handled	42- 49
Wine......................	22- 34

Probably other pieces. Colors, 150 percent higher than clear prices listed.

Jardiniere

Maker unknown, c. 1887, clear, nonflint.

Butter dish, covered	$29-38
Creamer	25-32
Spoonholder	21-28
Sugar bowl, covered	32-37

Possibly other pieces.

Jefferson's Number 251

Jefferson's Number 251

Jefferson Glass Company, Steubenville, Ohio, 1904. Plain, colored and opalescent.

Berry bowls, 8″, 6″, 4½″ ....$	22- 32
Butter dish, covered	38- 44
Condiment set	41- 51
Creamer.....................	22- 31
Cruet, handled (ill.)...........	34- 39
Jug, ½ gal....................	29- 37
Salt/Pepper, pr.	19- 24
Spoonholder	24- 32
Sugar bowl, covered	34- 42
Toothpick, blue, opalescent	
(rare)	115-120

Probably other pieces. Colors and opalescent 60 percent higher than clear prices listed.

Jefferson's Number 271

Jefferson's Number 271

Jefferson Glass Company, Follansbee, West Virginia, 1907. Crystal, blue, green, also gold trimmed, with gold rims.

473

(continued)

Butter dish, blue $44-54
Creamer 29-38
Jug, one-half gallon 36-47
Nappy, 4" and 8" 22-29
Pitcher, water, green 68-78
Spoonholder 22-29
Sugar bowl, covered 52-59
Tumbler (ill.) 32-42
Probably others.

Jersey

Jersey

McKee Bros., 1894. Clear
Butter dish, covered $44-52
Compote
  a. High standard 42-51
  b. Low standard.............. 42-49
Celery 28-38
Creamer 27-36
Goblet 27-37
Pitcher, ½ gal., small 47-58
Spoonholder 27-28
Sugar bowl, covered 39-47
Tumbler 24-32
Probably other pieces.

Jersey Swirl

Jersey Swirl

(Swirl): Windsor Glass Company, Pittsburgh, Pennsylvania, 1887. Clear and color: canary, amber, blue.
Butter dish, covered $49-58
Compote
  a. Covered 40-47
  b. Open 29-36
Creamer 32-42
Goblet
  a. Buttermilk (ill.) 29-36
  b. Regular size 29-38
Pitcher, water, buttermilk 48-50
Plate, bread.........¹.......... 24-34
Sauce 16-22
Salt dip...................... 12-21
Sugar bowl
  a. Covered 42-48
  b. Open 22-31
Tumbler 28-38
Wine....................... 22-32

Canary, 40 percent; blue or amber, 60 percent higher than crystal prices listed. Being reproduced in goblets, covered compotes, nappies, plates (2 sizes), salt dips and sauces.

Jewel and Dewdrop

Jewel and Dewdrop

(Kansas): Cooperative Flint Glass Company, 1870s; reproduced by U.S. Glass Company, in 1907 as Kansas pattern. Clear and opalescent.
Bowl, berry, 6", 7", 8½" $23-32
Butter dish 42-50
Cake stand, 8", 9", 10" 39-56
Celery 42-51
Compote
  a. Covered, high standard,
    deep bowl 54-64

b. Open, high standard 33-42
Creamer 48-57
Goblet (rare) 44-52
Pitcher, water (ill.) 42-52
Salt/Pepper, pr. 39-47
Spoonholder 42-52
Sugar bowl 47-58
Syrup 42-51
Toothpick holder 27-32
Tumbler 36-48
Wine 39-49

Probably other pieces.

Jewel and Festoon

Jewel and Festoon

(Loop and Jewel): Maker unknown, Ohio, late 1880s. Clear.

Bowls, several sizes $18-28
Butter dish, covered 29-39
Creamer 26-29
Goblet 26-34
Pitcher (ill.) 52-61
Relish dish 14-22
Salt/Pepper, pr. 18-28
Sherbet cup 15-22
Spoonholder 24-29
Sugar bowl, covered 34-43

Probably other pieces. Tumbler being reproduced.

Jeweled Heart

Northwood Glass Company, 1900s. Clear, colored, Carnival.

	Clear	Color
Butter	$55-64	$ 82- 92
Cruet, clear, colored		
(ill.)		39- 47
Lamp	44-49	77- 87

Pitcher 35-42   94-106
Pitcher,
  Carnival 168-178
Syrup 29-33   45- 55
Tumbler,
  Carnival 52- 62

Probably other pieces. Toothpick, goblet, creamer and sugar being reproduced.

Jeweled Heart

Jeweled Moon and Star

Jeweled Moon and Star

(Moon and Star with Waffle): Maker unknown, Ohio, 1880s. Clear and frosted moons, blue or red; amber and blue; red and amber.

Bowl, relish, oval $18-27
Butter dish, covered 34-42
Compote
  a. Covered 37-44
  b. Open 35-45
Goblet 38-49
Pitcher, water (ill.) 52-60
Sugar bowl, covered 38-47
Tray, water 32-40
Tumbler 28-37
Wine 26-35

Probably other pieces.

475

Jubilee

Jubilee

McKee Glass Company, 1894. Clear.

Celery vase $27-36
Compote
  a. Covered 35-44
  b. Open 23-34
Creamer 27-34
Goblet 36-44
Pickle dish 18-22
Pitcher, water (ill.) 42-52
Salt/Pepper, pr. 18-24
Spoonholder 24-34
Sugar bowl 32-39
Tumbler 22-29

Probably other pieces.

Jumbo

Jumbo

Canton Glass Company, Canton, Ohio, 1883. Clear. Also made by Aetna Glass Co., Bellaire, Ohio, same period.

Butter dish
  a. Round $250-300
  b. Oblong (rare) 320-380
Castor set, 3 bottles 320-345
Compote, covered 300-360
Creamer 240-260
Cup and saucer 140-180
Dish, covered, frosted 140-175
Goblet (rare) .... 500+
Spoonholder 130-160
Spoon rack (rare) (ill.) .... 550+
Sugar bowl, covered 280-340

Possibly other pieces. The spoon rack is one of the rarest pieces of pattern glass in America today. Prices are for Canton pieces.

King's Curtain

King's Curtain

Maker unknown, 1880s. Clear.

Butter dish, covered $40-50
Cake stand 38-48
Creamer 28-38
Goblet 27-37
Pitcher, water (ill.) 34-50
Plate 17-26
Salt shaker 16-26
Saucedish, flat 12-24
Spoonholder 22-29
Sugar bowl
  a. Covered 25-36
  b. Open 24-34

Probably other pieces.

King's 500

(Parrot): King, Son & Company, Pittsburgh, 1891. Clear, transparent blue, possibly other colors.

Bowl, berry, blue $40-50
Butter, coverd, cobalt, gold eyes .. 80-90
Cruet, blue (ill.) 65-75

King's 500

Photo: Mr. and Mrs. A.M. Zinkeler, Chattanooga, Tenn.

Probably the usual patterns, the usual prices for a glass of this date. The cruet shown is in a beautiful blue.

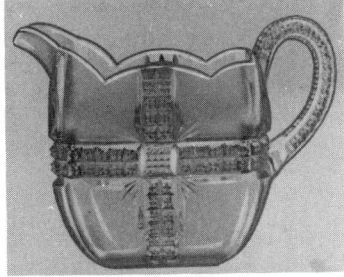

Klondike

Klondike

(Amberette; English Hobnail Cross): A. J. Beatty Company, Findlay Ohio, 1870s. Other companies, 1880s, one calling it Amberette. Clear or frosted with color — amber, lilac/gold.

Bowl, 6" sq.	$ 84- 92
Butter dish, covered	130-140
Compote, covered, 8"	150-160
Creamer (ill.)	107-112
Pitcher, square, tankard	130-140
Salt/Pepper, pr.	70- 80
Sauce, footed, flat, others	29- 39
Spoonholder	52- 62
Sugar bowl	
a. Covered	134-143
b. Open	92-105
Syrup	115-122
Toothpick holder, 2 types	110-121

Tray, square, 5½", 7", 8½"	....
Tumbler	....
Vase, bud, 8½" high	....

Many other pieces. Colors 100 percent higher than clear prices shown.

Knights of Labor

Knights of Labor

Bakewell, Pears & Company, Pittsburgh, 1879. Clear, canary, amber, blue.

Plate, bread (ill.)	$80-94
Mug	44-53

Colors, 65 percent higher than clear prices listed.

Krom

Krom

Maker unknown, c. 1830s, clear, flint.

Goblet (ill.)	$60-70
Whiskey, several sizes	22-34

Lacy Dewdrop

Co-Operative Flint Glass Company, Beaver Falls, Pennsylvania, c. 1890, clear, milk glass, non-flint. Possibly other colors.

477

(continued)

Bowl, berry	$18-27
Butter dish, covered	33-41
Creamer	28-37
Goblet	34-44
Mug	18-26
Pitcher, water	39-49
Spoonholder	18-26
Sugar bowl	
a. Open	16-24
b. Covered	38-48
Tumbler	12-22

Milk glass, 30% higher than clear prices listed. Probably other pieces.

Lacy Medallion

Lacy Medallion

U.S. Glass Company, 1890s. Souvenir-type, gilded in opaque white, sometimes with flowers painted on sides.

Cup	$27-37
Mug (ill.)	40-50
Toothpick	22-32
Tumbler	19-28
Wine	27-37

Other pieces.

Lacy Spiral

Lacy Spiral

(Colossus): Maker unknown, late 1880s. Clear.

Butter dish, covered	$34-44
Compote	
a. Covered	42-52
b. Jelly, open	27-36
c. Open	28-37
Creamer	29-39
Pitcher, water (ill.)	46-57
Spoonholder	24-34
Sugar bowl, covered	39-44
Relish dish	18-27

Probably other pieces.

Lady Hamilton
Photo: Mrs. Paul Brown, Chattanooga, Tenn.

Lady Hamilton

(Peerless): Richards & Hartley Flint Glass Company, Pittsburgh, 1875. Clear.

Celery vase
Compotes (22 different types were made)
Creamer, low and high stem
Goblet
Mustard jar
Spoonholder
Sugar bowl
Tumbler

Note: so many different types of each piece were made, it's impossible to honestly give specific prices. Just know your dealer!

"Lafayet"

Boat-shaped saltcellar: This is a rare piece because it's one of the few, if not the **only** piece of glass signed at the Boston & Sandwich Glass Company, Sandwich, Massachusetts.

"Lafayet"

No price given because there are few, if any, available today. Shown only because Sandwich made some of the finest glass the world has ever known.

Large Stippled Chain

Large Stippled Chain

Probably Gillinder & Sons, 1870s. Clear.

Creamer	$35-44
Goblet	26-36
Pitcher (ill.)	47-56
Sugar bowl	
a. Covered	37-47
b. Open	28-38

Probably other pieces.

Late Crystal

Richard & Hartley Company, 1888; also, McKee Bros., 1894, and U.S. Glass Company, 1898. Clear.

Late Crystal

Celery	$22-30
Compote	
a. Covered, low and high foot	38-47
b. Open, low foot only	28-36
Creamer	22-34
Egg cup	14-24
Goblet	27-36
Pitcher, water (ill.)	32-42
Salt/Pepper, pr.	18-24
Sauce, flat and footed	12-16
Spoonholder	19-27
Sugar bowl	34-44
Tumbler	22-32

Probably other pieces.

Late Diamond Point Band

Late Diamond Point Band

(Scalloped Diamond Point, Panel with Diamond Point): Central Glass Company, Wheeling. West Virginia, 1870s.

(continued)

Bowl, round, oval $18-24
Butter dish, covered 27-36
Cake stand, small, large 28-42
Cheese dish, covered 32-39
Creamer 22-30
Goblet 20-31
Pitcher (ill.) 44-52
Sugar bowl, covered, open 28-42
Probably other pieces.

Late Panelled Grape

Late Panelled Grape
Another of the "Grape" patterns, late 1890s. Clear.
Bowl, berry $19-28
Butter dish, covered 33-42
Creamer (ill.) 28-37
Dish, covered 22-30
Goblet 22-31
Pitcher, milk, syrup, water 34-44
Wine 22-31

Goblet being reproduced.

Late Panelled Grape, Variant

Late Panelled Grape, Variant
Maker unknown, 1890s. Clear, probably premium glass at grocery stores.
Bowl, berry $16-22
Butter dish, covered 28-37
Creamer (ill.) 26-37
Goblet 19-24
Pitcher
  a. Milk 32-41
  b. Syrup 29-34
  c. Water 29-42
Wine 14-19
Probably other pieces.

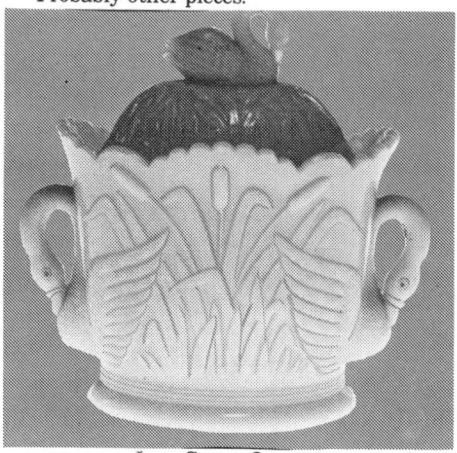
Late Swan, Opaque

Late Swan, Opaque
Westmoreland Specialty Company, Grapeville, Pennsylvania, 1891-1892. Opaque white and opaque turquoise.
Sugar bowl, covered
  a. Opaque white $70-80
  b. Opaque turquoise (ill.) 72-88
Probably other pieces.

Late Thistle
Pittsburgh, late 1890s. Clear.
Butter dish, covered $37-47
Cake stand, small 29-38
Compote
  a. Covered 41-52
  b. Open 29-38
Honey dish, covered 29-37
Pitcher, milk (ill.) 52-64
Sugar bowl 40-50
Tumbler 27-33
Probably other pieces.

Late Thistle

Lattice

Lattice

(Diamond Bar): King, Son & Company, Pittsburgh, Pennsylvania. 1880. Clear.

Butter dish	$50-60
Cake stand	40-57
Celery	37-47
Compote, covered, high standard	48-57
Cordial	27-34
Creamer	39-48
Egg cup	22-24
Goblet	29-37
Pitcher, water (ill.)	49-57
Plate, 6½", 7¼", 10", 12"	18-29
Platter, clear, "Waste not, want not"	44-56

Salt/Pepper, pr.	24-33
Sauce, flat, footed	15-22
Spoonholder	42-52
Sugar bowl	44-54
Wine	19-27

Probably others.

Leaf and Flower   Leaf Bracket

Leaf and Flower

Hobbs, Brokunier & Co., Wheeling, West Virginia. A Wheeling West Virginia product made in the 1890s. Clear, clear and frosted with amber or green flowers; red has been reported.

Bowl, finger or waste	$19-26
Butter dish, covered	42-54
Castor set	38-47
Creamer	24-32
Creamer, amber stained flowers	49-59
Pitcher, water (ill.)	43-50
Sauce, flat	14-19
Tray, celery	19-32

Probably other pieces. Clear and frosted, 30 percent higher; amber, green, 70 percent higher; red, 100 percent higher than clear prices listed.

Leaf Bracket

Indiana Tumbler & Goblet (National) Company, Greentown, Indiana, 1900. Crystal, opal, chocolate, Nile green.

Berry bowl	$42- 49
Butter dish	68- 79
Celery tray	42- 50
Creamer	52- 59
Cruet (ill.)	99-110
Salt/Pepper, pr.	47- 58

(continued)

Spoonholder 47- 58
Tumbler 39- 54

Probably other pieces. Chocolate, 80 percent higher; opal and Nile green, 30% higher than clear prices listed.

Pitcher 46-54
Relish, oval 19-24
Sauce, flat, footed 16-24
Spoonholder 18-29
Sugar bowl, covered 47-57

Probably other pieces.

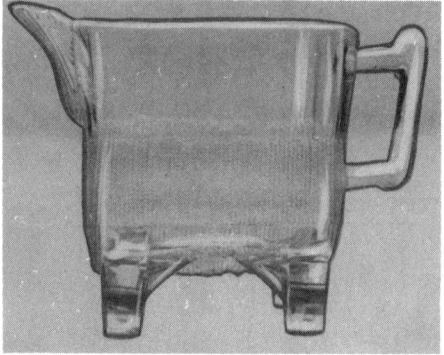

Legged Trough

Liberty Bell

Legged Trough

Maker and date unknown. How many pieces (creamer, sugar, tumbler, etc.) were made is unknown to this writer. It must have taken some doing to remove it from the mold! Knowers — **write!**

Lens and Star

O'Hara Glass Company, Pittsburgh, Pennsylvania, c. 1886, clear, non-flint.

Bowl, waste 24-34
Butter dish, covered 32-41
Celery 19-27
Creamer 29-42
Pitcher, water 34-41
Spoonholder 26-36
Sugar bowl, covered 38-48
Tray, handled 37-46
Tumbler 22-32

Probably other pieces.

Leverne

(Star in Honeycomb): Maker unknown, c. early 1870s, clear, non-flint.

Butter dish, covered $44-52
Celery 27-37
Compote
  a. Open 29-39
  b. Covered 47-56
Goblet 27-37

Liberty Bell

(Centennial): Gillinder & Company, Philadelphia. Made for 1876 Centennial. Rare in milk glass.

Butter dish, covered $133-154
Celery 90-100
Child's table set (4 pc.) 148-157
Compote, open, 6", 8" 90-110
Creamer
  a. Plain handle 83- 93
  b. Reeded handle 120-140
Goblet 52- 62
Pitcher, water 110-140
Plate, 6", 8", 10" 72- 82
Platter, 9¼" x 13", Independence signers' names on border (ill.) 240-248
Salt
  a. Celery dip, master salt .. 33- 42
  b. Shaker top, bell-shaped .. 76- 84
Salt/Pepper, pr. 36- 42
Salt shaker 77- 84
Spoonholder, pedestal base 86- 96
Sugar bowl, covered 110-118
Sugar bowl, open 88- 99

Probably other pieces. Milk glass, 150 percent higher than clear prices listed.

Liberty Bell Novelty Bank

This bell was made for the St. Louis Exposition in 1903.

Liberty Bell Novelty Bank

Liberty Bell bank (ill.) $38-46

Others were made and it gets confusing. If you like them, buy them.

Lightning

Lightning

(Chain Lightning): Tiffin Glass Company, Gas City, Indiana, 1890s. It was called Chain Lightning in the factory by the men. Clear.

Bowls, several styles	$15-27
Butter, covered	34-40
Celery vase	25-33
Compote	
a. Covered	38-47
b. Open	27-34
Creamer (ill.)	28-33
Goblet	24-34
Pitcher, water	38-48
Spoonholder	28-38

Probably others.

Lily-of-the-Valley

Lily-of-the-Valley

Sandwich, 1870s. Clear, etched.

Butter dish, footed, on three feet	$54- 65
Celery	49- 57
Compote, covered, high standard .	79- 92
Cordial	46- 54
Creamer, on three feet	59- 67
Cruet, tall stopper	59- 69
Dish, oval	32- 42
Goblet	45- 55
Pitcher, milk (scarce), water (ill.) .	92-102
Sauce, flat	18- 26
Spoonholder, on three feet	36- 44
Sugar bowl, on three feet	59- 69
Wine (scarce)	43- 52

Probably other pieces.

Lincoln Drape

Lincoln Drape

Sandwich, late 1860s. Clear, milk-white, sapphire blue (both rare).

Butter dish	$ 92-104
Celery	92-106
Compote	
a. Open, low standard	62- 72
b. Covered	65- 75
c. Flint	182-192

(continued)

Creamer	112-132
Decanter	94-107
Egg cup	50- 60
Goblet, w/tassel (ill.)	74- 84
Pitcher, water	210-230
Plate, 6″	60- 70
Spoonholder, flint	65- 75
Sugar bowl, open	92-106
Tumbler	41- 50

Probably other pieces. Colors, 45 to 75 percent higher than clear prices listed.

Lined Band Round Thumbprint

Lined Band Round Thumbprint

Maker unknown, c. 1860, clear, flint.

Champagne	$37-46
Compote, open	33-35
Goblet (ill.)	22-29
Tumbler, footed	17-26
Wine	28-39

Probably other pieces.

Lion

Lion

(Atlanta): Gillinder & Sons, Philadelphia, 1870s. Clear and frosted, milk glass.

Bread plate, frosted	$ 68- 78
Butter dish, 2 styles	105-108
Celery	110-115
Compote	
a. Covered, large, high standard	175-200
b. Covered, low, 5″, collared	140-160
Creamer, frosted lion on base	115-130
Goblet	110-130
Paperweight, milk glass, lions reclining	120-130
Pitcher	
a. Milk	172-182
b. Syrup, metal top	118-129
c. Water	112-114
Sauce, footed, small medium, large	22- 32
Spoonholder	82- 92
Sugar bowl, rampant lion finial (ill.)	130-145
Tumbler	92-120
Wine	108-115

Probably other pieces. Butter dish, celery, cordial, egg cup, goblet, water pitcher, sauce being reproduced. Don't buy it for genuine!

Lion and Baboon

Lion and Baboon

Maker unknown, a humorous design of the 1880s. Clear.

Butter dish, covered	$ 55- 62
Creamer	70- 80
Compote, covered	78- 87
Miniature 4-piece table set	115-132
Pitcher (ill.)	80- 90
Spoonholder	32- 44
Sugar bowl, covered	55- 65

Probably other pieces.

Lion's Head

Lion's Head

Miniature set possibly Gillinder & Sons, c. 1870s, clear, non-flint.

4-piece table set (ill.) $260-285
Cup/saucer (ill.)............. 44- 50

Little River

Little Owl

Little Owl

Bryce, Higbee & Company, Pittsburgh, mid-1880s. This is part of a "Menagerie Toy Set," which includes "Bear" covered sugar, "Fish" spoonholder, "Turtle" butter dish. Crystal, old gold, blue and white opaque, amber, other colors. You see too few of these to price them. Don't buy one of these as Sandwich, especially the owl.

Little River

Possibly Sandwich, 1870s. Clear, possibly colors.

Pickle castor $74-84
Pickle jar (ill.)................. 40-50

The scene shown in photo (windmill) is unknown to collectors. Probably other pieces.

Log Cabin

Log Cabin

Central Glass Company, Wheeling, West Virginia, 1875. Clear.

Butter dish .... $ 92-104
Compote, covered, on
  stand (ill.)................. 140-150
Creamer 72- 82
Mustard 52- 62
Pitcher, water 140-150
Sauce 29- 39
Spoonholder 62- 72
Sugar bowl (rare), covered 118-126

Probably other pieces.

485

Loganberry and Grape

Pitcher, water (ill.) 52-62
Salt/Pepper, pr. 20-30
Spoonholder 22-31
Sugar bowl, covered 35-41
Probably other pieces.

Loop

Loganberry and Grape

Dalzell, Gilmore & Leighton, mid-1880s. Clear.

Butter dish, covered $30-40
Celery 22-31
Creamer 32-40
Goblet 19-24
Pitcher, water (ill.) 32-42
Tumbler 19-27

Probably other pieces.

Loop

(O'Hara): O'Hara Glass Company, Pittsburgh, late 1850s or 1860s. Also made by Gillinder & Sons, 1860s, and by Portland Glass Co., Portland, Maine, 1870s. They called it Portland Petal.

Butter dish, covered $39-48
Cake stand 40-50
Celery 22-29
Compote
  a. Covered, high standard 52-61
  b. Open 34-41
Creamer, 6″ high 32-40
Egg cup 22-28
Goblet, 3 styles 18-36
Pitcher, water, applied
  handle (ill.) 54-64
Spoonholder 22-34
Sugar bowl
  a. Covered 38-47
  b. Open 28-38
Wine 29-39

Probably other pieces.

Long Maple Leaf

Long Maple Leaf

Possibly, Westmoreland Specialty Company, late 1800s. Clear.

Butter dish, covered $34-44
Celery 22-29
Creamer 29-37
Goblet 19-29
Mug with cap 24-34

Loop and Dart

Loop and Dart

Sandwich, early; Richards & Hartley, Portland Glass Company, Portland, Maine, 1860s. Clear.

Butter dish, covered, round
  ornaments $54-64
Celery vase, diamond band 48-58
Compote, 8″, low foot........... 48-57
Cordial...................... 47-56
Creamer, diamond ornaments .. 74-86
Egg cup, round ornaments 27-34
Goblet, buttermilk............. 38-50
Pitcher, water (ill.) 78-88
Plate, 6″ (rare) 70-80
Salt, footed 27-36
Spoonholder, round ornaments .. 44-54
Sugar bowl, covered 52-62
Tumbler, footed, water 47-57
Wine....................... 37-48

Probably other pieces.

Loop and Dart with Round Ornaments

Loop and Dart with Round Ornaments

Portland Glass Company, Portland, Maine, c. 1869, clear, non-flint, flint.

Butter dish, covered $44-53
Butter patty 18-26
Compote, covered 52-60
Creamer 42-51
Egg cup 27-57
Goblet (ill.) 34-44
Pitcher..................... 70-80
Spoonholder 27-32

Sugar bowl
  a. Covered 48-58
  b. Open 27-38

Flint, 25% higher than non-flint prices listed. See *Portland Glass,* Wallace-Homestead Book Company. Sauce being reproduced.

Loop and Moose Eye

Loop and Moose Eye

Maker unknown, c. 1870s, clear, flint.

Creamer $26-29
Decanter 34-46
Goblet (ill.) 36-45
Spoonholder 28-34
Sugar bowl, covered 36-46

Probably other pieces.

Loop with Dewdrops

Loop with Dewdrops

Earlier maker unknown; reproduced by U.S. Glass Company, 1892.

Bowl, 5″, 6″, 7″, 8″ $28-37
Butter dish, covered 45-54
Cake plate on stand, 9″, 10″ 56-62
Celery vase 52-61
Compote
  a. Covered, 5″, 6″, 7″, 8″,
     high foot 47-57

487   (continued)

b. Open, 5", 6", 7", 8",
   high foot 34-44
Creamer 42-52
Dish, oval, 7", 8", 9" 22-32
Goblet, knobbed stem 36-46
Mug, with cap.................. 27-37
Pitcher, syrup, water,
   ½ gal. (ill.) 42-52
Salt/Pepper, pr. 37-47
Spoonholder 41-50
Sugar bowl, covered 48-58
Tumbler 37-47
Wine........................ 33-43

Probably other pieces.

Loop with Stippled Panels

Loop with Stippled Panels

(Texas): U.S. Glass Company, 1900 and 1907. Crystal, crystal with gilded top, ruby in the body.

Bowl, berry, 7½", 8½", 9½",
   flat, footed...................$26-36
Butter dish 29-42
Cake stand, footed, 10", high
   and low standard 42-52
Celery 27-37
Creamer 26-35
Cruet, faceted stopper 29-38
Goblet 26-34
Pitcher, three pints (ill.) 32-39
Salt/Pepper, pr., large, small 24-32
Spoonholder 22-33
Sugar bowl, small 29-42
Toothpick holder 15-21
Tumbler 18-27
Wine........................ 22-29

Probably other pieces. Colors, same price.

Loops and Drops

Loops and Drops

(New Jersey): Maker unknown, c. 1890s, clear, ruby-flashed, non-flint.

Butter dish, covered (ill.) $49-59
Creamer 40-55
Goblet 32-42
Spoonholder 33-44
Sugar bowl, covered 47-57

Ruby-flashed, 50 percent higher than clear prices listed. Probably other pieces.

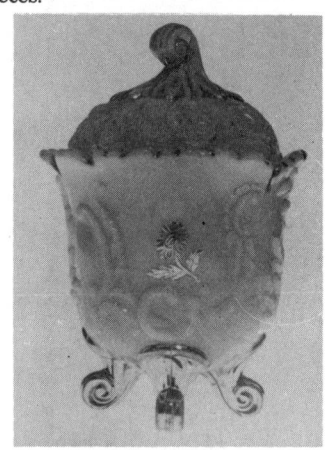

Louis XV

Louis XV

(Winged Scroll): Northwood Glass Company, Indiana, Pennsylvania, 1898. Custard, "Ivory and Gold," green, other colors.

	Color	Custard
Berry set		
a. Large bowl......	$87- 97	$145-156
b. Small bowl......	42- 52	80- 90
Butter dish, covered ..	80- 90	172-183

Compote		110-115
Creamer	70- 80	98-110
Cruet	75- 86	148-160
Pitcher, water	94-106	140-148
Salt/Pepper, pr......	55- 67	120-130
Spoonholder	69- 72	92-107
Sugar bowl, covered (ill.)	66- 76	112-132
Tumbler, water	52- 62	70- 80

Louisiana Purchase Exposition

Louisiana Purchase Exposition

The World's Fair held in St. Louis, Missouri, 1904, to commemorate the centennial of the Louisiana Purchase 100 years before. Plates and iced tea (or beverage) glasses were popular souvenirs. Crystal, crystal with frosted center, milk-glass.

Beverage glass	$30-40
Plate........................	30-40
Tumbler (ill.)	27-36

Probably other pieces.

Lutz

Lutz

McKee Bros., Jeanette, Pennsylvania, 1894. Clear.

Goblet	$27-37
Mustard jar..................	22-33
Pickle jar....................	22-33
Pitcher, water (ill.)	47-57

Probably other pieces.

William McKinley Campaign Items

William McKinley Campaign Items

Most were made by McKee & Bros. in 1896.

Bread plate, "His Will Be Done" (ill.)	$72-82
Goblet, bust..................	38-47
Gold tray	78-88
Mug (cup), covered	34-46
Plate, "Protection and Plenty" ..	52-63
Tumbler, clear	34-42
Tumbler, frosted	40-50

Other pieces.

Madison

Madison

Maker and date unknown, clear, flint.

Compote, covered	$62-70

489

(continued)

Creamer 88-98
Goblet 38-47
Spoonholder 40-50
Sugar bowl (base ill.) 81-90
Should be other pieces.

Magnet and Grape, Frosted Leaf

Magnet and Grape, Frosted Leaf

Sandwich glass, early. Clear glass with frosted leaf.

Butter dish $100-110
Celery 115-123
Champagne.................. 105-115
Compote, open (scarce),
   several types 110-120
Cordial..................... 88- 98
Creamer 96-107
Decanter with matching stoppers
   a. Pint 72- 82
   b. Quart 92-102
Goblet
   a. Knob stem (ill.) 70- 80
   b. Plain stem 62- 82
   c. Variant, large American
     shield 200-230
Salt, footed 40- 50
Saucedish, 4″ 28- 38
Spoonholder 44- 54
Sugar bowl, covered 92-108
Tumbler, water, whiskey...... 58- 68
Wine jug, two styles (rare) 64- 79

Creamer, goblet, covered sugar bowl being reproduced.

Magnet and Grape, Stippled Leaf

Sandwich glass, 1870s. Clear glass with stippled leaf.

Magnet and Grape, Stippled Leaf

Butter dish, acorn knob ......$ 80- 90
Compote, open 52- 64
Cordial..................... 63- 73
Creamer 105-115
Goblet, knob stem 68- 78
Pitcher (ill.) 120-140
Salt, footed 39- 50
Saucedish, 4″ 20- 30
Spoonholder 40- 50
Sugar bowl 79- 89
Tumbler 42- 53

Maine

Maine

(Panelled Flower, Stippled): U.S. Glass Company, Pittsburgh, early 1890s. Clear, emerald green.

Bowl, 6″, 7″, 8″ $29-39
Creamer 28-37
Dish, relish 15-20
Mug, handled 22-32
Pitcher (ill.).................. 40-50
Sauce, flat 15-27
Spoonholder 18-27
Sugar bowl, covered 27-39
Toothpick holder 18-27

490

Tumbler 22-32

Probably other pieces. Green, 100 percent higher than clear prices listed.

Maize

Maize

Libbey & Son Company, Toledo, Ohio, 1889. White opaque, yellow, clear, custard.

Bowl
  a. Berry, 9″ .... $ 80- 90
  b. Finger, 5″ 54- 64
Celery vase 104-118
Creamer 99-109
Decanter, pint, quart 99-108
Pitcher
  a. Syrup (ill.) 92-107
  b. Water 115-118
Spoonholder 75- 85
Sugar bowl 110-114
Toothpick holder 62- 74
Tumbler 66- 76

Probably other pieces. Clear, yellow, custard, 30 percent higher than white opaque prices listed. Being reproduced in many sizes and shapes. Careful here!

Manhattan

Manhattan

U.S. Glass Company, 1902. Clear, gilt in the sunken circles, red-flashed, amber.

Bowl, berry, 7″, 8″, 8½″, 9½″, 10″, 11″, 12½″ .... $ 22- 33
Bowl, punch, large 125-140
Butter dish 42- 52
Cake stand 46- 56
Celery vase, tall 33- 43
Compote, 9½″, 10½″ 42- 52
Creamer, individual, large 22- 29
Pitcher, ½ gal., tankard, water, syrup 37- 46
Plate, 5″, 9½″, 11″, 12″ 20- 30
Sauce, 5″, footed; 4½″, flat 16- 24
Spoonholder 18- 28
Sugar bowl
  a. Covered 44- 54
  b. Open, individual 19- 26
Tumbler, iced tea, water 19- 27
Water bottle 22- 32

Probably other pieces. Red-flashed 25 percent higher than clear. Amber 50 percent higher. Being reproduced in bowls, creamer and sugar, goblets, iced teas, plates, sherbets and wines.

Manhattan

Manhattan

Tarentum Glass Company, Tarentum, Pennsylvania, 1895, clear only.

Butter dish, covered (ill.) $32-42
Cake stand 29-39
Celery 16-27
Creamer 15-22
Pitcher, water 47-62
Spoonholder 16-27
Sugar bowl, covered 30-39
Wine 17-26

All standard pieces made.

Maple

(Hops Band): King, Son & Company, Pittsburgh, Pennsylvania, c. 1870s, clear.

Butter dish, covered	$34-54
Cake stand, large	42-52
Celery	34-44
Compote, covered	40-50
Creamer	27-36
Egg cup	26-32
Goblet	24-32
Pitcher	38-52
Salt, footed	24-34
Spoonholder	19-27
Sugar bowl	
a. Open	18-27
b. Covered	32-42

Probably other pieces.

Maple Leaf

Maple Leaf

Northwood Glass Company, 1890s. Custard, Carnival.

Berry set
a. Large bowl, stemmed, Custard	$138-140
b. Small bowl, stemmed, Custard	66- 76
Butter dish, covered, Custard	110-130
(same item, Carnival marigold)	58- 68
(same item, Carnival vivid)	88- 98
Creamer, Custard	72- 82
(same item, Carnival marigold)	34- 44
(same item, Carnival vivid)	58- 68

Ice cream set, Carnival
a. Large bowl, stemmed, marigold	40- 50
(same in Carnival vivid)	88- 92
b. Small bowl, stemmed, marigold	14- 19
(same in Carnival vivid)	26- 35
Pitcher, Custard	160-170
(same item, Carnival marigold)	58- 68

(same item, Carnival vivid) (ill.)	130-140
Spoonholder, Custard	84- 94
(same item, Carnival marigold)	37- 47
(same item, Carnival vivid)	60- 70
Sugar bowl, covered, Custard	89- 99
(same item, Carnival marigold)	32- 42
(same item, Carnival vivid)	55- 65
Tumbler, Custard	78- 88
(same item, Carnival marigold)	27- 37
(same item, Carnival vivid)	29- 39

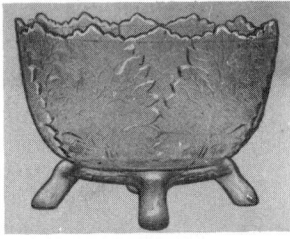

Maple Leaf

Maple Leaf

(Leaf): Gillinder & Sons, Greensburg Pennsylvania, late 1880s; they called it Leaf. Clear, canary, amber, vaseline, blue, sapphire, other colors.

Butter dish	$44-53
Celery vase	40-50
Compote	
a. Covered, high standard	78-88
b. Round, open, footed	52-62
Goblet	82-92
Pitcher, large, small	54-62
Plate, 10", 10½", Grant Peace	34-47
Sauce, 5", 6", footed	22-32
Spoonholder	27-37
Sugar bowl (ill.)	42-52
Tumbler	27-37

Probably other pieces. Colors, 40 to 60 percent higher than clear prices listed. Being heavily reproduced in various sizes and colors.

Marquisette

Co-Operative Flint Glass Company, Beaver Falls, Pennsylvania, c. early 1880s, clear, flint.

Butter dish, covered	$54-64
Celery	45-55

Compote
  a. Open 32-42
  b. Covered 60-70
Creamer 57-67
Goblet .... : 38-48
Spoonholder 44-52
Sugar bowl
  a. Open 44-56
  b. Covered 54-65
Wine 25-36
Probably other pieces.

Marsh Fern

Riverside Glass Works, Wellsburg, West Virginia, c. 1889, clear, non-flint. This was their "No. 327."

Bowl .... : $22-31
Compote, high standard 27-36
Creamer, tankard 29-37
Goblet 24-32
Spoonholder 18-29
Sugar bowl, covered 34-47
Other pieces.

Marsh Pink

Marsh Pink

Maker unknown, Ohio, 1880s. Clear, rare pieces in amber.

Bowl, open and covered $28-34
Butter dish, covered 29-36
Cake stand, small 37-47
Compote, covered 36-47
Jam jar 26-34
Pitcher (ill.) 38-47
Spoonholder 22-29
Sugar bowl, covered 27-36
Probably other pieces. Amber 150 percent higher than clear prices listed.

Maryland

Maryland

U.S. Glass Company, one of their "States" series. Clear, with gold.

Bowls $20-29
Butter dish, covered 35-42
Compotes, open 33-47
Custards 16-21
Creamer 24-33
Cruet 19-27
Honey dish 12-18
Goblet 22-32
Pitcher, water, with
  gold (ill.) 36-46
Plate, bread 18-27
Sauce 15-24
Spoonholder 28-38
Sugar bowl, covered 26-36
Tumbler 22-32
Wine 26-36

Mascotte

Ripley & Company, Pittsburgh, c. 1884, clear, plain or engraved. Reissued by U.S. Glass Company after 1891.

Butter dish
  a. Plain $49-57
  b. Horseshoe-shaped, marked
     "Maud S." (rare) 77-87
Celery 29-36
Compote
  a. Open 19-28
  b. Covered 36-44
Dish 22-28
Goblet 24-34
Sugar bowl, covered 52-62
Tumbler 24-34
Wine 18-27
Other pieces. Ripley prices listed.

Masonic

(Inverted Prism): McKee Glass Company, Jeannette, Pennsylvania, c. 1894, clear.

Bowl, berry $27-37
Butter dish, covered 37-48
Cake stand, high standard 34-44
Creamer 38-49
Pitcher, water................. 48-57
Spoonholder 39-49
Sugar bowl, covered 37-48
Tumbler 23-34

Probably other pieces.

Massachusetts

Massachusetts

U.S. Glass Company, 1898. Clear.

Butter dish, covered $42-51
Cruet 28-39
Dish, candy 26-39
Creamer 37-44
Pitcher...................... 68-78
Plate, 8″ 35-46
Shot glass 22-34
Table lamp 68-79
"Teapot" (intended as rum
  jug) (ill.) 74-83
Water carafe 48-54

Probably other pieces.

Medallion

(Spades, Hearts and Spades): Maker unknown, 1880s. Clear, yellow, amber, blue, apple green.

Butter dish $44-54
Cake stand 37-48
Celery vase 29-36

Medallion

Compote, covered, high
  standard 49-54
Creamer 29-38
Goblet 28-37
Mug 27-34
Pitcher, water (ill.) 39-49
Sauce, flat, footed 16-27
Spoonholder 30-40
Sugar bowl 32-41
Tumbler 21-31
Wine........................ 29-38

Probably other pieces. Yellow, amber, blue, 100 percent; apple green, 150 percent higher than clear prices listed.

Melrose

Greensburg Glass Company, Greensburg, Pennsylvania, c. 1890s, clear, plain or etched.

Butter dish, covered $38-43
Cake stand 34-44
Celery 27-34
Compote, covered, high
  standard, 6″, 8″ 44-56
Creamer, tankard 27-38
Goblet 19-28
Mug 15-27
Pitcher
  a. Quart 19-27
  b. ½ gal. 28-41
Spoonholder 19-29
Sugar bowl, covered 30-40
Tumbler 13-22
Wine........................ 16-27

Etched, 20 percent higher than clear prices listed. Other pieces.

Memphis

Memphis

(Doll's Eye): Northwood Glass Company, 1908-1910, clear, colors, Carnival.

Berry set (clear, colors only)
a. Large bowl .... $ 28- 38
b. Small bowl 15- 27
Butter dish, covered (clear,
colors only) 50- 60
Fruit bowl & base 48- 57
Pitcher
a. Syrup ... ,.............. 49- 58
b. Water 138-147
Punch set
a. Bowl & base 49- 58
b. Cup 14- 23
Spoonholder (clear, colors
only) 39- 49
Sugar bowl, covered (clear,
colors only) 39- 50

Colors, 25-75 percent; Carnival, 60 percent higher than clear prices listed. Probably other pieces.

Mephistopheles

Mephistopheles

Germany; also made in this country, late 1800s. Clear, frosted.

Ale glass, "Germany" $29-37
Goblet 36-44
Mug (ill.) 39-47
Pitcher, applied handle 49-58

Probably other pieces made.

Michigan

Michigan

(Loop with Pillar): U.S. Glass Company, c. 1893, clear, gilted, some pieces with painted decorations.

Bowl, berry, 7½", 8½", 10" $28-38
Butter dish, covered
a. Large 26-36
b. Small 35-44
Creamer
a. Individual 19-27
b. Large 29-36
Cruet 27-38
Goblet (ill.) 32-41
Pitcher, tankard.............. 34-44
Salt/Pepper, pr. 26-36
Spoonholder 27-37
Sugar bowl, covered 36-46
Tumbler 34-44
Wine........................ 27-37

Minerva

Sandwich glass, 1870s. Clear.

Butter dish, covered $79-89
Cake plate, on standard 82-92
Compote, high and low
standard 64-75
Creamer 54-64

495

(continued)

Minerva

Goblet 52-62
Marmalade jar, w/lid 42-52
Pitcher, water 68-78
Plate, small, closed handles, 9" .. 42-52
Platter, "Give Us This Day" 69-79
Sauce, flat round, footed
   round 24-34
Spoonholder 46-56
Sugar bowl, covered (ill.) 52-62
Probably other pieces.

Minnesota

U.S. Glass Company, c. 1898, clear, green with gold decoration.
Bowl
  a. Berry, round, 6", 7", 8" $28-39
  b. Flared edge, 4½", 7½",
     8½", 9½" 27-46
Butter dish, covered 44-54
Celery tray, 10", 13" 27-36
Compote
  a. Round, 6", 7", 8" 59-69
  b. Square, 6", 7", 8" 57-67
Creamer 32-46
Goblet 24-33
Pitcher, water 40-50
Sugar bowl, covered 44-58
Tumbler 19-29

Green with gold decoration, 25% higher than clear prices listed.

Mirror

McKee Brothers, Pittsburgh, Pennsylvania, c. 1870s, clear, flint.
Ale $29-38
Champagne 40-50
Compote, 6" 62-72
Cordial 40-50
Goblet 32-43

Mirror

Jar, pickle 39-48
Spoonholder 22-32
Tumbler (ill.) 40-50
Wine 50-60
Probably other pieces.

Missouri

Missouri

U.S. Glass Company, after 1891. Clear, blue, emerald green, canary, amethyst.
Butter dish, covered $36-46
Celery 19-28
Compote, high and low
  standard 29-39
Creamer 27-38
Goblet 26-37
Pitcher, pint, ½ gallon
  (ill.) 32-44
Spoonholder 19-28
Sugar bowl, covered 30-40
Tumbler 18-32

Probably other pieces. Blue, green, 50 percent higher; canary, amethyst, 100 percent higher than clear prices listed.

Mitred Bars

(Mitred Diamond Points): Bryce Brothers, Pittsburgh, c. 1885, clear, non-flint.

Bowl, oval	$15-24
Butter dish, covered	29-37
Cake stand	20-33
Celery	19-26
Creamer, covered	28-39
Goblet	20-32
Spoonholder	18-28
Sugar bowl, covered	32-42
Wine	19-27

Other pieces.

Monkey

Monkey

George A. Duncan and Sons, Pittsburgh, 1880s. Clear and opalescent.

Bowl, waste	$ 99-115
Butter dish, covered	120-132
Celery	49- 59
Creamer	85- 95
Jar, pickle	54- 63
Mug, 2 styles	68- 80
Pitcher (ill.)	148-160
Spoonholder	80- 90
Sugar	
a. Covered	121-132
b. Open	92-104
Toothpick holder	38- 48
Tumbler	58- 68

Probably other pieces. Opalescent, 35 percent higher than clear prices listed. Spoonholder and toothpick holder being reproduced.

Monroe

Maker unknown, made well before the Civil War. Clear and brilliant. Extremely rare in lamp. Shown here because too many patterns remain unidentified as to maker, etc. If you know, write to the Houston Museum, Chattanooga, Tennessee.

Lamp (rare) (ill.) .... $450+

Monroe

Moon and Star

Moon and Star

(Star and Punty): Sandwich, 1870s; Palace, Pioneer Glass Company, 1892; Wilson Glass Company, 1890, same name. Imperial, Cooperative Flint Glass Company, 1890s. Mold sold to Phoenix Glass Company, 1937. Many reproductions on market today. Clear, some

(continued)

pieces with color added, also milk glass.

Bowl, berry, 6", 12½"	$ 42- 52
Butter dish, covered	64- 74
Cake stand, 6" dia.	64- 74
Celery	45- 55
Compote, covered, 7", 8", 10", high standard	78- 88
Creamer	62- 72
Goblet, clear, frosted..........	42- 52
Pitcher, syrup, water (ill.)	140-152
Sugar bowl, covered, jeweled ..	58- 68
Tumbler, footed, flint	97-115
Wine.......................	52- 62

EVERY item being reproduced. Careful!

Morning Glory

Morning Glory

Sandwich, c. 1860s, clear, flint.

Compote, open	$172-190
Creamer (rare)	275-350
Egg cup	155-168
Goblet (ill.)	285-340
Wine.......................	158-168

Goblet and wine being reproduced in clear and in color.

Nail

Bryce Bros., Pittsburgh, 1885. Crystal glass with ruby stain, etched.

Bowl, footed....................	$10-20
Butter, covered	24-34
Creamer	22-34
Goblet	29-41
Pitcher, water, lemonade (ill.) ..	36-46
Sauce, footed	18-27
Salt/Pepper, pr.	15-28

Nail

Spoonholder	17-29
Sugar bowl	
a. Covered	28-40
b. Open	15-27
Tumbler	17-26

Probably other pieces. With ruby stain, 100 percent higher than clear prices listed.

Nailhead

Nailhead

(Gem): Sandwich, early; later, Bryce, Higbee & Co., Pittsburgh. Clear orange in the grooves, clear aquamarine.

Butter dish	$52-63
Cake stand, 4" high	62-72
Celery	58-68
Compote, covered, open, scalloped	55-62
Cordial.....................	36-39
Creamer	42-52
Goblet	33-42
Pitcher, water (ill.)	58-68

Plate, round, 9", square, 7" 44-54
Saucedish 21-29
Salt/Pepper, pr. 34-44
Spoonholder 44-53
Sugar bowl, covered, scalloped .. 58-64
Tumbler 33-43
Wine 19-27

Probably other pieces. Colors, 50 percent
higher than clear prices listed.

New England Pineapple

New England Pineapple

(Loop and Jewel): Boston & Sandwich
Glass Company, c. 1860s, clear, flint.
Colored pieces considered rare.

Butter dish, covered .... $ 58- 68
Champagne 48- 58
Compote, open 78- 88
Creamer.................... 98-118
Decanter, with or without
  stopper 99-116
Goblet (ill.) 52- 62
Sauce 19- 29
Spoonholder 48- 58
Sugar bowl, covered 115-125
Tumbler.................... 49- 59

Other pieces. Goblet and wine being
reproduced.

New York (Honeycomb)

Many firms made this pattern, among
them, Bakewell, Pears & Company, 1860s
on. Early in clear; later in yellow, blue,
amber, green, opalescent.

Bowl, 6", 7", 8", 9", 10" $27-38
Butter dish, New York 42-52

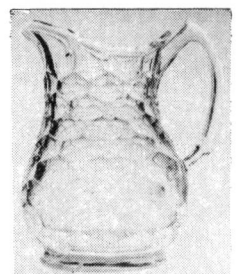

New York (Honeycomb)

Castor bottle, each............. 18-28
Celery, Laredo, flint 45-55
Creamer 41-51
Decanter, pint, quart 40-50
Goblet, flint.................. 36-46
Jug, one-half pint, pint, quart,
  3 pints 27-37
Pitcher, water (ill.) 50-60
Salt/Pepper, pr. 27-39
Spoonholder, non-flint 24-34
Sugar bowl 38-48
Tumbler, one-half pint, one-third
  pint, footed 26-36
Wine, claret.................. 28-39

Many other pieces. Colors, 40 to 60 percent higher than clear prices listed.

Niagara

Fostoria Glass Company, Fostoria,
Ohio, c. 1900, clear.

Bowl, berry $18-28
Butter dish, covered 28-39
Creamer 27-37
Pitcher
  a. Tankard 24-35
  b. Water, syrup 35-46
Spoonholder 21-30
Sugar bowl, covered 28-38
Tumbler 18-27

Other pieces.

Notched Bar

(Ball): McKee & Brothers, Jeannette,
Pennsylvania, c. 1894, clear, non-flint.

Bottle, castor $38-48
Butter dish, covered 64-73
Creamer 59-70
Cruet 42-53
Jar, jam 74-84
Spoonholder 29-39

(continued)

Sugar bowl, covered 63-73
Wine 43-53
Probably other pieces.

Nova Scotia Grape and Vine

Nova Scotia Grape and Vine

Nova Scotia, Canada, late 1880s.
Pitcher, water (ill.) $34-44
Tumbler to match 18-29
Probably other pieces.

Nursery Tales

A product of Pennsylvania, 1880s. Each piece shows different characters from old nursery tales. Clear and opal glass.

Child's 4-piece set (butter
dish, creamer, spoonholder,
sugar bowl), miniature
Clear $138-158
Punch set with 6 cups,
miniature
Clear 179-192
Sauce 38- 49

Opal, 100 percent more than clear prices listed.

Octagonal Beehive Deep Dish

Sandwich, early. Clear glass only, it is 9¼-inch in diameter and was used to hold a compote.

Beehive dish (ill.) $150-165
Compote to match
(extremely rare) 450-525

Odd Fellow

Probably Adams & Company, Pittsburgh, early 1880s. Clear. This firm spe-

Octagonal Beehive Deep Dish

Odd Fellow

cialized in selling their wares in Central and South America. If traveling there, look for Adams, if you know their patterns. Much has been found "South of the border."

Butter dish, covered $36-45
Cake stand, 8", 9", 10" 35-45
Celery 22-29
Creamer 26-34
Goblet, knob and round
stem (ill.) 22-32
Pitcher, large, small 38-48
Spoonholder 22-29
Sugar bowl 32-42

Many other pieces, some being reproduced, such as horseshoe-handled platter.

O'Hara Diamond

U.S. Glass Company, c. 1891, 1892, clear, plain, flashed with ruby stain.
Bowl, 8" $22-33

Celery 34-45
Creamer 28-37
Cup/saucer, custard 18-26
Goblet 26-36
Pitcher, tankard.............. 35-39
Spoonholder 27-37
Sugar bowl, covered 26-34
Tray, piecrust edge 24-37

Ruby stain, 40 percent higher than clear prices listed.

One-Hundred-and-One

One-Hundred-and-One

Probably Bellaire Goblet Company, Findlay, Ohio, late 1870s. Clear.

Butter dish $66-75
Celery 54-63
Compote, covered, high foot, 8" .. 58-68
Creamer 48-58
Goblet 44-53
Lamp, handled, flat 53-63
Pickle, oval, tapered 28-37
Plate
  a. 7", 8", 9", 10", 11" 26-44
  b. Bread, round, 11", "Give
    us this day" 62-72
Sauce, flat, 4" 19-28
Salt/Pepper, pr. 34-44
Spoonholder 46-54
Sugar bowl 48-58
Relish dish, oval, deep 19-29

Probably other pieces.

Opposing Pyramids

(Flora): Green Glass Company, Pittsburgh, 1889. Clear.

Butter dish, covered $29-38
Creamer 27-33
Goblet (ill.) 24-32
Pitcher, water................. 39-47
Sugar bowl, covered 32-41

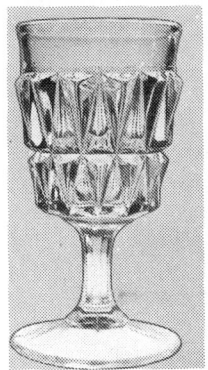

Opposing Pyramids

Tumbler 26-36
Wine......................... 17-24

Probably other pieces.

Optic

U.S. Glass Company, c. 1892, clear, often ruby stained or engraved or both.

Bowl, berry $17-24
Butter dish, covered 29-38
Celery 22-34
Creamer 26-34
Goblet 19-28
Pitcher, water................. 34-39
Spoonholder 19-27
Sugar bowl, covered 27-36
Toothpick holder 12-19

Ruby stained and/or engraved, 20 percent higher than clear prices listed.

Oregon

Richards & Hartley Flint Glass Company, Tarentum, Pennsylvania, c. 1888, clear, clear, flashed with ruby blocks, non-flint.

Butter dish, covered $51-61
Celery 40-50
Compote, covered 44-54
Creamer 36-44
Goblet 32-42
Pitcher, water................. 52-62
Sauce, footed 21-28
Spoonholder 28-39
Sugar bowl, covered 42-53

Ruby blocks, 50 percent higher than clear prices listed.

Oriental

Oriental

Probably La Belle Glass Works, Bridgeport, Ohio, 1875-1880. Clear.

Butter dish, covered	$40-48
Celery	50-60
Compote, covered	39-48
Creamer	33-42
Goblet	32-44
Pitcher	41-52
Spoonholder	42-52
Sugar bowl	
a. Covered (ill.)	42-54
b. Open	32-52
Tumbler	28-37

Probably other pieces.

Orion Inverted Thumbprint

Orion Inverted Thumbprint

Canton Glass Company, Canton, Ohio, 1894. Clear, amber, blue, green, milk-white, yellow, black.

Butter dish, covered	$33-42
Celery	27-37
Compote	
a. Covered	29-38
b. Open	26-36
Creamer	24-34
Pitcher, water (ill.)	39-49
Sauce, footed	17-27

Spoonholder	22-29
Sugar bowl	
a. Covered	34-43
b. Open	18-27

Probably other pieces. Milk-white, 25 percent; yellow, 45 percent; amber, green, 65 percent; blue, 100 percent higher than prices listed for clear.

Oval Loop

(Question Mark): Richards & Hartley Flint Glass Company, Pittsburgh, Pennsylvania, c. 1880, clear, non-flint.

Bowls, round, oval	$19-23
Butter dish, covered	37-47
Celery	28-38
Compote, covered	44-54
Creamer	20-28
Goblet	27-36
Pitcher	35-45
Shaker, sugar	27-37
Spoonholder	22-32
Sugar bowl, covered	32-42
Tumbler	27-37
Wine	22-28

Other pieces.

Oval Miter

McKee & Brothers, Pittsburgh, c. 1865, clear, flint.

Butter dish, covered	$48-58
Compote	
a. Open, 6″, 8″	42-52
b. Covered, high standard	62-71
Goblet	40-50
Sauce, flat	12-20
Spoonholder	28-37
Sugar bowl	
a. Open	46-56
b. Covered	54-64

Probably other pieces.

Oval Panels

Maker unknown, c. late 1880s, non-flint.

Goblet	
Clear	$22-32
Amber	26-37
Yellow	28-38
Blue	29-40

Other pieces?

Owl and Possum

Owl and Possum

Maker unknown, 1880s. Clear.

Goblet (ill.) $66- 76
Pitcher, water 94-106
Sauce, footed 28- 39

Probably other pieces.

Paling

Paling

Maker unknown, c. 1880s, clear, non-flint.

Butter dish, covered $22-28
Creamer (ill.) 19-27
Goblet 19-26
Spoonholder 14-21
Sugar bowl, covered 22-28

Other pieces.

Palm Beach

U.S. Glass Company, C. 1895, yellow, blue, non-flint.

Butter dish, covered $160-175
Creamer 75- 92
Pitcher, water 180-190
Sauce 37- 47
Spoonholder 82- 92
Sugar bowl, covered 150-162
Tumbler 69- 79

Blue, 20 percent higher than yellow prices listed.

Palm Leaf Fan

Palm Leaf Fan

Maker unknown, early 1890s. Clear.

Bowl, large $22-31
Butter dish, covered 26-39
Cake stand, large 26-37
Celery vase 20-36
Compote
  a. Covered 34-47
  b. Open 29-40
Creamer 22-31
Pitcher, water (ill.) 39-52
Sugar, covered 34-44
Wine 19-27

Probably other pieces.

Palmette

Maker unknown, c. 1870s, clear, non-flint.

Butter dish, covered $40-50
Cake stand 29-39
Celery 34-46

 (continued)

Palmette

Compote
  a. Covered, low standard 35-47
  b. Open, 8″ high 25-32
Creamer (with applied handle,
  rare) 48-57
Goblet 23-33
Pitcher (with applied handle,
  rare) 72-82
Salt, master (ill.) 21-31
Spoonholder 32-42
Sugar bowl, covered 40-50
Tumbler, water, footed 30-40
Wine 30-40

Probably other pieces.

Panama

Panama

(Fine Cut Bar): U.S. Glass Company, c. 1890s, clear, non-flint.
Butter dish, covered $22-32
Compote, covered 20-30
Cordial 12-18
Creamer 14-23
Decanter 22-24
Goblet 19-28

Salt/Pepper, pr. 12-22
Spoonholder 17-27
Sugar bowl, covered 26-37
Tumbler 16-27
Wine (ill.) 18-27
Many other pieces.

Panel and Cane

Panel and Cane

Maker unknown, 1890s. Clear.
Butter dish, covered $33-43
Celery vase 24-33
Goblet 22-28
Pitcher (ill.) 32-42
Spoonholder 17-27
Sugar bowl, covered 24-33
Probably other pieces.

Panel and Star

(Column Block): O'Hara Glass Company, Ltd., Pittsburgh, Pennsylvania, c. 1880, clear, non-flint.
Butter dish, covered $34-44
Celery 18-28
Creamer 18-27
Goblet 25-32
Jar, pickle 18-22
Pitcher 36-44
Sauce, footed 18-24
Shaker, salt 20-30
Spoonholder 18-28
Sugar bowl, covered 26-38
Other pieces.

Panelled Acorn Band

Sandwich, early; other factories later. Clear, opaque. Sandwich prices listed.

Panelled Acorn Band

Butter dish, covered $75-90
Compote
  a. Covered 72-82
  b. Open 52-62
Celery vase 70-79
Creamer, applied handle 50-59
Egg cup 37-47
Goblet 36-46
Pitcher (ill.).................. 72-82
Sauce, flat, footed 22-34
Spoonholder 32-42
Sugar bowl, covered 58-67

Probably other pieces. Goblet being reproduced.

Panelled Cable

Panelled Cable

Sandwich made a Cable pattern in the 1860s to commemorate the laying of the Atlantic Cable. There's a certain similarity between the Sandwich product and

Panelled Cable, except this was made much later, probably in the 1890s period. Sandwich closed its doors in 1888. Another of those "Who-where-when" patterns.

Panelled Cane

Panelled Cane

(Cane Column): Possibly A. H. Heisey, Newark, Ohio, c. 1897, clear, canary, amber, blue, non-flint.

  Butter dish, covered $23-33
  Creamer 28-37
  Goblet (ill.) 17-25
  Sauce, flat 8-15
  Spoonholder 17-27
  Sugar bowl, open 16-24
  Wine........................ 15-22

Canary, 75 percent; amber, 85 percent; blue, 100 percent higher than clear prices listed.

Panelled Cherry

Panelled Cherry

Northwood Glass Company, 1880s. "N" sometimes found in bottom. Clear, cherries red, leaves gold.

Butter dish, covered $82-92
Compote, covered, low
    standard 80-90
Creamer 51-61
Goblet 37-47
Pitcher
    a. Syrup 64-74
    b. Water (ill.) 78-86
Sauce, flat, footed 19-24
Spoonholder 38-48
Sugar bowl, covered 66-76
Tumbler 24-35

Panelled Daisy

Panelled Daisy

(Brazil): Bryce Brothers, Pittsburgh, Pennsylvania, c. 1888, clear, non-flint; amber, rare.

Bowl, waste $23-33
Butter dish, covered, footed 36-46
Cake stand, 8″, 9″, 10″, 11″,
    high standard 38-55
Creamer (rare) 48-59
Goblet 39-49
Pitcher
    a. Water 32-42
    b. Syrup 48-56
Plate, 7″ square (ill.) 27-37
Salt/Pepper, pr. 36-46
Spoonholder 43-53
Sugar bowl, covered 48-54

Amber, 300 percent higher than clear prices listed. Goblet being reproduced.

Panelled Dewdrop

(Striped Dewdrop): Campbell, Jones & Company, Pittsburgh, Pennsylvania, c. 1878, clear, non-flint. Two types: plain base; rows of dewdrops on base.

Panelled Dewdrop

Butter dish, covered $28-38
Celery 31-41
Cordial 19-27
Creamer 22-32
Goblet 31-39
Pitcher 40-48
Sauce 14-23
Spoonholder (ill.) 17-27
Sugar bowl, covered 26-36

Other pieces. Rows of dewdrops on base, 20 percent higher than plain base prices listed.

Panelled Diamond Cut and Fan

Panelled Diamond Cut and Fan

(Hartley): Richards & Hartley, late 1800s. Clear, amber, blue, canary.

506

Bowl	$14-23
Butter dish, covered	29-42
Cake stand	37-46
Celery	22-33
Compote	
a. Covered	39-47
b. Open	27-37
Creamer	28-37
Goblet (ill.)	22-31
Pitcher, water	40-48
Sauce, flat	12-18
Spoonholder	19-29
Sugar bowl	
a. Covered	29-39
b. Open	18-28
Wine	15-26

Probably other pieces. Colors, 100 percent higher than clear prices listed.

Panelled Forget-Me-Not

Panelled Forget-Me-Not

Bryce Bros., Pittsburgh, 1870s. (Regal): Clear, amber, yellow, blue, green.

Bowl, covered	$37-47
Butter dish, covered	36-46
Cake plate on standard	47-57
Celery	40-50
Compote, covered, high	
standard, 8″ high	53-63
Cordial	34-47
Creamer	28-39
Goblet	36-43
Jam jar	37-47
Pickle dish, oval	24-29
Pitcher, two sizes	42-52
Sauce, flat, round, footed	18-24
Spoonholder	33-43
Sugar bowl, covered	43-53

Probably other pieces. Colors, 40-50 percent higher than clear prices listed.

Panelled Grape (Number 507)

Panelled Grape (Number 507)

Kokomo Glass Manufacturing Company, Kokomo, Indiana, 1904. Clear, colors, rare in milk glass. Westmoreland reproduced it in crystal and milk glass.

Bowl, round, covered	$48-58
Butter dish, milk glass	48-57
Compote, covered	39-49
Creamer, milk glass	34-44
Pitcher, applied handle (ill.)	27-36
Sauce, footed and flat	14-23
Spoonholder, milk glass	20-30
Sugar bowl	
a. Covered, milk glass	29-37
b. Open, milk glass	22-32

Probably other pieces. Milk glass 50 percent higher than clear prices listed. All items made being reproduced.

Panelled Heather

(continued)

Panelled Heather

Maker unknown, early 1890s. Clear.

Butter dish $33-43
Cake stand 36-46
Compote, covered 40-50
Creamer 32-41
Goblet 28-38
Pitcher
  a. Milk 40-50
  b. Water (ill.) 41-52
Spoonholder 26-32
Sugar bowl, covered 34-41

Probably other pieces.

Panelled Hobnail

Panelled Hobnail

Bryce Bros., 1875-1885. Clear, amber, blue, opaque-white, vaseline, canary.

Butter dish, covered $26-36
Compote
  a. Covered 27-38
  b. Open 19-28
Creamer 26-33
Goblet 19-29
Pitcher (ill.) 30-40
Sugar bowl
  a. Covered 29-42
  b. Open 17-26
Wine 16-27

Probably other pieces. Amber, canary, opaque-white, 60 percent higher; blue, green, 80 percent higher than clear prices listed.

Panelled Honeycomb

Bryce, Walker & Company, 1880. Clear.

Butter dish $32-42
Celery 19-27

Panelled Honeycomb

Compote 32-43
Creamer 26-39
Goblet 22-29
Pitcher (ill.) 41-52
Spoonholder 18-27
Sugar bowl, covered 29-39

Probably other pieces.

Panelled Ivy

Panelled Ivy

Possibly Bryce Bros., late 1880s; later U.S. Glass Company. Clear, possibly colors.

Butter dish, covered $34-46
Cake stand 27-37
Celery 19-26
Compote
  a. Covered 42-52
  b. Open 26-35
Goblet 27-37
Pitcher (ill.) 39-52

Probably other pieces. If in color, at least 50 percent higher than clear prices listed.

Panelled Oak

Panelled Oak

Maker unknown, 1890s, early 1900s. Clear.

Butter dish, covered	$34-44
Celery vase	22-34
Creamer	32-38
Goblet	27-40
Pitcher (ill.)	42-54
Spoonholder	22-32
Sugar bowl, covered	34-44
Tumbler	19-29

Probably other pieces.

Panelled Ovals

Maker unknown, c. 1860s, clear, flint.

Butter dish, covered	$62-71
Compote	
a. Open	28-38
b. Covered	58-68
Creamer	57-69
Egg cup	47-54
Goblet	47-56
Spoonholder	44-55
Sugar bowl	
a. Open	17-29
b. Covered	42-52

Other pieces.

Panelled Pleat

Robinson Glass Company, Zanesville, Ohio, c. 1894, clear, non-flint.

Butter dish, covered	$24-34
Creamer	18-27
Goblet	16-28

Spoonholder	14-28
Sugar bowl, covered	27-37

Possibly other pieces.

Panelled Primula

Panelled Primula

Maker unknown, 1900s. Clear.

Butter dish, covered	$26-34
Cake stand	27-36
Celery vase	22-36
Compote	
a. Covered, high standard	37-47
b. Open, high and low	
standard	28-38
Creamer	19-27
Goblet	18-27
Pitcher, water (ill.)	29-42
Salt/Pepper, pr.	15-24
Spoonholder	17-27
Sugar bowl, covered	24-34
Tumbler	18-28

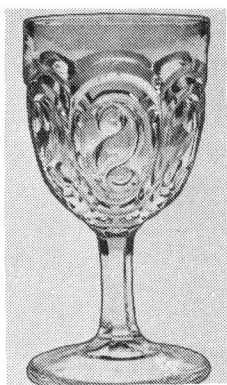

Panelled "S"

Panelled "S"

Maker unknown, 1880s. Clear.

Butter dish, covered	$29-39
Celery	19-27

(continued)

Compote 28-38
Creamer 24-34
Goblet (ill.) 22-32
Plate, 5″, 6″, 7½″............... 12-19
Pitcher, water................. 38-48
Spoonholder 19-27
Sugar bowl, covered 28-38

Probably other pieces.

Panelled Sawtooth

Panelled Sawtooth

(Fluted Diamond Point): Duncan & Miller Glass Company, Washington, Pennsylvania, 1880s. Clear.

Butter dish, covered $41-50
Cake stand 37-48
Celery 27-33
Goblet 28-38
Pitcher (ill.)................... 42-52
Spoonholder 19-26
Sugar
  a. Covered 34-44
  b. Open 26-36
Wine......................... 17-27

Probably other pieces.

Panelled Star and Button

Panelled Star and Button

(Sedan): Maker unknown, late 1880s. Clear.

Butter dish, covered $18-28
Creamer 17-26
Goblet 19-27
Pitcher (ill.)................... 26-38
Spoonholder 19-27
Sugar bowl
  a. Covered 22-32
  b. Open 17-26
Wine......................... 14-27

Probably other pieces.

Panelled Stippled Scroll

Panelled Stippled Scroll

Maker unknown, early 1900s. Clear, amber, blue.

Celery vase $20-30
Compote 32-42
Creamer 19-27
Goblet 26-29
Pitcher, water................. 40-50
Spoonholder (ill.) 20-30
Sugar bowl, covered 30-40
Tumbler 19-28

Probably other pieces. Color 40% more than clear prices listed.

Panelled Strawberry

Maker unknown, late 1890s. Clear, foliage and berries burnished gold; also, maroon to pink.

Butter dish $40-50
Celery 18-27
Creamer 28-38
Goblet 30-40

Panelled Strawberry

Pitcher (ill.) 48-60
Sauce, 5″, 6″, 6½″ 21-31
Spoonholder 27-36
Sugar bowl, covered 29-38
Tumbler 18-27

Colors don't affect price.

Panelled Sunflower

Panelled Thistle

Panelled Sunflower

Maker unknown, 1880s. Clear, blue.
Butter dish $30-40
Celery 22-29
Creamer 25-32
Goblet (ill.) 24-32
Spoonholder 19-27
Sugar bowl 26-36

Probably other pieces. Blue, 50 percent higher than clear prices listed.

Panelled Thistle

J. B. Higbee Glass Company, Bridgeville, Pennsylvania, 1910, possibly earlier. Clear.
Bowl, berry, 6½″, 7″, 8½″, 9″,
   footed $26-42
Butter dish 48-58
Cake plate on stand, large,
   small 41-52
Celery, 11″ 47-54
Compote, open, small, medium,
   large 39-54
Creamer, knob feet 36-46
Cruet 58-62
Dish, honey, oblong, oval,
   round 44-59
Goblet, two styles 40-52
Pickle dish, 7½″, 8¼″ 22-29
Pitcher, two sizes 48-67
Plate, 7¼″, 8¼″, 9½″, 10¼″ 38-49
Salt/Pepper, pr. 44-56
Spoonholder 36-47
Sugar bowl, 2 handles 43-52
Tumbler, water 38-48
Wine, two styles 29-39

Probably other pieces. With Bee mark 25 percent higher. Goblet, 7¼″ plate and salt being reproduced.

Panelled Wheat

Panelled Wheat

Hobbs, Brockunier & Company, Wheeling, West Virginia, 1871, crystal and milk glass.

(continued)

	Clear	Milk Glass
Butter dish, covered	$30-40	$34- 42
Compote		
a. Covered, footed	38-48	92-104
b. Open		36- 46
Creamer	19-24	34- 44
Goblet	18-27	82- 92
Pitcher, water, (ill.)		95-106
Sauce, flat	7-10	12- 17
Spoonholder	12-18	18- 27
Sugar bowl		
a. Covered	28-37	36- 46
b. Open	12-18	19- 24

Possibly other pieces.

Pansy and Moss Rose

Pansy and Moss Rose

Maker and date unknown. Clear.

Prices comparable to Panelled Strawberry.

Parrot

Parrot

(Owl in Fan): Possibly Richards & Hartley, Tarentum, Pennsylvania, 1880s. Clear.

Bowl	$37-46
Celery	22-32
Goblet (ill.)	38-47
Wine (rare)	42-52

Doubtful if other pieces were made.

Parthenon

(Egyptian): Sandwich glass, c. 1870s, clear, flint.

Butter dish, covered	$47-56
Celery	38-48
Compote	
a. Open, high, low standard	39-48
b. Covered, high, low standard	47-56
Creamer	39-48
Goblet	38-47
Pitcher, water.................	52-62
Platter	
a. Figure of a woman	52-62
b. Salt Lake Temple	54-63
Spoonholder	34-48
Sugar bowl, covered	47-52

Possibly other pieces.

Pattee Cross

(Broughton; Gloria): Maker unknown, c. 1900. In 1912, Sears, Roebuck listed it in their catalog under the name "Gloria." Clear, green, non-flint.

Butter dish, covered	$31-40
Celery	18-27
Creamer	22-32
Goblet	16-28
Pitcher	29-37
Sugar bowl, covered	27-36

Green, 40 percent higher than clear prices listed. Prices of 1900 pieces listed. Probably other pieces.

Pavonia

(Pineapple Stem): Ripley & Company, Pittsburgh, 1885. Clear, red-flashed, etched.

Butter dish, covered, etched	$52-62

Pavonia

Cake stand, etched
  a. Large 43-53
  b. Small 40-50
Celery 38-48
Compote
  a. Covered, high standard 68-78
  b. Open, high standard 60-70
Creamer, pedestal base, etched .. 40-50
Goblet, pineapple stemmed,
  etched 33-45
Pitcher, water, pineapple
  stemmed 52-62
Spoonholder (ill.) 29-38
Sugar bowl 47-58
Tumbler, etched 22-32
Wine 40-50

Probably other pieces. Red-flashed 25 percent higher than clear.

Peacock Eye

Peacock Eye

An early Sandwich pattern, clear, flint. Don't confuse it with Peacock Feather (Georgia).
Bowl, 8⅞″ dia. (ill.) $162-180

Peacock Feather

Peacock Feather

(Georgia): Originally an old Sandwich pattern. In 1907, U.S. Glass Company made same pattern and called it Georgia as part of their "States" series. Clear, blue, amethyst, other colors.
Bowl, berry $34-43
Butter dish, covered 39-48
Cake stand, 9″, 10″, 11″ 44-58
Celery boat 29-39
Compote
  a. Shallow, high standard 34-44
  b. Covered, deep, high
    standard 49-59
Creamer 52-62
Dish, oval.................... 27-37
Lamp, handles, oil, blue 76-87
Pitcher, water (ill.) 58-72
Salt/Pepper, pr. 40-50
Spoonholder 50-60
Sugar bowl, covered 50-59
Tumbler 29-40

Probably other pieces. Colors 50 percent higher.

Peerless

Richards & Hartley Flint Glass Company, Pittsburgh, c. 1875, clear, non-flint.
Bottle, castor $29-34
Champagne................... 38-50
Creamer, round, angular 37-47
Egg cup 22-31

(continued)

Goblet	28-38
Jar, pickle	40-50
Pitcher, water, ½ gal.	44-56
Spoonholder	19-28
Sugar bowl, covered	47-56
Tumbler	28-38

Many other pieces. Twenty-two compotes alone!

Pendelton

Pendelton

Maker unknown, late 1860s, early 1870s. Clear.

Butter dish	$34-44
Celery vase	24-33
Creamer	18-27
Goblet	22-31
Pitcher, syrup, metal cap (ill.)	34-44
Spoonholder	20-30
Sugar bowl, covered	29-41
Tumbler	19-27

Probably other pieces.

Pentagon

George Duncan & Sons, Pittsburgh, 1880. Clear.

Creamer, individual	$27-36
Creamer, tankard type	32-43
Pitcher, water, tankard type (ill.)	44-52

Other pieces probably exist in this pattern.

Persian

(Three Stories; Block and Pleat): Bryce, Higbee & Company, Pittsburgh, Pennsylvania, c. 1885, clear, non-flint.

Bowls, oval, 8″, 9″, 10″	$17-27
Butter dish, covered	40-50
Celery	30-40

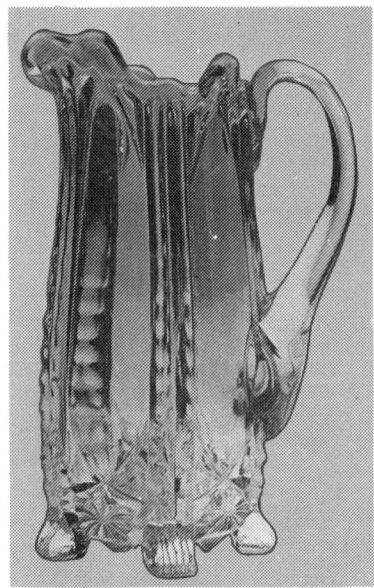
Pentagon

Persian

Creamer (ill.)	31-42
Goblet	28-38
Mug	28-38
Nappys, fruit, 6″, 7″, 8″	12-24
Pitcher, ½ gal.	38-50
Sugar bowl, covered	36-47

Many other pieces.

Pert

(Ribbed Forget-Me-Not): Bryce Bros., 1880. Clear.

Butter dish, covered	$32-41
Creamer (ill.)	28-38
Spoonholder	19-27
Sugar bowl, covered	29-36

Probably these pieces made for a whist table.

514

Pert

Petal and Loop

Petal and Loop

Sandwich, early; later produced by O'Hara Glass Company, Pittsburgh; they called it the "O'Hara" pattern (see Loop). The piece shown here is Sandwich; smaller petals and loop designs on base of standard.

Compote (ill.) $98-115
Dish, honey 30- 42

Philadelphia

New England Glass Company, c. 1860s, clear, flint.

Bowl, covered $27-37
Celery 32-41
Egg cup 26-36
Goblet 47-54
Spoonholder 27-39
Sugar bowl
  a. Open 22-29
  b. Covered 36-48

Wine 38-48
Possibly other pieces.

Picket

Picket

(London): King Glass Company, Pittsburgh, late 1880s. Clear, stippled.

Butter dish, covered $52-62
Celery vase 40-48
Compote
  a. Covered, 6", 8", high foot.... 49-59
  b. Open, high, low foot 34-44
Creamer 42-49
Goblet 33-49
Marmalade jar 34-39
Match holder 27-36
Pickle jar, with cover 40-50
Pitcher, water (ill.) 52-70
Salt, flat, oblong............... 12-21
Saucedish 18-29
Spoonholder 24-34
Sugar bowl, covered 51-62
Tray for water set 51-58

Pigs in Corn

(continued)

Pigs in Corn

Maker unknown, 1875-1885. Clear, goblet only.

    Goblet (ill.) $138-162

Pilgrim Bottle

Pilgrim Bottle

Variant; maker and date unknown. May come in colors or trimmed with ruby or gilt.

    Bottle (ill.) $55-68

Pillar

Pillar

(Loop): Bakewell, Pears & Company, Pittsburgh, Pennsylvania, c. 1850s, clear, flint.

    Ale (ill.) $52-64
    Bottle, bar, 7" 40-50
    Cordial 68-79
    Creamer 72-81
    Decanter, no stopper 50-60
    Sauce, flat 17-22
    Sugar bowl, covered 58-69

Should be other pieces.

Pillow and Sunburst

Pillow and Sunburst

(Elite): Westmoreland Specialty Company, 1891; again in 1896; again in 1917. Clear.

    Butter dish, covered $37-47
    Celery 26-38
    Compote
      a. Covered 40-50
      b. Open 22-32
    Creamer 28-37
    Goblet 28-39
    Pitcher, water (ill.) 39-49
    Spoonholder 18-27
    Sugar bowl 32-39

Probably other pieces.

Pillow Bands

Pillow Bands

Maker unknown. Clear and colors.

Berry bowl $27-37
Butter dish 36-45
Celery 26-34
Compote
  a. Covered 34-43
  b. Open 27-37
Creamer 19-27
Cruet, cobalt blue 39-49
Goblet 28-38
Pitcher (ill.).................. 34-44
Spoonholder 21-31
Sugar bowl, covered 27-37

Probably others. Colors 50 percent more than clear prices listed.

Pillow Encircled

Pillow Encircled

Maker unknown, early 1890s. Clear and ruby flashed.

Butter dish, covered $32-42
Compote
  a. Covered 40-50
  b. Open 31-41
Creamer 27-37
Dish, oval..................... 11-21
Pitcher (ill.).................. 36-42
Sauce 12-19
Spoonholder 18-27
Sugar bowl
  a. Covered 29-39
  b. Open 16-24
Tumbler 17-27

Probably other pieces. Ruby flashing, 50 percent higher than clear prices listed.

Pineapple   <small>Pineapple</small>

Hobbs, Brockunier & Company, Wheeling, West Virginia, 1886. Clear, opalescent, colors.

Butter dish, covered $42-53
Celery 28-38
Pitcher (ill.).................. 51-61
Spoonholder 28-38
Sugar bowl
  a. Covered 42-53
  b. Open 27-39

Other pieces. Opalescent and colors, 50 percent higher than clear prices listed.

Pineapple and Fan

Pineapple and Fan

Adams & Company, Pittsburgh; later by U.S. Glass Company, 1891. Clear, color.

Bowl, berry, 8", 9" $23-33
Butter dish, covered 42-52
Cake stand 28-38
Celery, medium, tall 27-38
Creamer, individual, large 24-34
Mug 22-32
Pitcher
  a. Half gallon, ¾ gallon,
    tankard 50-60
  b. One quart, one pint,
    water 40-50

(continued)

Sauce, 4″, 4½″ 12-19
Spoonholder, laydown type 27-33
Sugar bowl
  a. Individual, covered 29-42
  b. Large, covered 47-52
Tumbler, water, whiskey 24-34
Probably other pieces. Color, 50 percent higher than clear prices listed.

Pioneer's No. 15

Pioneer's No. 15

Pioneer Glass Company, Pittsburgh, Pennsylvania, c. 1890s, clear with ruby stain.

Butter dish covered $22-34
Compote, covered 27-37
Creamer 22-32
Goblet 19-29
Pitcher, milk 37-43
Salt/Pepper, pr. 15-23
Spoonholder 18-26
Sugar bowl, covered 22-32
Tumbler (ill.) 18-27
Wine 15-24

Probably other pieces.

Pioneer's Victoria

Pioneer's Victoria

Pioneer Glass Company, 1885. Crystal glass with ruby stain. Some pieces are engraved.

Butter dish, covered $32-42
Celery 24-33
Compote, high, low standards.... 27-36
Creamer 20-30
Egg cup 22-32
Goblet 19-27
Pitcher, water (ill.) 26-35
Sauce 18-27
Spoonholder 22-31
Sugar bowl 28-37

Probably other pieces. Ruby stain has no effect on price.

Plaid

Plaid

Maker unknown, rare pattern of the 1880s. Clear.

Celery $27-36
Creamer 24-36
Goblet 22-29
Pitcher, water (ill.) 39-48
Sugar bowl, open 24-36

Possibly other pieces.

Plain Tulip

Possibly Sandwich, 1850s. Clear.

Celery $22-34
Compote
  a. Covered, large, high
    standard 58-68
  b. Open, large............... 40-50
Creamer 37-47
Goblet 27-36

Plain Tulip

Pitcher
a. Syrup (ill.) 29-39
b. Water 48-58
Spoonholder 26-36
Sugar bowl 32-44
Tumbler 20-30
Wine 18-24

Probably other pieces.

Pleat and Panel

Pleat and Panel

(Derby): Bryce Bros., Pittsburgh, 1870s; they called it Derby; it is better known as Pleat and Panel today. Clear, amethyst, yellow, blue.

Butter dish, covered $40-50
Cake plate, square, on standard
  9″, 9¼″ 38-47
Compote, covered and open 46-52
Creamer 33-43
Dish, oblong and square 29-39
Goblet, 2 types 27-36
Lamp, 9¼″ high 38-44

Pickle dish 15-22
Pitcher, water, milk (ill.) 48-59
Plate, square, 3½″, 6″, 7½″, 8½″ .. 32-42
Platter, closed, open handles 37-47
Salt/Pepper, pr. 27-37
Spoonholder 26-36
Sugar bowl, covered 42-52

Probably other pieces. Colors, 75 percent higher than clear prices listed. 7″ plate, 7½″ plate and goblet being reproduced.

Pleating

(Flat Panel): Bryce Brothers, Pittsburgh; Gillinder & Sons, Philadelphia, c. 1880s. Reissued by U.S. Glass Company, c. 1891, clear, flashed in red.

Butter dish, covered $33-42
Cake stand 27-36
Celery 14-22
Compote
  a. Open 19-27
  b. Covered 34-42
Creamer 26-33
Pitcher, water................ 27-36
Spoonholder 26-36
Sugar bowl, covered 32-48

Flashed in red, 60 percent higher than clear; Bryce Brothers prices listed.

Plume

Plume

Adams Glass Company, 1874. Clear, red-flashed.

Bowl, berry, finger.............. $21-30
Butter dish, covered 40-50
Cake stand 42-52
Celery 35-45
Compote
  a. Covered 52-62
  b. Open, scalloped top 39-46

519

(continued)

Creamer 37-47
Goblet 27-38
Pickle 16-27
Pitcher, water (ill.) 52-61
Sauce 18-24
Spoonholder 40-50
Sugar bowl, covered 40-52
Tray, water 58-68
Tumbler 22-38

Probably other pieces. Red-flashed 25 percent higher than clear prices listed. Goblet being reproduced.

Plume and Block

Plume and Block

Richards & Hartley Glass Company, Tarentum, Pennsylvania, 1885-1891, clear, clear with ruby stain.

Butter dish, covered $32-47
Celery (ill.) 22-29
Compotes, 4″, 6″, 8″ 28-38
Creamer 21-31
Pitcher, ½ gal., gal. 44-54
Spoonholder 27-36
Sugar bowl, covered 34-44

Possibly other pieces.

Plutec

McKee Glass Company, Jeannette, Pennsylvania, c. early 1900s, clear, non-flint. All pieces marked "Prescut."

Bowl, nut $16-25
Butter dish, covered 22-34
Cake stand 30-40
Compote, covered 22-34

Plutec

Creamer 19-27
Dish, pickle 10-18
Goblet (ill.) 20-31
Pitcher, water 32-43
Spoonholder 21-31
Sugar bowl, covered 21-31

Many other pieces.

Pointed Cube

Pointed Cube

Maker unknown, c. 1880s, clear and frosted.

Decanter $25-35
Tray, wine 18-27
Wine (ill.).................... 16-27

Frosted, 20 percent higher than clear prices listed. Probably other pieces.

Pointed Jewel

Columbia Glass Company, Findlay, Ohio, 1880s; later U.S. Glass Company, 1892. Clear.

Pointed Jewel

Polar Bear

Butter dish, covered	$40-50
Creamer	19-27
Custard cup	9-18
Goblet	18-27
Pitcher (ill.)	32-42
Spoonholder	32-42
Sugar bowl	34-43
Tumbler	26-35
Wine	20-32

Probably other pieces.

Polar Bear

(Iceberg; Arctic; North Pole): Crystal Glass Company, Bridgeport, Ohio, 1880s. Clear; partly frosted.

Bowl, waste	$ 68- 74
Butter dish, clear	92-115
Creamer, clear	72- 92
Goblet	
a. Clear	110-126
b. Frosted	92-108
Pickle dish	40- 50
Pitcher, water, frosted (ill.)	210-240
Platter, oval, handled	97-110
Sauce	36- 47
Spoonholder	50- 60
Sugar bowl, covered	94-110
Tray, water, round, oval	158-172

Probably other pieces. Frosted, 10 percent higher than clear prices listed.

Popcorn

Sandwich, 1860s. Crystal only.

Butter dish	$72-80
Cordial	62-72
Creamer	74-83
Goblet, with and without ear	50-60

Popcorn

Pitcher, water (ill.)	79-86
Sauce	28-38
Spoonholder	56-66
Sugar bowl	75-85
Wine	37-47

Probably other pieces.

Portland

Portland

Middle-west, 1880s. Clear and with gilt.

Bride's basket in frame	$78-88
Butter dish, covered	40-50
Celery	32-42
Compote, covered, jelly	36-46
Creamer	40-50
Cruet (ill.)	27-37
Goblet	30-40
Jam jar	27-37
Pitcher, water	43-53
Punch bowl	42-60
Spoonholder	28-38
Sugar bowl	34-44
Sugar shaker	46-56
Tumbler	28-38
Wine	27-37

Many other pieces made.

Powder and Shot

Powder and Shot

Originally Sandwich; other makers unknown. Clear.

Butter dish	$66-76
Castor bottle	28-38
Celery	53-63
Compote, covered, high and low standard	74-84
Creamer	63-73
Egg cup	34-44
Goblet	62-80
Pitcher, water (ill.)	75-88
Sauce	22-32
Spoonholder	40-54
Sugar bowl	78-86
Tumbler	32-43

Pressed Diamond

Pressed Diamond

Central Glass Company, Wheeling, West Virginia. Clear, yellow, amber, blue (scarce).

Butter dish, covered	$39-50
Celery	36-47
Creamer	28-38

Compote	
a. Covered	40-50
b. Open	27-37
Goblet	26-36
Pitcher (ill.)	34-43
Spoonholder	18-24
Sugar bowl, covered	38-50
Tumbler	22-29

Probably other pieces. Yellow, 70 percent higher; amber, blue, 125 percent higher than clear prices listed.

Pressed Leaf

Pressed Leaf

(N.P.L.): Sandwich, early; Central Glass Company, Wheeling, West Virginia, 1881; McKee Bros., Pittsburgh, 1868, called it N.P.L. Clear.

Bowl, open, high and low foot 7″, 8″	$33- 43
Butter dish, covered	45- 55
Cake plate on stand	62- 72
Compote, covered, high, low standard, 6″, 7″, 8″	50- 60
Cordial	27- 37
Creamer	54- 64
Dish, oval, 5″, 6″, 8″, 9″	23- 33
Egg cup	28- 38
Goblet	29- 39
Lamp, applied handle	52- 61
Pitcher, water (ill.)	88-110
Sauce	24- 36
Spoonholder	40- 50
Sugar bowl	55- 65
Wine	54- 64

Probably other pieces.

Primrose

Canton Glass Company, Canton, Ohio, 1880s. Crystal, amber, canary, blue, apple

Primrose

green, opaque-white, turquoise, purple slag, opaque-black. Apple green and yellow, rarest colors.

Bowl, berry, round, deep	$28-37
Butter dish	46-52
Cake plate on standard	42-52
Compote, covered, 6″, 7½″, 8″, 9″	58-68
Creamer	44-54
Goblet, plain, knob stem	23-37
Pickle dish	22-31
Pitcher, water, milk (ill.)	54-63
Plate, 4½″, 6″, 7″, 8¾″, cake	22-34
Sauce, footed, 4″, 5½″	19-28
Spoonholder	40-50
Sugar bowl,° covered	44-54

Probably other pieces. Yellow and amber 55 percent higher; blue, 80 percent higher than clear prices listed.

Princess Feather

(Lacy Medallion; Rochelle): Sandwich called it Princess Feather; Bakewell, Pears, Blackwell & Company called it Rochelle. It was also called Lacy Medallion by U.S. Glass Company, late 1880s. Clear, opaque white.

Butter dish	$ 70- 80
Celery	50- 60
Compote	
a. Covered, 6″, 7″, high	
standard	78- 88

Princess Feather

b. Open, 8″, low standard	54- 64
Creamer	64- 73
Egg cup	37- 46
Goblet	44- 54
Honey dish	19- 28
Pitcher, quart, half gallon	110-132
Plate, 6″, 7″, 8″, 9″, cake	40- 50
Spoonholder	44- 52
Sugar bowl, open	72- 82

Opaque white, 50 percent higher than clear.

Printed Hobnail

Printed Hobnail

Maker unknown, 1880s. Clear, amber, canary, blue, green, amethyst.

Butter dish	$37-44
Celery vase	28-38

(continued)

Creamer	32-42
Goblet	33-43
Mug, handled	27-38
Pitcher, water	46-54
Saucedish, 4"	22-33
Spoonholder	34-44
Sugar bowl	40-50
Tray for water set	38-48
Tumbler	32-42
Wine	29-38

Probably other pieces. Amber, canary 60 percent higher; blue, green, amethyst, at least 125 percent higher than clear prices listed.

Priscilla

Priscilla

(Alexis; Sun and Star): Dalzell, Gilmore & Leighton Company, Findlay, Ohio, 1890s. Clear, with red dots.

Bowl, square, 8", flat, 10½", rose	$33- 42
Butter dish, covered	52- 62
Cake stand, 10" dia.	49- 58
Celery	34- 44
Compote	
a. Covered, 7"	62- 72
b. 5" high	30- 40
c. Open, 7½"	46- 56
Creamer	48- 58
Goblet	34- 43
Mug	25- 34
Pitcher, water	97-110
Spoonholder	33- 43
Sugar bowl, covered	52- 62
Toothpick holder	38- 58
Tumbler (ill.)	27- 38
Wine	40- 50

Probably other pieces. With red dots 40 percent higher than clear prices listed.

Rose bowl, compote, goblet, sauce, toothpick holder and wine being reproduced.

Prism

Prism

Maker unknown, c. 1860s, flint and non-flint. Don't confuse it with "Prism and Flute" — their trade name was also "Prism," a non-flint product.

Champagne	$42-52
Compote, open	42-51
Creamer	63-72
Decanter	50-60
Goblet (ill.)	42-51
Pitcher	68-79
Wine	40-50

Non-flint, 50 percent lower than flint prices listed. Probably other pieces.

Prism and Flattened Sawtooth

Prism and Flattened Sawtooth

(Ribbed Pineapple): Maker unknown, 1850s. Clear.

Goblet (ill.)	$52-62

Lamp 63-73
Spoonholder (or spill) 44-54
Sugar bowl, open 52-63
Probably other pieces.

Prism with Diamond Points

Possibly Sandwich Glass, early; or Midwest, c. 1860s, clear.

Butter dish, covered .... $ 68- 78
Compote, covered, knob stem .. 120-130
Cordial..................... 40- 50
Creamer 80- 90
Egg cup 39- 49
Goblet
  a. Plain stem 41- 52
  b. Knob stem 60- 70
Pitcher, 6½" high 82- 92
Spoonholder 52- 61
Sugar bowl, covered 60- 70
Tumbler 52- 62
Wine...................... 54- 64

Psyche and Cupid

Psyche and Cupid

Possibly Hartley Glass Company, Tarentum, Pennsylvania, 1880s. Clear.

Butter dish $54-64
Celery 52-62
Compote, high, low standard 59-69
Creamer 60-70
Goblet 34-44
Jam jar..................... 38-48
Pickle dish 27-37
Pitcher, water (ill.) 62-72
Sauce 22-32
Spoonholder 60-70
Sugar bowl 55-65
Wine...................... 29-39

Probably other pieces.

Quartered Block

George Duncan's Sons & Company, Washington, Pennsylvania, c. 1894, clear, non-flint; possibly clear with colored top.

Butter dish, covered $33-43
Cake plate, flat, high 27-37
Celery 22-32
Compote
  a. Low standard.............. 28-38
  b. High standard 30-40
Creamer, pt. 27-37
Dish, horseradish 18-23
Goblet 19-29
Spoonholder 17-27
Sugar bowl
  a. Open 15-28
  b. Covered 28-37
Tub, ice...................... 30-40

Many other pieces. If clear with colored top, 20 percent higher than clear prices listed.

Quatrefoil

Quatrefoil

Maker unknown, 1880s. Clear, apple green.

Bowl $18- 28
Butter dish, covered 37- 47
Compote, covered............. 33- 43
Creamer..................... 27- 37
Goblet (rare)................. 80- 90
Pitcher (ill.) 40- 50
Salt/Pepper, pr. 18- 29
Spoonholder 16- 27
Sugar bowl
  a. Covered.................. 27- 38
  b. Open 18- 24
Tumbler (some say it was never
  made) .... 98-140+

Colors, 75 percent higher than clear prices listed.

Queen   Queen Anne

Queen

(Sunk, Pointed Panel; Panelled Daisy and Button): McKee Glass Company, Jeannette, Pennsylvania, 1894; other factories same period. Clear, yellow, amber, apple green, blue.

Butter dish, covered $38-48
Compote
  a. Covered 42-52
  b. Open 30-40
Creamer 32-42
Goblet 29-39
Pitcher, water (ill.) 43-53
Sauce, oval 12-17
Spoonholder 21-31
Sugar bowl
  a. Covered 38-48
  b. Open 26-36
Tumbler 28-38

Probably other pieces. Yellow, 50 percent; amber, apple green, 60 percent; blue, 80 percent higher than clear prices listed.

Queen Anne

(Bearded Man; Santa Claus; Neptune): La Belle Glass Company, Bridgeport, Ohio, 1878. Clear.

Butter dish $50-60
Celery 40-50
Compote, covered, 7", 8" 58-68

Creamer 42-52
Pitcher, water, syrup (ill.) 70-80
Sauce, footed, 4½" 34-43
Spoonholder 37-47
Sugar bowl, open 42-52
Probably other pieces.

Quilt and Flute

Quilt and Flute

Maker and date unknown. Clear. Probably made for use as a container for mustard.

Creamer (ill.) $19-28
Mustard jar 16-26
Sugar bowl 22-31
Possibly other pieces.

Quixote

Quixote

Tarentum Glass Company, Tarentum, Pennsylvania, 1899.

Butter dish $40-50
Celery 21-31
Goblet 26-36

Pitcher (ill.) 48-52
Spoonholder 18-27
Sugar bowl 29-38

Probably other pieces.

Racing Deer

Racing Deer

Probably Indiana Tumbler & Goblet Company, late 1890s. Clear, chocolate.
Pitcher, water - chocolate $210-228
Pitcher, water - clear (ill.) 88- 99

Radiant

(Dynast): Maker unknown, c. late 1880s, clear, etched, non-flint.
Butter dish, covered $40-50
Cake plate 40-50
Celery 19-27
Compote
  a. Open 19-28
  b. Covered 40-50
Creamer 30-40
Goblet 29-39
Pitcher, syrup 40-50
Salt/Pepper, pr. 33-43
Spoonholder 19-27
Sugar bowl, covered 34-44
Tumbler 27-37
Wine 22-28

Clear, etched, same price. Probably other pieces.

Rainbow

McKee & Brothers, Pittsburgh, c. 1894, "Rose pink," gold decorated. McKee was the first of the manufacturers to use a permanent trademark, "Pres-Cut," 1894, in the glass.
Butter dish, covered $48-58
Carafe 40-50
Creamer 37-47
Goblet 34-43
Jar, cigar, gold or silver lid 33-42
Pitcher, water 78-82
Tumbler 29-36
Wine 27-34

Many other pieces.

Raindrop

Raindrop

Maker unknown, c. 1880s, clear, canary, amber, blue, light green (rare), non-flint.
Bowl (ill.) $16-25
Butter dish, covered 38-49
Compote, open, high, low
  standard 29-46
Creamer 30-38
Egg cup 20-30
Pitcher, syrup 33-43
Sauce, flat, footed 16-24
Tray, large 35-45

Canary, 70 percent higher; amber, blue, 100 percent higher; light green, 150 percent higher than clear prices listed.

Raspberry

Maker unknown, late 1870s. Clear.
Butter dish, covered $39-40
Celery 22-32
Compote
  a. Covered 31-41
  b. Open 20-30
Creamer 25-35

(continued)

Raspberry

Goblet	24-34
Pitcher, water (ill.)	39-49
Spoonholder	21-31
Sugar bowl, covered	34-44
Tumbler	25-35

Probably other pieces.

Ray

Ray

McKee Bros., 1894. Plain or engraved or ruby-stained or frosted on the plain parts.

Bowls, round, 6", 7"	$26-35
Celery vase, tall	28-38
Dish, oblong, deep, 7", 9"	24-39
Pitcher (ill.)	42-53
Plate, 6"	20-30
Saucedish, round, 4", 5", footed	17-26
Sugar bowl	
a. Covered	39-49
b. Open	26-36

Probably other pieces. Ruby-stained, 40 percent higher than clear prices listed.

Red Block

Red Block

Doyle & Company, reproduced by U.S. Glass Company, 1892 and later. Clear, blocks painted red.

Butter dish	$75- 88
Celery vase	62- 72
Creamer, large and individual	66- 77
Dish	
a. Cheese	93-110
b. Oblong, 8", 9", 10"	42- 52
Goblet	53- 63
Pitcher, water (ill.)	92-110
Salt/Pepper, pr.	50- 60
Spoonholder, double handled	36- 48
Sugar bowl	72- 81
Tumbler	36- 47
Wine bottle	54- 66
Wine glass	39- 49

Probably other pieces. Red, 25 percent higher than clear prices listed. Goblet and wine being reproduced.

Reticulated Cord

528

Reticulated Cord

Maker unknown, 1880s. Clear; color scarce.

Butter dish, covered $40-50
Cake stand, large 42-52
Celery vase 26-36
Creamer 34-44
Pitcher, water (ill.) 48-58
Relish 13-26
Spoonholder 22-32
Sugar bowl
  a. Covered 40-50
  b. Open 31-41
Tumbler 19-27
Wine........................ 18-26

Probably other pieces. Color, 150 percent higher than clear prices listed.

Ribbed Forget-Me-Not

Ribbed Forget-Me-Not

(Pert): Bryce, McKee & Company, 1880. Clear.

Butter dish, covered $36-46
Creamer 34-44
Cup, handled 19-29
Mustard jar with cover.......... 30-40
Pitcher (ill.).................... 43-53
Spoonholder 27-37
Sugar bowl, covered 36-46

Probably other pieces.

Rexford

Rexford

Tarentum Glass Company, Tarentum, Pennsylvania, 1912-1918, clear glass only. Pieces were made with flared, straight, or belled edges.

Butter dish, covered $26-36
Cake stand, 9¾" 24-34
Celery 22-32
Creamer 24-33
Goblet 23-29
Pitcher....................... 33-44
Spoonholder (ill.) 22-32
Sugar bowl, covered 30-40
Wine........................ 22-32

Many other pieces.

Ribbed Grape

Ribbed Grape

Maker unknown, possibly Sandwich, 1850s. Clear.

Butter dish, covered ....$ 82- 94
Celery vase.................. 51- 62
Compote
  a. Covered, 6", high
    standard 139-152
  b. Open, low foot 67- 77
Cordial...................... 64- 74
Creamer 133-140
Goblet 54- 64
Pitcher (ill.) 170-190

(continued)

Spoonholder	41- 50
Sugar bowl, covered	82- 92

Probably other pieces.

Ribbed Opal

Ribbed Opal

(Beatty Rib): A. J. Beatty Glass Company, Steubenville, Ohio, 1888. Crystal, amber, blue, canary, three opalescent colors.

Creamer, large	$34-38
Mug	26-36
Pitcher, water (ill.)	48-58
Relish	26-36
Sugar	
a. Bowl	39-49
b. Shaker	35-45
Tumbler, 2 types	34-44
Wine	26-36

Probably other pieces. Blue opalescent, 80 percent higher; yellow opalescent, 150 percent higher than clear prices listed.

Ribbed Palm

Ribbed Palm

(Sprig): McKee & Bros., Pittsburgh, 1868. Clear.

Butter dish	$ 80- 90
Celery	81- 93

Compote, 7", 8", 10", high,

low standard	71- 84
Creamer	82- 96
Dish, 6", 7", 8", 9", deep	40- 58
Goblet	43- 56
Lamp, three types	74- 84
Pitcher, 9" high, applied	
handle (rare) (ill.)	124-136
Saucedish, 4"	22- 32
Spoonholder	56- 66
Sugar bowl, covered	59- 72
Tumbler, water, whiskey	56- 67
Wine	57- 69

Probably other pieces. Color, 100 percent higher than clear prices listed.

Ribbon

Bakewell, Pears & Company, Pittsburgh, c. 1870, clear, frosted, non-flint.

Butter dish, covered	$ 45- 55
Compote	
a. Dolphin stem, scalloped	360-400
b. Round, rectangular bowl	155-180
Creamer	40- 50
Dish, cheese, covered	110-130
Goblet	42- 52
Spoonholder	36- 44
Sugar bowl, covered	48- 58
Tray, water	110-122
Wine (rare)	115-131

Other pieces.

Ribbon Candy

Ribbon Candy

(Figure Eight; Double Loop; Bryce): Bryce Bros., 1880s; U.S. Glass Company, 1898. Clear.

Bowls, various	$20-30
Butter dish, covered	40-50
Celery	31-41
Cruet	25-37

Cup	15-26
Creamer	32-42
Honey dish	21-31
Pitcher, water, milk, syrup	52-62
Sugar bowl	
a. Covered	36-46
b. Open	30-42
Tumbler	19-29

Probably other pieces.

Richmond

Richmond

Nickel Plate Glass Company, Fostoria, Ohio, 1889, early 1890s. Clear.

Butter dish	$33-43
Celery	24-34
Creamer	23-33
Compote	
a. Covered	44-54
b. Open	29-39
Creamer	32-42
Goblet	27-36
Pitcher, water (ill.)	44-54
Salt/Pepper, pr.	26-36
Spoonholder	22-32
Sugar bowl	39-49
Tumbler	24-34
Wine	23-33

Probably other pieces.

Richmond

Richards & Hartley Glass Company, Tarentum, Pennsylvania, 1885-1891, clear glass only.

Butter dish, covered	$30-40
Celery (ill.)	21-31
Compotes, 4″, 6″, 7″, 8″	16-39
Creamer	14-26
Goblet	20-29
Pitcher, qt., ½ gal.	38-49
Sugar shaker	17-26

Richmond

Sugar bowl, covered	27-39
Tumbler	18-29
Wine	21-31

Probably other pieces.

Ringed Framed Ovals

Ringed Framed Ovals

An "Oval" pattern originating at Sandwich Glass Company in the 1840s; clear, vaseline, apple green, flint.

Goblet	$69-76
Tumbler (ill.)	79-92

Vaseline, 25 percent; apple green, 40 percent higher than clear prices listed.

Ripple

(Ripple Band): Sandwich, last 1870s, clear, non-flint. Inferior as far as Sandwich glass is concerned.

Bowl, oval	$18-24
Butter dish, covered	27-38
Compote	
a. Open	24-34
b. Covered	33-42

531

(continued)

Creamer 31-41
Goblet....................... 22-39
Lamp 28-38
Salt, footed, oval.............. 14-26
Spoonholder 19-27
Sugar bowl, covered 36-46
Wine........................ 24-34

Probably other pieces.

Roanoke

Roanoke

Gillinder & Sons, Greensburg, Pennsylvania, 1885; later by U.S. Glass Company, 1898. Clear, amber, emerald green.

Butter dish, covered $36-46
Celery 26-36
Creamer (ill.) 27-37
Goblet 32-42
Spoonholder 19-28
Sugar bowl, covered 34-43
Tumbler 27-39
Water pitcher 42-52

Probably many other pieces. Colors, 200-250 percent higher than for clear prices listed.

Robin Hood

Robin Hood

Fostoria Glass Company, 1898. Clear.

Butter dish $32-43
Celery 31-42
Creamer (ill.) 33-41
Compote
  a. Covered 38-46
  b. Open 33-48
Goblet 29-39
Pitcher, water 42-52
Spoonholder 31-41
Sugar bowl 40-50
Tumbler 29-36

Probably other pieces.

Rock Crystal

McKee Glass Company, Jeannette, Pennsylvania, c. 1894, clear, colors, non-flint.

Butter dish, covered $28-39
Cake stand 20-30
Celery 22-32
Creamer 22-32
Cup, custard 15-27
Glass, sundae 10-20
Goblet 17-27
Pitcher...................... 29-40
Spoonholder 18-26
Sugar bowl, covered 22-34

Colors, 50 percent higher than clear prices listed. Many other pieces.

Roman Rosette

Roman Rosette

Bryce, Walker & Company, 1875. Reproduced by U.S. Glass Company, in 1892, again in 1898. Clear; few pieces in color; clear pieces sometimes decorated with ruby on vertical ribbing.

Bowl, 5″, 6″, 7″, 8″	$35-45
Butter dish, covered	44-54
Cake plate on stand, 9″, 10″ (rare)	68-78
Castor set	63-73
Celery	40-50
Compote, covered, high, low standard, 5″, 6″, 7″, 8″	58-69
Creamer, one pint	53-63
Goblet	32-42
Mug, large, medium	30-40
Pickle dish	28-39
Pitcher, water, half gallon, quart, syrup	44-55
Sauce, flat, footed	18-27
Salt/Pepper, pr.	34-44
Spoonholder	44-56
Sugar bowl, covered	52-62
Tumbler	41-50
Wine	44-53

Probably other pieces. Goblet being reproduced. Red color, 25 percent higher than clear prices listed.

Rope Bands

Rope Bands

(Clear Panels with Cord Band): Possibly McKee & Son, Pittsburgh, late 1870s. Clear; color, scarce.

Cake stand, large	$42-51
Celery	27-37
Compote, covered	40-50
Creamer (ill.)	26-36
Goblet	22-31
Platter	26-38
Sugar	
a. Covered	32-42
b. Open	25-35
Tumbler	19-28

Probably other pieces. Color, 150 percent higher than prices listed.

Rose-in-Snow

Rose-in-Snow

Bryce Bros., Pittsburgh, 1870s. Clear, amber, blue, yellow.

Butter dish, round, square	$69-82
Compote, covered, high low standard	75-84
Creamer, round, square	58-68
Dish, oval, large, small	44-54
Goblet	44-56
Mug	46-54
Pitcher, water, milk (ill.)	74-84
Plate, 5″, 6″, 7¼″, 9″ (5″ rare)	46-57
Sauce, flat, round, square	22-32
Spoonholder, round, square	49-59
Sugar bowl, round, square	48-58
Tumbler, water	46-56

Probably other pieces. Colors, 40-50 percent higher than clear prices listed. Pieces made in round and square shapes. Goblet, mug and 9″ plate being reproduced.

Rose Leaves

Rose Leaves

Maker unknown, c. 1880s, clear, non-flint.

Goblet (ill.) $28-32
Other pieces?

Rose Point Band

Rose Point Band

(Water Lily): Maker unknown early 1900s. Clear.

Butter dish $27-36
Celery 24-35
Creamer (ill.) 30-40
Goblet 22-32
Spoonholder 19-29
Sugar bowl, covered 32-42

Probably other pieces.

Rose Sprig

Campbell, Jones & Company, Pittsburgh, 1886. Clear, amber, yellow, blue.

Butter dish $42-54

Rose Sprig

Cake plate on stand 43-53
Celery vase 39-49
Creamer 36-46
Dish, three styles 30-40
Goblet 32-42
Mug, handled 37-47
Pitcher, water, two sizes (ill.) 46-56
Plate, 6½″, 10½″, square 28-38
Platter 36-46
Salt, sleigh 42-52
Spoonholder 30-40
Sugar bowl, covered 42-50
Tray, water 35-45
Tumbler 30-40

Probably other pieces. Colors, 40-50 percent higher than clear prices listed.

Rosette

Rosette

(Magic): Bryce Bros., Pittsburgh, called it Magic. Later produced by U.S. Glass Company, Tiffin, Ohio, who also called it Magic. Clear.

Butter dish, covered $47-57
Cake plates on stand, 9″, 10″, 11″ . 42-52
Celery 33-43
Compote
  a. Covered, high standard, 6″
     7″, 8″ 55-65
  b. Open, footed, 6″, 7″, 8″
     9″, 10″ 38-56

Creamer	37-48
Goblet	32-42
Pitcher, water, quart	
half gallon (ill.)	48-58
Plate, 7″, 9″, handled	34-47
Relish (fish shape)	32-42
Spoonholder	48-60
Sugar bowl, covered	47-59
Tumbler	22-29
Wine	30-40

Probably other pieces.

Rosette with Pinwheels

Rosette with Pinwheels

Possibly U.S. Glass Company, after 1895. Clear.

Butter dish, covered	$38-48
Celery	26-36
Creamer	31-41
Pitcher, water (ill.)	54-63
Spoonholder	27-37
Sugar bowl, covered	29-42

Probably other pieces.

Royal

Royal

Belmont Glass Company, Bellaire, Ohio, 1881. Clear.

| Butter dish | $47-56 |

Celery	24-36
Compote, covered 8″ high	33-42
Creamer	32-42
Goblet	29-39
Pitcher, water	42-52
Spoonholder	23-33
Sugar bowl, covered (ill.)	37-47
Tumbler	26-36

Probably other pieces.

Royal Crystal

Royal Crystal

Tarentum Glass Company, Tarentum, Pennsylvania, 1894. Clear, ruby flashed. Also known as Atlanta.

Butter dish, covered	$63-73
Celery	29-39
Compote, open, 7¾″	40-50
Creamer	25-35
Pitcher (ill.)	63-73
Sauce, flat	14-19
Spoonholder	27-37
Sugar bowl	
a. Covered	51-61
b. Open	28-39

Probably other pieces. Red or amber flashing, 50 percent higher than clear prices listed.

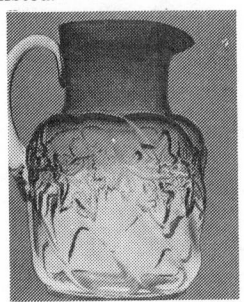

Royal Ivy

(continued)

Royal Ivy

Northwood Glass Company, Martins Ferry, Ohio, 1889-1890. Clear, deep pink/clear; deep pink/clear, acid finished; pink/clear, amber mottled.

Bowl, open, 7"	$ 42- 52
Butter dish, covered, clear to frosted	121-141
Creamer	40- 50
Pitcher	
a. Syrup	41- 52
b. Water	62- 72
Shakers	
a. Salt/Pepper, pr.	68- 80
b. Sugar	52- 62
Sugar bowl, covered	48- 57
Toothpick holder	42- 52
Tumbler	40- 50

Probably other pieces. All color patterns at least 150 percent higher than clear prices listed.

Ruffled Edge Hobnail

Royal Oak

Royal Oak

Northwood Glass Company, Martins Ferry, Ohio, 1889-1890. Flint, deep pink/clear; deep pink/clear, acid finished; pink/clear, amber mottled.

Prices same as Royal Ivy, flint and colors.

Ruffled Edge Hobnail

Maker and date unknown.

Bowl, finger	$26-26
Butter dish, covered	34-44
Celery	19-28
Creamer (ill.)	32-43
Sugar bowl, squat	42-51
Tumbler	20-30

Probably other pieces.

Ruffled Eye

Ruffled Eye

Indiana Tumbler & Goblet (National) Company, 1890s, this pattern is similar to Indiana's Dewey. Known to have been made in water pitcher.

Blue	$162-180
Amber	161-188
Green	141-152

Probably other pieces but not known to this writer.

Saint Bernard

Fostoria Glass Company, Moundsville, West Virginia, c. 1894, clear, non-flint.

Bowl, berry	$27-37
Compote, covered	41-51
Creamer	25-35

Many other pieces.

Sandwich Block

Sandwich Block

Sandwich, early

Piece shown in photo is blue perfume with stopper. Rare. No price available, but probably $425+.

Sandwich Covered Sugar

Sandwich glass, early. Not pressed glass in the truest sense as it's blown-molded but nevertheless absolutely beautiful and still to be found.

Covered sugar (ill.) $500-575

Sandwich Glass Sugar Bowl

Sandwich Glass Sugar Bowl

Sandwich, later period, blue, amethyst.

Sugar bowl with lid $270-290
Probably creamer to match.... 225-245

Sandwich Covered Sugar

Sandwich Spill

(continued)

Sandwich Spill

Sandwich glass, early 1850s. Another example of magnificent glass.

Sandwich Star

Sandwich Star

Sandwich, early. Clear and amethyst (rare).

Compote
  a. Covered, high standard .. $260-295
  b. Open, supported by 3
     dolphins, flint 625-675
  c. Amethyst, tall (rare),
     flint 780-880
Cordial, flint 260-295
Creamer, flint 260-290
Decanter, quart size 120-140
Goblet (rare), flint 345-375
Pitcher, flint (ill.) .... 975+
Relish dish 54- 64
Spill holder 68- 78
Spoonholder 52- 62

Probably other pieces.

Sawtooth

Sawtooth

(Roanoke): New England Glass Company, and Sandwich, 1860s. Later called Roanoke and made by Ripley & Company, Pittsburgh, 1885. Also made by U.S. Glass Co. (Gillinder-merge).

Bowl, berry .... $ 59- 70
Butter dish 78- 90
Cake stand, 9", 10" 52- 62
Celery vase 75- 84
Compote
  a. Covered, 6", 7", 8", 9",
     10", 11" knob stem 110-120
  b. Open, 6", 7", 8", 10" 62- 72
Creamer 92-102
Decanter, quart size 67- 77
Egg cup 49- 59
Goblet 52- 62
Pitcher, water, quart and
  ½ gal. (ill.) 78- 88
Sauce, 4", 5" 20- 30
Spill holder, octagonal 35- 45
Spoonholder 62- 72
Sugar bowl 78- 88
Tumbler, footed, water 40- 54

Probably other pieces. Goblet, iced tea, sherbet and wine being reproduced in pink. Yuk!

Sawtoothed Honeycomb

Sawtoothed Honeycomb

Steiner Glass Company, Buckhannon, West Virginia, 1906; again in 1908 by Union Stopper Company, Morgantown, West Virginia. Crystal; crystal with central honeycombs in ruby with rims in gold.

Celery $19-32
Creamer (ill.) 25-36
Goblet 24-36
Pitcher 47-60
Spoonholder 22-31
Sugar bowl, covered 36-42

Probably other pieces.

Saxon

Adams & Company, Pittsburgh, Pennsylvania, c. 1880, clear, plain and engraved, opal. Reissued after 1891 by the U.S. Glass Company.

Bowl, oval	$23-33
Butter dish, covered	34-44
Creamer	31-41
Compote	
a. Open	19-32
b. Covered	38-48
Goblet	26-36
Plate, 6″	27-40
Spoonholder	19-29
Sugar bowl, covered	32-42
Tumbler	33-43

Other pieces.

Scalloped Diamond Point

Possibly Central Glass Company, Wheeling, West Virginia, c. 1870s, clear, non-flint.

Bowls, round, oval	$17-27
Butter dish, covered	34-44
Cake stand, large, 10″	32-42
Creamer	36-46
Dish, cheese	36-46
Sauce, flat, footed	12-18
Spoonholder	19-27
Sugar bowl, covered	34-44
Wine	24-34

Probably other pieces.

Scalloped Prism

(Triple Bar): Doyle & Company, Pittsburgh, c. early 1880s, clear, non-flint. Originally called "No. 84" by Doyle. Reissued by U.S. Glass Company in 1891.

Butter dish, covered	$29-38
Goblet	16-27
Spoonholder	16-27
Sugar bowl, covered	29-42
Tumbler	12-23

Other pieces.

Scalloped Tape

(Jewel Band): Maker unknown, 1880s. Clear, amber, canary, blue, apple green.

Butter dish, covered	$32-42

Scalloped Tape

Cake stand	34-44
Celery	26-36
Creamer	29-39
Egg cup	18-27
Goblet	22-32
Pitcher, water (ill.)	42-52
Sauce	16-27
Sugar	
a. Covered	42-54
b. Open	32-42
Wine	19-29

Probably other pieces. All colored pieces at least 40 percent higher than clear prices listed.

Scarab

Scarab

Maker, date unknown, clear, flint.

Goblet (ill.)	$120-135

Other pieces? The goblet is beautiful!

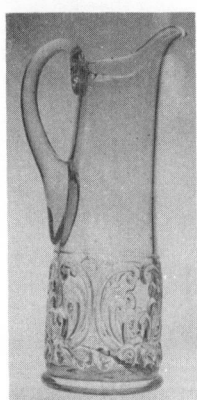

Scroll

Scroll

(Stippled Scroll): Maker unknown, 1880s. Clear.

Butter dish	$42-53
Celery	39-48
Compote, covered, high, low standard	58-68
Creamer	42-52
Egg cup	22-32
Goblet	29-41
Pitcher, tankard type (ill.)	42-52
Spoonholder	37-52
Sugar bowl	48-60
Tumbler	22-34
Wine	27-36

Scroll and Daisy

Scroll and Daisy

Northwood Glass Company, Opaline and Carnival; usual Carnival colors.

Compote, candy or jelly	$48-62
Creamer (probably a mustard jar, with lid, originally) (ill.)	36-45

Colors, 50 percent higher than crystal, marigold prices listed.

Scroll with Acanthus

Scroll with Acanthus

Central Glass Company, Wheeling, West Virginia. Clear, sapphire blue, purple slag. This pattern also was made by Northwood, only in the Mosaic or slag type. The prices shown are Northwood, 1902.

Creamer (ill.)	$70-80
Compote, jelly, tall, stemmed	63-75
Sugar bowl, open	72-84

Apparently these were the only pieces made in this pattern.

Scroll with Flowers

Scroll with Flowers

Central Glass Company, late 1870s. Clear, later made by Northwood in apple green, amber and blue. Possibly other colors made. Prices listed are for Northwood.

Butter dish $40-50
Cake plate, handled 49-59
Celery 42-52
Creamer 46-56
Egg cup, 2 handles 30-40
Goblet 37-47
Mustard, covered 40-50
Pitcher (ill.).................... 48-60
Salt/Pepper, pr. 34-44
Sugar bowl 50-60

Supposedly a rare pattern. Colors 50 percent higher than crystal/marigold prices listed. Probably other pieces.

Scroll with Star

Challinor, Taylor & Company, Tarentum, Pennsylvania, c. 1885, clear, non-flint.

Butter dish $30-40
Cup 15-24
Creamer 23-34
Goblet 25-35
Sauce 14-23
Spoonholder 18-26
Sugar bowl, covered 22-34

Probably other pieces.

Scrolled Spray

Scrolled Spray

Maker unknown, early 1880s. Milk glass. Possibly a Northwood pattern. Probably a mustard container with lid.

Creamer (ill.) $40-52

Blue, 100 percent higher than clear price listed.

Scrolled Sunflower

Scrolled Sunflower

Another of those patterns lost on the back roads of time. Possibly Northwood who made several "Scroll" patterns. Shown for identification only. If you know, tell me.

?

?

Because that's just what it is! An absolutely beautiful pattern. Maker and date unknown and no prices available. Anyone know its name?

Seashell

(Boswell): Maker unknown, c. late 1870s, clear, non-flint.

Butter dish, covered $31-42
Cake stand 27-37
Celery 22-32
Creamer 32-42
Goblet 26-36
Pitcher 29-39
Salt/Pepper, pr. 24-34
Spoonholder 25-35
Sugar bowl, covered 27-37

Probably other pieces.

Shell and Jewel

Butter dish, covered $48-58
Cake stand 42-52
Compote, open, high foot 41-50
Creamer 29-40
Pitcher, water (ill.) 42-52
Spoonholder 30-40
Sugar bowl 37-47
Tumbler 29-39

No goblet made. Probably other pieces. Colors 50 percent higher than clear prices listed.

Seesaw

Seesaw

Probably Gillinder & Sons, c. 1870s.
Plate, 10″ dia. (ill.).............$78-86

Serenade Plate

Indiana Tumbler & Goblet (National) Company, 1890s. Chocolate, white milk glass.

Serenade plate, large $132-142
Serenade plate, small 115-128

Prices given are for chocolate; milk-white, 50-60 percent lower.

Shell and Jewel

(Victor): Westmoreland Glass Company, 1893, originally called it Victor. Better known today as Shell and Jewel. Clear, blue, green.

Shell and Tassel

Shell and Ribbing

Shell and Ribbing

This is blown, 3-mold glass, probably very early Sandwich. Not Pressed Glass but we thought you'd like to see one of the rarest types of glass in the world.

Shell and Tassel

(Square): George A. Duncan & Sons; Shell and Tassel, Round: 10 years later, 1890, Duncan & Heisey. On the Round, the finial on the covered pieces was a dog in a reclining position. Prices given are for both.

Berry set, 7 pcs.	$ 83-	93
Butter dish, round, covered, dog finial	73-	83
Cake stand, large, small	50-	60
Celery vase, round, square	47-	57
Compote		
a. Covered	54-	64
b. Open, 4½", high standard	50-	60
Creamer, round, square	49-	59
Goblet, 2 types	40-	50
Pitcher, round, square (ill.)	51-	61
Platter, bread	62-	72
Salt shaker	27-	38
Spoonholder, round, square	40-	50
Sugar bowl, round, square	50-	60
Vases, pr.	124-138	

Probably other pieces. Colors, rare. 100 percent higher than prices listed for clear. Goblet being reproduced.

Sheraton

Sheraton

(Ida): Bryce, Higbee & Company, Pittsburgh, 1880s, called it Ida. Clear, amber, blue, green; and possibly yellow.

Bowl, berry	$30-40
Butter dish	38-48
Compote, covered	42-53
Creamer	30-40
Goblet	28-38
Pitcher, water	32-42
Sauce, flat	16-26
Sugar bowl, covered	42-52
Tumbler	26-36
Wine	19-27

Amber, blue, 100 percent higher than color prices listed. Probably other pieces.

Shimmering Star

Shimmering Star

Maker unknown, 1880s. Clear. Probably made at an earlier date also.

Butter dish, covered	$39-49
Cake stand	28-38
Pitcher (ill.)	34-44
Sauce, flat	12-19
Spoonholder	22-32
Sugar bowl	
a. Covered	47-57
b. Open	31-41
Tumbler	18-27

Probably other pieces.

Shoshone

Shoshone

(Victor; Blazing Pinwheels): U.S. Glass Co., c. 1895. Crystal, ruby-stained, emerald green.

Butter dish, covered	$33-43
Compote, covered and open, 7", 8½"	32-42
Creamer, 3½", 5" high (ill.)	26-36
Goblet	24-34
Mug	19-28
Pitcher, milk, several sizes	50-62
Spoonholder	19-28
Sugar bowl	29-39

Colors 100 percent higher than clear prices listed.

Shrine

Make unknown, c. 1880s, clear, non-flint.

Bowl	$24-33
Butter dish, covered	48-60
Compote, jelly	28-39
Creamer	47-59
Goblet	23-36
Sauce	8-18
Spoonholder	25-35
Sugar bowl	
a. Open	26-36
b. Covered	39-50
Tumbler	27-38

Probably other pieces.

Shuttle

Shuttle

Indiana Tumbler & Goblet (National) Company, 1900. Chocolate, clear, caramel.

	Chocolate	Clear
Cordial		$12-23
Creamer		37-47
Goblet		43-52
Mug (ill.)	$80-90	32-41
Pitcher, syrup	73-83	33-42
Punch cup	52-62	18-27
Salt/Pepper, pr.		37-46
Saucedish		16-27
Spoonholder	52-62	28-36
Tumbler	40-50	19-27
Wine	26-36	23-32

Caramel, 200 percent more than clear prices listed.

Singing Birds

Singing Birds

Northwood Glass Company, Wheeling, West Virginia, 1900s. Clear, Custard, Carnival, other.

Berry set		
a. Large bowl, marigold	$ 53-	64
Large bowl, vivid	70-	80
b. Small bowl, marigold	19-	29
Small bowl, vivid	31-	41
Mug, custard, marigold, vivid	29-	39
Mug, color, non-iridescent	32-	42
Sherbet, (custard) (rare)	48-	58
Butter dish, covered, clear	32-	42
Butter dish, covered, marigold	68-	78
Butter dish, covered, vivid	120-	134
Sugar bowl, covered, clear	40-	56
Sugar bowl, covered, marigold	47-	53
Sugar bowl, covered, vivid	68-	78
Creamer, clear (ill.)	39-	50
Creamer, marigold	42-	52
Creamer, vivid	64-	74
Spoonholder, clear	30-	40
Spoonholder, marigold	42-	52
Spoonholder, vivid	58-	68
Pitcher, marigold	72-	82
Pitcher, vivid	132-	148
Tumbler, marigold	27-	42
Tumbler, vivid	28-	39

Custard, Carnival, 100 percent higher than clear prices listed.

Single Rose

Probably Westmoreland Specialty Company, c. 1890-1900, clear, opaque white; sometimes colored, in rose and green, gilded.

Butter dish, covered	$40-52
Creamer	33-47
Spoonholder	25-36
Sugar bowl, covered	42-52

Opaque white, 25 percent; rose, 30 percent; green, gilded, 40 percent higher than clear prices listed. Possibly other pieces.

Siskyou

Siskyou

A member of the "Block" family, c. 1880s, clear, non-flint.

Same values as "Block and Fan" — see.

Slashed Swirl

Slashed Swirl

Riverside Glass Company, Wellsburg, West Virginia, 1891. Clear.

Butter dish, covered	$32-42
Celery	23-34
Compote	34-44
Creamer	19-27
Goblet	24-34
Pitcher, water (ill.)	44-54
Salt/Pepper, pr.	22-34
Sugar bowl	29-39

Tumbler 19-27
Wine 18-26
Probably other pieces.

Slewed Horseshoe

Slewed Horseshoe

Possibly Imperial Glass Company, Bellaire, Ohio, after 1906. Clear.

Butter dish	$32-41
Cake stand	28-38
Celery	23-36
Creamer	26-37
Compote	28-38
Goblet	22-29
Pitcher, water, syrup (ill.)	38-49
Spoonholder	15-26
Sugar bowl, covered	34-43
Tumbler	19-26

Probably other pieces.

Smocking

(continued)

Smocking

Sandwich Glass, 1840s. Clear.

Butter dish, covered ....$ 92-106
Compote, footed, open,
  6" high 102-112
Creamer, applied handle
  (rare)..................... 119-142
Goblet 72- 82
Lamp, 9" high............... 105-120
Spill, holder 50- 60
Sugar bowl, covered (ill.) 94-109

Probably other pieces.

Smooth Diamond

Smooth Diamond

Possibly McKee Bros., late 1880s. Clear.

Butter dish $34-44
Compote 29-39
Creamer 27-37
Goblet 26-36
Pitcher, water (ill.) 47-56
Sugar bowl, covered 38-48
Tumbler 24-36

Probably other pieces.

Snail

George Duncan & Sons, Pittsburgh, c. 1880s, clear. After 1891, by U.S. Glass Company, who added ruby color to the plain bands, sometimes engraving through the color.

Bowls, berry, finger $20-29
Butter dish, covered 27-37

Cake stand 28-38
Celery 24-34
Compote, covered 31-41
Creamer, two sizes 16-28
Goblet 22-32
Pitcher, water................. 29-54
Spoonholder 17-28
Sugar bowl
  a. Individual 15-22
  b. Large, covered 30-40
Tumbler 18-29

Ruby colored bands, 100 percent higher than clear prices listed. Many other pieces.

Snakeskin with Dot

Snakeskin with Dot

Maker unknown, late 1870s. Clear, occasionally found in deep blue and in amber.

Celery vase $27-37
Creamer 36-45
Goblet 28-38
Pitcher, water (ill.) 44-54
Plates, 4½" to 7" 19-27
Sugar bowl, covered 34-44

Probably other pieces. Deep blue and amber, 40 percent higher than clear prices listed.

Snow Band

(Puffed Bands): Maker unknown, c. early 1880s, clear, blue, possibly other colors, non-flint.

Butter dish $30-40

Compote
a. Open 19-27
b. Covered 32-42
Creamer 31-40
Goblet 17-25
Pitcher, water 34-44
Relish 18-27
Sauce, flat 12-28
Spoonholder 16-28
Sugar bowl, covered 32-41
Wine......................... 18-28

Blue, 40 percent higher than clear prices listed. Probably other pieces.

Snowdrop

(Ashland): Portland Glass Company, Portland, Maine, c. 1880s, clear.

Dish, ice cream, leaf-shaped $24-34
Goblet 27-37
Tray, ice cream 32-42

Should be other pieces.

Snowflake

Snowflake

Probably U.S. Glass Company, early 1900s. Clear.

Butter dish $38-49
Cake stand 44-54
Celery 21-31
Compote, covered, high, low
   standard 27-37
Creamer 28-39
Goblet 24-33
Pitcher
a. Milk (ill.) 47-57
b. Water 44-52
Spoonholder 20-28
Sugar bowl, covered 33-44
Tumbler 19-29

Probably other pieces.

Southern Ivy

Southern Ivy

Maker unknown, mid-1800s. Clear.

Bowl, berry $34-42
Butter dish, covered 42-52
Creamer 37-47
Cruet, small 43-53
Egg cup 28-38
Pitcher, water (ill.) 48-58
Saucedish, 4" 20-30
Spoonholder 29-39
Sugar bowl, covered 48-58
Tumbler, water 32-42

Probably other pieces made. No goblet made.

Spanish-American

Spanish-American

(Dewey): Bryce Bros., Pittsburgh. Clear, possibly colors, including milk white, 1890s.

Butter dish, covered $54-64
Celery 37-47
Compote 52-65
Creamer 38-47
Goblet 42-54

(continued)

Pitcher (ill.) 62-72
Spoonholder 26-36
Sugar bowl 60-70
Tumbler 39-49

Probably other pieces. At one time given away as a baking powder premium. Tumbler more scarce than pitcher. Don't confuse this "Dewey" with another that's also known as Flower Flange.

Spearpoint Band

Spearpoint Band

Maker and date unknown. Clear with ruby stain.

Butter dish $29-40
Creamer 28-37
Pitcher, water (ill.) 49-60
Sugar bowl, covered 34-47

Probably other pieces.

Spiral and Maltese Cross

Maker unknown, c. early 1880s, clear, non-flint.

Butter dish, covered $36-47
Creamer 22-32
Spoonholder 27-37
Sugar bowl, covered 36-46

Should be other pieces. We're always glad to hear from collectors and dealers alike. Constructive criticism is always welcome; it helps us produce a better price guide for *you*.

Spiralled Ivy

Another of the "Ivy" patterns, mid-1880s. Clear.

Spiralled Ivy

Butter dish, covered $31-40
Creamer 20-30
Pitcher, large, small 28-39
Sauce 14-21
Spoonholder 16-23
Sugar bowl, covered 28-38
Tumbler 18-27

Probably other pieces.

Spirea Band

Spirea Band

(Square and Dot; Squared Dot): Maker unknown. Clear.

Butter dish, covered $40-50
Cake stand 33-43
Celery 19-27
Compote
  a. Covered 44-54
  b. Open 36-46
Creamer 29-39
Goblet 23-33
Pitcher, water (ill.) 41-50
Platter 32-42
Salt/Pepper, pr. 30-40
Spoonholder 26-36
Sugar bowl, covered 34-44
Tumbler 21-29
Wine 19-29

Probably other pieces. Amber, canary, blue, 65 percent higher; green 100 percent higher than clear prices listed.

Sprig

Sprig

(Royal): Bryce, Higbee & Company, Pittsburgh, early 1880s. Clear, with and without sprig decoration.

Bowl, berry	$24-33
Butter dish	44-54
Cake stand	52-62
Celery	44-56
Compote	
a. Covered, high standard, 12″	52-62
b. Open, low standard	38-48
Creamer	44-52
Goblet	40-50
Pitcher, water (ill.)	54-64
Platter, oval	52-62
Sauce, flat, footed	22-32
Spoonholder	34-44
Sugar bowl, covered	49-59
Tumbler	29-39
Wine	32-42

Probably other pieces.

Squared Star

Maker unknown, 1890s. Clear.

Butter dish	$35-45
Creamer	27-37
Spoonholder (ill.)	24-34
Sugar bowl	37-46

Probably other pieces.

Squared Star

Squirrel

Squirrel

Indiana Tumbler & Goblet (National) Company, Greentown, Indiana, 1880s. Clear. Finials are squirrels.

Butter dish, covered, squirrel knob (ill.)	$ 97-115
Creamer	82- 93
Goblet (extremely rare)	375+
Pitcher, water	108-118
Sauce, footed, flat	39- 50
Sugar bowl	
a. Covered (ill.)	82- 94
b. Open	52- 64

Possibly other pieces. Chocolate (pitcher, water is known) would be 200 percent higher than clear prices listed.

S Repeat

Northwood Glass Company, then National Glass Company, Pittsburgh, 1903. Clear, colors: amethyst and gold; translucent sapphire; light green without gilt.

(continued)

S Repeat

Butter dish $42-52
Celery 26-36
Compote, high, low standard 44-54
Creamer 31-41
Goblet 32-42
Pitcher, water................. 52-62
Salt/Pepper, pr. 28-29
Spoonholder 26-36
Sugar bowl, covered 49-59
Tumbler (ill.) 47-57

Probably other pieces. Colors, 50 percent higher than clear prices listed.

Star and Dart

Star and Dart

Maker unknown, c. 1850s, clear, flint.

Butter dish, covered (ill.) $47-56
Creamer 36-44
Spoonholder 27-34
Sugar bowl, covered 42-52

Should be other pieces. A note to you nice people who have been kind enough to buy this *Price Guide*. IF you have information concerning **any** pattern, PLEASE, let's hear from you. IF you don't agree with the prices quoted, PLEASE, let's hear from you. IF you think the piece illustrated is a spoon-

holder rather than a celery (etc.), PLEASE let's hear from you. Constructive criticism is **always** welcome.

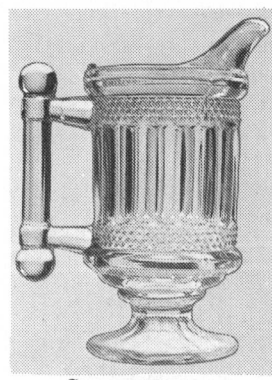

Star and Pillar

Star and Pillar

Possibly Nickel Plate Glass Company, 1891. Clear.

Butter dish, covered, also footed .. $58-69
Celery 35-46
Creamer 50-60
Goblet 38-48
Pitcher, water................. 73-83
Salt/Pepper, pr. 32-42
Spoonholder 31-42
Sugar bowl, covered 49-58
Tumbler 36-44
Wine......................... 29-39

Probably other pieces.

Star and Punty

Star and Punty

Sandwich, early. One of the finest patterns ever made at Sandwich. Clear.

Cologne bottle	$192-220
Creamer	215-235
Pitcher (ill.)	440-515
Sugar bowl	240-290
Whale-oil lamp	425+

Relatively few pieces made. Possibly a few more, but doubtful.

Star Band

Star Band

(Bosworth): A "new" glass as far as age goes; 1900s. Clear.

Butter dish	$24-34
Celery	17-27
Compote	28-38
Creamer	24-34
Goblet	18-28
Pitcher (ill.)	29-38
Spoonholder	19-27
Sugar bowl	21-34

Probably other pieces. As it gets older, it will probably become more collectible.

Star-in-Bull's-Eye

Star-in-Bull's-Eye

U.S. Glass Company, 1907, probably before. Clear, gold trim.

Bowl, berry	$20-30
Butter dish	33-43
Cake stand	32-42
Celery vase	17-26
Compote	
a. Covered	42-52
b. Open, 6″ high	32-42
Creamer (ill.)	19-28
Goblet	27-37
Pitcher, water	42-52
Spoonholder	21-31
Sugar bowl, covered	39-49
Tumbler	22-32

Probably other pieces.

Star in Honeycomb

Star in Honeycomb

Bryce Bros., Pittsburgh, late 1880s. Clear.

Butter dish, covered	$40-52
Compote	
a. Covered	44-54
b. Open	34-46
Cake stand	40-52
Creamer	33-43
Goblet	28-38
Pitcher (ill.)	31-41
Sauce, flat	15-26
Spoonholder	24-35
Sugar bowl, covered	42-52
Tumbler	29-38

Probably other pieces.

Star Pattern

Star Pattern

Not specific name; given only for filing purposes. No one can find it in any book. 8-pointed stars. Not made by U.S. Glass Company. Anyone know?

Star Rosetted

Star Rosetted

McKee & Bros., Pittsburgh, 1875. Clear.

Butter dish	$52-62
Compote, open, high, low standard	52-62
Creamer	42-53

Goblet	34-44
Pitcher, water	60-70
Plate, 10″, "A Good Mother" (ill.)	54-64
Spoonholder	40-50
Sugar bowl	51-61

Probably other pieces.

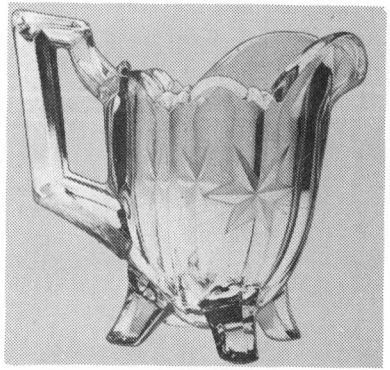
Starlyte

Starlyte

Lancaster Glass Company, Lancaster, Ohio, 1910. Clear.

Butter dish	$28-38
Celery vase	22-28
Compote	36-45
Creamer	27-34
Goblet	22-29
Pitcher, water (ill.)	38-48
Spoonholder	20-28
Sugar bowl, covered	40-50

Probably other pieces.

Starred Scroll

Starred Scroll

(Crescent and Fan): Maker unknown, c. early 1900s, clear, non-flint.

Butter dish, covered	$29-39
Celery	23-33
Jug, syrup (ill.)	42-51
Spoonholder	19-27
Sugar bowl, covered	34-45
Wine	17-26

Stars and Bars

Stars and Bars

(With Stippled Leaf): This is a clear glass of the late 1870s, or early 1880s. Most books show it without stippled leaf.

Butter dish	$34-44
Celery dish	21-31
Creamer	33-43
Dish, oval, 7″, 8″, 9″, 10″, 11″	19-32
Dollhouse set of creamer, butter dish, sugar, set	72-88
Goblet	24-35
Jam jar	24-33
Night lamp, small	30-40
Pitcher, milk (ill.)	46-56
Spoonholder	19-28
Sugar bowl, covered	33-43

Undoubtedly many more pieces.

Stars and Stripes

(Brilliant): Called Brilliant in an 1899 Ward Catalog.

Butter dish	$37-47
Celery	24-33
Compote	32-42
Creamer	30-40
Goblet	27-37
Pitcher (ill.)	40-50
Spoonholder	22-32

Stars and Stripes

Sugar bowl	34-44
Tumbler	19-28

Probably other pieces. Probably there are milk glass pieces; if so, 50 percent higher than clear prices listed.

Stippled Band

(Panelled Stippled Bowl): Maker unknown, c. 1870s, clear, non-flint.

Butter dish, covered	$39-48
Celery	18-28
Creamer	35-44
Goblet	25-35
Pitcher	37-47
Spoonholder	18-32
Sugar bowl, covered	41-52
Tumbler	18-27

Other pieces.

Stippled Chain

Stippled Chain

Gillinder & Sons, 1870s. Crystal.

Butter dish, covered	$38-47
Creamer	39-49

(continued)

Goblet	27-38
Pickle dish	25-34
Pitcher, water (ill.)	52-62
Salt, footed	18-27
Sauce	18-29
Spoonholder	40-50
Sugar bowl, covered	48-58
Tumbler	22-32

Probably other pieces.

Stippled Cherry

Stippled Cherry

Probably Lancaster Glass Company, 1880s. Clear.

Bowl, berry, 6″, 8″	$38-47
Butter dish	47-58
Celery	42-51
Creamer	42-52
Pitcher, water (ill.)	46-54
Plate, 6″, 9¼″, bread	27-37
Saucedish, 4″	16-27
Spoonholder	39-48
Sugar bowl, covered	48-58
Tumbler, water	22-32

Probably other pieces.

Stippled Daisy

Maker unknown, 1880s. Clear and stippled.

Compote, open	$37-47
Creamer	36-44
Relish, oval	22-31
Sauce, flat	18-27
Spoonholder	37-47
Sugar bowl	
a. Covered	41-52
b. Open	32-44

Stippled Daisy

Tumbler (ill.)	27-38
Wine	26-35

Probably other pieces.

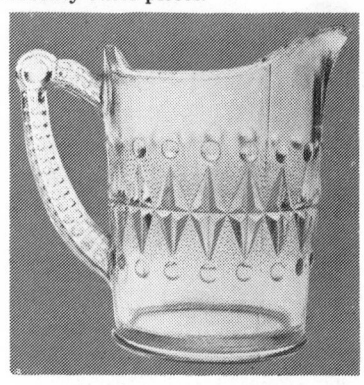

Stippled Dart and Balls

Stippled Dart and Balls

Another product of the 1890s. Clear.

Butter dish, covered	$33-44
Creamer	19-28
Goblet	19-27
Pitcher (ill.)	42-52
Sugar bowl, covered	32-42
Tumbler	19-27
Wine	22-32

Probably other pieces.

Stippled Double Loop

Made in Pennsylvania in the late 1880s. Scarce and in demand.

Stippled Double Loop

Butter dish, covered	$29-41
Creamer	22-32
Goblet	21-31
Pitcher (ill.)	39-51
Spoonholder	22-32
Sugar bowl, covered	34-44
Tumbler	20-28

Stippled Fleur-de-Lis

Stippled Fleur-de-Lis

(Frosted Fleur-de-Lis): Maker unknown, c. late 1880s; clear, amber, blue, green, milk glass, non-flint.

Butter dish, covered	$32-41
Cake stand	22-38
Creamer (ill.)	24-34
Goblet	22-32
Spoonholder	19-29
Sugar bowl, covered	30-40

Amber, blue, milk glass, 40 percent higher; green, 60 percent higher than clear prices listed.

Stippled Forget-Me-Not

Stippled Forget-Me-Not

Bryce Bros., 1880s, also Model Flint Glass Company, after 1891. Clear, color, extremely rare (amber, opal).

Butter dish	$39-47
Cake plate on stand, large, small	38-46
Celery	40-49
Compote, covered, 6", 7", 8"	51-63
Creamer	39-49
Goblet	36-47
Mug	21-31
Pitcher, small, large, syrup	40-50
Plate, baby center, 7", star center, 7", kitten center, 9"	32-44
Sauce, flat, footed	19-26
Spoonholder	40-50
Sugar bowl	52-59
Tumbler, bar, half pint, gill, footed	29-37
Wine	32-48

Amber, opal, 150 percent higher than clear pieces listed.

Stippled Fuchsia

Probably Sandwich, c. 1870s, clear and stippled, non-flint.

Butter dish, covered	$44-53
Compote	
a. Open	39-49
b. Covered	52-61
Creamer	44-52
Goblet	29-39
Pitcher	51-62
Spoonholder	24-33
Sugar bowl, covered	51-62

Probably other pieces.

Stippled Grape and Festoon

Stippled Grape and Festoon

Doyle & Company, Pittsburgh, 1870. Clear and stippled (this pattern with stippled background is the scarcest of the grape and festoon family).

Butter dish $68-78
Celery 63-73
Compote, covered, low
    standard 62-72
Cordial 39-50
Creamer 58-66
Egg cup 29-39
Goblet 38-48
Pitcher, water, applied
    handle (ill.) 70-80
Spoonholder 40-50
Sugar bowl, covered 48-60
Sugar bowl, open 37-48
Wine 28-34
Probably other pieces.

Stippled Leaf and Flower

Stippled Leaf and Flower

Maker unknown, 1870s. Clear.

Butter dish, covered $32-44
Creamer 33-42

Dish, sauce 15-24
Decanter, stopper 39-49
Goblet 28-37
Pitcher, water (ill.) 82-94
Spoonholder 26-38
Sugar
    a. Covered 50-60
    b. Open 28-34
Tumbler 29-39
Probably other pieces.

Stippled Medallion

Stippled Medallion

Union Glass Company, Somerville, Massachusetts, late 1860s. Clear.

Butter, covered $40-48
Celery 25-38
Creamer 32-41
Goblet (ill.) 26-36
Pitcher, water 42-52
Spoonholder 22-32
Sugar
    a. Covered 36-46
    b. Open 29-38
Probably other pieces.

Stippled Peppers

Sandwich glass, 1870s. Clear.

Creamer $29-39
Egg cup 16-24
Goblet 27-39
Pitcher, water 36-46
Salt, footed 14-20
Sauce 14-23
Spoonholder 17-28
Sugar bowl, covered 29-40
Probably other pieces.

Stippled Peppers

Stippled Sandbur

Stippled Star

Creamer (ill.)	60-71
Dish, oval, 8″	31-42
Egg cup	33-44
Goblet	38-49
Pickle dish	20-32
Pitcher	70-81
Sauce, flat, 4″, 6″	20-30
Spoonholder, 5½″ high	39-49
Sugar bowl, covered	52-62
Tumbler	24-34

Probably other pieces. Creamer, goblet, salt dip, sugar bowl and wine being reproduced in clear (original) and new colors.

Stippled Sandbur

(Stippled Star Variant): Maker unknown, early 1890s. Clear.

Bowl	$32-42
Butter, covered	30-40
Celery vase	19-28
Compote, covered	32-44
Creamer	19-29
Goblet	20-34
Sauce, flat	15-29
Spoonholder	19-24
Sugar bowl, covered	28-40
Wine	20-30

Probably other pieces.

Stippled Star

Gillinder & Sons, Greensburg, Pennsylvania, 1870s. Probably Sandwich, much earlier.

Butter dish	$54-63
Celery	39-49
Compote, large, small, high standard	59-70

Stippled Star Flower

Stippled Star Flower

(With the band, called Star Flower Band): Maker unknown, late 1880s. Clear.

Butter dish	$29-39
Celery	18-27
Creamer	19-29
Goblet (ill.)	22-32
Salt, footed	14-21
Spoonholder	18-29
Sugar bowl, covered	28-38
Tumbler	19-29
Wine	14-26

Other pieces.

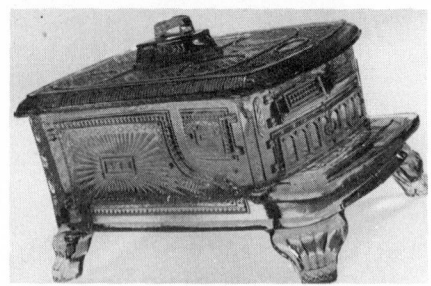

Stove

Stove

Maker and date unknown, clear, colors. A novelty of the late 1800s.

Clear (ill.) $97-116

Color, 100 percent higher than clear price listed.

Strawberry

Strawberry

Sandwich Glass, 1850-1860. Clear, opaque white (milk glass).

Butter dish, covered $64-76
Compote, covered, 8″ high,
  low standard 77-88
Creamer 52-62
Egg cup 30-40
Goblet 41-51
Honey dish 20-30
Pickle dish 23-33
Pitcher
  a. Syrup 42-52
  b. Water (ill.) 81-93
Salt, footed 22-31
Saucedish, flat 18-27
Spoonholder 42-51
Sugar bowl 48-59

Probably other pieces. Prices listed are for milk glass. Clear, 85-100 percent less. Egg cup and goblet being reproduced.

Strawberry Jar

Strawberry Jar

Don't confuse this with the Sandwich Glass Strawberry. This was a container for grocery products — mustard, etc. Possibly made by Specialty Glass Company and Indiana Tumbler & Goblet Company.

Strawberry jar (ill.) $31-42

Strigil

Strigil

Possibly McKee Bros., Pittsburgh, late 1880s. Clear.

Butter dish $32-42
Celery 22-32
Compote 41-51
Creamer 34-44
Egg cup 18-28

Goblet	22-32
Pitcher	52-62
Sauce	22-32
Spoonholder	19-27
Sugar bowl	40-50
Tumbler	20-26

Probably other pieces.

Strutting Peacock

Strutting Peacock

Possibly Westmoreland Glass Company, late 1880s. Clear, other colors.

Bottle, decanter type	$44-53
Butter dish, covered	47-56
Creamer, covered	32-42
Goblet	33-41
Mug, 4" high	19-27
Pitcher, half gallon (ill.)	60-72
Plates, 6", 7", 8", 9"	38-48
Spoonholder	29-40
Sugar bowl, covered	34-44
Tumbler, 4" high	27-37

Probably other pieces. Blue, purple, green, 50 percent higher; opalescent white or white Carnival, 125 percent higher; reds, 125 percent higher than clear/marigold prices given.

Stylized Flower

Stylized Flower

Challinor, Taylor & Company, Tarentum, Pennsylvania, 1885. "Mosaic glass" in brown and other colors. Also, crystal and opal. Only six pieces known in this pattern.

Butter dish	$39-50
Creamer	18-29
Pitcher	
a. Quart (ill.)	52-62
b. ½ gallon	42-54
Spoonholder	19-26
Sugar bowl, covered	38-44

Opal, 50 percent higher than clear prices listed.

Sunbeam

Sunbeam

McKee & Brothers, Jeannette, Pennsylvania, c. 1898, clear; later, emerald with gold decorations.

Bowl, berry	$16-27
Celery	15-19
Compote, jelly (ill.)	18-26
Creamer, individual	10-17
Sauce	7-17
Sugar bowl, covered	26-36
Tumbler	19-29

Emerald with gold decorations, 50 percent higher than clear prices listed.

Sunburst

McKee & Bros., 1898. Clear.

Butter dish	$39-49
Cake plate on standard, 2 types	32-43
Celery	27-41

559

(continued)

Sunburst

Compote, covered, low standard	42-52
Cordial	19-29
Creamer	32-41
Egg cup	22-32
Goblet	24-34
Pitcher, large, small	42-52
Plate, 6", 7", 11"	22-32
Spoonholder	26-36
Sugar bowl	39-50
Wine	19-27

Probably other pieces.

Sunflower

Sunflower

(Lilly); Atterbury & Company, Pittsburgh, 1881. Crystal, amber, blue, opal, mosaic glass.

Butter dish, covered	$54-62
Creamer	34-42
Goblet	22-34
Nappy	29-39
Pitcher (ill.)	52-62
Spoonholder	24-29

Sugar bowl	
a. Covered	47-57
b. Open	32-42

Probably other pieces. Amber, 50 percent higher; mosaic, 100 percent higher than clear prices listed.

Sunflower Container

Sunflower Container

Westmoreland Specialty Company or Specialty Glass Company. This is a creamer, originally made as a commercial jelly container.

Sunflower container (ill.) $29-40

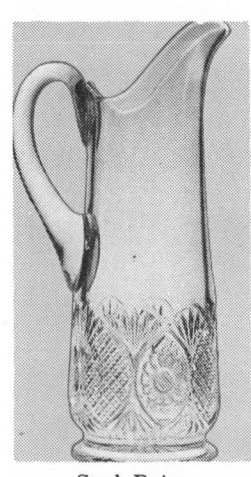

Sunk Daisy

Sunk Daisy

Co-Operative Flint Glass Company, Beaver Falls, Pennsylvania, 1898. Clear and green.

Butter dish, covered $29-40
Compote 32-42
Creamer 22-34
Goblet 24-36
Pitcher (ill.)................... 41-52
Sugar bowl, covered 22-31
Wine....................... 16-27

Probably other pieces. Green, 50 percent higher than clear prices listed.

Sunk Diamond and Lattice

Sunk Diamond and Lattice

Maker unknown, 1885-1890. Clear.

Butter dish $29-39
Celery vase 24-33
Compote
  a. Covered 34-46
  b. Open 17-29
Creamer 20-30
Pitcher, water (ill.) 32-41
Salt/Pepper, pr. 18-29
Spoonholder 18-27
Sugar bowl, covered 33-43
Tumbler 20-30

Probably other pieces.

Sunk Honeycomb

Another of the many "Honeycomb" patterns; this one of the late 1880s. Clear as well as with a ruby top.

Creamer, clear $39-49
Cruet with stopper 38-48
Decanter, 12½" high, original,
  stopper, ruby top............. 59-69

Sunk Honeycomb

Pitcher, water, ruby top 72-82
Spooner, ruby top 40-50

Sunken Buttons

Sunken Buttons

Maker unknown, Ohio, late 1880s. Clear, canary, amber, blue.

Butter dish, covered $29-40
Compote
  a. Covered 34-46
  b. Open 32-42
Creamer 27-37
Goblet 26-38
Pitcher, syrup (ill.) 38-48
Platter 29-41
Salt/Pepper, pr. 21-31
Sugar bowl
  a. Covered 36-46
  b. Open 30-40
Wine....................... 21-31

Probably other pieces. Canary, 50 percent higher; amber, blue, 125 percent higher than clear prices listed.

561

Swag with Brackets

Swag with Brackets

Jefferson Glass Company, Steubenville, Ohio, late 1800s. Clear, green, opalescent, gold trim.

Butter dish, covered	$37-47
Celery	21-31
Creamer	22-34
Pitcher, water (ill.)	39-48
Spoonholder	19-29
Sugar bowl, covered	44-52
Tumbler	21-32

Probably other pieces. Green opalescent 90 percent higher than clear prices listed.

Swan

Swan

Maker unknown, 1880s. Clear, light amber, yellow, deep blue. Possibly Westmoreland.

Butter dish, covered, 5" dia.	$80-91
Creamer	62-71
Dish, oval, covered	48-58
Goblet	62-72
Marmalade jar, covered, swan finial	64-74
Pitcher, water (ill.)	69-82
Sauce, footed, round, flat, 4"	18-27
Spoonholder	44-54
Sugar bowl, covered	60-70

Probably other pieces. Amber, yellow, 45 percent higher; blue, 65 percent higher than clear prices listed.

Swan with Tree

Swan with Tree

U.S. Glass Company, Gas City, Indiana, late 1880s. Clear.

Goblet	$40-49
Pitcher, water (ill.)	53-63

At least these two pieces; possibly more.

Swirl

(Jersey Swirl): Windsor Glass Company, Pittsburgh, c. 1887, clear, amber, blue, yellow.

Butter dish, covered	$39-50
Cake stand	42-52
Celery	38-44

Compote, covered 42-52
Creamer 37-47
Goblet
  a. Buttermilk, large 34-44
  b. Regular 29-39
Pitcher, water 42-52
Spoonholder 40-50
Sugar bowl, covered 39-49

Yellow, 30 percent; amber, blue, 50 percent higher than clear prices listed. Many repros in the colored glass; also in clear buttermilk goblet.

Swirl and Cable

Swirl and Cable

Possibly Sandwich, mid-1850s. Clear.

Creamer $34-44
Pitcher, milk (ill.) 57-69

Probably other pieces.

Swirl and Diamond

(America): Riverside Glass Works, Wellsburg, West Virginia, called it America. Also made by Riverside's successor, American Glass Company, Anderson, Indiana, in 1899. Crystal.

Bowl $16-25
Butter dish, covered 39-49
Creamer 24-34
Pitcher, water (ill.) 50-60
Sauce, flat 16-26
Spoonholder 19-29
Sugar bowl
  a. Covered 40-50
  b. Open 22-34

Probably other pieces.

Swirl and Diamond

Sydney

Sydney

Fostoria Glass Company, 1905, possibly earlier. Clear.

Butter dish, covered $36-46
Celery 18-27
Compote
  a. Covered 38-48
  b. Open 27-37
Creamer 22-32
Goblet 27-37
Molasses jug 18-27
Pickle dish, 6″, 8″, 9″ 14-24
Pitcher (ill.) 49-59
Salt shaker 14-28
Spoonholder 16-27
Sugar bowl, covered 38-48

Probably other pieces.

Syrup Jug with Applied Handle

Syrup Jug with Applied Handle

Maker and date unknown. Bird on lid, Britannia lid.

Syrup jug (ill.) $42-51

Anyone have information on it?

Tackle Block

Tackle Block

Maker unknown, c. 1840s, clear, flint.

Goblet (ill.) $52-61

Possibly other pieces.

Tall Argus

Maker unknown, 1850s. Clear.

Goblet ....$ 74- 82
Pitcher, water (ill.) 134-156

Possibly other pieces.

Tall Argus

Tape Measure

Tape Measure

(Shields): Portland Glass Company, early 1870s. Clear.

Butter dish $42-52
Goblet 29-40
Pitcher, water (ill.) 59-70
Sauce, flat 17-27

Probably other pieces.

Teardrop and Tassel

Teardrop and Tassel

(Sampson): Original name was Sampson, made by Indiana Tumbler & Goblet Company, 1890s. Better known today as Teardrop and Tassel. Clear, blue, amber, opaque white, green yellow.

	Amber	White	Nile Green
Butter dish	$92-102		$198-220
Creamer	58- 68	$ 40- 50	215-240
Goblet (rare)	55- 65		
Pitcher (ill.)	450+	220-245	355+
Relish tray	60- 70		
Spoonholder	49- 59	48- 58	
Sugar bowl, covered	58- 68	57- 67	130-142
Tumbler	42- 52		
Wine	61- 71	110-130	

	Blue	Green	Clear
Butter dish	$82- 92	$ 88- 98	$ 52- 62
Creamer	52- 62	58- 68	46- 56
Goblet	52- 62	54- 64	42- 60
Pitcher, (ill.)	275+	200-235	60- 70
Relish tray	52- 62	58- 68	40- 50
Spoonholder	52- 62	48- 56	40- 48
Sugar bowl	62- 72	60- 70	58- 68
Tumbler	29- 39	38- 48	33- 43
Wine (rare)	54- 64	58- 68	40- 50

Probably other pieces.

Teardrop and Thumbprint

Teardrop and Thumbprint

Ripley & Company, Pittsburgh; later, U.S. Glass Company, early 1900s. Plain or engraved, clear, blue; pattern on blue enameled on white.

Bowl	$17-27
Butter dish, covered	34-43
Cake stand	38-48
Celery	19-27
Creamer, covered	22-33
Compote, open	24-34
Goblet	20-30
Pitcher, water (ill.)	49-62
Sugar	
a. Covered	34-44
b. Open	22-30
Wine	18-29

Probably other pieces. Blue, 100 percent higher than clear prices listed.

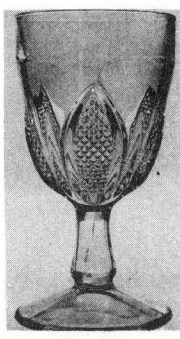

Teasel

Teasel

Bryce Bros., Pittsburgh, 1870s. Clear.

Butter dish, covered	$39-49
Cake stand	29-42
Celery	17-27
Compote	28-38
Creamer	27-37
Cruet	22-32
Goblet (ill.)	24-32
Sauce, square footed	12-19
Spoonholder	18-29
Sugar bowl, covered	34-40

Probably many other pieces.

Tennessee

U.S. Glass Company, 1900. One of their "States" series. Clear.

(continued)

Tennessee

Butter dish $40-50
Cake stand 42-51
Celery 18-27
Creamer 20-30
Goblet 22-34
Jam jar........................ 20-30
Pitcher, water (ill.) 52-62
Relish, oval 18-27
Spoonholder 18-32
Sugar bowl, covered 29-41
Tumbler 21-34

Probably others.

Tennessee Mug

Tennessee Mug

So-called camphor glass, American flag, 16 stars on one side, Cherokee rose on other.

Mug (ill.) $26-36

Texas

(Loop with Stippled Panels): U.S. Glass Company, c. 1900, as "No. 15,067." In their 1907 catalog, given name of "Texas." Clear, clear with gilded top; also with ruby in the body.

Butter dish, covered $34-45
Cake stand 38-48
Compote, open 22-32
Creamer 19-27
Goblet 28-37
Pitcher...................... 36-46
Spoonholder 19-27
Sugar bowl, covered 28-38
Tumbler 15-22

Color, gilded top, 50 percent higher than clear prices listed. Other pieces.

The Bedford

The Bedford

Fostoria Glass Company, Moundsville, West Virginia, 1901-1905. Clear. Over 60 pieces were made in this popular pattern.

Butter dish $33-43
Celery vase 18-28
Creamer 29-39
Goblet 26-36
Pitcher (ill.).................. 38-48
Spoonholder 17-29
Sugar bowl 34-44
Tumbler 24-34

Many other pieces.

The Fox and the Crow

Indiana Tumbler & Goblet (National) Company, late 1890s.

Pitcher, water, clear (ill.)...... $130-150

Probably tumbler to match.

The Fox and the Crow

The Regent

The Regent

H. Northwood and Co., Wheeling, West Virginia, 1880s. Clear, blue-green, amethyst (extremely rare), decorated with gold; also in crystal. Clear prices given.

Bowl	$ 49- 60
Butter dish	88- 98
Compote	110-122
Creamer	75- 88
Cruet set	125-155
Pitcher, water (ill.)	120-140
Salt/Pepper, pr.	58- 68
Sherbet	40- 44
Spoonholder	62- 72
Sugar bowl	88-110

Probably other pieces. Colors, 40 percent to 250 percent higher than clear prices given.

The States

U.S. Glass Company, 1905. Clear, some pieces gold trimmed.

Butter dish, covered	$38-48

The States

Celery	27-37
Compote, 7", open	28-37
Creamer	30-40
Dish, handled, round...........	20-30
Pitcher, water, gold trimmed	40-52
Plate, large	26-37
Sugar bowl, covered	34-44
Toothpick holder	14-26
Tumbler	17-26

Probably other pieces. Gold trim doesn't affect price of clear prices listed.

The Summit

Thompson Glass Company, Uniontown, Pennsylvania, c. 1895, clear, flint.

Butter dish, covered	$54-64
Celery	42-52
Creamer	47-57
Pitcher, large, tankard	64-74
Spoonholder	37-47
Sugar bowl, covered	52-62

Possibly other pieces.

Thistle

Thistle

(Pillar and Bull's Eye): Bakewell, Pears and Company, 1875. Crystal.

Bowl, berry, covered	$42-52

(continued)

Butter dish, covered 50-60
Cake plate on standard 60-70
Compote
  a. Covered, high standard 52-62
  b. Open, low standard, 8" 42-52
Cordial 41-51
Creamer 48-59
Egg cup 28-39
Goblet 39-49
Pickle dish, tapered at one end .. 22-32
Pitcher (ill.) 60-72
Plate, 10¾" dia. 29-40
Sauce, flat, deep, 4" 19-27
Spoonholder 42-52
Sugar bowl, covered 62-72
Tumbler, footed, water 38-52
Wine 40-50

Probably other pieces.

Thousand Eye

Thousand Eye

(Daisy; No. 11): Richards & Hartley, 1888, called it Daisy; New Brighton Glass Company, New Brighton, Pennsylvania, 1889, also máde it. It's also No. 11 in an old Adams Glass Company catalog. Clear and just about every color.

Bowl, banana $42-52
Bowl, berry, waste 34-44
Butter dish, knob, plain stem 52-63
Cake stand, knob, plain stem 50-60
Compote, open, covered 57-67
Creamer, knob, plain stem 53-63
Goblet, knob stem 42-52
Pitcher, small, large knob,
  plain stem 54-64
Spoonholder, knob, plain stem .. 32-42
Sugar bowl, knob, plain stem 54-63
Tumbler, jelly, water 28-39

Many other pieces. Amber, yellow, blue, 40 percent higher; apple green, 60 per-

cent higher than clear prices listed. Cruet, plain stem, goblet, hat (match holder), mug, 8" sq. plate, tumbler and wine being reproduced.

Threading

(Threaded): Maker unknown, c, late 1870s, clear, non-flint.

Butter dish, covered $27-38
Compote
  a. Open 18-27
  b. Covered 33-43
Creamer 24-34
Spoonholder 25-38
Sugar bowl
  a. Open 14-26
  b. Covered 31-41

Probably other pieces.

Three Birds

Three Birds

Dalzell, Gilmore & Leighton Company, Findlay, Ohio, 1880s. Clear.

Pitcher, water (ill.) $48-59

Probably tumbler and other pieces to match.

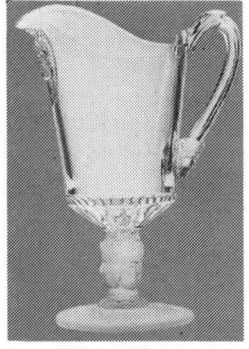

Three Face

Three Face

(The Sisters): George A. Duncan's Sons, Pittsburgh, 1878. Clear and crystal-with-frosted-faces. Some pieces etched and engraved.

Butter dish	$132-148
Cake stand	
a. 8", 9½"	92-110
b. Frosted base	128-140
Celery, pedestal base	97-110
Celery, scalloped top	72- 82
Compote	
a. Covered, large	190-220
b. Covered, 6", small	130-145
c. Open, high standard	96-110
Creamer, 2 styles	107-118
Goblet	92-115
Pitcher, milk, etched	230-275
Pitcher, water ½ gal.	
(rare) (ill.)	280-325
Salt/Pepper, pr.	77- 87
Spoonholder	130-140
Wine	78- 88

Probably other patterns. Butter dish, cake stand, champagne, 6½" covered compote, claret, creamer, goblet, lamp, sauce, salt/peppers, spoonholder, sugar bowl, wine, being reproduced. Advice is cheap. This advice won't cost you a thing: DON'T BUY IT! Some dealers sell the new for the same price as the old! ALL pieces being skillfully reproduced.

Three-in-One

Three-in-One

(Fancy Diamonds): Imperial Glass Company, Bellaire, Ohio, c, late 1880s, clear, non-flint.

Bowl	$19-27
Butter dish, covered	26-36
Creamer	22-38
Goblet (ill.)	17-29
Spoonholder	19-27
Sugar bowl	
a. Covered	28-38
b. Open	22-34
Wine	14-28

Probably other pieces.

Three Leaf Clover

Three Leaf Clover

Maker and date unknown. Any information on this lovely piece of flint glass would be deeply appreciated.

Three Panel

Three Panel

Hartley & Company, Tarentum, Pennsylvania, 1888. Clear, canary, amber, blue.

(continued)

Bowl, 8½" $42-52
Butter dish, covered 44-54
Celery 42-52
Compote, open, 7", 8½", 9", 10",
　　low standard 38-47
Creamer 36-46
Cruet 34-44
Goblet 29-38
Mug 28-38
Pitcher, water (ill.) 44-58
Sauce 19-28
Spoonholder 34-44
Sugar bowl 42-52
Tumbler 32-42

Probably other pieces. Colors, 60-100 percent higher than clear prices listed.

Tic-Tac-Toe

Tic-Tac-Toe

Maker unknown, c. late 1880s, clear, non-flint.

Goblet (ill.) $22-32
Salt, master, footed 8-18

Should be other pieces.

Tiebacks

Tiebacks

Boston & Sandwich Glass Company, c. 1850s, opalescent. They were used to hold the window curtains in place.

2" dia., pr.....................$42-52
3" dia., pr. (ill.) 52-62
4¼" dia., pr.................... 61-71

Tiny Lion

Tiny Lion

Maker unknown, Ohio, early 1880s. Clear; clear and frosted.

Butter dish, covered $35-42
Celery, 2 handles (ill.) 44-54
Compote 44-53
Creamer 28-38
Pitcher, water 50-60
Spoonholder 19-28
Sugar bowl
　a. Covered 34-44
　b. Open 28-37

Probably other pieces.

Tom Thumb — Humpty Dumpty Mug

Tom Thumb — Humpty Dumpty Mug

(Humpty Dumpty shown): Maker unknown, a novelty of the 1880s. Clear only.

Mug (ill.) $45-55

Torpedo

Tree of Life

Torpedo

(Pygmy, Fisheye): Thompson Glass Company, Uniontown, Pennsylvania, 1889. Clear.

Bowl
   a. Berry, 8" $35-44
   b. Rose, 4" (scarce)........... 42-52
   c. Open, 8", 8¼", 9", 9½",
      flared rim 37-47
   d. Waste, scalloped top....... 28-38
Butter dish, covered 56-66
Cake stand, 9", 10" 52-62
Compote
   a. Covered, jelly, 4" 50-60
   b. Open, jelly, flared rim 44-54
   c. Covered, 6", 7", 8" 63-73
Creamer, flat, footed, large
   and medium................. 42-52
Decanter 48-60
Goblet 44-54
Pitcher, milk, syrup, water
   10⅞", 11½", 12" (ill.) 58-70
Salt, individual, master 19-27
Sauce, 4½" footed honey, 3½"
   flat honey 16-27
Salt/Pepper, pr., 2¼" high,
   3" high 34-40
Spoonholder 29-40
Sugar bowl, covered 62-72
Tumbler 48-59
Wine........................ 33-39

Undoubtedly other pieces.

Tree of Life

Portland Glass Company, Portland, Maine, c. 1867. Clear, amber, blue, purple, canary, green and etched.

Bowl, flat, 8", 10", finger $27-36
Butter dish, hand/ball on cover ... 48-58

Celery vase 49-59
Compote
   a. Open, 10", "Davis" 62-72
   b. Covered 78-88
Creamer 62-72
Goblet 50-60
Pitcher, water (ill.) 60-70
Spoonholder 34-44
Sugar bowl, covered 50-60
Tumbler, footed 32-44
Wine......................... 38-50

Probably other pieces. Colors, 50-100 percent higher than clear prices listed. Some pieces came in a plated holder. No change in value. Some pieces signed "P.G. Co. Patent." Others, "Davis" (woven in design).

Tree of Life with Hand

Tree of Life with Hand

George A. Duncan's Sons, 1884. Clear, blue. Probably other colors.

Bowl, finger .... $ 26- 36
Butter dish, covered 62- 74
Celery 42- 52
Compote, covered 115-124
Creamer 52- 62
Dish, berry 24- 34

(continued)

Plate, berry 29- 39
Saucedish 27- 37
Sugar bowl
  a. Covered 92-102
  b. Open 42- 52

Probably other pieces. No goblet seems to have been made in hand stem.

Tree of Life with Sprig

Tree of Life with Sprig

Portland, Glass Company, Portland, Maine, 1870s. Clear, possibly colors.

Butter dish $39-50
Celery 29-39
Creamer 32-42
Spoonholder 22-32
Sugar bowl, covered 38-48
Syrup jug, top missing (ill.) 29-40

Probably other pieces. Creamer has little wheels at base; other pieces don't. Don't let this confuse you.

Triangular Prism

Triangular Prism

Maker unknown, c. 1850s, clear, flint and non-flint.

Bowl, shallow $16-27
Butter dish, covered 40-50
Celery 39-48
Compote
  a. Low pedestal 18-27
  b. Tall pedestal 24-37
Cup, handled 12-21
Goblet, ladies' or gents' (ill.) 40-50
Salt, master, footed 19-30
Spoonholder 30-40
Sugar bowl, covered 42-52
Tumbler 16-27
Wine 32-42

Flint, 25 percent higher than clear prices listed. Probably other pieces.

Triple Triangle

Triple Triangle

Doyle & Company, Pittsburgh, Pennsylvania, c. 1885, clear and ruby-stained.

Butter dish, covered $34-44
Cup, punch 12-22
Creamer 22-32
Goblet (ill.) 42-52
Mug 32-42
Sugar bowl, covered 36-46
Wine 28-40

Ruby-stained, 20 percent higher than clear prices listed. Other pieces.

Troubadour Scene

Indiana Tumbler & Goblet (National) Company, late 1890s. See colors with price.

Troubadour Scene

Chocolate ....$	71- 82
White milk	40- 50
Blue milk	52- 63
Nile green	53- 63
Clear	44- 54
Amber (ill.)	120-132

With lip, regular size, 100 percent higher. Large steins, 350-400 percent higher.

Tulip with Sawtooth

Tulip with Sawtooth

(Tulip): Bryce, Richard and Company, Pittsburgh, c. 1854.

Butter dish ....$	72- 84
Celery vase	54- 64
Compote	
a. Covered, large high	
standard	121-141
b. Covered, small, high	
standard	94-107
c. Open, large	94-115
d. Covered, low standard....	70- 82
Creamer	98-112
Decanter, half pint, pint,	
quart	62- 74
Goblet, knob stem, 7″ high	40- 50
Jug	
a. Pint	92-107
b. Quart	129-139
Pitcher (ill.)	140-150

Spoonholder	32- 42
Sugar bowl	90-100
Tumbler, footed, water	40- 50
Wine (being reproduced)	42- 53

Probably other pieces.

Twin Teardrops

Twin Teardrops

Maker unknown, c. 1890s, clear, non-flint; possibly in emerald green.

Celery ....$	21-31
Compote, open (ill.)	27-34
Cruet	22-34
Dish, banana, flat	19-27
Plate, 7″ square	18-28

If emerald green, 100 percent higher than clear prices listed. Should be other pieces.

Twinkle Star

Twinkle Star

(Frost Flower): U.S. Glass Company, 1901. Clear, clear and frosted. Six-pointed stars on **inside** of glass.

Butter dish, covered ....$	36-46

(continued)

Celery 24-34
Creamer 28-38
Goblet 27-37
Pitcher, water (ill.) 48-58
Spoonholder 22-33
Sugar bowl, covered 27-36
Tumbler 21-40

Probably other pieces.

Two Band

Two Band

Maker unknown, c. late 1880s, clear, non-flint.

Butter dish, covered $29-39
Creamer (ill.) 24-34
Goblet 18-27
Spoonholder 22-32
Sugar bowl, covered 31-41
Also made in child's set:
Butter dish, covered 64-74
Creamer 50-60
Spoonholder 51-63
Sugar bowl, covered 68-82

Probably other pieces in adult size.

Two Panel

(Daisy in Panel; Daisy in Square): Richards & Hartley Flint Glass Company, Tarentum, Pennsylvania, c. 1880s; clear, apple green, amber, blue, canary.

Bowls, 3 sizes $22-32
Butter dish, covered 37-47
Celery 28-39
Compote
  a. Covered, open, high
    standard 29-46
  b. Open, low standard 28-38

Two Panel

Creamer 34-44
Goblet (ill.) 26-36
Lamp 42-52
Mug 19-32
Pitcher 38-48
Spoonholder 40-50
Sugar bowl, covered 44-58

Apple green, 80 percent; canary, 60 percent; amber, blue, 50 percent higher than clear prices listed. Many other pieces. Goblet being reproduced, especially in color.

Umbilicated Sawtooth

Umbilicated Sawtooth

Another of the Sandwich patterns.
Bowl, 8″ $22-29
Butter dish, covered, on
  pedestal (ill.) 44-53
Egg cup 26-35
Plate, 6″ 19-27
Salt, master, footed 14-27
Sauce 7-12
Tumbler 22-32
Wine 19-27

Probably other pieces.

Unique

Unique

Co-Operative Flint Glass Company, 1898. Clear.

Butter dish	$31-40
Celery vase	25-35
Creamer	28-38
Goblet	19-32
Pitcher	
a. Syrup metal cap (ill.)	24-34
b. Water	38-47
Spoonholder	19-27
Sugar bowl, covered	24-34
Tumbler	18-29

Probably other pieces.

U.S. Rib

U.S. Rib

(Rib): U.S. Glass Company, 1900. Green glass with gold rims; possibly crystal and other colors.

Butter dish	$52-62
Celery	30-40
Creamer (ill.)	38-48
Pitcher, water	60-70
Spoonholder	22-34
Sugar bowl, covered	42-52
Tumbler	28-38

Probably other pieces. Crystal 50 percent less than green prices listed.

Valentine

Valentine

(Trilby): U.S. Glass Company, Pittsburgh, late 1870s. Clear.

Butter dish	$ 44- 53
Celery	30- 40
Cologne bottle	24- 33
Creamer	24- 33
Goblet	28- 42
Match holder	19- 29
Pitcher, water (ill.)	132-151
Tumbler	34- 46

Victoria

Victoria

Bakewell, Pears & Company, early 1860s. Clear, canary, possibly other colors.

Bowl, 8½" dia. (ill.)	$ 80- 90
Butter dish, low foot, 8"	80- 90
Cake stand	
a. 9"	80- 90
b. 15"	122-156
Celery	28- 38
Dish, sweetmeat	62- 73

Compote
a. Covered 130-147
b. Open 32- 44
Creamer 97-115
Sugar bowl (scarce) 165-195

Possibly other pieces. Colors, 128-165 percent higher than clear prices listed.

Victoria

Bakewell, Pears & Company, early 1860s. Clear, canary, possibly other colors.
Bowl, 8½" dia. (ill.) ....$ 80- 90
Butter dish, low foot, 8" 80- 90
Cake stand
a. 9" 80- 90
b. 15" 122-156
Celery 28- 38
Dish, sweetmeat 62- 73
Compote
a. Covered 130-147
b. Open 32- 44
Creamer 97-115
Sugar bowl (scarce) 165-195

Possibly other pieces. Colors, 100-150 percent higher than clear prices listed.

Virginia

Virginia

(Galloway): U.S. Glass Company, 1901 Glassport, Indiana. Clear, red-flashed.
Butter dish, covered $43-52
Celery 34-44
Compote
a. Covered, footed, 6", 7", 8" 52-62
b. Open, footed, 6", 7", 8" 40-50
Creamer, individual, large 39-49
Goblet 37-47
Pitcher, half gallon tankard,
water 48-58

Sauce, flared, 4"; straight,
4", 4½" 18-24
Spoonholder 27-37
Sugar bowl
a. Covered, large 44-53
b. Open, small 29-39
Tumbler 34-44
Wine 28-38

Probably other pieces. There are several "Virginia" patterns; don't get them confused, price-wise. Red-flashed, 25 percent higher than clear prices listed.

Waffle

Waffle

Bryce, Walker & Company, Pittsburgh, Pennsylvania, 1860s.
Butter dish, covered ....$ 68- 79
Celery, 9" high (ill.) 58- 68
Champagne goblet........... 62- 74
Claret 40- 50
Compote
a. Open, large, high
standard 59- 70
b. Open, small, high
standard 52- 62
c. Open, small, low
standard 48- 58
Creamer, pint and quart
(rare) 118-132
Decanter, pint and quart 49- 68
Goblet, knob stem 44- 54
Pitcher, water (rare) 9½"
high 92-107
Spoonholder 54- 64
Sugar bowl, covered 92-107
Tumbler, water, whiskey 62- 74
Wine 56- 66

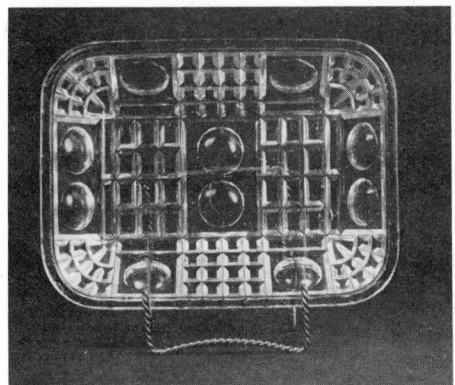

Waffle and Thumbprint

Waffle and Thumbprint

Possibly New England Glass Company or Sandwich, early; later, Ohio Valley, c. 1850s, 1860s, clear, flint and non-flint.

Bowl, rectangular (ill.) . . . . $ 42- 52
Butter dish, covered 120-137
Cordial 72- 90
Creamer 118-140
Decanter
  a. Pint 70- 80
  b. Quart 82- 92
Goblet 67- 77
Sugar bowl, covered 128-140

Non-flint, 50 percent lower than flint prices listed. Possibly other pieces.

Waffle with Fan Top

Waffle with Fan Top

Maker unknown, c. 1880s, clear, non-flint.

Goblet (ill.) $24-34

Another member of the "Waffle" family. There should be other pieces.

Washboard

McKee & Brothers, Pittsburgh, c. 1897, clear, canary, blue, non-flint.

Bowls, round, oval $19-28
Butter dish, covered 22-32
Cake stand, large 32-42
Creamer 27-37
Goblet 28-38
Pitcher 42-52
Sauce, flat 9-14
Spoonholder 19-27
Sugar bowl, covered 26-37

Colors, 35 percent higher than clear prices listed. Probably other pieces.

Washington

Washington

New England Glass Company, Cambridge, Massachusetts, c. early 1860s, clear, flint.

Butter dish, covered, on
  pedestal . . . . $ 82- 92
Celery 80- 90
Compote, covered, tall 120-140
Cordial 84- 94
Creamer 92-108
Egg cup 52- 63
Goblet 70- 85
Pitcher
  a. Syrup 120-145
  b. Water 230-255
Sugar bowl (base ill.) 162-182
Tumbler 57- 69
Wine 80- 90

Possibly other pieces.

Washington Centennial

Gillinder & Sons, Philadelphia, c. 1876, clear, non-flint.

Bowl, oval	$ 29- 42
Butter dish, covered	110-118
Celery	60- 73
Champagne	52- 72
Creamer	95-120
Goblet	48- 62
Pitcher, water	97-110
Platters	
a. Washington's head	120-140
b. "The Nation's birthplace"	127-153
c. Carpenter's Hall	118-127
Relish, flat, oval, marked "Centennial 1776-1876"	42- 52
Sugar bowl, covered	102-117
Wine	50- 60

Probably other pieces.

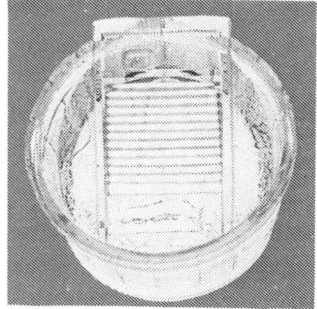

Washtub Soap Dish

Washtub Soap Dish

Maker and date unknown. A novelty item of the 1860s. Clear glass; also canary, amber, blue.

Washtub, clear	$39-53
Washtub, canary or amber	52-68
Washtub, blue (rare) (ill.)	71-81

Water Lily

(Frosted Magnolia): Dalzell, Gilmore & Leighton Company, Findlay, Ohio, c. 1890, clear, non-flint.

Butter dish, covered	$ 70- 80
Cake stand, large	72- 82
Creamer	59- 71
Goblet	69- 79
Pitcher, syrup	128-140
Sauce, flat	19- 27
Sugar bowl, covered	62- 73

Probably other pieces.

Waterfall

Waterfall

O'Hara Glass Company, Pittsburgh, 1880s. Clear, light blue, canary.

Butter dish	$34-44
Celery	23-33
Compote	40-50
Creamer	22-32
Goblet	24-34
Pitcher, water (ill.)	52-62
Spoonholder	24-34
Sugar bowl, covered	36-47

Probably other pieces. Colors, 50 percent higher than clear prices listed.

Waterlily and Cattails

Waterlily and Cattails

Northwood Glass Company, later Fenton, 1889. Clear, colored w/opalescence (blue, green Carnival glass). Lavender (rare). Northwood prices given.

Butter dish, covered	$44-52
Celery vase	22-32
Creamer	31-41

Goblet 27-38
Pitcher, water (ill.) 44-54
Plate, 9", 10" 29-39
Spoonholder 28-37
Sugar bowl, covered 44-53
Tumbler 24-39

Probably other pieces. Sapphire and purple 100 percent higher than clear prices listed.

Way's Colonial

Way's Colonial

Maker unknown, c. 1840s, clear, flint. Possibly Central Glass Company, c. 1870s.

Sugar bowl, covered $54-64
Tumbler (ill.) 34-47
Whiskey, handled 33-46

Wedding Bells

Wedding Bells

Fostoria Glass Company, Moundsville, West Virginia, 1900. Clear, amethyst gold, possibly green, pink flashed, flint.

Butter dish, covered $42-52
Celery 22-34
Creamer 32-42
Compote, covered, high, low
  foot........................ 39-49
Cruet, with stopper 36-46
Egg cup 20-30
Goblet 40-50
Pitcher, half gallon tankard (ill.) . 60-72
Spoonholder 26-37
Sugar bowl 34-44
Tumbler 22-28

Probably other pieces. Colors, 60 percent higher than clear prices listed.

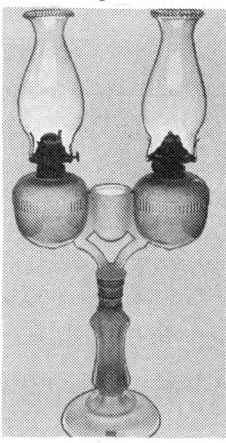
Wedding Lamp

Wedding Lamp

On July 14, 1870, Daniel C. Ripley patented a mold for producing twin-fountain oil lamps, both by pressing and blowing. Extremely rare today, the one shown here is on display at the Houston Museum, Chattanooga, Tennessee.

Lamp (rare) (ill.) ....$575+

Wedding Ring

Wedding Ring

Maker unknown, 1870s. Clear.

Champagne	$18-27
Creamer	28-39
Decanter	29-39
Goblet	22-38
Pitcher, syrup (ill.)	34-48
Wine	19-27

Probably other pieces.

Westward Ho!

Westward Ho!

(Pioneer; Tippecanoe): Gillinder & Sons, Philadelphia, about 1879. It was originally called Pioneer; also Tippecanoe, this last name was never popular. Clear, frosted. Be careful! Heavily reproduced.

Butter dish, covered, standard	$146-167
Celery	115-135
Compote	
a. Covered, 6", high standard	210-250
b. Covered, 6", low standard	160-188
c. Oval, 9"	143-163
Creamer	128-142
Goblet, frosted	77- 87
Jar, jam, covered (scarce)	176-184
Pitcher, milk	220-248
Pitcher, water (ill.)	190-210
Sauce, 4", footed	36- 46
Spoonholder	93-106
Sugar bowl, covered	162-195
Wine	110-130

Probably other pieces. Butter dish, 6" compote, 9" compote, cordial, goblet, clear and frosted, water pitcher, sauce, wine being reproduced. Goblets originally clear or frosted. Being reproduced in amethyst, blue green, clear and frosted.

Wheat and Barley

Wheat and Barley

(Duquesne; Hops and Barley; Oats and Barley): Original trade name was Duquesne and it was made by Bryce Bros., Pittsburgh, late 1870s, early 1880s. It was also called Hops and Barley; also Oats and Barley. Clear, amber, blue, yellow. Reproduced by U.S. Glass Company, 1889.

Butter dish, covered	$39-48
Cake stand, 8", 9", 10"	43-54
Compote	
a. Covered, 7", 8", high standard	49-59
b. Open, high standard	40-50
Creamer, plain and footed	38-48
Goblet	32-42
Pitcher	
a. Water (ill.)	33-43
b. Milk, syrup	28-38
Plate, 7", 9"	29-39
Sauce, footed, 4", flat	16-27
Salt/Pepper, pr.	32-38
Spoonholder	31-41
Sugar bowl, covered	38-48
Tumbler, footed, water	34-44

Probably other pieces. Canary, amber, 50 percent higher; blue, 65 percent higher than clear prices listed.

Wheat Sheaf

Maker unknown, late 1870s. Clear.

Butter dish	$29-38
Celery vase	22-32
Compote, low standard	33-47
Creamer	28-36
Goblet	22-31

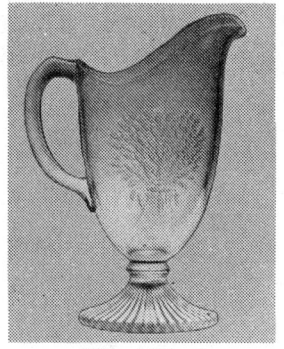

Wheat Sheaf

Pitcher, water (ill.)	35-45
Spoonholder	22-34
Sugar bowl	32-42
Tumbler	22-32

Probably other pieces.

Wheel in Band

Wheel in Band

Maker unknown, 1870s. Clear.

Butter dish, covered	$36-46
Celery	23-33
Creamer	27-37
Goblet	26-36
Jam jar, covered	30-40
Pitcher, water (ill.)	48-58
Spoonholder	19-27
Sugar bowl, covered	28-38
Wine	19-29

Probably other pieces.

Whirled Sunburst in Circle

Maker and date unknown, 1890-1895. Clear.

Whirled Sunburst in Circle

Butter dish, covered	$38-48
Creamer	29-39
Pitcher, water (ill.)	50-64
Spoonholder	19-29
Sugar bowl, covered	33-44

Probably other pieces.

Wigwam

(Teepee): Iowa Glass Company, Iowa City, Iowa, c. late 1880s, clear, non-flint.

Butter dish, covered	$42-61
Creamer	29-39
Goblet	37-46
Spoonholder	28-35
Sugar bowl, covered	48-56

Probably other pieces.

Wild Bouquet

Wild Bouquet

Northwood Glass Company, 1902. Custard glass, gold trim, colors.

Bowl, berry, large	$ 49- 59
Bowl, berry, small	28- 38
Butter dish, covered	39- 52

(continued)

Compote 52- 64
Cruet 51- 61
Pitcher, water (ill.) 110-130
Tumbler 29- 41
Probably other pieces.

Wild Rose and Lady Lamp

Wild Rose and Lady Lamp

Riverside Glass Company, Wellsburg, West Virginia. The Millersburg Glass Company, Millersburg, Ohio, made nine of these lamps to honor the wives of the company officials. When Millersburg went out of business in 1914, Riverside Glass Company somehow obtained the Wild Rose and Lady lamp mold. Millersburg had the familiar wild rose and honeycomb on the outside of the lamp; Riverside has these on the underside. Also, Riverside had "Riverside Clinch on Collar" in raised letters on the outside at the base. All these lamps, both Millersburg and Riverside are highly collectible today.

Lamp, Millersburg (rare) (ill.) . . $ 590 +
Lamp, Riverside 180-198

Wild Rose with Bow-Knot

Maker unknown, late 1880s. Clear, colors, frosted.

Bowl $29-39
Butter dish 32-41
Creamer 28-39

Wild Rose with Bow-Knot

Pitcher (ill.) 44-74
Sauce 14-26
Spoonholder 22-34
Sugar bowl, covered 48-59
Tumbler 29-42

Probably other pieces. Water pitcher had cover, meaning it was originally made as condiment holder — mustard, jelly, etc. Colors, 50 percent higher than clear prices listed.

Wild Rose with Scrolling

Wild Rose with Scrolling

Possibly Dithridge & Company, Pittsburgh, 1870s. Clear; possibly opaque white, other colors. It's almost as if this miniature table set were made for the "wee people." Tiny and dainty.

Butter dish, covered (ill.) $61-72
Creamer 47-57
Spoonholder 29-41
Sugar bowl, covered 58-72

Probably other pieces.

Wildflower

Wildflower

Adams & Company, Pittsburgh, 1874; other factories later; reproduced by U.S. Glass Company, 1898. Clear, canary, amber, blue, green, amethyst, vaseline.

Butter dish, collared base,
covered $40-50
Cake stand, large, small 38-54
Celery 38-48
Compote
  a. 6″, 8″, covered, high
    standard 44-54
  b. 8″, low standard 39-46
  c. Open, high standard 34-47
Creamer 32-42
Goblet 27-37
Pitcher, water (ill.) 49-62
Sauce, flat, round, square 18-27
Salt/Pepper, pr. 34-44
Spoonholder 32-46
Sugar bowl, covered 36-44
Tumbler, water 27-38
Wine........................ 29-34

Probably other pieces. Amber, yellow, blue, 50 percent higher; green, 100 percent higher than clear prices listed. Goblet, 10″ plate, round, flat sauce, tumbler, wine being reproduced.

Willow Oak

(Oak Leaf; Stippled Star; Acorn; Thistle; Wreath): Bryce Bros., Pittsburgh, made it in the 1880s and called it Wreath. It is also known by the other names listed here. Clear, amber, blue.

Willow Oak

Bowl, waste, berry $32-46
Butter dish 72-80
Cake stand, 8½″ 40-50
Celery 33-46
Compote, covered, 7½″, 9″, high
standard 42-62
Creamer 32-46
Goblet 22-32
Mug 28-38
Pitcher, large, small 48-62
Plates, 7″, 9″, closed handles 19-29
Salt/Pepper, pr. 22-29
Sauce, flat, footed, round 14-16
Spoonholder 22-31
Sugar bowl, covered 38-54
Tumbler 24-34

Probably other pieces. Amber, 50 percent higher; blue, 80 percent higher than clear prices listed.

Wiltec

(continued)

Wiltec

McKee & Brothers, Pittsburgh, Pennsylvania, c. 1890s, clear, flint.

Butter dish, covered	$36-45
Creamer	28-40
Spoonholder	22-32
Sugar bowl, covered (ill.)	32-42

Obviously other pieces.

Windflower

Windflower

Maker unknown, late 1870s. Clear.

Butter dish, flat, covered	$64-74
Celery	44-53
Compote, covered, high, low standard	64-76
Cordial	40-50
Creamer	44-56
Egg cup	32-42
Goblet	39-52
Pitcher, water (ill.)	69-78
Salt, footed	33-44
Saucedish, 4″	19-28
Spoonholder	33-43
Sugar bowl, covered	54-66
Tumbler, water	42-49
Wine	44-55

Probably other pieces.

Wooden Pail

(Oaken Bucket): Bryce Bros., 1880s. Clear, amber, blue, canary. Probably a container for candy, mustard, baking

Wooden Pail

powder, coffee. Bryce Bros. called it their "Bucket Set." Made in miniature and full size. Amethyst, rare!

Butter dish, covered	$54-64
Creamer	38-48
Pitcher (ill.)	44-54
Spoonholder	22-33
Sugar bowl	
a. Covered	38-48
b. Open	27-37

Undoubtedly other pieces. Miniature same price as large. Yellow, amber, 60 percent higher; blue, 85 percent higher; amethyst, 275 percent higher than clear prices listed.

Woodflower

Sandwich, 1870s. Clear and stippled.

Creamer	$54-64
Goblet	52-62
Sugar bowl, covered	72-81

Probably other pieces.

Wreath and Shell

584

Wreath and Shell

Albany, Indiana, Glass Company, late 1880s. Opaque colors.

Butter dish, covered \$72-82
Rose bowl (ill.) 50-59
Tumbler 61-71

Probably many other pieces.

Wyoming

Wyoming

(Enigma): U.S. Glass Company, Gas City, Indiana, 1907. Crystal, colored glass, including mosaic glass.

Butter dish \$28-38
Cake stand, 9″ 34-44
Creamer 22-34
Goblet 28-38
Pitcher, milk, water (ill.) 34-46
Spoonholder 19-28
Sugar bowl
  a. Covered 33-43
  b. Open 27-36
Tumbler 19-28
Wine........................ 19-23

Probably other pieces.

X-Log

X-Log

(Prism Arc): Maker unknown, c. mid-1880s, clear, non-flint.

Bowl, vegetable, oval (ill.) \$14-20
Butter dish, covered 28-38
Cake stand 34-44
Creamer 32-42
Goblet 19-28
Mug 17-26
Spoonholder 18-27
Sugar bowl, covered 28-38
Wine........................ 19-27

Probably other pieces.

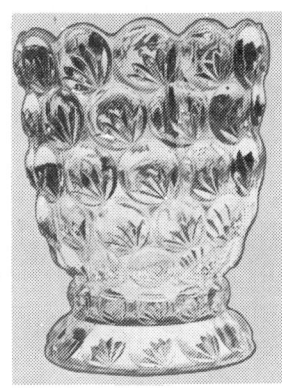
Yale

Yale

(Crow-Foot): McKee Glass Company, Jeannette, Pennsylvania, 1894. Clear.

Butter dish, covered \$34-44
Cake stand 29-36
Celery 28-38
Compote 34-44
Cordial...................... 19-26
Creamer 28-39
Goblet 27-36
Pitcher
  a. Syrup 24-34
  b. Water (ill.) 36-47
Plate........................ 23-34
Saucedish, 4″, 6″............... 14-22
Salt/Pepper, pr. 28-34
Spoonholder 21-32
Sugar bowl, covered 29-42
Tumbler 19-27

Probably other pieces.

Yoked Loop

Yoked Loop

(Scalloped Loop): Maker unknown, c. 1860s, clear, flint.

Goblet $28-39
Sugar bowl
  a. Covered 42-56
  b. Open (ill.) 27-37

Should be other pieces.

York Colonial

York Colonial

Possibly Sandwich, c. 1850s, clear, flint; also opalescent, amethyst, blue. Later, Central Glass Company, c. 1870s, clear, non-flint.

Ale footed $51- 61
Celery........................ 88-100
Compote, covered.............. 92-105
Creamer...................... 96-104
Goblet........................ 62- 71
Sugar bowl (base ill.) 51- 61
Tumbler...................... 33- 44

Colors (rare), 200 percent higher than clear prices listed. Central Glass pieces, 50 percent lower than Sandwich prices listed.

York Herringbone

York Herringbone

Maker unknown, late 1880s. Clear; clear with ruby stain. Souvenir pieces sold at 1893 World's Fair.

Celery $28-38
Creamer, green, individual
  (ill.) 42-54
Spoonholder 38-49

Probably other pieces.

Yuma Loop

Yuma Loop

O'Hara Glass Company, late 1850s or early 1860s. Clear, flint. Contemporary of Loop (O'Hara)! Same values.

Zigzag Band

Zigzag Band

Possibly Gillinder & Sons, 1870s. Clear.

Butter dish, covered $32-42
Celery vase 19-29
Creamer 26-37
Goblet 23-38
Pitcher, water (ill.) 48-58
Spoonholder 19-29
Sugar bowl, covered 34-44
Tumbler 27-37

Probably other pieces.

Zipper Slash

Zipper Slash

George A. Duncan's Sons, Washington, Pennsylvania, 1893. Stained ruby-red above pattern; sometimes in yellow.

Butter, covered $48-58
Creamer 39-48
Spoonholder 26-37
Sugar bowl (ill.) 52-62
Wine........................ 28-37

Probably other pieces. Yellow, 50 percent higher; with souvenir marking, 50 percent less than clear prices listed.

Zipper

Richards & Hartley Glass Company, Tarentum, Pennsylvania, c. 1880s, clear, non-flint.

Butter dish, covered $25-36
Celery 18-29
Compote
  a. Open 17-28
  b. Covered 32-44
Jar, jam, covered 37-47
Pitcher, water................. 36-46
Sugar bowl
  a. Open 19-29
  b. Covered 38-48

Probably other pieces.

Glass Companies

* Adams & Company, Pittsburgh, 1861; joined U.S. Glass Company in 1891 as Factory A.

Aetna Glass & Manufacturing Company, Bellaire, Ohio, 1880.

American Glass Company, Anderson, Indiana, 1889.

Anchor-Hocking Glass Company (see Ohio Flint Glass Company).

* Atterbury & Company, Pittsburgh, about 1858.

Bakewell & Company (also called Bakewell & Page), 1809.

Bakewell & Ensell, Pittsburgh, 1807.

Bakewell, Page & Bakewell, 1824.

* Bakewell, Pears & Company, 1836.

Bay State Glass Company, Cambridge, Massachusetts, about 1849.

Beatty, Alexander J. & Sons, Steubenville, Ohio, about 1850. Moved to Tiffin, Ohio in 1890.

Beatty-Brady Glass Company, Steubenville, then to Dunkirk, Indiana in 1898. Both taken over by the U.S. Glass Company; Factory S at Steubenville, and Factory T at Tiffin.

Beaumont Glass Company, Martins Ferry, Ohio, 1895. Sold to Hocking Glass in 1905.

Beaver Falls Co-Operative Glass Company, Beaver Falls, Pennsylvania, 1879.

Beaver Falls Glass Company, Beaver Falls, Pennsylvania, 1887.

Bellaire Goblet Company, Bellaire & Findlay, Ohio, 1878; merged with U.S. Glass Company in 1891. Both plants were moved to Tiffin, Ohio under the name Factory M.

Belmont Glass Company, Bellaire, Ohio, 1866.

* Boston & Sandwich Glass Company, Sandwich, Massachusetts, 1825.

Boston Silver-Glass Company, East Cambridge, Massachusetts, 1857.

Brilliant Glass Works, Brilliant, Ohio (originally called Novelty Glass Company), 1880.

Bryce, McKee & Company, Pittsburgh, 1850.

Bryce, Richards & Company, Pittsburgh, 1854.

Bryce, Walker & Company, Pittsburgh, 1865.

Bryce Bros., Pittsburgh, 1882. Taken over by U.S. Glass Company around 1889 and named Factory B.

Bryce Bros. again entered the business Hammondsville, Pennsylvania, 1896.

Bryce, Higbee & Company (also known as Homestead Glass Works), Pittsburgh, 1879.

J. B. Higbee Glass Company, Bridgeville, Pennsylvania, 1900.

* Excelsior Glass Works, Wheeling, West Virginia; moved to Martins Ferry, Ohio in 1879 under the name Buckeye Glass Company.

National Glass Company, Cambridge, Ohio, 1901 (also called Cambridge Glass Company).

Campbell, Jones & Company, Pittsburgh, 1865.

Canton Glass Company, Canton, Ohio, 1883; factory moved to Marion, Indiana in 1894. In 1899 it joined with National Glass Company. In 1903 the factory site changed to Cambridge, Ohio. Another Canton Glass Company was founded in Marion, Indiana in 1904.

Jones, Cavitt & Company, Ltd., Pittsburgh, 1886.

GLASS COMPANIES

*Central Glass Company, Wheelng, West Virginia, 1863. (Famous for their Coin pattern.) Joined U.S. Glass Company in 1891 as Factory O.

Challinor, Taylor, Ltd., Tarentum, Pennsylvania, 1884-1894.

Columbia Glass Company, Findlay, Ohio, 1886; incorporated into U.S. Glass Company in 1891 as Factory J.

Consolidated Lamp & Glass Company, Pittsburgh & Coraopolis, Pennsylvania, 1894.

Co-perative Flint Glass Company, Beaver Falls, Pennsylvania, 1889.

*Crystal Glass Company, Pittsburgh, 1868; later moved to Bridgeport, Ohio, in 1882.

Craig & Ritchie, Wheeling, West Virginia, 1824 or 1826 — said to be the first plant in the U.S. for pressing glass. Before Sandwich on Cape Cod.

R. B. Curling & Sons (originally called Curling, Price & Company), Pittsburgh, 1827.

Dalzell, Gilmore & Leighton Company, Findlay, Ohio, 1888.

Diders, McGee, Brilliant, Ohio, date unknown.

Dithridge & Company, Pittsburgh, 1860s; also a factory at Martins Ferry, Ohio.

Doyle & Company, PITTSBURGH, ⅓—¾¾: PURCHASED BY Phoenix Glass Company, Phillipsburgh, New Jersey in the early 1880s. In 1891, firm was purchased by U.S. Glass Company, known as Factory P.

Dugan Class Company, Indiana, Pennsylvania in 1892 (originally known as Indiana Glass Company).

*George Duncan & Sons, Pittsburgh, 1874; George A. Duncan & Sons, Washington, Pennsylvania, 1894; Duncan & Heisey Company, 1886-1889, Pittsburgh; Duncan & Miller Glass Company, Washington, Pennsylvania, 1870s — U.S. Glass Company's Factory D.

East Liverpool Glass Company, East Liverpool, Ohio, 1882.

Elson Glass Company, Martins Ferry, Ohio, 1882.

Enterprise Glass Works, Ravenna, Ohio, 1878.

Fenton Art Glass Company, Martins Ferry, Ohio, 1906; factory moved to present location in Williamstown, West Virginia, in 1906. The firm is still in business.

Findlay Flint Glass Company, Findlay, Ohio, 1888.

Fort Pitt Glass works — better known as Dithridge & Company.

Fostoria Glass Company, Fostoria, Ohio, 1887; the factory was moved to Moundsville, West Virginia in 1891, and is still in operation today.

Franklin Flint Glass Company, Philadelphia, 1861.

Gillinder & Bennett, Philadelphia, 1863.

*Gillinder & Sons, Philadelphia, 1867; later sold to U.S. Glass Company and named Factory G.

Graham Glass Works, Brilliant, Ohio, 1895.

Greensburg Glass Company, Greensburg, Pennsylvania, 1889 (previously operated as Brilliant Glass Works, Brilliant, Ohio).

A. H. Heisey Glass Company, Newark, Ohio, 1895.

GLASS COMPANIES

Hemingray Glass Company, Cincinnati, Ohio & Covington, Kentucky, founded in Cincinnati around 1848.

Hipkins Novelty Mold Shop, Martins Ferry, Ohio, 1884.

*Hobbs, Brockunier & Company, Wheeling, West Virginia, 1863; factory known as J. H Hobbs Glass Company. Taken over by U.S. Glass Company in 1891, calling their new acquisition Factory H.

Homestead Glass Works, Pittsburgh, 1879.

Huntington Glass Company, Huntington, West Virginia, 1891. Originally called Central City until incorporated as Huntington in 1909.

C. Ihmsen & Company, Pittsburgh, 1850s.

Imperial Glass Company, Bellaire, Ohio, 1901. Still in business today.

Indiana Glass Company, Dunkirk, Indiana, 1897. Joined National Glass Company merger in 1899.

Indiana Tumbler & Goblet Company, Greentown, Indiana, 1894. In 1899, firm merged with nineteen other factories to become National Glass Company.

Jefferson Glass Company, Steubenville, Ohio, 1901; moved to Follansbee, West Virginia in 1907.

Jenkins Glass Company, Greentown, Indiana, 1894.

Jersey Glass Company, Jersey City, New Jersey, 1825.

Jones, Cavitt & Company, Pittsburgh, 1884.

*Keystone Tumbler Works, Rochester, Pennsylvania, 1897.

King Glass Company, Pittsburgh, 1880. This firm was absorbed into the U.S. Glass Company in 1891, thereafter known as Factory K.

King, Son & Company, Pittsburgh, 1869.

Kokomo Glass Company, Kokomo, Indiana, 1899. It was destroyed by fire but rebuilt in 1906 as the D. C. Jenkins Glass Company.

*La Belle Glass Company, Bridgeport, Ohio, 1872.

Lancaster Glass Company, Lancaster, Ohio, 1915.

Model Flint Glass Company, Findlay, Ohio, 1888.

Mosaic Glass Company, Fostoria, Ohio, 1887.

Muhleman Glass Works, LaBelle, Ohio, 1888.

National Glass Company, Bellaire, Ohio, 1877. Not the National Glass Company.

New Brighton Glass Company, New Brighton, Pennsylvania, 1884. Originally known as American Ferroline Company.

*New England Glass Company, Cambridge, Massachusetts, early 1800s. Later New England Glass Works.

Nickel Plate Glass Company, Fostoria, Ohio, 1888. Joined the U.S. Glass Company in 1891, becoming their Factory N.

Northwood: Union Glass Works, Martins Ferry, Ohio, 1887; Elwood City, Pennsylvania, 1890; Indiana, Pennyslvania, 1895; Wheeling, West Virginia, 1901 (this factory is probably where he made most of his Carnival Glass.)

Novelty Glass Company, LaGrange, Ohio, 1880; later became U.S. Glass Company's Factory T.

*O'Hara Glass Company, 1848. Joined U.S. Glass Company in 1891 as Factory L.

Ohio Flint Glass Company, Lancaster, Ohio, 1899. Soon merged with the National Glass Company — out of these combines emerged today's giant Anchor-Hocking Glass Company.

Oriental Glass Company, Pittsburgh, early 1890s.

Phoenix Glass Company, Monaca, Pennsylvania, 1880.

Pioneer Glass Company, Pittsburgh, 1891.

Portland Glass Company, Portland, Maine, 1864.

*Richards & Hartley Glass Company, Tarentum, Pennsylvania, 1884-1893.

*Ripley & Company, Pittsburgh, 1866; joined U.S. Glass Company in 1891 as Factory F.

Riverside Glass Company, Wellsburgh, West Virginia, 1879.

Robinson Glass Company, Zanesville, Ohio, 1893.

*Rochester Tumbler Company, Rochester, Pennsylvania, 1872.

Steiner Glass Company, Buckhannon, West Virginia, 1870s.

Tarentum Glass Company, Tarentum, Pennsylvania, 1894-1918.

Thompson Glass Company, Uniontown, Pennsylvania, 1889.

*Union Glass Company, Somerville, Massachusetts, 1851.

U.S. Glass Company, 1891. (See Factories A-T).

Specialty Glass Company, East Liverpool, Ohio, 1889.

West Virginia Glass Company, Martins Ferry, Ohio, 1861.

Westmoreland Glass Company, during World War I.

Westmoreland Specialty Company, early 1890s.

Windsor Glass Company, Pittsburgh, 1887.

Whitla Glass Company, Beaver Falls, Pennsylvania, 1887. In 1890 the company reorganized as Valley Glass Company.

NOTE: There were probably many other glass companies, but as some stayed in business less than a year, and since many never published a catalog or advertised their products in newspapers, etc., the above list gives a fairly comprehensive list of the "better known" producers of pressed glass in the United States from 1824 until the early 1900s.

About the Editor

Robert W. Miller has written twelve books to do with antiques and collectibles in the past nine years, all published by the Wallace-Homestead Book Company in Des Moines, Iowa.

Mr. Miller is a member of the Appraisers Association of America, a past editor of The *Antique Trader Weekly* and holds membership in many of the world's leading organizations specializing in antiques.

A consultant to museums and historical societies, worldwide, when he isn't lecturing in Europe or the United States or autographing his many books at the nation's better antiques shows, he can be found at home in Panama City Beach, Florida.

For information concerning Mr. Miller's lecture rates contact him at Post Office Box 14111, Panama City Beach, Florida 32407.